A HISTORY

OF

MARION COUNTY,

SOUTH CAROLINA,

From Its Earliest Times to the Present, 1901.

By W. W. SELLERS, Esq.,
of the Marion Bar.

Southern Historical Press, Inc.
Greenville, South Carolina

Originally printed 1902

New Material Copyright 1996 by:
Southern Historical Press, Inc.

All rights reserved. No part of this publication may be reproduced, stored in a retrieval system or transmitted in any form or by any means without the prior permission of the publisher.

SOUTHERN HISTORICAL PRESS, INC.
PO BOX 1267
Greenville, SC 29601

ISBN #0-89308-699-1

Printed in the United States of America

CONTENTS

CHAPTER I.
  Settlement 1
CHAPTER II.
  Section I. Location and Boundaries........................ 6
  Section II. Its Surface and Soil, Its Rivers and Lakes, Its In-Land Swamps 15
  Section III. Its Soil and Productions...................... 17
  Section IV. Stock Raising................................. 29
CHAPTER III.
  Section I. Its Educational, Political and Judicial History...... 33
    Graduates of Colleges................................. 50
    Political History 52
    Queensboro Township 78
    Plat of the Welch Grant (First)....................... 81
  The Early Settlement of Marion County.................... 104
    Some Families mentioned:
      Godbold 117
      Evans 125
      Giles 135
      Britton, Fladger. etc............................... 137
      Crawford 142
      Murfees 147
      Berry.. 148
      Saunders 157
      Gibson 159
      Page 162
      Ayres.. 166
      Ford 167
      Hays 170
      Elvington 173
      Scott 175
      Owens 175
      Gaddy 176
      Lupo and Arnett 178
      Rogers 178
      Perritt 183
      Edwards 185
      Nichols 189
      Hutchinson 191
      Barfield 191
      Goodyear 192
      Tart 193
      Bryant 197
      Watson 199

Reaves	206
Grice	208
Roberts	209
Ellerbee	213
Fore	218
Mace	221
Finklea	223
Haselden	223
Bass	225
Hamer	232
McKenzie	235
Manning	238
Jones	241
Cottingham	246
Hamilton	247
Braddy	249
Clark	252
Harrelson	255
Martin	258
Henry	261
Huggins	263
Hayes	267
Dew	271
Nicholson	275
Jackson	276
Galloway	281
Sherwood	281
Alford	282
Greenwood	284
McInnis	285
Stafford	287
Blue	289
Baker	290
McPriest	291
McKellar	291
McKay	292
McCormick	293
McArthur	299
McIntyre	300
McKinly	307
McLellan	308
Sinclair	314
McDuffie	315
Campbell	320
Butler	327
Moody	330

Harllee	342
Woodberry	355
Stackhouse	358
Wayne	366
Legette	369
Gasque	373
Brown	373
Gilchrist	382
Easterling	384
Lane	386
Bethea	395
McMillan	421
Miller	425
Spencer	427
Williamson	429
Wall	432
McEachern	435
Carmichael	437
Baker	445
Davis	448
Stanley	455
Harrel, in Britton's Neck	456
Altman	456
Whaley	457
Richardson	457
Stevenson	462
Craven	463
Thompson	464
Kirton	464
Philips	465
Owens	466
Rowell	468
Giles	471
Coleman	472
Norton	475
Lewis	480
Fowler	483
Shooter	484
Campbell (of Maiden Down)	486
Atkinson	488
Fladger	491
Smith	492
Flowers	502
Mullins	506
Gregg	510
Collins	512

    Wiggins, of Wahee 516
    Shaw 518
    Dozier 521
    Foxworth and Boatwright 522
    White and Monroe 525
    Snipes 528
    Wilcox 536
    Young 537
    Johnson 538
    Sellers 543
The Negro 546
Towns of the County.. 550
    Marion. 551
    Nichols and Mullins 553
    Latta and Dillon...................................... 555
    Hamer and Sellers 559
The Denominational Churches............................... 560
Clerks of Court for Marion County, from 1800 to 1900....... 564
Sheriffs for Marion County from 1800 to 1900............... 565
Representatives in the Legislature.......................... 566
Senators from 1800 to 1900................................. 568
Ordinaries and Probate Judges from 1800 to 1900.......... 568
Proprietary Governors 568
Lawyers practicing at Marion from 1800 to 1900............ 570
Volunteers in Confederate Army............................ 572
    Company L, 21st Regiment Infantry, C. S. A............ 572
    Company H, Orr's Regt. Rifles S. C. V., C. S. A....... 577
    Company F, 4th Regt. Cav. S. C. V., C. S. A........... 581
    Company E, Gregg's 1st Regt. S. C. V., C. S. A........ 585
    Company I, 8th Regt. Inf. S. C. V., C. S. A........... 590
    Company H, 8th Regt. Inf. S. C. V., C. S. A........... 593
    Company I, 1st Regt. Inf. (Hagood's) S. C. V., C. S. A.. 596
    Company L, 10th Regt. Inf. S. C. V., C. S. A.......... 599
    Company L, 8th Regt. Inf. S. C. V., C. S. A........... 602
    Company I, 21st Regt. Inf. S. C. V., C. S. A.......... 605
    Company E, 23d Regt. Inf. S. C. V., C. S. A.......... 609
    Company Gregg's Battery, Co. D, Manigault's Battalion
        Artillery S. C. V., C. S. A......................... 613
    Company H, 23d Regt. Inf. S. C. V., C. S. A.......... 620
    Company D, 10th Regt. Inf. S. C. V., C. S. A......... 626
    Company F, 10th Regt. Inf. S. C. V., C. S. A......... 628
    Company I, 6th Regt. Cav. S. C. V., C. S. A.......... 631
    Company D, 25th Regt. Inf. S. C. V., C. S. A......... 632
    Company E, 26th Reg. Inf. S. C. V., C. S. A.......... 636
    Company I, 10th Regt. Inf. S. C. V., C. S. A......... 639
    Company D, 7th Battalion S. C. Reserves............. 642
    Company of Militia, last called into service........... 644

PREFACE

Within the last ten or twelve years the author has been solicited to write a history of this, Marion County, and by many whose opinions and judgment he much valued; but then being much engaged in the practice of the law, he could not find the time to engage in and complete such a work. Furthermore, he felt a diffidence in his abilities to perform the task with satisfaction and credit to himself. January, 1898, he concluded to retire from the active practice of his profession, for the reason, first, that his sense of hearing became much impaired; and secondly, because of his age, then near eighty years old. He retired, and since that time has taken no new case, and confined himself only to old cases then pending in the Courts of Marion, Florence and Horry Counties; cases, too, that his junior partner had had nothing to do with and knew but little about. Those cases were in due time mostly ended. After this work in the Courts was practically accomplished, and having fair health and strength for one of his age, physically and mentally, he determined to undertake the work, and for the last eighteen months has been engaged principally in its performance, and he herewith submits it to the people of the county, and it will be for them to say whether he has succeeded well or has failed to meet expectations. Such as it is, it is his own work. Its subject matter, the language used, the style, manner and composition are all his own. He has not borrowed from another author without giving to that other full credit by placing the language used in quotation marks, and referring to the author by name and page. He acknowledges his indebtedness to Dr. Ramsay's History of South Carolina, to Bishop Gregg's History of the Old Cheraws, to the Lives of General

Marion written by M. L. Weems, and General Horry, and the same by W. Gilmore Sims, to the Statutes at Large as published by Dr. Thomas Cooper, and to perhaps other sources. He is further indebted to many of our citizens for information as to families that he could not otherwise have obtained.

It may be found that he has made mistakes. It will be a wonder if it is not so found. He expects no other. In mentioning families, it is mainly genealogical. All genealogy is history, and he trusts that families for the next three or four generations, at least, may be able to trace their ancestry back to and including what is herein written; that it will not be then, as he has found it in his inquiries of persons, when writing this history, that some of them of superior intelligence did not know who their grand-father was. Many of the old families have become extinct by death or removal. The author may have omitted to notice some that now exist. Where that is the case, it was because the author knew nothing or but little about them, and could not ascertain anything in reference to them. He tried to get a list of the graduates of literary colleges from Marion County, but some of them did not answer inquiries. Hence he had to depend on memory. Marion may well congratulate herself on the number and character of her young and older men of learning. She is fast coming to the front in that line, as well as in many other lines. He has furnished a list of all the Clerks of the Court, Sheriffs and Probate Judges or Ordinaries from the earliest times of her existence as a Judicial District. Also, a list of her Senators in the Legislature and Representatives. Further, a list of all the lawyers that have practiced in Marion since 1800. He has also procured and inserted a list of all the Governors of the province, proprietary and royal, while a province, and all after it became an independent State down to the present time, and last, but not least in importance and in its numbers, a list of all the companies that went from Marion to the Confederate War. This list embraces West Marion, including all company officers, what became of them, killed in battle or died of disease or wounds; whether living or dead now, so far as is known, and much other information concerning our brave boys during that momentous struggle. All of which the author trusts may be of interest to many, very many, of the present generation.

The author, now in his eighty-fourth year, submits what he has done in this regard as his last work on the stage of life. It has been a labor of love for the county in which he has spent most of his life, and for any errors, omissions and failures he asks the indulgence of its people, to whom he herein and hereby respectfully dedicates the result of his labors.

W. W. SELLERS.

Sellers, S. C., August 27th, 1901.

A History of Marion County

CHAPTER I.

The first permanent settlement made in South Carolina was by a few emigrants from England, under the direction and patronage of William Sayle, at or near Port Royal, in 1670. William Sayle was their first Governor. These colonists, for some reason or another, became dissatisfied with their location at Port Royal. They removed, in 1671, up the coast and settled on the west side of the Ashley River, opposite the present site of the city of Charleston, and there laid the foundation of old Charleston. This site was not wisely chosen, as it could not be reached by ships of heavy burden, and therefore it was abandoned. "A second removal took place to Oyster Point, formed by the confluence of Ashley and Cooper Rivers. There, in 1680, the foundation of the present city of Charleston was laid, and in one year thirty houses were built." Of the number and names of these first settlers of South Carolina, no records have been kept and preserved; only two names have come down to us, that of William Sayle and Joseph West. William Sayle dying in 1671, Joseph West was appointed as his successor, August 28, 1671. He was succeeded by Sir John Yeamans, April 19th, 1672, and he was succeeded by Joseph West, 13th August 1674, who held the office till 26th September, 1682, when he was succeeded by Joseph Morton, and on September 6th, 1684, Joseph West was appointed Governor for the third time. (1 vol., Statutes at Large, pp. 17, 18 and 19.) The first slaves introduced in South Carolina were brought hither by Sir John Yeamans from Barbadoes, one of the West India Islands, in 1671. Sir John Yeamans was an Englishman, though he came from Barbadoes to Carolina. Had he not been an Englishman, he would not have been appointed Governor of the province. The writer infers that he left England at or about the time the emigrants left England under William Sayle for Carolina, and who landed at Port

Royal the year before, to wit: 1670. The writer further infers that Sir John Yeamans went by Barbadoes for the purpose of getting a cargo of slaves to be carried to Carolina, and that Yeamans and Sayle understood one another. A sad day for the country! Thus the germ of near two hundred years' contention in America was planted, which culminated in a bloody four years war between the States of America, from 1861 to 1865. The results of this nucleus of slavery are still felt among us, and is perplexing the brain of our best and ablest men, and will, perhaps, for ages to come. There is no doubt a providence is in it all, and He who rules and determines the destinies of men and nations, may and will bring good out of the seeming evil.

The government of Carolina (both North and South Carolina) had been granted by two charters by King Charles the Second, to certain English noblemen, to wit: to "Edward, Earl of Clarendon, High Chancellor of England, and George, Duke of Albemarle, Master of our Horse and Captain General of all our forces, and well beloved William Lord Craven, John Lord Berkley, our right trusty and well beloved Counsellor, Anthony Lord Ashley, Chancellor of our Exchequer, Sir George Content, Kn't and Baronet, Vice Chamberlain of our household, and our trusty and well beloved Sir William Berkley, Kn't, and Sir John Colleton, Knight and Baronet, being excited with a laudable and pious zeal for the propagation of the Christian faith, and the enlargement of our empire and dominions, have humbly sought leave of us by their industry and charge to transport and make an ample colony of our subjects natives of our Kingdom of England and elsewhere within our dominions, unto a certain country hereafter described in the parts of America not yet cultivated or planted, and only inhabited by some barbarous people who have no knowledge of Almighty God." This charter, of which the above quotation is the first section, was granted 24th March, 1663; and on the 30th June, 1665, the said Charles the Second granted to the said parties named in the first charter the same territory, to wit: all the lands lying between the 31st and 36th degrees of north latitude, and between the Atlantic Ocean on the east and the South Seas (Pacific Ocean) on the west, including what is now the States of North Carolina and South Carolina, giving to the said named proprietors larger rights and powers than in the first charter. (See 1st and 2d charters, 1 vol., Statutes at Large of South Carolina, pp. 22 to 31, and pp. 31 to 40.)

Under these charters, the Lords Proprietors drew up, or had it done, five different constitutions for the government of the province, but it does not appear that any one of them was ever adopted and ratified by the Assembly, except in part, and except those drawn up by the celebrated John Locke, and then only in part; but notwithstanding the rejection of parts of all of them by the Assembly, the government established by them moved along with some success, and without serious friction, for a period of forty-nine or fifty years, until 1719, when a revolution (bloodless) took place under the administration of Robert Johnson, Esq., as Governor, and threw off and repudiated the government of the Lords Proprietors, thinking they would be better protected in their rights under the King. They first offered the government to Governor Robert Johnson, provided he would administer it in the name of the King, instead of in the name of the Lords Proprietors. He refused so to do, whereupon the Assembly offered the governorship to Col. James Moore, son of the former Governor, who accepted the position and took upon himself the government of the province. Accounts of the trouble in the province being sent to England, King George the First appointed Francis Nicholson Governor of the province, to act until the matter was decided between the Lords Proprietors and the King. Facilities for communicating and conferring together across the Atlantic were not what they are now, and it took several years to consider and come to an agreement. At last, in 1729, the second year of the reign of George the Second, they came to an agreement by which seven of the proprietors agreed to surrender to the Crown their title and interest in the province, which agreement was duly signed by the several Lords Proprietors, and which surrender was confirmed by an Act of Parliament. Robert Johnson was commissioned under the broad seal of England as Governor of the province, and his Excellency arrived in the province in December, 1730; and henceforth for more than fifty years the government of the province was administered under the Crown of England.

Lord Carteret (afterwards Lord Granville), the eighth Proprietor, resigned on the 17th September, 1744, all pretensions to the government and his eighth part of the right to the soil of Carolina. Commissioners were appointed on his part and on the part of the King to lay off his part to him, which they did next adjoining Virginia. In 1729, the province of Carolina was divided into North and South Carolina, and the boundaries between the two provinces were fixed by an order of the British Council.

Hardship and privation were doubtless the lot of the first settlers of the province, so numerous that all cannot even be imagined in this day and time. The number of the first emigrants were unknown, as no record of them has been kept. There could not have been many: "There could not, however, been many, for all of them together with provisions, arms and utensils requisite for their support, defence and comfort, in a country inhabited only by savages, were brought from England to Carolina in two vessels." (Ramsay's History of South Carolina, vol. 1, p. 1.) To increase the population was the general primary object. Think of it. A country of vast extent, and a vast wilderness roamed over by savages and wild animals; no roads or bridges across the rivers and other inland streams; nowhere to go; no means of communication with the rest of the world except by the stormy Atlantic, and to cross it took from one to two months. The first settlers were of necessity taught that valuable lesson, self-reliance. They were obliged to go to work building rude houses for habitation, also to cut down and clear up lands for cultivation, to make crops for another year. They were necessarily obliged to stay close together, by the laws of self-preservation, being surrounded by hostile and murderous savages. Wherever they were or at whatever they were engaged, they had to carry their arms, and be always on the lookout for an attack from their savage enemies. In Ramsay's History of South Carolina, pp. 18 and 19: "They were obliged to stand in a constant posture of defence. While one party was employed in raising their little habitations, another was always kept under arms to watch the

Indians. While they gathered oysters with one hand for subsistence, they were obliged to carry guns in the other for self-defence. The only fresh provisions they could procure were fish from the river or what game they could kill with their guns."

The young colonists being thus situated and necessarily confined within such narrow limits, were extremely anxious that other settlers should come in. The proprietary and regal governments were also anxious to the same end, and, therefore, they held out great inducements to the people in Europe and elsewhere to migrate to the new province of Carolina, by offering bounties in money and land to all (being Protestants) and especially poor Protestant families, to emigrate to Carolina. By the inducements held out to the people of the old world by various parties, many emigrants were induced to venture into the province from England, Scotland, Wales, France and Germany—transportation and supplies in many instances furnished. The several bodies of emigrants coming into the province at different times, from different countries, and other provinces or States, besides individual emigration or families from the more northern States, and the natural increase of the population, raised the number of the inhabitants from the mere handful that came in 1670, as hereinbefore stated, to 345,591 in 130 years, or in 1800. (Ramsay, 1 vol., p. 14.) During this period, 130 years, the government was first proprietary, then regal, and lastly from regal to a representative government, a "government by the people and for the people," under which we are now living and have lived for 124 years, and which the writer hopes will be perpetual for all time to come. From 1696 to 1730, there were not any additions made to the population of the province by the emigration to it of any large bodies of settlers, only by an occasional adventurer to the province from other provinces.

I have here given a general view of the State in its first settlement; the hardships and privations of its early inhabitants; its changes of government, &c., without going into details, as preliminary to the subject to be brought to view in the proposed history of this, Marion County.

CHAPTER II.

Location and Boundaries—Surface and Soil—Its Rivers and Lakes—Its Inland Creeks or Swamps.

SECTION I.

Marion County, as originally laid out, is in about latitude 34 north, and longiture 3 west from Washington. A line commencing at a stake on the North Carolina line, about one and a half miles from McInnis' Bridge over Little Pee Dee River, running a southwest course to and across the Great Pee Dee River to Lynch's Creek (river), dividing it from Marlborough County, on the east side of the Great Pee Dee, and from Darlington County, on the west side of said river. From the point where said line intersects Lynch's River—said Lynch's River is the line down to its confluence with the Great Pee Dee on its west side; thence down the said Great Pee Dee to its confluence with Little Pee Dee; thence up the Little Pee Dee to its confluence with Lumber River; thence up Lumber River to its intersection with the North and South Carolina line; thence up the said North Carolina line to the beginning stake above McInnis' Bridge. Its boundaries may be thus described: on the north by Marlborough County; on the northwest by Darlington County; on the west and southwest by Lynch's River; on the southwest and south by Great Pee Dee; on the east by Little Pee Dee and Lumber River; on the north and northeast by North Carolina.

Since the formation of Florence County, in 1888, Great Pee Dee forms its southern and southwestern boundary. It covers between nine and ten hundred square miles (estimated) now, or since the formation of Florence County. In length, from the northwest to southeast, it is about seventy miles—some of our people have to travel thirty-five or forty miles to reach the Court House. In breadth, from east and northeast to west and southwest, it is about thirty miles, on the line of the Atlantic Coast Line Railroad; from that line southward it gradually narrows to a point at the confluence of the two Pee Dees. The line between Marion and Marlborough is estimated at eighteen to twenty miles long, and on the North Carolina side at thirty-one or thirty-two miles (estimated). For political and county government purposes it is divided into fourteen (formerly eighteen) townships, as nearly equal in area as may be, having regard to creeks or swamps, public roads and other well known marks or division lines. Their names are Marion, Reaves, Hillsboro, Carmichael, Manning, Harlleesville, Bethea, Moody, Kirby, Wahee, Rowell, Legette, Britton's Neck and Woodberry. Of these, Marion, Reaves, Harlleesville and Manning are the most populous, and have the greatest amount of taxable property within them. These townships were laid out under the State Constitution of 1868, and Acts of the General Assembly made in pursuance thereof, and are yet continued under the Constitution of 1895, and subsequent legislation. The taxable property of these several townships, including the two graded schools in Marion and Manning Townships, is hereto appended, as shown from the County Auditor and County Treasurer's books for the year 1899. Also, the population of each of said townships:

	Taxes 1899.
Bethea Township	$209,701
Britton's Neck Township	99,659
Carmichael Township	282,910
Harlleesville Township	418,039
Hillsboro Township	287,542
Kirby Township	296,429
Legette Township	136,661
Manning Township	498,605
Marion Township	745,235
Moody Township	260,147
Reaves Township	434,107
Rowell Township	79,065
Wahee Township	315,371
Woodberry Township	18,298
	$4,081,768

The above shows the total taxable property for Marion County in the year 1899, exclusive of poll taxes. There are at least two thousand in the county, at one dollar each, $2,000.

Never before in the history of the State were townships or subdivisions of the counties made or laid out for civil purposes, but only for military and church purposes. Our people, from the earliest settlement of the State down to the present time, have been a military people, as the legislation of the State shows. From the very first, when the first Legislature, or Parliament as it was then called, met in Charleston (1674), they provided as best they could with their scanty means for the defence of the colony against the hostile incursions of the Indians. Although no Act or Acts of the provincial Legislature of the province are to be found until 1682—eight years after the first Legislature, in 1674—yet we are bound to infer that there were during that period some Act or Acts passed for the protection of the infant colony against hostile attacks from the bordering savages, which were hovering round and watching for an opportunity to successfully attack and destroy the pale-faced intruders from off the land, and whom the Indians thought to be enemies, and whose presence, in their estimation, boded no good to them. Hence we may infer that the attention of the first legislators was directed to the organization of the militia by appointing a Commander-in-Chief or General, Colonels, Captains, Lieutenants, &c., and for an enrolment of the militia. From that time on to the Revolution, numberless enactments of the Legislature were passed perfecting the organization of the militia of the former, as may be seen on examination of the Statutes at Large, by Dr. Thomas Cooper, under authority of the Legislature, and on down to 1841, when the compilation of Dr. Cooper was published, and even down to the present time, 1900. The tenth volume of said compilation is an index to the nine preceding volumes. The index to the militia laws of the province, and now the State, covers twenty pages. Our people have always manifested a martial spirit, not only on paper by legislation, but in actual service in times of war. I will not herein undertake to enumerate the valiant deeds of her sons in all the wars through which they have freely spilled their blood—in all of which, whether in the right or not, they believed they were right.

In 1832 and 1833, Acts were passed reorganizing the militia of the whole State. By those Acts the muster beats (townships) in every county were laid out, and a thorough reorganization of the militia of the State effected. Every muster beat formed a company, eight companies formed a regiment, four regiments formed a brigade, two brigades formed a division, and five divisions covered the State. For each division a Major General was elected, for each brigade a Brigadier General was elected, and for each regiment a Colonel, a Lieutenant Colonel and a Major were elected, and for each company a Captain and three Lieutenants were elected; also, a staff for each field officer was appointed. The field officers for divisions and brigades were elected by the Legislature. Colonels of regiments and all officers below him were elected by the people. An Adjutant was appointed for each regiment, and an Adjutant and Inspector General for the whole State was elected. The Governor for the time being was Commander-in-Chief of the militia of the whole State, including cavalry and artillery regiments. Brigade encampments were provided for in each of the two brigades, to be held for five and six days every two years. The brigade encampment for the 8th brigade, in which the regiment (32d) from Marion was, was held every two years on the west side of Great Pee Dee, near Godfrey's Ferry. At these brigade encampments the Governor and his staff; the Major General and his staff of this (4th) division; the Brigadier General and his staff; the Colonels of the eight regiments composing the 8th brigade; all the Adjutants of the several regiments; the Lieutenant Colonels and Majors; all the Captains and Lieutenants of all the companies in the brigade, were required to attend, each in his prescribed uniform, from Lieutenant up to Governor. These brigade encampments were for drill, exercise and inspection. The horses of the field officers were required to be richly caparisoned, according to rank, the higher the officer the richer the uniform and horse-trappings. They had their tents and camp equipage. The expense of all this was borne by each officer, so far as his uniform and horse-trappings were concerned. The transportation of all this equipage was in wagons (no railroads in those times).

The subdivisions of the district into company beats (townships) in Marion District were as follows: High Hill, Maiden

Down, Berry's Cross Roads and Harlleesville formed what was the upper battalion; Marion or Gilesboro, Britton's Neck, Big Swamp and Jeffreys formed the lower battalion. The companies in each beat were required to meet for "drill, exercise and parade" every two months, or six times in the year. In each battalion there had to be a battalion muster once a year, and a general muster of the regiment, composed of the two battalions, was required to be held once a year. Every ablebodied man in each beat was enrolled and required to do militia service, between the ages of eighteen and forty years. Many other requirements, not necessary to mention, were contained in the law. The organization was seemingly perfect—at least on paper—and continued to exist until the Confederate war. The offices, from highest to lowest, were eagerly sought—our people were ambitious to obtain military honors or distinction, notwithstanding they were mere empty titles. There was no money or pay in any of them, except the Adjutant and Inspector General of the State. Every officer equipped himself and served his country at his own expense. As a general rule, they took pride in their positions and showed off to best possible advantage—and especially the field officers. The writer recollects an illustrative remark made by the late John C. Bethea, in reference to the late Col. James R. Bethea, while he was Colonel of this (the 32d) regiment. He bought a fine horse for $200 and fine horse-trappings, a uniform for himself of fine material, trimmed in the manner prescribed by law for an officer of his rank. The total outfit cost him from $400 to $500. He was elected Colonel while a single man. He was also fond of hunting, and kept a kennel of hounds—five or six. Pending his colonelcy he married, and in due process of time his wife bore him a son, whom he named Jesse; the Colonel was very proud of his boy. There were four objects which the Colonel delighted in above all things else, to wit: his wife, Mary; his son, Jesse; his horse, Hughwarra, and his dogs—these were his pets and nearest his heart. John C. Bethea, a relative and neighbor of the Colonel, observing these idols of his, said: "It was difficult to tell which of the four the Colonel worshipped most." Said though, "he thought the boy, Jesse, was first, and his horse, Hughwarra, was next; and he did not know which came next, whether it was Mary or the dogs." This play of humor upon Col. Bethea illustrates the martial pride and spirit of the whole State, inclusive of Marion District. It permeated the whole people. The higher militia offices were sought most generally by men of means, able and willing to incur the concomitant expense. They were sometimes sought by men of small means, but such was the militia *mania* of the people and times, that men with little means would stake all they had or could procure for the sake of the empty honors consequent upon military titles and preferments. Some of the bitterest contests that ever occurred in Marion District for office, were inspired by this military spirit. This was much more commendable than the scramble of the present day, between scheming politicians for office because of the money there is in it. From 1833 to 1860, Marion District had her full share of the high positions in the military of the State. I will name such of them as are remembered since 1833: Before 1833, Marion had her Brigadier Generals, Thomas Godbold and William Woodberry; Brigadier General E. B. Wheeler, Brigadier General William Evans, Brigadier General Elly Godbold; Major General W. W. Harllee; Colonel Thomas Harllee, Colonel James R. Bethea, Colonel John J. George; Majors W. H. Moody, William Ford, D. J. Taylor, Samuel McPherson, R. G. Howard, James S. Rogers, John A. Breeden, Woodward Manning and D. W. Edwards. The Majors and Brigadier Generals went up by regular gradations from the lower positions of Major and Colonel. The Colonels rose from lower position to that of Colonel. All except Colonel Thomas Harllee, who was the first Colonel elected upon the reorganization of the militia under the Acts of 1832 and 1833. He was elected, as the writer has always understood, from the ranks. By those Acts, all previous commissions were vacated. The election was just after the heated struggle for and against Nullification. In Marion District, the parties for and against Nullification were about equal in strength. The Nullifiers carried the District by a narrow majority. In 1834, when the reorganization actually took place, the smouldering fires of the Nullification struggle were again lighted up and burned with their original fury. Each party put up their supposed strongest man for Colonel. The Nullifiers brought out Thomas Harllee, a modest and unassuming man—a man who had never asked for office, and never did afterwards (he had previously been elected a delegate to the Nullification Convention in 1832, unsought by him). *He was a man of great natural popularity, a magnetic man.* The Opposition or Union party brought out as their candidate for Colonel, John T. Ervin, then a resident citizen of Marion District, but afterwards moved to Darlington. He was a man of wealth, with winning and graceful manners, a magnetic man. They both had many strong and monied friends—either could command as much money as he wanted. These two champions entered the race—the most heated and exciting race, perhaps, the county has never had. The district was stirred from centre to its utmost limits; in every nook and corner, the aged and decrepit were hunted up and brought to the polls on the day of election. Doubtless, much money was spent by the respective parties during the campaign, and on the day of election. When the votes were counted, it was ascertained that Ervin had beaten Harllee *one vote*. The election was protested by Harllee's friends, and of course more than one illegal vote was found. The election was set aside and another election was ordered. The parties entered the second race with renewed determination and vigor, nothing left undone that was within human compass. The second election was held, and when the votes were counted, it was ascertained and so declared that Harllee had beaten Ervin by twenty-six votes. No protest was made, and Harllee became Colonel of the 32d Regiment. Colonel Thomas Harllee was not fitted for such an office—it was not congenial to his nature. He held the office, however, with credit to himself and satisfaction to his numerous friends for a few years, and resigned and returned to the pursuits of private life. He was of a retiring dispositon, modest and unassuming—the district honored itself in honoring him. He was older than the late General W. W. Harllee, and never married. In 1844 or 1845, he sold out at Harlleesville and went to Charleston, and there went into a factorage and commission business with a man named Carson, under the firm name of Carson & Harllee. He lived only a short while after this, and died universally loved and respected wherever he was known.

Among the Majors of the two battalions, the oldest by virtue of his seniority became Lieutenant Colonel. The writer may not have mentioned all the Colonels and Majors in Marion District since the reorganization in 1834—the omission arises not from intention, but from his want of memory—he has no record to look at.

Other heated contests were common in companies and battalions. The most noted of these was between Captain John J. George, of Berry's Cross Roads beat, and Captain H. B. Cook, of the Maiden Down beat, for Major of the upper battalion, which occurred by the promotion of Major James R. Bethea to the Colonency of the regiment. This was about 1842 or 1843. The first election, Captain Cook beat Captain George six votes. George protested the election, which was set aside and another election ordered. At the second election, George beat Cook seven votes. It was protested and set aside, and a third election ordered—at which Captain Cook declined to enter the race, and Captain Henry Rogers, of the High Hill beat, became the candidate. At this third election, Captain George was elected by a hundred majority. This contest, though confined to the upper battalion, was exciting, and a full vote was polled. Major George was finally promoted to the Colonelcy of the regiment, which he held for several years.

Enough has been said to show the martial spirit of our people even in times of peace, and it continues down to the present day—though it seems to the writer that the present organization of the militia of the State is not calculated to awaken and arouse and foster the martial ardor and spirit of the people as did the former organization of the State militia, and especially that of 1833 and 1834, which the writer thinks the best ever devised here or elsewhere for a citizen militia. As already stated, every able-bodied man from eighteen to forty years of age was enrolled. At each petty muster the roll was called, and defaulters marked and afterwards court martialed; and unless he had an excuse deemed sufficient by the court, he was fined, and if not paid an execution was issued against his property and lodged with the Sheriff; and if no property sufficient to satisfy the execution and costs, he could be arrested and put in jail, and kept there until he was thence discharged according to law. This provision of the law forced attendance, and there were few defaulters without sufficient excuse. Along in this line a ludicrous occurrence once happened at roll-call at Harlleesville on a petty muster occasion, which I will relate. During roll-call the name of Ephraim Taylor, the father of our late respectable fellow-citizen, Morgan Taylor, was called; he did not answer—was not present. Ephraim's brother, Thomas, was in line, and he (Thomas) hollered out, "He could not come, he had no breeches to wear." This produced a general laugh along the whole line.

Another incident, at the same muster ground, of a different character, had a sad ending. In July, 1842 or 1843, at a petty muster, one Yates Cottingham, the grand-father of our Henry C. Cottingham, at Dillon, was at the muster that day. The old gentleman, a harmless man, had one failing, and but one—he was passionately fond of liquor; if he had any other failing, the writer never heard of it. He went up to a cart or wagon where whiskey was to sell (for in that day any one might sell liquor with impunity, although against the law), several were standing round; old man Yates expressed a strong desire for some liquor, and said he could drink a quart, if he had it, without taking it from his head; whereupon some one in the crowd said to him, "Yates, if you will drink it I will pay for it." The whiskey was measured in a quart cup and handed out, the old gentleman took it and turned it up to his mouth, and there held it until he had drained the quart cup. After drinking it, he turned and walked off towards Colonel Thos. Harllee's store, a few steps off, walked up the steps and to a long board in the piazza; he lay down on the board and never rose again. In the afternoon the people broke up and left for their homes. About sunset, after the people had all gone, Colonel Harllee closed up the store and went up to his house, perhaps a hundred or more yards away. Colonel Harllee said when he closed his front door, he saw old man Yates lying there on the bench; did not go to him nor did he call him—that the old man was only tight and was asleep; that the old gentleman would wake up during the night and go home, only a mile or so away.

That he had seen him many times drunk and asleep upon that bench; that the old gentleman would wake up during the night and go home. Col. Harllee heard or knew no more till the next morning, when a negro went to his house, and told him the old man was dead. He immediately went down to the store and found the old man dead and rigid—so much so that they concluded that he died before night the evening before. An inquest was held and the facts found about as herein stated. The old man, Yates Cottingham, was the uncle by marriage of Colonel Harllee—Yates' wife was his aunt. It is supposed that there are not many now living who were there that day, hence the writer speaks of it as a sad occurrence at a petty muster in that day and time, and that the incident may be transmitted to posterity and have an influence for good upon the present and future generations.

SECTION II.

Its Surface and Soil, Its Rivers and Lakes, Its Inland Swamps.

The surface of Marion County is generally level. It is undulating gently in the upper portion of the county, and is undulating more or less on the rivers and inland swamps in every part of the county, which affords fall enough for proper and effective drainage, but not enough to produce damage to the cleared land by washing from excessive floods of rain. It is a well watered region. It has on its west side Great Pee Dee, its western boundary, and its tributary streams. It is intersected in its whole length by Little Pee Dee, where said river is not a boundary, and Lumber River is a boundary in part on the east. In the upper part of the county it has the two Reedy Creeks, Big and Little Reedy Creek. They both rise in Marlborough County, and running in a southeasterly direction come together just above the town of Latta, and make Buck Swamp, which continues to run the same course, or rather a little more east, for fifteen or more miles, and pours its waters into Little Pee Dee, near or just above what was formerly called Norton's Landing, and is now known by that name, though long since it has ceased to be a public landing. These creeks and Buck Swamp have several small tributaries laterally emptying themselves into them, to wit: Hannah Bethea's Mill Branch into the Big Creek; the Clark Mill Branch and Cana Branch into Little Reedy Creek; Gin House Branch and Peter's Branch into Buck Swamp; Robert's Mill Branch and Maiden Down, with its tributaries, into Buck Swamp, lower down. There are good lands on all these streams, and well watered by them. There are, perhaps, other small tributaries not herein mentioned. There are many tributaries to Little Pee Dee, on both sides, which water the sections through which they flow. Shoe Heel is one almost as large as Little Pee Dee; Hays' Swamp another; Maple Swamp another; Catfish, another inland swamp, has its rise in Marlborough County, and traverses for near forty miles the county from north to northwest to south and southeast, and empties into Great Pee Dee seventeen or eighteen miles below Marion C. H. It has some tributaries, not so many as Buck Swamp, to wit: E. J. Moody's Mill Creek, Smith's Swamp, Bull Swamp and others. Catfish waters a large portion of the country, and has some very fine lands (mostly sandy) watered by it and its tributaries.

Lumber River has a large tributary from the upper end of Marion, to wit: Bear Swamp, with its tributaries, Gaddy's Mill Creek, Cowper's Swamp and Alligator Swamp. It empties into Ashpole, and Ashpole empties into Lumber River just above Nichols' Depot, in the eastern portion of the county. There are two Reedy Creeks, with their tributaries, below Marion, coming together above Legett's Mill, emptying into Little Pee Dee. There is the Back Swamp, which breaks out of Little Pee Dee not far below Gilchrist's Bridge, and runs down somewhat parallel with the river for ten or fifteen miles and flows into the river again. This swamp may have been originally, or in the long past, the river itself. Reasons for this theory are only conjectural, not conclusive. Lower down is Cypress Creek, flowing into Little Pee Dee from the west. Upon all of these streams are good lands, with sufficient natural drainage, and aided by the many artificial ones, makes the lands adjacent most desirable for agricultural purposes. Nature has done as much for us in Marion County as perhaps any other county in the State, with as few drawbacks, and it remains for its people to avail themselves of these many natural advantages, and to improve upon them; and if the same progress and improvements are made for the next fifty years as has been made for the last fifty, the county will probably take the highest stand, agriculturally, among the many agricultural counties in the State. They are already vieing with each other for the highest distinction. An ambition to excel in agricultural life is everywhere apparent, not only here in Maron, but all over the State.

SECTION III.

Its Soil and Productions.

The soil of the county is varied, some parts sandy and light, other parts a dark gray soil or loam, others a dark brown soil, and some places black. The different soils here mentioned rest on a clay foundation, except the sandy or light soils, and even some of these are underlaid with clay. The different soils vary in thickness, as also in fertility, from one inch to six inches, and in some places even more than six inches, to wit: in swamp or bay lands. The lands of every description are more or less fertile, and respond more or less abundantly to the labor of man in plentiful harvests. The sandy or light lands lie mostly on Catfish and Little Pee Dee. The gray soil is mostly found on Buck Swamp, and its tributaries; and below Marion in all parts or neighborhoods after leaving Catfish and Little Pee Dee for two or three miles, also in the Mullins region, and in Hillsboro and Carmichael, after getting off from the river as above indicated. The dark brown soil is mostly near the Great Pee Dee River, and the Grove lands in Wahee Township. The black in swamps and bays. The agricultural productions of the county are varied—most or all of the cereals, such as corn, wheat, rye, oats, rice and barley. Vegetables in great abundance are successfully grown in every portion of the county, made for domestic use and some for shipment; of the latter, peas, beans, cabbage and strawberries are becoming, over and above domestic use, a money crop. Strawberries, in particular, are raised for shipment with reasonable profit, and are increasing in value every year. The cultivation of these vegetable crops for shipment gives needed employment to many that otherwise would be unemployed. Women and children find work to do, which they can perform, and thus become contributors to their own support, rather than consumers only. Irish and sweet potatoes are generally made mostly for domestic use, some for shipment. Watermelons and canteloupes grow well here, only for domestic use. The great money crops are cotton and tobacco. It is only within the last few years that tobacco has been grown here as a money crop, and its production has been rapidly increased, giving employment to hundreds that formerly were unemployed from July 1st to September in every year. In the cultivation, curing and grading tobacco, to which stemming has recently been added, hundreds in the county, every season, are busily employed. There are perhaps hundreds of tobacco barns in the county and others are now going up. At Mullins, there are three tobacco warehouses; at Nichols, one; at Marion, two; at Latta, two, and at Dillon, two, with prize houses at each point named, in number and size sufficient to accommodate the business needs of the trade. It is estimated that there were made and sold at these different tobacco warehouses in 1899 ten millions of pounds; many of the farmers shipped their tobacco to Danville, Va., Richmond, and other markets. Tobacco is fast becoming one of the staple crops of Marion County, and there is no telling to what proportions it may attain.

Tobacco has been raised as a money crop for export in this country, ever since the first settlement at Jamestown, Va., in 1607. Its cultivation in this State began only a few years ago, and still later in this, Marion County. It has so far, in this county, brought fairly good prices, which, together with the low price of cotton, stimulates its production. Most of the arable lands in the county are well adapted to its growth and maturity, and much of the land makes tobacco of a very fine quality, and it commands the highest prices. Its cultivation as a money crop has, perhaps, come to stay. The leading staple crop of the county is cotton—the lands are well adapted to its growth and maturity. Its production prior to 1793 was quite limited, not only in Marion County, but in the State, and we might say throughout the cotton belt.

From the first settlement of the State, in 1670, to 1793, for near one hundred and twenty-five years, the export of agricultural products was confined to rice and indigo. The rice crops were mostly raised on the coast or in tide-water lands, where it is yet the leading money crop. It was never raised to much extent in Marion County; only raised for domestic use. A few old rice plantations were in the lower part of the county, contiguous to the river. Rice was shipped thence to Charleston, the only market for it in the State, and thence shipped to Europe.

Cotton has been the chief money crop of the State for one hundred years or more. It succeeded indigo. Although cotton has been known for more than two thousand years, or since the days of Herodotus, who wrote that "Gossypium (cotton) grew in India which instead of seed produced wool" (Ramsay's, vol. 2, p. 119), yet through all ages from that remote period cotton was grown only for domestic use. Now it is an article of universal use, and it may be said, clothes the world. Of cotton, there are two kinds—the long staple, or black seed, and the short staple. The former is restricted as to production to confined limits, to the sea islands and parts adjacent. The lint is easily separated from the seed, and is used for manufacturing the finer classes of goods. The latter, or short staple cotton, grows well in all the cotton belt in this country, and is used in making the coarser fabrics, such as are in common use everywhere, and the lint is hard to separate from the seed, and can be done with facility only by the use of saw gins. The difficulty of separating the lint from the seed furnishes the reason it was not planted and cultivated as a money crop in South Carolina till about the first of the nineteenth century, or about one hundred years ago. The saw gin was invented in 1793, by Eli Whitney, a Connecticut school teacher, then teaching in Georgia. This invention, and its success in the purpose for which it was intended, suddenly gave a stimulus to the production of cotton in the South. "Whitney's invention has had more influence on the industry, wealth and political condition of this country than any other labor saving machine ever constructed in America." Previous to that time only small quantiites of cotton had been made in the South. Almost every one planted a little patch for domestic use, and that little was freed from the seed by the fingers. A grown hand could not pick more than a pound a day, and did well to pick that much. This was tedious, and so expensive that none but the rich could afford to buy it. (American History, by Montgomery, p. 196): "By the use of Whitney's machine, one man could clean in a single day a thousand pounds." Now, at this writing, 40,000 pounds may be cleaned of seed and packed and hooped for market in one day. The same author says: "In 1784, we had exported (from the cotton belt) eight bags, or about 3,000 pounds of cotton to Liverpool. The cotton was seized by the English custom officers on the ground that the United States could not have produced such a prodigious quantity, and that the captain of some vessel must have smuggled it from some other country. Ten years after Whitney had put his machine into operation (1803), we were exporting over 100,000 bags of cotton, or more than 40,000,000 pounds, and every year saw an enormous increase. The effect at home was equally marked. Hundreds of cotton mills for the manufacture of cotton cloth were built in New England. At the South, the raising of cotton became immensely profitable, and planters gave more and more land to it. Up to this period, many men in both sections of the country had deplored the holding of slaves. They had earnestly discussed how to rid the country of what was felt to be both an evil of itself and a danger to the nation. The invention of the cotton gin put a stop to the discussion in great measure; for now the Southern planters and Northern manufacturers of cotton both found it to their interest to keep the negro in bondage, since by his labor they were both rapidly growing rich. Few, even of the ablest minds, of that time realized what we all see to-day; that in the end free labor is cheaper, safer and better than any other." The author says: "To sum up, Whitney's great invention of 1793 did four things: (1) It stimulated the production of cotton and made it one of the leading industries of the country. (2) It increased our exports immensely. (3) It caused the building of great numbers of cotton mills at the North. (4) It made a large class, both North and South, interested in maintaining slave labor." In a note to the foregoing quotation, the author says: "Whitney received fifty thousand dollars for his invention from South Carolina, besides something from several other Southern States." Such was the impetus given to the production of cotton by the invention of Whitney, that, in the short space of two years, South Carolina, in 1795, exported to England cotton to the value of £1,109,653 (Ramsay's History of South Carolina, vol. II., p. 120). What an enormous increase! The author does not say how many bags or how many pounds were shipped, nor what it brought per pound—he only gives the total value, which is equivalent to $5,000,000. The increase in production must have been fabulous, or prices of the staple must have been fabulous. We suppose South Carolina must have gone into its production with a vim, as she bought the right to use it for $50,000, and "Munificently threw open its use and benefit to all its citizens." (Ramsay, II. vol., 121.) The invention of the Whitney saw gin was and is the greatest invention of modern times. From that time to this it has been the means of expanding our commerce to vast proportions. Has been the means not only of clothing the civilized world, but it gives remunerative employment to millions, and by which they obtain their daily bread. It overshadows every other invention of any age, ancient or modern. Many other inventions since Whitney's, of immense use, are now to be counted, but they sink into insignificance when compared with the result of the Whitney saw gin. Machinery for the manufacturing of cotton cloth soon followed, first in England, then in the United States, and they are now to be found in every civilized country of the world. It has enterprized and vitalized almost every other useful art which contributes to the happiness of man in every clime. Its production has increased from eight small bags crudely put up, exported previous to Whitney's invention, and which was seized by the custom house officials in Liverpool, on the ground that so much cotton could not have been made and exported in the United States, and, therefore, was smuggled from some other country, to the prodigious number of 11,000,000 bales much heavier than those seized as smuggled. Cotton has been called "King," and that is no misnomer. The writer will not now enter into a discussion of the question as to whether cotton is entitled to that high distinction to wear the title of "King."

Marion County, if she has not been *magna pars fui,* she has been *minime pars fui,* not in a disparaging sense of the latter term. She has done and is doing her full share in utilizing the benefits of Whitney's inventive brain. From a wilderness, say, 170 years ago, she has converted much of her territory to fertile fields, and including that part of her territory now in Florence County, she makes at least 50,000 bales of cotton.

The first great article of export from Carolina was rice, raised mostly on tidewater lands. The second was indigo. The first indigo seed was introduced into South Carolina by "Miss Eliza Lucas, the mother of Major General Charles Cotesworth Pinckney. Her father, George Lucas, Governor of Antigua (one of the West India Islands), observing her fondness for the vegetable world, frequently sent her tropical seeds and fruits to be planted for her amusement on his plantation at Wappoo (near Charleston). Among others he sent her some indigo seed as a subject of experiment. She planted it in March, 1741 or 1742; it was destroyed by frost. She repeated the experiment in April; this was cut down by a worm. Notwithstanding these discouragements, she persevered, and her third attempt was successful. Governor Lucas (her father), on hearing that the plant had seeded and ripened, sent from Montserrat a man by the name of Cromwell, who had been accustomed to the making of indigo, and engaged him at high wages to come to Carolina and let his daughter see the whole process for extracting the dye from the weed. This professed indigo maker built vats on the Wappoo Creek, and there made the first indigo that was formed in Carolina. It was but indifferent. Cromwell repented of his engagement as being likely to injure his own country, made a mystery of the business, and with the hope of deceiving, injured the process by throwing in too much lime. Miss Lucas watched him carefully, and also employed Mr. Deveaux to superintend his operations. Notwithstanding the duplicity of Cromwell, a knowledge of the process was obtained. Soon after Miss Lucas had completely succeeded in this useful project she married Charles Pinckney, and her father made a present of all the indigo on his plantation, the fruit of her industry, to her husband. The whole was saved for seed. Part was planted by the proprietor next year at Ashepoo, and the remainder given away to his friends in small quantities, for the same purpose. They all succeeded. From that time the culture of indigo was common, and in a year or two an article of export. Soon after the dye was successfully extracted from the cultivated plant, Mr. Cattel made a present to Mr. Pinckney of some wild indigo, which he had just discovered in the woods of Carolina. Experiments were instituted to ascertain its virtues. It proved to be capable of yielding good indigo, but was less productive than what had been imported. The attention of the planters was fixed on the latter. They urged its culture with so much industry and success, that in the year 1747 a considerable quantity of it was sent to England; which induced the merchants trading in Carolina to petition Parliament for a bounty on Carolina indigo * * * Accordingly, an Act of Parliament was passed in the year 1748 for allowing a bounty of six pence per pound on indigo raised in the British American plantations, and imported directly into Britain from the place of its growth. In consequence of this Act the planters applied themselves with double vigor and spirit to that article, and seemed to vie with each other who should bring the best kind and greatest quantity of it to market. Some years indeed elapsed before they found out the nice art of making it as good as the French; but every year they improved in the mode of preparing it and finally received great profit as the reward of their labors. While many of them doubled their capital every three or four years by planting indigo; they, in process of time, brought it to such a degree of perfection as not only to supply the mother country, but also to undersell the French at several European markets. It proved more really beneficial to Carolina than the mines of Mexico or Peru are or have been either to old or new Spain. In the year 1754, the export of indigo from the province amounted to 216,924 pounds, and shortly before the American Revolution it had arisen to 1,107,660 pounds. In the Revolutionary War it was less attended to than rice. In the year 1783, it again began to be more cultivated—2,051 casks of indigo was exported, and it continued to form a valuable export for some years; but large importations of it from the East Indies into England so lowered the price as to make it less profitable. Near the close of the eighteenth century it gave place to the cultivation of cotton." (Ramsay, II. vol., 118 and 119.) Eli Whitney's invention of the saw gin, in 1793, put a complete stop to the making of indigo—just so soon as the Whitney invention was introduced. From 1747 to 1793, many fortunes were made by raising and exporting indigo. It is true, that in this part of the province (what is now Marion County), other pursuits were remunerative. Stock raising was a money making business, and that, with indigo, during the period indicated, made many men rich—rich for that day and time and especially in the lower end of the county and on the Great Pee Dee River, where the range for stock was seemingly inexhaustible, and where the lands were well adapted to the production of indigo. As late as 1876, and since that time, the writer hereof, on a visit to old Ark Church, thirty-three miles below Marion Court House, in some old fields which had been thrown out on what was formerly General Woodberry's plantation, saw stalks of indigo growing about in those old fields four or five feet high, limbed out vigorously, so much so that it attracted his attention. On getting to the "Ark," where he met a crowd of the citizens, and during his stay he inquired of some one—he thinks William Woodberry, son of the old General Woodberry—how it was that there was so much indigo growing in those old fields. The answer was, that in former times the people planted much indigo in that region for market, and although its culture had been abandoned for years, yet it had perpetuated itself from year to year, and was there regarded as wild indigo. The writer has seen it in various places in the county and in Robeson County, N. C., adjoining Marion County, when a boy and even since manhood; but always supposed it to be wild indigo, until better informed by reading the early history of the State, and what he was told by Mr. William Woodberry in 1876 as to that then growing in that part of the county. In 1848, the writer bought the place on which he soon afterwards settled, in the fork of the two Reedy Creeks, about three miles above the town of Latta. Most of the lands that had been cleared had been thrown out; that one field, which it was said had been cleared more than a hundred years, not a stump in it, right in the Big Creek, and a point of the field ran down as it were into the creek, so that the creek was on three sides of the point. On that point the writer saw several stalks of indigo very luxurious in growth; the land was rich, and he then supposed it was wild indigo. The land was soon taken in and the indigo destroyed. He now supposes it was the cultivated indigo, and that it perpetuated itself as did that in Woodberry Township. Old Colonel Elisha Bethea, who was born and raised near by, informed the writer that the Murfies, from Great Pee Dee, of whom more will be said hereinafter, used to bring their stock out there on account of the reed range in those creeks every winter; that they penned them in that field above spoken of, and it was said marked 300 calves every spring. Old Colonel Elisha Bethea further said that his father, old Buck Swamp John Bethea, of whom more will be said hereafter, after he came there marked often 100 calves every spring. It is not difficult to infer that some of the previous owners of the place planted and raised indigo for market on those lands, and when abandoned and the land thrown out, the indigo sprang up every year, and thus perpetuated itself, and had continued to do so year after year till 1850, when the writer saw it there, as above set forth. It is certain that indigo was planted and cultivated as a money crop within the bounds of what was afterwards Marion District and is now Marion County. "Fortunes were made rapidly by its cultivation." (Gregg's History of the Old Cheraws, p. 112.) In a note appended, the same author (Gregg) says: "As an illustration of the value of the crop, it may be mentioned that General Harrington sent three four-horse wagon loads to Virginia, and with the proceeds of the sale bought from fifteen to twenty negroes." The same author (p. 112) says: "It brought at one time $4 to $5 per pound." In a note to the same he says: "The account sales of one cask of indigo shipped to London from the Pee Dee in 1766, shows that it commanded 2s. and 3d. per pound, amounting to £37 4s. and 3d., the bounty on it, £3 13s. and 4d.; the total expense of the shipment from Charleston £3 6s. and 4d."

Many people in the county continued to plant it for domestic use long after it was abandoned in 1793 as a money crop. Our mothers and great-grand-mothers were necessarily obliged to keep up its culture, with which to dye their thread which was woven into cloth to clothe their families with. In the latter part of the eighteenth and first part of the nineteenth centuries, there were no cotton mills; every family had to manufacture its own cloth, whether of wool or cotton. It was not until far in the nineteenth century that manufactured cloth could be bought because of its scarcity and because of its price, and a vast majority of our grand-mothers were thus forced to make their own cloth, and many of them preferred the domestic article to the manufactured. They were provided with their spinning wheels and cotton cards, their reels and warping bars, their slags and weaving harness and their looms. Every family was of necessity possessed of these implements for making cloth, and indigo blue was indispensible in coloring their thread, and hence every family had their annual patch of indigo, and all were familiar with the process of extracting the dye from the indigo weed. All were scientists to that extent. As a safeguard to this species of domestic property, the law of the land threw around it its protecting aegis. In 1823, our State Legislature passed an Act exempting from levy and sale under execution to every family certain property of the execution debtor, to wit: One pair of cards, one spinning wheel and loom, and other articles (I have not the Act before me), showing the necessity of these articles to every family. Many of our mothers did not give up the making of cloth for their family's use for many years after 1823, and a few not until after the Confederate War, and there may be some that yet continue to make their own homespun. Every mother had her indigo patch; it was as indispensible to her as was her vegetable garden. The writer's mother never did abandon the home industry of making cloth entirely, up to the time of her death, in 1868; she had her little indigo patch every year; she spun and wove her own cloth while she lived. The blockade of the war did not affect her in that regard—she had her wheel and cotton cards, loom, &c., and she knew how to use them. Being cut off from all commerce with the outside world for four years, many of our people were put to it to supply clothing to their families. They had no implements for making cloth for domestic use. To get cards was the greatest trouble—they could not be had except through blockade runners, and only at enormous prices. Few had any of the old spinning wheels or looms and other necessary implements for making cloth, and when they were procured or made, many did not know how to use them. These troubles of our people are better remembered by many now living than can be expressed. In the writer's mother's case, she was in no way nonplussed, as she had all the apparatus for making cloth, and knew how to use them. Such women were in demand during the war blockade. They could teach their less provident neighbor women how to make indigo and how to extract the dye; how to card and spin the cotton into thread, and how to dye it, not only with indigo blue but with other improvised dyes; how to warp it and put it through the slays and harness, and then how to weave it. We cannot now well see how the people could have gotten along without these domestic and provident mothers and grand-mothers. Bless their memory! Though many of them are dead, yet they live in recollection at least, "honored and sung." The prettiest dresses for ladies, the writer ever saw, were of homespun tastefully streaked and striped with domestic dye, and made in the style of the times, and worn by our mothers and daughters on public occasion, at church, &c., only. They were admired by all and appreciated by all. This latter sentiment was what, in the main, imparted to them beauty and high adornment. For the first thirty years or more of the nineteenth century, the housewives of the country made cloth to sell to the merchants, who in that day and time bought it, especially where it was paid for in trade. The writer's mother, when he was a boy, would make cloth, and carry it to Fair Bluff, Leesville and Lumberton, N. C., and sell it or barter it for other goods with the merchants. The prices paid for it were remunerative, depending on the quality of the cloth, ranging from 25 cents to $2 per yard—the latter price for the finest jeans cloth. In connection with this subject, the making and selling or bartering of home-made cloth, I will relate an incident which occurred when I was a boy, from the year 1828 to 1832. My mother and one Susan Rosier, a maiden lady rather above the marriageable age, a near neighbor and who went by the name of "Sookey Rosier," and though near neighbors, the State line divided them, my mother living on the North Carolina side of the line and Miss Rosier on the South Carolina side. Each made a piece of cloth for sale. They carried it to Fair Bluff, N. C., and offered and did sell it to a merchant doing business there, by the name of Colin McRae, a young man from Marlborough District. My mother sold hers, I think, at 30 cents per yard, and Miss Rosier was offered 40 cents per yard for hers. She said she could not take that for hers; the merchant said that was all he could give for it. She said she set her price on her cloth before she left home, and if she did not get that, she would carry it back home. McRae, the merchant, asked what was the price fixed; she replied, "A quarter and seven pence a yard," and if she did not get that she would carry it back home. McRae, the merchant, said to her, "Madam, I have offered you more than that—that 40 cents was more than 'a quarter and seven pence;'" to which she replied, "You can't fool me; if I do not get 'a quarter and seven pence' for it, I will carry it back home." My mother, standing by, said to her, "He has offered you more than that;" to which Miss Rosier replied, "I know better than that; I am not going to be fooled by any of you." Whereupon McRae said to her, "Well, I will give you 'a quarter and seven pence' a yard for your cloth rather than you shall carry it back home with you," which was her price. And she went home satisfied. A remarkable instance of gross ignorance (*crassa ignorantia*). "A quarter and seven pence" was only thirty-seven and a half cents. However, notwithstanding her gross ignorance, she knew how to make good cloth—she had been trained in that art. The family, not many years afterward, sold out and removed to some other parts, and so far as that family is concerned, the name has become extinct in Marion County. S. S. Rozier at Dillon, we think, is of a different family. The family of "Sookey" Rosier lived on Cowpen Swamp, which rises in North Carolina, and runs south and empties into Bear Swamp, just below Page's Mill, and just above Bear Swamp Baptist Church. The Rozier place was on the west side of said Cowpen Swamp, and was afterwards bought by Zany Rogers, an older brother of our respected fellow-citizen, Captain Robt. H. Rogers; and I suppose Zany Rogers died there. The writer has not seen the place in sixty-five or more years. It is a fine region in upper Marion, in Hillsboro Township, and was, when the writer last saw it, almost wholly undeveloped, but now, it is learned, that it is greatly developed and fast coming to the front.

SECTION IV.

Stock Raising.

From the first settlements in South Carolina down, even to the present time, a period of more than two hundred years, stock raising for market has been a profitable pursuit in all the State, and especially in the lower or eastern portions of the State, in which Marion County is located. Intersected as it is, by the Pee Dee and Lumber Rivers, with numerous inland creeks, swamps and bays, it afforded a splendid and extensive range for cattle and hogs. Luxurious bodies of reeds were in the swamps and low grounds of the three rivers, and in the inland swamps and bays of the county; the uncleared uplands everywhere covered with a heavy annual crop of nutritious grass in summer for cattle to browse upon; the swamps, and especially the river swamps, teeming with acorns, and the pine woods bearing every year quantities of mast—pure mast. The enterprising and sagacious settler quickly saw the money in it, and at once utilized the bounties of nature around him, which he could do without much labor. All he had to do was to watch and attend to his stocks of cattle and hogs, and feed them just enough to keep them gentle. The range was sufficient to maintain and fatten for market large droves of cattle and hogs with little or no expense or labor. In the first instance, he had to have a road to market, and the means of crossing rivers and other inland streams. With these facilities he was in easy reach of Charleston, his only market in the State. These facilities were not long in being procured and established. Bishop Gregg, in his history, page 76, says: "Stock raising was the most profitable business, and laid the foundation of fortunes which rapidly increased." Stock raising in Marion County, from its earliest settlement, was a common and very profitable business, and some of the largest fortunes made in the territory now embraced in this county were made by raising stock and carrying it to market. In Bishop Gregg's History, p. 110, he says: "The stock was driven to Charleston and other places on the coast, as well as to more distant markets. Large numbers of cattle were sent from Pee Dee to Philadelphia." The same author further says, on page 68: "Stock raising was the most profitable business, Charleston affording a good market for all that the industrious settlers could carry thither." This was about 1735. In a note to page 110, the same author says: "It is related of Malachi Murphy, who drove many beeves annually to Philadelphia, that on one occasion he was the owner of a famous beast called 'Blaze Face,' of great size and unusual sagacity, which he sold in Philadelphia. On the night of his return home to Pee Dee, and soon after his arrival he heard the low of 'Blaze Face.' He had escaped and followed close upon the track of his owner, swimming rivers and distancing all pursuers. Mr. Murphy drove him a second time to Philadelphia, and again he returned. Such a spirit was worthy of a better fate, but did not shield the bold rover. He was taken a third time to Philadelphia and came back no more. This was related to the author by the late John D. Witherspoon, of Society Hill." This same Malachi Murphy (Murfee, originally spelled), was one of the four brothers, who settled on the Great Pee Dee about 1735, at a place then called Sandy Bluff, afterwards known as Solomon's Landing, and is just above the railroad crossing, and of whom more may yet be said—became very wealthy from stock raising, and of whom Bishop Gregg, p. 72, says: "Of these, Malachi became the most wealthy. He is said to have given one hundred slaves to each of three sons. He died before the Revolution." He took up large bodies of land up and down the Pee Dee River. Malachi Murphy, senior, had also three daughters. It is naturally to be supposed that he provided for his daughters as well as for his sons, and if so, he was certainly the wealthiest man in the Pee Dee section of the province. We have no account that he made his money in any other way than by stock raising, yet we are bound to suppose that having as many slaves as he had, he employed them, or most of them, in other pursuits, perhaps in raising and preparing indigo for market, at that time, from 1747 to 1793, a lucrative business. He must have been an extraordinary man, full of pluck and energy, together with sound judgment. It was related to the writer fifty years ago, when he first settled in the fork of the two Reedy Creeks which make Buck Swamp, by Colonel Elisha Bethea, that in former times the Murfees (suppose Malachi) drove their stock to that place to raise them on the range in the two creeks and Buck Swamp, which was then very fine and is yet good. That Malachi Murfee would or did mark and trim as many as 300 calves there in a spring. And he further told the writer that his father (Buck Swamp John Bethea) in early times marked and trimmed as many as 100 calves of a spring, and raised a great many hogs in the swamp every year, and drove to Charleston every year a large drove of cattle and hogs. That the hog range kept good until the "big storm" of 1822, which blew down most of the oaks, and thus the acorn crop was destroyed or cut off. Old Buck Swamp John Bethea became wealthy, mostly from raising stock for market. He died in 1821. More will be said of the Murfees and Buck Swamp John Bethea hereafter.

We suppose stock raising was the business of most of the early settlers of the county, and especially in that part of Marion County called Britton's Neck. The settlers down in that region became wealthy, and outstripped the upper end of the county for near a hundred years in the pursuit and accumulation of wealth. When the writer can first remember, the wealth of the county was mostly in its lower end, and the upper end of the county was comparatively poor. These conditions are now and have been for the last half century reversed. The greater wealth is to be found in the upper end of the county. This state of things may be accounted for, in great part, because of the greater agricultural enterprise among its people, and because of the failing of the stock range in the lower end of the county; and because of the more numerous and better schools in the upper end, and the more general diffusion of knowledge among the people of that section; and lastly, the facilities of transportation and commerce and trade conditions are better, and have been so for a period of years, than in the lower section. For the last few years, however, the lower section of the county shows signs of upheaval in these respects, and ere long, if she progresses as she has for the last fifteen or twenty years, she may claim her place, her section of the county, to be equal with that of the northern section. She has lands of equal fertility, and all they need is intelligent and energetic culture, and to build up and foster her schools, public and private.

Pursuits, other than stock raising, and other than agricultural, have necessarily occupied the attention of the people of Marion County, more or less, for, perhaps, one hundred and sixty-five years, subordinate to and consequent upon those leading pursuits. Tradesmen of various kinds have sprung up amongst us. Blacksmiths, until within the last few years, were to be found in every community, were in great demand, and found constant and remunerative employment. They have been supplanted of late by imported work from outside the county. This imported work is better adapted to the uses of the farmer than the former domestic work, hence the blacksmith is driven out; and the same of the wheelwright—his occupation is gone; his work is superseded by imported productions along his line of work, and hence he is driven out. The house carpenter and brick mason holds his own; they yet find remunerative employment, and thereby make a living. The turpentine and lumber industry in the county are and have been very extensive. How many of them have succeeded in making money, is not known. It may be said only a few have made a fortune. While they have succeeded admirably in destroying our very extensive and beautiful pine forests to such an extent as to threaten, and in the near future to bring about a timber famine. To the writer it looks like vandalism. The face of the whole county will soon be denuded of timber, and neither the county as a section of the country nor its people will have anything to show for it. No valid consideration left in its place, no *quid pro quo*.

CHAPTER III.

SECTION I.

Its Educational, Political and Judicial History.

No scheme was ever inaugurated in South Carolina for the general education of the public, until it was provided for in the Constitution of 1868. The reconstruction was made and adopted, not by the intelligence of the State, but under the restraints of the sword by "carpet-baggers" and a few renegade whites, contemptuously called "scallawags," and ignorant negroes. Yet, with respect to education, it was quite an improvement upon the Constitutions of 1790 and 1865, neither of which fundamentally made any provision for the education of the masses. From the earliest times it seems to have been a matter of concern to establish and to have schools for the education of the masses. As early as 1710, the Provincial Legislature passed an Act to found such schools; and again in 1712, another Act was passed, extending and amplifying the system. In both of these Acts there was a provision that no one should be employed as a teacher or schoolmaster in the public schools of the province unless he belonged to the English or Episcopal Church. (Statutes at Large, vol. II., p. 342, and vol. II., p. 390.) Under each of these Acts, sixteen persons were named as Commissioners, every one of whom belonged to the Church of England, and who were empowered and directed to found said schools, to buy land, to erect school houses, to employ teachers, and so forth, and to be paid for out of the public treasury. These two Acts, or rather the latter one, remained the law for free schools in the province and the State till 1811, when another Act was passed. (V. Statutes at Large, p. 639.) The title of this Act is as follows: "An Act to establish free schools throughout the State." The first section of this Act reads as follows: "Be it enacted by the Honorable Senate and House of Representatives, now met and sitting in General Assembly, and by the authority of the same, That immediately after the passing of this Act, there shall be established in each election district within this State a number of free schools equal to the number of members which such district is entitled to send to the House of Representatives in the Legislature of the State." Under this Act, Marion District, a large district territorially, could only have two free schools within her borders, as she then was only entitled to two Representatives in the State Legislature; but the little parishes in the lower part of the State, some of them not having more than twenty-five or thirty voters in them, could have three free schools, as each of them, by the Constitution of 1790, was entitled to three Representatives in the State Legislature. (Constitution of 1790, I. vol. Statutes, p. 184, and amendments *sequens*.) Those parishes were the creation of the Church of England, under the proprietary and regal governments of the province, and their power and influence were retained by the Constitution of 1790. In the Convention of 1790, its members equaling the number of Senators and Representatives in the Legislature to which each parish and district or county was entitled under the Constitution of 1778, was 158 of the Church of England (Episcopal), and 68 belonged either to that church or to some other. Thus it is easy to see what influence dominated the Convention of 1790, that made the Constitution of that year. The Constitution of the United States and its amendments, made in 1787, and ratified by a Convention of South Carolina, May, 1788—Article I. of its amendments reads thus: "Congress shall make no law respecting an establishment of religion or prohibiting the free exercise thereof." This amendment made it necessary for South Carolina to disestablish her establishment of the Church of England. Article VIII. reads thus on that subject: "The free exercise and enjoyment of religious profession and worship without discrimination or preference shall forever hereafter be allowed within this State to all mankind; provided, that the liberty of conscience hereby declared shall not be so construed as to excuse acts of licentiousness, or justify practices inconsistent with the peace or safety of this State." (Vol. I., Statutes at Large, p. 191.) For near one hundred years the people of the State, including all Dissenters, had been taxed to buy lands (glebe) for Episcopal Churches to build churches in the different parishes, and to pay the rectors or preachers of that church their salaries.

Dissenters were deprived of the right to hold office and of the right to various employments within the State, while a member of the Church of England had the exclusive right by law to seek and to hold office, and to enter into and assume any employment whatever. The first step taken towards the establishment by law of the Church of England in the province of Carolina was in 1698, when an Act "to settle maintainance on a minister of the Church of England in Charlestown," was passed. This Act did not seem to awaken any suspicion and alarm among the Dissenters; but the precedent thus set paved the way for further Acts in favor of that church. In Dr. Ramsay's History of South Carolina (vol. 2, pp. 3 and 4), we find the following, and the author can do no better than to give it in his own words: "In the year 1704, when the white population of the province was between 5,000 and 6,000, when the Episcopalians had only one church in the province, and the Dissenters three in Charleston and one in the country, the former were so far favored as to obtain a legal establishment. Most of the proprietors and public officers of the province, and particularly the Governor, Sir Nathaniel Johnson, were zealously attached to the Church of England. Believing in the current creed of the times, that an established religion was essential to the support of civil government, they concerted measures for endowing the church of the mother country and advancing it in South Carolina to a legal prominence. Preparatory thereto they promoted the election of members of that church to a seat in the provincial Legislature, and succeeded by surprise so far as to obtain a majority. The recently elected members soon after they entered on their legislative functions took measures for perpetuating the power they had thus obtained; for they enacted a law which made it necessary for all persons thereafter chosen members of the House of Commons to conform to the religious worship of the Church of England, and to receive the sacrament of the Lord's Supper according to the rights and usages of that church. This Act passed the lower House by a majority of one vote. It virtually excluded from a seat in the Legislature all who were Dissenters, erected an aristocracy, and gave a monopoly of power to one sect though far from being a majority of the inhabitants.

The usual consequences followed. Animosities took place and spread in every direction. Moderate men of the favored church considered the law as impolitic and hostile to the prosperity of the province. Dissenters of all denominations made a common cause in endeavoring to obtain its repeal." They used every means within their power to obtain its repeal. They not only tried to get their own Legislature to repeal the obnoxious law, but they petitioned the Lords Proprietors, and failing there, they went to the House of Lords in Parliament, and finally to Queen Anne, but all to no purpose. The law remained of force until the Revolutionary War, and even down to the time of the Constitution of 1790. And it will be seen that that Constitution did not afford entire and complete relief; that through its parochial system of representation in the Senate and House of Representatives, the Episcopal Church has to a great extent controlled the legislation of the State from that time, 1790, all the way down to 1868; when by that Constitution the parish system was broken up and the State freed from the domination of the Episcopal Church. Though the white people of the State had no sympathy with the Convention that made the Constitution of 1868, yet many of its provisions are a great improvement upon the Constitution of 1790—notably the destruction of the parish system; the emancipation of married women as to their rights of property, and perhaps other improvements not necessary to mention. Such legislation betokens superlative arrogance and self-assumption. It was oppressive and a tyranny. When the government prop is knocked from under them they fall. They have had to stand upon their merits for the last hundred years, and they have dwindled down to a small element in the body politic, their members are a mere handful when compared with the members of the various dissenting denominations. All honor, however, to many of the noble people who were and are identified with that branch of God's church. Their position of undue influence in the State's affairs was the result of early environments, and its best and most conservative followers recognized the injustice of the system in vogue before the war, and were willing that it should be abolished, as it was inimical to the best interests of their church.

Under the Act of 1811, $300 was appropriated to each school. Under the Act of 1814, $37,000 was appropriated for the free public schools, and continued from year to year up to the war. How much of this $37,000 appropriated for free schools since 1814 was apportioned to Marion District is unknown, as no permanent record thereof seems to have been kept by the Commissioners. If any was kept, it is inaccessible—it was, however, a mere pittance, and did but little good. The four counties—Beaufort, Colleton, Charleston and Georgetown—having most of the parishes within their borders, and having the greater representation in the Legislature, hence they shared most of the appropriation, while the rest of the State got but little of it, and were little benefited by it. It was provided in said Act of 1811, that all should send to said schools, rich and poor alike, free of expense; and further, that if the money appropriated was insufficient to pay for all attending said schools, a preference should be given to the poor, or the children of indigent parents. The result was that the poor in many instances did not attend those schools, parents were not able to furnish books and clothing for their children; and many of them being poor and ignorant themselves, were careless and indifferent about educating their children. Whether there were any public schools, public or private, in Liberty or Marion District prior to the beginning of the nineteenth century, we cannot say, nor can we with certainty say there were schools in Marion District before 1814. We can only say there was legislation to that end as to free public schools, but whether our people availed themselves of it or not, we can only conjecture. We, however, suppose their little "old field" schools were opened for short terms in some neighborhoods, with teachers possibly competent to teach the rudimentary branches of an education, and which each succeeding generation has improved upon during the whole of the nineteenth century, and has brought it up to its present high standard; and as evidence thereof, the log cabin school houses with, in many instances, only a dirt floor, have been succeeded by large and commodious school buildings, and in some places brick buildings, in almost every section of the county, and they are all well patronized; and we have teachers fully competent to instruct and to prepare the youth of both sexes for college. The progress in educational enterprise has kept pace with the progress in material and industrial enterprise. Much might be said in amplifying the contrast between our conditions educationally now and one hundred years ago, but space will not permit and the field is too large. In 1814, the Marion Academy Society, at Marion Court House, was given the power of escheators and also its perquisites up to $2,000. It seems it had been incorporated before, but the writer has not been able to find the Act of incorporation, and hence he cannot give the names of the corporators. A school was established there under its provisions, and has been kept up with more or less success from that time to the present. At that school many men of the past generation who have been prominent in the affairs of the county and State, and in the industrial walks of life, were educated, and it exerted an influence for good all over the county. The writer can only mention a few of the many who went there, and got the education and training that fitted them for life and its activities and responsibilities. All of them have passed off the stage of life. Hugh Godbold, General William Evans, Dr. Charles Godbold, Asa Godbold, General E. B. Wheeler, Colonel Levi Legette, C. D. Evans, Colonel D. S. Harllee, Dr. Robert Harllee, General W. W. Harllee, John C. Bethea, Elisha C. Bethea, W. B. Rowell, General Elly Godbold, Nathan Evans, General N. G. Evans, Reddin W. Smith, all men of mark and character, and a host of others younger, all of whom got their training and early impressions from that school, taught by such men as the Rev. Joseph F. Travis, Rev. Tracy R. Walsh, and W. H. Witherow. We are not yet done harvesting from the seeds planted and cultivated in that school; its fruits are still being gathered. And it has been succeeded by one of the best and most successful graded schools, perhaps, in the State. A large and commodious brick building has been erected, and the school established under the laws prescribing the manner of regulating such schools. It is largely patronized, and has a strong corps of teachers, and is equal, perhaps, in its curriculum and course of study to one of our colleges a hundred years ago. There a young man or woman is prepared to enter the Freshman Class in the South Carolina College, or any other college—quite an advance on the schools of the eighteenth century.

Not many years after this—perhaps in the thirties—an academy was built at Harlleesville, and a school established there, and for more than sixty years a good school has been kept up at that point. It has told upon the intelligence and high standing of that community. Its teachers have generally been men of learning, character and scholarly ability. It has awakened a spirit of industrial pursuits and industrial arts, perhaps, unsurpassed anywhere. It has moulded character—high character—in both male and female. It has energized its citizens and made them the peer of the citizens of any community. They have no cause to blush when they say, "I am from Little Rock, Marion County." They are proud of their citizenship and homes. The school was founded by Herod Stackhouse, Isaac Stackhouse, Allen Gaddy, Cade Bethea, John Braddy, and last, but not least, by Colonel Thomas Harllee—though he never married and had no children to send to school, yet he was liberal to any call for the betterment of his people, the uplifting of them and putting them upon a higher plane in civilized life. His hand and heart were ever open to any such enterprise. Those substantial and open-hearted men have been succeeded by a better informed community, their efforts have been crowned with success far beyond expectation. They are all gone to their reward, but their works survive, and yet remain to bless and build up generations yet to come.

The next high school, in the order of time, in the county was Pine Hill Academy, near Sellers, on the Florence Railroad, built in 1841. It was erected by Major James Haselden, John C. Ellerbe, Isham Watson, Henry Berry, James Tart and the Widow Moses Mace, and perhaps others. The first teacher in that school was John H. McDonald, a brother of D. J. McDonald, who afterwards merchandised at Marion for years, and who married a Miss Crawford, a sister of the late W. H. Crawford. The next teacher at Pine Hill was the late A. Q. McDuffie, Esq., who taught there several years and had a large and flourishing school. The writer hereof, in 1842, went to school there to John H. McDonald, and in 1844, to A. Q. McDuffie. The latter was his last teacher. The old academy yet stands as a monument to the enterprising men who built and established it, still dispensing its influence for good to the third and fourth generations of the men who founded it. It has done much for the community in which it is located, and has furnished many men and women who have been prominent in the affairs of the State and county, and among them our Governor, the late William H. Ellerbe.

The next high school, in the order of time, was Hofwyl Academy. It was built in 1853, and was burned by an incendiary in 1855. This academy was built and the school established there by Captain E. C. Bethea, Colonel James R. Bethea, John R. Bethea, Rev. Samuel J. Bethea, Stephen Fore, Captain C. J. Fladger, Joseph D. Bass and W. W. Sellers—all of whom have passed "over the river of death" except the writer. After the burning in 1855, another and better building was erected on the same spot by the same parties, at once, and the school reopened with competent teachers, and was very popular in its day. It attracted patronage from beyond the limits of its immediate neighborhood. From below Marion Court House, the late W. F. Richardson sent two of his daughters up there— Miss Augusta, who afterwards married James H. Godbold, and who now resides about fifteen miles below Marion, and Miss Alice, who afterwards became the second wife of John H. Hamer, of Little Rock. She is now dead, leaving five children surviving her, Ed. Hamer, of Little Rock, and Dr. Tristram B. Hamer, now in the far West, Mrs. Neill A. Berry, of Sellers, and Mrs. Lawrence Manning, in the Little Rock section, and John H., now about twenty-one years old. Also, G. W. Woodberry, of Britton's Neck, sent his daughter, Julia, to the Hofwyl School. She afterwards, I think, married a Mr. Brown, and is yet living, and reared a nice family. James Jenkins sent his daughter, Ella, his only child, to Hofwyl. She afterwards married B. F. Davis, below Marion; they raised a large family of sons and daughters; the mother died some years ago. Miss Mary E. Watson, daughter of the late James Watson, near Marion, went up to the Hofwyl School. She afterwards married Jessie H. Gibson, below Marion; both are now living, and have raised a family of sons and daughters ready to take their places in society, and to fill them with respectability and success, as their parents have done. Dr. F. M. Monroe went to school there, perhaps the last school he ever attended before reading medicine; he boarded at Captain James W. Bass', together with one Willie Sheckelford, son of John B. Sheckelford, below Marion. He came to a sad end in North Carolina. Dr. Monroe is now well known in the county as one of our best physicians, a respectable and prominent citizen of hich character and a Christian gentleman. From the Little Pee Dee section there were H. M. Stackhouse, now a very prominent citizen of Marlborough County, lately its State Senator, a progressive and successful farmer, well posted in the concerns of his county, State and nation. Also, his brother, Robert E. Stackhouse, who died while a young man a few years afterwards—very promising. J. G. Haselden, who died a few days ago, near Sellers, attended the Hofwyl School, perhaps the last school to which he ever went. He became a prominent and useful citizen, a progressive farmer, raised a family of four children, three sons and a daughter, all of whom survive him. He represented his county one term in the State Legislature. His sons are the Hon. J. D. Haselden, L. M. Haselden and L. B. Haselden, now in Clemson College; and his daughter, Carrie Haselden. His son, L. M. Haselden, took a literary course in the South Carolina College, and another in the law department of that institution, from which he graduated with highly distinguished honors. F. M. Godbold also went to school at Hofwyl at the same time that J. G. Haselden was there. They both boarded at the writer's house. Soon after leaving the Hofwyl School, F. M. Godbold went to the Cokesbury School, in Abbeville District, where he soon married a Miss Vance, had several children as the fruit of the marriage, when his wife died. He afterwards married another Miss Vance, a cousin of his former wife, and they now together live three miles above Marion Court House. He is now farming. Others from the Little Pee Dee section came to the Hofwyl School, to wit: John C. Clark and his brother, R. K. Clark. John C. seemed at school to be a cowardly boy; other boys in school, it was said, imposed on him more than ordinary among school boys, and he would not assert himself so much as to resent it. Afterwards, when the war commenced, John Calvin Clark volunteered in Company L, 8th regiment South Carolina troops, and was Second Lieutenant in that company. In one of the many battles in which that regiment was engaged, John Calvin, for some reason or other, was in command of his company, and was killed in advance of his command, while calling on his men to follow him, telling them to *come on,* not to go on. Thus a truly brave boy fell at the head of his command, in a position that tried men's souls; while others of his command, perhaps, in school, and then in battle with him, if they did not exactly show the "white feather," did not manifest the bravery of schoolboy days. All honor to the true, manly courage of John Calvin Clark. R. K. Clark, a brother, who went to school at Hofwyl, grew up to manhood and went into the war towards the last of it, and from the writer's knowledge of him was equally as brave in the performance of duty as was his brother, John Calvin. After the war he married Miss Nannie Stackhouse, a daughter of the then late Wesley Stackhouse. He went to farming, which he continued to follow with some success till 1876, when he was nominated in that memorable campaign for Clerk of the Court, and was elected. He served four years in that position with credit, and made an excellent Clerk. At the end of his term he was a candidate for renomination, but failed to get the nomination, and J. Albert Smith was nominated and elected. For reasons which it is not necessary to state, he failed to get the nomination. It was not that he had not made an efficient Clerk. He was soon afterwards appointed County Treasurer, which position he filled with great credit and to the entire satisfaction of his people. He held it for a year or two, and resigned it and moved upon his plantation in upper Marion, where he successfully farmed until 1888, when he died, leaving his widow, who has since died, and three sons and four daughters, of whom Luther Clark, now in Marion, is one, and Hon. W. A. Brown's wife is another. Do not know of the remaining five.

There is another batch of Hofwyl pupils from abroad that I must notice. They were from Marlborough County, viz: Joseph Steed, who died at old man Philip Bethea's, where he boarded while going to school. There was, also, R. Y. Henegan, son of ex-Governor B. K. Henegan, Henry Baggett and Peter Baggett. R. Y. Henegan is yet living, near Florence, and is one of the many good citizens of that county, and prominent in his community; married, I think, a Miss Waring, a highly respectable family. The writer saw Bob a few days ago, with his daughter, a beautiful girl, at Florence. Time is snowing on the head of R. Y. Henegan, the Hofwyl schoolboy. The two Baggett boys, Henry and Peter, the writer knows nothing of. Thinks Henry Baggett went to Charleston after the war, and went into, perhaps, a factorage and commission business, under the firm name of J. H. Baggett & Co. I think, Peter Baggett was killed or died in the war. All these from abroad showed the popularity of the school. Such was its efficiency that it drew to it the favor and patronage, not only of its neighborhood, but others from a distance. The first teacher in that school was William McDuffie, a cousin of the late A. Q. McDuffie, Esq. The next was Harris Covington, a very scholarly man and a good teacher. He had his sister with him one or two years of his three or four years. The next was the late W. J. McKerall, for two years. He had his sister with him the last year, 1859. Harris Covington succeeded W. J. McKerall in 1860 and 1861. During 1861, Covington volunteered in C. J. Fladger's company, was First Lieutenant in that company and went off to the war. Then followed Archibald McGrogan, a young man from North Carolina, who continued the school till 1865. Next was Colonel J. W. St. Clair, who continued till 1868. John C. Sellers taught the school in 1869. John A. Kelly taught there in 1870, and Philip Y. Bethea, in 1871, which was the last school taught at Hofwyl. The community became bare of children—so much so, that it was deemed proper to close it, and no school has been taught there since. The school made its mark there, and for about twenty years was the pride of the community, and did much in building up the neighborhood. It turned out many boys and girls that made our best citizens, surpassed nowhere. The writer, it is to be hoped, will be pardoned for having said so much about the Hofwyl School. He was *magna pars fui,* one of its founders, and one of its constant promoters and patrons. All his children except the youngest were educated at that celebrated school, the foundation was laid there. Two of his sons graduates, one at the South Carolina College, the other at

Wofford College, both citizens among you, and stand in character and attainments the peers of any. He has a right to talk, to feel proud, to be grateful, that he lived when he did and was enabled to accomplish the little he did for his community and for his own children. Let the coming generation do as well—yea, better—for their posterity than did the Hofwyl community in their day and time. So may it be.

The next high school, in chronological order, was the Mullins School, established some twenty-five or thirty years ago. This school for several of its first years did not prosper or succeed well, owing to dissensions and some ill feeling among its patrons; but time with its soothing and harmonizing influence has hushed its bickerings, and mollified and wiped out the former ill feeling that existed among its patrons, and it now presents a harmonious and united front, and they have a school there now of high standing and equal, perhaps, to any in the county, well attended, popular and doing a good work, a great deal for that community. They have a corps of competent teachers, and no reason why it should not continue to prosper and grow in its power for good. It, with other influences for the uplifting of the community, is making the Mullins people a great people, a moral and Christian community. The school, the two Sunday Schools there, one Baptist, the other Methodist, the two churches, Baptist and Methodist, under the hand of the highest supreme power, have achieved a revolution for good, so much so, that the most sanguine among them twenty-five years ago never dreamed or thought of. The writer will not draw and present the contrast any further. It is easier to conceive it than to tell it.

The next high school, in the order of time, as remembered, was at Dalcho, near the Catfish Baptist Church, in Bethea Township. It is a part of the old Hofwyl Academy. It was established some twelve or fifteen years ago, has been and is yet a very flourishing school. It is well attended, they have kept the best of teachers there and it is telling for good on that whole community, raising the standard of morality, widening the circle of social life, elevating and inspiring Christian character and Christian endeavor. The school has much to do with it.

The next school (high school), in chronological order, is the Dothan School, another part of the old Hofwyl Academy. It, too, is a school of high standing, well patronized; they employ and keep the best teachers in it. Some years ago the promoters and principal patrons built a large and commodious academy building there at a cost of $1,600. A year or two after it was constructed, they had some public school exercises there one night in very warm weather—they had no fire except lighted lamps; it was burned down about 1 or 2 o'clock, together with books, seats, blackboards and other school furniture, a total loss with no insurance. It was and is yet believed that it was an incendiary fire. Not daunted thereby, they went back into the old school house near by, a house less pretentious and less commodious, and continued the school, and have kept it up to the present day. It is in a good community. They are doing a good work there, training and fitting the youth of that place for higher education, if they desire it, and to take their respective places in future society and in future business life.

The next high school, in the order of time, is the Hopewell School, situated in the "Fork" neighborhood, between Little Pee Dee and Buck Swamp. This school the writer has heard is a first class school. Its chief promoters and patrons are D. D. McDuffie, Dempsy Lewis, T. B. Rogers, Ferdinand Rogers, David S. Edwards and perhaps others. It is well attended, has a strong corps of teachers, is doing much in building up and improving the community, and giving to its people a higher and better tone, inspiring their local pride and promotive of good morals.

Another high school established about the same time was the Gaddy School, located near or at Gaddy's Mills, in Hillsboro Township. Its chief patrons are Captain R. H. Rogers, Joseph R. Oliver, Barfield Rogers, T. B. Hays, W. S. Lupo, A. B. Carmichael, Samuel T. Gaddy, B. F. Edwards and perhaps others. They keep a good school there, employ good teachers, and are doing much for building up and elevating their community. The school, together with the two churches, Piney Grove (Baptist) and Union (Methodist), are improving the morals of that community, and qualifying and fitting the present rising generation for a favorable entrance upon life's arena.

The next high school, in the order of time, is the school at Latta. A school had been established there, or just above the town, some years before the Florence Railroad was constructed, not very pretentious, but was said to be a good country school. It, too, was a part of old Hofwyl. When a town sprang up (Latta), it seemed to quicken and inspire an ambition for better and larger school facilities, and hence the establishment of the present popular high school. The writer does not know whether it is called "a graded school" or not, he has since learned that it is a graded school. It, however, does not matter—the school is established and has a high character. They have a good building, well attended, and the school is in high favor with the town and surrounding country. They have a first class teacher at its head, who is sowing the seeds of knowledge there that will spring up and bear good fruit in that community years to come in the rising and coming generation. They are touching chords that will vibrate not only in future years but in and through eternity. That school, with the three churches (Methodist, Baptist and Presbyterian) located there, will, in the near future, if they continue to nurse them and strengthen them, elevate that people far above present conceptions, and future generations will echo with the praises of their ancestry. It being a growing town, it is difficult to say who are the leaders in their school enterprise; therefore, the writer will ascribe it to all the good citizens of that place.

At Dillon, on the Florence Railroad, is a most excellent graded school. It is only of few years standing, and already will compare favorably with any like school, perhaps, in the State. The town of Dillon itself is only eleven or twelve years of age. It has now from 800 to 1,000 inhabitants. It is a very enterprising place, located in a fine section of the county, and surrounded on all sides by one of the best farming regions in the State, its prospects for becoming a city in the near future are bright and cheering. They have started right. They have established a fine graded school, and built a commodious brick building for the school. The school is largely attended. They keep a corps of good teachers, who are doing a good work, giving entire satisfaction to the patrons. The session now closing for the present scholastic year, 1899 and

1900, discloses the fact that the enrolment of scholars in the white school for this session is 180. What will it be ten years hence? Doubled, if the town continues to grow as it has in the last ten years.

All the foregoing schools are and were, including Hofwyl, which no longer exists, first class schools, largely attended, ran for the whole year and from year to year. At any one of them a boy could be prepared to enter the Freshman Class in any college in the State, and even higher than that—to enter the Sophomore Class, as was done in one instance at least.

It will be noted that all these first class schools are in the upper end of the county—Marion is in the centre—and goes to verify what the writer said in a former part of this book, contrasting the progress made by the upper end as compared with that of the lower end. It is there said that one of the causes was that the upper end had more and better schools than in the lower end. The writer would not say a word in disparagement of the people in the lower end, but he is merely stating what is apparent to any one—a fact, the truth. Far from it, the writer hopes that by stating this particular fact, the people of the lower end will be stirred up to follow the example set them by their fellow-citizens of upper Marion. Thus far, in pursuing this subject, the educational history of the county, the writer has only referred to the high schools, some near a hundred years old, others a half century and more, and others for a shorter period. It is not to be inferred from this that there are and were not other schools all over the county of less note, and which have done a great deal of good, and are still doing so. Those schools may be said to be auxiliaries to the higher schools. They are not only to be found in upper Marion, but in lower Marion as well, and they are as useful in their limited sphere as are the higher schools. In them, limited in duration and in calibre as they are, they teach and instruct the youth attending them in the fundamentals of an education. In them the foundation is laid for the superstructure. If they go no further, that much is effected, and by self-effort and self-improvement, such may become useful and intelligent citizens, otherwise the foundation thus laid gets no higher and the recipient relapses back to his natural condition, and his ambition, if he had any, is dwarfed, and he never rises any higher than "a hewer of wood and a drawer of water," lives in the very lowest walks of life unnoticed and dies in the same way. The common schools have been in the county from the earliest times—at least, from the writer's earliest recollection. He went to school in this county (upper Marion), on the road leading from Harlleesville to Fair Bluff, N. C., between Bear Swamp and the North Carolina line, in 1832, near seventy years ago, and he remembers seeing the late General Woodberry pass there. He was electioneering for Sheriff. He stopped at the school house and talked with the teacher, Daniel McLellan, an uncle of our present County Auditor, F. T. McLellan, also to some young men there, scholars and voters, to wit: the late Elgat Horn, Daniel Horn and Alexander Johnson, all now dead. General Woodberry was in fine humor and adapted himself to his then surroundings. He was elected Sheriff and went into office in April, 1833, and served his term, four years, as the Sheriff's office shows. By the then Constitution (1790), he was not eligible for a second term, until the expiration of another four years. That was the only time the writer ever saw General Woodberry, a man of great versatility and of marked character. More may be said about General Woodberry in a subsequent part of this book. That school house was built of logs, about twenty feet long and sixteen feet wide, a dirt floor, a dirt chimney. One log was cut out of the back end so as to give light; the log below that had some holes bored in it with a two-inch auger. Large pegs, a foot or more long, were driven into those auger holes, and then a plank laid on those pegs and nailed to them. This served for our writing desks. That schol building and its appliances were about such as were, in that day and time, used in many or most of the schools in the country. The means of the people were limited, and the spirit of progress and improvement was equally as limited. Occasionally you would find a man of more elevated views, as to schools, but standing alone, he could do nothing to improve the prevailing conditions. It was not until about 1840, that signs of a better day, in these respects, began to show themselves, and from that time to the present signs of improvement have been multiplying and spreading, until the whole country is permeated with a spirit of education, even in sections of the county where, heretofore, great indifference was manifested. A wholesome sentiment on the subject is prevailing. The fundamental provisions in the Constitution of 1868 and of 1895 have been and are potent factors in kindling and energizing a strong and healthy sentiment in favor of education. The Legislature has wisely and liberally constructed the machinery for public education. The laws foster and care for the common schools; the common schools evolute the higher schools, and by an ascending gradation the higher schools evolute colleges. There is no excuse now, nor can there be any, for illiteracy and ignorance among our people, white and colored. Both races, under the law, share equally in the liberal appropriations made by the Legislature for school purposes, and the funds provided seem to be equitably distributed. School funds raised by taxation and in some other forms, for the year 1899, and distributed under the law to the schools of Marion County, amounted to $11,502.13. In this amount is included $1,500 poll tax; this last item is an estimate, as the precise amount could not be arrived at. The county is laid off into fifty-five school districts and schools established in each school district. They are designated by numbers from one to fifty-five. According to the report of the County Superintendent of Education, there were enrolled in the different schools through the year 7,638 attending those schools, white and colored. The school funds collected and paid out as above stated are nearly one-third as much as was the appropriation for the public schools each year for the whole State a year from 1811 to the war. And besides the amount thus collected and paid to the public schools of the county, in which rich and poor share alike, in many neighborhoods there are pay schools, that are kept up from year to year; or after the public funds are exhausted, the schools are continued on and paid for by the private funds of the patrons. Thus it is easy to be seen how much greater are the educational advantages of to-day than they were fifty years ago and before that time. Few there were a half century ago that had an opportunity to "rub their backs against a college wall." Now our college graduates may be counted by the dozens. Our young men and women, too, are fitted to fill any station in life, public or private. What improvement! Rapid strides are making towards the goal of universal knowledge. In the next generation there will be found few who cannot read and write.

Graduates of Colleges.

From Davidson College, N. C.

A. Q. McDuffie (dead).
William McDuffie (dead).
D. W. Bethea (dead).
D. W. Bethea, Jr.

From Chapel Hill, N. C.

Gewood Berry, 1846 (dead).
J. Hamilton Evans, 1854 (dead).
John H. Hamer, 1856.
Missouri R. Hamer.
William D. Carmichael, Jr.

From Greenville University, S. C.

Rev. Joseph H. Dew, 1890.
W. C. Allen, 1900.

From the Citadel Academy, Charleston, S. C.

Lieutenant Colonel W. P. Shooter, 1859 (dead).
A. J. Howard, J. T. Coleman, 1886.
A. G. Singletary, 1890.
A. S. Manning, 1892.
S. W. Reaves, 1895.
T. W. Carmichael, 1896.
Herbert Rogers, 1900.

Wofford College, S. C.

There have been ninety matriculates from Marion County. The following graduated:

Bond E. Chreitzburg, 1869.
Marcus Stackhouse, 1871.
James T. Brown, William A. Brown, Wilbur F. Smith, 1874.
W. J. Montgomery, 1875.
Henry M. Wilcox, T. B. Stackhouse, 1880.

Philip B. Sellers, 1882.
W. M. Lester, 1884.
J. E. Ellerbe, J. Marion Rogers, 1887.
E. P. Taylor, 1888.
R. L. Rogers, 1889.
J. G. Baker, 1890.
P. P. Bethea, 1892.
P. H. Edwards, W. M. Ellerbe, 1894.
J. R. Rogers, B. B. Sellers, W. F. Stackhouse, 1895.
C. H. Barber, C. C. Leitner, L. B. Smith, 1896.
T. L. Manning, W. B. Evans, 1897.
C. H. Leitner, 1898.
G. E. Edwards, 1899.

South Carolina College.

From this College I have no report. My son, John C. Sellers, wrote to Professor R. Means Davis, who was a classmate of his in that College, for a report. The Professor replied that he would do so, but has never sent it. My grand-son, Wallace D. Sellers, who was in the South Carolina College in 1899-1900, procured a catalogue of the Euphradian Society up to 1859, which shows the matriculates from Marion County, but who and how many of them graduated is not shown, as follows: Robert H. Gregg, 1808; Ezra M. Gregg, 1817; Jeremiah Brown, 1819; Charles Godbold, 1819; D. Reese Gregg, 1825; John H. Latta, 1826; C. D. Evans, 1836; G. Cooper Gregg, 1836; O. S. Gregg, 1838; R. G. Howard, 1848; Evander Gregg, 1837; E. M. Davis, 1848; R. C. McIntyre, 1851; G. M. Fairlee, 1853; J. C. McClenaghan, 1854; D. McIntyre, 1854; S. A. Gregg, 1855; W. J. Singletary, 1856; Walter Gregg, 1857; C. E. Gregg, 1859. Those of the above who it is certainly known graduated are: C. D. Evans, R. G. Howard, R. C. McIntyre, G. M. Fairlee, W. J. Singletary. Those graduating there since the war are: John C. Sellers, Hezekiah Johnson, Robert P. Hamer, Jr., W. M. Hamer, P. A. Wilcox, J. S. McLucas, Walter H. Wells, Luther M. Haselden, Henry Mullins.

Wake Forrest, N. C.

The graduates from this College, as ascertained, are: Dr. C.

T. Ford, Rev. Rufus Ford, Julian Dew, Baker Ford, Lila Cottingham.

The graduates from Marion in female colleges are equally as numerous as in the male departments. I have not the list of them. In education, Marion County will rank as high, according to her population, as any county in the State. She is now fully awake to her interest in that regard.

Political and Judicial History of Marion County.

The first divisions of the territory of the Province (State) were for purposes of "Church and State," to wit: parishes, counties and districts, partly political for representation in the Legislature, and partly judicial for the establishment of courts of justice for the convenience of the people and the administration of law, in conformity to the then existing laws of England, and for military purposes and the protection of the colonists against the hostile incursions of the Indians.

As early as 1682, twelve years after the first settlement of the province, it was deemed advisable to "divide the province, or rather the settled portions of it, into counties, and accordingly there were laid out, Berkeley, embracing Charleston and the space around the capital, extended from Seewee (Santee) on the north to Stono Creek on the south. Beyond this to the northward was Craven County, and to the southward Colleton County, all extending thirty-five miles from the coast. Shortly after this Carteret County was added." Subsequently Craven County was greatly extended, so as to embrace all the territory between Santee River and the Wateree up to the North Carolina province line; thence down the dividing line between North and South Carolina to the Atlantic Ocean, and thence the seacoast to the mouth of Santee River. At the time of this division, Craven County was much the largest of any of these counties, and was so sparsely settled that it was not particularly noticed. But twenty years afterward it was described as being pretty well inhabited, the Huguenots having settled on the Santee. About which time it sent two members to the General Assembly of the province. It took its name from William, Earl of Craven, one of the Lords Proprietors, and long retained it. (Gregg's History of the Old Cheraws, pp. 31 and 32.) The same author says: "The first parochial organization in Craven County was under the Act of Assembly of 1706, commonly called the Church Acts, passed for the establishment of religious worship according to the Church of England and for erecting churches. It divided the province into ten parishes, of which Craven County constituted one, by the name of St. James Santee." (Statutes at Large, vol. II., p. 330.) The Circuit or District Court Act of 1768 divided the provinces into seven judicial districts, to wit: Charleston, Beaufort, Orangeburg, Georgetown, Camden, Cheraw and Ninety-Six. (Statutes at Large, vol. VII., p. 199, section II.) Each one of those districts covered three or more counties. By the Act of 1785, those districts were divided into counties. One district, Georgetown, was divided into four counties—Winyaw, Williamsburg, Kingston and Liberty. (Act of 1785, Statutes at Large, vol. IV., pp. 662 and 663, section I.) By the County Court Act of 1785 (vol. VII., Statutes at Large, p. 211), County Courts were established with limited jurisdiction. Courts to be held every three months in each county where established, by seven Justices of the Peace, or a majority of them. The Circuit Courts for our county (Liberty) were held in Georgetown. No County Court was ever held in any of the counties composing the Georgetown District. The 11th section of the County Court Act of 1785, appoints and empowers the County Court Judges to select sites for court houses and jails of the several counties, and to contract for and build the same. As no County Court was established in Liberty County (now Marion), no court house or jail was built therein. No one had any power to contract for and to build, hence it was not until years afterwards that a court house and jail were erected in Liberty or Marion County. The Constitution of 1778 fixed the representation for the district east of the Wateree at two members in the Legislature, which so continued until the Constitution of 1790. The district east of the Wateree included Lancaster, Kershaw, Sumter, Clarendon, Darlington, Chesterfield, Marlborough, Marion, Williamsburg, Kingston and Georgetown, and also included the parishes of St. James Santee, Prince George Winyaw, All Saints, Prince Frederic and St. David, to each of which Representatives were assigned as follows: St. James Santee, six; to Prince George Winyaw, four; to All Saints, two; to Prince Frederic, six, and to St. David, six—making twenty-four Representatives from the parishes named as within the district east of the Wateree; while the whole district, exclusive of the said parishes, had only ten Representatives. (I. vol., Statutes at Large, p. 140, 13th section.) By the said Constitution of 1778, each parish and election district throughout the State elected a Senator. No provision was made for the district east of the Wateree, except Prince George Winyaw and All Saints. They together could elect a Senator. There were some few other exceptions. No Senator or Representative was eligible unless he professed the Protestant religion. There is no evidence of any change in the law or Constitution in regard to representation until the Constitution of 1790 was made and adopted, and which became necessary in order to make our Constitution conform to the Constitution of the United States.

The Act of 1785 had created or established Liberty County (now Marion). The Constitution of 1790 recognized it, so far as to assign to it two Representatives in the House, and assigned to it and Kingston (Horry) together one Senator. Whilst all the little parishes in the low country each had three Representatives, except All Saints, which had but one, and Charleston, including St. Philip and St. Michael, had fifteen Representatives. Such counties as Williamsburg, Marlborough, Chesterfield, Darlington, Chester, Fairfield, Richland, Lancaster, Kershaw, Claremont, Clarendon, Union, Spartanburg and Greenville had only two Representatives each. In the Senate, Charleston (including St. Philip and St. Michael), had two Senators, each and every parish had a Senator, while Winyaw and Williamsburg together had one, Liberty and Kingston one, Marlborough, Chesterfield and Darlington together had two Senators. Fairfield, Richland and Chester together had one. Lancaster and Kershaw together had one. Claremont and Clarendon together had one. (See article I., sections 3 and 7, Constitution 1790, I. vol., Statutes at Large, pp. 184, 185 and 186.) Article XI. reads as follows: "No Convention of the people shall be called unless by the concurrence of two-thirds of both branches of the whole representation. No part of this Constitution shall be altered, unless a bill to alter the same shall have been read three times in the House of Representatives and three times in the Senate, and agreed to by two-thirds of both branches of the whole representation; neither shall any alteration take place until the bill so agreed to be published three months previous to a new election for members of the House of Representatives; and if the alteration proposed by the Legislature shall be agreed to in the first session by two-thirds of the whole representation in both branches of the Legislature after the same shall have been read three times on three several days in each House, then, and not otherwise, the same shall become a part of the Constitution." (I. Vol., Statutes at Large, page 192.)

The Constitution of 1790 was of force, and the people of the State lived under it, without alteration or amendment, for twenty years. The amendment ratified in December, 1808, which did not go into effect till 1810, made some change in the basis of representation. Population and taxation were the basis, and if there was a deficiency in either population or taxation, or of both, there was a provision for some representation, as will be seen. And representation varied every ten years, according to the population as shown by the census every tenth year, which was provided for, and the taxation for each decade might show. The amendment of December, 1808, was as follows: "The House of Representatives shall consist of one hundred and twenty-four members, to be apportioned among the several election districts of the State according to the number of white inhabitants contained and the amount of all taxes raised by the Legislature, whether direct or indirect or of whatever species paid in each, deducting therefrom all taxes paid on account of property held in any other district, and adding thereto all taxes elsewhere paid on account of property held in such district. An enumeration of the white inhabitants for this purpose shall be made in the year one thousand eight hundred and nine, and in the course of every tenth year thereafter, in such manner as shall be by law directed; and Representatives shall be assigned to the different districts in the above mentioned proportion by Act of the Legislature at the session immediately succeeding the above enumeration.

"If the enumeration herein directed should not be made in the course of the year appointed for the purpose by these amendments, it shall be the duty of the Governor to have it effected as soon thereafter as shall be practicable.

"In assigning Representatives to the several districts of the State, the Legislature shall allow one Representative for every sixty-second part of the whole number of white inhabitants in the State; and one Representative also for every sixty-second part of the whole taxes raised by the Legislature of the State. The Legislature shall further allow for such fractions of the sixty-second part of the white inhabitants of the State, and of the sixty-second part of the taxes raised by the Legislature of the State, as when added together they form a unit.

"In every apportionment of Representatives under these amendments, which shall take place after the first apportionment, the amount of taxes shall be estimated from the average of the ten preceding years; but the first apportionment shall be founded upon the tax of the preceding year, excluding from the amount thereof the whole produce of the tax on sales at public auction.

"If, in the apportionment of Representatives under these amendments, any elective district shall appear not to be entitled, from its population and its taxes, to a Representative, such election district shall, nevertheless, send one Representative; and if there should still be a deficiency of the number of Representatives required by these amendments, such deficiency shall be supplied by assigning Representatives to those election districts having the largest surplus fraction, whether those fractions consist of a combination of population and taxes, or of population or of taxes separately, until the number of one hundred and twenty-four members be provided.

"No apportionment under these amendments shall be construed to take effect in any manner, until the general election which shall succeed such apportionment.

"The election districts for members of the House of Representatives shall be and remain as heretofore established.

"The Senate shall be composed of one member from each election district as now established for the election of members of the House of Representatives, except the district formed by the parishes of St. Philip and St. Michael, to which shall be allowed two Senators as heretofore."

Such was the Constitution of 1790 and amendments of 1808, made with reference to representation in the State Legislature. Taking into consideration the time when it was framed and the circumstances which brought it about, the persons composing the Convention and the historic facts antecedent thereto and leading up to it, the most casual reader cannot fail to see its purpose. It was to secure and perpetuate the power of those who had dominated the State from 1704 up to that time (1790) a period of, say, eighty-five years. It is well understood by those who have read and kept up with the history of the State, to what party allusion is here made. The Church of England, the Episcopal Church, is meant. In 1704, that church secured legal establishment. (Vol. II., Statutes at Large, page 236, *et sequens*.)

The caption of the Act is, "An Act for the establishment of religious worship in the provinces according to the Church of England, and for the erecting of churches for the public worship of God, and also for the maintenance of ministers and the building convenient houses for them." There are thirty-five sections of the said Act, covering ten pages. The said several sections cannot here be given in full, for the want of space. It was, however, provided that lands should be taken up or bought upon which to erect the churches and for church-yards, cemeteries, out-houses, &c., and to have built thereon the church and all necessary out-buildings, together with convenient and commodious parsonages and chapels of ease, and to employ ministers or rectors at such salary as might be agreed on, and all to be paid for out of the public treasury. At this time there was only one Church (of England), St. Philip, in Charleston, and the same provisions were made for all such Episcopal Churches that might be erected in future; though at that time, and, perhaps, at all times since, the Episcopalians were greatly in the minority, yet they managed to hold to this advantage, laying off parishes till the Revolution, and erecting churches to the number of twenty-four, mostly on the coast or in the low country. (Ramsay, II. vol., p. 5.) Thus the Episcopal Church gained political ascendancy and held it till the

Revolution or until 1790, having all their church expenses paid by the public, besides other advantages, their religion costing them but little comparatively, while dissenting denominations had to build and maintain their own churches or do without them, if too poor to buy and build and support their own ministers—a most iniquitous arrangement, unjust and tyrannical. Many amendments to the law were subsequently made, but none to weaken their political power and advantage. They held it with a death-like grip. The Revolutionary War brought no change in the law. It may have diminished some of its rigors, but no repeal of the obnoxious law. No disposition was manifested after the Revolutionary War ended to repeal the unequal and unjust laws. There is a considerable difference between "skinning and being skinned." They had been extracting money from the people to support their religion for more than one hundred years—very pleasant to them, but very unpleasant to the taxpayers. The Constitution of the United States was made in 1787, and was submitted to the States for ratification or rejection. The Convention of South Carolina called for the purpose ratified and adopted the United States Constitution in May, 1788. Having ratified that instrument, she of necessity was obliged to put herself in line with it. Hence a Convention of the State to frame another Constitution was called, and the Constitution of June, 1790, was the result. South Carolina was in a dilemma. She had either to give up her legislation in favor of the Episcopal Church—so dear to the hearts of its adherents, though iniquitous and oppressive to all other classes—or remain out of the Union formed by the Constitution of the United States. She chose between the two evils the former, and retained the latter position which she had assumed in 1788, by ratifying the Constitution of the United States. Being shorn of her discriminating power, hitherto exercised in favor of the Episcopal Church, and to the discomfort and injury of all dissenting denominations, she determined to hold on to the political power she had obtained and wielded for near a century. She had the Convention of 1790 called to frame a new Constitution, and in that to perpetuate her political power and influence, through parochial representation. The low county parishes dominated that Convention. Its membership was composed of delegates from each parish and district as provided for representation in the Legislature under the Constitution of 1778, as hereinbefore stated. They outnumbered all other delegations at least two to one; they could and did make a Constitution just such as suited the views of the low country, and thereby in the fundamental law of the State perpetuated their power and influence in the Legislature. They fixed representation so as thus, under the forms of law, to control and influence the legislation of the State. The Constitution of 1790 in this regard is "iron bound" and "rock ribbed." No future Convention of the people could be called, or any amendment or alteration made in that Constitution, unless it was by bill, introduced in the Legislature, and read three times, on three several days, in both the Senate and House of Representatives, and upon its second and third readings, must be agreed to by two-thirds of the whole representation in each house. And this is not all. The proposed alteration or amendment, after being thus agreed to, must be published previous to a new election for members of the House of Representatives; and if the alteration proposed by the Legislature shall be agreed to in their first session by two-thirds of the whole representation in each branch of the Legislature, after the same shall have been read on three several days in each house, then, and not otherwise, the same shall become a part of this Constitution. Thus it is seen that the low country, by means of their parochial representation, secured to themselves the power to control the legislation of the State, and also to prevent any legislation which looked to the curtailment of their power. They kept and maintained their power until after the war between the States, the Confederate War. First by the Constitution of 1865, made under the auspices of Governor B. F. Perry, and under the proclamation of Andrew Johnson, then President of the United States. The Constitution of 1865 broke up the parish system of the low country and destroyed its power, so long enjoyed and originally so oppressively exercised. We were not allowed to live under the Constitution of 1865. A maddened and fanatical Congress of the United States disagreed with Andrew Johnson, the President, as to his method of restoring the late seceding States to proper relations to the Union, and passed the Reconstruction Acts of Congress, putting the South under a military government. The President, Andrew Johnson, vetoed those Acts, and the Congress readopted and passed them over his veto by a two-thirds vote of that body. Those Acts divided the Southern States into military divisions, and put a commanding general over each division, to carry out at the point of the bayonet, if necessary, those Acts. Many among us remember too well the hardships and rigors of the enforcement of those Acts. Burdensome and annoying as they were, our people, with a fortitude unequaled, bore them all in mute obedience to the "powers that be" until they were consummated by the Constitution of 1868—a Constitution made by carpetbaggers, scalawags and negroes. That Constitution, odious as it was, and with it at the time the intelligence of the State had no sympathy, yet it did, as did the Constitution of 1865, strike a deathblow to parochial representation in the Legislature of the State, and thereby the citizens everywhere in the State were relieved of the parish system, and its unjust and discriminating power—in the interest of a favored class, and against all others equally concerned and equally entitled to a fair share of the benefits of legislation.

It may be asked, why so much space is given to the discussion of this subject? It is answered by saying that it affected the people of Marion County to her injury. Marion County was, and has been all the time, an integral part of the State, and whatever affected the State, affected her *pro tanto*. To some few people, the revelations here made are news, and to many they are already familiar. Such political machinery can never again set itself up in South Carolina. The schoolmaster is, and has been, abroad in the land. The people are too intelligent, and know and appreciate their rights too well ever to allow of such again.

The first legislative notice taken of Marion District by that name is to be found in the Act of 1798, 1st section, 7th vol. Statutes at Large, page 283, by which the name was changed from Liberty County to Marion District, on page 284 of the said 7th vol. of the Statutes at Large. In the said first section of the said Act are the following words: "One other district to be named Marion District, to comprehend the county now called Liberty County, according to its present limits." This section of the Act changes the name in some instances, as well as also the counties, to be called districts for the whole State. By section II. of the said Act, Courts were established in the following words: "That in each of the said districts by this Act established, there shall be held, from and after the first day of January, in the year of our Lord one thousand eight hundred, by one or more of the Associates Judges of this State for the time being, and at such places as shall be appointed by or under this Act, a Court of Sessions, and a Court of Common Pleas, to possess and exercise, respectively, each Court, in its respective district, the same power and jurisdiction now held and exercised by the several Circuit or District Courts of this State in their respective districts, and shall sit at the times following, that is to say: for Marion District, at Marion Court House, on the first Mondays in March and October in every year." The fourth section of the Act distributed the Courts into circuits. "And that the several Courts of Marion District, Darlington District, Marlborough District, Chesterfield District, Fairfield District, Kershaw District, and Sumter District, shall form one other Circuit, to be named the Northern Circuit, and that the Solicitor of the said Northern Circuit shall attend each of the Courts of the said Northern Circuit, and prosecute therein, respectively, all suits and prosecutions on behalf of the State, according to the usage and custom of the existing Circuit Courts of the State." These Courts were made Courts of record, juries provided for, Clerks and Sheriffs to be appointed, and their duties prescribed. The County Courts after 1st January, 1800, to have no jurisdiction, original or appellate, of any causes, civil or criminal, and after 1800, all causes, civil or criminal, pending in the County Courts were transferred to the Court of Sessions or Common Pleas, as the case might be, to the Courts hereby established. It was further enacted, "That from and after the first day of January, one thousand eight hundred, the several Courts of General Sessions of the Peace, Oyer and Terminer, Assize and General Gaol Delivery and of Common Pleas, now established and held in this State, shall be, and the same are hereby, forever abolished; and that all suits, appeals and indictments then depending in any of the said Courts (except the Court of Charleston District, in which the business already commenced shall be continued in the District of Charleston, established by this Act), shall be transferred in the manner following, that is to say: when any district shall contain two or more of the districts established by this Act, the suits, appeals and indictments depending in the superior Courts of law of such districts shall be transferred to that new district established by this Act, within such district, wherein the defendant or appellee resides; and where there are two or more defendants or appellees residing in different new districts within the limits of such district, then to such one of the said new districts as the plaintiff or appellor shall direct, and where more of the defendants or appellees reside in such district, then to such of the new district therein as the plaintiff or appellant shall direct; and all indictments to the new district where the offence was committed, and all the said suits and indictments shall be continued, proceeded on and determined in the respective Courts to which they shall be transferred as aforesaid; and all records of the said Superior Courts hereby abolished shall be transferred to the nearest district established by this Act, there to be kept and continued."

(Section XI. of Act of 1798, 7th vol. Statutes at Large, an Act to es*ablish an uniform and more convenient system of judicature.) Section XXIII. of said Act appoints Commissioners to locate court houses and gaols, and to superintend building the same, and for Marion District, the following named gentlemen were appointed: "Colonel John McRae, Dr. Thomas Wickham, John Ford, John Orr, Benjamin Harrelson, James Crawford, Thomas Harley and James Rie; that they be, and are hereby, appointed Commissioners for the purpose of fixing on a convenient and central location whereon to establish and build a court house and gaol in the District of Marion, and to superintend the building of the same." A very good Commission as is supposed. The men appointed set about the work they were appointed to perform. They only had the year 1799 to perform the work assigned them—the time was too short, with the facilities then to be had for such undertakings. By the terms of the Act, the first Court was to be held first Monday in March, 1800. Tradition informs us, that the first Court held in the county, and under the terms of this Act, was held about two miles below the present court house, just across Smith Swamp, on the plantation owned and occupied by Colonel Hugh Giles, afterwards owned and occupied by the late Samuel Stevenson, and now by W. W. Baker. The very spot where the house stood was shown the writer by Mr. Stevenson while he owned it. The new court house then in course of construction was not in condition to be used; therefore, this little log house, probably sixteen feet square, was improvised for holding the first Court ever held in the county. Philip Bethea, the father-in-law of the writer, told him often that he attended the first Court held. It is supposed that the court house was completed during the year—that court house is still in existence and in a good state of preservation. It was located somewhere on the public square not far from where the present court house stands—a wooden building. It was occupied as a court house until 1823, when it was replaced by a brick building, which was built that year and was located about the place where the new fire-proof building, lately constructed for the Clerk's office and for the Probate Judge now stands. The records in their offices are deemed most important, and hence this latter building, made fire-proof for the protection and safe preservation of those records. The court house erected in 1823 of brick was of good material, but was found to be too small and contracted for convenience, and not adapted to the requirements of the growing county; hence the present commodious and substantial brick building was constructed in 1853 and 1854, and it is well adapted to the purposes for which it was built, except that the entrance door should have been placed in the northern end of the building instead of the eastern side, where it is. The throng coming in and going out where it now is, produces noise and confusion—very often to the disturbance of the Court, to attorneys, parties and witnesses engaged. Furthermore, a cold east wind, when the door is open, comes rushing in from the door, to the great discomfort and annoyance of all within, and necessitates keeping the door closed, which it is almost impossible to do, as persons are frequently passing in and out, and the opening and closing the door every minute causes confusion. If the entrance was at the north end, much or all of these objections would be obviated.

As already stated, the first court house was a wooden structure, which, doubtless, did very well as an initiatory court house, but was soon found to be insufficient for the purposes of its erection, and the powers that then were, had the brick one of 1823 built. Who the contractor was for the one built in 1800, we have not been able to find out. The contractor for the one built in 1823 was Enos Tart, a prominent man in his day. The court house of 1800 was sold or given to the late Thomas Evans, Sr., who moved it out of the public square and reconstructed it on his own lot, and converted it into a commodious dwelling. The house still stands on said lot, and now belongs to the Hon. T. C. Moody, and is occupied at this writing by said Moody and Stephen G. Miles and family. The house, though one hundred years old, seems to be perfectly sound and still in a good state of preservation. The writer supposes it was built of the very best material; if it had not been it would have gone to decay before this time. It was built before the day of turpentine vandalism. It is an evident fact, that the timber from which the turpentine has been extracted soon rots—its very life is taken from it. It is like taking the blood from the animal, man included; life is destroyed, and soon goes into a state of decay. One hundred years ago the uses of turpentine had not been discovered, nor had the cupidity of man been excited to the destruction of our pine forests.

The court house of 1823 remained intact for about ten years after the new or present court house was erected. The rooms below were rented by the Commissioners of Public Buildings to lawyers and others for offices. They were occupied as such until the year of 1861. Who the Commissioners were is not now remembered. In the winter of 1864 and 1865, one O. R. Smith, claiming to be a quartermaster, was stationed at Marion, and was there during the year 1864 and 1865, till the surrender of General Lee. During the latter part of his stay he claimed to have bought for $5,000 (Confederate money) the old court house (of 1823), upon condition that he was to remove it. He took down the building and shipped off the brick, iron and stone steps, &c., that he did not sell to individuals in town. What he received for it is unknown, whether anything or not. Whether he ever paid for it or not, and to whom paid, is also unknown. There has never been any accounting for its proceeds, or any accounting called for, by the Court or other authority. In the minds of many it has been doubted whether he ever paid anything for it. There was no one authorized to sell it. No Commissioners of Public Buildings were then in existence. If there were any, they were disorganized and had no power to sell. The old court house sold was built by the State and not by the county, hence it belonged to the State and not to the county. The Legislature alone had the power to sell or to authorize and direct its sale, which the Legislature had not done. The pressure of the war was upon us. Civil affairs were not much looked after or attended to. Everything in relation to civil affairs were much disorganized, it may be said were disintegrated. Confusion and disorder prevailed everywhere. Matters more vital occupied our attention—our very existence was threatened. Some there were who took advantage of the conditions then existing; they were on the make, and were not very scrupulous as to how they made it. We do not say that this old court house transaction was one of those cases, but we do say that the circumstances surrounding and attending the transaction are enough at least to excite a reasonable suspicion. The said O. R. Smith, the so-called Confederate Quartermaster, left just when Sherman's raid passed through the upper end of the county, and carried two wagons loaded with corn and bacon, which he had not gathered as an official, but took it from the warehouse at Marion, and which had been gathered and stored there by the Post Quartermaster's Department, the writer hereof being in charge of it, and who remonstrated with said Smith about it. Smith's reply to him was with an oath, "That you, corn, bacon and all, would be in the hands of the Yankees in two weeks. D—n it all, he was going to take care of himself; he was going to get away and carry what he could." This prediction of Smith then seemed probable. The writer saw Smith about four or five years afterwards, and has heard since that he was dead. He was from Warrenton, N. C.,

The first jail was built about the time the first court house was built; it is not known by whom it was built. It is supposed the Commissioners appointed for the purpose by the Act of 1798, *supra,* had the jail built as early as practicable. It was located northwest of the present court house on the public square. The writer saw it while standing. Did not then observe it as he would now. It remained there and was used until about 1846, when it was replaced by the present jail, located at the lower end of Main street.

The court house and jail located according to the Act of 1798, formed or made a nucleus for the building up a county town, at and around the court house. We do not know who resided near the county seat before the court house was erected; as we are informed by tradition, Colonel Hugh Giles, a distinguished character during the Revolutionary War, lived just over Smith's Swamp, south of the site of Marion Court House. It was for him that the village of Marion was first called Gilesboro, and was so called till away up into the thirties, and even after that by some of the older people. The town of Marion was not incorporated until long after. At the time of which we are now writing, we suppose others were in the vicinity. These were descendants of John Godbold, who settled just below where Marion Court House now stands, of whom more will be said hereinafterwards; also, the descendants of Nathan Evans, who was one of the early settlers of that region, of whom more will yet be said. In connection with the name of Gilesboro, the writer will relate what his father-in-law, Philip Bethea, told him. Before Marion Court House was located and established as the county seat, there were no public roads leading to it, from the upper end of the county. The court house being located there, it became necessary to lay out and build roads to the seat of justice. The road now leading from Marion up by Moody's Mill, and on up by what is now Ebenezer Church, and on up by John Bethea's (now John C. Bethea's plantation), and on up to Harlleesville (now Little Rock), then owned by Gibson (Stephen, the writer believes), was ordered by the road authorities to be laid out, opened and put in condition for travel. In cutting out and opening the road, the overseer in charge of the work had much trouble in getting those liable to perform road duty to work; the hands, the poorer white people, alleging that they did not want to work and build a road for old Colonel Giles and John Smith, who lived where Moody's Mill now is, to go up to old John Bethea's to drink cider (old John Bethea made quantities of cider and peach and apple brandy) ; that no one else wanted the road or would use it, the white hands alleging that they did not want the road. He said that such was the opposition that it almost amounted to a rebellion, and that the law had to be invoked in order to get the work done. The road is one of the most useful roads we have in the county, and none so poor that he would not be affected by closing it up, and would not have it abandoned. The writer's informant, Philip Bethea, was a man grown at the time, and a son of old John, the cider maker, and one of the road hands. We have a few such people among us yet, and perhaps always will have them—men having no public spirit, and care for no one but themselves.

Courts of Equity, prior to the Revolution, were held by the Governor and his Majesty's Council, or a majority of them. By the Act of 1721 (VII. vol. Statutes at Large, p. 163), it was provided that the Court of Chancery should always be open for the transaction of business within the jurisdiction of that Court, "but the days and times of full and solemn hearing shall be four times in every year, that is to say, on every Thursday next after the Court of Common Pleas is directed to meet and sit in Charleston, and shall at such times sit *de die in diem* until the business ready for said Court shall be finished." It was further provided, "that all the officers of the said Court should reside in Charleston." All Courts were held then only in Charleston. This was an ample arrangement at the time and answered all the purposes of said Courts. Charleston was then the State, and at that time was convenient to the settled parts of the province. Some modifications or amendments to the Act of 1721 were made in 1746, which it is not necessary to notice. In regard to the Courts of Equity, no special changes were made until 1784, after the Revolution. In that year the Legislature passed an Act abolishing the former

Courts or Equity and conferring all its powers and duties on three Judges or Chancellors, to be elected by the General Assembly, and to be commissioned by the Governor. (It will be remembered that in 1784 there was no such thing at "His Majesty's Counsel.") The powers and duties of the Courts were the same as under the Act of 1721. The change was made to suit the conditions then existing. The Court established by this Act, 1784, was to be held only in Charleston. The three Chancellors provided for in this Act, and elected by the Legislature, were John Rutledge, Richard Hudson and John Matthews.

The next Act of the Legislature to establish a Court of Equity within this State is the Act of 1791. (VII. vol. Statutes at Large, p. 258.) The first section of which provides: "That all laws now of force for establishing the Court of Chancery within this State, be, and they are hereby, declared to be and continue of force in this State, until altered or repealed by the Legislature thereof," &c.

The second section of this Act, 1791, after reciting the great inconveniences to the remote inhabitants of this State resulting from the fact that the Court of Equity is held only in one place within the State, to wit: Charleston, enacts: "That all future sittings of the Court of Equity for the full and solemn hearing of cases shall be held at the times and places hereinafter directed, that is to say: At Columbia, for all causes wherein the defendant shall reside in Camden, Orangeburg or Cheraw Districts, on the 15th days of May and December; at Cambridge, for all causes wherein the defendant shall reside within the District of Ninety-Six, on the 5th days of May and December; and at Charleston, for all causes wherein the defendant shall reside in either of the Districts of Charleston, Beaufort or Georgetown (our district), on the second Monday in March, the second Monday in June, and the third Monday in September, and the same days in every succeeding year," &c. It further provided that each and every Judge should ride the Circuit, unless prevented by sickness or other unavoidable disability.

The next Act in regard to the Equity Courts is the Act of 1799 (VII. vol. Statutes at Large, at page 297), which divides the districts as then established into four Equity Circuits, to be called the Eastern, Northern, Western and Southern. Marion County was placed in the Eastern Circuit; the Courts of Equity for this Circuit were to be held for Marion and Georgetown, at Georgetown, on the first Monday in February in each and every year.

The next Act in reference to the Courts of Equity is that of 1808 (VII. vol. Statutes at Large, p. 304). Section 1 of said Act divides the State into three Equity Circuits, viz: the Southern, Northern and Western. Our county, Marion, is placed in the Northern Circuit, composed of Georgetown, Horry, Marion and Williamsburg, which shall form one other Equity District, to be called the Georgetown District, the Courts of Equity for which shall be held at Georgetown, on the first Monday in February and June in every year. This Act of 1808 also provides for the election of two additional Chancellors to be commissioned and perform the same duties as the present Chancellors. The two elected were Henry Wm. DeSaussure and Theodore Gaillard.

The Act of 1824 established an Appeal Court for both law and equity, to consist of three Judges. It also divided the State into four Equity Circuits. Marion District was assigned to the Fourth Circuit, and the Courts to be held for "Georgetown, at Georgetown, for the Districts of Williamsburg, Horry, Marion and Georgetown, on the first Monday after the fourth Monday in January, to sit for two weeks, should so much be necessary." (VII. vol. Statutes at Large, section IX., p. 327.) From which it appears as well by this Act of 1824 as by the Act of 1808, *supra,* that from and after the year 1799, the business of the Equity Courts for this section of the State was on the decrease, for by the Act of 1799, only Georgetown and Marion were united for equity purposes; while by the Act of 1808 and 1824, Georgetown, Marion, Williamsburg and Horry were united for the same purpose.

The Act of 1825, VII. vol., p. 330, was amended so far as to allow the Court of Equity to sit twice a year for the Georgetown (Marion) Equity District instead of but once, one week at each term, if so much be necessary.

By the Act of 1833, it appears that Marion and Williamsburg

Districts were detached from the Georgetown Equity District, and that the Court sat in each separately, to wit: for Marion District, to commence the Thursday after the first Monday after the fourth Monday in January, and to continue in session three days, unless the business be sooner disposed of." The Act of 1833, for the first time in the judicial history of Marion District, recognized Marion as a coequal in her relations to the Courts of Equity with the other districts of the State.

The Act of 1824, entitled "An Act to revise and amend the judiciary system of this State," with some amendments thereto, continued to be the law regulating both the Courts of law and equity, together with the Court of Appeals, composed of three Judges, until 1835, when the Act of that year, 1835, entitled "An Act to reform and amend the judiciary system of this State," was passed. By this latter Act, the Appeal Court as then existing was abolished, and its powers and duties were transferred to a Court of Appeals, composed of all the law Judges and all the Chancellors in the State, sitting in banc; that no Chancellor or law Judge who had tried the cause on Circuit should sit upon hearing the appeal thereon. That the Courts of Common Pleas and General Sessions, and also the Equity Courts, should be arranged into circuits. One circuit was called the Eastern Circuit, in which Marion was placed. Courts of Common Pleas and General Sessions were to be held at Marion Court House for Marion District, on the third Monday after the fourth Monday in March and October each and every year thereafter for one week at each term, unless the business of the said Courts respectively shall be sooner dispatched. And the several Courts of Equity in the State shall hereafter be holden twice annually at the following periods, that is to say:" * * * and "at Marion Court House, for Marion District, on the Thursday next after the second Monday after the fourth Monday in January, and the Thursday next after the third Monday in June, in every year, for three days at each term, unless the business of the said Courts shall, respectively, be sooner despatched. (Act of 1835, VII. vol. Statutes, pp. 335 and 336.)

Another Act of 1836 was passed, entitled "An Act to organize the Courts of this State. That the several Courts of law and equity in this State shall hereafter be held at the times and places as follows, that is to say: For the Eastern Circuit, at Marion Court Hause, on the fourth Monday in March and October." This was for the Court of Common Pleas and General Sessions. For the Court of Equity, "at Marion Court House, on the third Monday in January." By this Act, "all appeals from the Courts of law shall be heard and determined in a Court of Appeals, consisting of the law Judges, and that all appeals in equity shall be heard and determined in a Court of Appeals, consisting of the Chancellors. That said Courts shall meet at the same time and be held as follows, that is to say: at Charleston, on the first Monday in February, and at Columbia, on the first Monday in May, and fourth Monday in November." (Act of 1836, VII. vol. Statutes, 339 and 340.) By this Act also was created the Court of Errors, as follows: "That upon all constitutional questions arising out of the Constitution of this State or the United States, an appeal shall lie to the whole of the Judges assembled to hear such appeal. That an appeal shall also lie to the whole of the Judges upon all questions upon which either of the Courts of Appeal shall be divided, or when any two of the Judges of the Court shall require that a cause be further heard by all the Judges. That the Judges of law and equity, when assembled as aforesaid in one chamber, shall form a Court for the correction of all errors in law or equity in the cases that may be heard before them, and that it shall be the duty of the Judges to make all proper rules and regulations for the practice of the said Courts," &c. In this latter Court, Marion District figured in two of the cases, involving the constitutionality of the stay law, as it was called, passed in December, 1861, and continued from year to year till 1866, inclusive. The two cases were the State *vs.* Carew, 13 Richardson Law Reports, p. 398, represented by Mr. Lord, of Charleston, and the case of Barry *vs.* Iseman, 14 Richardson Law Reports, p. 161, represented by A. C. Spain for plaintiff-appellant, and W. W. Harllee and W. W. Sellers for defendant-respondent, from Marion. The cases were argued together in the Court of Errors before all the Judges and Chancellors "assembled in the same room," at May Term, 1866, in Columbia, S. C. As to the case of the State *vs.* Carew, opinion by the venerable Chancellor Duncan, then Chief Justice, the stay law was held to be unconstitutional. Judge A. P. Aldrich *dissenting*. As to the case of Barry *vs.* Iseman, from Marion, opinion by Judge Monroe, the stay law was held to be constitutional. No dissent. The essential difference between the two cases was this: in the case of the State *vs.* Carew, the contract was made before the passage of the stay law, hence its passage was held to be an impairment of the obligation of the contract. In the case of Barry *vs.* Iseman, the contract was made after the passage of the stay law, and hence its passage was held not to be an impairment of the obligation of the contract, and, therefore, constitutional. The contract was made in reference to existing law. (Constitution of the United States, article I., section 10; Constitution of the State, 1790, article IX., section 2.)

The Circuit Courts, both of law and equity, continued about the same, as provided by the Act of 1836, *supra,* until the war. In 1859, a separate Court of Appeals, consisting of three Judges, was again established for the hearing and decision of all cases of appeal, either at law or equity. The Court of Errors remained as before. The Judges of the Court of Appeals, as organized in 1859, were John Belton O'Neall, Chief Justice, Job Johnston and F. Wardlaw, Associate Justices. F. Wardlaw died in 1860 or 1861. Chief Justice O'Neall and Job Johnston died during the war, upon which Chancellor B. F. Dunkin was elected Chief Justice, and D. L. Wardlaw and John A. Inglis were elected as Associate Justices, which positions they held with distinguished ability, until the upheavals of reconstruction put them out. It can be truthfully said that the judiciary of South Carolina from the earliest times as a State, have been filled, both Circuit and Appeal Courts, by men of high character, distinguished alike for integrity, dignity, learning and ability. Many of them would have done credit to any country, in any age of the world. Their names stand prominent on the rolls of fame. Such a galaxy of eminent names is scarcely to be seen anywhere. Where all are so eminent, it would seem to be invidious to mention any. Without disparaging others, the writer cannot forbear to mention some. From the Revolution down to the war of the States, John

Rutledge, Henry Wm. DeSaussure, Hugh Rutledge, Thomas Waties, Joseph Brevard, Samuel Wilds, Jr., Abraham Nott, Charles Jones Colcock, Langdon Cheves, William Harper, David Johnson, John S. Richardson, John Belton O'Neall, Joseph J. Evans, Job Johnston, B. F. Dunkin, D. L. Wardlaw, Frank Wardlaw, John A. Inglis and George W. Dargan. To this list of eminent jurists others might be added. Of such an array of legal talent as this, any people might justly be proud. Most of these Judges performed circuit as well as appeal duty. Their names are imperishable. It may be said that the judicial system of the State was perfected with and by the Act of 1836. Some slight amendments were made to it in after times, and up to "reconstruction." That unparalleled event affected great and radical changes in the judiciary system of the State. It abolished the Court of Equity as a separate Court, and with it the venerable name of Chancellor. It transferred all its powers, jurisdiction and duties to the Court of Common Pleas. The same Judge administers both law and equity—the former with a jury, the latter without a jury—the conscience of the Judge being in place of a jury. A Court of General Sessions, which has jurisdiction of all criminal matters, is also established, and is administered by the same Judge. Hence, we now have a three-sided Court; one side is called the law side, another side is called the equity side, and another side is called the criminal side. Thus centering in one man's hand jurisdiction of every possible right or wrong to be redressed, cognizable among a highly civilized people. Whether for the better or not, such is the now judicial administration of law in our State, and such it has been for more than thirty years—so since the making of the Constitution of 1868. That Constitution was made and adopted for the government of the people by a class of men who did not understand the situation or the wants of the people of the State. Those who were well qualified by education and a knowledge of the needs of the people, were shut out of the Convention of 1868, called to make an organic law for the State. It was made by a few foreigners called "carpet-baggers," a few white men, natives of the State, renegades, called "scalawags," and a horde of ignorant negroes— whom the carpet-baggers voted like so many cattle. It was made really only by fifteen or twenty men, who had no sympathy with or for the heretofore ruling element of the State. It was made rather to humiliate and punish the better class of the people than for their future benefit. Its purpose was to perpetuate the power of themselves, to aggrandise and enrich the "carpet-bag" and "scalawag" few, out of the hard earnings of the former rulers, the former owners of the property of the people. In other words, it was to put the "bottom rail on top" and keep it there. The Constitution-makers of 1868 did make some improvement upon the Constitution of 1790 in the abolition of the parish system of representation in the State Legislature, in emancipating married women as to their ownership of property and their right to control it independent of their husbands.

Marion County has been an essential factor in all this. Whatever affected the State for good or evil affected her. She has borne her troubles and misfortunes with marked equanimity—she has subordinated herself to the powers that be, and has ever been in favor of law and order. Her people are a law-abiding people—lynch law finds no place among us. Her citizenship, as a whole, are composed of honest, industrious men, who live by honest means, who are enterprising, each in his vocation trying to live and let others live. She is fast coming to the front among her sister counties in the race for distinction and preferment—a model county. If she progresses through the twentieth century, as she has during the nineteenth century now closing, she will have attained a prominence in everything that makes a people great, prosperous and happy. Her resources are unbounded and not yet half developed. These, used as they may and will be, by her people for another century, will make her a star of first magnitude among the many stars of the commonwealth, and her citizens, when they travel, will be proud to say, "I am from Marion County, S. C." The officials of the county, Senators and Representatives in the State Legislature, her Clerks of Court, her Sheriffs, her Ordinaries and Probate Judges, her Commissioners and Masters in Equity, will be hereinafter given, and, perhaps, the names of other county officials, since days of "reconstruction."

Political History.

Prior to the Revolutionary War, the territory now embraced in the County of Marion, including that portion of it on the west side of the Great Pee Dee, now embraced in the County of Florence, was unknown as a political or judicial division of the State, then a province of Great Britain. Bishop Gregg, in his History of the Old Cheraws (a tribe of Indians), does not mention Marion County or District as of early formation. Wherever he speaks of it, he speaks of it as what it was at the time of his writing; for instance, as what is "now called Marion District." That eminent writer's purpose was mainly to write a history of Chesterfield, Marlborough and Darlington, and what he says about Marion County is only incidental.

The English government, from the earliest settlement of the province of Carolina, had manifested a deep interest in the colony, and was anxious to strengthen it by emigration. Great inducements were held out to the poor of European nations to emigrate to Carolina in various ways—by offering bounties in lands and in other ways. Prior to 1730, there were few, if any, settlements in what is now Marion County. It appears by well authenticated tradition that there were a few settlements within its territory, concerning which notice will be taken hereinafterwards. Bishop Gregg, in his history, on page 42, says: "From 1696 to 1730, although its population gradually increased, no large addition was made at any one time to the inhabitants of Carolina. About the latter year (1730), a new scheme was adopted to promote the settlement of the province, which proved successful beyond the most sanguine expectations of the government. Governor Johnson was instructed 'to mark out eleven townships, in square lots, on the sides of rivers, consisting each of twenty thousand acres, and to divide the land within them into shares of fifty acres, for each man, woman and child that should come over to occupy and improve them. Each township was to form a parish, and all the inhabitants were to have an equal right to the river. As soon as the parish should increase to the number of one hundred families, they were to have the right to send two members of their own election to the Assembly, and to enjoy the same privileges as the parishes already established. Each settler was to pay four shillings a year for every hundred acres of land, excepting the first ten years, during which term they were to be rent free.' Governor Johnson issued a warrant to St. John, Surveyor General of the province, empowering him to go and mark out these townships; but he having demanded an exorbitant sum of money for his trouble, the members of the Council agreed among themselves to do this piece of service for their country." (Noble on the part of the Council.) "Accordingly, eleven townships were marked out by them in the following situations: two on the River Altamaha, two on Savanna, two on Santee, one on Pee Dee, one on Wackamaw, one on Wateree and one on Black River." The writer does not understand how it was that two townships were to be laid out "on the River Altamaha," as that is a river of the afterwards Province of Georgia, and Georgia was not then settled, 1730-1731, and was not settled until two years afterwards (1733). The Province of South Carolina did not at that time, nor at any time since, have any jurisdiction beyond the Savannah River. It must have been the Edisto River, which may have been at that time called the "Altamaha River." The writer cannot otherwise account for it. "The township on the Pee Dee was called Queensborough, and to the time of its being marked out, 1731-1732, or a period a little subsequent, is to be assigned the date of our first settlements. There was no delay in the execution of this work (of marking out the townships), which had been committed to the Governor by his Majesty's government, for building up its waste places and the more speedy settlement of the province." Bishop Gregg further says, on page 44: "From the annexed plot or draft, Queensborough appears to have been laid out on the Great Pee Dee, but a short distance above the mouth of Little Pee Dee River, embracing a part of what has since been known as Britton's Neck (a narrow strip of land between the two rivers), and extending also on the west side of the Great Pee Dee." He says further: "But for this plot, most unexpectedly found, the exact location of Queensborough Township could not have been determined." On page 45, he further says: "On the 14th February, 1734, it was ordered that the several persons who have laid out the several townships do prepare a rough draft or plan of a town to be laid out in each township containing about 800 acres, out of which a common of 300 acres, to be laid out in the back part, and the remaining 500 to be laid out in half-acre lots, to be a convenient distance from the river." This was done accordingly, and the town for Queensborough Township was located on the west side of the Great Pee Dee, as the writer supposes, not far from Godfrey's Ferry. The township covered 20,000 acres, and lay on both sides of the river. How far it extended up the river is unknown, nor how far on each side, as the plot does not show the number of chains to the mile. The town thus laid out and located on the west side of the river in Queensborough Township seems never to have been settled as a town. Bishop Gregg says that up to 1734 no settlement was made in Queensborough Township.

Queensborough Township.

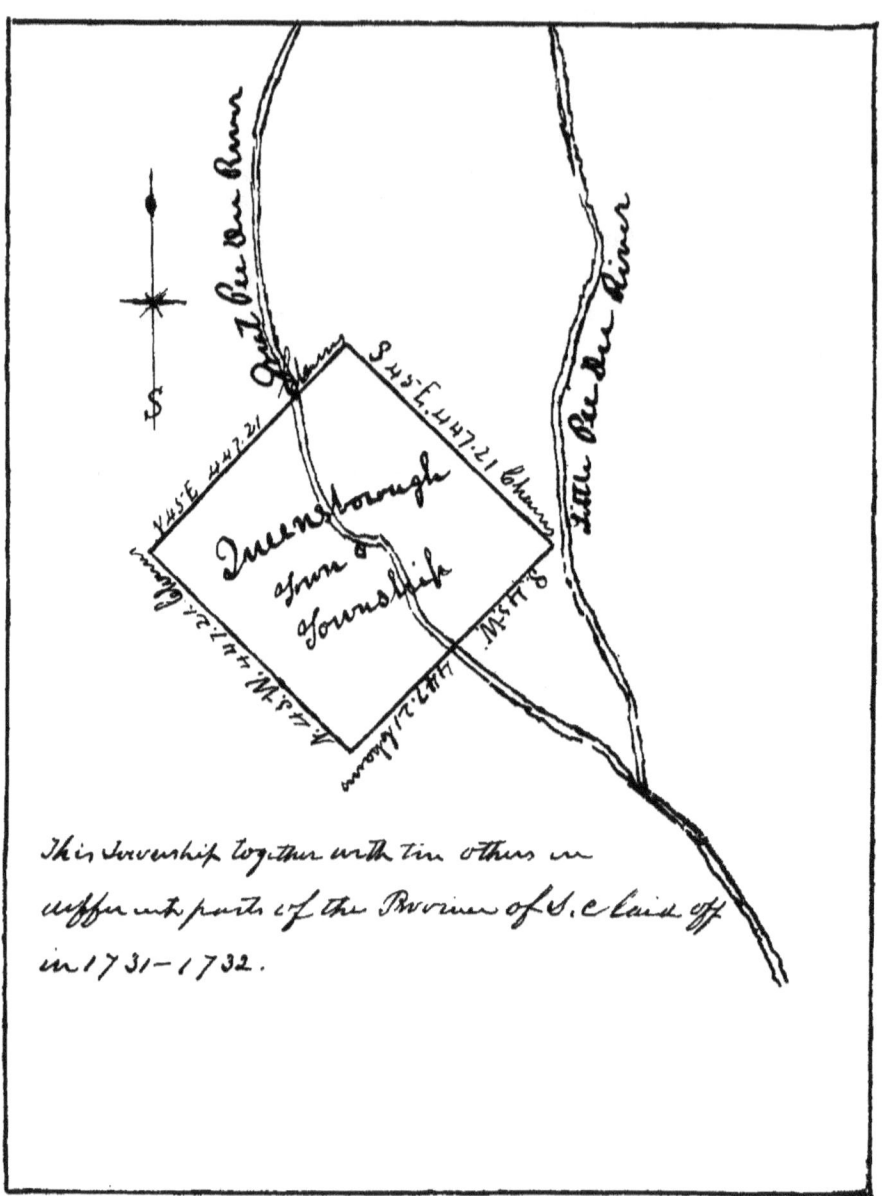

This township, together with ten others in different parts of the Province of South Carolina, laid off in 1731-1732.

Bishop Gregg says, on page 45: "The inducements held out in connection with the township, appear to have led to a visit of some of the Welsh from Pennsylvania for the purpose of exploration and settlement, and to removal very shortly after of the colony, which was destined to form so important an element in the history and progress of the region of the upper Pee Dee." He says, on page 47: "The first visit of the Welch to Pee Dee appears to have been made in the latter part of 1735 or early in the following year. It led to a remarkable act of favor on the part of the Council, to induce the colony to come. Wishing on their arrival to settle in a body, and be possessed of ample and exclusive privileges as to the occupancy of the soil, they petitioned the government that an extensive tract of land might be appropriated to their sole benefit for a certain period. This appears from a message of the Lieutenant-Governor to the lower House of Assembly, 2 February, 1737, in which he said: 'The late Lieutenant-Governor, with the advice of his Majesty's Council, thought it would tend to the service and strengthening of the province to grant the petition of several natives of the principality of Wales, in behalf of themselves and others of their countrymen, who intended to settle in this province from Great Britain and Pennsylvania, praying the land near the fork, above the township (Queensborough) on Pee Dee River, might be reserved and set apart for their uses, and Mr. John Ouldfield being thought a very proper person, was employed for that service.' The petition here referred to bore date August 13th, 1736, having been favorably received by the Council, his Majesty's Surveyor-General, James H. St. John, Esq., was instructed to have the said tract laid out. Accordingly he directed a precept to John Ouldfield, bearing date November 16th, 1736, 'to admeasure and lay out for the Welsh families that were to be imported to this province a tract of land, containing in the whole one hundred and seventy-three thousand eight hundred and forty acres, situated and being in Craven County. Ten thousand acres, being part thereof, lying within the limits of the township of Queensborough, on the north side of Pee Dee River. The remainder of said tract lying on the south side of said river and abutting and bounding to southeast on the reserved land of the said township of Queensborough, and all other sides on vacant lands, as are supposed.' The survey was made, and a plot thereof returned 29th Nov., 1736, of which a copy is annexed." The tract thus surveyed extended up the river on both sides only a short distance above Mar's Bluff. It was not adapted to the wants of the Welsh people, the petitioners. They petitioned again the government for a further extension of the tract up the river, and after due consideration of this petition, the authorities granted it, by which it was extended up the river, to and even above the North Carolina State line, to the branches of said river, to wit: "Yadkin and Uwhare or Yadkin and Rocky River," a distance of over one hundred miles by the course of the river, and included a territory of eight miles on each side of the river the whole way. Thus the Welsh had exclusive privileges over an immense territory, probably half million of acres. This proves both the anxiety and benevolence of the government, and the Welsh were not slow in availing themselves of such unprecedented advantages. This extension of their grant was dated 8th February, 1737. This first grant to the Welsh was afterwards extended up to North Carolina line, eight miles on each side of Pee Dee River.

A Plat of the Welch Grant (First).

Containing 173,840 acres. November 16th, 1736. Scale of copy Plat, 320 chains per inch.

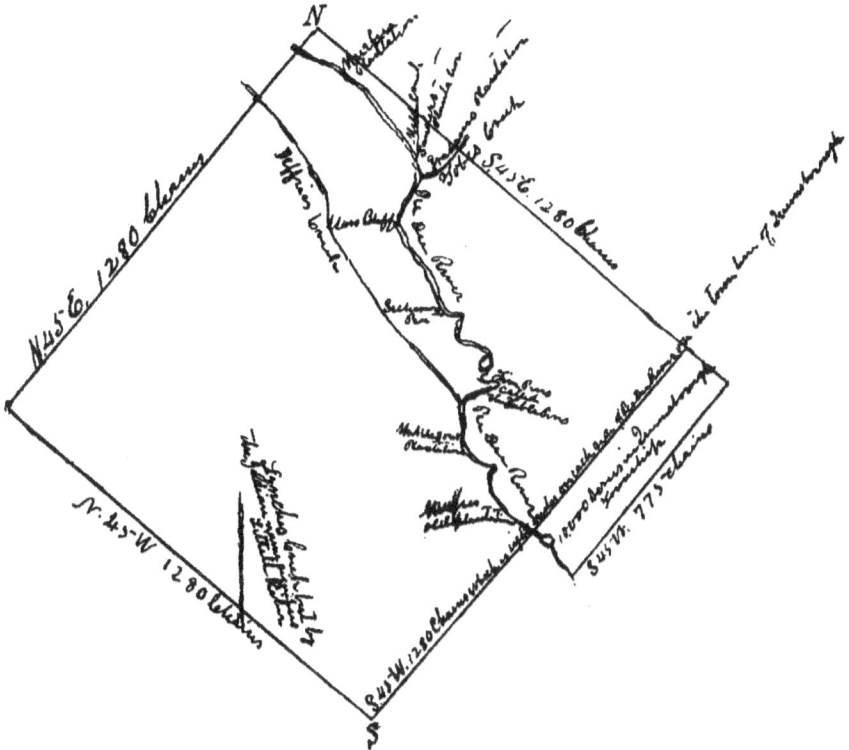

"South Carolina.

"By virtue of precept to me directed by James H. Johns, Esq., His Majesty's Surveyor General, bearing date 16th November, 1736, I have measured and laid for the Welsh familys that are to be imported to the province, a tract of land containing in the whole one hundred and seventy-three thousand eight hundred and forty acres, situate and being in Craven County. Ten thousand acres being part thereof, lying within the limits of the township of Queensborough on the north side of Pee Dee River. The remainder of said tract lying on both sides of said river. Butting and bounding to the southeast on the reserved lands of the said township of Queensborough, and all other sides vacant lands as is supposed, and hath such shape, form and marks as are represented by this delineated plot thereof. Given under my hand, 29th day of November, 1736, per me. (Signed)

"Deputy Surveyor."

NOTE.—This copy made May 22, 1859, from original plat in Secretary of State's office by White & Ramsay, Deputy Surveyors.

These bodies of land were not civil or political divisions, but only tracts laid out to induce emigrants to come in and settle them. It was to increase the population, to begin the development of the vast resources of the soil, to raise products not only for home consumption but for exportation to Charleston and to England.

As to Queensborough Township, the laying it off was for the double purpose of inducing emigrants to come in and settle it up and to obtain lands cheaply, and in the Act or order of the Governor and Council for laying it and ten other townships ordered to be laid out at the same time, it was provided that so soon as the population in any township should amount to a hundred families, that such township should constitute a parish, and be entitled to two representatives in the General Assembly. To this extent it was a civil or political division. Whether any of the eleven townships laid off at that time, 1731-2, availed themselves of this political provision or not, is not known. It is very certain that Queensborough Township did not.

Marion County was designated for the first time as a civil or political division by the Act of 1785, and was called Liberty. Prior to that time, it formed part of the large county of Craven; but Craven County, as such, never had any representation in the General Assembly. For political purposes, it was called the District East of the Wateree, and as such was entitled to two Representatives. (Constitution of 1778, I. vol. Statutes at Large, page 140, section 13.)

The politics of the Province of South Carolina up to the Revolutionary War were intensely British. After the Revolution, they did not take definite shape, as far as can now be gathered, until about the date of 1800, when her policy tended to support the views of Alexander Hamilton—who, though an advocate for the adoption of the Federal Constitution of 1787, and a Federalist, yet he believed in a latitudinous construction of that instrument. He believed in a strong executive government. Hamilton was not alone; many able and truly patriotic men had the same views. John Adams and the Pinckneys, of South ·Carolina, ranged themselves on that side. They were, doubtless, honest in their opinions, laboring for the good of the country. In the presidential campaign of 1800, the contest was bitter and intensely exciting. Thomas Jefferson, the great apostle of Republicanism (Democratic) of that day, and John Adams, Aaron Burr and perhaps others, headed the two parties, Republicans and Federalists. There was no election by the people; hence, under the Constitution, the election devolved upon the House of Representatives, in which, as the writer understands it, they voted by States; each State counted one vote, and in that way the small States of Rhode Island and Delaware were as strong as the larger States—Virginia and New York. The House balloted thirty-seven times before an election was made. The race in the House was between Jefferson and Burr, each getting eight votes—South Carolina voting for Burr. On the thirty-seventh ballot, South Carolina and Tennessee voted blank; the result was, eight for Jefferson and six for Burr. Jefferson was declared elected President and Burr was declared elected Vice-President. It thus appears that South Carolina voted for thirty-six ballots for Burr and against Jefferson, the great leader of the Democracy of 1800. And though dead for three-quarters of a century, Jefferson is now the beau ideal of the Democracy of 1900. How it was that they then voted with the Federalists and against Democracy, has never been explained. Such is the record of history. In every presidential election since that time, except one in 1832, South Carolina has invariably voted for the Democratic candidate.

We have no means of ascertaining what were the politics of Marion County in 1800, but we presume they were in line with the balance of the State. On several occasions since that time, the people of Marion County have been divided on political issues, and have had some very bitter contests among themselves. The first, in the order of time, was in 1832, on the question of Nullification—that is, to decide whether or not South Carolina should nullify and make void within this State the tariff laws passed by Congress, and to resist by force, if necessary, the collection of the Federal revenue within this State. It raised a storm, a very tempestuous one, from the mountains to the seaboard, Marion included. One party was called Nullifiers and the other Union men. Marion District was aroused as it had never been before from its centre to its utmost limits. Each party had its candidates for delegates to the Convention. I do not know who the candidates were on the respective sides, but do know who were elected. The Nullifiers carried the county by a few votes—say thirty. Colonel Thomas Harllee, General William Evans and Alexander L. Gregg, from West Marion, were elected. The Convention convened in Columbia on the 19th November, 1832, and passed and adopted an ordinance of Nullification on the 24th November, 1832. (I. vol. Statutes at Large, pp. 329-333.) This Convention had in it many able men, and true patriots, such as R. W. Barnwell, Pierce M. Butler, C. J. Colcock, F. H. Elmore, Robert Y. Hayne, William Harper, Job Johnston, George MacDuffie, Stephen D. Miller, Charles C. Pinckney, Thomas Pinckney, John Lide Wilson, F. H. Wardlaw, R. Barnwell Smith (Rhett) and many others. Most of the Union delegates refused to sign the ordinance. The Convention issued a strong and stirring address to the people, setting forth their grievances and their rights and the proposed remedy. The die was cast. Preparations to resist by force were hastily made, war seemed imminent. Andrew Jackson was President of the United States. He issued a proclamation, Congress passed a force bill and everything looked like war. South Carolina seemed determined, and set about making the best preparation possible for defence. Turmoil and strife existed and permeated the whole State—brother arrayed against brother, father against son, neighbor against neighbor. Those were fearful times. The more thoughtful among us were scheming how to throw oil on the troubled waters, and to avoid a collision. Just at this juncture of affairs a ray of hope dawned upon us. The State of Virginia, seeing the danger, intervened in the interest of compromise and peace. With a view to its accomplishment, she sent as an agent or a commission to South Carolina the Hon. Benjamin Watkins Leigh, and he, with the aid of Hon. Henry Clay, the great pacificator of the United States in Washington, stayed the advance of grim-visaged war so close upon us, and brought about a compromise. Congress passed an Act for the gradual reduction of the tariff, the *casus belli,* down to a revenue standard—which South Carolina accepted, and repealed her ordinance of Nullification. Thus was averted, for a period of near thirty years, a bloody fratricidal war. (I. vol. Statutes at Large, p. 390, *et sequens.*)

In repealing the ordinance, the Convention excepted from its operation the Act entitled "An Act further to alter and amend the militia laws of this State, passed by the General Assembly of this State on the 20th day of December, 1832." Thus preserving and manifesting a military spirit, which has ever characterized the State. The stirring times of the Nullification struggle intensified the military ardor of our people, referred to more at large in the former part of this history, and opened the way for the contest a year or two later, in this (Marion) district, between Thomas Harllee and John F. Ervin for the colonelcy of the newly-organized 32d regiment of the South Carolina militia, and gave an impetus to and fanned into a flame the military spirit of the people, which continued with unabated ardor for years, and culminated in the founding of the Arsenal Academy in Columbia, and Citadel in Charleston. The Arsenal was preparatory to the Citadel, and they were largely patronized until they were broken up by the war of 1861-1865. Those schools turned out many useful and distinguished men, versed in military affairs, and prepared to take the lead in the bloody contest of 1861-1865. Since the war (1882), the Citadel has been reorganized and is doing well, has an extensive patronage, and is turning out every year young men well educated and, especially in the arts of military life, prepared and equipped for service in any rank of military life, and competent to fill the highest positions in the army or honorable positions in civil life. It is one of the best schools in the State. The names of the sons of Marion County graduating therein are hereinbefore given.

Not long after the Nullification struggle, the Whig party in the United States was formed. In 1836, that party nominated for the Presidency Hugh L. White, of Tennessee, and the Democrats nominated Martin VanBuren, of New York. VanBuren was elected. In that campaign, South Carolina was not much divided—she voted for VanBuren. In 1840, the Whig party had become very formidable. They nominated for the Presidency that year, William Henry Harrison, of Ohio, and for the Vice-Presidency, John Tyler, of Virginia. The Democrats nominated Martin VanBuren, of New York, for a second term, and Richard M. Johnson, for the Vice-Presidency. This campaign was called the "Log Cabin, Hard Cider, Coonskin and Red Pepper" campaign. In Nashville, Tenn., they actually built a log cabin, put it on wheels, with a barrel of hard cider planted in the top of it, a picture of their candidate pictured on it astraddle of the barrel with a quill in his mouth sucking the cider from the bung of the barrel; coon-skins and red pepper were hung all round the cabin, and the whole drawn through the streets of Nashville by four white horses. It was said in the newspapers of the day that Parson Brownlow, a Methodist preacher, and editor of a leading newspaper in Nashville, rode on top of the cabin, sucking cider out of the barrel with a quill, and gnawing the coon-skins—thus parading himself and his candidates through that refined city. And such emblems and "clap-trap" as that carried the election, not only in Tennessee, but in the United States. William Henry Harrison was, doubtless, a patriot and good man. The whole thing was gotten up, promulgated and carried through by his partisans, who were hungry for the "plums" of Federal patronage. Unfortunately for the Whig party, President Harrison lived only a month after his inauguration, and John Tyler, the Vice-President, became President, and proved to be about as good a Democrat as most public men belonging to the party. It is said that history repeats itself. John Tyler was with the Whig party only on one question, that of internal improvements by the government, and was nominated for the Vice-Presidency as a matter of policy—that is, to carry Virginia, then a large State, in the electoral college. Virginia then included what is now West Virginia. So in 1864, during the war, the Republicans nominated Andrew Johnson, a war Democrat, for the Vice-Presidency on the ticket with Abraham Lincoln, as a matter of policy to mollify the South and to carry not only Tennessee, Johnson's State, but perhaps other Democratic States, against George B. McClellan, the Democratic candidate. They succeeded in the election, but Lincoln lived only a little over a month after inauguration, and Andrew Johnson became President. The Republican Congress was caught just like the Whig Congress, elected in 1840, was by John Tyler. Tyler vetoed the favorite Acts of the Congress of 1841-2, and the party in Congress were not strong enough to pass them over the veto by a two-thirds vote. Not so in Andrew Johnson's case. He vetoed the Reconstruction Acts of Congress, and the Republicans were strong enough to pass them over the veto by a two-thirds majority. Johnson did all he could to save the South from the horrors of reconstruction, but the Congress was too strong for him. They tried to impeach him, and came within one vote of succeeding in their mad effort. Andrew Johnson was far from being the man the South would have wanted for President. The South, however, owes him a debt of gratitude, though in his grave, for what he strove to do in her favor. Too many Thad. Stevens then in Congress, whose hearts were bent on revenge.

In the Log Cabin, Coon-skin and Red Pepper campaign of 1840, Marion District was about equally divided between the Democrats and the Whigs. There were strong men on both sides. The Whig candidates were, for the State Senate, Benjamin Gause, and for the House, David Palmer, Henry Davis and Dr. Daniel Gilchrist. The Democratic candidates were, for the Senate, Addison L. Scarborough, and for the House, John C. Bethea, Hugh Godbold and William T. Wilson. The people were wrought up to the highest point. VanBuren's administration of the government was too extravagant. His administration of the government had cost on an average $60,000,000 a year. That was paraded in the newspapers and all through the country as being enormous. Another fad circulated was that he slept on a $1,500 bedstead, and had other conveniences in proportion. When, now sixty years after that period, an administration of the government costs on an average of $500,000,000 a year, when not engaged in a foreign war. Our people are standing all this reckless expenditure of money now, when our fathers and grand-fathers could not stand $60,000,000. President VanBuren's extravagant administration, together with the coon-skin and hard cider "clap-trap," hurled VanBuren from power. What shall be done now in the campaign of 1900? In 1840, the result in Marion District was the election of Benjamin Gause to the Senate by eighteen votes; David Palmer, Henry Davis and John C. Bethea were elected to the House. Among the six candidates for Representatives, there were not fifty votes between the highest and the lowest of the six.

In the campaign of 1844, the Whigs and Democrats had another contest in Marion District. The respective parties had each its candidate for the Presidency. James K. Polk headed the Democratic party, and Henry Clay led the Whig party. Polk was elected President. The respective parties had each its candidates in Marion. Ex-Governor Dr. B. K. Henagan was the Democratic candidate for the Senate; John C. Bethea, Barfield Moody and Chapman J. Crawford were the Democratic candidates for the House of Representatives. Senator Benjamin Gause was a candidate for re-election to the Senate as the Whig candidate; William H. Grice, John Woodberry and N. Philips, Esq., were the Whig candidates for the House. The campaign was conducted with spirit and dogged determination—every exertion possible was made by each party for success. The result was that the Democratic ticket carried the county by a majority of 200 or more. The writer remembers that Henagan's majority over Gause was 204. The campaign that year (1844) lacked the "Coon-skin and Red Pepper" clap-trap of 1840 to give it success. The class of men carried by such clap-trap in 1840 were generally such as could be swerved and seduced from that path by silent and effective influences, no doubt used, which were powerless in 1844. The writer remembers hearing a remark made by Colonel W. H. Grice, one of the defeated candidates for the House, at Marion on the second day of the election, when it was ascertained that the Democratic ticket was elected entire, to this effect: That such a thing had never before been heard of—the entire delegation from a district, Senator and Representatives, all belonged to one family. The Senator, Dr. B. K. Henagan, and Representatives, Bethea, Moody and Crawford, were all connected with each other by blood or marriage. The wife of Barfield Moody was the aunt of John C. Bethea and Chapman J. Crawford, Bethea and Crawford were first cousins; Crawford's father and Bethea's mother were brother and sister, and Moody's wife was a sister of Crawford's father and also of John C. Bethea's mother; Bethea's name was John Crawford Bethea. The Senator-elect, Dr. B. K. Henagan's, mother was a Bethea. The result of the election verified Colonel Grice's remark; yet it was not a preconcerted arrangement,—it was only a happen so.

The election laws, at that time and for years before and after until the war, provided that elections should be held one day at each poll, including the court house poll, in the district, and on the next day the election should continue to be held at the court house. That on the second day, the managers from the out or country polls, or a majority of them, were required to carry in the votes from the out polls, respectively, to be counted whilst the election was going at the court house poll, and at the close of the court house poll it was counted and the result for the whole district was then declared. The practical operation of this arrangement of the election laws of the State opened the door to all sorts of combinations on the second day at the court house poll. Many times the candidate or candidates elected on the first day of election were beaten on the second day. Not more than half the votes would be polled at the court house on the first day, and many from the out polls would not vote the first day, but would go to Marion the second day, and after hearing from, perhaps, all the polls in the district as to how the election went the day before, were ready to form combinations to elect or to defeat certain candidates, and vote accordingly. A heavy vote was thereby cast on the second day. It was not then, as now, an elector could vote at any precinct in the county, provided he could identify himself to the satisfaction of the managers, and take the required oath that he had not voted in the election at any other voting precinct. The having one day's election at the out polls and two at the court house, was wrong in policy, as it often operated to defeat the will of the people; but allowing an elector to vote at any poll in the district, wherever he might happen to be on day of election, was right and good policy, and ought to be so now in 1900, provided he showed his registration certificate and takes the required oath. And it ought to be extended further. An elector ought to be allowed to vote at any precinct in the State for Governor and other State officers, and for a Representative in Congress at any voting precinct in his Congressional District, provided he identifies himself to the satisfaction of the managers by the production of his registration certificate and by other evidences, and takes the required oath. It often happens that a man's business or family necessities compel him on day of election to be somewhere else other than at his own poll. If so, by the law as it now is, he is disfranchised, he is deprived of his right to vote. Our election and registration laws ought to be amended so as to avoid such disfranchisement. Every man ought to have, and does have, the right to have his voice in choosing the makers and administrators of the law under which he lives, unless by crime or other disability he has forfeited that right.

After the campaign of 1844, there was a lull in party strife, and each party seemed to merge into the other party; discrimination ceased and men were seemingly elected to office without any reference to past party affiliations till 1851 and 1852. In 1851, it was proposed to hold a Convention of the Southern or slave-holding States at Montgomery, Ala., to consult as to the most advisable course to protect themselves against the aggressions of the North on the institution of slavery. South Carolina was for separate State action, whether any other State joined in or not. When I say South Carolina was for separate State action, I mean that was the proposition—Separate State Secession or Co-operate Secession—Secession or Co-operation. A popular election was held to elect delegates to the proposed Convention at Montgomery, Ala. It aroused a furor in the State. Excitement and strife permeated the whole State, from the mountains to the seaboard. The Co-operation party, as it was called, was in favor of secession, provided they could get the co-operation of the other slave States, or a majority of them; the Separate State Action party were in favor of the secession of South Carolina, whether any other Southern State seceded or not. Each party put out their respective candidates for delegates. The contest was bitter and strong; animosities were engendered, party feeling was strained to its utmost tension. I do not recollect who the respective candidates were. The Co-operation party carried the district by thirty-five majority, and that party carried the State by a considerable majority. The Montgomery Convention was never held, and thus the matter ended; but the feelings, the animosities and jealousies engendered and aroused were not allayed, or seemingly modified, but continued through the next year, 1852, as bitter and unrelenting as ever. Each party was unwilling to trust the other, and each party had out its candidates for the Senate and House the next year, 1852, in this, Marion District, and it was so throughout the State. Dr. Robert Harllee was the candidate of the Secession party for the Senate, and C. J. Crawford was the candidate of the Co-operation party for the same office. I do not remember the names of the candidates for the House. Dr. Harllee was elected to the Senate over Crawford by 171 majority. Dr. William R. Johnson, Colonel W. W. Durant and William S. Mullins were elected to the House of Representatives. Dr. Johnson was Secessionist, Durant and Mullins were Co-operationists. The Secession party had four candidates for the House to carry, and hence they elected but one of their ticket, Dr. Johnson. The bitterness engendered by the campaign gradually cooled down, and harmony and good feeling were restored. The party for Separate State Action believed and felt assured that if South Carolina acted alone, the other slave States would of necessity follow. The Co-operation party thought otherwise—that South Carolina should act only in conjunction with the other slave States. Both parties, doubtless, were honest. One party wanted to act at once, the other party wanted to go slow, being more cautious. The writer believes that if we had acted then, either separately or unitedly, there would have been no attempt at coercion. The anti-slavery feeling of the North was not then as strong as it was in 1860 and 1861. It was intensified and became more fanatical in each succeeding year from 1852 to 1860. Franklin Pierce was elected President in 1852, and a Congress in accord with the views of Pierce. Instead of coercion, some scheme of compromise would have been suggested and adopted, by which war would have then been averted, at least for a time, and maybe for all time. Slavery was bound to go, sooner or later, either peacefully or by the scourge of war. After 1851 and 1852, there were no questions or issues to divide our people in South Carolina. But for the constant agitation of the slavery question in Congress, the people of the State were quiet and at ease. No division among themselves, nothing to disturb their equanimity of a political character.

Marion District, during the last decade before the war between the States, was steadily progressing on the different lines of civilized life to that proud eminence to which she has since attained, and which she now occupies. When the tocsin of war was sounded, she responded to the call of her section with an alacrity and an enthusiasm not excelled by, perhaps, any district in the State. However much she may have heretofore been divided and torn by factional issues and factional strife, she was almost a solid unit for the war, as the rolls of the companies from Marion District will show, hereinafter published. It is true, there were a few on Maple Swamp and in the lower part of Hillsboro Township, and perhaps a few in the Great Pee Dee slashes in Kirby Township, who failed and refused to respond to their country's call, but the great bulk of the young and middle-aged, and some passed the age of active military service, obeyed their country's call from motives of patriotism, and went to whatever place they were assigned, and wherever the exigencies of the times and service required, and sealed and demonstrated their devotion to their country's cause with their life's blood. Many left home and family and friends, never to return. The casualties of our late war with Spain and now going on in the Philippines, are but a bagatelle to the casualties in the Confederate War. In some of the great battles in Virginia and elsewhere, the casualties on each side ran up into the thousands. The casualties were generally much greater in the Federal army than in the Confederate army. All were Americans—all had learned the arts of warfare in the same school, and why should the casualties have been greater in the Northern army than in the Southern? The Northern army had greatly the advantage in numbers, in the character and calibre of their arms, in equipment of their soldiers and in their means and resources of every kind for successful war. It can be accounted for only upon the assumption that the Southern people as a whole have more pluck, more indomitable courage, more intrepidity and more dogged endurance than has the Northern people. With equal means, equal numbers and resources, the South would have won, and the war could not have lasted more than two years. Above all, our cause was just; the slavery question, although the proximate cause of the war, was subordinate to the great cause of the right of self-government, self-control. The Southern people were and are a homogeneous people, a chivalrous people—more of the Cavalier than the Puritan or Round-head, and under equal conditions make the best soldiers. Hence it was that the South resisted the overpowering forces of the North so successfully for so long a period—four years. The North never did whip the South by combat on the field, but by exhausting us and our resources. The world's history does not furnish a single example of such heroic endurance against such odds so successfully for so long a time, and Marion District did her full share in every way during the unparalleled struggle. She may truthfully say, *magna pars fui,* to the full extent of her capabilities. The war over, her men who had escaped the casualties and diseases and deaths incident and consequent upon it, having lost all, *save honor,* returned to their desolated and impoverished homes, with nothing to begin life again but strong arms and stout hearts. They found property gone (and what little remained had but little value), destitute homes, ragged children, in many cases no bread and other necessaries of life, and nothing to buy with. Their condition in many instances was deplorable indeed. Their poverty and want were more appalling than the enemy they had faced for four long years. The prospect for living, for recuperation, was most gloomy. Our people, nothing daunted, went to work with such scanty means as they had or could procure, entered the school of hardship and self-denial with a hearty good will, and in a comparatively short time acquired the means necessary to supply their natural needs, and continuing to ply their energies under adverse circumstances, the horrors of reconstruction under an insolent soldiery, the people of the district gradually recuperated, and not only supplied natural and pressing wants, but after reconstruction, though on a radical basis, began to accumulate the means of life, as well as many of its comforts and enjoyments, and occasionally a surplus. Our troubles did not end by reconstruction, so-called, and the State Constitution of 1868. The institution of civil government did not displace the military, but it was continued for eight or nine years, or till April, 1877. Before every election, and at the meeting of the Legislature, so-called, a body of armed soldiers was sent here, for the purpose of intimidation, and to awe our citizens at the polls and, as the "powers that be" said, to protect the voters of the Republican party at elections, and to prevent as many Democrats as possible from exercising their right to vote. And on the meeting of the Legislature, the soldiers were the doorkeepers, and allowed no one to enter, as a member, except such as were known Republicans; and some from counties, for instance, Horry County, where after the first three or four years it was impossible to elect a Republican. The soldiers were the judges of the election and election returns, and were the actual returning boards of both county and State; were judges of not only the election of members to the House and Senate, but also of their qualifications; and the only qualification necessary for admission to a seat in either House, if a white man, was that he was a Republican, a "carpet-bagger" or "scalawag;" if a negro, that his skin was black or tan colored. So far as the negro member was concerned, he was nothing more than a puppet in the hands of those who led and controlled the body, and at least five-sixths of the members were negroes. There were a few leading negroes, such as W. J. Whipper, of Beaufort, Beverly Nash, of Richland, S. A. Swails, of Williamsburg, Henry E. Hayne, of Marion, H. J. Maxwell, of Marlborough, and some other negroes, who were the lieutenants of such men as Scott, Moses, Leslie, John J. Patterson, H. C. Corbin and the Mackeys, and perhaps some others. These latter did the planning as to when and how to steal, and their lieutenants put the plans into execution. The ignorant rabble in the Legislature were voted as occasion might require. Such a carnival of plunder, under the forms of law, was never witnessed before. Open and shameless bribery was the order of the day, and the bribes were paid from the public treasury. Every man had his price—verifying the assertion of Robert Walpole, of England. The bribes paid in South Carolina were from $5,000 down to $200. Every man was paid according to his supposed influence. Henry E. Hayne, first a Senator from Marion County, and then Secretary of State, built a fine house in Marion, now owned and occupied by Mr. James Baker, and had it finely furnished. Whilst he was hauling up the furniture from the depot at Marion, the writer heard him say that it (the furniture) was a present to his mother from a friend of hers. Each one of those mentioned above, including B. F. Whittemore, a Massachusetts carpet-bagger, representing Darlington County in the Senate, received $5,000; others $2,000, $1,000, $500 and $200. I would mention the names of some of the scalawags in Marion, but out of respect to the families or descendants of some of them, the writer forbears, knowing that the present generation is not responsible for what was then done.

When the white people, the taxpayers of the State, got possession of the Legislature and the executive departments of the government by the election in 1876 (ever to be remembered), a Fraud Commission was appointed to investigate and unearth the frauds and stealage for the then past eight years. One Josephus Woodruff, who had been and was Clerk of the Senate, turned evidence against his party, or against the party who had been in power. It seems he kept a little book, called at the time a "whirligig book," in which many of the stealings were entered—I suppose it was stenographically entered—each man's name, and how much he was paid, and what he had been paid. When that Committee made its report, our own people were astonished. They knew that fraud and stealing had been going on, but to what extent was unknown. A stampede from the State of many of the leaders, white and colored, took place at once. Whittemore, then in the State Senate from Darlington, fled never to return; the same of Moses (F. J., Jr.),

R. K. Scott, H. E. Hayne, S. A. Swails, and, in short, the whole gang of the leaders, the biggest rogues, fled the State, and in a few months time they were all gone. "A guilty conscience makes cowards of us all." Henry E. Hayne left Columbia and went down to Marion, his home, and where his mother lived, and was so badly frightened that he did not spend the night there, but left the same night and, as the writer understands it, has never returned. "He left his country for his country's good." We can spare him. The particular stealings above mentioned were not all, by many, that occurred during the eight years of radical rule and high carnival. These were the bribes given and taken to pass a certain financial scheme by which the State was robbed and to be robbed of millions. In the early part of their career they did not seem so rapacious—more modest in their actings and doings; but as time went on, the disguise was thrown off, and they became familiar with crime and theft; and growing more rapacious, they did not hesitate to take it by thousands, when at first they were afraid of being caught, and being somewhat squeamish, they would take only by littles, by hundreds; now in or near the end of their reign, they could and did take it by thousands; and no doubt thinking that their hold on the State could not be broken—that their lease of power was well secured to them for all time to come, or at least for a long time—they were the more ready to embark into stealing enterprises on a large scale. Hence this voracious greed for money could not be satiated with small amounts. It took more and more to satisfy them. Wresting the State from them in 1876 was a complete surprise to them—they had no idea of defeat. On the 15th August, 1876, D. H. Chamberlain, their candidate for Governor, said in a public speech in Marion that day, that the Republican party would carry the State by 40,000 majority. In other words, that he would be elected by that majority. There are many now living who heard him say it. Hence the Hampton campaign success was a great and fatal surprise to them.

In 1868, at the first election under the Constitution of that year, Henry E. Hayne, a mulatto negro, was elected to the State Senate. I am not certain as to who were elected as Representatives, but think it was B. F. Thompson, Ebben Hays (white) and W. S. Collins (white); the white men were called scalawags. In 1870, only Representatives were elected. The Democrats put out a ticket that year and succeeded in electing it, to wit: Rev. Joel Allen, F. A. Miles, Dr. Thomas R. Bass and John C. Sellers. They were elected by a majority of from 150 to 180. They would, doubtless, have been counted out by the Returning Board for the county, had they not been put in fear. Some half dozen or more of our citizens, headed by Major S. A. Durham, waited upon R. F. Graham, C. Smith and others, leading lights of the Radical party, the night before the returns of election were to be canvassed the next day, and told them that they knew the Democratic ticket entire was elected, and if they were counted out, the lives of the canvassers would be taken at once. Major Durham and his associates were appointed a committee to wait on the Board of Canvassers, and so say to them, by an *impromptu* meeting of citizens in the town of Marion. This prompt action on the part of the Democrats had the desired effect, and thus saved Democratic representation to and from the county. Our Representatives could do nothing in the Legislature when they were there. They could only watch the Radicals and block, as far as possible, any hurtful legislation attempted. There were only about twenty Democrats in that Legislature.

In 1872, the Democrats and Republicans each had their tickets in the field for Marion County. A strong effort was made, but the Republicans having the whole machinery of election in their hands, succeeded by fraud and by counting in their candidates. William S. Mullins was the candidate for the Senate on the part of the Democrats, and C. Smith on the part of the Radicals. Henry E. Hayne, the former Senator, was elected that year Secretary of State. The Democrats elected every one of their candidates, but they were all counted out, and the Radicals counted in. Kukluxism had been doing its bloody work in some parts of the State, and the power of the United States was being invoked to suppress and punish it, and that to some extent awed our people and deterred them from going as far in 1872 as they would have gone in 1870. Hence the counting out of our candidates in 1872 was submitted to. We had a full Radical set of county officers and Senator and Representatives. Incompetency in office and greed for money ruled the times. Crime was everywhere rampant, not only in Marion County, but throughout the State. The State was called the "prostrate State"—she was powerless everywhere. In 1872, three negroes, Jonas Deas, Lawrence Mills and Enos Reeves, were elected County Commissioners for Marion County. Ignorant and corrupt, they knew nothing whatever about the duties of the office, nothing about finances, except to steal them. For the year 1874, they fixed the county taxes so high that they, with the State levy, made the taxes for Marion County $100,000, whereas they should not have exceeded $40,000, county and State. In consequence of which a public meeting of the citizens and taxpayers was held at Marion on salesday in January, 1874. The Legislature was then in session; our situation was discussed, and resulted in appointing a committee of our citizens to go to Columbia and memorialize the Legislature on the subject, and to pray that body for relief. The committee appointed to perform that duty was composed of Major A. J. Shaw (afterwards Judge), A. Q. McDuffie, J. M. Johnson, T. C. Moody and W. W. Sellers. The committee repaired to Columbia. We consulted our own delegation and the leaders, or some of them, in the House and Senate, and heard their suggestions. We drew up a strong memorial for the House and Senate, setting forth our grievances and the relief sought, in a respectful manner, avoiding or refraining from saying anything that would give offence or exhibit any partisan feeling—remembering the old adage, "that when your hand is in the lion's mouth, it won't do to twist his tail." We had the memorial printed and placed copies in the hands of our delegation, and they were introduced simultaneously into the House and Senate, and were referred to the respective Judiciary Committees of the House and Senate. By appointment of those Committees we went before them and were courteously received. Major A. J. Shaw, the Chairman of our committee, was our spokesman before the Judiciary Committees. The facts were very fully stated, both in the memorials and in the statements made by Major Shaw. We remained in Columbia about a week, talking with different members of other delegations and with our own, when we left and returned home, feeling very well assured that our mission there would be successful. The final result was the passing of an Act for our relief, and a reduction was made of the taxes for that year from fifty to sixty per cent., and was so arranged as to benefit only those taxpayers whose property was valued too high. For on inspection of the Auditor's books, there were those whose property was not valued too high and, of course, those did not share in the reduction. It saved some of our people a great deal, while it saved to others less. It saved to General William Evans over $200, to William S. Ellerbe near $250; one Mr. Sinclair (whose first name is not remembered) was assessed at $89 amount to be paid, and by the reduction made it was less than $30. Thus it ran, some saving much and some less. All this trouble and expense were incurred by the ignorance and incompetency of the three negro County Commissioners for the county, and it is not improbable that they desired a heavy collection of taxes that they might have a larger pile to steal from. This is inferred from the fact that they were afterwards indicted for embezzlement of the public funds, tried by a Republican Court, prosecuted by a Republican Solicitor and a jury, a majority of whom were negroes, and were convicted and sentenced to terms, each, of imprisonment for a number of months not now remembered—some for longer terms than others. Jonas Deas, the Chairman of the Board, got the longest term.

In 1874, there was a sort of compromise in Marion County between the parties, by which the white people of the county had two Representatives and the Republicans two. The Representatives elected that year were ex-Chancellor W. D. Johnson and Colonel R. G. Howard, and William E. Hayne and Anthony Howard—the two former for the whites and the two latter for the Republicans. During that legislative term Judge Green (a Republican) died, which left the Third Circuit without a Judge. His place was filled by the election of A. J. Shaw, Esq., then a resident citizen of Marion, and a Democrat. The Representatives from Marion voted for him, and it was said, and truthfully said, that W. E. Hayne, one of the Republican Representatives from Marion, did his best for the election of Shaw as Judge, and was fully appreciated by the citizens of

Marion and of the Third Judicial Circuit, and also by the people of the State. Daniel H. Chamberlain, Republican, was Governor from 1874 to 1876, and during his term as Governor there were two other vacant judgeships, and W. J. Whipper and Franklin J. Moses, Jr., were elected to fill those vacancies, at which the whole State was very much mortified and humiliated; but, to the surprise and great relief of the white people of the State, Governor Chamberlain refused to commission them, on the ground of their want of moral character, and thus the State was saved from the infliction. Chamberlain was a man of courage, otherwise he would not have dared to refuse their commissions. Chamberlain was a decent Republican and a gentleman. He had been first elected Attorney General of the State and then Governor by the Republican party. It took courage to oppose the will of the Legislature expressed in the election of said men as Judges. Very few in the party, if any, would have thus flown in the face of the party as Chamberlain did. He was a Northern man, a graduate of Yale College, a fine scholar and a brainy man. He did many things while Governor which the white people favored, and by which he ingratiated himself into the favor of many of our good and leading men. In the campaign of 1876, Chamberlain was again nominated by the Republicans for a second term as Governor. The people of the State were sick and tired of Radical carpet-bag rule, and anxious to make the fight for its overthrow. Many good men in the State were fearful that if the fight was made that it would fail, and our condition would thereby be made more intolerable; that as Chamberlain had made a pretty good Governor, we had better acquiesce in his nomination and election, than to run the risk. This was the idea of many very good men, who were opposed to making the contest. "The Straightouts," as they were called, were for making the contest, and gain all or lose all; that if they were beaten, it could not and would not make our condition any worse. Strong men were on each side of the question. A Democratic State Convention was called to meet in Columbia on 15th August, 1876. Each and every county in the State was represented in the Convention, and the election of a Chairman or President of the Convention was made the test of the strength of the respective sides. The "Straightouts" nominated General W. W. Harllee, of Marion, for Chairman, and the Chamberlain men nominated C. H. Simonton, of Charleston (now Judge), for Chairman. Upon a strict party vote, General Harllee was elected Chairman by thirteen majority. The Convention made nominations for Governor, Lieutenant-Governor and State officers, including Solicitors, and perhaps Congressmen. General Wade Hampton was nominated for Governor and W. D. Simpson for Lieutenant-Governor. The Chamberlain men wheeled right into line. They were just as good men as the "Straightouts," only were not as sanguine as to results as were the "Straightouts." The delegation from Marion were all "Straightouts," the only county in the Pee Dee section that sent such. The whole State was a unit, and in a blaze with enthusiasm. Never before within the memory of the writer was there such unanimity and such united effort. The campaign meetings were attended by the whole people throughout the State. No "coon-skins, hard cider or red pepper clap-trap" were resorted to. Nothing but red shirts, and cavalcades, and bands of music, marked the campaign. To defeat the Radical party and to rescue the State from its clutches were the aim and end to be attained. To do this, it was necessary to carry a great portion of the negro vote, and we did carry enough of it to turn the scale. A red shirt was the badge, and it was not uncommon in Marion to see in the cavalcades of the day as many as fifty to a hundred negroes, mounted on horseback in the cavalcades, with red shirts on, in procession with the white folks. The red shirts and horses in most instances were furnished them by the white people. He was then committed to the Hampton ticket, and could not go back on it. The business of the country was for the time pretty much abandoned. Men rode day and night with the red shirt insignia of the times on. No doubt, that some excesses were committed by the less considerate of our people, but not often to the injury of the common cause. Speech-making to gatherings of the people was the order of the day, and they were attended by the people in crowds. Never before in the memory of man, had there been such intensified determination manifested. It was not much less than a struggle for life. Chamberlain, the Republican candidate for Governor, in a speech delivered at Marion on the very day of the meeting of our Convention in Columbia, said that he would carry the State by 40,000 majority, we suppose he was about correct, counting every negro voter a Republican. To elect our ticket we must carry with us more than 20,000 negro voters—and we think that many were carried. The Hampton ticket was on white paper, the Radical ticket was on pink colored paper—all kept secret from the opposite party. A few days before the election, Captain Daggett, of Horry, managed to get hold of one of their tickets, it was immediately sent to Charleston (*News and Courier*), thousands of them were printed with the names of our candidates on them, and on the morning of election day they were at every voting precinct in the State. That discovery and its immediate sequel was a protection to the negro voter for the Hampton ticket. There were many negroes willing to, and wanted to, vote that ticket, but were afraid to do so—were afraid of their own people, and especially of their neighborhood leaders; and doubtless thousands of those red tickets, with the Hampton candidates' names upon them, were that day (7th November, 1876), voted. Those red tickets turned the election, by which the people of the State were redeemed from the curse and hateful, ruinous rule of the carpet-bagger, scalawag and the ignorant negro. How or by what means Captain Daggett came into possession of that red ticket, with its eagle emblem upon it, we do not know, nor do we care to know. The tickets were sent to leaders in every county in the State, with an injunction of secrecy, to let no white man see them or to get hold of them. No doubt Captain Daggett knew the leaders in his county, Horry—he knew who was approachable and by what means. He accomplished his purposes for the good of his adopted State, and thereby his State was redeemed. To him should be erected a monument in the hearts of the people of the State more enduring than brass and marble. He was afterwards honored by the citizens of Horry with a seat in the State Senate, an honor not at all commensurate with the daring courage which animated his patriotic bosom to do or to die. Captain Dagget has been dead for several years, has gone to his reward—*"Requiescat in pace."* The election in the

State for Governor was pretty close. Hampton's majority, as claimed and his claim was sustained, was 1,134. Marion County was carried overwhelmingly for the Hampton ticket. Marion did her full share in the contest and she did no more than the other counties in the State—all were strained to the utmost. There were elected in the State, also, majorities for the Senate and House of Representatives. There were bitter contests in the Supreme Court for the offices. Chamberlain and State officers on his ticket claimed to have been elected. For a while there were two Houses of Representatives, each organized with a Speaker and other officers. Both bodies, for two or three days, had possession of the Representative Hall, both Speakers-elect occupied the Speaker's chair. William H. Wallace was Speaker of the Democratic House, afterwards a Judge. E. W. M. Mackey, of Charleston, was Speaker of the Republican House. They clashed and blocked each other for two or three days and nights without leaving the House—took their meals there, furnished by the respective friends outside. In the meantime, thousands of our people had assembled outside the State House. Every man was well armed and ready for the fray. A company of United States soldiers were stationed in Columbia, and a detachment of them was in the State House with their guns and bayonets. General Hampton made a speech from the steps of the Capitol to our people, in which he assured them he would be Governor, and advised that they commit no act of violence nor provoke any hostilities. His head was cool and level. Such was the confidence the people had in him, they took his advice and left for their homes. Our legislative House quietly withdrew from the Capitol building and went to some other house in town and held their sessions there. The Court was composed of F. J. Moses, Chief Justice, a Republican, A. J. Willard, a carpet-bag Judge, though an able man, and J. J. Wright, a negro Judge. This Court, constituted as it was, or a majority of them, decided the various questions springing out of the late elections in favor of the Democrats, and when Rutherford B. Hayes, the President-elect, was inaugurated to the Presidency, the military troops were ordered to leave Columbia, and did leave. Chamberlain at once vacated the executive chamber, and left the whole

State House open for the Democratic Legislature and Democratic State officials. Thus ended the struggle, and thus ended the reign of the carpet-bag government, to the great joy and satisfaction of the people. This consummation proved the sagacity and wisdom of our leader, Wade Hampton, when he advised, in his speech above alluded to, the people to do nothing rash, to be quiet and to go home, with his assurance that he would be Governor. But for the magic of his name and character, the State might have been till this day under Republican rule, and maybe the rule of the bayonet. This much has been said about carpet-bagism, reconstruction, the profligacy of the Radical regime, and the State's redemption in 1876, not so much for the present generation, as most of them were the subjects and actors, and participants in the governmental occurrences of the last twenty-five or thirty years, but that some faint sketch of it might be put in book form, for the sons and daughters of the next and future generations to read and ponder. The one-hundredth part has not been told—in fact, it can never all be told.

The Early Settlement of Marion County.

This part of the Province of South Carolina, Craven County, was not much settled until about 1735. When Queensborough Township was laid off wholly in Marion County, in 1731 and 1732, there was not a settlement within it; but below that township, and between the two rivers, Great and Little Pee Dee, according to well authenticated tradition, there were some settlements before that time. Mr. M. M. Lowrimore, of Woodberry Township, has furnished the writer with some interesting facts about the first settlement of that part of the county, Britton's Neck, below the old Britton's Neck Church of the present day (about which church more may be said hereinafter). The writer is also indebted to Mrs. Margaret F. Johnson, widow of the late Hugh R. Johnson, near Nichols, S. C., and who was the daughter of the late General William Woodberry, of Britton's Neck, for valuable and interesting information about the Woodberry family. From these two sources, viz: letter of Mr. M. M. Lowrimore and letter of Mrs. Margaret F. Johnson, the writer gleans the following:

"Some time in the early part of 1700, there came from Ireland some people by the name of Michalls, 'not McAll,' and settled on a point of land now called the 'Tan-yard.' Their occupation in their native land was that of tanners. After coming to this country, finding game so numerous, they became great hunters, and to carry on their trade they erected a tan-yard just one mile above the mouth of Little Pee Dee River, on the bank of the Great Pee Dee. They killed game, then plentiful of all kinds and sorts, bought hides from others, tanned them and sold the leather to the early planters in that region and on the Waccamaw Neck. What became of the Michalls is unknown; the signs of the tan-yard erected by them were there for many years afterwards, and may be seen there even yet. The place is known now as the 'tan-yard.' The name of Michall is now extinct in the county." Mr. Lowrimore says: "About 1710, there came over a goodly number from Great Britain, and thereby they were called the Brittons or Brittains." This would imply that the whole colony, whatever might be their individual names, were called the "Brittons" or "Brittains." The time of this settlement antedates the settlement made twenty-five years afterward, as spoken of by Bishop Gregg in his book, p. 69 There possibly may have been two emigrations in those early times to that part of the county (Craven). Mr. Lowrimore says: "They commenced settling at the lower mouth of Jordan's Lake. Their occupations were planting corn, peas, potatoes, rye, oats, wheat and flax, raised hogs, sheep, goats and cattle; lived high on fish and honey, and wore otter-skin coats." If Mr. Lowrimore is correct, and the writer sees no reason to discredit him, this applies to the colony of 1710, called "Brittons" or "Brittains." Mr. Lowrimore further says: "About 1734, a number of Lowrimores with their wives came over from Ireland. Their trade was blacksmith and house carpentering. My great-grand-father was the blacksmith. Some of them went off to the rice countries and got rich, and lost it all by bad management. My grand-father, W. James Lowrimore, was a blacksmith, which trade my father, Robert Lowrimore, learned." The writer regrets that he has not been able to see Mr. Lowrimore, and learn more of the Lowrimore family—

whom they married, how many children they raised, and their names, and what their successes in life were, and what has become of them. The writer has met with the present M. M. Lowrimore in times past, but not lately. He is advancing in life, perhaps seventy years old, an excellent man, in fact, no ordinary man, considering his want of opportunities and his environments. He and his immediate family are the only ones by the name known now to be in the county. In his very interesting letter to the writer, he says nothing about his family, except as above quoted, and nothing at all about his own immediate family, or whether he has any children or otherwise. There are several of the name in Horry County, who the writer supposes to be lineally or collaterally related to him. M. M. Lowrimore is a patriot and true man; if he has any family of his own, he is too modest to say anything about them. He is a remarkable antiquarian, and it is natural with him, not acquired, as his early educational opportunities were quite limited. Mr. Lowrimore continues: "Later on came a Capps, a farmer; next a family of Augustines, bee-tree hunters and hunters generally. This is on a lonely island between Jordan's Lake and the Great Pee Dee. Also an adjacent island was settled by a family of Hunters, a hunter by name and by trade. These islands go by the names of Augustine and Hunter's Islands. In 1734, came in a family of Kibber (or Kibler), occupation as others. All this on the Great Pee Dee. On Little Pee Dee, a man from England settled near its waters, by the name of Parker. Next a family of Colemans and a man by the name of Jerry Touchberry; the Brittons at Hickory Hill. Next on the Little Pee Dee River, a family of the Woodberrys, who raised hogs and cattle for market, made indigo, met the trading vessels and changed off indigo pound for pound of negro weighed naked (so much for the Woodberrys). Next the Okes did likewise also. About 1760, the Munnerlyns (Irish), farmers and stock raisers, planted indigo, rice, oats, wheat and tobacco, raised orchards, beat cider." Mr. Lowrimore proceeds: "Next was a number of Williams—I know not where from. They lived chiefly by raising stock and driving it to market. Near the Great Pee Dee, a family of Rays, near the place that you know that is called Ray's

Causeway, on the road leading from Britton's Neck to the Ark Church. Also, the old Jenkins lived in there, too. There is where old Mrs. Jenkins drank the toast to the British officer, when she told him she had three sons in the war, and she wished that she had three thousand. Another settlement which I forgot to note was old James Crockett, an old Englishman, came and settled on Little Pee Dee, near what is known as Pawley's Camps, the place where old Tory Pawley hid when old General Marion was ransacking this part of the country for the Tories. But the said Crockett obtained a warrant, and in 1734, he took up and had granted to him a tract of land. I have had the old plat and grant in my hand many times. This then was called Craven County. I have not gone above the road leading to Britton's Neck Church. The Graves that lived on the road, you can get knowledge of them and the old Davises and Mapp Claff." The old gentleman, Mr. M. M. Lowrimore, closes above quoted letter in these words, *verbatim et literatim:*

"Mr. Sellers, I take great pleasure in replying to you it was a Great strain on the mind, I did as best I could under the present circumstance please write to me if it is any profit to you or not, excuse mistakes and blunders, as I am no Grammareon In those old days the rattlesnakes were numberous I give you a receipt for the cure of Rattlesnake bite take one handful of parsley leaves one of Hoar hound leaves, beat up and squice (or) squix through one pint of new milk, add a lump of allum as big as a hulled hickory nut, give at draught" (he doesn't say how much) "When this you remember an old friend." Yours M. M. Lowrimore."

"address Smiths Mills, S. C."

The writer cannot adequately express his appreciation of the above quoted letter, coming from the man it did. Now as to the different settlers mentioned in Mr. Lowrimore's letter. The Michalls, of "tan-yard" notoriety, have long since disappeared. It is not improbable that the name Michall, as given by Mr. Lowrimore, is the same as Mikell (a family), noticed by Bishop Gregg, pages 89 and 90, and notes, as coming to the Upper Pee Dee in 1756, two brothers, John and William. The difference is in the spelling, but *idem sonans.* One of these was killed during the Revolutionary War by a Tory; the other survived that struggle. John, the elder brother, settled on the west side of the river, a few miles above Long Bluff. Gregg says he became a Major in the Revolutionary War, and was a man of decided character. It is not stated by Gregg where the Mikells came from, and it may be when the Michalls broke up from the "tan-yard," that they moved up the river on the west side in 1756, as stated by Bishop Gregg. At any rate, the suggestion is made for what it is worth. There are no Michalls in Britton's Neck now, nor has there been within the memory of the writer. As to the Lowrimores, the writer has already said all he knows about them. Now as to the colony of English spoken of by Lowrimore as coming into Britton's Neck about the year 1710, and coming from England, "thereby" called "Brittons" or "Brittains." They were different from the Brittons by name, as settling down there about 1735 or 1736, by Bishop Gregg (page 69), who says: "About the time John Godbold came to Pee Dee, two important settlements were made in that region. One of these was in Britton's Neck, twenty miles below Mar's Bluff and forty miles above Georgetown." "It was composed of the families of Britton, Graves, Fladger, Davis, Tyler, Giles and others. They came directly from England as one colony." Further notice of this colony will be taken by the writer hereinafter. As to the "Brittons" mentioned by Mr. Lowrimore, of 1710, and those mentioned by Bishop Gregg, of 1735, are they the same, or were there two emigrations by the name of Britton? Both may be correct, or one of them is in error, and if so, which one? Neither Bishop Gregg nor Mr. Lowrimore were cotemporaries with the Brittons, and, therefore, both depended on information derived from tradition. Bishop Gregg was a man of scholarly ability; Mr. Lowrimore was to the "manor born," a lineal descendant of some of the "Lowrimores with their wives," who came there in 1734 from Ireland, and M. M. Lowrimore got his information in the traditions of his family, handed down from the great-grand-father to the grand-father, and from him to the father, Robert Lowrimore, and from the father, Robert, to the son, M. M. Lowrimore. Bishop Gregg obtained his information (traditional) from the late Hugh Godbold, of Marion District—says so, in a note on page 69.

The writer will not undertake to decide between them, but leaves it to the reader to decide for himself.

As to the Capps, spoken of by Mr. Lowrimore as coming later, who he says was a farmer, the writer supposes he is and was the progenitor of the family by that name now living, and has been for a century, below Marion Court House. If he was not the progenitor of them, it is altogether unknown what became of the one mentioned by Mr. Lowrimore. As to the Augustines and Hunters, mentioned by Mr. Lowrimore as settling there in those early times, the writer knows nothing; he is not informed as to what became of them. No such name as Augustine is now in Marion County, nor has there been since his recollection. The name has disappeared; as also the Hunters, so far as Marion County is concerned. There are Hunters in Florence and Darlington Counties, who, it is not improbable, descended from the Hunter family or families, mentioned by Mr. Lowrimore as settling in Britton's Neck.

Mr. Lowrimore says, in 1734, a family by the name of "Kibler or Kibber" came in and settled there; that name is also extinct in Marion County. He says all the foregoing settlements were made on the Great Pee Dee. He says: "On Little Pee Dee, a man from England settled near its waters by the name of Parker. Next a family of Coleman, and a man by the name of Jerry Touchberry; the Brittons at Hickory Hill." Parker is a name that has been long and favorably known in Marion County; the Parker family reside on the west side of the Great Pee Dee, in what is now Florence County, formerly in Marion. There is also a family of Parkers in Marlborough County, quite respectable. The family in both counties have extensive connections, and are here to stay. In the absence of other information, it is probable that the family in both counties sprang from the one who settled about 1734 in Britton's Neck. The name of Touchberry is not in Marion County now. The name of Britton is also extinct in this county, and has been for years, though they have connections here not bearing the name. Time and circumstantial conditions effect wonderful changes—at least, in 165 years—and often leave no trace or remembrance of families or conditions. All terrestrial things are transitory and passing into the shades of oblivion.

Mr. Lowrimore says: "Next on Little Pee Dee River, a family of the Woodberrys (came), who raised hogs and cattle for market, made indigo, met the trading vessels and changed off indigo pound for pound of negro weighed naked."

The writer received a letter from Mrs. Hugh R. Johnson, who was a daughter of the late General Wm. Woodberry, of Britton's Neck, in which she says: "The Woodberrys (two brothers), Richard and Jonah, came from Socastee—I can't give the date; they settled in Britton's Neck, where they found several brothers by the name of Britton, who were large land and slave owners. Richard Woodberry, my grand-father, married Miss Lizzie Balloon, on Black River. They brought up two sons and three daughters; one of the sons was my father, the well known General Wm. Woodberry. General Woodberry was born January 10th, 1788, and died January 31st, 1851. I have heard my father say that about 1815, the Brittons sold out and moved to Sumter County, except Dr. Tom Britton, who had married Margaret, one of the General's sisters; she died childless. Fannie, another one of the sisters, married Sam. Wilson; she also died without children. The other sister married the Rev. Jeremiah Norman, of North Carolina; Mrs. John Woodberry and Mrs. James Jenkins, and Samuel Norman, of Horry, were their children. Richard Woodberry, the General's only brother, married Miss Desda Davis; their children were John and Washington, Mrs. Benjamin Gause and Mrs. John Gause. General Woodberry's first wife was Miss Hannah Davis; they had four children, all dying quite young. His second wife was Miss Sarah Johnson, of Horry; they brought up four sons and four daughters, all of whom except one daughter married and reared families, but I expect you know as much about them as I do."

Mr. Lowrimore says: "Next the Okes did likewise all"—that is, as I construe it, they did like the Woodberrys—"raised hogs and cattle for market, made indigo, met the trading vessels and changed off indigo pound for pound of negro weighed naked." As to this name, "Okes," there is no record of such name in the county anywhere, as the writer has ever seen. The name may be included in the word "others," mentioned by Bishop Gregg, on p. 69, where he mentions the settlement in

Britton's Neck of 1735, and gives the names of several of those early settlers there and concludes with the words "and others." The name has entirely disappeared, if it ever existed. Mr. Lowrimore says: "About 1760, the Munnerlyns (Irish), farmers and stock raisers, planted indigo, rice, oats, wheat and tobacco, raised orchards, beat cider." They settled in Britton's Neck; there are none there now by that name. It is very probable that the Munnerlyn family, the Rev. Thomas M. Munnerlyn, who lived up near Ariel Church for many years, and raised a family there, and died there some twenty years ago, was a descendant of the Munnerlyn spoken of by Mr. Lowrimore. The Rev. Thomas M. Munnerlyn had a son, Thomas W. Munnerlyn, who became an itinerant Methodist preacher, and who died in 1898 and was buried at Smithville, S. C. (Minutes of the Conference, 1899, held at Orangeburg, S. C.), a son named George, who emigrated West some years ago, and a daughter, who married the late R. Z. Harllee; he and wife are both dead. The Munnerlyn family were quite respectable in their day; none bearing the name now in the county, that the writer is aware of. A branch of the old Munnerlyn family is in Georgetown. B. A. Munnerlyn, of Georgetown, is a first class business man and stands high with all who have business with him. Mr. Lowrimore mentions the Williams as being early settlers in Britton's Neck, on the Great Pee Dee; that they raised stock and drove it to market. There are several Williams down in that region or portion of the county now, but the writer has no personal acquaintance with them. They have the reputation of being a peaceable and quiet people, unostentatious, and unpretending in their manners and habits.

Mr. Lowrimore mentions a family of Rays, who settled near the place that is called Ray's Causeway, on the road leading from Britton's Neck to the "Ark" Church. There are no Rays down in that section now. There are Rays in the upper end of the county, but they are not of that family. What became of them is unknown. Mr. Lowrimore further says: "Also, the old Jenkings lived in there, too, there is where old Mrs. Jenkins drank the toast to the British officer, when she told him she had three sons in the army, and she wished she had three thousand." This colloquy between Mrs. Jenkins, who it seems was at that time a widow, and the British officer, is related in full in the Life of Marion, written by Brigadier General Horry and Rev. M. L. Weems, pages 220-222. It is as follows: "It was not for the British and Marion to lie long at rest in the same neighborhood. After a short repose, Colonel Watson, with a stout force of regulars and Tories, made an inroad upon Pee Dee, which was no sooner known in our camp, than Marion pushed after him. We presently struck their trail; and after a handsome day's run, pitched our tents near the house of the excellent widow, Jenkins, and on the very spot which the British had left in the morning. Colonel Watson, it seems, had taken his quarters that night in her house; and learning that she had three sons with Marion, all active, young men, he sent for her after supper, and desired her to sit down and take a glass of wine with him. To his request, a good old lady of taste and manners could have no objection; so waiting upon the Colonel, and taking a chair which he handed her, she sat down and emptied her glass to his health. He then commenced the following conversation with her: 'So, Madam, they tell me you have several sons in General Marion's camp; I hope it is not true.' She said, 'It was very true, and was only sorry that it was not a thousand times truer.' 'A thousand times truer, Madam!' replied he, with great surprise. 'Pray, what can be your meaning in that?' 'Why, sir, I am only sorry that in place of three, I have not three thousand sons with General Marion.' 'Aye, indeed! Well, then, Madam, begging your pardon, you had better send for them immediately to come in and join his Majesty's troops under my command; for as they are rebels now in arms against their king, should they be taken they will be hung as sure as ever they were born.' 'Why, sir,' said the old lady, 'you are very considerate of my sons; for which, at any rate, I thank you. But, as you have begged my pardon for giving me this advice, I must beg yours for not taking it. My sons, sir, are of age, and must and will act for themselves. And as to their being in a state of rebellion against their king, I must take the liberty, sir, to deny that.' 'What, Madam!' replied he; 'not in rebellion against their king? Shooting and killing his Majesty's subjects like wolves! Don't you call that rebellion against their king, Madam?' 'No, sir,' answered she; 'they are only doing their duty, as God and nature commanded them, sir.' 'The d—l they are, Madam.' 'Yes, sir,' continued she, 'and what you and every man in England would glory to do against the king, were he to dare to tax you contrary to your own consent, and the Constitution of the realm. 'Tis the king, sir, who is in rebellion against my sons, and not they against him. And could right prevail against might, he would as certainly lose his head as ever King Charles the First did.' Colonel Watson could hardly keep his chair under the smart of this speech; but thinking it would never do for a British Colonel to be rude to a lady, he filled her glass, and saying, 'he'd be d—d if she were not a very plain spoken woman at any rate,' insisted she would drink a toast with him for all that. She replied she had no objection. Then filling the glasses round, he looked at her with a constrained smile, and said, 'Well, Madam, here is George the Third.' 'With all my heart, sir,' and turned off her bumper with a good grace. After a decent interval of sprightly conversation, he called on the widow for a toast, who smartly retorted, 'Well, sir, here's George Washington.' At which he darkened a little, but drank it off with an officer-like politeness. The next morning early, we left the good Mrs. Jenkins, and burning with impatience to give Watson another race, we drove on Jehu-like." Mrs. Jenkins was a noble lady, full of the fires of patriotism, and had the courage, inspired by it, to speak her mind in almost the presence of royalty—at least, in the presence of and to a representative of it—and yet she did not forget the proprieties of her sex. She did not hesitate to express her sentiments, though pointed, yet with the calm dignity of a true and virtuous woman. She assuredly got the better of Colonel Watson, which he did not rudely resent. It may be inferred from his rank and position that he had the instincts of a gentleman, and though she stung him to the core, he treated her with much respect and due consideration. She, doubtless, loved her sons with all the ardor of her soul, yet she was willing to surrender them to her country's call, to resist its invaders, to fight for its liberties and, if needs be, to die in its cause. The writer does not know how many sons she had; he does know, however, that she had, in addition to the three noble boys in Marion's army, another boy, James, then a lad of fourteen or fifteen years, who at an early age entered into the ministry, joined the Methodist Conference, and engaged in a warfare against the devil and sin—a much more formidable enemy than was the King of Great Britain. He joined the Conference in 1792, and was an itinerant preacher for the balance of his life, or as long as he was physically able. He was a pioneer preacher. In those early times of Methodism, the South Carolina Conference included the States of North Carolina, South Carolina and Georgia. Previous to 1800, there was but one Presiding Elder's District covering the whole territory of the Conference. In that year, the whole State of South Carolina was made a District, and James Jenkins was appointed the Presiding Elder. He became a strong preacher, and was distinguished through life for his great pulpit strength, and for his deep and devoted piety. He was an effective preacher wherever he went, and filled the most important positions in his Conference. He lived to the age of eighty-three. In his old age he became blind, and had to be led about by some one. The writer saw him and heard him preach two masterly sermons at a camp meeting in Brownsville, Marlborough County, S. C., in 1841. It seemed to the writer that he knew the Bible and hymn book by heart. He gave his hymns as though he was reading them from the book, and would state the number and page, and during the sermon would quote from the Bible, book, chapter and verse. It was simply wonderful. It was evidence that he had made the Bible and its contents a lifelong study. He died 24th June, 1847, and was buried in Camden, S. C. A distinguished son of Marion County, born and reared by a noble and historically distinguished mother; thus verifying the adage, that "all great men had great mothers." W. J. Crosswell, Superintendent of Southern Express Company, of Wilmington, N. C., and J. J. Crosswell, Route Agent of same company, Fayetteville, N. C., are grand-sons of the Rev. James Jenkins.

Mr. Lowrimore gives us the name of another early settler in Britton's Neck, by the name of James Crockett, in the following words: "Another settlement which I forgot to note was old James Crockett, an old Englishman, came and settled on

Little Pee Dee, near what is known as Pawley's Camp, the place where old Tory Pawly, hid, when old General Marion was ransacking this part of the country for the Torys; but the said Crockett obtained a warrant, and in 1734, he taken up and had granted to him a tract of land. I have had the old plat and grant in my hand many times." This was probably the progenitor of the celebrated David Crockett, of frontier fame in the wild West, seventy-five or eighty years ago. Davy Crockett was a great hunter in those early times. He wrote a book containing his own biography—his life and adventures with the Indians and wild, ferocious animals, his hair-breadth escapes, always the hero of his own stories; his candidacy for and election to Congress; a ludicrous account of his introduction to and interview with President Andrew Jackson. Crockett was exceedingly humorous, and could tell most ludicrous stories. His dress was made of the skins of the animals he killed; wore a cap made of a coon-skin, with the tail hanging down his back. It has been forty or fifty years since the writer read his book, and remembers some of his exploits as he told them, but cannot tell any of them like Crockett told them in his book. He cannot put the "spice in and gravy on," as Crockett did. He will, however, venture to insert one of his exploits here. Crockett says one day he was hunting in a swamp or bog, and he found a den of young bears. They were in a large hollow stump some twenty feet or more high; he could hear the young bears in the stump. He determined to get at them and destroy them. He sat "Betsy," his rifle, which he called Betsy, down against a tree, and then climbed up the hollow stump to the top. He looked down the hollow and could see the young bears in their bed at the bottom, but he could not reach them. He got into the top of the hollow, his feet downwards, and with his hands hold of the top of the broken tree—like going down into a well feet foremost; swinging by the top of the curb with his hands, he let himself down as low as he could—his feet not reaching to the bottom; he turned loose and down he dropped in among the young bears. The young bears became frightened at his intrusion among them, and set up a terrible screaming. The old she bear being off a little distance in the swamp. The mother bear, hearing the distress cries of her young, came to see what was the matter. She climbed up the stump and looked down to see her young ones and to see what was the matter, and saw Crockett down there among them; she, enraged, turned tail downward and climbed down. Crockett was in a very serious dilemma—a maddened mother bear coming down upon him among her young ones. Crockett, always ready with some expedient, jerked out of a side pocket in his clothes his hunting knife, which he always carried, and which was long and sharp-pointed, then made ready for the contest with the maddened mother bear. As soon as she approached near enough, he grabbed her by the tail with one hand and with the knife in the other, he plunged it into her hind parts. She tried to turn upon him, but could not do so; he kept plunging the knife into her. She made for the top of the hollow, in order to extricate herself from Crockett and the knife, Crockett hanging on to her tail and using the knife constantly; she soon carried him out. She went down the stump to the ground, carrying her tormenter with her. He turned her loose and sprang to "Betsy," his rifle, close by, and fired on her, and thus dispatched her. The above is substantially the story as told by Crockett, but is not related as Crockett himself told—in fact, no one could tell it as he did. His book was full of such stories—he was always the hero. He may be a descendant of the Britton's Neck Crocketts. If so, he has immortalized the name. This "Nimrod" of the West was a unique character, a wonderful man. The name is now extinct in Marion County; what has become of them is unknown. It is likely that the family removed West, and hence the celebrated "Davy Crockett."

There are other families in Woodberry Township, but the writer is little acquainted in that region, and, therefore, can say nothing about them. The Hucks family, down there—W. W. Hucks and his brother, Robert Hucks—are prominent men in their community, industrious and thriving citizens; they are in middle life, have families, and are doing well and quite respectable. They are sons of the late John R. Hucks, who has been a resident citizen for many years. I think he came from Horry County. The old gentleman was a very patriotic man; volunteered in 1837, in a company raised in Horry, and went in General Harllee's Battalion to the Seminole War in Florida; and when the Confederate War came on, though past age, he volunteered into the Confederate service and went to Virginia and remained, as the writer thinks, in the service to the end. Few there are who would have done so; as he was not subject to conscription, and is, therefore, entitled to the greater honor. I think he is dead—died lately in his ninetieth year. His sons and family are and may be justly proud of him. I think the old gentleman Hucks had some daughters, but how many, and who they married and where they are, is unknown to the writer.

GODBOLD.—John Godbold was the first who came to the region of Marion Court House. Bishop Gregg, p. 68, says: "He was an Englishman, and had been long a sailor in the British service. Though advanced in years at the time of his arrival, such was his enterprising energy that he succeeded in accumulating what for that day was a large property. He settled in 1735, about a half-mile below the site of the present village of Marion, being the first adventurer to that locality." * * * "During the French and Indian wars, Mr. Godbold was plundered of almost all the personal property he had gathered. Of thirty negroes, twenty-two were taken from him and never recovered; a trunk of guineas, the fruits of many years' labor, was rifled. He married, after his arrival on Pee Dee, Elizabeth McGurney, by whom he had three sons, John, James and Thomas, and two daughters, Elizabeth and Anne, from whom the extensive connexion in Marion have descended." To this Bishop Gregg appends a note, in which he says: "Of his sons, John, the oldest, married Priscilla Jones, and had three sons, Zachariah, John and Jesse. Of these, Zachariah was a Captain in the Revolution; James, the second son (of the first John), married Mourning Elizabeth Baker, by whom he had six sons, John, James, Zachariah, Cade, Abram and Thomas. Of these, John and Zachariah were Lieutenants in the Revolution. Thomas, the youngest son, was the father of the late Hugh Godbold, of Marion. Thomas, the third son (of the first old John), married Martha Herron, and had four sons, Stephen, David, Thomas and Elly. Of these, Thomas was the father of Asa Godbold, of Marion, and Elly, who left a son bearing his name." Bishop Gregg, in a note to this note, acknowledges that he got his information, and also much other valuable information, from the late Hugh Godbold, and to whom the Bishop pays a very high compliment. Thus it will be seen that all the Godbolds now in the county, or that have been for many years in the county, and connections through the females, are derived directly from the first old John, who was an Englishman, and not only in the county, but in the State and perhaps in the United States. Many of the descendants of old John emigrated to the Western States. More than forty years ago the writer was in Alabama and Mississippi, and he found Godbolds in those States; also in Texas, thirty years ago. The writer supposes that, counting the seven or eight generations of them down to the present time, they, perhaps, would number thousands. There are not very many now in the county bearing the name, but their connexions are numerous, and could scarcely be counted, if the attempt to do so was made. As a family, they have always stood high as men of decided character, pluck and energy. General Thomas Godbold, the grand-son of the first old John, had three sons, John, Hugh and Charles, all now dead; yet were and are known to many now living. The late Hugh Godbold was a remarkable man. The writer, on one occasion, heard the late Julius Dargan, of Darlington, say of Hugh Godbold, that he had mind enough, if he had been educated, to be President of the United States—a very high compliment, coming from the source it did. Charles Godbold was a graduate of the South Carolina College; studied medicine, but died soon after graduation; never married. Neither Hugh nor Charles left any children. John, the other son, never amounted to much—his habits were not good; his matrimonial connection was not such as to promote his social standing. He lived to a ripe old age. Some of his grand-children are among us now; and some of them are doing much to elevate their branch of the family. The first old John Godbold, Bishop Gregg says, lived to be more than a hundred years old, and died in 1765, a member of the Church of England. Thomas, the third and youngest son of the first old John, and who married Martha

A HISTORY OF MARION COUNTY. 119

Herron, had four sons, Stephen, David, Thomas and Elly. Stephen was the father of the late Stephen G. Godbold, was a well-to-do citizen, and lived in Wahee Township, I think, on the place where Dr. D. F. Miles formerly lived; he died there. He left but two children; married twice; the late Stephen G. Godbold was a son of the first wife, and by the second wife he had a daughter, who is now the widow of the late John F. Spencer, and owns and resides upon her father's patrimony. The late Stephen G. Godbold, a most worthy and estimable man, settled near by his father; married and had an only child, a daughter, who married the late Francis A. Miles. Mrs. Miles inherited the entire estate of her father, Stephen G. Godbold. Mrs. Miles was the mother of several children; three sons, David Franklin, Samuel A. C. Miles and Stephen G. Miles, and, I think, two daughters, Mrs. W. L. Durant and Mrs. Lide, of Darlington. Of these, Dr. Samuel A. C. Miles and Mrs. Lide are dead; both leaving children. Dr. D. F. Miles is now Clerk of the Court at Marion, and resides there, has a farm in Wahee; is an amiable, worthy gentleman, and a very efficient and accommodating Clerk. Stephen G. Miles is merchandising at Marion, resides there, and has a farm in Wahee, which seems to be run successfully; a very energetic, worthy citizen. Mrs. Durant was left a widow, with six or seven children (small); she lives on lands inherited from her mother; has raised her children respectably, and it is said they are promising; Mrs. Durant is a very excellent lady—a woman of strong sense and full of energy. These Miles are the great-grand-children of old Stephen Godbold, who was the grand-son of the first old John Godbold. Mrs. Spencer, the daughter of old Stephen Godbold, and who lives on lands he gave her, has ten living children, all grown, and all married, except a son, Nathan. Mrs. Spencer is a worthy lady, of sound, practical sense, and very energetic; she is a great-grand-daughter of the first old John Godbold. Thomas, a brother of old man Stephen, married I do not know whom; but he had a son named Thomas, who married Nancy Gasque. The fruits of this marriage were a daughter, who married a Mr. Harrington, I think, of Georgetown; and sons, Asa Godbold, Jehu, Robert, Thomas, Alexander, Charles, Thomas and

William H., and another daughter, named Martha Ann. Thomas Godbold, the father of these latter, died in 1836 or '7. Asa Godbold, the eldest son of this family, married, in 1828, Miss Sarah Cox, a most excellent lady; the fruits of this marriage were Mary Jane, James, Thomas W., Asa, Sarah, Anne, Eliza and F. Marion. Asa Godbold, Sr., was a very energetic, persevering man, sharp and shrewd, was elected Ordinary after the death of General E. B. Wheeler, in 1859, which position he held by successive elections until the reconstruction period, and he, like all others of the old regime, was relegated to the rear. His daughter, Mary Jane, married Captain Mat. Stanly, of Mexican War and Confederate reputation, and resides ten or twelve miles below Marion Court House. Captain M. B. Stanly is an importation from Darlington. When a young man he volunteered and went to the Mexican War, was with General Taylor in the several battles around the city of Mexico, and in the storming and capture of that city. When the Confederate War began, he was made Captain of the first company that left Marion, 4th January, 1861, and went to Charleston and joined the first regiment (Maxcy Gregg's), and remained Captain of the company until after the reduction of Fort Sumter, 13th April, 1861. Captain Stanly has several children, two sons and one daughter, who are the men and women of the present generation, and all doing well. James Godbold, son of Asa, Sr., married a daughter of the late W. F. Richardson, below Marion. He has reared a family of two sons and three daughters, the names of whom the writer does not know. Asa Godbold, Jr., married Miss Sallie Ellerbe, sister of the late Captain W. S. Ellerbe; he died a few years ago, leaving a large family of sons and daughters; the sons are Walter, William, James C., Lawrence and Luther; the daughters, Alice, Mollie, Anne, Victoria, Bessie and Daisy; of the sons, Walter and William are married; of the daughters, Alice, Mollie, Anne and Victoria are married; Bessie and Daisy are unmarried. Of the sons, Walter married a Miss Williams, near Nichols, S. C.; William married his cousin, Lucy Ellerbe, sister of the late Governor Ellerbe. Of the daughters, Miss Alice married Rev. J. Thomas Pate, now stationed at Florence; Miss Mollie, J. B. Moore, of Latta,

S. C.; Miss Annie married James Harrel, of Cheraw, S. C.; Miss Victoria married W. H. Breeden, of Campbell's Bridge, S. C. The late Thomas W. Godbold, another son of Asa Godbold (senior), was no ordinary man; clear-minded, energetic and industrious; never married; died about a year ago, at the age of sixty-five. F. M. Godbold, the youngest son of Asa Godbold (senior), married, first, a Miss Vance, in Abbeville County, to which county he removed, and there remained till a few years ago, when he returned to his native county, where he now resides; by his first wife he had several children; and she dying, he married another Miss Vance, a cousin of the first wife. Sarah Godbold, second daughter of Asa (senior), married Colonel E. B. Ellerbe, uncle of the late Governor Ellerbe; he some years back moved to Horry County, where he now resides; has a large family. Annie Eliza Godbold, the youngest daughter of Asa (senior), married Edwin A. Bethea, now of Latta; they have several children, sons and daughters; one daughter married to W. C. McMillan, of Marion, but now residing in Columbia, and is said to be doing well; one son, Asa Bethea, is in Texas; the other children are all with their parents at Latta.

We have noticed the families of Stephen and Thomas Godbold, grand-sons of the first old John. Stephen and Thomas had two other brothers, David and Elly. What became of David Godbold and his family, if he had any, is unknown to the writer. The other brother, Elly, had and left a son named Elly, and one named Stephen, usually called Captain Stephen, and one named Ervin M. The son, Elly, afterwards known as Sheriff Elly, and then as General Elly Godbold, was born in 1804. His early educational opportunities were very limited; he could scarcely write his name. The writer had hundreds of business transactions with him while Sheriff for three terms, and never knew him to write anything but his name—never saw any writing said to be his, except his name; he could barely write it, yet he was the most remarkable of men; nature had endowed him with strong intellectual powers, mental acumen and astuteness; he was well versed in human nature; could look in a man's face and know all about him—could almost read his thoughts. He was elected Sheriff for three terms, and served in that office for four years each term, with entire satisfaction to the people and with credit to himself. During those terms the business of the office was very heavy, as his books will show. He was a model Sheriff, though he could do nothing in the office himself—never pretended to make a settlement with any party; he had his clerk to do all the office business; don't think his handwriting appears in or on any book kept in his office during his three terms, nor on paper belonging to the office, except in matters where it was required by law for him to sign his name *in propria persona*. He was run a fourth time for Sheriff, during the Radical regime in 1872, by the white people of the county, and elected, but, like all others of his party in that election, was counted out. He was a successful manager of men; he knew every man, knew his inclinations and almost his thoughts; he knew his weak points, as well as his strong ones, hence he knew how to turn his innate knowledge of men to advantage. He had military ambition, and rose in the militia of that day by regular gradations from the Captaincy of a company to Brigadier General of the Eighth Brigade, S. C. militia, and performed the duties of that position with satisfaction to all concerned (see *supra*). He was twice married; first, to Miss Flowers, by whom he had three sons, Huger, David and Zachariah, and two daughters. Huger married a daughter of Stephen White, by whom he had several children, sons and daughters, when his wife died and left him with her children; the sons, or rather two of them, went West; one, Waties, is here yet, and married, and lives over Catfish, in Wahee Township; one of the daughters married a Mr. Game, and another married Truman Foxworth; a third one is yet single. The father, Huger, though a widower for thirty years, has not married again; he is about seventy-five years of age, has been in Washington for eight or ten years; is in the public printing office. Though seventy-five years old, he looks about as young as he did thirty years ago; sprightly as a boy, has no gray hairs. General Elly Godbold's son, David, was in the Confederate War, and was killed or died in it. His son, Zack, married and had four children; his wife died; he went off, left his children, all small, married again—don't know what has become of him. His son, D. E. Godbold, the eldest, grew up, took care of his sisters; one of the sisters married some one; another sister died, a young woman; the youngest sister is yet single; D. E. Godbold is now at Mullins, merchandising, in partnership with W. McG. Buck, and seems to be doing fairly well. D. E. Godbold married a Miss Young, daughter of the late Johnson B. Young; he is Mayor of the town of Mullins, is steady, a first rate business man and is bound to succeed. He is very much like his grand-father, General Godbold; he deserves much credit for his success, so far, and especially for the care he has taken of his orphan sisters. General Elly Godbold was a successful man; he accumulated a large property. He told the writer just before the war that he had fifty negroes (children) that were not large enough to work in the field. His wife died some years before the war. He remained a widower until the 16th February, 1874, when he married the Widow Kelly, then in Marion; she was forty-five years old and he was seventy—born in 1804. He died suddenly, 12th June, 1874, not quite four months after the second marriage. What became of the General's brother, Stephen T., or Captain Stephen, as he was called, the writer knows not. He was, by no means, such a man as his brother, the General. Ervin M. married Miss Foxworth; is dead; left several children. Recurring back to the sons and grandsons of the old first John, a majority of them must have died childless or removed to other parts. The old first John, as has already been stated, had three sons, John, James and Thomas. John had three sons, Zachariah, John and Jesse. What became of these last three is not stated, and is altogether unknown. The second son of old John was James; James had six sons, John, James, Zachariah, Cade, Abraham and Thomas. No account whatever is given as to these or their posterity, except Thomas, the youngest, who was the father of the late Hugh Godbold, as before stated, and who became a Brigadier General of the militia, and was quite a prominent man in his day; he died in 1825. Thus, five of the grandsons of the old first John seem to have no representatives or descendants in this country. The third son of the old first John was named Thomas, and he had a son named Thomas. This latter Thomas was the father of Asa Godbold (senior), of whom we have already had something to say. It seems that this last Thomas had seven sons, who have already been named; only three of them were married; Asa (senior), Robert and William H.; the others lived in single blessedness, and they are all dead, leaving no representatives. Robert married and died, leaving only a daughter. Of Asa (senior) and his family, we have already spoken. The only one not yet noticed is William H., the youngest; he was a doctor, and a most excellent and worthy man; he married, first, a Miss Mendenhall, of North Carolina; she died in about a year, leaving no offspring; after the usual lapse of time in such cases, the Doctor married a second time, a Miss Hunt (Mary E.), from about High Point, N. C., a highly accomplished lady—a woman of a fine and a cultivated mind. By her the Doctor had four children, two sons, Thomas N. and William H., and two daughters, Mattie and Mary L.; the Doctor died when these children were all small; the mother, with the courage of a Spartan, with her limited means, raised her children respectably, and gave them all a fairly good education; she is yet living. After some years she married Captain J. C. Finklea (Confederate), by whom she had one child, a son; who died, however, at the age of four or five. The eldest son, Thomas N. Godbold, married on the 10th January, 1888, the youngest daughter, Mary, of the writer. She has three children living, Thomas Carroll, Anna and Mary E. The second son of Dr. W. H. Godbold, who was named for his father, married, about 1886, a Miss Mattie Beaty, daughter of Hon. James C. Beaty, of Horry County. About seven years ago, he disappeared from home, and has not been heard of since; he left his wife and four small children, two sons and two daughters; his wife and the children are doing fairly well. Dr. Godbold's oldest daughter, Mattie, married J. E. Stevenson; she died three or four years ago, and left three children, two sons and a daughter; Mary L., the youngest daughter of the Doctor, married Richard Davis, below Marion; they are doing very well.

There is one circumstance worthy to be noted in the Godbold family, and that is the name Thomas. The first old John had a son by that name; and his son, James, who had six sons, one of whom was named Thomas, and who became General Thomas Godbold. The third son of old first John was named Thomas, and he had a son named Thomas, called "Tom Cat," not in derision, but to distinguish him from his cousin, Thomas (the General); and in most branches of the family, from those early days till the present time, the name Thomas is to be found, and now at this time there are four or five Thomas Godbolds in the family. The late Ervin Godbold, youngest brother of General Elly, as already stated, married a Miss Foxworth, by whom he had five or six children; he was a quiet, inoffensive man, unaspiring, and had the respect and confidence of his fellow-citizens. One of his daughters became the wife of the late S. G. Owens, Clerk of the Court; she died, and Owens died. Ervin M. Godbold left a son, Thomas, keeping up that name. The writer has dwelt upon the Godbold family to a greater extent than he otherwise would, because the first settlement made about Marion Court House was made, as hereinbefore stated, by John Godbold. It runs over a period of 165 years, and yet the Godbolds are here, by themselves and by their respectable connections, while many who came and settled in other parts of the county, about the same time and before and after, have disappeared; their names have become extinct, either by misfortune, deaths or removals.

EVANS.—The next family the writer will notice, is the Evans family. Bishop Gregg says, on page 75: "Nathan Evans was a Welshman, and settled on Catfish. He either came from the Welsh Neck above, soon after his arrival there, or was one of those who went first to the lower part of the Welsh tracts, and remained there. Lands in the neighborhood of Tart's Mill (now Moody's) were granted to Nathan Evans." Bishop Gregg, in a note on same page, says: "Nathan Evans was the grand-father of the late Thomas Evans and General William Evans, of Marion. The father of General Evans was also named Nathan, and was a man of upright character through life." Nathan Evans' arrival and settlement on "Catfish" was soon after the arrival and settlement of John Godbold, in 1735. Gregg further says: "David Evans, a son of Nathan, was a Captain in the Revolution, and a man of note. He died childless. About the same time, two families of James and Lucas came down the river and settled on Catfish; with the latter of these the Crawfords and Evans intermarried. Soon after a family of Bakers came from Newbern, N. C., to Pee Dee. One of this name married a daughter of Nathan Evans. William Baker was prominent in the Revolution, and marked for his devotion to the cause of liberty." Thus the foundation of the Evans family, so far as Marion County is concerned, is laid in old Nathan Evans. We are not informed whether he had sons other than David and Nathan, and no account of any daughter, except that one of the name of Baker married a daughter of Nathan Evans. His son, Nathan, was the only one to perpetuate the name. The writer thinks he married twice (the second Nathan). His first wife was a Godbold, by whom he had a son, the late Thomas Evans, and two daughters, Mrs. R. J. Gregg and Mrs. Colonel Levi Legette, there may have been other children of the first marriage. Nathan Evans' second wife was a Miss Rogers (first name not known), a daughter of old Lot Rogers, of upper Marion. By his second wife he had three sons and a daughter. The sons were the late General William Evans, Nathan Evans and Gamewell Evans; the daughter, Elizabeth A., married Alexander Murdock, of Marlborough County. The late Thomas Evans married a Miss Daniel, a Virginia lady, a most excellent woman, and a woman of more than ordinary culture for her day and time; the fruits of this marriage were ten sons and one daughter. The father, Thomas Evans, was quite a prominent man in his day—Representative and Senator from his county in the State Legislature, Commissioner in Equity, and a useful man generally; he died in middle life—I think, in 1845; the names of his sons, as remembered, were Chesly D., Thomas, Nathan G., James, Beverly, Jackson, William, Asa, Alfred and Woodson; the daughter, Sarah, who married R. L. Singletary, on the west side of Great Pee Dee, who has children grown and married. Chesly D. Evans graduated at the South Carolina College, I think, in 1839, studied law and was admitted to the bar in 1841; went into practice, and was elected Commissioner in Equity, which position he held for years; he was a delegate to the Secession Convention in 1860, was quite a scholarly man and a good lawyer, though not much of an advocate; he married, in 1850 or 1851, Miss Jane Haselden, and reared a family of seven sons and one daughter. The sons were Junius H., Chesly D., Walker, Samuel, Frank, Leon, Nathan and David (called Tris Magistas); and a daughter, Bettie. Of these, Junius is a practicing lawyer at Marion; married Miss Florence Durant, and has three or four children. Chesly D. married a Miss Wells; he is dead, and left three children. Samuel Married an English lady, and is dead; he left two children. Walker married a Miss McDougal, in upper Marion, and is farming and doing well. Frank is in Spartanburg at the head of a graded school, and is highly esteemed. Where the other two, Nathan and David, are unknown, having left Marion. Leon died when a youth. Chesly died in May, 1897, at the advanced age of eighty years, being born 10th January, 1817. Thomas Evans, second son of Thomas Evans (senior), grew up, studied law, practiced for several years, and was appointed (I think, by President Pierce,) United States District Attorney for South Carolina, which position he filled for four years with credit to himself and satisfaction to the public. He married late in life (don't remember whom), settled down in Britton's Neck at a place called Oakton, and soon thereafter removed West and died there. Nathan G. Evans, and third son of Thomas Evans (senior), was educated at West Point and went into the regular army of the United States, and when the war between the States broke out, loyal to his section, he threw himself on the side of the South and was soon appointed by President Davis a Brigadier General, and won distinction on many fields, and especially at the battle of Leesburg or Ball's Bluff, where he pursued the Federals to the river, completely routed them, and besides killing many, others sprang off the bluff into the river and were either drowned or killed in the water. (Rise and Fall of the Confederate Government, 1 vol., 437.) General N. George Evans (called Shanks at home), married about the close of the war a Miss Gary, of Edgefield, or Abbeville, and by her had sons and daughters, the number and names unknown, think three sons; one of whom, John Gary Evans, is now an ex-Governor of the State; he removed to Edgefield after his marriage, and died there several years ago. A true South Carolinian and a gallant soldier, his face was ever to the front. James E. Evans, another son of Thomas Evans (senior), was a doctor, and did service in the war as a surgeon; married a Virginia lady, and after the war returned to South Carolina, located as a physician at Little Rock, in his native county, and remained there doing a good practice for several years; then removed to Florence, and continued his practice there till the present time. He is eminent in his profession, is Secretary to the State Board of Health, and President of the State Board of Medical Examiners for the examination of applicants to practice in the State, as required by law—quite a distinguished position; he is a man of high character and of excellent morals; has a family, children grown, the number and names unknown; has a daughter married to Hon. F. B. Gary, present Speaker of the House of Representatives of the South Carolina Legislature, and at present a candidate for Governor of the State. Another son of Thomas Evans (senior), William, who was in the navy under Admiral Semmes on the Alabama, during the war, and an officer of what rank is now unknown, and was perhaps a graduate of the Naval Academy at Annapolis, Md.; he was a brave Carolinian, and a staunch supporter of the Confederacy; he never married, and died some years ago and was buried in his native town. Two other sons of Thomas Evans (senior), Jackson and Beverly, left this country years ago and went West; they were unmarried when they left Marion; don't know what has become of them. Another son, Captain A. L. Evans, now Deputy Clerk of the Court, of Thomas Evans (senior), volunteered early in the war, and remained in it to the last, a gallant soldier, contending for the rights of his section; he was Adjutant in his brother's, N. G. Evans, brigade, and went through all the battles in which it was engaged during the war, from Virginia to Mississippi, always at his post and did his full duty; he married a daughter of the late Horatio McClenaghan, and by her has had five children, two sons and three daughters; one daughter married. Two other sons of Thomas Evans (senior), were Alfred and Woodson. Soon after the war, Alfred, a young man, went West; I have lost sight of him, and cannot say what has become of him. Woodson, the youngest son, just as he was entering into manhood, sickened and died. That family of Evans did much for the "lost cause;" their whole soul was in it and went down with it, not whipped, but simply overcome by the number and resources of the enemy.

General William Evans, a son of Nathan, the second, by his second marriage, was born in 1804, grew up to manhood and married Miss Sarah Ann Godbold, daughter of General Thomas Godbold; settled down at the place just north of Marion, and went to farming; he succeeded well in his chosen occupation and amassed a large property; he had only two sons, James Hamilton and William Thomas; the latter is now the Sheriff (second term) of the county; and seven daughters, viz: Catharine, Mary, Eliza Jane, Louisa, Ann M., Rosa and Margaret. The oldest son, James Hamilton, was a graduate of the University of North Carolina. He married Miss Amelia Legette, daughter of Rev. David Legette, and lived to a few years back and died childless. William Thomas grew up to manhood, just in time to strike the war; he was in college, left it and came home, volunteered and went into the war and made a good soldier, remained in it till the last; came home and married a Miss Stith, of Wilson, N. C.; by her he had one child, a daughter; soon after his wife died; he has not remarried; his daughter, however, grew up, raised by her grandmother, Evans, and married Henry I. Gasque; had two children for him, a daughter and a son; she died three or four years ago, leaving her two children and husband. Thus it appears that the name of Evans, so far as the sons of the General are concerned, will become extinct, unless the Sheriff, W. T. Evans, should marry again and thereby perpetuate his name. General Evans' oldest daughter, Catharine, died not long after reaching her womanhood, unmarried; his daughter, Mary, married A. J. Requier, a lawyer, who afterwards moved to Mobile, where Requier became distinguished as a lawyer, a man of erudition; his wife, Mary, died in Mobile, Ala., I think, childless; his daughter, Eliza Jane, married Dr. Dixon Evans, of Fayetteville, N. C.; by the marriage she did not change her name, but preserved her identity as an Evans. Dr. Dixon Evans died at Marion a few years ago, leaving three sons and three daughters; of the sons, Charles E. Evans, now of

Marion, is the eldest, who married Sophie Miles, daughter of Dr. D. F. Miles, Clerk of the Court. The next son, William A., grew up and went West; his whereabouts is unknown to the writer. The third and last son of Dr. Dixon Evans is named Joseph, a young man, unmarried. Of Dr. Evans' daughters, the eldest is the wife of B. R. Mullins, of Marion; the second daughter, Kate, married W. H. Cross, Cashier of the Merchants and Farmers Bank at Marion; she died three or four years ago, and left two or three children. Another daughter, Amelia, married a Mr. Glover, of Fayetteville, N. C. General Evans' daughter, Louiza, married, first, a Mr. McEachern, of North Carolina; by him she had two daughters, when McEachern died. The widow, in a few years, married Rev. W. C. Power, an itinerant Methodist minister, and by him, I think, she has six children, three sons and three daughters; one daughter and two sons, W. C. and John M., married, but do not know to whom. Rev. W. C. Power married in 1867. He has continued in the itinerancy thence to the present time; stands high in the Conference, has filled many important stations, has been a Presiding Elder for twenty years; he is a close thinker and an able minister, a very methodical man. I have heard it remarked by several that he ought to have been a bank president—he is a good financier. The two McEachern daughters both married; the eldest, Lilly, married John M. Power, a nephew of the Rev. W. C. Power; I do not know what has become of them; the younger McEachern daughter, Mary, married a Mr. Tesky, of Charleston; he is a merchant in his home city, and is said to be a prosperous man. General Evans' daughter, Anna M., married Colonel John G. Blue, of North Carolina; he was a graduate of the University of North Carolina and a lawyer; Colonel Blue was a man of good sense and mentally much above the ordinary, and especially when aroused; and had he applied himself to his profession, as some do, he doubtless would have attained an enviable position in the profession; he would have been where there is always room plenty—that is, at the top; he went into the war early as a private, and rose by successive steps to a Lieutenant Colonelcy; he was brave and patriotic; had a high sense of duty; very temperate in all his habits except one, and in that was very intemperate, and that was in the use of tobacco, and its excessive use probably shortened his life; he was a candidate for the Legislature in 1876 and was elected and was a member of the famous "Wallace House" of that year, and was re-elected for several terms thereafter, and was a very useful member of that body; he was very cool and deliberate, and his judgment good; he had the confidence of his fellow-members. Some ten or twelve years ago his health failed him, and after lingering for several months he died in Richmond County, N. C., his old home place, to which he had gone for recuperation; he died rather unexpectedly; his widow and the younger members of her family live on their homestead, near Marion. Colonel Blue raised three sons and five daughters; his eldest son, William E. Blue, is yet single and lives with his mother, and carries on the farm, and is now County Treasurer; he is a young man of fine talents and of good character. Another son, Rupert, is a doctor, and has for several years been a surgeon in the United States Army, and stands well as such; he is, or was, somewhere in the West, attending to the duties of his position. Another son, Victor, graduated some years ago, in the Naval Academy at Annapolis, Md., and has been in the navy ever since his graduation, and is now Flag Lieutenant, and has gone, it is said, in the newspapers, on a war ship to China as Flag Lieutenant. He acquired celebrity and distinction by heroic deeds in the late Spanish-American War, and is well on the road to an Admiralship, the highest honor that can be attained in that branch of his country's service—a Marion boy, of whom Marion and the whole State are justly proud; he is a fine specimen of manhood physically; he recently married a daughter of some naval Captain. Of Colonel Blue's daughters, one, Miss Sallie, married Peter John, of Marlborough County; another, Miss Ida, married Mr. James John, of North Carolina, a brother to Peter. The Johns are good men and well-to-do. Another daughter, Miss Effie, married Edward B. Wheeler, of Marion, a very worthy native and citizen. The two other daughters, Miss Kate and Miss Hettie, are unmarried—worthy of some good man. Miss Kate has obtained some celebrity as a writer, and is quite literary in her taste. Another daughter of General Evans, Miss Rosa, married Captain Duncan McIntyre; did not live long after her marriage, and died childless. The youngest daughter of General Evans, Miss Margaret, or Maggie, as she was called, married in the latter part of the war the late Major S. A. Durham, and by him she had three children, two daughters and a son. The son, Cicero A. Durham, now living in Marion, married Miss Kate McKerall, daughter of the late Captain W. J. McKerall; they have no children. The two daughters of Major S. A. Durham, Miss Eunice and Miss Marguerette, are unmarried.

General William Evans was a prominent man in his day. He was a large and active man, handsome and of fine address, and much of a man physically. He was chosen as one of the delegates to the Nullification Convention in 1832, and was one of the signers to the Ordinance of Nullification passed by that body. About that time he was elected Brigadier General of the militia. In 1838, he was elected to the House of Representatives from his county and served a term; he was again elected to the same position in 1846, and served another term. General Evans was a man of fine sense, but not a scholar; he devoted himself almost exclusively to his farm, at which he succeeded well, made a large property in lands and slaves, and kept out of debt. At the time of emancipation he owned over one hundred slaves. It seemed that everything he touched "turned to gold"—it prospered in his hands. He died sitting on the steps of his front piazza, suddenly, on the 6th June, 1876, at the age of seventy-two years.

Nathan Evans, a younger brother of General Evans, and a grand-son of the first old Nathan, was born in 1805; was a worthy man and an excellent citizen; a gentleman of fine taste, affable and very popular with everybody; he married a Miss Baker, below Marion, a daughter of William and Annise Baker; by whom he had four children, two sons, William B. and Nathan, and two daughters, Lizzie and Ann Eliza. The Baker wife died. After a reasonable time, he married again, Miss Harriet Braddy, of upper Marion; by her he had four children, two sons, Julius and Lawrence, and two daughters, Martha, called "Pat," and Fannie. His second wife died about 1878 or 1879, of cancer; she suffered for a long time the most intense agonies. He married no more, lived on his farm until 12th February, 1885, when he, too, passed away. His son, William B. Evans, was a Captain in the war, a true and valiant soldier. In one of the battles in Virginia he was badly wounded, shot through one of his lungs—which at the time was thought to be mortal; but to every one's surprise, he recovered. After recovery he returned to his command and continued therein to the surrender of Johnston's army, 26th April, 1865. He came home and soon after married Miss Maggie Haselden, a daughter of Major James Haselden; she lived but a short while and died childless. He afterwards married Miss Sue Berry, a daughter of Elihu Berry, a niece of his first wife, by whom he has had three sons and five daughters. The sons are William Boyd, James Aubrey and Thomas Baker; the daughters are Mamie, Emma, Nellie, Lucy and Gary Lee, all unmarried, except his oldest son, William Boyd Evans, who has recently married a Miss Heyward, in Charleston. W. Boyd Evans is a graduate of Wofford College; he was Private Secretary to Governor Ellerbe up to the death of the Governor, 2d June, 1899; he has also recently graduated in the law department of the South Carolina College. With it all, including his recent marriage, he is well equipped for life, and sets out on its tempestuous sea with ballast, rudder and sails. The other children, sons and daughters, of Captain Evans, are all with him; the sons and two eldest daughters are grown, the rest are small. Captain Evans is a very worthy citizen, a man of good morals, and a good man in his family—in short, he is a high-toned gentleman; he is a farmer.

Nathan Evans' daughter, Lizzie, by his first wife, married the late W. W. Braddy, and by him had several children; they are all dead, except two—Sue, the wife of Professor Coleman, in the Citadel Academy, in Charleston, and a son, Wightman Braddy, a young man just grown. Mrs. Lizzie Braddy had a daughter named Walker, who married J. W. Davis, of Marion. They moved to Alabama, where Walker died, as is said, and left three sons, Willie, Hicks and Elbert. Their father, J. W. Davis, has married twice since his first wife, Walker Braddy, died. These three Davis boys are direct descendants of Nathan Evans, whose family we are now noticing. Nathan Evans had another son by his Baker wife, named Nathan; he grew up to manhood and died unmarried. He had also another daughter by the Baker wife, named Ann Eliza; she married a man by the name of Cole and died childless. As already stated, Nathan Evans (the third) had by his second wife, Harriet Braddy, two sons, Julius and Lawrence; and two daughters, Martha (called Pat) and Fannie. Julius grew up to manhood, merchandised a few years at Marion, in partnership with his brother-in-law, Richard Jordan, who had married his sister, "Pat." The firm was not successful. In the meantime, he had married a Miss   by whom he has had four sons and a daughter. He removed to Tallahassee, Florida, where he now resides.

Richard Jordan, of Horry, married Miss "Pat" Evans, and after the failure of the mercantile firm of Jordan & Evans, as above indicated, Mr. Jordan remained in Marion a few years, variously engaged, and then removed to Georgia and started a business there (turpentine and merchandise), at which, it is said, he has succeeded well. He has a considerable family, seven daughters and one son. Mr. Jordan is a first-rate business man, full of push and energy—by no means an idler; if he cannot succeed at one thing, he tries another; he tries again and does not give up. Nathan Evans' (the third) son, Lawrence, married some girl in Horry County some years ago, and has been lost sight of. Miss Fannie, the youngest daughter of Nathan Evans, by second wife, went out to Georgia with her brother-in-law, Jordan, and married a Mr. Applewhite; she has also been lost sight of.

Nathan Evans (the third) was one of nature's noblemen; had great good sense, was energetic and upright in every respect; always lent his ear to a tale of suffering; had a kind and sympathetic heart, and would help his neighbor in distress, if it was in his power, often to his own injury; he injured himself and family by becoming surety for others. He lived on his splendid farm, which he managed to keep, till his death; he was a very popular man, more so than his brother, the General; yet he never aspired to the honors of office but once, and then not of his own motion; but being urged by his numerous friends, he became a candidate for Representative in the State Legislature in 1858, and though the contest was heated, he was triumphantly elected at the head of the ticket, and served a term in the House. Faithful to his trust, he retired from public life in the full confidence of his people, and could never after be induced to become a candidate again—he loved his home and family too well; the pursuits of home life were more congenial to his nature.

"About 1735," as stated by Bishop Gregg, p. 69: "two important settlements were made in that region (Marion District); one of these was in Britton's Neck, twenty miles below Mar's Bluff, and forty miles above Georgetown. It was composed of the families of Britton, Graves, Fladger, Davis, Tyler, Giles and others. They came directly from England as one colony; and being members of the Established Church, one of their first acts was to erect a house for the worship of God. Their minister, Dr. Robert Hunter, came with them, and is supposed to have died there. He was succeeded by the Rev. Mr. Allison." In a note on the same page, Bishop Gregg, in regard to the church built there at that time, 1735, says: "This building was of black cypress, with a brick foundation, and is still to be seen (1859), or was a few years since, in a good state of preservation, on the road leading from Port's Ferry to Potato Bed Ferry, on Little Pee Dee. About the year 1780, the congregation having long been without a minister, and doubtless very much broken up by the troublous times of the Revolution, united with the Methodist, and the building passed into the hands of the latter, by whom it has since been retained. Charles Wesley is said to have once preached in it. The name of one of these families subsequently became distinguishd in the person of Hugh Giles, who took a prominent part in this region during the Revolution. He was the son of Robert Giles."

GILES.—Of Colonel Hugh Giles, something has already been said in these pages, and something more may yet be said herein. Of the church here spoken of, it is the Britton's Neck Methodist Church now—of course, not the original building, but on the same plat of ground, and is supposed to be the oldest church in the county. I think it likely that Francis Asbury (Bishop) in his travels round and through the country preached in it more than once. The writer has not the life of Bishop Asbury now before him, but he read it years ago, and remembers the fact stated in it, that he preached in the Britton's Neck Church perhaps more than once. Bishop Gregg says it was built of black cypress, with a brick foundation. The question may arise in the mind of the reader, where did they get the brick from? Had they, then and there, the appliances for making bricks? The answer is, they had not; they brought the brick with them from England. Many of the first brick houses or brick chimneys in Charleston and other portions of the low country, were made of brick imported from England, and some of the first settlers brought the brick with them. Brick afforded a capital ballast for the ships, then sailing vessels. The writer, in the spring of 1900, visited Jacksonboro, in Colleton County, thirty-seven miles below Charleston, to see his youngest daughter, Mary S. Godbold. He stayed there three weeks, and while there he was invited one afternoon to take a carriage ride into the country with old Mrs. Goodman and her daughter, Miss Edith, and a Miss Coburn, school teacher; of course, he accepted the invitation; went out westward about five miles to the ruins of an old Episcopal Church in what was formerly known as St. Bartholomew's Parish. The two side walls were both down and most of the brick had been removed; the back end wall was to a great extent down and bricks removed; the front end wall was nearly intact. The old lady Goodman said the bricks were brought from England—that was the tradition. They seemed to be as hard as iron; the writer tried to make an impression on or an incision with his knife, but could not do so. The cement between them was equally as hard. Upon the front wall, about fifteen or twenty feet from the ground, was an inscription dimmed by the action of time so that the writer could not read it; but those in our party whose eyes were younger could read it thus: "12th November, 1754." Those brick, said to have been made in England, are much harder than any brick now made in this Southern country. The brick of this old St. Bartholomew

Church, put there some twenty years after the old brick in the Britton's Neck Church, spoken of by Bishop Gregg, corroborates the tradition that in the early times of the Province of South Carolina, the settlers either brought their brick with them from England, or imported them from that country after their arrival.

BRITTON, FLADGER, ETC.—Of the Brittons we have already spoken; none of the name now in the county. The Graves have also become extinct in the county; tradition says they were a good people and prosperous. The name Fladger has also become extinct in the county, except one female, a daughter of the late C. J. Fladger, named Sallie Maria, unmarried, and lives with her half-sister, Mrs. R. B. Game, near Mullins. Of the Fladgers, however, they may be noticed herein further on. Of the Davis, of whom there are many, they will be noticed further on. Of the Tylers, they must have removed or disappeared many years ago, as the writer has never heard the name in the county; there are some of the name in Horry County, who probably are descendants of those spoken of by Bishop Gregg. Of the Giles, something has already been said, and more may be said of them hereafter. "And others," a term used by Bishop Gregg, does not afford us much light. It may mean many or it may be only a few; nor does the term identify any one in particular. "And being members of the Established Church, one of their first acts was to erect a house for the worship of God. Their minister, Dr. Robert Hunter, came with them, and is supposed to have died there. He was succeeded by the Rev. Mr. Allison." It will be remembered that hereinbefore it has been stated on the information of Mr. M. M. Lowrimore, that a family of Hunters, hunters by trade as well as by name, about this time, 1735, came and settled down there on Hunter's Island, so named from the Hunters settling there. This is corroborative of what Bishop Gregg says, as above stated. No one of that name has been known in the present limits of Marion County for years; but families by that name have been known in West Marion, now in Florence County, in all these years, and there may be some over there now by that name. It is probable that the family first settling in Britton's Neck, in the progress of time, moved higher up the river on the west side, and those over there are descendants of the Hunters of Britton's Neck. "Dr. Robert Hunter came with them, and is supposed to have died there. He was succeeded by the Rev. Mr. Allison." The Allisons have been long known on the lower Pee Dee. The late James H. Allison, a very reputable gentleman, lived and reared a family on Great Pee Dee—I suppose, on the west side, and died there some years ago. One of his sons or grand-sons married a daughter of our late fellow-citizen, Captain William H. Crawford, and moved out to Georgia some few years back, and it is said he is very prosperous there in his business—is getting rich. It is an old and respectable name of the county, though the name is extinct in the county now, so fas as is known. A ferry on the Great Pee Dee, just above Port's Ferry, or just below, bears the name of "Allison's Ferry." The two ferries are not more than a mile apart.

Bishop Gregg, page 70, says: "The other settlement referred to was made at a point on the east bank of the river called Sandy Bluff, two and a half miles above Mar's Bluff. A few traces of it are yet to be seen at several points immediately on the high bank of the river. The families of Crawford, Saunders, Murfee, Crosby, Keighly, Berry, and shortly after the Gibsons, made up this community. Sandy Bluff extended up the river about three miles. With the fertile uplands running out for some distance, and a rich swamp on the opposite side, and supplied, too, with numerous springs of good water, this locality was in many respects admirably adapted to the wants of the infant colony." * * * "These settlers built their houses, as did the Welsh above, immediately on the bank of the river, and in close proximity to each other, for the convenience of water, of social intercourse, and their mutual protection against the Indians. It was also more healthy than locations further from the river, as experience has proved. They were from England and Ireland, and having landed at Charleston, found their way to Georgetown, and thence up the river, attracted by the bounties which the government had offered. Like their neighbors in Britton's Neck, they erected a building for public worship according to the rites of the Established Church.

Faint traces of this early structure were to be seen a few years since. The brick used for the foundation were brought up the river (the settlers thus transporting themselves and their stores), and were of superior quality. The Rev. Wm. Turbeville came with this colony, and was their pastor. He was a well educated man, and had a high reputation as a preacher. Eminent also for piety and devotion to his work, he retained the confidence and affection of the people in an extensive region of the country to the close of a long life. One of the incidents related in connexion with him is singularly illustrative of this feeling. Such was the genral confidence in his piety and the efficacy of his prayers, that he was sent for from considerable distances during the pressure of any general calamity, to make intercession to God in behalf of the people. On one occasion, about the year 1760, during the prevalence of a fearful drought, there was a general meeting at Bass' Mills to pray for rain." (I suppose then known as Hulon's Mills.) "Mr. Turbeville was sent for. He answered the summons and, as tradition relates, before the sufferers had reached their homes, the heavens were opened and copious rains came down. Mr. Turbeville had no children. Several brothers came with him, of whom some descendants are now (1859) to be found in Marion. He lived at Sandy Bluff until after the year 1800, then removed to the west side of the river, near Mar's Bluff, where he married a second time, and died about 1810, at the advanced age of 103 years." Bishop Gregg says further, in a note, page 71: "Mr. Turbeville was a poor man through life. It is said that William Allston, grand-father of Governor Allston," (I suppose, R. F. W. Allston,) "who lived at that time near the Wahees," (a few miles below Mar's Bluff,) "complained to Mr. T., on one occasion, of his wearing such coarse garments. Mr. T. told him, he got but little for preaching and could not afford to dress better. Whereupon Mr. Allston gave him a black suit and silk gown, on condition that he was not to use them except in preaching and on other public official occasions."

This last is a most remarkable story. Here is a man of fine education, young and vigorous, with a wife, but no children to support and educate, preaching for what, we suppose, was and became a rich church—a church, too, supported by taxation and a church to which, I suppose, Allston himself belonged, or at least attended, lived near by, and the Murfees, Saunders, Crawfords and Gibsons, all rich men, so says Bishop Gregg, and yet did not pay their pastor enough to enable him to appear decent in the pulpit. This presents a strange condition of affairs, and does not speak well for his congregation; though rich, yet niggardly stingy, and very much detracts from their otherwise high standing. Mr. Turbeville, in his apparent poverty, was in truth more wealthy than all of them put together. He evidently had the saving grace of God in his heart, and in his physical make up had the elements of an unusually long life, which was abundantly more valuable than gold and costly apparel. He, after suffering poverty and its pangs here for one hundred and three years, was taken into "Abraham's bosom." What became of his wealthy parishioners, is not known. Bishop Gregg says: "Mr. Turbeville had no children. Several brothers came with him, of whom some descendants are now to be found in Marion." These were the foundation and origin of the Turbeville family in Marion. Of these, old William Turbeville, then in the prime of life, sixty years ago, lived in the neighborhood of Ebenezer Methodist Church, within the bounds of what was then called the Cross Roads Beat Company—a military division. The writer remembers very distinctly a very spirited contest for the Captaincy of the Cross Roads Beat Company, in 1840 or early '41, between William Turbeville and W. H. Moody. The respective candidates and their friends worked for their favorites as zealously as if the election had involved the safety of the State or an income of thousands of dollars. The military spirit of the State, in those times, has been noted in preceding pages of this book. The result of the election was in favor of W. H. Moody by thirteen votes. There were three brothers of that generation of Turbevilles—William, Absalom and John. William, not long after the contest for the Captaincy of the Cross Roads militia company, moved down into Britton's Neck, and there died in a good old age, left a son, Asa, and one named William. Asa Turbeville is one of our most respected citizens in the Britton's Neck section. A daughter of his married J. H. Bostick, in that section, another worthy and upright man, and is doing well. Absalom Turbeville, a brother of old William, lived on and owned the place just below Ebenezer, where the late John C. Campbell lived and died. Absalom left one daughter. John Turbeville lived and owned the place on the northeast side of Ebenezer, died only a few years ago; he left sons and daughters. Of his sons, George and Samuel are still living, but not on the lands of their father. The late William Dillon, a brother of J. W. Dillon, of the town of Dillon, married a daughter of John Turbeville, and by her had several sons and daughters. William Dillon and wife are both dead, and I think most of their children—parents and children all died of consumption. I do not know that all are dead, but many of them are. Another branch of the Turbeville family was the father of the late old William Turbeville, of Marion; he is dead. Bethel Turbeville, another brother, is also dead. One of them, do not remember which, left a son, Edward, called Ned Turbeville, a blacksmith, who died young, leaving a family; what has become of them is unknown. There was another brother of Bethel, who lived over Catfish, in Wahee, a very noisy man, especially at elections, when enthused by the *spirits* of the occasion; his name was Robert, familiarly called Bob; he is dead. Recurring to the William Turbeville who ran for the Captaincy in 1840, as before stated, he left another son, named Stephen, who is one of our most worthy citizens; lives on Buck Swamp. The wife of the late Samuel Johnson was a daughter of old "Captain" William, and is still living, but has no children. Beverly Culbreath, merchant of Marion, married, first, a daughter of Asa Turbeville, and she died, and he has married another daughter. These three old Turbevilles about Ebenezer Church were not rich, yet they were not poor—"they lived at home and boarded at the same place," as the saying goes. They were honest, hard-working men.

Of the settlement at Sandy Bluff, the names Saunders, Crosby and Keighly, as also that of Murfee, are now extinct in Marion County. Never have heard of the name Keighly; that family must have removed to other parts. The name Crosby, the writer has heard of; in fact, he has seen a man by that name from Alabama, who said he was born in Marion

County, and was a half-brother of the late John C. Legette, of West Marion; this was fifty years ago; his name was William Crosby. The name Saunders has long since disappeared from the county. I have been informed, however, there is a Peter Sanders, who lives below Marion Court House, who is, doubtless, a descendant of the Saunders spoken of; he is a good citizen and has been Assistant Door-keeper of the House of Representatives in Columbia for the last several years. The writer in his law practice for more than fifty years has seen grants of large bodies of land in Marion District to John Sanders, supposed to be a descendant of the family at Sandy Bluff; the grants spoken of were for lands lying between Catfish and Great Pee Dee, in the neighborhood of Antioch Church and Berry's Cross Roads.

Bishop Gregg, p. 71, says: "Of the settlers at Sandy Bluff, the Murfees, Sanders, Gibsons and Crawfords accumulated the largest properties, and became most prominent. John Crawford, the first of that name, had three sons—James, John and Hardy. James, the eldest of them, amassed a large fortune for that day, and maintained through life a high character for integrity. He was a Captain in the Revolution, and a valiant soldier in the cause of liberty." In a note, the Bishop says: "He was the grand-father of the late Chapman J. Crawford, of Marion." Thus we have the origin of the once extensive family of Crawfords, so far as Marion County is concerned—to whom they married and what children they had, we are pretty much in the dark. Bishop Gregg says, on p. 75: "About the same time, two families of James and Lucas, came down the river, and settled on Catfish. With the latter of these, the Crawfords and Evans intermarried." Who of the Crawfords intermarried with the Lucas family, and whether they were males or females, is now unknown, and perhaps past finding out, and the same may be said of the Evans and James.

CRAWFORD.—James Crawford, the grand-father of the late Chapman Crawford, had a son named James, the father of Chapman; whether there were other sons or not, is not now known; there were daughters—the wife of old Osborne Lane was one; the first wife of old William Bethea was another, who was the mother of the late John C. Bethea; another daughter married a man by the name of Porter; she was the grand-mother of Robert P. Porter, now living at Marion. James Crawford, the father of Chapman J. Crawford, married Miss Rachel Nevils, and by her had two sons, Chapman J. and William H., and three or four daughters; one married Peter P. Johnson, of Fayetteville, N. C.; one married D. C. Milling, of Darlington, and one married D. J. McDonald, long a merchant at Marion, and Representative from Marion in the State Legislature in 1850, and finally failing in his business, removed to Arkansas. James Crawford, the second, was a very prosperous man, left a large estate, and died in the prime of life. His widow, Rachel, married Dr. Cherry, and by him had several daughters; one of them married, first, Dr. Richard Scarborough, of Marion; he soon died childless, and his widow then married Major O. P. Wheeler, and after some years he died, and she remained his widow for several years, when she died. Another daughter of Mrs. Cherry became the wife of the late C. Graham, of Marion; she died before he did, and left an only child, a son, Herbert C. Graham, now residing in Marion. Another daughter, Sarah Jane, became the wife of Dr. J. Hamilton Wheeler, who died and left her a widow with two children, Ed. B. Wheeler and Tiston C. Wheeler, now residing in Marion; their mother, Sarah Jane, still lives. Dr. Cherry, a most excellent and upright man, died away back in the '40's; he was a well-to-do man. The sons of James Crawford, the second, were Chapman J. and William H. Crawford. Chapman was an ambitious, energetic and enterprising man; married, first, a Miss Jolly, an only child of Joseph Jolly, a very wealthy man in West Marion; she died, leaving an only child; he married again, and the second wife died, and he married a third time. I think he had two or three children in all. Dr. Ross married the daughter by the Jolly wife; Junius H. Law, of Darlington, married a daughter by one of his other wives. By his energy and push and by his marriages, he made property and left a large estate at his death, which occurred in November, 1852, when only in the prime of life; he lived fast (not in the sense of a dissipated life) and went through life in a hurry. His younger brother, Wm. H. Crawford, grew up and married a Miss Durant, sister of Rev. H. H. Durant, of the South Carolina Conference of the Southern Methodist Church; he married, 10th February, 1840, the same day of Queen Victoria's marriage to Prince Albert. Captain Crawford started out in life with fine prospects; he went into a large mercantile business at Marion, in partnership with his brother-in-law, D. J. McDonald, who had had some training for such business—a man of push and enterprise, but lacking in business judgment. The firm seemed to do well for a few years and then began to go down, and finally failed altogether, and Captain Crawford's whole property was swept out, and he with his family were left penniless. McDonald emigrated to Arkansas, and was said to have built up again; but Captain Crawford remained poor to the day of his death; he lived in Marion until three or four years ago, when he moved to Georgia, and died there about two years ago, eighty years of age. Captain Crawford was a good man, but the reverses to which he had been subjected soured his disposition, and he became apathetic as to all mankind; he left two sons, George and William, who are the only hope of perpetuating the name in that branch of the Crawford family. George Crawford is married and has children, whether sons or daughters, is unknown to the writer; William is yet single. The connexion is yet large, but the name, like many others, may become extinct at least in that branch of the family, in another generation or two. What changes are wrought in one hundred and sixty years! The first James Crawford married a second time, and had a daughter, Sallie, who became the wife of the late Barfield Moody, a prominent man in his day in Marion, of whom more may be said hereinafter. Recurring to the late Chapman J. Crawford, it is proper to say that he was elected to the lower House of the Legislature in 1844, as hereinbefore stated, and again in 1846, and served two terms. In 1852, he was a candidate for the Senate against Dr. Robert Harllee, and after a very heated campaign, he was beaten by 171 majority, and, like Horace Greeley in 1872, did not survive the campaign more than a month. It was thought and said by some that his defeat killed him or contributed to his death; he was a very ambitious man.

We have traced one branch of the family of old John Crawford, who was one of the first settlers at Sandy Bluff (afterwards called Solomon's Landing, and perhaps later called Bird's Landing). Old John Crawford had three sons, James, John and Hardy. We have traced it through James, the eldest; of John and Hardy's posterity we know not how they ran. There have been other Crawfords here, but whether from John or Hardy, or both, we can't say; for instance, James, called Cype, lived upon and owned the grove lands, now owned by the estates of Governor Ellerbe and James G. Haselden; Cype Crawford died there, back in the '40's; never married. He had a brother, Willis Crawford, who married Sallie Bethea, and raised a large family, and died in 1851, in what is now Bethea Township; his sons were James, Hardy B., Thomas C., Willis G., William and Gibson G. Crawford; his daughters were Rhoda and Margaret. Of Willis Crawford's sons, James died before he was grown; Hardy B. married a Miss Platt, and went to Mississippi years ago, and is yet living, and is said to be doing well; Thomas C., well known and now living in Florence County, and one of the best of her citizens, married, first, a Miss Morgan, of Charleston, who died a year or two after marriage, childless; he married again, 16th May, 1866, Miss Carrie R. McPherson, in West Marion (now Florence), where Thomas C. Crawford has ever since resided, and where he now resides.* His wife died suddenly about a month ago, childless. Willis G. Crawford was a doctor; married a Miss Morgan, of Charleston, a sister of his brother Thomas' wife. Not long after his marriage he was on a fox chase, and galloping his horse through the woods, his horse bogged down and threw the doctor, whose gun was lying across his front, and in the fall of his horse and himself, the gun was discharged and he was killed; he left no child. William Crawford died unmarried, some years after the war. Gibson G. Crawford married a daughter of the late Colonel James R. Bethea; the fruits of the marriage were two sons, James G. and Samuel B., and two daughters, Jessie and Mary; the sons are now young men. James G. married, a week or two ago, a Miss Evans, of Society Hill; the daughter, Jessie, married

---

*Thomas C. Crawford died since writing the above.

W. Ellis Bethea, who lives at Latta; Samuel B. and Mary are yet single, and live at Latta with their father, G. G. Crawford. Of the two daughters of Willis Crawford, Rhoda married Henry Easterling, about 1850, and he was killed in the war; the widow, Rhoda, is also dead; she left three sons, Willis C., Thomas and Frank; and two daughters, Ella and Florence. The three sons are married—Willis C. to a Miss Legette; they have a family, some of them grown and married. J. Frank Easterling married a Miss Watson, daughter of the late Samuel Watson. Thomas Easterling went to Florida, where he married, has children, and is Sheriff of the county in which he lives. The Easterling boys are men of character and doing fairly well. Of the two daughters of Henry Easterling and his wife, Rhoda, Ella married Leroy Bethea, a son of Captain D. W. Bethea; they live in Marlborough, and are doing well; I know not of their family. Florence Easterling, the other daughter, married Robert McPherson, in West Marion; she is dead; left one child, a son. Margaret Crawford, the youngest daughter of Willis Crawford, never married; she died a few years ago. "Cype" and Willis Crawford had another brother—think he was a brother—named Gadi. The writer never saw him; he died unmarried. There was another family of Crawfords, descendants of old John, but in a different branch of the family—Hal Crawford and a brother, named John, and two sisters, the wife of Cross Roads Henry Berry, and Mercy Bass, wife of Joseph Bass (senior). Berry's wife was named Charity. Hal Crawford married and went West; John Crawford never did marry. I suppose they are both dead. "Cype" and Willis Crawford had a sister, named Rhoda, who became the wife of the late Hugh Godbold; she has been dead some years, and left no children. There were two Crawford brothers from Alabama of the same family, named John H. Crawford and Dr. James Crawford; they were here during the '40's. John H. married a Sarah Ann Moody, oldest daughter of the late Barfield Moody. They went back to Alabama. The wife of John H. died, leaving a son, named Albert, but was called Dock Crawford; he came back to this State and lived here for years; was a merchant at Marion, and was County Auditor for a while, but resigned the office. It was said he went crazy or became a lunatic, and in a lucid interval went or started back to Georgia, and died, it was said, crazy in the woods. He was the nephew of our fellow-citizen, E. J. Moody.

MURFEE.—Bishop Gregg, p. 71, says: "Of the Murfees there were four brothers, Moses, Malachi, Maurice and Michael. Of these, Malachi became the wealthiest. He is said to have given one hundred slaves to each of three sons; he died before the Revolution. Maurice had a son bearing his name, who was destined to occupy a prominent place in the subsequent history of the Pee Dee." Maurice Murfee, of the second generation, was a Colonel in the Revolution, and did valiant service for his country. He was an ardent Whig, of daring and reckless courage; he was a man of violent passion, so much so, as to lead him to the commission of violent and brutal acts; he killed his uncle, Gideon Gibson, in a fit of anger, and for which he had no valid excuse or even palliation; he was a violent man through life, and finally died in prison for debt. Malachi Murfee, of the second generation, was a Captain in the Revolution; he was wounded and escaped at Bass' Mill in a fight with the Tories; another account says he was killed. He was a first cousin of Colonel Maurice Murfee. The Murfee family must have been numerous, not only in the name, but also in its connections. There were four brothers of them to start with; they all had descendants, males as well as females. They intermarried with the best families in both ways, males and females, and by the third and fourth generations must have been numerous. We have no account of their emigration to other parts, and yet in a period of one hundred and fifty years, the name (from that family) has entirely disappeared, and their connections are unknown. The last one of them has disappeared. Mrs. Arline Mooneyham, *nee* Murfee or Murphy, died childless, about ten years ago, in the Pee Dee slashes; she was the last; she had no children or known relations to inherit her lands—some 600 or 800 acres in the slashes; she made a last will and gave all she had to Dr. J. E. Jarnigan; he attended her in her last illness. Such are the results of the action of time. Change and decay pervade all things terrestrial. The present actors in the drama of life, in a few years will have passed into the forever beyond, and their successors will not know, in many instances, that a particular one lived.

BERRY.—Another settler at Sandy Bluff (Solomon's Landing), mentioned by Bishop Gregg, was a Berry. He does not say what his name was, or anything else about him. The writer takes it for granted that he is the progenitor of the extensive family by that name, in the county, and such supposition is not in conflict with the traditions of that family, but rather corroborate it. The writer a few years ago, and not long before her death, talked with old Mrs. Fama Tart, who died in her ninety-fourth year, and who, as she said, was the grand-daughter of the first Berry in this region of country, and she said his name was Andrew Berry—a small man in stature; he settled at Sandy Bluff, on Pee Dee River. How long he remained or who he married, is not known; but, according to Mrs. Tart's statement, he had and raised a family of ten children, six sons and four daughters. From the Berry family and its connections is derived much of our citizenship. The sons of old Andrew were six. Henry and Stephen were both known to the writer. Henry was a man of family, and had lands granted to him on Little Reedy Creek in 1786; he married a Miss Hays, and settled on said Reedy Creek; he raised two sons, Dennis and Slaughter, and four daughters. Dennis and Slaughter married sisters, two daughters of David Miles, an old citizen of upper Marion. Of the four daughters, Elizabeth married Bryant Jones; Fama married Nathan Tart; Martha, called Pattie, married John M. Miles; and Mary married William Rogers. The father, Henry Berry, was a capital man and intelligent for his day and time; he served as Justice of the Peace for some years, evidenced by his official signature to the probate of deeds for record seen by the writer; he accumulated a good property for his time; he founded or built the Catfish Baptist Church, not where it now stands, but back from its present location on Little Reedy Creek. In his old age he divided out his property among his children, and then lived among them himself till his death, about 1853 or

1854; he was over ninety years of age at his death. His brother, Stephen, also lived to a great age—perhaps as old as his brother, Henry. I do not know whom he married; he raised a considerable family, only two sons, and several daughters; his sons were Henry (known in later times as Cross Roads Henry), and Andrew Stephen Berry; he was a good citizen, an honest man, bore a good character through life, but not as useful a man as was his brother, Henry—perhaps, not so well educated; he died about 1862. Dennis Berry, the oldest son of old Henry, raised only one son, Frank A. Berry, who died childless, a few years ago. Dennis Berry lived to an advanced age, over eighty; he, too, was a Justice of the Peace in his day—but few in his locality competent for such position, and still fewer in his father's day. The second son of old Henry Slaughter, and youngest child, as before stated, married a Miss Miles; he raised a small family—two sons, Charles and Henry, and two daughters; he and his family removed to Florida in 1854 or 1855. Elizabeth, daughter of old Henry, married Bryant Jones, the father of our fellow-citizen, Henry Jones, and the late F. D. Jones and James E. Jones; the two latter are dead. James E. never married; and two daughters, Nancy and Polly. Fama Berry, who married Nathan Tart, born in 1791, and died in 1884, was a most remarkable woman, physically and mentally. The writer went to see her a year or so before she died; she was very large and corpulent, suppose she weighed 250 or more; she said she had never in her life been sick but little, and had never taken any medicine, except what she prescribed for and could procure for herself; her mental powers were unimpaired and her memory of persons, families and events excelled anything of the kind I ever met with. I wrote her obituary and published it in the "Marion Star" newspaper, soon after her death. She was not sick when she died, as it was told the writer by her son-in-law, Wilson Hays—who called in a physician to see her, who said the fat had overgrown the heart so as to prevent its action, and no relief was possible. Fama Tart raised several sons, Enos, James H., H. Tart, Thomas E. and Gadie, and several daughters. The sons are, perhaps, all dead; also the daughters, except Jane, who married Willis Waters, who lives in

Florence County; and Wilson Hays' wife. H. H. Tart, who was an excellent and energetic man of high character in his sphere of life, died last year, about seventy-eight years of age. Fama Tart's children and great-grand-children, and even another generation of them, are numerous. Pattie Miles has been dead for years, the third daughter of old Henry. If there are any of her children or grand-children now in the county, it is unknown to the writer, except the widow of H. H. Tart, deceased, and her children and grand-children, all of whom are unknown. Mary, called Polly Rogers, wife of the late William Rogers, has been dead for more than twenty years; she was the youngest daughter of old Henry Berry; she has several descendants now in the county, to the third and fourth generations. Our good citizens, Philip B. Rogers and Lot B. Rogers, are sons of hers; and of her daughters, Mrs. Mastin Stackhouse, Mrs. D. F. Berry and Mrs. Maggie Ivey are still living. Of the dead and the living they, perhaps, number more than a hundred, among the Hays, Stackhouses, Lewis, Adams, Berrys and others, her descendants are to be found. To trace all from old Andrew down through males and females is and would be an impossibility; if it could be done, it would run up into thousands. Heretofore in this work the writer has in most cases pursued that course—that is, commencing with the first settler and tracing it down through every branch of the family to the present generation, male and female—which in many instances is very difficult and in some cases impossible, for want of knowledge; but he will have to abandon that mode for want of space and time, and in a book of the size contemplated, the fourth part could not be told. Andrew Berry, a grand-son of the first Andrew, and brother of Cross Roads Henry, lived to the advanced age of eighty-nine, and died only a few years ago; was a harmless, inoffensive man; raised by two wives several sons and daughters—Captain Stephen F. Berry and Bright Berry by the first marriage—(the latter of whom is now dead, leaving a considerable family, sons and daughters, names unknown); and by the second marriage, Henry, Nathan, Joseph and two other sons, nicknamed "Close" and "Tight." Nathan married a daughter of Daniel A. Platt, and died, leaving a son named David. Joseph Berry married his brother Nathan's widow, and has a considerable family. Of the brothers, "Close" and "Tight," the writer knows nothing, and can, therefore, say nothing more. Andrew Berry had several daughters, but knows not to whom they married; no doubt but that there is a numerous progeny from Andrew (second) Berry, but they are unknown to the writer. Cross Roads Henry Berry, a grand-son of the first settler, Andrew, and a brother of Andrew, the second, became the most noted of any of the Berry family, except, perhaps, his Uncle Henry, already referred to. He was born January 13th, 1796, and died 9th July, 1876, and was cremated, July 11th, 1876, near his home.

Cross Roads Henry Berry was a man of fine business sense, honest and upright in all his various dealings with his fellowman; he applied himself strictly to his own business (farming) and succeeded therein, not for show and ostentation at county and State fairs, but for profit. He settled on 150 acres of land, acquired through his wife, Charity Crawford (then unimproved), and with very little means otherwise began life at the Cross Roads, afterwards and yet called Berry's Cross Roads, where he lived and where he spent his whole life, and there and thereabouts made his large property. He entered into no schemes of speculation; he at first acquired slowly but surely; he took care of what he made and kept adding to it, making it larger and larger year by year; lived well at home, but without ostentation; made most of what he used on his plantation; he acquired a large landed estate around him, more than ten thousand acres, most of which he deeded to his children before his death; his lands were very valuable; he avoided debt through life; he raised to be grown five sons and three daughters. The sons were Cade, Gewood, Elihu, James and Stephen, all of whom are now dead, except James, who lives on the old homestead of his father. Cade Berry, the oldest son, never married; he died more than twenty-five years ago; Gewood, a graduate of the University of North Carolina, and the only one of the family to whom a collegiate education was given, married Joanna Ellerbe, a daughter of the late John C. Ellerbe, and a sister of the late Captain W. S. Ellerbe; the fruits of this marriage were five sons and a daughter; the daughter died in childhood, the sons were all raised to be grown. Three of the sons, John H., Edward Burke and Thomas Wickham Berry, are among our best and most respected citizens; the two others, William E. and Ashton, emigrated West; William E. Berry is dead, leaving a family somewhere in the Western States. Ashton lives in Florida, and is doing well, as is said. Elihu Berry married, first, Miss Jane Haselden; and she, after having three children, Sallie, Sue and James H., died. Elihu married, a second time, to Miss Mary Ellen Hays, a daughter of the late John C. Hays, and by her had four daughters and two sons. The sons are E. Lide Berry and Eugene Berry, the latter now a minor; the daughters, Telatha, Emma, Lucy and Leila. Telatha married J. W. Davis, of Marion, removed West, and is now dead, leaving two little daughters, twins, who are now being raised by their Grand-mother Berry; Emma, the next daughter, married Dow Atkins, who is one of our good citizens; Lucy and Leila are both young girls—one at the Columbia Female College, the other at Rock Hill. E. Lide Berry, a very worthy young man, is yet single. James Berry, a son of Cross Roads Henry, the only survivor of the family, resides on his father's old homestead, advancing far into life, sixty-seven years of age, a very successful farmer and exemplary citizen; he married Miss Harriett Alford, a daughter of the late Neill Alford, and has raised a large family of sons and daughters. The sons are Robert A., Neil A., Henry, James, Quincy and Downing; the daughters are Telatha, Julia, Florence and Etta—all married, except Florence and Downing. Robert A. and James are doctors, residing and practicing their professions in Birmingham, Ala., and are said to be doing well. Robert A. married a Virginia lady, a Miss McChesney; James married a Miss Carpenter, of Charleston; Henry married a Miss Deer, of Marion; Quincy married a Miss Oliver, of Marion, and daughter of Squire D. J. Oliver; Downing is yet single. Of the daughters of James Berry, Telatha married a Mr. Guy Lovejoy, and is in some of the Western States; Julia married Mr. Ed. R. Hamer, who resides at Little Rock; Miss Etta married a Mr. Drayspring, of Birmingham, Ala.; Miss Florence is yet unmarried. Of Elihu Berry's children by his first wife, Jane Haselden, Miss Sallie married Willis Fore; they raised five children, three sons and two daughters. The sons are Linwood, Tracy and Willis. Linwood married a Miss Dudley, of Marlborough; Tracy married a Miss Hays, daughter of our fellow-citizen, H. R. Hays; Willis is yet unmarried. Of the two daughters, Janie married James Dudley, of Marlborough; Rebecca, the younger daughter, married John C. Hays. The second daughter of Elihu, Sue, married our respected fellow-citizen, Captain W. B. Evans; they have several children, sons and daughters, noted among the Evans family. Of the children of Elihu Berry by his first wife, is a son, James H. Berry, one of our energetic and prosperous farmers; he has been married twice. His first wife was Miss Mollie Stackhouse, daughter of the late Colonel E. T. Stackhouse; she died some years ago, leaving seven children; the husband, James H. Berry, married, a second time, a daughter of John H. Davis, of Marion. Of the sons of the late Gewood Berry, John H. married Miss Madge Fore, a daughter of Tracy R. Fore; they have only one child living, a daughter. Edmund Burke married Miss Mary Manning, daughter of the late Thomas J. Manning; they have only one child living, a boy, named for his father, Edmund Burke. Thomas Wickham Berry, the youngest son of Gewood Berry, married Miss Tommie Manning, a sister of Edmund Burke's wife; they have several children, all girls; they are in the Little Rock community. Stephen Berry, the youngest son of Cross Roads Henry Berry, married Miss Euphemia Watson, a daughter of the late old Isham Watson; Stephen died in about a year after his marriage, childless. His widow married the late F. D. Jones, of Marion, and raised a family of five daughters and one son, about whom more may be said hereafter; Mrs. Jones is also dead. Of the daughters of Cross Roads Henry Berry, Mary, the eldest, married Stephen Fore, 20th February, 1845. The writer was one of his best men upon that pleasant occasion. Stephen Fore and wife are both dead; he died 11th March, 1881; Mrs. Fore died some four or five years ago; the fruits of their marriage were five daughters and four sons, viz: Flora, Amanda, Florence, Annie and Ida; the sons are George, Oliver Cromwell, J. Russell and Clarence. Flora, the eldest daughter, married James D. Bethea, who survives her, she having died two or three years ago; she left several daughters and three sons, viz: Mary, Blanche, Maude, Clara, Maggie and Leslie, all of whom are grown. Blanche and Maude are married—the former to Dan Dillon, the latter to Chalmers Biggs; the other girls are single. The sons are Kemper, Charles and Lonnie; of these, Kemper, the writer thinks, is married, and is in the city of Washington, in the employ of the government in some of its departments; Charles is about grown; he and his younger brother, Lonnie, remain with their father and unmarried sisters. Amanda, the second daughter of Stephen Fore and wife, Mary, married David S. Allen; she died some years back, and left at her death four girl children, the oldest of whom, Mary, is the wife of John D. Coleman, a very excellent man and worthy citizen; her three sisters all live with her. D. S. Allen, the father, married a second time; his wife is the sister of his son-in-law, John D. Coleman. The writer is curious to know what kin the children of D. S. Allen, by his second wife, are to the children of John D. Coleman, the son-in-law of D. S. Allen? The third daughter of Stephen Fore and wife, Mary, Florence by name, married D. McL. Bethea; she died in May last, leaving seven children, six daughters and one son, named James Stephen; the daughters are Estelle, Nellie, Lutie, Annie, Ida and Florence Alline; Nellie, the second daughter, lately married Mr. Maurice Manning, a promising young man; the other children are with their father, the youngest about two years old; the son, James Stephen, is about fifteen or sixteen years of age. D. McL. Bethea is a very prosperous man. Annie, the fourth daughter of Stephen Fore, married Willie Watson, son of William Watson, deceased; they have ten children, seven sons and three daughters; the sons are Lawton, Julian, Burke, Hoyt, Jasper, Pratt and Memory; the daughters are Nora, Pauline and Alma—all single and live with their parents. The two oldest sons, Lawton and Julian, are in Wake Forrest College, in North Carolina. Ida, the fifth daughter of Stephen Fore, married Mr. Emerson M. Duffie, at Marion, who is a genius in machinery, and is the owner of the extensive iron works in the town of Marion; he is not only a useful man in his profession, which he took up within himself and brought it up to its present perfection without serving any apprenticeship; he may truthfully be called a natural genius, but he is a most excellent man every way—full of energy, pluck and perseverance, reliable in every phase of life. They have five or six children of both sexes, none grown, names unknown to the writer. The oldest son of Stephen Fore is George Fore, one of our best and most worthy citizens; he married a Miss Ford, daughter of the late Elias B. Ford. George Fore has three children; two sons, Baker and Joseph, and one daughter, Kate—all grown and unmarried. The oldest son, Baker, is a graduate of Wake Forrest College, and is a promising young man.* The second son of Stephen Fore is J. Russel Fore; he and the fourth son, Clarence Fore, have never married; they live together on the father's old homestead; one of James D. Bethea's daughters, their niece, stays with them and keeps house. Each of these boys has his own place, runs his own farm, and makes his own money. J. Russel is reputed to have money ahead; he is much older than Clarence, and has been working for himself much longer, and hence has accumulated more money. Oliver Cromwell Fore, the third son of Stephen Fore, married Miss Jennie Lassiter, a very smart woman, as well as a good woman; they have four children, two boys and two girls, all small; Cromwell has been in the iron works of his brother-in-law, McDuffie, for several years, and is supposed to have learned much about machinery and how to make or repair it. Cross Roads Henry Berry's second daughter, Telatha, married Dr. Willis Fore, a brother of Stephen Fore, *supra;* she lived only a few years, and died childless; Dr. Fore himself survived his wife only a few years, when he died, not having remarried. Cross Roads Henry Berry's third and youngest daughter, Virzilla by name, married the late John Mace; the fruits of the marriage were two daughters, Lucinda M. and Maggie Ellen; their mother died when they were quite young, aged eight and and six years respectively; they were raised without any mother by their father; he never remarried; the girls grew up to womanhood, and the younger, Maggie Ellen, married John C. Sellers, 23d December, 1869; four years afterwards, Lucinda

---

*Since writing the above, George Fore has died.

M. married William G. Edwards; both Lucinda M. and Maggie E. are dead; the latter died 26th April, 1888, the former died in 1896. Maggie left six children surviving her, viz: Lucy, Benjamin B., Annie, Wallace D., Leila and Maggie Ellen (called Pearl), the latter only three days old at her mother's death; she was taken by her aunt, Rachel Norton, who has kept her till the present time; she is now thirteen years old. Lucinda M., wife of William G. Edwards, left at her death five children, three daughters and two sons; the daughters are: Mary, now the wife of J. Dudley Haselden; she has two children, both sons; also, Maggie and Carrie Edwards. The two sons are Henry A. Edwards and Samuel Edwards. Henry, the elder son, after taking a two years course in Wofford College, went to Vanderbilt University, Tenn., and took a three or four years course in the medical department of that well equipped institution, and is now a young "M. D."

Captain Stephen F. Berry, son of the late Andrew Berry, and nephew of Cross Roads Henry, married a Miss Jones, and raised a large family of sons and daughters, the names of whom (or all of them) the writer does not know. His oldest son, Henry, married a Miss Cottingham, and has a family; another son, Wylie, married a daughter of H. C. Dew, and is doing fairly well; he has one child, a daughter. Another son, Benjamin O., was for a while an itinerant Methodist preacher; married some lady, to the writer unknown; he did not do well, was finally expelled from the Conference and has disappeared. Another son, G. Raymond Berry, married a Miss McIntyre, and having a fair education, he has taught school most of the time since his majority, and has a good reputation, both as a citizen and as a teacher; he is very popular, and has lately been elected as County Superintendent of Education. Captain Berry has other sons unmarried and living with him, names unknown—think one of them is named Wade Hampton; he has four married daughters; one married Albert Rogers, who is doing well and a good citizen, has children—how many is unknown. Another married John B. Hamer, a very energetic, pushing man; I think he has five or six children. Another married James S. Hays, and is doing well; Hays is an energetic, persevering man, and prosperous;

he has several children. Another daughter married a man by the name of Wright, who recently died at Latta; don't think he left any children.

Another family of Berrys may be noted, to wit: Samuel J. Berry's family. The first old Andrew, that settled with the Sandy Bluff colony about 1736 or 1737, it will be remembered, had six sons and four daughters, according to tradition, through old Mrs. Fama Tart, a grand-daughter of old Andrew. Mrs. Tart was a living walking genealogical dictionary, and a memory equally as wonderful. Of the six brothers, four lived to be grown and raised families, to wit: Henry, her father, Stephen, John and Andrew; I think another was named Samuel; the sixth name not remembered. The Samuel J. Berry's family, mentioned above, was a direct descendant from either John or Andrew. Samuel J. Berry died some years ago, leaving a family of three sons, Madison, Wilson and Stephen, and perhaps some daughters; he was a volunteer soldier in the Florida Seminole War, in a company from Marion, commanded by Captain   and formed a part of the battalion commanded by Major W. W. Harllee. The writer procured a pension for Samuel J. Berry's widow, which she yet, if living, receives from the United States government. Samuel J. Berry was an unpretentious man, a quiet and peaceable citizen, honest to the cent, but little known outside his neighborhood; his three sons, Madison, Wilson and Stephen, are of like character, honoring their departed father and perpetuating his name and many virtues. There are other Berrys, descendants of the first old Andrew, of less note than those herein mentioned, and unknown to the writer. Their connections, through the female line, are very extensive and permeate pretty much the whole of the upper end of the county; many have gone West. The name will not soon become extinct. Of the four daughters of the old first Andrew Berry, two of them married Dews, one of them a Hays, and the other did not marry—if she did it is not known to whom. Of these more will be said hereafter.

SAUNDERS.—In the settlement made at Sandy Bluff, the name of Saunders appears. John, George and William

Saunders were the first of the name there. Bishop Gregg, on p. 71, says: "Of the settlers at Sandy Bluff, the Murfees, Saunders, Gibsons and Crawfords accumulated the largest properties." The name Saunders has become extinct in Marion County—not one of the name in the county, to the knowledge of the writer. One John Saunders took up large grants of land between Catfish and Great Pee Dee. "They came from England. John Saunders had two sons, George and Thomas. George was the father of Nathaniel Saunders, who became a man of some note, and was the father of the late Moses Saunders and Jordan Saunders, in Darlington" (Gregg, p. 73). In a note to the same page, the Bishop says: "George Saunders came to an untimely end; in connection with which a singular incident is related. He was engaged on a Sunday in cutting down a bee tree, a cypress, in the swamp on the opposite side of the river. As the cypress fell, the limb of an ash was broken off, and being thrown with violence on the head of Saunders, killed him instantly. An ash afterwards came up at the head of his grave and grew to a large tree, being regarded by the people as a standing monument of the judgment sent upon him for the violation of the Lord's day, which led to his end. It is but a few years since that the last vestige of this famous ash was to be seen. Near the spot are faint traces of the burial ground of the Sandy Bluff settlement." The descendants of this Saunders family have all played out. Between fifty and sixty years ago, Tobias Saunders and Smithey Saunders, brother and sister (neither one ever married), lived on the road leading from Berry's Cross Roads to Marion, near the end of Pigeon Bay, just below where the Florence Railroad crosses said bay; they were descendants of old John Saunders, to whom much land had been granted; the little hut of a house in which they lived stood on land granted to their ancestor; they were invalids, and lived by begging and by the charity of the neighbors. The writer used to see them at his father-in-law's many times begging, and the old man would give them a shoulder of meat and half bushel of meal, as much as they could carry. The sister was the stronger of the two; they were imbecile, and especially the brother, and harmless; they ultimately died there. Such are the sad changes in families.

GIBSON.—Among the early settlers at "Sandy Bluff" were the Gibsons. Gregg, p. 73, says: "Of the Gibsons, Gideon and Jordan were brothers. The latter (Jordan) went to the West as a companion of Daniel Boone. Gideon Gibson came with his father from Virginia to Pee Dee. There is a public record of a grant to him for 550 acres of land as early as April, 1736. He settled at a place called Hickory Grove, five miles from Sandy Bluff, on a large and fertile body of land, long after noted as the most valuable in that region." In a note to the same page, Gregg says: "He (Gideon Gibson) was the grand-uncle of the late Captain John Gibson, of Darlington. Gideon Gibson had three sons" (p. 74); "of these, Stephen became wealthy, and removed to Georgia about the year 1800. Roger, another son, removed to the West before the Revolution." Bishop Gregg says nothing about the third son of Gideon Gibson, does not even mention his name. The writer supposes his name was Tobias Gibson, who became a Methodist traveling preacher, joined the Conference in 1792, from Marion County, and died in 1804, at the age of thirty years, and was buried at Natchez, Miss. (Minutes of the 111th session of the South Carolina Annual Conference of the M. E. Church, South, held in Abbeville, S. C., December 9-14, 1899.) According to this, he was born in 1774; he may have been a grand-son of Gideon Gibson. In 1781 (February), Gideon Gibson was killed at his own house by Colonel Maurice Murfee; Gideon Gibson was the uncle of Murfee. Colonel Maurice Murfee, though a staunch Whig and a daring and gallant soldier, yet was a very violent man, and especially so when in liquor. Bishop Gregg, p. 354, says: "Lower down, on the east side of the river, the Tories made frequent incursions from Little Pee Dee, finding co-operation on the part of some in that immediate region. The Whigs were driven in some instances to acts of cruel retaliation. One instance of the kind is related of Colonel Maurice Murphy. He was a man of ungovernable passion, which was often inflamed by strong drink. On the occasion alluded to, he went to the house of a noted Tory, named Blackman, then somewhat advanced in years, and inoffensive. He had, however, several sons who were active against the Whigs. Murphy's real object, doubtless, was to discover where these and others of their companions were. Having tied Blackman, he asked him who he was for; and upon his replying 'for King George,' gave him fifty lashes. The question was repeated, with the same reply, and the like punishment inflicted until the fourth time, when, upon finding the old man unyielding, Murphy was compelled to desist. Blackman lived on Catfish, and the place is yet called 'Tory's Camp.' Gideon Gibson, the uncle of Murphy, blamed him for his conduct on the occasion. Subsequently, Murphy stopped, with his company, at Gibson's for breakfast, and while there the subject was resumed. A quarrel ensued, and as Murphy mounted his horse to start off, Gibson followed him to the door and said something offensive, whereupon Murphy shot him dead. Three of Gibson's sons were present in Murphy's company, and were men of undaunted courage; but knowing his violent temper and desperate resolution, did not interfere. Nothing was done to Murphy afterwards on account of it." From this it would appear that Jordan Gibson, the brother of Gideon, must have been the grand-father of the "late Captain John Gibson, of Darlington." Jordan Gibson went off "West as a companion of Daniel Boone," but we suppose he returned to Carolina, Gregg says, *supra,* that Gideon Gibson was "the great-uncle of Captain John Gibson, of Darlington." Stephen Gibson was a son of Gideon; he lived prior to 1800, and owned a large body of land in and around Harlleesville, in this county. About the latter date, he sold his lands there and removed to Georgia (Gregg). The writer remembers in his long practice of law to have seen the deeds from Stephen Gibson to Thomas Harllee. He may have been the father of Tobias Gibson, the preacher hereinbefore referred to. Captain John Gibson lived in Marion County and owned large bodies of land therein, near Mars Bluff Ferry, on both sides of the river; he had two sons, Ferdinand S. Gibson and James S. Gibson; I think he married a Miss Savage. The lands on the east side of the river, and perhaps some on the west side, went to his son, Ferdinand, whose first wife was a Miss Godfrey, and his second wife was Miss Constantine McClenaghan; he died at Marion Court House, 12th May, 1867, childless. He was considered very wealthy before the war, had two hundred or more slaves; he was involved in debt, his lands were sold under proceedings to marshal his assets and for the payment of his debts, and thus that valuable property has passed entirely out of the hands of the family; his widow got dower out of it; she afterwards became the wife of Dr. D. S. Price; she died some years back, leaving some four or five children—think three sons and a daughter; the latter is now the wife of W. G. Mullins.

James S. Gibson, brother to Ferdinand S., married a Miss DuBose, of Darlington; he inherited from his father, Captain John Gibson, that large and valuable plantation, on the west side of Great Pee Dee, near Mars Bluff Ferry. James S. Gibson died not long after his brother, Ferdinand; he was a better manager, or at least more fortunate in the results of the war, and saved his large landed estate for his two sons, Knight and Nathan S.; the latter is now in possession of those lands. Knight Gibson married a daughter of Dr. C. H. Black, by whom he had, I think, four children; Knight Gibson died in the latter part of 1885 or 1886; what has become of his children is unknown. Nathan S. Gibson is certainly rich in lands and may be so otherwise; he is unmarried, and is almost fifty years of age. This is in Florence County, formerly Marion County.

Another quite respectable family of Gibsons are below Marion Court House. The first known of them was Squire David Gibson, who was a very worthy man and good citizen. Think he came from Scotland—at any rate, he was a Scotchman; his tongue betrayed his nationality. It has been said of him that he was on the stand as a witness in some case, that the occasion and circumstances suggested the question to be asked him, if he believed in ghosts, spirits, &c., and the old gentleman, in the honesty of his heart, replied that he could not say that he did, but that when he passed by a graveyard at night he always kept a sharp lookout. The writer does not know whom he married, but he raised four sons, if no more, James, Allen, Jessee and Albert; the first and last of these are dead, but left families; Allen and Jessee yet survive, and are among our best people, quiet and unpretentious, honest and straightforward in all their movements and dealings with their fellow-men; engage in no local strife or bickerings; keep clear of lawsuits; attend strictly to their own business and let the business of others strictly alone; it may be said, "with masterly inactivity." Observation teaches that it takes a pretty smart man to do this. Jessee Gibson and Allen Gibson married sisters, daughters of the late James Watson, and, doubtless, make good housewives, and are raising up families "in the way they should go." James Gibson died many years ago and left six or seven children; his oldest son, about twenty years of age, was killed on Main street, in Marion, more than twenty years ago; a horse ran away with a cart which the young man was driving, and threw him out near where the Bank of Marion now stands, his head striking an elm root on the sidewalk, which crushed his skull. The writer was in fifteen feet of him when he fell, and was the first one to get to him; others soon came up and among them a doctor; he breathed sturtously for five or ten minutes and then expired. A sad and sudden ending. Albert Gibson died a few years ago, leaving a family of children, none grown at the time; he was one of our progressive, good citizens; his family are not known to the writer.

PAGE.—Another pretty extensive family in the county are the Pages; they are mostly on Bear Swamp and Ashpole, near the State line, and Buck Swamp and Little Pee Dee. Of the old Pages known to the writer, there were Joseph, Solomon and Thomas, and perhaps David. Joseph died about the first of the nineteenth century, leaving three sons and several daughters; his wife was a Miss Horn; his sons were Joseph and Abram and John W. The son, Joseph, settled on the paternal homestead, just across the State line, in North Carolina, owning lands, however, in both States; he married a Miss Connerly, a North Carolina lady; died many years ago, quite a thrifty man, leaving two sons, Joseph and Timothy, and four daughters; his large landed property descended to his two sons, Joseph and Timothy. Joseph is dead, leaving sons and daughters, unknown to the writer. Timothy raised a considerable family, sons and daughters, and is still living. Timothy's sisters, all older than he and his brother, Joseph, married well; one an Elvington, one a Lewis, one a Connerly, and another, the youngest, Civil, married William H. Oliver, of North Carolina, and became the mother of two of our most respected and worthy citizens, to wit: the late Joseph R. Oliver and the late Dr. Wm. A. Oliver, both quite prominent, whose descendants, sons and daughters, married and single, are among us now, treading in the footsteps of their honored and beloved sires. Abram Page, the second son of the first old Joseph, married Miss Alice Nichols, of Columbus County, N. C., and sister to our late respected fellow-citizen, Averett Nichols, of Nichols, S. C. He settled on Ashpole, below the mouth of Bear Swamp, on the place now owned by the Widow T. B. Braddy, and where she resides. Abram Page raised five sons and one daughter; the sons were David N., Averett, Abram B., Joseph N. and Dock, as he was called, and one daughter, Ava. David N. died in early manhood; I do not think he married; Averett moved into North Carolina; I do not know whom he married, nor of his family; Abram B. Page, well known by his cotemporaries, settled and merchandised for many years at Nichols, S. C., and apparently did well for years, but finally failed, lost his mind, was carried to the Asylum at Columbia, S. C., and after staying there for a while, returned home and soon thereafter died; he never married; his fine property in and about Nichols was all sold and has gone into other hands. Joseph N. Page, of Page's Mill, settled there many years ago; he married a daughter of the late Elias B. Ford, by whom he had and raised only one child, a daughter, who in recent years married a Mr. L. W. Temple, of Raleigh, N. C., who has a family of several children. Joseph N. Page was a very safe man, accumulated a considerable property, which was all clear at his death, a few years ago. Dock Page, the youngest brother, and who inherited the old homestead, married Miss Addie Ayres, daughter of Thos. W. Ayres, and lived on the old homestead until a year or two ago, when he sold it to Mrs. Braddy, as herein stated, who now occupies it. Dock Page has a considerable family, unknown to the writer. Ava Page, the only daughter of Abram Page, married James D. Oliver, many years ago; they removed to Texas; nothing further is known of them. John W. Page died in middle life, and left two children, a son, Augustus Page, and a daughter, who married the late Aaron Oliver. Augustus Page married a Miss Page; he died childless. Solomon Page lived and died on Bear Swamp, on the road from Lumberton, N. C., to Nichols, S. C.; his wife was a Miss Ford; he raised a considerable family, sons and daughters; the sons were Eli, Joseph, James E., David and John F., all of whom were our citizens thirty or forty years ago, but all now dead, each leaving a family of sons and daughters. They and their descendants and connections are numerous, and especially in that part of the county. Three of the sons, Eli, John F. and David, married three sisters, Misses Bennett—somewhat remarkable. Thomas Page married and settled on the south side of Little Pee Dee, on the place where S. L. Page now resides; I do not know who his wife was; he raised one son, an only child, his name was William; he married a Miss Smith, daughter of old Samuel Smith, who lived and died about 1843, just below "Temperance Hill," on the road from Buck Swamp Bridge to Marion Court House. That marriage connects the Page and Smith families. Captain William Page was an excellent citizen and a very successful farmer, and accumulated a large property; he died in 1859; he left four sons, Samuel T., John S., William J. and Pinckney Page; the latter married a daughter of the late John L. Smith; he was killed or died in the war; left three children, I think, a son and two daughters; I do not know much about them. John S. Page married Miss Louisa Bass, and died about the beginning of the war, and left four or five children. William, a son of John S., was killed in 1873 or '4, in a posse of Sheriff Berry's, in trying to make an arrest. One of the daughters is now the wife of C. J. McColl, a cotton buyer at Mullins, S. C. The oldest son of Captain William Page, Samuel T., got into some trouble, in 1865, with the military authorities then stationed in Marion; he sold out his plantation, now owned by J. Robert Reaves; eluding the "Yankees," he went West, and for years it was not generally known where he was—he was in Mississippi; he remained there for twenty years or more, when he returned to Marion with his wife; she soon died, and he has been with his son, John K. Page, and still lives with him; he is in his eighty-third year. John K. Page, with whom the old gentleman lives, is a very trustworthy man, a good manager and very prosperous. William J. Page, another son of Captain William Page, resides on his father's old homestead; he married, first, a Miss Grice, by whom he had eighteen children, and raised sixteen of them to be grown, sons and aughters, most of whom are married; they are all unknown to the writer, except the oldest son, J. Lawrence Page, a Magistrate for years, and a very good one, and a useful man; he lives on the homestead of his great-grand-father, Thomas Page; he has children grown and married unknown to the writer, except the second wife of John K. Page. William J. Page is over three score years and ten, but vigorous and active, a good citizen. Old Captain William Page had several daughters; one married Joseph Deer (the name now extinct in Marion County); Deer died, and the widow married Rev. John B. Platt, of the South Carolina Conference; I think she had two sons and three daughters by the Deer marriage; Wm. P. Deer and John were the sons; Mrs. William Watson, one of the daughters, still survives; one other daughter, Ellenora, never married, and is dead; the last daughter, Elizabeth, married John E. Elvington. By the Platt marriage, she had a son, R. B. Platt, a Magistrate, near Mullins, S. C., and two daughters, Mrs. B. Gause Smith, and the late Mrs. Dr. C. T. Ford; they all have large families. Another daughter of Captain William Page married D. W. Platt; they moved to Mississippi, fifty years ago or more. Another daughter married George J. Bethea, and still survives; she had two sons, William A. Bethea and John D. Bethea, and several daughters; I do not know whom they married, except that one married W. B. Ellen and one married W. Joseph Watson, and is dead, leaving several children. Another daughter of Captain William Page married the late Samuel Watson, and is dead; she left at her death, W. Joseph Melton, S. P. and Stonewall C. Watson, and two daughters, Sophronia and Maggie. W. Joseph Watson removed to North Carolina. Melton is dead, without child or children; he married a daughter of the late Charles Moody, who still survives. Sophronia was the first wife of John K. Page; she left two sons, Samuel and Ernest. Maggie married Frank Easterling, a very worthy citizen, and is doing well. Another daughter of old Captain William Page married Levi H. Hays, and was the mother of our very worthy fellow-citizen, W. B. Hays, in Hillsboro Township.

AYRES.—Another family in the northeastern section of the county is the Ayres family. Of this family the first known to the writer was the Rev. William Ayres, and two brothers, Darius and John, usually called Jack Ayres. Rev. William Ayres was a Baptist preacher; stood well among his clerical brethren, and was dearly beloved by the laity of his church; he married a Miss Shaw; the fruits of the marriage were our esteemed fellow-citizens, Thomas W. Ayres and Enoch S. Ayres, and several daughters—three or four. Thomas W. Ayres is well known to the county; was County Commissioner perhaps two terms, some years ago, and a prominent member of the Baptist Church; he did valiant service in the war—he and two of his sons were in the war together; his two sons were killed, as the writer has been informed, on the same day and in the same battle. Thomas W. Ayres married a Miss Williamson, in the Gapway neighborhood, a sister of Joseph Williamson. Besides the two sons killed in the war, he has three other sons, John and Pendleton G. Ayres, two excellent citizens, and a younger son, named Robert; he has several daughters, one married Dock Page, as hereinbefore stated, and one named Sallie, who died while off at school at Limestone Springs; not known as to the other daughters. Pendleton G. Ayres married a Miss McMillan, in the Mullins community. John Ayres married Miss Susan Page, a daughter of Timothy Page, and has a house full of children, so said. Robert Ayres has gone to Georgia and, I think, has married out there. Enoch Ayres, one of our best citizens, youngest son of Rev. William Ayres, married a Miss Tyler, in Horry County; the fruits of the marriage are three sons and four or five daughters; the sons are William, Elias and Lennon; his daughters all married but one, Erma; two in Kentucky, or are there now; one of them married a Baptist preacher named Rockwell; she was reputed to be a very intellectual lady. Another daughter married a Mr. Renfroe, of North Carolina. Of the daughters of Rev. William Ayres, one, Catharine, married Major H. B. Cook; they moved to Horry, raised a considerable family, sons and daughters; both are now dead. Another daughter married Buck Watson; they moved to Horry just after the war; both are dead. Another daughter married Levi Grainger, of Horry. I think another daughter died unmarried, during the war, with smallpox—I am not sure of it. Rev. William Ayres and wife both died of smallpox during the war. His brother, Jack Ayres, came home from the army, and after getting home the disease broke out on him and he died of it, whence it spread in the neighborhood, and several others, perhaps a dozen or more, died of it. Jack Ayres never married. Darius Ayres, brother of Rev. William, died in early life, leaving two sons, Darius and another, whose name the writer has forgotten (they both went to school to him). The elder boy, Darius, grew up, and the last heard of him by the writer he was a Baptist preacher in North Carolina. I do not know whence the Ayres sprang; I think, from the name, and their complexion and their general make-up, that their progenitors were from Wales, in South England, and may have been part of the Welsh settlement on Great Pee Dee, who came from Pennsylvania and Delaware to South Carolina, in 1735 or '6, and afterwards.

FORD.—The Ford family, in upper Marion, were among the first settlers in upper Marion. In the appendix to Ramsay's History of South Carolina, on page 302, volume 2, he says: "There have been many instances of longevity in the county between Little Pee Dee and Catfish Creek, about sixty miles north of Georgetown; six very old men died there since the year 1800. One of them, James Ford, died in or near 1804, at the age of one hundred years. The others are James Munnerlyn, Moses Martin, Rockingham Keene, Michael Mixon and William Watson, who all died upwards of eighty years of age. James Munnerlyn served in the office of Constable at eighty-six years, walked fifty miles to serve a process and returned home again in less than thre days." Where the Fords of Marion originally came from, is unknown. The James Ford mentioned above by Dr. Ramsay, must have been here two hundred years ago; and without better or other information, the writer will assume that either he or some other contemporary Ford were the progenitor or progenitors of the extensive family by that name. The first one known to the writer, in about 1830, was Preserved Ford, universally called Zarv Ford; he was then seventy-five or eighty years of age, may be older; he lived on the west side of Gaddy's Mills, then called Ford's Mills. It was at an association held at the old Saw Mill Church, on the east side of the mills—the church was old and dilapidated. It was there that I first saw him, and never saw him afterwards. He was a well-to-do man, and prominent in his day; he had three sons, Jessee, William and Charles. Major Jessee Ford, the eldest son, represented the district in the Legislature in the twenties—I do not know the precise date.* He was Major in the militia; his first wife was a Miss Townsend, of Robeson County, N. C.; by her he had two sons, the late Elias B. Ford and Allen Ford; his second wife was a Miss Watson, a daughter of Scarcebook Watson, above Nichols, on the road from Nichols to Lumberton, N. C.; by the second wife he had several sons and daughters; the sons, as their names are remembered, were Watson, Jessee, Thomas, David and Charles Ford. The war and emigration have removed them all, except Jessee, who is now an old and respectable citizen in the community of his birth, and has raised a family, unknown to the writer. The daughters of Major Jesse Ford, as remembered, were Elizabeth, Mary, Caroline and Virginia. Elizabeth married William H. Hays; by him she had several children; Mary married John I. Gaddy, and died in a year or two childless; Caroline married Dr. George E. Shooter, and raised a large family, unknown; I do not remember what became of Virginia. Major Jesse Ford may have had other daughters. Elias B. Ford, a most excellent and kind hearted man, born in 1809, married, 9th February, 1830, Miss Jane Herring, of Robeson, N. C., a woman of good property and one of the best of women; the fruits of this marriage were three sons. "Sandy" Ford, for a long time in Marion, and very prominent as a business man, now resides in Ander-

---

*Jessee Ford was elected a Representative in 1820. See list of Representatives in latter part hereof.

son County.* Dr. C. T. Ford, of Mullins, and Rev. Rufus Ford, a prominent minister of the Baptist Church, and now resides in Marlborough, and several daughters. Neill C. McDuffie, Sheriff, married two of them; D. D. McDuffie married one; Joseph N. Page married one, and George Fore married one; one unmarried and one dead, names not remembered. Elias B. Ford lost his wife, the mother of these children, and he married, a second time, the Widow Helen Pitman, who had four Pitman children, two sons and two daughters; the sons were killed or died in the war, and one of the daughters died during the war, all unmarried; the other daughter, the youngest, Amanda, married the late Joseph R. Oliver, and had by inheritance a good property. Elias B. Ford had no child or children by his second marriage; he died some years ago, greatly missed by the poor of his neighborhood. Allen Ford, the second son of Major Jessee Ford by his Townsend wife, married a Miss Falk, of Robeson; she died childless in a few years, and he removed to the West many years ago. Major William Ford, the second son of old man "Zarv" Ford, married a Miss Thompson; he was a well-to-do man; had not many children; the writer does not remember but one, a daughter, Sallie, who had a personal distinction, seldom, if ever, met with—she had a black eye and a blue one; a very pretty girl; she married John R. Watson, who occupied and owned his father's homestead, on the road from Nichols to Lumberton, N. C.; he died, leaving six or seven children together with his widow; the children all small; the widow managed well and raised a very nice family, sons and daughters—mostly daughters; the mother died some years ago, much respected while living. Major William Ford may have had a son, not now recollected; he had another daughter, as now remembered, who became and is now, the wife of Captain R. H. Rogers. Old man "Zarv" Ford's third and youngest son, Charles, died after arriving at manhood, unmarried. There was another old Ford, by name of George, who lived just below Tabernacle Church, on the road leading from Bear Swamp to Allen's Bridge, on Little Pee Dee; he was related to those other Fords, at least collaterally; he was a very energetic man and accumu-

---

*Moved to Texas.

lated some property; I never knew much of him; he was not a very old man when he died. I know that he left two sons, William and Nelson Ford, and know that he had three daughters, if no more, to wit; second wife of William Goodyear, Sr.—her name was Elizabeth; also the wife of the late Benjamin Shooter—her name was Mary; she was the mother of the Shooter family, a numerous family, and among them the gallant Colonel W. P. Shooter, who was killed in the severe battle of Spottsylvania Court House, in May, 1864. A family noted for its gallantry in the war. Colonel Wm. P. Shooter and two of his brothers (names not remembered) fell on the same day and in the same fight. Another daughter was the wife of Anthony Cribb, and became the mother of our W. T. Cribb and of Dempsy Cribb, Jr.; the latter is dead. W. T. Cribb is a respectable and good citizen, a brave soldier in the struggle for the "Lost Cause," and so was his brother, George T. Cribb. He lost a leg in the contest, and yet lives. Of the sons of George Ford, William (familiarly called "Little Bill Ford"), as now remembered, married, first, a Miss Lupo; he raised some family by her, the names and number not now known to the writer. "Little Bill Ford" has been dead some years, and perhaps his Butler wife. Nelson Ford lived to an advanced age, eighty or more, has not been dead many years; he was a most excellent man and worthy citizen; he married a Miss Lupo, and raised a family, how many is not known; one of his sons, named Hardy, lives near Nichols, and is a most excellent man and one of our best citizens. The Ford family, as a whole, were good people, and extend down two or three generations further than herein traced; for the want of information and personal acquaintance, the writer can go no further. They did their duty fully in the war, and demonstrated to their country a patriotism and courage of which the present and coming generations may be proud. Their connections are extensive.

HAYS.—Another family of note in Hillsboro Township is the Hays family. The common ancestor of that family was Benjamin Hays; I do not know who his wife was; he raised a considerable family of sons and daughters; the sons, as remembered, were James, Jessee, William H., Joseph B. and Levi H. Hays; the daughters, as remembered, were Mrs. Elias Allen, the mother of the late Rev. Joel Allen, and Thompson Allen, of Marlborough County; Mrs. Samuel Smith, of Buck Swamp, who died in 1857, and Mrs. John Martin, of Buck Swamp and Maiden Down; there may have been other daughters. These sons and daughters are all dead, some of them for many years, but were the stock of a numerous progeny—down to a second and third and even to a fourth generation; many of them unknown to the writer, and, therefore, can say but little about them. James Hays married a daughter of Matthew Jones, of Robeson; he raised a large family of sons and daughters; the names of these sons, as remembered, were Reaves, Henry and James R.; they were older than the writer, and all are dead. One of them was the father of our respected fellow-citizen, above Buck Swamp Bridge, W. D. B. Hays—the upper bridge is meant. There are several bridges across Buck Swamp now. The bridge near Page's was, for a long time, the only bridge on the swamp, and acquired the name of Buck Swamp Bridge; and when we say Buck Swamp Bridge, that bridge is meant. I do not know to whom these sons of James Hays were married. Jessee Hays married a Miss Elvington, and raised a large and respectable family. William H. Hays married, first, a Miss Thompson, and from that marriage sprang children, one named Lewis, as now remembered; his wife died, and he then married Miss Elizabeth Ford, daughter of Major Jessee Ford; this wife had children unknown to the writer; the Ford wife died, and he married, a third time, a Miss Elvington, by whom he had children, how many is unknown. Joseph B. Hays, the father of our much respected and substantial fellow-citizen, T. B. Hays, married a Miss Gaddy, daughter of old Ithamer Gaddy, near Gaddy's Mills; the fruits of this marriage were three sons, as now remebered, E. Wilson Hays, Aleck and T. B. Hays; E. Wilson Hays is now dead; he married, first, Miss Elizabeth Ann Rogers, a sister of our fellow-citizen, Lot B. Rogers; he had several children by this marriage; one of them is Gamewell Hays, who has removed to the West, and another is O. C. Hays, who lives near Little Rock; he married a daughter of

Owen Jackson, in the Judson section of the county, and he has a large family; Wilson Hays married, a second time, a daughter of the late Matthew Martin; she bore some children to him, how many is unknown. E. Wilson Hays was a very respectable man and excellent citizen; he died a few years ago of a cancer on his face. T. B. Hays married Sarah Nance, daughter of Everet Nance, of Robeson County, N. C., and by her had four children, Orilla, now the wife of Olin Edwards, Ina Rembert and Tristam. Rembert recently graduated at Wofford College, and is now engaged in farming; the first wife dying, T. B. Hays married, a second time, his cousin, Miss Walker Hays, daughter of Wm. B. Hays, by whom he has one child. Aleck Hays married Elizabeth, daughter of the late Colonel John Roberts, and lives at the forks of the road just below the residence of Captain Wm. J. Page; he raised a large family, all of whom are grown; one of his sons (name not remembered), married a daughter of Hiram Lee; another, Murray, married a daughter of Mrs. Zilpha Floyd; Mattie married a D. V. Coleman, of Columbus County, N. C., and removed to Georgia several years ago; Annie and Fanny are unmarried. Joseph B. Hays had some daughters; I do not know how many; one married the late T. B. Rogers, in the Fork, and is still living; they raised a considerable family; of the sons, J. Marion Rogers is a preacher of the South Carolina Conference, Methodist Church, South; he graduated with distinction at Wofford College some years past; another son, Herbert, graduated in the Citadel Academy last year, 1899. Another daughter of J. B. Hays married a Mr. Booth; think she is a widow. Another daughter of Joseph B. Hays became the wife of Solomon Edwards, in the Fork; she has an only daughter, who is now the wife of that excellent citizen, Kirkland Fort, with whom Mrs. Edwards lives, her husband having died many years ago. Another daughter, rather late in life, married Archie Thompson, and resides in Robeson County, N. C. Joseph B. Hays was a useful man in his day in his community; he was a Magistrate for many years. Levi H. Hays, the youngest son of old Benjamin, married a daughter of Captain William Page, near Buck Swamp Bridge; he raised a family, how many is not known; our respected and highly esteemed fellow-citizen, William B. Hays, is a son of Levi H. Levi H. Hays was a most excellent man and useful citizen in his neighborhood in his day; he served as a Magistrate for several years, and gave general satisfaction in that responsible and indispensable position; he preceded some of his older brothers to the grave.

The Hays family, of Hillsboro, have held their own about as well as any family in the county. They are and ever have been a peaceable, orderly and law-abiding people; honest, industrious and frugal, attend strictly to their own business, and do not meddle with the business of others; their name seldom appears on the journals of the Courts. An incident may here be related in reference to the old man, Benjamin, told to the writer sixty-five years ago. It runs thus: At a night meeting held in the neighborhood, some brother was called upon to pray (the name forgotten), and in his prayer, among his many petitions, one was that the good Lord would send down a thunderbolt from heaven and strike old Ben Hays' heart and make him sell his "backer" (tobacco) cheaper. From this incident several inferences may be drawn. The reader is left to draw his own conclusions. There is another family of Hays in Hillsboro, perhaps related collaterally; if so, they have greatly degenerated from their common ancestry—at any rate, so little is known of them that the writer cannot trace them.

There is another family of Hays in Kirby Township, which will be noticed herein further on.

ELVINGTON.—The Elvington family are to be found in Hillsboro. There were two old Elvingtons, brothers, of some note in Hillsboro—John and Jessee. The descendants of both, with their connections, are numerous; some of them are in the West. Old John Elvington lived on the road from Gaddy's Mills to Nichols; he raised a large family, sons and daughters; of the sons, Zadoc Elvington still survives, and lives near the old homestead; has no children; had two sons, whom he lost in the war. In some respects he is a prodigy, which will not be further alluded to. He has made and has money, which it is said he does not much enjoy, except the satisfaction of knowing that he has it. He married one of the ten daughters of the late John Goodyear (all of whom, it is said, were good women, and made industrious and frugal housewives). Old man John Elvington was a good citizen. His other sons were William, John (commonly called Jack), and Owen. They are all dead. Owen was the father of our excellent and thrifty good citizen, George W. Elvington; there may have been another son or two, not now remembered. He had several daughters; one the wife of the late Henry Huggins; one the wife of the late James Scott (she still survives); one the wife of the late Eli Scott, and perhaps others. The old gentleman was remarkable in one respect; he told the writer, when he was over seventy years of age, that he never saw a seed-tick or a red-bug in his life; spectacles did him no good, yet his eyesight had not failed him and he could see as well in his old age as he ever could; his eyes were very peculiar—did not look like the ordinary eye—they sparkled or twinkled. Old man Jessee Elvington lived and died on Bear Swamp; he was an old man seventy years ago; a good manager and snug farmer; he raised a considerable family, sons and daughters. Three sons, Giles, Hughey and John E. Giles Elvington married Miss Mary Ann Page, daughter of Joseph Page, just in North Carolina; Giles Elvington lived till after the war, and died an old man, after having married a second time. By his first wife he raised several children, sons and daughters, none of whom are now known to the writer. Giles Elvington owned the plantation where Dr. William A. Oliver lately died; he, like his father, was a good manager—at least, during his first wife's lifetime, and he and family were highly respected. Hughey Elvington married one of the ten girls of John Goodyear, hereinbefore mentioned, and she is now the wife of Wilson Lewis, of Horry, and weighs 260 pounds, as she recently told the writer. Hughey Elvington was a good citizen. John E. Elvington married a Miss Deer (Elizabeth Ann), daughter of Joseph Deer; her mother was a Page, and he inherited the old homestead of his father; he has been dead several years; raised a family quite respectable. A daughter of his is now the wife of William J. Williamson, who it is supposed has grown children. The several daughters of old Jesse Elvington married; one married the late Elgate Horn, who raised a large family, entirely unknown; another daughter married William

B. Grantham, of North Carolina; they are both dead and died childless. I do not know whom the other daughter of old man Jessee married. The Elvingtons and their connections are numerous, and all sprang from the two old men, John and Jesse Elvington.

SCOTT.—The Scott family, in Hillsboro, are not very extensive. Old man Pharaoh Scott lived near Tabernacle Church, on the road from Gaddy's to Nichols; he was a harmless, honest and inoffensive man; he raised three sons, Thomas, James and Ely. Thomas married and moved West, many years ago; James married Miss Sallie Elvington, daughter of old John Elvington; James Scott is dead, but his wife, Sallie, still survives; he raised a large family, sons and daughters, all unknown except the oldest son, Giles Scott, who is now a worthy citizen of that community. Ely Scott also married Miss Appie Elvington, daughter of old man John Elvington; by her he had one daughter; his wife died, and he married another one of the ten daughters of John Goodyear—an excellent woman she was; I think she is dead; she left two daughters; Ely Scott is also dead. Old Pharaoh Scott had one daughter, named Patience; she married Jerry Campbell, near Mullins; Jerry and wife are both dead; they left two sons, K. M. Campbell and Rev. Ely Campbell, citizens of Reaves Township, and much respected. Pharaoh Scott had a brother up about the High Hill, whose name is forgotten; he had sons, William and Ervin, and perhaps others, and there are members of that family now in that neighborhood, two of whom, John L. and William, are known. Ervin Scott married a daughter of old Jessee Elvington; he was an energetic, persevering man; he died in middle life, and left a family. I know nothing of them—nor is anything known of William Scott's family.

OWENS.—The writer knows but little of the Owens family, in Hillsboro. Reddin Owens, who died two years ago, at the advanced age of ninety-four, was a son of old Shadrack Owens, of the Fork community; he had another son, named Lot Owens; he was in Hillsboro for the last sixty years or more, and raised a considerable family; he was an honest, well meaning man; of his family nothing is known, except a grand-son, James Owens, who resides near where his grand-father died.

GADDY.—Another family in Hillsboro, is the Gaddy family. Old man Ithamer Gaddy was the first known; his wife, Charity, was a Miss Pitman, sister of old man Hardy Pitman, who seventy-five years ago lived near by, and was a prominent citizen; the name Pitman is not found in the county. Old man Ithamer Gaddy was a most excellent man, quiet and inoffensive, a Christian gentleman; he raised a large family, five sons and two daughters; the sons were William, James, Hardy, Allen and Silas; the daughters were Elizabeth and Mary (Polly, as she was called). William Gaddy married Miss Sallie Jones, on Catfish, daughter of old man John Jones; raised a large family of sons and daughters, to wit: John I., Levi, Israel, Joseph, Samuel T. and Charles B.; the daughters were Elizabeth, Ann, Mary and Sarah. John I. Gaddy married Miss Mary Ford; he and his wife both died in a few years, perhaps childless. Levi Gaddy was a very steady, level-headed young man, and bid fair to succeed well in life; he went into the war, and was killed or died of disease or wounds, never came back. Israel Gaddy married in North Carolina and settled there; know nothing of his family, if he had any; Joseph died unmarried; Samuel T. Gaddy, one of our good citizens, married a daughter of the late Harman Floyd, of Nichols, S. C., the fruits of the marriage are one son, Walker, and two daughters—one the wife of W. B. Atkinson, the other the wife of Franklin Rogers; the son, Walker, married a lady in North Carolina. Charles B. Gaddy, the youngest son of William Gaddy, married one of Colonel John Roberts' daughters; three sons and one daughter are the results of the marriage. Charles B. Gaddy died suddenly, a few weeks ago, on the old homestead of his father. Of the daughters of William Gaddy, Elizabeth Ann, the eldest, married Elias Grantham, who was killed near Campbell's Bridge, in the discharge of his duty during the war, it was said, by Nicholas Gaddy, a first cousin of his wife. They raised a family of several children, sons and daughters, who are now living on, and near, the place of their birth; the mother died a year or two ago. William

Gaddy's second daughter, Mary, married a Mr. Inman, of North Carolina; I know nothing further of her. Sarah, the youngest daughter, married D. C. McKinly, who is dead; she has two sons, William and John McKinly, living, and one daughter married, another dead. William Gaddy and wife died in a few days of each other, of typhoid fever, in August, 1850; William Gaddy was an industrious, energetic and trustworthy citizen. James Gaddy married Elizabeth Jones, another daughter of old man John Jones; he settled just across the State line, in Robeson County; raised a large family; I know nothing further of them. Hardy Gaddy married Miss Winnie Humphrey, of Robeson, a very smart, business woman; they are both dead; they raised a family, four sons and three daughters; the sons were Nicholas W., J. Maston, Richard M. and Duncan; the daughters were Anna Jane, Charity and Lizzie. Richard M. went to Virginia some years ago, and is now a citizen of that State; Nicholas M. removed several years ago to North Carolina, and is now a resident citizen of that State; J. Maston died a few years ago, at Marion Court House, and left one son, William, and two daughters—one the wife of Joseph A. Baker, the other the wife of Thomas Monroe, of Marion; I do not know what has become of the son, William. J. Maston Gaddy married twice; first, a Miss Fladger, the mother of his children; the second wife was a Widow Gregg, daughter of General Elly Godbold; she is also dead. Duncan Gaddy, youngest son of Hardy Gaddy, married a Miss Miller, and lives near Gaddy's Mills; I know nothing of his family. Of the daughters of Hardy Gaddy, Anna Jane married a Mr. Inman, of Robeson; Lizzie married A. B. Carmichael, son of old Sheriff Carmichael, and lives on the homestead of her grand-father, Ithamer Gaddy, and has a family; I know nothing of the family. Charity married our good fellow-citizen, R. L. Lane, who resides near Dillon, S. C.; he has several sons and one daughter. Hardy Gaddy was an excellent and very safe man, prudent and successful in his vocation. Allen Gaddy married a Miss Stackhouse, an aunt of Colonel E. T. Stackhouse, and raised a considerable family; he and wife have both been dead for years; I know not much of the family; had a son, Herod Gaddy; I do not know what has become of him—think he is in Marlborough; another son, John W., who is a good citizen and lives now at Bingham; another son, named Tristran, I don't know what has become of him. The widow of the late David Ellen was a daughter of Allen Gaddy; she married twice; first, a Manship, of Marlborough, and after his death she married the late David Ellen, an old man when she married him; he died in 1876; she lives with her son, John H. Ellen, a very energetic and prosperous farmer, in the Dothan neighborhood; she had two daughters by the Manship marriage—one is the wife of Peter P. McCormac, the other the wife of Woodberry Norton. Silas Gaddy, the youngest son of old Ithamer Gaddy, married a Miss Caldwell, in North Carolina, and first settled near his father; after the birth of several children, he emigrated Westward. Of the daughters of Ithamer Gaddy, the oldest married Joseph B. Hays, as hereinbefore stated; the second daughter, Mary (or Polly), married Lysias Stackhouse, son of Herod Stackhouse; they raised one son, John W. Stackhouse, and some daughters, perhaps only two. The son, J. W. Stackhouse, has been dead about thirty years; left a family, all grown; one of the daughters married Thomas Ammons, a descendant of Joshua Ammons, of Revolutionary fame; I do not remember who the other daughter married; the third and last daughter married Owen Grantham, of Robeson County, N. C.; some of her descendants are now living in Marion; the wife of W. C. Foxworth is a grand-daughter of Owen Grantham and wife, Elizabeth Grantham, *nee* Gaddy. The writer has seen six or seven generations of that Grantham family.

LUPOS AND ARNETTS.—There is, and was, a family of Lupos and Arnetts in Hillsboro, but do not know enough of them to trace their genealogy. Some of them went to school to the writer, sixty-six years ago—1834 and 1835. They were an honest and hard-working people, primitive in their modes of living and habits, as most people were in that day and time. What is said about the Lupos and Arnetts may be said about the Horn family.

ROGERS.—The Rogers family, in Hillsboro, is a very extensive family, taken in connection with the Rogers in the Fork and Mullins region, whence they all sprang; there is, perhaps, not a more extensive family in the county. Dew Rogers. a way back in the twenties, went from the Fork over into what is now called Hillsboro, having married over there, a Miss Mary Barfield; he bought land and went to work; he was a very energetic, persevering and frugal man; made money, bought other lands, negroes, &c., and raised children; the children reached the number of sixteen or nineteen, mostly sons; the names of some of them, as remembered, was Zany, Jesse, Henry, Ebenezer, Dew, Barfield and others, and lastly, our esteemed and worthy fellow-citizen, Captain Robert H. Rogers—the youngest son; some of them are yet living, and it may be supposed they are keeping up the name and perpetuating it to the second, third and fourth generations. Captain Henry Rogers (familiarly called "Captain Tarleton"), a brother of old Dew, married a Miss Thompson, and came over from the Fork about the same time Dew Rogers came, and settled on the Lewis Thompson homestead, his wife's father, and lived and died there some years ago; he also raised a large family of sons and daughters, and about them the writer knows but little. R. R. Hays, of Dillon, is a grand-son of "Captain Tarleton." These two old Rogers are the trunks of the family, so far as Hillsboro is concerned. They had two brothers left in the Fork, Ebenezer and Alfred; the latter was a Baptist preacher; I do not think he ever married. Ebenezer Rogers died in the Fork a few years ago, leaving a numerous progeny. The Rogers family in Hillsboro, in the Fork and in the Mullins region are all related to each other in greater or less degree—had a common ancestor, whose name is unto the writer unknown. The numerous branches, each becoming, as it were a new trunk, are so varied that it is impossible, with the limited information at hand, to take each branch up *seriatim* and trace them, with their numerous descendants, down to the present time; want of time and space, together with the want of information, forbid the undertaking. As a family they are peaceable, harmless, inoffensive and law-abiding; in so large a family, of course, there are, and must be, some exception, but they do not affect the general rule. As a family, they are honest in their sentiments and convictions; in their modes of life they are somewhat primitive and unostentatious; patriotic to the core, as evidenced by the numbers they and their connections furnished to the Southern army in the war. Their names do not often appear upon the dockets of the Courts, civil or criminal, and this said, is saying much for so large a family. There are two other families of Rogers in the county—one in the Dothan neighborhood and one in Britton's Neck; neither of which, or both together, are not so large and numerous as the family just mentioned. Of the Britton's Neck family, the writer knows but little. There was, years ago, an old gentleman in the Britton's Neck section by the name of Silas Rogers; of his family the writer knows nothing; also, Major James S. Rogers (militia Major), lived and died a few years ago in that section—a man rather prominent in his day, a good citizen and quite reputable, and was for years a fair representative of his family and of his section; he left some family, but of them the writer knows nothing; nor does he know whether he was lineally or collaterally related to old man Silas Rogers, or not, and, therefore, can say nothing more. Of the Dothan family, one Lot Rogers, from Virginia, came to South Carolina about the close of the Revolutionary War; he married a sister of old Buck Swamp John Bethea, named Nannie, whether before his arrival in South Carolina or after, is not now known; he settled and lived and died just above Dothan Church, on the road leading from Dothan to Little Rock, formerly called Harlleesville; he raised a large family—think, mostly sons; of these, only Timothy and William were known to the writer; others of them went West; one daughter only known to the writer; she became the wife of Nathan Evans, and the mother of the late General William and Nathan Evans, as hereinbefore mentioned. Timothy Rogers, a most excellent man and worthy citizen, married Sarah Bethea, a daughter of Sweat Swamp John Bethea, and settled where Dr. J. F. Bethea now lives; they raised a large family of sons and daughters; of the sons, John B. Rogers emigrated to the West many years ago—not, however, until after he married a Miss McRee, and had some family. Trestram B. Rogers married a Miss Parnell; had some family when he removed West, and Lot B. Rogers married a Miss Thwing, had some family and removed to Texas, I think. These three all dead; I know nothing of their posterity. Two other sons, Jesse and Cade B. Rogers. Jesse married, first, Miss Harriet Bethea, daughter of the late Parker Bethea, by whom he had three children, two sons and one daughter. Two sons, David S. Rogers, of "Free State," who married a Miss Pipkin, of Marlborough, and who has had twenty children born to him by the same wife, seven of them are, however, dead; D. S. Rogers is quite a good citizen and prosperous man. Albert S. Rogers, the other son, married a daughter of Captain Stephen F. Berry, has a considerable family, sons and daughters, how many is unknown. Albert Rogers is also doing well. Their sister, Alice Rogers, married Holden Bethea; they live in the "Free State," and are said to be doing well; have a family of children. Jesse Rogers married, a second time, the Widow Anna Rogers, below Marion; his wife was the widow of his cousin, Evan Rogers, who will be mentioned hereinafterwards; he (Jesse) died, leaving no issue by his second marriage. Cade B. Rogers, the youngest son of old man Timothy Rogers, still survives, and, as far as is known, the only survivor of that large family; he married, first, a Miss George (Nancy); by her he had two daughters and one son; one of the daughters married a Mr. Butler, on north side of Little Pee Dee; can say nothing of their family, if they had any; the other daughter married Herod Gaddy, and lives in Marlborough. The son, Henry G. Rogers, married a Miss Pipkin, settled in Marlborough, and is dead; I can say nothing of his family. Cade B. Rogers' first wife died, and he married a second time, a Widow Morris, of Florence County; no children by this latter marriage. Of the many daughters of old man Timothy Rogers, the oldest married Daniel McInnis; both dead and childless; the second, Mary, married the late Rev. Samuel J. Bethea, and is dead; the next, Miranza, married Thomas C. Bethea; the next, Harriet, married Arch'd K. McLellan; the next, Elizabeth, married Daniel A. Platt; the next (name forgotten) married Levi Gasque; and the next (name forgotten) married William E. Brown, of Marlborough; all dead, and left families except Mrs. McInnis. Mrs. T. C. Bethea, Mrs.

Levi Gasque and Mrs. William E. Brown went West many years ago; those remaining here raised large families, and they and their descendants now form a good portion of our population. Old Lot Rogers' youngest son, William, and perhaps his youngest child, born in 1799, inherited the old homestead of his father, and is now owned by his youngest son, our good fellow-citizen, Lot B. Rogers; he married the youngest daughter (Mary) of old Henry Berry, as hereinbefore stated; he and wife lived and died on his father's homestead at an old age—not many years ago; the fruits of the marriage were sons, Charles, Evan, Frank, Philip B. and Lot B., and daughters, Elizabeth Ann, Mary Ann, Nancy and Margaret. Of the sons, Charles emigrated West, and, doubtless, is dead; nothing, however, is known of him by the writer; Evan grew up and married Miss Anna Legette, daughter of Colonel Levi Legette, below Marion, and where Evan Rogers settled. He was killed on Sunday, 1st of October, 1855, by a man by the name of Harrelson, who was tried the next week after at Court in Marion, and very ably defended by the late Chancellor Inglis and Julius A. Dargan, two very eminent and able lawyers, and was convicted and sentenced to be hanged on a certain day fixed; before the day appointed for his execution he escaped from jail; a large reward, two hundred dollars or more, was offered for his recapture and delivery at the jail in Marion by General Elly Godbold, then Sheriff; great efforts were made to find and recapture him, but all in vain; about eighteen months thereafter he was recaptured in Columbus County, N. C., brought back and lodged in the jail in Marion, and at the succeeding Court, in March, 1857, he was re-sentenced or a new day assigned for his execution, and he was accordingly hanged by the then Sheriff, N. C. McDuffie, on the 5th day of June, 1857. The third son, Frank, grew up to manhood and went to Louisiana, and died there many years ago. Philip B., the fourth son, now one of our prosperous fellow-citizens, married a Miss Gaddy, daughter of Allen Gaddy, and raised a considerable family, sons and daughters, who are among us now as citizens and wives of our citizens, and are known. Philip B. Rogers' wife died some two or three years ago; he is now a widower—I do not know how long he will remain such.* Lot B. Rogers, the youngest son of William Rogers, is now a leading and successful farmer among us; he married Miss Adaline Townsend, daughter of the late Jacob Townsend, and sister of D. A. Townsend, of Union, one of the Circuit Judges of the State; by that marriage a large family resulted, of sons and daughters, and among them are four sets of twins—all the latter are living except one—some grown and some married, and some of them yet minors. Having succeeded well in life, Lot B. Rogers has so far educated his children well, and they are promising; he himself has represented his county in the State Legislature, besides holding other public positions in the county by the suffrages of his fellow-citizens, and in every one of them has discharged his duty faithfully and to the satisfaction of his friends. William Rogers died in 1874, at the age of seventy-five years; his wife survived him a few years and she died.

PERRITT.—Another numerous family of the county is the Perritt family. Of the old Perritts, there were four brothers known to the writer, viz: David, Joseph, Jesse and John. David only has left posterity; he married a Miss Smith, a sister of old Mr. Hugh Smith, and he in turn married a sister of David Perritt (this latter is according to information, may be wrong). The old man Perritt raised a family, mostly sons, David B., Needham, William, Bennett, Jesse, John E. and Asa, and one daughter, if no more. David B. Perritt married Miss Martha Edwards, daughter of the late Rev. David Edwards, and by her had several children, sons and daughters; and they in turn have perpetuated the name and connections to a second and, perhaps, third generation, and of whom the writer knows nothing. Needham Perritt married a Miss Moody, sister of the late Joshua W. Moody, a man highly esteemed for his many good qualities and noble traits of character. Needham Perritt is dead; he left a considerable family, sons and daughters, and they (the children) have become fathers and mothers, and extending down to another generation or more. William Perritt married a Miss Carmichael, daughter of the late Dugald C. Carmichael, of Buck Swamp

---

*Philip B. Rogers has since married to a lady in North Carolina.

and Maiden Down; William Perritt is dead, and left a son, Morgan, and three daughters, who, it is supposed, are among the present inhabitants of the country, unknown to the writer. Bennett Perritt married a Miss Powers, sister of our esteemed fellow-citizen, Mitchell Powers; he raised a family, about whom the writer knows but little; one daughter married James Sanderson, who has been dead for years; his widow still lives, and has raised her family respectably, and is said to be doing well; she has two sons grown; one daughter married Hugh Price, a prosperous citizen in that neighborhood; he has a family, about whom the writer knows nothing. Another daughter married Frank Huggins; he and she have both left the country, and their whereabouts unknown. If Bennett Perritt had any sons, it is unknown to the writer. Jesse Perritt, another son of old David, the writer has not been able to get anything concerning him; whom he married and whether he had any family or not, is unascertainable; it is said that he is dead. Another son of old David Perritt is our very worthy fellow-citizen, John E. Perritt; he married, first, a Miss Campbell, a daughter of the late Wm. S. Campbell, and raised a large and respectable family, mostly daughters, and two sons, A. J. A. Perritt and Arvington Perritt. A. J. A. Perritt moved to Darlington County some years ago, and since he has been there has held several positions of honor and trust, to wit: County Superintendent of Education, Representative in the State Legislature and a member of the State Constitutional Convention, all of which positions he has filled with credit to himself and satistory to his constituents; he married a daughter of the late Rev. John W. Murray, of the South Carolina Conference of the Methodist Church, South. Arvington Perritt left the county a single man and went to Texas; nothing further is known of him. Of John E. Perritt's daughters, one married our excellent fellow-citizen, Jerry Lambert; another married W. C. Bracy, of Dillon; another married a Mr. Keith; another married a Mr. Smith, below Marion, think a son of Reddin W. Smith. I think there is another one or two daughters, whether married or not, is not known. Asa Perritt, the youngest son of old David, was a Lieutenant in Captain S. A. Durham's company in the late war; he married a daughter of the late

Rev. David Edwards, and removed West not long after the war; nothing further is known of him. Of the three brothers of old David Perritt, Joseph never married; he has been dead many years. Jesse married Mary Dew, daughter of old Christopher Dew; they had no children; she died, and he married a second wife, the widow of Elias Townsend; she had been the widow of Alfred Kirven, and was originally Elizabeth Tart, daughter of old Enos Tart, a notable man in his day, and of whom something may be said hereinafter; by her he had no child or children; both have been dead for some years. John Perritt, the youngest brother of old David Perritt, died in 1840 or 1841, a young single man, from the bite of a rattlesnake; he was with a surveying party about the Marlborough line, and in toward the Great Pee Dee River, when the snake bit him; there was no house near them and no doctor near; he was carried two miles to the nearest house and a doctor was finally procured, but too late; he died that same night; a young man of fine character and good habits, and was spoken well of by all who knew him. Thus it seems that the very large family of Perritts and their many connections of the present day, and now in the county, sprang from old David Perritt, on or near the Ten Mile Bay; he was an energetic and persevering man, exceedingly frugal and thoughtful; would not be in debt, paid as he went, and made a good property by saving it; was a good and law-abiding citizen; he lost his wife in his old age; married some one, name not remembered, and left her a widow; I think she drew a pension after his death for his services in the War of 1812—I think he drew it in his lifetime. Few men anywhere have a larger connection than he has from himself. They and the Perritt connections are numerous, and are an honest, well-meaning people; ambitious only to live honestly and to let others live, and are primitive in their modes of life.

EDWARDS.—The Edwards family, on Buck Swamp, is another family of some note. Tradition informs us that Richard Edwards came to South Carolina from Virginia soon after the Revolutionary War; that he was originally from England, or rather his ancestors; that during the Revolution he was shot in the head and his skull was fractured; that the fracture was trepanned with gold, and from that fact was generally called "Gold-headed Richard or Dick Edwards." We are not informed who his wife was; he raised a family of sons and perhaps daughters, the daughters are unknown; his sons were Richard, David, Samuel and Henry—who became stocks for families, more or less numerous, now in the county; they settled on Buck Swamp. Their father, "Gold-headed Dick," lived to a great age, and was a man of some means. Richard, the oldest son, a local preacher of the Methodist Church, had only two children—a son, the late Captain L. M. Edwards, and another, whether a son or daughter, is unknown. Captain L. M. Edwards was noted in his day; he died a few months ago, and left a large family, sons and daughters; he was married twice; his first wife was a Miss Martin, sister of the late A. Martin and, I think, a cousin of Captain Edwards; by her he had sons and daughters; sons, Richard, Albert, Enos and Hamilton, all of whom are married, and have families, are good citizens and doing fairly well. By Captain Edwards' second wife, the Widow Fort, originally a Miss Lewis, he had sons—P. H. Edwards, Marion, Olin and Bonnie; of these, Marion is dead; P. H. Edwards married a daughter of Dr. C. T. Ford; Olin married a daughter of T. B. Hays; Bonnie is yet single. Captain Edwards had some daughters by each wife; one married Samuel Roberts; one married a Nicholson; and perhaps other daughters, unknown. Of his first sons, Richard married a Miss Martin, his first cousin; Albert Edwards married a Miss Roberts; Enos Edwards married Miss Hays, and Hamilton Edwards married Miss Ida Smith. These are all now citizens of the county, and performing their duties as such. Rev. David Edwards, second son of "Gold-headed Dick," a capital man, married into the extensive family of the Rogers; his wife was a sister of "Captain Tarleton" and of Dew Rogers, both of them before spoken of herein; by his marriage he had and raised fourteen children, six sons and eight daughters; the sons were Carey, Andrew, David, Richard, Robert and William; the daughters were Harriet, Elizabeth, Sallie, Martha, Nancy, Alice, Emaline and Mary. Of the sons, Andrew, Richard and Robert are dead; of the daughters, Sallie,

Martha, Alice and Emaline are dead; the dead ones, however, all married and left families. I do not know who Andrew married; he was a Baptist preacher; he left the county; I know nothing of his family. Richard married Miss Caroline Martin, and left two sons, B. F. Edwards and Austin Edwards. Robert married Sarah Lewis, and left two sons, George and Stanly; they went to Texts some years ago; George died in Texarkana, and was Mayor of that city at the time of his death, and was otherwise a prosperous man; he being a single man, his property was inherited by his only brother, Stanly Edwards, who was also in Texas, is yet there, and is said to be wealthy and a good citizen of the "Lone Star" State. Of the dead daughters, Sallie, the wife of Stephen H. Martin, left two sons and a daughter; the sons were Mack Martin and David Martin. The daughter married Perry J. Williams, and is dead. Martha Edwards married David B. Perritt, and is dead, leaving a considerable family. Alice married Solomon Bryant, and is dead—died in the Asylum. Emaline married Hugh Bryant, and is dead; she also died in the Asylum in Columbia. Alice and Emaline both left families, who are now among us. Of the sons of David Edwards, only three survive, to wit: Cary, David W. Edwards, of Mullins, and William. D. W. Edwards married a Miss Carmichael, daughter of old Dugal Carmichael, on Buck Swamp, and has three children; two sons, E. C. Edwards, our very excellent fellow-citizen, and County Superintendent of Education, and Melvin Edwards, also a good citizen; and a daughter, Catharine, who is now the wife of Robert Rogers, a prosperous farmer. D. W. Edwards married a second time; her name is unknown. William Edwards married Miss Nancy Owens, of the Fork. William Edwards, like two of his sisters above mentioned, is afflicted with lunacy, and has been in the Asylum two or three times, but is now at home; he has a family. The oldest daughter, Harriet, married the late Richard Moody; she still survives, with a numerous family. Carey Edwards, the oldest son, married Miss Martha Mace, 5th March, 1845—the writer was at the wedding; four children are the fruits of said marriage, two sons, John and James, and two daughters, Melvina and Jane—the latter is dead, died in the Asylum. Carey Edwards still survives, an old man, and lives with his son, John; his wife has been dead many years. James married a Miss Davis, in Wahee; he has a family of four children. Melvina is an old maid, enjoying the sweets of single blessedness. John married his cousin, a daughter of Solomon Bryant, and lives on the homestead of his mother. Elizabeth married John Thompson, of Britton's Neck. Thompson is dead; of his family little is known. Nancy married Asa Pruitt, and removed West many years ago. Mary married, first, Ebb. Smith; he went into the war and was killed or died of disease—has never returned; his widow married George Lane, and between the two husbands raised a considerable family, who are now among our citizens; the writer knows but little of them. Samuel Edwards, the third son of "Gold-headed Dick," married a Miss Martin, sister of Matthew, Jr., and the late Aaron Martin; he lived and died in the Fork, and raised a family, how many the writer does not know; he was a prosperous and excellent man. He had a son, Renselaer, who died some years ago, and left a family—the number is not known, nor do I know who the mother was. He has another son, David S. Edwards, now a prominent and prosperous farmer in the Fork; he has a large family of sons and daughters; I think his wife was a Miss Carmichael. D. S. Edwards is an enterprising and public-spirited man; he is doing a good part by his children in the way of education; one of his sons, G. Emory Edwards, graduated in Wofford College recently with distinction; since his graduation he has been teaching at Dothan, and gives full satisfaction to his patrons. D. S. Edwards has two daughters, promising girls and graduates of the Winthrop Female College; he is doing abundantly better for his children than those of the former generations. It is greatly to be wished that we had many more like him with regard to education. Another son of Samuel Edwards was Solomon, who died many years ago; he married a daughter of Joseph B. Hays and left one daughter, who is now the wife of Kirkland Fort. Samuel Edwards had a daughter, Civil, who married Daniel W. Carmichael, and they have raised a numerous family of sons and daughters, who will be further noticed when we come to speak of the Carmichaels. Samuel Edwards, I think, had another daughter, who married an Owens, in the Fork; nothing is known of them. Another son of "Gold-headed Dick," named Henry, the youngest, married a Miss Gerald, and had one son, Levi, who lives in the Gapway neighborhood. Henry Edwards' habits were not good; he drank excessively, never did much in life, and, no doubt, was a source of much trouble to his relations. It seems to the writer that there was another son of "Gold-headed Dick," perhaps the oldest one, by the name of Solomon; nothing, however, is known of him or of his family, if he had any—I am not certain there was such an one. The Edwards family and its connections are numerous; they are quite respectable, and stand fair among their fellow-citizens; seldom in the Courts. Since writing the foregoing account of the Edwards family, the writer has learned that Captain L. M. Edwards had a brother, named Enos, who married and died, leaving a son, Frank Edwards, who lives in the Pleasant Hill neighborhood, and is one of our good citizens. It may be further added, that B. F. Edwards, in the Gaddy neighborhood, and Austin Edwards, in the Latta community, great-grand-sons of "Gold-headed Dick" Edwards, are prominent and thriving men of our county.

NICHOLS.—The Nichols family, so far as the county is concerned, sprang from old Averett Nichols, of Columbus County, N. C. His youngest son, Averett, born 8th March, 1803, settled in Marion County in 1830; he married a Miss Burney, of Columbus County, N. C.; he located near what is now called Nichols, in the woods, apparently a poor place, lived there during his long life, and died there at the age of near ninety-three, on the 7th January, 1896; he raised a family of ten children, eight daughters and two sons; the sons, McKendree (called Kendree) and Averitt Burney. Kendree was a very promising young man, unmarried; went into the Southern army as a Lieutenant, and was killed, as I think, in second Manassas, 30th August, 1862. A. B. Nichols, a prominent and progressive citizen, merchant and farmer at Nichols, S. C., married a Miss Sophronia Daniel, and has a family of children, how many is unknown—he is doing his full duty in that respect, as well as in every other; he is a first class man, and safe in every way. Averitt Nichols' oldest daughter, Mary, married Isham H. Watson, and is now a widow, and childless; his daughter, Lucy, married a Mr. Lawson; they emigrated to Texas many years ago, and, I suppose, are contributing their share to the population and wealth of that great State. Sarah (or Sallie) married our modest but successful fellow-citizen, J. Thomas Jones; she has been dead many years, but left several sons and daughters, all of whom are now among us; I do not know the names of all the sons; Eli is one, Beverly another, Kendree, Evander and Robert Boyd, maybe another one or two. There are four daughters, Lucy Ellen, who married J. B. Williams; Lola, who married William E. Hewit; Catharine, married David N. Bethea; and Miss Fannie is yet single. Of this family, it may be said, they are all first class citizens, doing well and law-abiding. Anne Nichols married the late T. B. Braddy, who was killed by D. W. McLaurin, in 1881; he left a son, Oscar Braddy, by his Nichols wife; he and his mother reside in Hillsboro Township, and, I suppose, are doing fairly well. Fannie Nichols married our respected fellow-citizen, Jacob W. Smith, and has several children; I do not know how many; he lives in Latta. I know his son, Alonzo Smith, who is a progressive and first class young business man, and promises to become one of the leading men of the county. Miss Rebecca Nichols, youngest daughter of Averitt Nichols, never married; she was, after the death of her mother, the controling spirit and manager of the female department of the household until a few years ago, she unexpectedly and suddenly died; she was a charming young woman, just the sort to have made a good housewife. There were two other daughters, who died about maturity and unmarried. Averitt Nichols was a very exemplary man; he had the faculty in large degree of attending to his own business and of letting other people's business severely alone; the result was that he amassed a large property, raised a large and respectable family; would not go in debt—paid as he went; he was never in a hurry or in a flurry about anything; had in the Bank of New Hanover, Wilmington, N. C., several thousand dollars when it failed some seven or eight years ago, and which was mostly lost. In his later days the old gentleman partially lost his mind, and his affairs, financial and otherwise, were managed by his son, A. B. Nichols. The old man was never informed of the loss of his money by the failure of the bank; he died not knowing anything about it.

HUTCHINSON.—There is a family near Nichols, by the name of Hutchinson. John Hutchinson is a very worthy citizen. I do not know anything of his ancestry, or where he came from; he has children grown and married; a daughter married a Barfield, who lives in the neighborhood, and is doing well.

BARFIELD.—The Barfield family, in part, live in Hillsboro. They are descendants of Barrett Barfield, who in the thirties resided in Hillsboro, just below Gaddy's Mill, and on the plantation now owned by his grand-son, Captain R. H. Rogers; he had by the same wife, and raised them to be grown, twenty-two children, sons and daughters; he, with most of his family, removed West. Writ Barfield, a son, and an excellent citizen, remained, and several of his daughters, who had married—one to Dew Rogers, one to Ebenezer Rogers in the Fork, one to Love Goodyear—they also remained and all raised large families. Writ Barfield was a very worthy citizen, raised a considerable family, several sons; they and their posterity now are among our people, not personally known to the writer; and he supposes that old Barrett Barfield, their ancestor, was a son, or brother, or nephew of the celebrated Tory, Captain Barfield, of Revolutionary fame; which appellation, Tory, is now no longer a derisive name—at least, so far as the Barfield family is concerned; some of the best soldiers we had in our late Confederate War were of that family, of that name and its connections of Barfield blood. The writer may have something to say further on in this book in regard to the word Tory, as an appellation of derision or contempt. Captain Barfield as a leader, though on the losing side in the Revolution, is spoken of as a brave man, fighting for what he believed to be right. A distinctive characteristic of the Barfield family, and especially of the females, was their beauty—perfect in form and features, of medium size and great activity. The men were as agile as a deer. It was said of one of the sons of old Barrett, named Thompson, that he could cut a double summersault—that he could walk along and cut a dozen without stopping. In a tustle or a fight, they were hard to handle, even by larger men and of greater strength. Miss Appey Barfield, the youngest daughter of old man Barrett, was as beautiful a woman as ever the writer looked at, weighed about one hundred and twenty-five or thirty, was perfect in form and as pretty as the fabled Venus. The last time the writer saw her was in February, 1835, not long before her father left this country. Writ Barfield, the father of the Barfields, now in Hillsboro, lived to be more than eighty years of age.

GOODYEAR.—The Goodyear family, so far as Marion County is concerned, sprang from William Goodyear, who died in 1800. His wife, I think, was a Ford or a Grainger; his sons or grandsons were the late John Goodyear and Love Goodyear, both dead. John Goodyear had only one son, who was killed or died in the war; he raised ten daughters, of whom something has already been said herein. Love Goodyear died in 1851, and left a family of sons and perhaps daughters; the sons, as remembered and known, were William, Elias and Harman. William Goodyear, now an old man and very worthy citizen, lives near Nichols, and has raised a family who are now among our people and known. I do not know what became of Elias, whether dead or alive; Harman, I think, is dead. There is one, Madison Goodyear, if alive, whose son he is, or was, is not now remembered. Some six or eight years ago, the writer received a letter from a lady in the State of Washington or one of the Dakotas, the wife of a Lieutenant in the regular army of the United States, stationed out there in the far West, who signed her name "Grace Goodyear ————" (the last name not remembered, and the correspondence is mislaid). This lady said she belonged to the family of Goodyears in this county, or was collaterally related to them; that she had been referred to me as an antiquarian and genealogist; she said she was trying to trace her family, the Goodyear family, back to a Goodyear (John, I believe), who was Lieutenant-Governor of Connecticut, then a province of Great Britain, about 1690. The writer made what investigation he could, and wrote the result to her, which she received and acknowledged its receipt in very complimentary and appreciative terms. I have heard nothing from her since. The Goodyear family are, doubtless, of English extraction, and were among the early settlers of the country. There is now in the city of New York a very wealthy family of that name, and a strong company called "The Goodyear Rubber Company," and the Goodyears of this county are, doubtless, of the same family.

TART.—The Tart family was formerly a very noted family—at least, in the person of old Enos Tart. There were three brothers of them as known to the writer, Enos, John and Nathan. Of these, Enos was the most prominent; he lived on and owned the plantation and mill latterly known as E. J. Moody's. Who the father of these three brothers were, is not known to the writer. When that mill was built, and by whom, is not known. In Gregg's History it is spoken of as "Tart's Mill, about six miles above Marion Court House." It is reasonable to presume it was among the first mills in the county, except, perhaps, "Hulins," on Catfish, afterwards Bass' Mill. (Gregg, p. 359.) The mill was, before the Revolution, the property of John Smith, whose daughter, tradition informs us, was the mother of Enos Tart and brothers. This John Smith was the progenitor of most of the Smiths (numerous) now and since that time in the county. Enos Tart was a most remarkable man, a giant in strength and size, weighing about three hundred pounds and not over corpulent. It is related of him that he could interfere between two men fighting, and take one combatant with one hand in the collar and with the other hand the other combatant, and hold them apart; they could not break his hold, and he would hold them apart, until each promised him that they would desist, and each go his way and quit the fight. He was a man of such remarkable equanimity of temper, that a man might curse and abuse him for everything he could think of, and call him all sorts of contemptuous names, and he would not resent it, but laugh at his would-be adversary. It is related of him that on one occasion old man Cade Bethea so cursed and abused him at Marion Court House, calling him by every contemptuous name in the catalogue, and daring Tart to resent it, which Tart did not do, and as usual laughed at old Cade. On that night, as Tart was going home, he came up with old man Cade by the side of the road, down dead drunk. Tart alighted, went to him and took him home with him, and stripped him and put him to bed, old man Cade being unconscious all the while. Next morning, the sleeping Cade, so furious the day before, awoke and found out where he was; he got up and manfully acknowledged his error; that he was whipped by Tart's kindness, and was ever afterwards a close and constant friend of Tart's. Enos Tart, according to tradition, was never known to strike any man, and the reason given for it was, that he was afraid to strike a man for fear he might kill him; Tart knew his physical power. He was a kind-hearted and generous man, and befriended all as far as he could; he was a very popular man, and could not be beaten before the people. He was more than once a Representative of his district in the State Legislature; was Sheriff of the county, and Clerk of the Court when he died, in 1828. Enos Tart married a Miss Susanna Johnson, of the county; the results of the marriage were four or five daughters and three sons. One of his daughters married Jack Finklea; one married Willis Finklea; one, Elizabeth, married, first, Alfred Kirvin, and had two children for him, two daughters, when they separated, and years afterwards, after Kirvin died, she married Elias Townsend; some years afterward, Townsend died, and she married Jessee Perritt; by neither of the last marriages had she any offspring; they lived together for some years, and they both died in a week of each other. Of her Kirvin children, the oldest, Lucinda, died just as she was budding into womanhood. The other daughter, whose name is not remembered, married James Fore, and had four children, three daughters and a son; of these, two of the daughters married Berrys—Stephen Berry and William Berry; the other daughter married Powers, a son of Mitchel Powers. The son, Thomas E. Fore, is now one of our good citizens, and has a family. Susan Tart, the fourth daughter, married a Mr. Brown, of Brownsville, in Marlborough; after having two children, a son and a daughter, the father and mother both died; the children grew up and emigrated West. Jane Tart, the youngest daughter of old Enos Tart, married another Brown, of the same family; he soon after died, leaving no offspring; the widow again married Humphrey Lester; the results of this marriage were two children—a daughter, Mary, now the wife of M. Stackhouse, and a son, Robert H. Lester, now among us, with an increasing family; he married a Miss Proctor, of Little Rock. Soon after the birth of these two children, Humphrey Lester died, and Jane became a widow the second time; she again married our esteemed fellow-citizen, E. J. Moody; the fruits of this latter marriage were two sons, Thomas E. and Neill C. Moody, and two daughters. Thomas E. married a Miss Little, daughter of the Rev. L. M. Little; he soon died childless. Neill C. Moody never married, died three or four years ago. The daughters, Virginia and Maggie, both married. Virginia married Douglas McIntyre, of Marion—a noble woman she was; she died some years ago, leaving three or four children, the oldest of whom, Janie, married Robert Proctor; they have left the State. McIntyre married again, a Miss Fore, and has his first children with him now, except Janie. Maggie Moody married Dr. D. I. Watson; they removed to Southport, N. C., have several children, and are said to be doing well. It may be truthfully said of Mrs. Jane Moody, who died some years ago, that she was the excellent of the earth; high-toned, and above all had a good and kind heart, beloved by all who knew her; and if any of her children or grand-children should turn out badly, it will not be the fault or failings of the mother; she left an influence that will tell upon her offspring sooner or later. Old Enos Tart had three sons, Enos, Nathan and Thomas E. Tart. Enos, the oldest, died a young man, in 1844, before his mother; he was a very promising young man, a graduate of the University of Virginia, a Chesterfield in his manners and deportment; he had many of the qualities of his father; had he lived, would, doubtless, have become prominent, and filled a large space in the public eye. Soon after Enos Tart, Jr., died, Thomas E., the youngest brother, accidentally shot himself with a pistol, from which he died in a few minutes. Three or four years after that sad event, Nathan Tart, the middle son, died. The sons of old Enos all died unmarried, so that the name, so far as old

Enos was concerned, was entirely cut off. Enos Tart was not a very old man when he died; he was a man of business, accumulated a large property and left his family in good condition; he was the contractor for and built the old brick court house in Marion, in 1823, which was torn down and removed, in 1864, during the war. That court house stood about the spot where the new building lately erected for the Clerk and Probate Judge's offices now stands. There are many now living who remember the old brick court house; it was constructed on the "Mills" plan of court houses for that day and time. Of the brothers of old Enos, John and Nathan, John Tart, I think, married a Miss Crawford; he raised two sons and some daughters; the sons were James and Enos Tart—the name Enos runs down to the present generation in every family. James Tart's brother, Enos, was called "Dog Enos," for distinction. Why they gave him so unsavory a name is not now known. The writer has seen him, or saw him, about sixty years ago; he was regarded as a bully on the muster fields of that day; I do not know what became of him. James, the older brother, was a very respectable man and good citizen; he married Miss Julia Ann Smith, and raised a large family of sons and daughters, all of whom are now dead, except the youngest son, Enos Murchison Tart, who married in Columbus County, N. C., where he settled and now resides. John W. Tart, the oldest son of James, married a daughter of Rev. Samuel J. Bethea, raised a large family of sons and daughters, who are now among us as citizens of the county; he died on April 14th, 1875, of a cancer on the tongue. A daughter of James Tart, Amelia, married the late John C. Campbell, near Ebenezer Church, where he and she both died a few years ago; they raised a large family of sons, and two daughters, perhaps eight or ten sons. Some of the sons, two or three, are dead, leaving no family, and one of the daughters is also dead, unmarried; the others are among us, and are respectable citizens. James Tart died during the war, on the place near Moody's Mill, now owned by the estate of the late Governor Ellerbe. James Tart had some sisters, two of whom married Birds, Joseph Bird and Hugh Bird, and one married a Malloy—all of whom are dead. Nathan Tart, the youngest brother of old Enos, married Fama

Berry, a daughter of old Henry Berry, as already herein noted; by their marriage a considerable family resulted of sons and daughters. Nathan Tart died in middle life and left his widow, Fama, and children. Fama Tart, as heretofore noted, was one of the most remarkable women that the writer ever saw. Of this family of Tarts, I think I have already written. Nathan and Fama Tart also had a son, named Enos, who was called by way of contradistinction, "Russell Enos." The name is continued down for two or three generations further.

BRYANT.—Another family may be here noticed. The Bryant family is an old family. Jesse Bryant is said to have been the first of that name in the county; he came from England, as it is said; he married a Miss Turbeville, supposed to have been a sister of Rev. William Turbeville, who, according to Bishop Gregg (pp. 70 and 71), came over about 1735, and settled at Sandy Bluff, on the Great Pee Dee, with the colony then and there settled, as their minister. "Several brothers came with him, of whom some descendants are now to be found in Marion." It may be presumed that sisters came too, and that one of them married old Jesse Bryant. Old Jesse had sons, William, Stephen and Jesse. Of these, William married Rebecca Miller; he lived and died some twenty-five or thirty years ago, on the road just above Ebenezer Church, at the age of eighty-nine. Whether William, Stephen or Jesse was the oldest, is not known. Old Billy Bryant raised a large family, four sons and several daughters. Of the sons, John M. Bryant was the oldest; he died some years ago, at the age of eighty-three; he married a Miss Drew, below Marion, and raised a large family—sons, Eli, Solomon, David, Pinckney and Hugh Bryant; and daughters, Mrs. David Johnson, Mrs. Hardy Johnson and Mrs. Addison Lane. Eli Bryant went West. Solomon Bryant married a daughter of Rev. David Edwards, first, and then a Miss McDonald. I do not know who David married; he has a son, named Curtis Bryant. Pinckney Bryant married, had a large family and is dead; I don't know who his wife was. Hugh Bryant married a daughter of the late Rev. David Edwards, and has a family; these are now our fellow-citizens, and are contributing their share towards populating and improving the conditions of the county. John M. Bryant was a solid, number one man, honest, truthful and reliable. Jesse Bryant, son of the first Jesse, went West. Stephen Bryant was the father or grand-father of F. D. Bryant, Esq., of the Marion bar. One of the daughters of the first Jesse was the wife of the late Charles Taylor. One of the sons of old William Bryant, named William, was a Baptist preacher; he went to Horry, and became the head of a family there. Also, did Stephen, the father of F. D. Bryant. Old man William Bryant was a simple-minded gentleman, honest and straight; he acted for many years as a Constable; and I heard it related of him that on one occasion, having a Magistrate's execution to levy on the property of another, the old man went to the cowpen of the execution debtor to levy upon a bull yearling therein; that the old man's idea was, that in order to make the levy, as required by the mandate of the execution, he had to lay the execution upon the back of the yearling. Accordingly, the old man went into the cowpen, armed with the execution, and took after the yearling, and after running him a while caught him by the tail, and he and the old man had it round and round the pen, the yearling bellowing; at last the old man got him hemmed in a jamb of the fence and held him, till he laid the execution on the yearling's back; when the old man said, "I levy upon this yearling in the name of the State of South Carolina." Another incident showing the simplicity of the old gentleman was, that he used to plant and cultivate two and three stalks of corn in a hill. Some one asked him why he did so, saying to him that one stalk in a hill would make more corn than the two or three. The old gentleman replied, that when he cultivated only one stalk in a hill, he never made corn enough to do him; but when he cultivated two and three stalks, he always made plenty; that when he fed his horse, he always gave him ten ears at a bait; that ten little ears would go as far as ten large ones; that two or three stalks in a hill would make more in number than one stalk. Many of the Bryants of Marion have emigrated to other sections of the country. The writer is not reasonably certain that this account of the Bryant family is correct in every particular—it is, however, in accord with the information obtained.

WATSON.—Another family that may here be noticed, is the Watson family. The progenitor of this family, so far as Marion County is concerned, was Barnabas Watson, on Buck Swamp, who was the great-grand-father of our now fellow-citizens of the county. Old man Isham Watson was the founder, it may be said, of the family on Catfish, in name and fortune. Barny Watson, his father, was married twice; whether he had a child or children other than Isham, by his first wife, is not known. Isham Watson married and settled on Catfish, near where Antioch Church now stands, in the first part of the nineteenth century, a poor man; his wife was Miss Mary Hays, a sister of the late John C. Hays; the results of the marriage were five sons, Matthew, James, Isham H., Samuel and William; and seven daughters, Nellie, Nancy, Elizabeth, Mary, Verzella, Fama and Jane; all raised to be grown and all married, and all now dead, except the daughters, Mary and Jane. Matthew Watson married Miss Celia Easterling, in 1839; and raised a large family of sons and daughters; the sons are David E., Isham E., Silas, Enos and Robert; and daughters, Martha, Lavina, Kate and Hortensia. David E. Watson married Miss Rose Bass, and has now living two sons and one daughter. Silas Watson married a Miss Page, daughter of W. J. Page, and has a family of sons and daughters, some of them grown. Isham E. Watson married Miss Beulah Emanuel; he moved to Florence and has several children, sons and daughters; he is in the dairy business. Enos Watson married Miss Theodocia Emanuel, sister of Isham E. Watson's wife; the two brothers married two sisters—both married the same evening. Enos Watson's wife is dead, leaving five children, the oldest of whom, Henry, by name, went into the Cuban war, thence to the Philippines, and perhaps now in China. Robert Watson married a Miss Walling; he died four or five years after marriage, and left two or three children; the whereabouts of his widow and children are unknown. Martha, the eldest daughter of Matthew Watson, married the Rev. Alfred Pitman, in North Carolina, and resides there. Lavina, the second daughter, married a Mr. McNeill, in North Carolina, and is dead, leaving children. Kate Watson married Tracy R. Fore, they have several children, one, a daughter, married to John H.

Berry. Hortensia Watson married Thomas J. Bass, who was killed some years ago by the falling of a tree, leaning over the path which he was traveling; he left four sons, all young men, now among us; their mother resides at Latta. James Watson, the second son of Isham Watson, married Miss Elizabeth Jones, daughter of Bryant Jones, of Wahee; the fruits of the marriage were several sons and daughters. James, the eldest, married Miss Flora Lane, and has several children, sons and daughters. Edward B. Watson married Miss Addie Bethea, a daughter of the late John R. Bethea; they have several children. Joseph F. Watson, a physician, married in Darlington; I don't know to whom. Cicero Watson, I think, is still single. Charles, I think, is married, and he and two single sisters live together on the old homestead of his father. James Watson's oldest daughter, Mary, married Jesse Gibson, below Marion; they have a family, how many is not known. The next daughter, Sarah, married Allen Gibson, brother of Jesse; they also have a family, of how many is not known to the writer. Another daughter married W. H. Daniels, of Mullins; they have two or three children. Two daughters of James Watson, Telatha and Drusilla, are yet single, and live with their brother on the old homestead. Isham H. Watson, the third son of old man Isham, married a Miss McDuffie, sister to the late Sheriff McDuffie; by her he raised three children, two sons and a daughter; the sons were George E. and Duncan I., the latter named for his two grand-fathers, Isham Watson and Duncan McDuffie; the daughter (Janie), married our fellow-citizen, J. D. Montgomery. Isham H. Watson's first wife died of small-pox during the war; he married again, Miss Mary Nichols, who survives him, childless. George E. Watson went West, and married there; some months after marriage, Geo. E. died suddenly, and left his widow, to whom a posthumous daughter was born, who takes and has the name of her father, George Elmore; the widow and daughter are both now in Marion. Samuel Watson, the fourth son of old Isham, married, first, a Miss Page, and by her had sons, W. J. Watson, Melton, S. P. Watson and S. C. Watson, and two daughters, Sophronia and Maggie. W. J. Watson married his first cousin, a Miss Bethea, moved to Mt. Airy, N. C.; his wife is dead; he has seven children. Melton Watson married a Miss Moody, daughter of the late Charles Moody, and soon after died childless; his widow still survives. Samuel Watson's first wife died, and he married a Miss Roberts, daughter of the late Rowland Roberts, and by her had five children, when she died; he married a third time, a Miss Price, sister of the Rev. Willie Price, of the Baptist Church; by her he had one child, a boy, named Albert. The children of his last two marriages are unknown to the writer; they are, however, here among us, and are of the present generation. S. P. Watson, third son of Samuel, married a Miss Bryan, near Little River, in Horry County; is a physician; he left a few days ago, with his family, for Oklahoma; he practiced medicine in Latta, and left his beautiful and comfortable home in Latta unsold; he sold his plantation to J. K. Page; he has seven children; he made a trip to that far off land last winter, and bought thirty acres of land in the suburbs of Oklahoma City, at $90 an acre; the city is growing so fast that his place is no longer in the suburbs, but is now in the city; his purchase has already quadrupled, and there is no telling what his thirty aches of land will be worth in the near future; the city now has 20,000 inhabitants. S. C. Watson, the fourth son of Samuel Watson and youngest by his first wife, married a Miss Stackhouse, daughter of Wm. R. Stackhouse; he has five children. William Watson, the fifth son and youngest of old man Isham's sons, married Miss Cherry Deer, daughter of Joseph Deer; the results of the marriage were four sons, John G., William E., Furman and D. Maxcy Watson; and three daughters, Ellen, Pauline and Norma. William Watson, the father, died some years ago. The son, John G. Watson, married a Miss Emanuel, and by her has several children; he resides in Marion, and is now one of the division chief liquor constables of the State. William E. Watson, the second son of William Watson, deceased, married Miss Annie Fore, daughter of the late Stephen Fore, and by her has had twelve children, one dead, eight sons living and three daughters. Furman Watson married Miss Linnie Bond, and has two children, two sons. D. Maxcy Watson, the youngest son of the late William Watson, married Miss Lucy B. Sellers, daughter of John C. Sellers, and grand-daughter of the writer; they have no children. Of the daughters of the late William Watson, the eldest, Ellen, married Addison Bass; they have several children, sons and daughters. The second daughter, Pauline, married, first, Rev. Mr. Price, a Baptist minister; he died a few years ago, leaving one child, a daughter, named Annie Hamer; the widow married, a second time, Charles W. Wiggins, of Dillon; they have no children. Norma, the youngest daughter, married Benj. B. Sellers, son of John C. Sellers; they have two children, a son and a daughter—Harry and Margaret Ellen. As to the two daughters of the late Samuel Watson by his first marriage, Sophronia and Maggie, Sophronia married John K. Page, a first class citizen; she died some four years ago, leaving two sons, Samuel and Ernest. Samuel is now in Baltimore, in a medical college; Ernest, a lad, is yet at home. The second daughter, Maggie, married Frank Easterling, a very worthy man; they have two children, sons, Rupert and Henry. Of the daughters of old Isham Watson, Nellie, the oldest, married Frank A. Berry, in 1839; she died, together with her infant, in 1840; both were buried together in the same grave. Frank A. Berry lived a widower for perhaps thirty years or more, when he married Verzilla Watson, sister of Nellie, then an old maid; she died childless, a few years ago; her husband preceded her to the grave a year or two. Nancy, the second daughter, married Rev. Joel Allen; they raised a large family of sons and daughters; the sons were James (killed in the war), William, Joel I., David E. and Frank; the daughters were Annie, Maria, Eugenia and Alice. Of the sons, William married a Miss Cox, of Florence; they have a large family of children, sons and daughters, and live on the old homestead. Joel I. married, first, Miss Helen Bass; she died, and left four or five children, sons and daughters; Joel I. married, a second time, a lady near Ridgeway, S. C., named Lulie Meredith; by her he had three children, when she died, and he is now a widower again, with two sets of children, eight in number. Joel I. Allen, like his father, is a Baptist preacher, and has charge of the Baptist Church at Dillon, and resides there; is a fair preacher, and has one quality that many preachers do not have—his sermons are short and sensible, and when he gets through he quits—he does not turn round and thrash the straw over again or rehash it; he is a good man. David E. Allen married Elizabeth (Bettie) Bethea, a daughter of Philip W. Bethea; has raised a family of eight or nine children, sons and daughters; some of them are married and have families. Frank Allen emigrated some years ago to Greenwood, S. C., and married there—can't say to whom; he is a first class man. The Allen boys are all good men, straightforward and reliable. Of the daughters of the Rev. Joel Allen, Annie Maria, the oldest, married Dr. Andrew J. Bethea, son of Rev. S. J. Bethea; he died in 1881, and left three sons and two daughters; the sons are Herbert, Percy and Andrew, and are all young men of fine character. Andrew is now in Wake Forrest College, N. C.; all unmarried.* Of the daughters, the oldest, Nettie Bethea, married Rev. Pierce F. Kilgo, a Methodist preacher of the South Carolina Conference, and is now stationed at Williamston and Belton, and is said to be a fine preacher; they have several children. Georgia, the younger daughter, married W. T. Bethea, her first cousin, who is, and has been, for several years, agent for the Atlantic Coast Line Railroad Company at Dillon, and has been Mayor of the town for three or four years. They have three children, sons, and are doing well. W. T. Bethea is the grand-son of the writer. Eugenia, a daughter of Rev. Joel Allen, married Preston L. Dew; they moved to Greenwood several years ago, and are said to be doing well; they have several children. Alice Allen, the remaining daughter of Rev. Joel Allen, married her cousin, Furman Allen, of Marlborough; they are doing well, and have a large family, sons and daughters. The Allen family under consideration herein are most respectable, good citizens, worthy to be emulated. Elizabeth Watson, third daughter of old man Isham, married the late George W. Reaves, being his third wife; by him she had five children, three of whom died children; two were raised a son, J. R. Reaves, and a daughter, Mary E. Robert Reaves is one of our leading fellow-citizens, on Buck Swamp; he married a Miss McMillan, in the Mullins community, and has raised a large family—I think, thirteen or fourteen

---

*Herbert Bethea has recently married Miss Eva Manning, daughter of the late Houston Manning.

children, sons and daughters; he is doing a good part by his children in the way of education. Charles is a leading merchant of Mullins. Samuel W. is a graduate of the Citadel, and is a promising young man.* Robert, another son, is a graduate of a dental school, and has located in Marion for the practice of his profession; he is also a promising young man. Of J. R. Reaves' daughters, the older ones are well educated and stand well; one or two of them married, to whom unknown; several not yet grown.† Mary married Dr. N. C. Murphy, who died several years ago; she is a practical business woman, a good manager in her business and farm affairs; she has three sons and two daughters; both daughters are married, one to a Mr. McMillan, the other to a Mr. Cain, of St. Matthews. Mary, the next daughter of Isham Watson, married James B. Legette, and still survives; they raised a large family, mostly girls—only two sons, Salathiel and Andrew. The oldest daughter, Sarah Ellen, married a Mr. Cadell, a one-legged man; they left the county—I think they are now in Florence; they have a family, how many not known. Another daughter married D. S. Cottingham, and is doing well; of their family the writer knows nothing. Another married W. C. Easterling, of "Free State;" they have several children, five daughters and two sons; the oldest daughter married; I do not know anything of their family. Of the two sons of James B. Legette and Mary, his wife, the oldest, Salathiel, accidentally shot himself several years ago, unmarried. The younger one, Andrew, married a Miss Moore, a daughter of Alfred Moore, of Marlborough; he lost his wife some months ago, and left him with, I think, seven children. Fama Watson, another daughter of old man Isham Watson, married, first, Stephen Berry, youngest son of Cross Roads Henry Berry; he lived about a year, and died childless; the widow afterwards married the late Fred. D. Jones, of Marion; the fruits of this marriage were one son, Presley, and five daughters. Presley Jones married a Miss Sparks, of Marlborough, and has four children. The oldest daughter, Costa, married a Mr. Hunter, of Marlborough, who died a few months ago, and left five

---

*S. W. Reaves is now a professor in Clemson College.

†Mary Reaves, a graduate of Winthrop, died of typhoid fever recently.

or six children. Alice Jones married L. W. Oliver, of Marion. Sallie, Theodocia and Cora, young ladies, are yet single, and live at the old homestead. The father and mother are both dead. Jane Watson, the youngest daughter of old Isham, married John M. Mace, and yet survives; they live in the Friendship neighborhood, and have a large family of sons and daughters; the sons are Thadeus, Stephen, Moses, Samuel, John C. and Cornelius, and one son dead; daughters, Elizabeth (Bettie) and Mary. Thadeus married a Miss Eugenia Gasque, daughter of our excellent fellow-citizen, Arny Gasque, and Moses Mace married another daughter, Miss Emma. Stephen Mace married Miss Julia Philips, daughter of our late fellow-citizen, F. Marion Philips. Samuel Mace married a Miss Carter, and John C. Mace married a Miss Griffith, I think, of Edgefield County. Neill Mace is yet unmarried. Of these sons of John M. Mace, John C. Mace and Samuel are both doctors; one, John C., located at Marion, and running a drug store, and is Coroner of the county; Samuel Mace is located at Loris, in Horry County, and is said to be doing well there, and is a fine physician. Of the two daughters of John M. Mace, the oldest, Bettie, is married to Furman Wall; the younger one, Mary, is yet unmarried. It is supposed (the writer does not know) that all these young Maces that are married have families, more or less numerous, perpetuating the name and family connections, and also contributing to an increase in the population of the county, and industriously adding to the county's wealth and prosperity. This closes the notice of the Watson family, so far as is descended from the old man, Isham. In many respects, the old man, Isham, was an extraordinary man; he made a large fortune, raised his large family respectably—industry, frugality and economy were the prominent characteristics of his career; these, with his great good sense, gave him success in life; he died of erysipelas, in 1864, over three-score and ten years of age. Barney Watson, his father, married a second time, I do not know to whom; by this marriage he had two sons, Barney and Meredith, and some daughters. Barney and Meredith are both dead, and left families, about whom the writer knows nothing. Barney and Meredith were hard-working, honest men, but did not succeed in life as did their older half-brother, Isham. The father, old man Barney, had two brothers, Needham and Thomas; I do not know what became of Thomas. Needham Watson married and had a family—at least, one son, named Wickham, who lived in the Temperance Hill neighborhood. Wickham married and had a family, how many is unknown; one son, named Kerigan—what became of him is unknown; he was not remarkable for his beauty; if there had been such a club as an "Ugly Club," he would have stood a fair chance to have been its president. Wickham Watson was a remarkable man physically, in respect to which the writer will say nothing. There are some Watsons in Britton's Neck, whether related to these Watsons on Catfish is not known; of them, however, the writer knows nothing. There was another family of Watsons in what is now known as Hillsboro Township, and of whom something has already herein been incidentally said. Seacebook Watson came from Virginia, and settled on the road leading from Nichols to Lumberton, N. C., more than one hundred years ago; he succeeded well in life, raised a large family, sons and daughters; the sons, Michael, Thomas and John R., were known to the writer. Michael and Thomas went to North Carolina, married sisters, Smithy and Kitsey Ham, very excellent women, and each raised respectable families; they were just across the line, and many of their descendants are now in South Carolina. John R. Watson, the youngest son, married Miss Sallie Ford, who had the phenomenon of a black eye and a blue one; they lived on the old homestead of his father, and had a large family of four sons and several daughters. John R. Watson died in middle life, and left his widow and children, many of them small; the widow managed well and raised her family respectably, and died a few years ago; some of them are now in the county, and among our best people. If all these Watsons and their thrice multiplied connections, hereinabove referred to, were destroyed, it would cut a mighty swathe in our county population. There may be, and perhaps are, some few families larger or more numerous, but not many—the name will not soon become extinct.

REAVES.—Another family to be here noticed is the Reaves

family. The first known of this family was Solomon Reaves, a Baptist preacher. The writer heard him preach when a boy, about 1829, at an association at Porter Swamp Church, in Columbus County, N. C., about five miles from Fair Bluff, N. C.; he was then an old man, white hair and red face; he had a son, named Charles—he may have had other sons, but Charles is the only one that concerns Marion County; he married a Miss Hodge, sister of the late Dr. Samuel Hodge, in the Gapway neighborhood; by her he had two sons, George W. and Robert H. Reaves; he may have had other sons and daughters. His first wife dying, he married Miss Mary Griffin, of North Carolina, near Fair Bluff; no offspring by this second marriage. Charles Reaves died in 1861 or 1862, leaving his widow and a large estate of lands and negroes; he died intestate, his property, real and personal, descended under the law to his widow and two sons, one-third each, the widow getting the old homestead. Some years after that, the widow married the late Colonel John T. Harrington, who died some years back, and left Mrs. Harrington a widow for the second time; no child or children; she still survives and is still a widow on the old Reaves homestead, now in her eighty-seventh year—somewhat a remarkable woman for her age. Of the sons, George W. Reaves married four times—not being a very old man at the time of his fourth marriage; he was born in 1811, and died, I think, in 1896 or 1897; his first wife was a Miss Carmichael, of what is now Carmichael Township, a sister of the late Neill C. Carmichael; she lived only about a year, and died childless; he married, a second time, a Miss Brown; by her he had some children, how many is not known. There were one or two sons by this marriage, who were killed or died in the war, and a daughter, who married some one, and soon became a widow; I know nothing more of her. His Brown wife died, I think, in 1846 or 7; he married in a few months, Miss Elizabeth Watson, who has hereinbefore been spoken of; by her he raised two children, James Robert Reaves and Mary E. Reaves, now Mrs. Murphy—heretofore noticed. The Watson wife died, and he married a Miss Rogers, of the Fork, a daughter of the late Captain John Rogers; by her he had and raised four sons, George R. Reaves, John Reaves, William Reaves and Edward

Reaves; the latter is a Baptist preacher of high standing, and is pastor of some church in the upper part of the State. These sons of George W. Reaves are all respectable and valued citizens, and are a part of the bone and sinews of the county, married and contributing their full share to the citizenship and general prosperity of the county. The father, George W. Reaves, was a good citizen and a prominent church man, weighed, avoirdupois, three hundred pounds, or more. His brother, Robert H. Reaves, was for many years a prominent merchant at Marion; he married a daughter of old Colonel W. H. Grice, who still survives, and lives upon and owns her patrimonial estate in Wahee Township. R. H. Reaves, the last years of his life, retired from mercantile pursuits, and went on his farm in Wahee, where he accidentally fell from his piazza some years ago and broke his neck; he raised a family of four sons and perhaps two daughters; of the sons, two, Henry and Thomas, died young men, unmarried; Augustus and James still survive; the former unmarried, lives with his mother; the latter married, and lives in Sumter County; has a family, and is said to be doing well. Of the daughters, Miss Sallie, the oldest, has never married, and lives with her mother. The younger one, name not remembered, married a Mr. Lide, in Darlington. R. H. Reaves was a good and successful merchant for many years, but in the wind-up of his mercantile affairs, did not seem to have made much, but saved his plantation and negroes; he was a man of equable temperament, and never seemed to be in a hurry; he represented the district in the Legislature just after the war in 1866—before Reconstruction commenced or before it got under way.

GRICE.—Just here may be noticed the Grice family, to which Mrs. Reaves belonged. Colonel W. H. Grice was originally from Horry County; he came to Marion away back in the twenties or thirties. In former times he had represented Horry in the House and had been Senator from Liberty (Marion) and Kingston before 1810; he was a well read man for his day; he had three children, one of whom was Mrs. Reaves, above spoken of. His youngest daughter, Ellen, became the third wife of the late Colonel W. W. DuRant, well known in Marion, having been in the town perhaps all his life; she was respected by all who knew her, and loved for her many good qualities; she raised several daughters and one son to be thirteen or fourteen years of age (Thadeus, I believe), who accidentally shot himself twelve or fifteen years ago. These daughters of Colonel DuRant have all married and have families, except, perhaps, two, who reside in the old DuRant homestead, near the town, all doing well and quite respectable. Colonel William H. Grice had only one son, Augustus E. Grice, quite a literary man and a fine speaker; he was elected Sheriff of the county in 1876; he lived about two years, and died during his term of softening of the brain; he married, late in life, a Miss Tanner, and left a considerable family. Perseus L. Grice, our present fellow-citizen, and quite respectable, is one of his sons—perhaps the oldest; one of his daughters is the wife of J. T. Dozier, the late nominee of the Democratic party of Marion for County Supervisor.* Of the others of the family of Sheriff Grice, the writer knows nothing. Colonel William H. Grice died in 1854, leaving a good property in both town and country to his children; he was up to the times in his day, a very honest and reliable man, very cautious and prudent. The old court house of 1823 had a large crack in its northwest corner, and such was the prudence of Colonel Grice—excited, perhaps, by his fear—that he would not go up into the court room when it was crowded, unless from strong business compulsion; whether it was dangerous or not, the writer cannot say; he was in it many times when it was packed with people.

ROBERTS.—The next family now to be noticed is the Roberts family. The first of them known to the writer was Redden Roberts and Norton Roberts. They settled on Buck Swamp, near Buck Swamp Bridge. I do not know who the wife of either was, but both married and raised families. Redden Roberts had sons, William D., James, Rowland and Giles. The latter went into the Confederate army, and died of disease, unmarried. William D. Roberts married Lishia Manning, a daughter of old John Manning, and had and raised a considerable family, sons—John M. Roberts and William Roberts; they

---

*J. T. Dozier was elected and is now the County Supervisor.

both have families unknown. Daughters of Wm. D. Roberts—Penelope, and perhaps another, married sons of Charles Taylor, both of which Taylors were killed or died in the Confederate War. Another daughter, Julia Ann, married A. H. Harrelson, who has a family of several children. Another, Lispia Ann, married Captain Thomas E. Tart; Tart is dead. Another (name not remembered) married Dugal C. McIntyre; McIntyre is dead; left a family of several children, and the widow still survives. Another married an Avant; he is dead, his widow survives; there were no children. And one other daughter (name not remembered) still unmarried. James Roberts, second son of old man Reddin Roberts, married Sallie Goodyear, only child of old Mr. William Goodyear; he raised a considerable family; he is and was a very excellent citizen; little is known of his family. A son of his, Henry Roberts, is a capital man and good citizen; I do not know whether he is married or not; I think he lives on his father's old homestead. One of James Roberts' daughters married A. C. Oliver, of Robeson County, N. C.; they have considerable family. Another daughter married Albert Edwards, of this county; think they have but one child, a daughter, who is said to be quite a scholar and a fine teacher. Another daughter is the wife of Albert Shooter. James Roberts had other children, not known to the writer. James Roberts was a good man and unexceptional citizen—honest and truthful. Rowland Roberts, third son of Reddin Roberts, married Miss Mary Smith, daughter of the late Samuel Smith, senior, of Buck Swamp; they raised a family of sons and daughters—the oldest, I think, was Pinckney, who went into the Confederate War, and was killed or died of disease, unmarried. Roger married, first, a daughter of Colonel John Roberts; they had four or five children, boys and girls, when their mother died, and Roger married again—I do not know whom. Giles, another son, married Miss Hays, daughter of Wilson Hays. Samuel and Stephen, I think, both married daughters of Captain L. M. Edwards; they all have families, are good citizens, and are doing their share towards building up and forwarding the interest and welfare of the county. Rowland Roberts' daughters, two of whom are only known by the writer; one married the late Samuel Watson (his second wife, I think); her name was Bettie; she died some years ago, leaving five children, named Mary, Lamar, Judson, Elliott and Carrie. Mary is married to Albert Allen, a son of Elmore Allen, of Marlborough County. Albert Allen resides in North Carolina. Elmore C. Allen, of Latta, married the other daughter of Rowland Roberts, named Sallie; resides at Latta, and has several children, neither age or sex is known. Elmore Allen is one of the well-to-do citizens of the town and county; he and his wife are first cousins, their mothers being sisters. Of the daughters of old Reddin Roberts, one married Harllee Bethea, who removed to Florida many years ago— know but little of his family; had a son named Reddin, a very promising young man. Another daughter married Henry Hays, of Hillsboro, who has been dead several years; he left a son, our good fellow-citizen, W. D. B. Hays, near Mount Andrew Church; he married his first cousin, a daughter of Harllee Bethea; they have only one child, a daughter; I suppose she is grown, name not known. Another daughter of old man Reddin, his youngest, named Zilpha, married C. P. Floyd, of Nichols; he was killed on the railroad between Mullins and Nichols, some twenty-five or thirty years ago; he left several children, sons and daughters. Mrs. Floyd now lives on the homestead of her father, an excellent lady and capital manager; has raised her children in credit and respectability— three sons and three or four daughters. The sons were Charles P., Henry Bascom (called Battie), and Giles R. Floyd. Charles P. was killed some twenty or more years ago by a man by the name of Anderson, near Campbell's Bridge. The writer was employed to prosecute Anderson, who was convicted of manslaughter and sentenced to two years in the State penitentiary. Henry Bascom married a Miss Stackhouse, daughter of the late Wm. R. Stackhouse, and is one of our good citizens. I believe Giles R. is married; don't know to whom; he is afflicted with asthma. The writer can truly sympathise with him, as he has had that most distressing of diseases, off and on, for twenty-five years. Of her daughters, the two oldest, Cornelia and Minnie, married North Carolina men, where they reside, and, therefore, cannot tell anything about their families. Think Minnie is dead. Roberta married Lewis S. Bethea, above Latta, and is doing well. There is one, perhaps, two daughters yet unmarried, and yet with their mother. Reddin Roberts had another daughter, who never married; her name was Martha Ann; she is dead. Old man Reddin Roberts was an excellent, quiet citizen; was wealthy before the war, especially in negro property. It was said of him that when he married he had one negro girl about grown, that his wife had one, and on the night of their marriage, his wife's girl had a child; that from these two girls, at emancipation, he had and had given off some to his children together eighty slaves; that during his married life he had sold two and had bought three, or *vice versa*—showing how fortunes might be made by raising negroes. It was said he did not work his negroes hard, and fed and clothed them well, hence his negro women "bred like rabbits," as the saying is. He was an exemplary man, lived at home and kept out of debt. Norton Roberts resided on the first settled place south of Buck Swamp Bridge; don't know to whom he married—think, however, his wife was a Miss Johnson; he, with all his family, except his oldest son, Colonel John M. Roberts, went to Louisiana a way back, perhaps, in the forties, and it is said, don't know with how much truth, that one of his sons became Governor of Louisiana. I have learned from the Hon. James Norton, that Norton Roberts' mother was a Miss Norton, sister of James Norton's grand-father, hence his name, Norton Roberts. Norton Roberts married Martha Norton, who was the mother of Colonel John M. Colonel John M. Roberts, his oldest son, married Miss Franky Mace; by her he had seven daughters and no son. One of his daughters died unmarried. His oldest daughter, Elizabeth, married Alexander Hays, son of Joseph B. Hays, and brother to our T. B. Hays; they have raised a large family of sons and daughters, unknown to the writer. Another daughter, Joanna, married Thomas Finklea, a son of old "Corn-making Willis Finklea." Finklea is dead; suppose they raised a family. Another daughter married Roger Roberts, already mentioned herein. Another daughter married Charles B. Gaddy, who died a few weeks ago, suddenly, hereinbefore mentioned. Another daughter, Louisa, married John M. McColl, now one of our best and most reliable citizens; they have only one child, a daughter, Fannie; married to a Mr. McNeill, of North Carolina. One other daughter, named Emelia or Mille, has never married, and still living. Colonel Roberts was eminently a good citizen, a successful man every way, with only an ordinary common school education. In the late unpleasantness, he volunteered early, raised a company and went into the war as a Captain, and upon the reorganization of the regiment was promoted to Major, and then to Lieutenant Colonel. In the battle, Seven Days Fight around Richmond, or at Second Manassas, or at Sharpsburg, in 1862, was wounded in the thigh by a Minie ball or piece of shell. He came home, the wound became gangrenous, and he died, to the regret of all who knew him, both in and out of the army; he was a good soldier, a good officer, beloved by his company and regiment, a growing, rising man at home and in the army; and though comparatively a young man, had accumulated a good property, and left it unencumbered and his family in good condition. Had he lived, there was no public position within the gift of the people that he might have aspired to, that he could not have obtained; he was exceedingly popular.

ELLERBE.—The next family to be noticed is the Ellerbe family. Two brothers, Thomas and John Ellerbe, came to South Carolina about 1740. Thomas Ellerbe applied to the Council for lands, about which he had some trouble; and Bishop Gregg says, on page 63: "Mr. Elerby was doubtless successful in the end, as he remained in that neighborhood and became the owner of extensive landed possessions, a large portion of which has remained in the family to the present day." And in a note to this, Gregg says: "The mill site referred to in the petition of Thomas Elerby was, doubtless, that on Juniper Creek, of which some signs yet remain, near the road leading from Cheraw to Society Hill. A grist and saw mill, at all events, were there, and in successful operation some time before the Revolution." Resuming the text, Bishop Gregg further says: "John Elerby, a brother of Thomas, came with him to Pee Dee, and settled on the east side of the river. He either returned to Virginia or removed elsewhere at an early period. Thomas Elerby brought a good property with him and was probably the first slaveholder on the upper Pee Dee. Some years prior to the Revolution he had a large number, at least for that day. This family emigrated from England to Virginia. The name is still known in England, and is spelt as it appears in our early records. Not long afterwards, however, it was changed to its present form, Ellerbe. Thomas Elerby, who married, as already stated, Obedience Gillespie, had two sons, Thomas and William, from whom the extensive family on the Pee Dee have descended." In a note to this, page 63, Bishop Gregg traces the progeny of William and Thomas Ellerbe down to his own day and time, or near it. So far as Marion County is concerned, the first of the name in this county was John C. Ellerbe, of the same family spoken of above. He married a Miss Wickham, daughter of Dr. Thomas J. Wickham, a man of much note in his day in Liberty or Marion; she was wealthy and perhaps the only child; at any rate, John C. Ellerbe married her and came down into Marion and settled on her property, and lived and died there; he retained her property and increased it; not an old man when he died—he died some time in the forties; his widow survived him, and afterwards married ex-Governor B. K. Henagan; no offspring from the marriage; they both died in a few years. John C. Ellerbe left his family in good condition; his large property went, as the law then was, mostly to the Henagans—that is, the personal property; the large landed estate went to the heirs of the widow, who, I think, survived him. By John C. Ellerbe's marriage, he had and raised three sons and three daughters. The sons were William S., Richard P. and Edward B.; the daughters were Joanna, Julia and Sallie. The son, William, married Miss Sarah Haselden, daughter of Major James Haselden; the fruits of this marriage were four sons and nine daughters. Of the sons, William H. Ellerbe married Henrietta Rogers, daughter of the late Henry Rogers, of Marlborough County; the fruits of this marriage were six children, five sons and one daughter; one son dead. He was a very successful man in more ways than one—succeeded well in his occupation as a farmer in the acquisition of property. In the political revolution of 1890, he was on the winning side, and by the help of good friends, to the manor born, was nominated and elected Comptroller General of the State; was re-elected without opposition in 1892. At the end of his term, in 1894, he was a candidate for Governor, but was defeated by John Gary Evans, of Aiken. In 1896, John Gary Evans not being a candidate for re-election as Governor, Wm. H. Ellerbe was again a candidate, with opposition, and was triumphantly elected. In the meantime, a new State Constitution had been made, which changed the time for the meeting of the General Assembly, so that Governor Ellerbe was not inaugurated till January, 1897. With his administration there was much dissatisfaction; his health had failed him, and in 1898, he was again a candidate for re-election, but had numerous and strong opposition—so much so, that he failed to get the nomination in the first primary, but led all others. In a second primary he was, however, nominated by over 4,000 votes. In November afterwards, at the general election, he was elected to a second term. Miles B. McSweeney, of Hampton County, was elected Lieutenant-Governor. They were inaugurated as Governor and Lieutenant-Governor, 18th January, 1899. Such by this time was the Governor's state of health, that he could do but little work in his laborious office, and lingered from bad to worse till 2d June, when he expired in his old home—the home in which he was raised. Thus his eventful career was ended, and the Lieutenant-Governor, by operation of the Constitution, became Governor, and took the oath of office on the night of the 4th June, 1899, and has filled out the unexpired term of the deceased Governor Ellerbe. McSweeny has just been elected to the next full term. Thus the world goes. This was the second death of a Governor while in office in the history of the State—Governor Patrick Noble died in office, in 1840, and Dr. B. K. Henagan, then of Marlborough, afterwards of Marion, being the Lieutenant-Governor, filled out Governor Noble's unexpired term. J. E. Ellerbe, the next son of the late Captain W. S. Ellerbe, and now one of our fellow-citizens, has not been as successful, in any way, as his deceased brother, the late Governor Ellerbe; he has great energy and persistent pluck, and is an impressive public speaker; he married Miss Nellie Elford, of Spartanburg, an elegant lady; the fruits of the marriage are four children, two sons and two daughters. J. E. Ellerbe is yet comparatively a young man; has represented his county in the lower House of the Legislature; was chosen as a delegate to the State Convention for making a new Constitution for the State, and served in that body; he has three times been a candidate for Congress, but has failed to receive the nomination; his opportunities have been better than those of his brother, the late Governor; he graduated in 1887, at Wofford College; the Governor only spent two years in college (Wofford); nevertheless, he outstripped his younger brother in the race of life for wealth and honors. Don't know what J. E. Ellerbe may do or become in the lines indicated in the future. Cash Ellerbe, the third son of Captain W. S. Ellerbe, is a young single man, highly respectable, a good farmer and business man, and promises to be a first class man every way—nothing to hinder it. Herbert Ellerbe, the fourth and youngest son, about twenty-five years of age, unmarried, was unfortunately killed on the railroad, on the 3d or 4th of August, 1899. Of the daughters of Captain W. S. Ellerbe, the oldest, Mary, married Dr. Ellerbe, of Cheraw; by him she had two sons, W. M. Ellerbe and Thomas, and a daughter, Estelle, when he died suddenly, while his children were yet small; the widow has raised and educated them, who are all now grown; her sons are promising young men, and the daughter a charming young lady, all unmarried. Another daughter (don't know the names of some of them nor the order in which they come,) married her cousin, James H. Manning, and has a large family, sons and daughters; Manning is a very prosperous farmer. Another married Charley Rogers, of Marlborough, in the Brownsville neighborhood, likewise a prosperous man; they have a family, how many is not known. Another married Stephen G. Miles, a good farmer, and is a merchant at Marion; they have a large family, sons and daughters—I think, mostly daughters. Another married Dr. S. A. C. Miles, who is dead; the widow has four children, all daughters. Another married her cousin, Willie Godbold, who is not wanting in push and energy; they have some two or three children. Another married Hon. T. C. Moody, of Marion, and is dead, childless. Two daughters, Misses Omega and Eva, are yet unmarried. The Widow Ellerbe and her family, the Widow Miles and her family, together with their brother, Cash Ellerbe, and two single girls, all live together on their father's homestead. Richard P. Ellerbe, second son of old John C. Ellerbe, married Elizabeth Lamb, a very pretty woman and quite a belle in her day; they remained here for several years, and had several children; he did not succeed well; some years ago they went to Florida, where Mrs. Ellerbe died; what has become of Richard P. or his children is not known. Edward B. Ellerbe, the youngest son of old John C., inherited the old homestead of his father, where J. E. Ellerbe now resides, a very fine plantation; he married Miss Sarah Godbold, a daughter of old Asa Godbold; he did not succeed well; sold his place to his brother, William, and moved off, and finally went to Horry County, where he now resides; raised a large family, sons and daughters, about whom the writer knows but little. John C., his eldest son, is in Venezuela, South America, as the writer has been informed. Of the daughters of old John C. Ellerbe, Joanna, the oldest, married the late Gewood Berry; the results of which were five sons raised, viz: John H., William E., Edmund Burke, Ashton and Thomas Wickham Berry; of these, John H., Edmund Burke and Thomas Wickham are now among us, and are among our best citizens, doing well and highly respected. Julia Ellerbe, second daughter of old John C. Ellerbe, married our respected fellow-citizen, Charles Haselden; by this marriage is three daughters; one married and dead; Anne and Mary both yet single; and six sons, James, C. Edgar, Samuel, Thomas, Alonzo and Guy. Of these, James and C. Edgar are married; James married a daughter of the late F. C. Dew, lives in the "Slashes." C. Edgar married a Miss Dusenberry in Horry. Samuel has gone West. Thomas, a fine and much respected young man, suicided last winter at Clio, S. C.; no cause known. Alonzo is here, a very nice young man, unmarried. Guy, the youngest, is said to be in Florida. The youngest daughter of old John C. Ellerbe married Asa Godbold, Jr., and is now a widow; she has ten or twelve children. Of this family the writer has already hereinbefore spoken, and it is not necessary to be repeated or added to. The late Captain W.

S. Ellerbe was a most excellent man and a capital manager of affairs; he attended to his own business, and left his family in good condition; his wife survived him but a short while.

FORE.—The Fore family will be next noticed. The first Fore known to the writer was Joel Fore; he was an exemplary man, and a good quiet man, unpretentious, and strictly honest— a man who seemed to measure every word, and practical in his management in every day life; he married a Miss Finklea, and raised a considerable family, sons and daughters. Five of his sons, Thomas, Daniel, Willis, Stephen and Alfred, were best known in the county.* Others of them, when young, went West, and one of them, named James, it was said, became very wealthy. Thomas, the eldest of the sons, was born in 1805; he lived to a great age—I think the age of eighty-eight. Thomas married a Miss Gasque, and settled on a little place on the northeast side of Catfish, at what is now called Ellerbe's crossing, and there, on about sixty-four acres of land, he raised a family of eight sons and three daughters, and did it respectably; he purchased other lands after his children were practically raised; his sons were Elly, Thomas, Daniel, James, Tracy R., Willis and Edward M. Fore; his daughters were Elizabeth Ann, Rebecca Jane and Eugenia. Of his sons, Elly, Thomas and Daniel emigrated to Louisiana, young men. James Fore, a son, married, first, a Miss Kirvin, and by her had three daughters and a son, Thomas E. Fore; the latter is now living on the place where his grand-father settled. Of James Fore's daughters, they have already herein been noticed in the notice of the Tart family. His Kirvin wife dying, he married a daughter of the late Bryant Lane, named Henrietta; by her he has some children, how many is not known; they have removed to Columbus County, N. C. Tracy R. Fore married Miss Kate Watson, daughter of the late Matthew Watson, who has hereinbefore been noticed in the notice of the Watson family. Willis Fore married Miss Sallie Berry, daughter of the late Elihu Berry; they have five children, three sons and two daughters; the sons are Linwood, Tracy and Willis; the daughters are Janie and Rebecca. Willis Fore's family has

---

*John, Joel and James, three others, went West.

already been noticed in the notice of the Berry family. Willis Fore was killed some years ago, by a fall in getting off of a moving train at Marion depot. Edward M. Fore married a daughter of Charles Haselden, named Maggie; they had four children, one daughter and three sons; he was murdered in the Slashes some years ago; his widow did not turn out well, and died; the daughter is married and in Columbia; the sons are scattered. Of the daughters of old man Thomas Fore, Elizabeth Ann, the oldest, married the late Colonel E. T. Stackhouse; they are both dead; raised a large family—sons, James, William and Walter F. Stackhouse; daughters, one the wife of James H. Berry, dead; left seven children; another, the wife of Houston Manning; she and her husband both dead; left three children, two sons and a daughter, Austin and Maurice; the latter married Nellie Bethea, daughter of D. McL. Bethea. The daughter, named Eva, unmarried.* Another the wife of Neill Alford; they have several children. Another the wife of W. J. Montgomery, Esq., of the Marion bar; they have several children, mostly girls. Another the wife of T. C. Covington; they have several children. Of the sons, James Stackhouse married a Miss McAlister; they have several children. One son, Laneau, married Mary Miles, the daughter of Dr. D. F. Miles, the efficient Clerk of the Court. There are other sons and daughters, how many and names unknown, except a son named Lacy. William Stackhouse, of Dillon, married a daughter of B. F. Davis; they have some children, how many is not known. James Stackhouse is Senator-elect from Marion to the State Senate. W. F. Stackhouse, the youngest son of Colonel E. T. Stackhouse, lately married a Miss Waller, of Greenwood, S. C.; is a member of the Marion bar, and promises to attain to a place in the front. The second daughter of old man Thomas Fore, Rebecca Jane, married Dr. W. W. Hamilton, of Marion, a dental surgeon and farmer, and a first rate man; they have only one child, a son, named Thomas, and now nearing manhood. The third and last daughter, Eugenia, never married; she died a few years ago. Daniel Fore, another son of old man Joel, was a tailor by trade—which in his day was a profitable business; he made a suit for the writer in

---

*Miss Eva Manning, since writing the above, married Herbert Bethea.

1843. He did not marry till somewhat late in life; he married, first, the Widow White, who was the daughter of old man Isaac Stackhouse, and sister of the late Colonel E. T. Stackhouse; by her he had one child, a daughter, the wife of Rev. Maston Gasque; when she died, he married, a second time, a Miss McDuffie, sister of the late A. Q. McDuffie; by this marriage he had two sons, John A. Fore, now of Dillon, and one named Baker, who died a young man, and, I think, three daughters; one of them dead; another became the second wife of Douglas McIntyre, and has some children; another daughter yet single—she and her mother live with Mr. McIntyre. Daniel Fore died some years ago, in a good old age; his son, John A. Fore, married a Miss Gibson, daughter of the late Albert Gibson, below Marion; they have five children, sons and daughters. Dr. Willis Fore, another son of old man Joel Fore, married Miss Telatha Berry; she lived only a few years, and died childless; he lived a widower for several years, and died in 1864. Another son of old man Joel was Stephen, who married Miss Mary Berry, the oldest daughter of Cross Roads Henry Berry; his family has already been noted in the notice of the Berry family hereinbefore. Alfred Fore, the youngest son of old Joel, married Miss Martha Ann Mace, daughter of the late Moses Mace; they had some children, don't know how many; one son I knew, A. M. Fore, a promising and growing man; he died a few years ago—left some family. Alfred Fore, the father, went into the Confederate army, and was killed or died. Of the daughters of old Joel Fore, there were two, Mary Ann and Elizabeth. Mary Ann married Samuel Campbell, and died, leaving one child. Elizabeth married Hugh Finklea, her cousin; he died, left her a widow, without any child; she again married, Bennett Jordan, below Marion; they had no child or children; she died some years ago. The Fores, as a family from old Joel down, had the peculiarity of being particular and exceedingly cautious in all they said or did, either in social or home life; honest, truthful and upright, straight in all their dealings with the world around them, economical, industrious and frugal—they came as near living to themselves and of themselves as any family within the writer's knowledge.

MACE.—Another family will now be noticed, the Mace family. The grand-father of the late John Mace was named John Mace, who came from Maryland in the time of the Revolutionary War, being a widower, with one child, a son, named John, then a small boy; the old gentleman married a Widow Crawford; by her he had no offspring; he died and his widow again married a Mikell. The son, John, grew up and married, first, a Miss Franky Finklea, a sister of old "Corn-making Willis Finklea;" by this marriage he had five children, Matthew, Moses, Elizabeth (Betsy), Mary (Polly) and Martha (Patsy); his first wife died, and he married again, a sister of his first wife, named Martha (Patsy); by the second marriage he had Franky, John, Massey, Sallie, James and Rhoda; of all these children by both marriages, Matthew, the oldest, never married, and died with a good property, about 1853. Moses married Miss Drusilla Miles, a daughter of David Miles, the grand-father of Dr. D. F. Miles; by this marriage he had six children, Martha Ann, John M., Verzilla, Gregory, James and Mary. Martha Ann has already been noticed in or among the Fore family, and John M. was noticed in or among the Watson family. Verzilla married William C. Bethea, and after having several children, they moved to Texas, where father and mother, and perhaps some of the children, died in an epidemic of yellow fever; and Frank A. Miles and others of their friends made up money and sent out to that far-off State (Dallas, Texas, I believe,) and brought the surviving children back to this State and county; they have grown up, but what has become of them is not known to the writer. Dr. Gregg Mace and his brother, James, both went to the Confederate War, and both were killed or died of disease, both unmarried. Mary Mace married a man by the name of Adams, and left the State; don't know anything further of her. Elizabeth Mace married the late John H. Moody; by this marriage there was only one child, a daughter; she grew up and married the late Major S. A. Durham; only one child, a daughter, was the result of this latter marriage; she grew up and married a Mr. Gorham, of North Carolina, to which State they went; nothing further is known of them. Mary (Polly) married Hal Crawford, and went West; nothing further is known of them. Martha

(Pattie) married Cary Edwards; of her and her family notice has already been taken in or among the Edwards family. Franky, the oldest child by the second marriage of old John Mace, married Colonel John Roberts; of their family notice has already been taken in or among the Roberts family. John Mace (the late) married Verzilla Berry, of whom notice has already been taken in or among the Berry family. Massey, a daughter, married the late David Monroe; by her he had one child, a daughter, when his wife died; the daughter grew up, and married a Mr. King, in North Carolina; nothing further is known of her. Sallie Mace married Wesley White; by this marriage was a son, James White, and several daughters. James White is still unmarried. Another son, William, older than James, was killed or died in the war. Of the daughters, one married Hugh Davis, and is a widow, with several children; another daughter, Susan, married Joseph Game, and has no children; another married Benjamin Philips, and is now a widow, with several children; another married Thomas Hargrove; they have several children; and there are two unmarried daughters, Martha and Sallie. James Mace, brother to the late John Mace, died in 1846, when a young man, unmarried. Rhoda Mace, the youngest by old John Mace's second marriage, married William S. Lewis; by this marriage five children were born and raised, Sarah, Evan, Joel, Wesley and Anne. Sarah Lewis married Robert Edwards, and has been noticed in or among the Edwards family. Evan Lewis did not marry till late in life; he married a Miss Avant, and I suppose has some children; he is one of our good citizens. Joel Lewis went West, and is said to be doing well. Wesley Lewis married Miss Addie Potter, of Marion, turned out badly, and has gone West; his wife is now at Marion; she has three children, a son, Charles, who is in Georgia, but provides for his mother and sisters—a dutiful son; the two daughters are with their mother, living on a place in town, which her son, Charley, bought for her, and paid $300 for it, and provides for her in other ways. All the sons and daughters of old John Mace are dead. One daughter of Rhoda Lewis above forgotten; her name was Anna; a charming woman, as it was said; she married, first, Marion Avant, who was killed or died in the war, left one child; the widow, after the war, went to Wilmington, and there married a Mr. Wilson, by whom she has one child, a daughter, now a grown young lady; her son, Willie Avant, was a locomotive engineer for the Atlantic Coast Line for many years; he died last August, leaving a widow and some children. Moses Mace died in 1836 or 1837. John Mace died in 1885. Matthew Mace died about 1854, and James Mace died about 1846. The Maces as a family are and were energetic and prudent managers of affairs, economical and frugal, held to what they had and added to it all they could, peaceable and quiet people, not ambitious of public favor.

FINKLEA.—Another family, once numerous and somewhat prominent, but now reduced in numbers to but a few, are the Finkleas; they have been much reduced by emigration. There were two old Finkleas in the early times in the county—John Finklea and "Corn-making Willis." John Finklea, whose wife was a Crawford, with his numerous family, went to Alabama, and died there about 1850. Captain J. C. Finklea, a grand-son, now in Wahee Township, is the only representative of that branch of the family. Of "Corn-making Willis" family, the only remaining ones bearing the name are Hardy Finklea, of Latta,* who has one son, named Willis; and Alfred Finklea, who has three sons, John, Alfred and Hugh; and a son of Thomas Finklea, deceased, named Neill. Upon these depend the perpetuation of the name in the county, and not only the name, but the reputation of it. Captain J. C. Finklea is sixty-three years of age, and has no child or children, and it is not presumable that he ever will have any.

HASELDEN.—Another family to be noticed is the Haselden family. There were three Haselden brothers, John, William and James; don't know which was the older, nor is anything known of their ancestors. John Haselden married Elizabeth Godbold, daughter of old General Thomas Godbold; by this marriage three children were born and raised, Cyrus B. Haselden, Hugh G. Haselden and Jane Haselden; don't know which was the older. John Haselden, the father, died, and the widow

---

*Hardy Finklea, since writing the above, died.

married the late David Monroe, and by her had two sons, Colonel James Monroe, of Confederate fame, and our respected fellow-citizen, Dr. F. M. Monroe, of Latta. Cyrus B. Haselden married Miss Labennon Bass, daughter of the late old Joseph Bass; by this marriage one child was born, and the mother died, and a few months afterwards the child died. The grand-father, Bass, had died before the death of Mrs. Haselden. Thus, by three successive deaths, Cyrus B. Haselden, the husband and father, became the *heres factus,* one of the heirs of the large estate of Joseph Bass, and as such received in property and money from $10,000 to $15,000. There were ten of the Bass heirs, including C. B. Haselden; he soon after married Miss Sallie Finklea, a niece of the writer's wife, and by her he had five children, Lucy, John, Maggie, Fannie and Frank. In the meantime, Cyrus B. Haselden went through with all his property, and whilst his children were all small, the youngest, Frank, about two years old, he took the train one night (not letting his family know anything about it) and left; he went to Arkansas, and has not been seen in this country since. His wife and her children were taken by her mother, Mrs. Margaret Finklea, and the children were raised respectably and in good credit; they all married respectably and all doing well. The other brother, Hugh G. Haselden, volunteered in the Confederate army, and was killed or died in the same; he married, I think, a Miss Foxworth, and had some children, one or two sons, who are among us, but whose name or names is or are unknown. Jane Haselden, a very pretty girl, married, in 1850, Hon. C. D. Evans, of the Marion bar, and has had and raised seven sons and one daughter; they have been noticed hereinbefore in or among the Evans family. Mrs. Jane Evans is now a widow, and an excellent lady she is. Of William Haselden's family, the writer can't say anything; they are, if living, in Darlington, Florence and Williamsburg Counties. Of Major James Haselden and family, the writer can speak with some certainty. Major James Haselden married Mary Godbold, another and the youngest daughter of old General Thomas Godbold; the fruits of the marriage were Charles, Anna, Sarah, Jane, James G. and Maggie—all now dead except Charles and Anna. Charles Haselden married

Miss Julia Ellerbe, and notice of their family has already been taken herein or among the Ellerbe family, not necessary to repeat it; and the same may be said as to Sarah's family, already spoken of among the Ellerbes. Of Jane and her family, notice has already been taken in and among the Berry family. Of James G. Haselden and his family, now here among us—he married Miss Rebecca Dudley, of Marlborough County, an excellent lady; the fruits of the marriage are James Dudley Haselden, Carrie Haselden, Luther M. Haselden and Lawrence Benton Haselden; of these none are married except James Dudley Haselden; he married Miss Mary Edwards, a very nice girl; they live in her patrimonial home, and have two children, sons, named J. Dudley and William E. Haselden, an infant. The grand-father, Major James Haselden, and the son, James G. Haselden, and the grand-son, J. Dudley Haselden, have all been honored by the people of the county with a seat in the State Legislature—the latter, or grand-son, twice. James G. Haselden died at his home on the 20th April, 1900. Major James Haselden died in 1864, at the age of fifty-nine. Major Haselden in many respects was a model man, and excellent farmer, a good neighbor and a very successful man; he was modest and unassuming; a man of fine sense and good humor, of good habits and genteel in demeanor and appearance; he accumulated a large property, wholly unencumbered at his death, and was divided among his heirs without the interposition of any Court; he was greatly missed in his community. The Haselden family are not long-lived. The writer heard Charles Haselden say when he was sixty-nine, that he was the oldest Haselden he ever knew. J. G. Haselden was sixty at the time of his death.

BASS.—The Bass family will be next noticed. The first Bass of which the writer has any information was Joseph Bass; he married a Miss Jones, sister of John Jones, Bryant and Thomas N. Jones. By the older people, her contemporaries, she was spoken of in very high terms as an excellent lady, industrious and frugal, ever looking with a keen eye to the welfare of her household, and with all, and above all, was a pious, good woman—truly a "mother in Israel;" they settled on Catfish, on the road leading from Berry's Cross Roads to Harlleesville, now the property of James Berry, and is yet called the "old Bass place;" they raised a family of sons and daughters; the sons were Joseph, Bryant and Robert, and three or four daughters, names unknown. The old people accumulated a good property for that day and time. Of the sons, Joseph, the oldest, married Miss Massey Crawford, and first settled just below the present town of Latta, on the place now owned by the Widow Thomas J. Bass and her four sons; afterwards he moved to the place where the late Captain James W. Bass lately lived and died. Joseph, the second, raised five sons and six daughters. The sons were James W., Joseph R., Enos, Thomas R. and John C. Bass; the daughters were Elizabeth, Harriet, Laura, Helen, Adarezer and Lebanon. Of the five sons, James W. Bass married late in life Miss Lucy Moody, daughter of the late Barfield Moody; by this marriage they had and raised to be grown, C. G. Bass, Edgar, Robert, George F., T. Leon, Lucius and Rufus. The widow, Lucy, died a few years ago, suddenly. The second son, Joseph R., married Miss Amelia Moody, a daughter of the late Elizabeth Moody, of Buck Swamp, and settled on the land now covered in part by the town of Latta, and died there in 1866, leaving four children, two daughters and two sons— Araminta and Rosa, and Addison L. and Thomas J. Araminta, the oldest, married Hugh Ellis, and lived only a year or two, and died childless. Rosa married our fellow-citizen, David E. Watson, and has already been noticed in or among the Watson family. Addison L. Bass married Miss Ellen Watson, daughter of the late William Watson, resides now at Latta, and has been already noticed in or among the Watson family. Thomas J. Bass, the youngest son, married Miss Hortensia Watson, daughter of the late Matthew Watson, who has already been somewhat noticed herein in or among the Watson family. But his death was so tragic and unusual that I deem it proper in this place to notice it more particularly. He was a juryman in Marion, at a June term of the Court, about fifteen years ago, and was discharged from the Court on Tuesday evening; he went home in perfect health and vigor. On the next afternoon he left home to go to the postoffice, just across

Buck Swamp, at the Bailey Ford, and went a footpath around the plantations next to the swamp, it being a nearer way—a path that I suppose he had traveled five hundred times. He passed by a negro house by the side of the swamp and went to the well and drew some water and drank it; a negro woman saw him at the well. He left the well and went some two or three hundred yards to a point where a pine tree had, years before, fallen and lodged on the limb of another tree, over the path, and as he passed under the lodged tree, it broke loose from its moorings and fell upon him; and he was found that night, on the ground under the fallen tree, which fell upon him and crushed him to instant death. The tree where it struck was more than a foot through and was heavy—don't suppose he knew what struck him. It is supposed that he had walked under that lodged tree perhaps five hundred times. Such a thing would not happen again in perhaps a million of times. Thus was the tragic end of Thomas J. Bass, the youngest son and child of Joseph Bass, the third. He left his widow and four sons, Carl, Tracy, Luther and Thomas, now promising young men. Tracy is now the agent of the railroad at Sellers, S. C. The father was an energetic and persevering man—cut off in middle life. Again recurring to James W. Bass' family, his son, C. G. Bass, a boy scarcely grown at the death of his father, in 1876, took charge of the family and its circumstances; his father was much in debt at the time of his death; he had been the guardian of his infant niece, Helen Bass, who had a good property; she had grown up and married the now Rev. Joel I. Allen, about the time of Captain James W. Bass' death. Captain Bass' widow administered upon his estate. Joel I. Allen called upon the administratrix for a settlement of his guardianship account with his ward, Helen, and which Allen estimated at near $10,000 due his ward—cash received, negro hire, &c. One item in the account was $3,315 cash received at one time from the Commissioner in Equity, in March, 1860, which, with interest, amounted to about $8,000. Allen, not wishing to break up Captain Bass' family, offered to take $3,315, without interest, and receipt in full. The then advisers of the administratrix, not being safe and good advisers, she declined Allen's proposition. He then filed a complaint against her as administratrix and her children for an account of the guardian's transactions, and after two or three years' stiff litigation, a decree was rendered in favor of the ward for about $8,000. Defendant threatened an appeal and neglected to prosecute it till it was too late, submitted to the decree. Allen, then, in the magnanimity of his heart, not desiring to break up and beggar Captain Bass' family, offered to take the $3,315 as at first offered, without interest—notwithstanding the hot litigation and the hundreds paid out in counsel fees, loss of time and so forth, much to Allen's credit. Defendants agreed to pay the compromise. There were other debts of Captain J. W. Bass—one to F. W. Kerchner, of Wilmington, N. C., in judgment, I think, for about $1,400, compromised for $800. C. G. Bass, then hardly grown, took charge of the farm, and by his untiring energy and good management in three years' time paid up the indebtedness of his father's estate, and saved his valuable plantation, lands and other property for his mother, himself and younger brothers. These things are mentioned herein to the everlasting credit of Rev. Joel I. Allen and Cornelius G. Bass. Notwithstanding this sacrifice on the part of these two gentlemen, they both have prospered, and are among our best citizens. C. G. Bass married his cousin, Miss Lula Deer; the result of their marriage is one son, yet a little boy. Enos Bass, the third son of Joseph the second, died a young man, unmarried, before his father. Thomas R. Bass, the fourth son of Joseph the second, grew up and studied medicine, and located in West Marion (now Florence County), on Lynch's River; married a Miss Carter, raised a nice family of sons and daughters, and accumulated a large property, educated his children, was a good citizen and useful man; was a Representative from Marion County in the Legislature of 1870; died some years ago, much respected and largely regretted by his people; his family is scattered—don't know enough about them to particularize. John C. Bass, the fifth and youngest son and child of Joseph the second, born in March, 1835, yet survives, and lives near Latta; he is the only survivor of that large family, male or female; he married, first, Miss Hannah Jane Bethea, daughter of the late Levi Bethea; they lived together for many years, when she died, childless; he married, a second time, a lady whose name is not now remembered; she died at her first accouchement, neither she nor the child surviving; John has not married again—apparently the name will die out or disappear, so far as he, John C. Bass, is concerned. Of the daughters of Joseph the second, the oldest, Elizabeth A., married Rev. S. J. Bethea, his second wife; only one child to live, was the fruit of this marriage, born October 7th, 1857, now the Rev. S. J. Bethea, of the South Carolina Conference of the M. E. Church, South; she was a most excellent woman, died a year or two ago. Harriet, the second daughter, married the late John R. Bethea, 2d February, 1842. The writer was one of the guests at the marriage. The results of this marriage were two daughters, Almira, now the wife of Joseph Allen, of Latta, and Addie, now the wife of Ed. B. Watson; and five sons, Joseph J. Bethea, our well known and much respected fellow-citizen of Latta, who married his distant cousin, Carrie Bethea; they have no children. Lewis S. Bethea, whose first wife was a Miss McPherson, of West Marion, and who died some years ago, leaving five or six children; Lewis married, a second time, Miss Roberta Floyd, a daughter of Mrs. Zilpha Floyd, near Campbell's Bridge; there are two or three children from this last marriage. Harris C. Bethea, a third son, became a Methodist traveling preacher, and after traveling for several years, by some means or other, unknown to the writer, he quit the Methodist Church and ministry, joined the Baptist Church, and became and is now a minister in that denomination; he married some lady in Sumter County, and there now resides; know nothing of his family. Another son, Walter E. Bethea, now a citizen of Latta, married a Miss Rouse, of Williamsburg County, an excellent woman; they have no children. Thomas C., the fifth and youngest son of the late John R. Bethea, sickened and died when about twenty-one years of age. Laura Bass, the third daughter of Joseph the second, married her first cousin, David S. Bass; she had and left one child only, Helen, when she died; that child from early girlhood was raised by her guardian, Captain James W. Bass, and became the first wife of Rev. Joel I. Allen, as hereinabove mentioned; she left five children. David S. Bass afterwards married a Miss Powers, and went off to Georgetown County; know nothing further of him. Helen Bass, the fourth daughter of Joseph the second, married W. H. Smith, of Buck Swamp; by him she had two children, daughters, and then died; those daughters grew up, and one married Lawrence Sessions; they raised a considerable family, now young people among us, quite respectable; the other married a Mr. Moody, son of the late Hugh Moody, whose name the writer has forgotten; know nothing further of them. Adarezer, the fifth daughter of Joseph Bass the second, married her first cousin, James E. Coxe, of Marlborough, and raised a family of four children, two sons and two daughters; Mrs. Coxe died in the spring of 1900; they being in Marlborough, the writer can trace the family no further. Lebanon Bass, the sixth and youngest daughter of Joseph the second, married Cyrus B. Haselden, as hereinbefore stated in and among the Haselden family, to which reference is made. Joseph Bass the second, notwithstanding his large family of eleven children, all raised to be grown, by his energy and frugality amassed a large fortune for his day and time; he died intestate, in 1854; his estate was valued at $150,000, unencumbered; his wife, Massey, preceded him to the grave, in December, 1846. The Bass family, back to Joseph the first, including all the descendants, as far as known, have been noted for their large hospitality. Joseph the second, gave away more at his table in one year than some of his equally well-to-do neighbors did in a whole lifetime; he and all his sons were close and tight on a trade, exacting to the last cent; but go to their homes, and their hospitality was most lavish. Of the eleven children, John C. Bass, now sixty-five years old, only survives. Of the other sons of Joseph the first, Bryant Bass married Miss Jane Rogers, daughter of old Eli Rogers; by her he had five children, three sons and two daughters, and died before reaching middle life, well-to-do and prosperous. Of his sons, David S. has already been spoken of; the other two sons, William and Robert, emigrated West in early manhood; know nothing further of them. Of the two daughters, Louisa and Anna, the former married John S. Page, who died in first of the war, as already noticed in or among the Page family; he left some sons and two daughters; one of the sons, William, was killed in Sheriff Berry's *posse*, twenty-five or thirty years ago, as already stated; think another son or two went to parts unknown. One daughter married Joseph Smith, from whom she was divorced in the seventies, while that law was in force; don't know where she is or what has become of her. The other daughter of John S. Page and wife married C. J. McColl, now of Mullins, a prosperous man and good citizen; has been a cotton buyer for years and is still thus engaged; they have a family of children to the writer unknown. Robert Bass, the third son of Joseph the first, married Miss Mahala Deer; by her he had four children, one son and three daughters; he died when quite a young man; like his brothers, he was prospering at the time of his death; the widow married again; don't remember to whom; they removed West in the forties; know nothing of them since. Of the daughters of Joseph the first, one married old Daniel Platt, who died in 1839 or '40; she was the progenitress of all the Platts in the county, from that time until now, and there have been many and their connections, yet the name Platt is now extinct in the county, except R. B. Platt and children of Mullins. Another daughter, Nancy, married a Mr. Coxe, of Marlborough; Coxe died, leaving her a widow, well-to-do, with three sons, Edwin, James and Robert; the eldest and youngest both died unmarried; Robert was a doctor; James Coxe is still living, a well-to-do citizen and highly respectable. Another daughter of old Joseph the first, Dicey, married a Tart, whose name is now forgotten; they went West. Recurring to the children of Bryant Bass: his youngest daughter, Anna, married Samuel Smith, son of old Samuel Smith, on Buck Swamp; she is still living, and has raised several children, daughters and sons; one the wife of Dr. Connelly; one the wife of R. B. McLean, of Dillon—McLean married two of them; she has three sons, young men, unknown to the writer. Bryant Bass' widow married Salathiel Moody, and by him had two children, a son and a daughter; the son was idiotic and died; the daughter grew up, and married Mack Martin; think they went West—at any rate, have lost sight of them. Recurring to the family of Captain James W. Bass; his second son, Edgar, married, a few years ago, a Miss McIntyre, of Carmichael Township, and immediately left for Georgia; it was said that at the time of their marriage their joint weight, avoirdupois, was over 500 pounds. The third son of Captain J. W. Bass, Robert A., is a physician; married his first cousin, a daughter of Robert Moody, of Richmond, Va.; resides at Latta, and has two or three children; George F. and Lucius Bass, sons of Captain J. W. Bass, have gone from the county, and can say nothing about them. T. Leon Bass married Miss Beulah McColl;* has only one child, a son, resides at Dillon, is a dispenser of liquor, under the law, and is also merchandising; he is apparently doing well; sober and a very pleasant gentleman and highly respectable, except so far as the odium which attaches to liquor sellers affects him.

HAMER.—The next family to be noticed is the Hamer family. So far as Marion County is concerned, the Hamer family is an importation from Marlborough County. The late Robert C. Hamer, son of John Hamer and wife, Mary (Polly), of Marlborough, married, in 1830, Mary (Polly) Bethea, daughter of Tristram Bethea, in this (Marion) County, and settled on the road leading from Harlleesville to Rockingham, about five miles above Harlleesville, where he resided till his death, February, 1878 or 1879; by the marriage he raised three children to be grown; Elizabeth Ann, John H. and Robert P. Hamer; he had another son, named Tristram, who when about grown sickened and died; his wife died when Robert P. was quite a child; the father never married again, but remained a widower until his death; a maiden sister of his kept house for him, and looked after his children. His daughter, Elizabeth Ann (Betsey Ann, as she was called,) married a Mr. Thompson, of Robeson County, N. C.—think his name was John; he died and left his widow with three children, one daughter and two sons. The daughter (Mollie, I believe,) married her cousin, L. D. Hamer, of Marlborough; of the two sons, John C. Thompson married a Miss Smith, of Alabama; the other son, Tristram Thompson, married Miss Flora Bethea—daughter of Dr. J. F. Bethea; by this marriage two sons were born, Frank and Tristram; their father died six or eight years ago, with measles, or rather a relapse of that disease; his widow moved to Dillon,

---

*She is now dead.

and she died suddenly some two years ago, leaving her two boys surviving; their grand-father, Dr. J. F. Bethea, took them to his home, where they now are. The widow, Elizabeth A. Thompson, married Lemuel Thompson, a cousin of her first husband; by this, her second marriage, she had and raised three children, two daughters, Mary and Charlotte (Lottie), and one son, Robert. Mary is the wife of Adolphus Stackhouse, now a resident citizen of Sumter County. Charlotte married Dr. P. N. Timmerman, of Edgefield or Bamberg County, but now a resident citizen of Marion County. Lemuel Thompson, a most worthy man and quiet, unpretending citizen, died about a year ago, leaving "Betsey Ann" a widow for a second time. Her son, Robert Thompson, married a Miss Woodley, of Marlborough, and is among our best and most progressive citizens, a young man of promise. John H. Hamer, the oldest son of old Robert C., married, first, Miss Missouri Bethea, daughter of the late William S. Bethea; she died in a year or two, leaving an infant son, Missouri Robert, now one of our best citizens, a graduate of the University of North Carolina, and who married a Miss Townsend, of Robeson; they have only one child, a son, named John David, for his two grand-fathers, John H. Hamer and David Townsend. After the death of his first wife, John H. Hamer married Miss Alice Richardson, daughter of the late Wm. F. Richardson, below Marion; by this marriage he had five children, three sons and two daughters; the sons are Edward R., Tristram and John H.; the daughters are Mary and Orianna. Of the sons, Edward R. married Miss Julia Berry, daughter of James Berry; they have several children. Tristram Hamer is a physician, and left the county a few years ago, a single man, and went to Texas, where he still is, as it is said. John H., Jr., is a young man, and still resides with his father. His daughter, Mary, married Neill Berry, one of our progressive citizens, and has three children. Orianna Hamer is the second wife of Lawrence Manning; they have no children. After the death of his Richardson wife, John H. Hamer married the Widow Fannie Lyles, of Anson County, N. C.; she was originally a Fladger, of Marion, a daughter of the late Captain C. J. Fladger. Robert P. Hamer, the youngest son of old Robert

C. Hamer, lives at old Harlleesville, now called Little Rock; he married a Miss McCall, of West Marion, a daughter of old William McCall. Robert P. has raised a large family of ten or twelve children, sons and daughters; think he has lost a son and a daughter, both grown or about so. His older sons: Robert P. Hamer married a Miss McCollum, daughter of the late Brown McCollum, and lives at Hamer, on the "Short-cut" Railroad, and is one of the most thorough-going, progressive men of the county; though a young man, is already a rich man for our section of the country; he has some four or five children. James Hamer, another son of Robert P., married a Miss Breeden, of Marlborough; don't know whether they have any offspring or not. Brooks Hamer, another son of Robert P., married a Miss Bennett, daughter of John Bennett, in upper Marion; don't know whether they have any children or not. William M. Hamer, another son of Robert P., yet single, is quite prominent in business circles, is reputed to have made money, and very clear-headed in business—a promising young man. A daughter of R. P. Hamer married T. B. Stackhouse, of Dillon, Cashier of the Bank of Dillon; also has a good farm near by; well qualified for business, a first class business man every way, and stands fair with all who know him; he has one child, a daughter. Robert P. Hamer has other sons and several daughters, unmarried, some grown. Old Robert C. Hamer was a very successful man in life; he accumulated a large property, and left his children in good condition for the battle of life, so far as means are concerned. In his numerous dealings with men he was always prompt and strictly honest, acting "on the plumb and parting on the square;" he was frugal and economical, and made his money by gradual accretions; liberal in his views of life and with his means to every commendable project for the good of his community and advancement of his people. Much more might be said of him, but space will not permit. It is not in good taste to speak of the virtues and good traits of the living, remembering the old adage, "Never speak of one's virtues to his face, nor of his faults behind his back;" but as to this family I will venture one remark: wherever you find a Hamer, phrenologically speaking, you will find the bump denoting acquisitiveness fully developed, strong and prominent; and when it is mixed with old William McCall's family, it adds to its development and strength. Another branch of the Hamer family, imported from Marlborough, is a Widow Hamer and sons, John B. Hamer, Charles Hamer and Jesse Hamer, with a deaf-mute sister, in Kirby Township. John B. Hamer was first imported and married a daughter of Captain Stephen F. Berry; by her he has several children; he lives in Bethea Township. Charles Hamer recently married a daughter of Wilson Berry. Jesse and the mute sister live with their mother. This branch of the family are collaterally related to those in Harlleesville community; they all came from the same common stock, old man John Hamer, of Marlborough, whose wife was a daughter of old Thomas Cochrane, and sister to the writer's mother-in-law, Rachel Bethea. This branch of the Hamer family seems not to have succeeded in life so well as the Harlleesville branch, yet they have many of the same characteristics.

McKenzie.—Another family will here be noticed—the McKenzie family. The first known was old Robert McKenzie; he settled and lived there till he died, near where Dothan Church now stands; don't know who his wife was; he raised a family, some of whom the writer knows nothing of. He had a son named John and one named Asa; he had a daughter named Dilla and one, his youngest child, named Mary (Polly); may have had others, perhaps did have. Old "Bobby," as he was familiarly called, was one of the principal founders of Dothan Church, where first located, and also where it now stands. It was first located on the road from Harlleesville to Mars Bluff, opposite the dwelling of John C. Bethea, and for several years in the first of the nineteenth century camp meetings were held there; the camp ground was above the road leading to Harlleesville, between the cross of the roads and Little Reedy Creek; it was called Bethea Camp Ground; camp meetings were held there as late as 1808 and 1809. The grand-father and father of the writer was there at a camp meeting in August, 1808 or 1809. This the writer got from his father, Jordan Sellers. The circumstances as related were, that they were at camp meeting there and heard that Levin

Sellers, a brother of my father, and traveling preacher of the Methodist Church, had died on Cypress Circuit, in the low country, and my grand-father proposed going down there after his dead son's horse, books, clothing, &c.; that old John Bethea, Robert McKenzie and others dissuaded him, on account of his age and the hot weather, from going, but to send his son, my father, which he did, and my father went accordingly, and got his brother's horse, saddle-bags, &c., and carried them home. This church building was not then called Dothan, was then called Bethea's Church. About 1830, most of the congregation moved to the place now and since called Dothan, and first built a log church. The writer was there at church in 1832, then a lad, and saw old "Bobby McKenzie;" he was a very pious man. Of his sons, John, called "Jackey," married Emery Jackson, a daughter of old Edward Jackson, the first of that name on Catfish. "Jackey" and Emery raised a considerable family, as remembered—Robert, James, Elisha and David J., and several daughters, names not remembered. Jackey died and left Emery a widow, with her children, and who died a very old lady, since the Confederate War. Robert, the oldest son, married a Miss Sallie Kenady, and raised a considerable family, mostly sons, John W., Eli, Allen, Frank and David, and two daughters, Sarah Ann, the name of the other not remembered. John W. McKenzie married, first, a Miss Brigman, daughter of the late Thomas Brigman, who had several children, and died; he married, a second time, I don't know to whom. Eli McKenzie married a Miss Spivey, daughter of Isaac Spivey; think she is dead, leaving several children. Allen McKenzie married another daughter of Isaac Spivey; she died, leaving several children, and he married again, a Miss Jackson, daughter of the late Reuben B. Jackson, who has one child. Frank McKenzie married a Miss Spivey also. David McKenzie married a Miss Allen, daughter of the late Joseph Allen, of Buck Swamp; he and his wife are both dead, leaving some children, don't know how many; the children are cared for by their uncle and guardian, Herod W. Allen. Of the daughters of Robert McKenzie, the oldest, Sarah Ann, married Ervin M. Jackson; she had, perhaps, two children, a son, Thomas Jackson, who now lives in the Dillon community; she died some years ago. The other daughter of Robert McKenzie married Kenneth Hargrove; know nothing more of them. Robert McKenzie and his wife, Sallie, both died some years ago; the sons are all industrious and progressive men, all successful farmers and good managers. Of old "Bobby McKenzie's" other son, Asa, the writer knows nothing; of his daughters, Dilla, married Owen Jackson, a hard-working, honest man; he lived and died on the road from Dothan Church to Harlleesville, on the place now owned and occupied by Missouri Hamer; he raised a considerable family of daughters and one son, Ervin M. His oldest daughter, Elizabeth, never married; two daughters married William T. Jackson, and died childless; another one is the wife of Hugh P. Price, and has no children. I think there were other daughters, not now remembered. His son, Ervin M., married Sarah Ann McKenzie, as already stated. Old "Bobby McKenzie's" youngest daughter, Mary (Polly), married the late David Ellen, of grateful memory; the fruits of this marriage were Ritta, Zimri, Robert M., William B., Wesley, Elijah, Mary Jane and Martha Ann. Ritta married Isaac Price, who many years ago emigrated to Mississippi with his family, and died; I think his widow is still living, and it is said that she and her children are all doing well and are highly respected. Isaac Price (called Peter) was an older brother of Hugh P. Price, of Maple notoriety. Zimri M. Ellen married Miss Margaret Little, a sister of the late Rev. John R. Little; was an industrious, thriving man; he died in November, 1890, childless; his widow, a first-rate, good woman, still survives, and is doing well. Robert M. Ellen married Miss Mary Wilson, of Marlborough, sister of Rev. John B. Wilson, a Presiding Elder now in the South Carolina Conference; Robert M. died some twenty years ago, leaving two or three children; his widow went back to Marlborough; married again—don't know to whom, or what has become of her or her children. Wesley and Elijah Ellen both went into the war, young single men, and both were killed or died. William B. Ellen married Miss Amanda Bethea, daughter of George J. Bethea; he owns the old Ellen homestead at Dothan; has raised a family of five children, three sons and two daughters; he is a hard-working, well-to-do man, and a good citizen in every way; don't know the names of his children, except the oldest son, James; he is married, don't know to whom; he is depot agent and telegraph operator somewhere—I think, on the Central Road, in Clarendon County. Mary Jane did not marry; Martha Ann married William Bundy, of Marlborough; have lost sight of her and Mary Jane—they are somewhere in Marlborough County, near Red Bluff. Mary (Polly) Ellen, first wife of David Ellen, was no ordinary woman for business; she died 14th November, 1854. Old man David married again, 17th September, 1857, the Widow Charles Munship; the fruit of the marriage was and is John H. Ellen, near Dothan, an excellent manager and successful farmer and a first-class citizen; he married a Miss Moody, daughter of the late Richard Moody, of Buck Swamp; has three children, a son now in Wofford College.

MANNING.—Another family now to be noticed is the Manning family. The first known of them was old John Manning; he came from Virginia; married a sister of old Buck Swamp John Bethea, whether before or after his arrival in South Carolina, is not known—perhaps, before he came. Nothing is known of his family or progeny, except one son, whose name was John; who John, Jr., married is not known, but he married some lady and settled where his father lived, on Buck Swamp, where John D. Bethea now lives. It is now remembered that his wife was a Miss Lee, a name now almost extinct in the county. There yet remains James W. Lee and his son, Calvin Lee, fairly good citizens of the county. If there are others of the name in the county, the writer knows not of them. John Manning, Jr., raised a considerable family of sons and only one daughter, Lisha, who became the wife of the late William Roberts, and who has been somewhat noticed in or among the Roberts family. Of the several sons of John, Jr., none will be noticed here except Meely and Woodward, as the others, Ira, James and, I think, one named John, emigrated West. Meely married Miss Mary (Polly) Kinney, of Marlborough, and settled, lived and died in that county. Woodward married a sister of Meely's wife, and first settled on Buck Swamp, but afterwards moved to Marlborough and lived there for years, and then moved back to Marion, and lived on his father's old homestead till he died, some years ago. Meely Manning raised a large family of sons and two daughters; the sons were Eli, Thomas J., William, James, John, Frank, Houston and Holland. These, though born and raised in Marlborough, many of them came back to Marion and became citizens of their mother county. The two daughters were Sarah Jane and Gerona. Eli, the oldest, married Miss Amanda Bethea, a daughter of Tristram Bethea, of Floral College; he settled and lived in Marion County, raised two sons, Thomas B. and Eli. Thomas was a doctor; he practiced medicine some years at Little Rock; he married a Miss Carnes, of Sumter; he emigrated Westward. Eli, a promising young man, went West. Eli Manning was an excellent man and citizen; he died some years ago; think his widow went West with her sons. Thomas J. Manning married Miss Anna Haselden, a daughter of the late Major James Haselden. Thomas J. Manning was killed by the deserters, whom he, with others, was hunting in Donahoe Bay, in the latter part of the war; he left his widow, Anna Manning, and five children, three daughters and two sons, in good condition, so far as the means of life were concerned; the widow managed well, and raised her children quite respectably, and all are married and doing well. Her oldest daughter, Lettie, married Dr. J. H. David, now of Dillon, S. C., an excellent business man and very prosperous; they have five or six children. The next daughter, Mollie, married E. Burke Berry, an excellent citizen and very prosperous man; they have but one child, a son, who bears his father's name, E. Burke, Jr. The youngest daughter, Tommie, married Thomas Wickham Berry, and has four or five children, all daughters; he, too, is doing well and prospering. The eldest son, James H. Manning, a thorough-going business man and progressive farmer, married his cousin, a Miss Ellerbe, daughter of the late Captain W. S. Ellerbe; they have several children, unknown to the writer. The younger son, Lawrence Manning, one of our good citizens and reliable men, married, first, a Miss Malloy, of Chesterfield; she died childless, and he married, a second time, Miss Orianna Hamer, daughter of John H. Hamer; they have no children. Mrs. Ann Manning yet survives, and stays with her son, Lawrence. William Manning married Miss Martha Jane Stackhouse, daughter of the late Wesley Stackhouse, about the beginning of the war, settled in Marion County; he went into the war early, and was killed at second Manassas, 29th or 30th August, 1862; he left one child, a daughter, named Willie; her mother afterwards married her cousin, Milton Stackhouse, of Marlborough—or, rather, they went to Marlborough and still reside there; her daughter, Willie Manning, was well educated, and is now a professor or teacher in some high school or college; has not married; James Manning married a Miss Covington, and lived in Marion for years, and then went back to Marlborough; have lost sight of him and his family. Houston Manning married a daughter of Colonel E. T. Stackhouse, resided in Marion till his death, some years ago; he died in Baltimore under a surgical operation there and then performed on him; he was one of our best citizens; he left his widow, who has since died, and three children, two sons and a daughter. One of the sons, Maurice, recently married Miss Nellie Bethea, daughter of D. McL. Bethea. Austin, the older brother, is yet single; both are promising young men. The daughter, Miss Eva, is yet unmarried, and is a pretty girl. Holland Manning married, first, a Miss Gibson, of Richmond County, N. C., or of Marlborough County, S. C.; he settled and lived in upper Marion until after the death of his wife, by whom he had four or five children; he then married Miss Clara Bethea, daughter of the late Colonel James R. Bethea; since that marriage he has resided on his second wife's place, still retaining his place in upper Marion; he has two children by his second marriage, both daughters; three or four of his first children are married—don't know to whom. Meely Manning's oldest daughter, Sarah Jane, married Captain D. W. Bethea; by this marriage, two sons, Le Roy and D. W. Bethea, Jr., bearing his father's name, were raised. Le Roy, the older one, resides in Marlborough, on his mother's patrimony; D. W., Jr., resides on his father's homestead, in Marion. Sarah Jane, the mother, died more than twenty years ago. Le Roy and D. W. Bethea, Jr., both have families; are good citizens and promising young men. Their father, D. W. Bethea, Sr., married, a second time, a Miss Brunson, of Darlington; no offspring as a result of the marriage; he died a year ago. Of the sons of Meely Manning remaining in Marlborough, are John, who became a Methodist preacher, and Frank Manning, who was a Captain in the war, and has two or three times represented his county in the Legislature. The youngest daughter, Gerona, married a Mr. McLean, has a large family, and resides in Marlborough. Meely Manning amassed a large property, died during the war, negroes were emancipated; his large landed estate was unencumbered; he left his family in good condition.· Woodward Manning left but two children, daughters, Rebecca and Sallie; he had a son, who lived to be grown, named Robert, but who died in early manhood, before the war. Rebecca, his oldest daughter, married, first, Frank Bethea, who died January 2d, 1860, leaving one child, a son, who died soon after his father. The widow married, a second time, Simeon P. McCormac; by him she had three sons. Simeon went to the war and died of measles, and her three boys all died in one week with diphtheria; so far as children were concerned, she was where she started—childless. After the war some time, she married a third time, James McIntyre; by him she had an only son, who is now one of our fellow-citizens. Woodward Manning McIntyre, a large, fine-looking man; he married a Miss Atkinson, of North Carolina, and has one or two children. Rebecca, his mother, still lives, and is an excellent woman. Sallie Manning married John D. Bethea; they live on the old Manning homestead; they have four or five children, don't know whether sons or daughters. Woodward Manning died some years ago, and left his two daughters in comfortable condition; he did not make property like his brother, Meely; they were both harmless, inoffensive men and attended to their own business; for years Woodward drank excessively, but quit entirely a few years before his death.

JONES.—The Jones family will next be noticed. The writer has some difficulty in ascertaining and assigning properly the remote ancestry of the Jones family in Marion County. To the writer three old Jones—John, Bryant and Thomas M. Jones—were known; but Bishop Gregg, in his history, goes further back than the writer's knowledge, and if Bishop Gregg is correct, the father of the three above named was John Jones, a brother of the noted Tory, Captain Joseph Jones, who led the Tory party to the killing of Colonel Kolb, in April, 1781. Time, the great leveler, together with the conduct of our people during the late war, has measurably put an end to the odious distinction between Whig and Tory of the Revolution, and properly so, too. The descendants of many of the Tories of the Revolutionary War are now among our best people, and of highest respectability; and further, many of the soldiers in our late war, descendants of Tories, were as good soldiers as the Confederacy had. I need not specify, because it is generally known and well understood, and hence the term, Tory, as a derisive term, ought to be no longer named. Bishop Gregg says, on page 360: "Accordingly a company of about fifty Tories collected at the place now known as Tart's Mill, six miles above Marion Court House. The leader was Captain Joseph Jones, a native of that neighborhood, &c." This company, led by Joseph Jones as Captain, went over to where Society Hill now stands, and killed Colonel Kolb, plundered and burned his house. In a note to page 361, Gregg says: "John Jones, a brother of the Tory Captain, was seen on the return of the party as they passed old John Bethea's, riding Colonel Kolb's horse and saddle, with a feather-bed tied before him." Bishop Gregg, on page 367, further says: "Captain Jones, the leader, which surprised Colonel Kolb, was a man of some note. He possessed a good property, and was ingenious to a remarkable degree. He is said to have made the first surveyor's compass ever used in Marion District. Notwithstanding his course during the Revolution, he continued to live on Catfish until about 1802, and then removed to Colleton District, where he died not very many years since." It is presumed (in the absence of more definite information) that either Captain Joseph Jones, or his brother, John Jones, was the progenitor of these Jones on Catfish, or the family in question. Rather suppose it was John and not Joseph Jones. The killing of Colonel Kolb in the manner in which it was done, and the plundering of his premises, was most certainly a horrid crime, and a severe blow to the cause of independence in South

Carolina—at least, for a while; but yet we are obliged to admit that it was not without provocation. It was merely retaliatory. Colonel Kolb with his men had just been down on Catfish, in the region of the Jones, and had killed several of the Tories, so that if honors were not even, conduct and conditions were about equal. The writer takes it for granted that one of these Jones was the father to the three brothers, John Jones, Bryant Jones and Thomas M. Jones. John Jones lived on the road leading from Isham Watson's crossing of Catfish to Marion Court House, not more than half a mile from the crossing. The writer stayed all night at his house in 1838, went there in company with the late William Gaddy, a son-in-law of old man Jones. Old man Jones had two sons, John D. and Samuel (if there were other sons, the writer never knew or heard of them). There were two daughters, Sallie and Elizabeth, who married two of the Gaddys, William and James, and have already been noticed among the Gaddy family. John D. Jones married, first, a Miss Avant, below Marion, and settled on the north side of Little Pee Dee, where his son, John Thomas Jones, now resides; he was a local preacher in the Methodist Church, and a most excellent man and manager of affairs; he raised only three children, a daughter, Mary, and two sons, James A. and John Thomas. The two latter went to school to the writer in 1834 and 1835. James A., the older, married a Miss Huggins, a daughter of Solomon Huggins, and by her had several children—one a son, J. O. Jones, a promising and worthy man, the others not known. The father, James A., went into the Confederate War, and was either killed or died in the war; his family are about Nichols. John Thomas Jones married Miss Sallie Nichols, as hereinbefore stated in the notice of the Nichols family; is yet living, a first-rate, practical man and a worthy citizen; he raised a family of six sons and four daughters. The sons are Evander, Eli, Beverly, Kendree, R. Boyd and another, name forgotten, all young men of promise; four of them have families, two unmarried—good people. Of the daughters, one married J. B. Williams, of Nichols; one W. L. Hewit, of Marion; one D. N. Bethea, in upper Marion, and Miss Fannie is unmarried. Taken altogether, there are no better people in the county than they are.

Mary Jones, the daughter of John D. Jones, married John Huggins (familiarly called Jack); they raised several children. He (John Huggins) was a local preacher in the Methodist Church, a capital and good man; he died years ago, suddenly one morning, as he rose from his knees at family prayers; he raised a considerable family, mostly sons, George W., John, Dock and Charles—may have been others. George W. married a Miss Porter, daughter of Rev. John A. Porter; he moved to Georgia some years since; know nothing further of him. Dock Huggins married a Miss Johnson, daughter of the late Hugh R. Johnson; they have a family, names and number unknown—a well-to-do citizen. Don't know to whom John and Charles married, if at all. Know of but two daughters, Zilpha and Miss Louisa, now at Dillon; Zilpha married a man by the name of Blackwell; he and family have gone to parts unknown. A daughter of Blackwell, raised by her aunt, Miss Lou Huggins, married Mr. E. L. Moore, of Dillon. Miss Louisa Huggins, a nice woman, has never married. "Jack" Huggins may have had other sons and daughters, unknown to writer. Old John Jones had another son, Samuel; he emigrated West many years ago. John D. Jones married, a second time, to the Widow Walters; by her he had no children; she survived him—don't know what has become of her. Bryant Jones married, late in life, Elizabeth Berry, daughter of old Henry Berry the first, as hereinbefore stated, and settled down in Wahee on the "Grove" lands; they raised a family of three sons and three daughters. The sons were Henry B. Jones, Frederic D. Jones and James E. Jones; the daughters were Elizabeth, Nancy and Mary (Polly). Henry B., the only survivor of the family, married a Miss Hood, second cousin to him, and lives on his patrimonial estate; he raised a family of six children, two sons and four daughters; the sons are Frank and Charles. Frank married a Miss Sessoms, and has a coming family, is a quiet, good citizen. Charles is unmarried. One daughter, Hattie, married a Mr. Bowen, a son of Dr. Bowen; don't know where they are or what they are doing. The other three daughters are single and with their parents. Frederic D. Jones married the Widow Stephen Berry, whose maiden name was Fama Watson. Fred. D. Jones and his family have already been noticed in or among the Watson family. James E. Jones died some years ago, unmarried. Elizabeth Jones married the late James Watson, and has already been noticed in or among the Watson family. Nancy Jones married William A. Brown; they raised five children, three sons and two daughters. One of the daughters married Calvin Dew; she and her husband are both dead, childless. The other daughter died unmarried, though grown. Of the sons, Edward is a physician and citizen of Latta; he married Miss Victoria Martin; they have some children; don't know how many. John Brown, the second son, married a Miss Turbeville, daughter of our good citizen, Stephen Turbeville. William Brown married a Miss Bowen, daughter of Dr. Bowen, of Florence County, and have several small children. Mary Jones (called Polly) married B. W. Jarnigan, of North Carolina; he lived and died in the neighborhood of his marriage, three or four years ago; his wife also died soon after; they had and raised two children, a son and a daughter—Dr. J. E. Jarnigan and Sarah Ellen. Dr. Jarnigan married Miss Alice Bailey, of Fairfield County; his wife lived several years, and died childless. The Doctor still remains a widower, much to his own disgust and surprise to his friends; he was physician to the State Penitentiary for three or four years, and was Consul to Honduras, appointed by President Cleveland, for two or three years, and was recently elected to represent the county in the State Legislature; has had much experience in affairs and more of observation in his life, and is well equipped for the position he now occupies. His sister, Sarah Ellen, married A. J. Matheson, of Marlborough, who is now a very wealthy man, engaged in mercantile and agricultural pursuits—succeeds in everything he touches, and turns it to gold; they have eight children living, sons and daughters—several of them married. Thomas M. Jones emigrated with his family to Alabama more than fifty years ago. A sister of John and Bryant Jones married old John Blackman, became his second wife. Another sister married Christopher Dew the second, and by him she had two children, Frederic C. and John A. Dew, both dead. Frederic left several children, sons—John Foster, Philip and Christopher; and daughters—don't know; one the wife of James Haselden. John A. Dew married a Miss Hays, daughter of old Levi Hays, but had no children; his widow still survives.

COTTINGHAM.—The Cottingham family will next be noticed. Andrew Cottingham and his brother, Daniel Cottingham, are importations from Marlborough County. Andrew Cottingham was the son of Conner Cottingham, born the 4th January, 1818, as he told the writer himself, and is still active and strong for a man of his age—a first rate citizen; married, I think, a Miss Sinclair; has made a good living; has raised six enterprising and respectable sons, J. C. Cottingham, Daniel C. Cottingham, A. J. Cottingham, Elkanah Cottingham, William Cottingham and A. J. C. Cottingham; most or all of them, except A. J. C., are married or have been married. Elkanah settled and lived in West Marion; his wife died two or three years ago; don't know whether he has remarried or not—think he has several children. Daniel C. Cottingham married a Miss Legette, daughter of the late James B. Legette, and lives in the "Free State" section of the county—a good citizen and is doing well. J. C. Cottingham married a Miss Legette, of Marlborough County; has raised a nice family, doing well; has a son, promising young man, a graduate of Wake Forrest College, N. C. A. J. C. Cottingham lives at Dillon, one of the leading merchants of the town; has made money—enterprising and progressive; he does not marry fast—pays a great deal of attention to ladies, and especially to the younger ones, but never gets to the "sticking point." The Cottinghams are all first class citizens, energetic and progressive, doing their share in the general make-up of the county, so far as the development of the county's resources are concerned. We would like to make other such importations from Marlborough County or elsewhere as the Cottingham family have proven themselves to be. Andrew Cottingham raised one daughter, who married W. J. Carter, of Dillon, a worthy and useful man; they have several children, sons and daughters, and are prosperous. If there are other daughters, the writer does not know them. Daniel Cottingham, a brother of Andrew, is another good citizen of the county, but I don't know enough about them to specify and give them a place herein *seriatim*. One of Daniel

Cottingham's daughters married Henry Berry, a son of Captain Stephen F. Berry. Another is the wife of our progressive fellow-citizen of Latta, John L. Dew; have only one child.

There is another family of Cottinghams, not of recent importation, that must have a place herein. I mean old Yates Cottingham, whose sad end has already been noticed. Yates Cottingham married a sister of old Thomas Harllee; where he came from is not known; his only fault was that he inordinately loved liquor; by his marriage he had a son, Stewart Cottingham; there may have been others—never heard of any others. Old Yates had daughters also—one, at least, the mother of the polite and accommodating barber now at Dillon, Henry Cottingham; don't know who his father was. Stewart Cottingham was a very reliable and very worthy man; don't know who his wife was; he had a son (and, perhaps, others), named Thomas (a Harllee family name), who married and raised a family, unknown to the writer; he died a few years back.

HAMILTON.—Another family to be noticed is the Hamilton family. This is an old family in the county, never noted for being over-pretentious, but plain, honest, hard-working people. As known to the writer, there were two brothers, William and John, in the prime of life a hundred years ago; don't know to whom either of them was married. Of William Hamilton and his family the writer knows more than of John and his family. William Hamilton had two sons, Whittington and William. Whittington married a Miss Herring, by whom he had several sons, John, Arthur, Stephen, Tobias, William Warren and Whittington; and some two or three daughters. Of the sons, John married and raised several children, sons and perhaps daughters; the sons were Allen, Perry, Ira, John H. and Bryant. Allen married a Miss Price, by whom he has a large family of children, how many not known. Perry died unmarried. Ira married a Miss Surls, daughter of A. B. Surls, of Dillon. Bryant is unmarried. Arthur Hamilton married a Miss Hyatt, and by her had only one child, a daughter, now the wife of Talley Martin; know nothing of Martin's family. Stephen Hamilton married and has sons, Dayton V. and William K.; a daughter, the wife of Angus Moore; they all have families. Tobias went to Horry after the war; never married; accumulated a nice property, which went mostly to his brothers and sisters. Dr. William W. Hamilton, now of Marion, married Miss Rebecca J. Fore, daughter of the late Thomas Fore, by whom he has only one child, a son, named Thomas F., now nearing manhood, with a fine prospect for life ahead of him. Whittington Hamilton married his cousin, a daughter of Henry Jackson, and by her has several children, two sons and, perhaps, three daughters. The sons are Whittington, Jr., and Warley. Whittington, Jr., married, but his wife died childless, a year or so ago; Whittington, Jr., is now a widower. Warley married a Miss Waters, and has some two or three children; he resides at Dillon, an energetic and enterprising young man. Whittington Hamilton's daughters—two or three are married, but to whom is not known; has one single one with him. Of old man John Hamilton's family, the writer knows but little; he had two sons, John and Tristram, both are dead. John married a daughter of old man Alexander Henderson, a unique character fifty years ago; by the marriage there are two sons, Jasper and Tristram, two excellent men and good citizens; both married. Who Jasper's wife was is not known. Tristram married Miss Nellie Bethea, a daughter of E. Bethea, of Latta, S. C.; they reside at Dillon; have two or three children, and are doing well. Of the daughters of old John, also of his son John, or of Tristram, I know nothing, and, therefore, can say nothing about them. William Hamilton, a son of old William, married twice; who his first wife was is not known; his last wife was a Miss Moody, a daughter of the late Rev. Hugh Moody; by her he had and left several children; know nothing further of them. Of the daughters of old William, I can only speak of two of them. One married William Jackson, called "Fire-coal Bill;" both are dead. "Fire-coal Bill" had six sons in the war, and all gallant soldiers—Robert, Levi, Owen, Malcolm, others, names not remembered. Another daughter married Elisha McKenzie, and raised a large family, sons and daughters; but of their children the writer is not informed and can say nothing. The Hamilton family, taken as a whole, are good people, taking into consideration their time and environments. They lived on Maple Swamp and its borders, and that region of the county was, up to the war, the "dark corner" of the county—not scarcely civilized. Since the war a new order of things has obtained on Maple, and it is now one of the best sections of the county, a progressive and up-to-date population. The Hamilton family was true to the Confederacy from beginning to the end. "Fire-coal Bill" Jackson had six boys (half Hamilton) in the war, and no better soldiers followed the flag than they. Dr. W. W. Hamilton went into it as a Second Lieutenant and came out as a Captain of his company. Heard one of his comrade Captains say of him, that he (Captain Hamilton) was one of the coolest men he ever saw in battle; that he went on all occasions without hesitation and without trepidation wherever he was ordered, it mattered not how dangerous the position. He is a kind-hearted man and a real gentleman, and is an honor to his name and family; and while saying this, the writer would not disparage others of his family.

BRADDY.—The Braddy family will now be noticed. John Braddy, the first known in the county, married Martha (Patty) Bethea, daughter of John Bethea, and sister to old Tristram and Cade Bethea; he raised a considerable family of sons and daughters. The sons were John B., Luton C., Tristram B., William W. and Robert B. Braddy, and of these, Robert B. alone survives;* the daughters were Elizabeth, Harriet and Kittie. John B. Braddy married Miss Mary Crawford, a lovely girl, raised by Hugh Godbold, a niece of his wife, Rhoda; they remained a few years in Marion and then went to Alabama; had two children when they left. Braddy and wife are both dead. Luton C. Braddy grew up and studied medicine and located near Holmesville, on the North Carolina line; he was a young man of fine presence and promise, a picture of health, robust and strong; he took brain fever and died therefrom in three or four days, unmarried. T. B. Braddy married, first, a Miss McKinnon, of Robeson County, N. C., and by her had three sons, Daniel McK. Braddy, Luton C. Braddy and Adolphus Braddy, and a daughter, Alice Braddy,

---

*Now dead.

when his wife died; and he married, a second time, Miss Anne Nichols, a daughter of old Averitt Nichols, and by her he had one son, Oscar, who has already been mentioned among the Nichols family. T. B. Braddy was shot and killed by D. W. McLaurin, in November, 1881. McLaurin was tried for it on the charge of murder, and was acquitted. As the writer was employed by the sons of Braddy to assist the Solicitor (Dargan) in the prosecution of the case, he will forbear saying anything further of the homicide. Daniel McK. Braddy married, and they have now only one child, a daughter. Luton C. Braddy married, and has several children, all girls but one, Adolphus Braddy, who died suddenly some few years ago, unmarried. The daughter of T. B. Braddy, Miss Alice, is still unmarried. Daniel McK. and Luton C. Braddy are excellent and good citizens, energetic and prosperous. William W. Braddy, a fine specimen of the physical man, married Miss Lizzie Evans, a daughter of the late Nathan Evans, by whom he had several children, sons and daughters. Walker Braddy, his oldest daughter, married J. W. Davis, of Marion; they emigrated to Alabama, where she died, leaving some children. William, his oldest son, died about the time of his majority, unmarried. Another son, Robert, died when a lad. His daughter, Susan, married J. T. Coleman, a professor in the Citadel Academy, in Charleston; they reside there, and have one son, named Walker. His youngest, a son, named Wightman, two weeks old at his father's death, is a young single man in Charleston, and belongs to the "Grip-sack Brigade" of commercial travelers, and, I suppose, is doing fairly well; his mother still survives. W. W. Braddy was elected Clerk of the Court in 1868, and held that position at the time of his death, November 29th, 1872. S. G. Owens had been elected as his successor in office, but had not qualified and entered upon the duties of the office at the time of Braddy's death, but did so in a short time afterwards. Horace Greeley died the same day that Braddy did, 29th November, 1872. R. B. Braddy, the youngest child and son of old John Braddy, still lives; he married, first, a Miss McKay; she had one child for him, a daughter, and then died. After some years he married again, a Miss Wishart, of North Carolina; they had five or six children, sons and daughters. The oldest daughter married a Mr. McQueen, of Horry, where they now reside. Another daughter, named Hattie, married to some one not now known. His youngest daughter was an infant when her mother died; she was taken by Mrs. J. R. N. Tenhet, of Marion, and raised; is now a young lady, and instead of taking her true name, Braddy, she takes the name of Tenhet—Miss Ethel Tenhet, so her name appears in the Columbia College catalogue, where she graduated. His sons, Edgar and Otho, and another, have left the county and perhaps the State, all unmarried. The old gentleman moves about among his children. His daughter by his first wife married some gentleman in North Carolina; saw her father a few weeks ago coming up from Marion on the train, he and his son, Edgar, were on their way to see her in North Carolina. The eldest daughter of old John Braddy, Elizabeth, married Mr. Jefferson Williams, of Marlborough, in February, 1830; by this marriage several children were born; only one, Benjamin, now survives; he formerly lived in Marion, a merchant, failed; he went to Sumter County, and there married a Miss McFadden, an only child of her parents; he resides in Sumter, on the patrimony of his wife, and is said to be succeeding well. "Ben," as he was called, had a good deal of the "get-up" in him, and was an honorable boy. The second daughter of old John Braddy, Harriet, was a very pretty girl, very popular, but did not marry young; she finally married Nathan Evans, a widower, below Marion, and lived and died there, where B. F. Davis now resides; by her marriage she had four children, two sons, Julius and Lawrence, and two daughters, Martha (Patty) and Fannie; she died about 1879, with cancer. Her oldest daughter married Richard Jordan, of Horry, a first-rate business man; he merchandised several years with his brother-in-law, Julius Evans, as a partner; they finally failed, and each at different times went to Georgia or Florida. It is said that Jordan has succeeded well in his new home, and has raised a nice family, mostly girls; two of them were here on a visit to their uncle, Captain W. B. Evans, in 1899; they were fine looking. Julius Evans married and went to Florida, and is said to be doing well; one of his daughters, Miss Edna, was also on a visit to her uncle, Captain

Evans, in the summer of 1900, on her way home from Winthrop College. Lawrence Evans, the second son of Harriet Evans, *nee* Braddy, married in Horry, don't know what has become of him. The younger daughter, Fannie, went out to Georgia with her sister, Mrs. Jordan, and married some one out there; have lost sight of her. The Braddys, as a family, were very ardent in their disposition and attachments, and were very good citizens, and self-asserting.

CLARK.—Another family to be noticed is the Clark family, Malcolm and Kenneth, two brothers, citizens on Little Pee Dee, near where the town of Dillon now is. The writer can trace them no further back than themselves; but is satisfied they were of Scotch origin; they both had and raised families. Malcolm married a Miss McCollum, of Robeson County, N. C., about 1839 or 1840, a very excellent lady, a sister of the late Brown McCollum's father; don't know how many children they had—think there were three sons and two daughters—Martin Luther, John Calvin and Robert Knox Clark. The two daughters (names not known), one married the Rev. Duncan McDuffie; she died, leaving some children; one son, named Archie. Duncan McDuffie married again, and now lives in Florence County; has been School Commissioner of that county; a worthy, good man. The other daughter of old Malcolm married a Mr. Gasque, from about Marion, who died in a few weeks after his marriage; his widow had a posthumous son, named Robert K. Gasque; don't know what has become of either him or his mother. Of the sons of old Malcolm, Martin Luther died when about grown, unmarried. John Calvin was a Lieutenant in the Confederate War, and was in command of his company in some battles in Virginia, and was killed in front of his command, calling out to his men, "Come on, come on," not go on; he was one of the many brave men from Marion in that eventful struggle, made by the South for Southern independence. John Calvin Clark, when a boy at school at Hofwyl Academy, was considered by his school comrades, or some of them, at least, as a coward, and was so branded; yet he was anything else but cowardly when duty required the exercise of true courage; his courage was not of the school-boy sort or the muster field kind; but was true courage—the courage to do right, the courage to do his duty, however dangerous the position might be. Robert Knox Clark, late Clerk of the Court, was the second son of old man Malcolm, well known to many now living; he, too, was not a coward, either in war or in peace; he married Miss Nannie Stackhouse, daughter of the late Wesley Stackhouse; by the marriage they had three sons and four daughters. The sons were Martin Luther, Robert Knox and John Calvin—the same names that his father, old Malcolm, gave to his sons. The four daughters were Dora, Eliza, Lilly and Nannie, the latter about two years old when her father died, in 1888. Martin Luther Clark, the oldest son, is now at Marion, editor of the "Marion Star" newspaper. The next two sons, Robert K. and John Calvin, the writer has lost sight of; don't know what has become of them. Of the oldest, Dora, has never married. Eliza, the second daughter, married the Hon. William A. Brown, below Marion, and has several children. Lilly, the third daughter, married a Dr. Smith, son of Dr. E. B. Smith, below Marion; don't know the results of the marriage. John Calvin, the youngest son, and Nannie, the youngest daughter, are barely grown. It is due to the memory of the late R. K. Clark to say that at the age of seventeen, he volunteered and went into the army in Captain C. J. Fladger's company, and in January, 1863, was transferred to the Arsenal Academy, in Columbia; remained there that year and in January, 1864, was transferred to the Citadel, in Charleston, and remained there during the year 1864, and was then transferred back to the army, where he remained till about the end of the war, when he came home and undertook to avenge his father's death— who was killed by deserters on 12th March, 1865—which he in great part succeeded in doing. It was after this he was married. In 1876, he was elected Clerk of the Court, which position he filled with credit to himself, for four years; he was then appointed County Treasurer, which position he held for one or two years, and resigned, and retired upon his farm, where he lived till 1888, and died thereon; he was likewise a man of true courage; he had the courage to say no, which every man does not possess. The old man, Malcolm, died game. He was passing up the road from Marion, on Sunday after Sherman's "bummers" had passed through the upper end of the county, 12th March, 1865, and came upon a crowd of deserters, who were cooking in Samuel Page's lane, near where J. R. Reaves now lives. The old man had his gun, and on approaching the crowd cooking, and recognizing who they were, one of them, the leader, said to him, "Old man, put down your gun and surrender." He did neither, but fired in among them; the one he aimed at jumped behind his horse, and Clark's load entered the horse, and killed him; whereupon others of the crowd seized their guns and fired upon the old man and killed him. The deserters left him and the dead horse there in the road, and they lay there two days before they were removed. The few old men then in the community were terrorized by Sherman's bummers and the emboldened deserters to such an extent that they were afraid to remove old man Clark and the dead horse out of the road, and give the old man a burial. The circumstances of the killing were told, afterwards, by one of the deserters to a friend, and that friend informed the writer. Kenneth Clark, a brother of old Malcolm, was a first-rate man and good citizen; don't know whom he married; he had a son, John Clark, and one or more daughters; the old gentleman is dead. His son, John, is on the old homestead, a first-class citizen, a good soldier in the war, has never married; is prosperous and quite respectable, drives a fine horse and a fine buggy, is fully able to take care of some man's daughter as a wife, but does not seem to have much fancy for such a life. Old man Kenneth Clark was also a brave man—could here relate an incident in his life in proof of his courage, but space will not permit. Those who knew him will indorse him, not as a coward, but as a brave man.

There is another Clark, Pinckney Clark, two or three miles east of Marion; don't know anything of his parentage, or where he came from; he has a family, think grown and married, sons and perhaps daughters; he is obscure, makes no noise in the world, inoffensive and works for his living. His family, now poor and obscure, may in the future develop into prominence—who can tell! The writer could name parents within his day, who were as obscure as Pink Clark's family, whose children are now prominent citizens among us. Such developments often occur. It also happens that those prominent in the present, go down into obscurity and dwindle away in the second and third generation—"There is a providence that shapes our ends, rough-hew them as we may."

HARRELSON.—Another family now to be noticed is the Harrelson family. Of this family, on Buck Swamp and Maiden Down, the writer cannot say much, for the want of information; he cannot trace them genealogically. They are somewhat numerous in name and in their connections, and in former times more prominent than they now seem to be. In 1798, Lewis Harrelson and John Ford were elected as Representatives of Liberty County (now Marion) in the State Legislature. (Gregg's History, page 459.) Also, in the Acts of the Legislature of 1798 (section 7, p. 289,) we find Commissioners appointed "for the purpose of fixing on a convenient and central situation, whereon to establish and build a court house and gaol for the District of Marion and to superintend the building of the same;" and among them we find the name of Benjamin Harrelson; and it may be supposed that he and Lewis Harrelson, the member of the Legislature that year from Liberty or Marion, were brothers, and it is to be presumed that the best men were selected for the Legislature and for locating and building the court house and gaol for the county. Hence the Harrelson family of that day was prominent and among the first people of the county. From these two Harrelsons, and, perhaps, others of the family whose names have not been preserved in the records of the times, have descended all the Harrelsons of the county from that time to the peesent. The writer only wishes that he could trace them down to the present generation. The writer remembers that in July, 1835, he ate supper one night at the house of an old man, Hugh Harrelson (I believe, was his name), where the Widow Lewis Harrelson now resides, near the lowest bridge on Buck Swamp; he had daughters grown. The writer could tell why he was there and who went there with him, and the circumstances of the occasion, and what happened in that family two or three years afterwards, in connection with one who went there with him, but all that is not necessary in a book of this kind. The writer was then only seventeen years of age. These old Harrelsons were men of high character and stood well among their people, and from them descended the large family with their connections, which now inhabit the county. Although those of the present day may not be as prominent as their ancestors, yet all the way through, they have been law-abiding, industrious and honest people, part of the bone and sinew of the county. The late Lewis Harrelson, near Miller's Church, married Miss Mahala Rogers, and by her had six or seven children, sons and daughters, all minors at his death. The oldest son, Charles, is quite a promising young man; the names of the others not remembered; they are soon to take their places in society. The late Lewis Harrelson had a brother, John Harrelson, who died or was killed in the war; he left two daughters, both married and have families; their names not remembered. Lewis and John Harrelson had a sister, Mary Jane, who married our capital citizen, W. T. Cribb; she died a few years ago, childless. There are other Harrelsons in the county, collaterally related. George Harrelson, near Mullins, is an exceptionally good man, and is doing well. Another branch of the family is on the Back Swamp, above Ariel. Old man Hugh Harrelson, down there, was a well-to-do man; married a Miss Smith, of Horry, and raised a family of five sons and five daughters. John E., Hugh G., David J., Samuel and another not now remembered; the daughters were Mrs. William J. Atkinson, Mrs. James Atkinson, Mrs. Prudence Johnson, Mrs. John D. Sessions, and Miss Theresa, who died unmarried before her father. The old gentleman left a last will and testament and, by means which it is not necessary to state, it got into the Courts, and it was in some form or another in the Circuit and Supreme Courts of the State for twelve or fourteen years. This is stated from the personal knowledge of the writer, as he had to do with the litigation from start to finish. Of the old man Hugh Harrelson's sons, Hugh G. married, I think, a Miss Williamson, and died young, leaving his widow and some children; don't know what has become of them. John Ellis Harrelson married, and raised a large family of children, sons and daughters, who are among our citizens now; some unknown, but those that are known are good men and prospering. Ham Harrelson, a son, is one of the leading citizens of his community. John E. Harrelson died about two years ago; he was an energetic and persevering man, and substantially a good citizen. The other sons of old Hugh Harrelson all died unmarried and childless. It is assumed that these Back Swamp Harrelsons are of the same family as the Buck Swamp Harrelsons; that they are all collaterally related; that they all had the same common ancestor. Lewis, Hugh and Benjamin seem to be family names from the early times down to the present; that events and circumstances separated them, though not far apart, in the same county. In the absence of other and better information, the writer is bound to assume that they are all of the same family originally, and sprang from a common ancestor in the first settlement of this part of the State, Marion County. At all events, they are here and have been from time immemorial, and have been and are quite respectable. Another branch of the same family are those on the north side of Little Pee Dee River. They are certainly of the same family as those on Buck Swamp and Maiden Down. Zephaniah and Stephen Harrelson, two old men, resided on Bear Swamp and Cainey Branch, near the Gaddy Mills, sixty-five or seventy years ago. Stephen Harrelson raised a large family of sons, nine or ten, who are among us now, and are respectable, good citizens; don't know the names of all of them, but name such as are remembered—John R., Alfred H., James W., Joel and Hugh only are remembered; another one is a Baptist preacher. Of these, Alfred H. Harrelson married a daughter of William Roberts, and has a family of sons and daughters; he is an industrious and prosperous man and a law-abiding citizen. James W. lives near Mullins, is also a quiet and worthy citizen. John R. (called Jack) raised a considerable family, died years ago. One of his daughters was the second wife of Dr. George E. Shooter; another is the wife of John Altman. Joel Harrelson has raised a family, is a progressive, good citizen, and is well to do; don't know to whom he married. They were all good soldiers in the war, did their duty there and are doing the same now, in time of peace. Don't know anything of old man Zephaniah Harrelson's progeny; he died many years ago, a respectable, good man in his day; don't think he had many children. A daughter of Stephen H. married Neill B. McQueen; is now a widow; she is an extra smart woman, if alive yet.

MARTIN.—Another family will here be noticed, to wit: the Martin family. This family is somewhat extensive, both in name and its connections. The first Martin in the county, of which the writer has any knowledge or information was Matthew Martin; have not been able to learn who his wife was. He lived in the Maiden Down section, and raised a family of four sons and two daughters, and, perhaps, other daughters, to the writer unknown; he was a thrifty man, and accumulated a good property as a farmer for his day and time. His sons were John, Matthew, Stephen H. and Aaron; daughters' names unknown. John Martin married a Miss Hays, daughter of old man Benjamin Hays, on north side of Little Pee Dee; by her he had and raised a family, how many is unknown. He had a son, Alexander Martin, now in Horry County; he married a Miss Cribb, daughter of Anthony Cribb; he went years ago to Horry County, raised a family and they are in that county. John Martin had some daughters. One married Dempsey Cribb, Jr.; another married a Mr. Baker, and another married a Mr. Lovet; know nothing further of them. John Martin died before the war, freezed to death. Matthew Martin, Jr., married a daughter of Captain John Rogers, in the Fork; by this marriage he had and raised four daughters, names not known. One married Jesse Butler, who moved to Darlington, and is dead; he had a family of several children—one son, named Charles; suppose they are all in Darlington now. Another daughter married E. W. Hays, of Hillsboro, and is now a widow; she has some children. Another daughter married R. B. Platt; she is dead; think she left some three or four children. Another daughter married a Mr. Nicholson (Archie); they are raising a family, prospering and doing well. Aaron Martin, the youngest son of old Matthew, Sr., married a daughter of Captain John Rogers, in the Fork; they are now both dead, but left a family of two sons and seven daughters; the sons were Mitchel M. Martin and Valentine Martin.

Mitchell married Miss Lizzie Smith, daughter of the late Stephen Smith; the fruits of the marriage are four sons—Vance, Victor, Clyde and Mitchell. Of these, Vance married Miss Florence Owen, daughter of the late Rev. John Owen, who was accidentally shot and killed a few weeks ago; they have two children, a son and a daughter. Victor Martin lately married a Miss Pepper, of Southport, N. C. The two younger boys, Clyde and Mitchell, are with their mother. Mitchell Martin died some years ago, at Mullins, S. C., where his widow now resides. Valentine Martin, the youngest son of Mr. Aaron Martin, married Miss Margaret Norton, daughter of the late John Norton; to this marriage twelve children have been born, ten of whom are living—seven daughters and three sons. One son, Donald, is grown; and five daughters, Lilly, Pensy, Maggie, Kate and May; the other names not known. Of the daughters of Aaron Martin, the eldest, Anne, married her first cousin, Richard Edwards, a notice of whom has already been taken in or among the Edwards family. The second daughter, Louisa, married W. H. Daniel, of Mullins; for him she had three children—one son, Robert, and two daughters, Katie and Mary. Katie married George Reaves, and has two or three children. Robert Daniel married Minnie Bethea, a daughter of Dr. John J. Bethea, who died childless, and Robert is now a widower. Mary Daniel, the youngest, died in early womanhood, unmarried—quite a charming young lady. Katie Martin married Perry J. Williams, of Nichols, S. C.; by him she had two or three children, when the father died and left her a widow; she afterwards married and went off to Georgia. Emma Martin, another daughter of Aaron Martin, married J. Oscar Daniel, of Mullins, by whom she had several children, when he died; she afterwards married William Leith; whether there was any offspring by the Leith marriage, the writer does not know; she died, and Leith, after a time went off West; don't know what became of her children by Oscar Daniel. Ida Martin married B. F. Elliott, of Marion, and by this marriage a daughter and a son were born. The daughter is very promising, and is now in the Salem, N. C., Female School. The son is a mere boy; name not known. Victoria Martin married Dr. Edward Brown, now of Latta, S. C.; by this marriage three sons and one daughter are born, all yet children. Mary Martin married a Mr. Cole, from North Carolina; they left immediately for Georgia; don't know anything further of them. Stephen H. Martin, a brother of John, Matthew and Aaron Martin, not mentioned in the order of their ages, married a daughter of the late David S. Edwards, and by her had several children, and then died. Two of his sons, "Mack" Martin and David Martin, grew up, and "Mack" married Miss Josephine Moody, a daughter of the late Salathiel Moody; they had some family, how many is not known—a son, named Robert, who was rather an extra keen and sensible young man. The family went West some years ago, and it is said are doing well in that region. David Martin went West also; have heard nothing of him since. Stephen H. Martin had a daughter, named Sue, who married Perry J. Williams, of Nichols (first wife); she had some three or four children, and died very suddenly, without any apparent cause. "Mack" Martin, her brother, became the guardian of her children, and took them and raised them; the oldest, a daughter, Maggie, became the wife of Benjamin M. Carmichael; they are raising a family. "Mack" Martin, their guardian and uncle, managed in some way to turn the boys, three (I think), and their means over to Carmichael and wife, and went West; after this Carmichael and wife have had charge of them. The writer has understood that two of the boys are graduates of Wofford College, or if they did not graduate they matriculated in that college, and went for a while, perhaps, two years or more. Hope they will do well, as they were orphans, indeed. Two daughters of Matthew Martin, Sr., are only known of; don't know their names. One married the late Samuel Edwards, and the other married his nephew, Captain L. M. Edwards; both of whom have herein already been noticed in or among the Edwards family. The Martin family thus far noticed are an unpretending people, hard-working, honest, good citizens, satisfied with themselves, regardless of what others might think or say. Matthew, Jr., and Aaron married sisters, good women, and by industry and frugality accumulated a good property, and left it unencumbered for their children.

There are other Martins in the same section of the county,

and the writer's information is (whether true or not) that they are no relation to those above mentioned; some of them I know nothing about, and, therefore, can say nothing concerning them. The late William Martin married, first, a daughter of the late Rev. Moses Coleman—a mighty good woman, as it is said; she had for him several children; don't know how many. The sons, Daniel, William P. and Charles Betts Martin, now among our good citizens, and doing well. Daniel Martin married a Widow Chreitzberg, whose maiden name was Game, a daughter of our excellent man and fellow-citizen, Robert B. Game; they have no children. Daniel is a hard worker, a good man, and is doing well. William P. Martin, another brother, is and has been for several years in the railroad service as section master at and near Mullins; has made some money and saves it; he married a Miss Rushing, the daughter of Henry Rushing, also a railroad man; they have, as I am informed, several children, whether sons or daughters the writer does not know. Charles Betts Martin, another brother, is one of our citizens, but whether married or not is not known. Their father, William Martin, married a second time, but to whom is not known; he died a year or so ago, and left a widow with children, about whom the writer knows nothing. William Martin had by his first wife a daughter (may have had more), named Julia; she married Joseph M. Price, a nephew of the writer; think they have five or six children, sons and daughters. Price is now above Columbia in the railroad service as section master. There are other Martins in the community that the writer would like to notice, but for the want of knowledge or information he cannot do so. The Martins and their connections are very numerous, and many of them quite respectable.

HENRY.—Another now to be noticed is that of our respected fellow-citizen, John E. Henry. This family is not very extensive in name or connections. The grand-father of John E. Henry was named John; I suppose he lived at Marion; he married some lady, I think, a Miss Dudley, sister of the late Colonel Dudley, a prominent member of the bar for years at Bennettsville, S. C.; by the marriage two children were born—

a son, the late David S. Henry, and a daughter, whose name I have forgotten. The father died, and the late Addison L. Scarborough married the Widow Henry, and for him she had two children—a son and a daughter—Richard and Mary F. Richard Scarborough became a doctor, married a Miss Crawford or Cherry; died a young man, childless, and his widow afterwards married the late Major O. P. Wheeler; both are dead and left no child. Mary Scarborough married the late James J. Harllee, a member of the Marion bar, but did not practice much after his marriage—devoted himself mainly to his large farm near Marion, which his wife inherited from her father, A. L. Scarborough. In 1861, J. J. Harllee and wife sold their plantation, near Marion, now owned by the daughters of the late Fred. D. Jones, and took their negroes and money, &c., and emigrated to Arkadelphia, Ark., where they remained, I suppose, during the war. J. J. Harllee was killed about that time, as it was said, by a horse running away with him; his widow, Mary F., was left poor by the war and by other causes—extravagance mainly, as it is said. A girl that had never known what it was to need or want anything, both before and after her marriage, was reduced to penury and want. This the writer knows from correspondence with her after the war and information obtained from others. Our correspondence was in reference to her claim for dower in certain lots in the town of Marion, which he brought action for and recovered, and sent the money to her. She had no child; she afterwards married a "Yankee" officer from Wisconsin, a widower, with four children, whose name was F. M. Chrisman. This marriage, I suppose, took place during the Reconstruction period in Arkansas. David. S. Henry, the son of John Henry, grew up and married a Miss Telatha Flowers, and by her had only one child, a son, our energetic and enterprising fellow-citizen, John E. Henry, who married Miss Charlotte Bethea, a daughter of the late Levi and Mary Ann Bethea; they have several children, sons and daughters—one son named Sheppard, one named John (called Jack), and Patrick, and a daughter named Mary, who married Mr. Augustus Alford; they moved to Georgia, have several children, and are said to be doing well. The sons, Sheppard and Jack, emigrated West somewhere, and, I suppose, looking out for themselves. John E. Henry and wife have another daughter grown, whose name, I believe, is Ella; besides these there are other children, younger. John E. Henry is an enterprising man, and is apparently doing well; they own and occupy the old homestead of Mrs. Henry's paternal grand-father, old William Bethea. The sister of David S. Henry married the Rev. Tracy R. Walsh, a strong preacher in the Methodist Conference, who is dead; his family are scattered through Marlborough and Chesterfield Counties.

HUGGINS.—Another family may here be noticed—the Huggins family. The first known of this family were John Huggins and Willis Huggins, not brothers, but first cousins.* Old John Huggins lived at Huggins' Bridge, on Little Pee Dee; he married a Miss Campbell, sister of Gadi and Theophilus; he raised a considerable family of sons and one daughter— if there were other daughters, the writer never heard of them; the sons were Solomon, Henry, John, Theophilus, George, Enos and Ebben. Solomon Huggins married some one to the writer unknown, and raised a family, of whom I know nothing. Henry Huggins married a Miss Elvington, daughter of old man John Elvington, of whom mention has already been made herein. Henry Huggins had a son, Theophilus, now one of our good citizens, on Little Pee Dee; he married some one to the writer unknown, and has raised a considerable family. Henry Huggins raised one daughter, Martha, and, perhaps, others. Martha married James A. Jones, an older brother of our excellent fellow-citizen, J. T. Jones, and her family has already been mentioned herein, in or among the Jones family. There may have been other sons and daughters of Henry Huggins; if so, the writer knows nothing of them. Henry Huggins and wife died many years ago. Another son of Henry Huggins is now remembered, Thomas A. Huggins, who married and raised a family, not known to the writer; Thomas A. Huggins died a few years ago, quite an old man. John Huggins, Jr. (Jack, as he was called), has already been mentioned

---

*John Huggins and Willis were first cousins. Their fathers were brothers; their grand-father was the common ancestor, and, I suppose, was the first Huggins in the county, about 1740 or 1750.

in and among the Jones family; his wife was Mary Jones, a sister of our J. T. Jones. Theophilus Huggins and George W. Huggins became Methodist traveling preachers in the South Carolina Conference, and both died therein. George W. Huggins never married, and died young—in Conway or Horry—to which circuit he was then assigned, in 1835. In the minutes of the Conference of 1899, in the chapter entitled "The dead of the South Carolina Conference, 1788 to 1900," George W. Huggins is put down as joining the Conference in 1833; that he died October, 1835, at the age of twenty-seven, and was buried in Horry County. As to the place of his burial, it is a mistake; he was buried at Huggins Bridge, on Little Pee Dee—not more than a hundred yards from the place of his birth. The writer attended his funeral and knows whereof he speaks. Theophilus Huggins continued in the itineracy until his death; he married some one unknown to the writer; think he died in the North Carolina Conference. Enos Huggins, a very vigorous and athletic young man, sickened and died when young, unmarried. Dr. Ebben Huggins, a dental surgeon, married and settled in Horry County, just below Galivant's Ferry; he raised a large family—or, rather, had one— he dying before the younger ones were raised. Old John Huggins' daughter, Mary (Polly as she was called), married the late Stephen Smith; by the marriage several sons and daughters were born; the sons were, and are, Ebenezer, George W., S. Elmore, Benjamin Gause, S. Whiteford and J. Emory Smith, and another, named Augustus, who was killed during the war on a train near Florence; and daughters, Mrs. Mitchell Martin, Mrs. George W. Rogers, Mrs. J. C. Harrelson and Mrs. Celia Atkinson. Ebb Smith was killed or died of disease in the war. George W. Smith, one of our steady and progressive citizens, married a Miss Nance; the fruits of the marriage are several sons and daughters; some of them married and have families coming on, the names of all of whom are not known. One daughter of George W. Smith married Allen Lewis. A son, Augustus, at Mullins, married a Miss Dill. Bonham Smith married a Miss Lewis. Another daughter married Hampton McMillan; another daughter married a Mr. Nye. Benjamin Gause Smith, another progressive and prosperous citizen, married a Miss Platt, daughter of the late Rev. John B. Platt; they have, I think, ten children, seven sons and three daughters; the older sons are L. Boyd Smith, Rembert Smith and others, names not remembered. The two oldest daughters, Florence and Leila, are married. Florence to W. F. Norton; they have no children. Leila married P. S. Cooper, a first-rate business man at Mullins; they have had two children, both dead. The third daughter, Polly, named for her grand-mother, now a little girl. L. Boyd Smith married a Widow Gibbes, in Macon, Ga.; they are living at Mullins; he is in the saw mill business; is a graduate of Wofford College. S. Elmore Smith, a first-class business man and an excellent citizen, married a Miss Montgomery, of Williamsburg County; has a large family, sons and daughters, mostly daughters. Has one daughter married; she married a Mr. Love, of Wilmington; think they are now residing in Mullins; has a son grown, named Eugene; has other daughters grown. S. Whiteford Smith married a Miss Boatwright, daughter of the late Thomas W. Boatwright; by this marriage are two children—a son, Fleming, who, I think, is married, and a daughter, whose name is Bessie; think she has arrived at womanhood. Whiteford Smith is a business man and good farmer; was County Superintendent of Education for four or six years; retired from that position and was immediately elected as a Representative of his county in the State Legislature. In whatever position he has been placed, he has met public expectation—a man of strict integrity every way, and perfectly reliable. J. Emory Smith, the youngest son of old Stephen and Polly Smith, married a Miss Williamson, a daughter of Joseph Williamson, and has a family coming on. It seems that J. Emory has not succeeded so well as his older brothers; he is young and may yet win, outstrip them in the race of life. Mrs. Lizzie Martin and her family of four sons have already been noticed herein or among the Martin family. Mrs. George W. Rogers, another daughter of Polly Smith, *nee* Huggins, has raised a nice family of sons and one daughter; the writer is not posted as to the particulars of this family. I know three of the sons, Leroy, Lucean and Chalmers; they are promising young men, and in the race of life will be very apt to be among the winners in the race. Leroy married a Miss Gore, in Wilmington; she died a few days ago, leaving an infant. Chalmers Rogers married Miss Laura Smith; they have two children. Willis Huggins, the cousin of old John Huggins, whose progeny we have been tracing, was a very respectable and good citizen; married some one and raised a family—one son and three daughters. The son, Jesse Huggins, was a promising young man; was Captain of the Maiden Down militia company, a position then much sought by our best men; he was killed by John Martin, hereinbefore mentioned; he never married. Willis' daughters were Nancy, Elizabeth and Polly. Nancy Huggins married the late John Norton, father of the Hon. James Norton; she had three children, one son and two daughters. The son is John W. Norton, now of Mullins; he married, first, a Miss Carmichael; by her he had one child, a daughter, named Ira, who was killed by the band-wheel of a gin, when a girl; he afterwards married the Widow Carmichael; by her he had one daughter, named Minnie, who died when about grown. The second wife died, and he married, a third time, a Miss Ivey; by whom he now has four children, two sons and two daughters, all small. John W. Norton went through the Confederate War. Some years before the war he enlisted in the regular army of the United States and served in the frontiers for five years. Lizzie Norton married Aaron Oliver, of Robeson County, N. C., by whom she had three sons and four daughters. One of the latter died unmarried; another daughter is now the second wife of John C. Sellers. Mrs. Lizzie Oliver is dead. The second daughter of old John Norton and his wife, Nancy, married Lewis Huggins; her name was Caroline; they had several children, sons and daughters. Lewis Huggins and family emigrated to Georgia some years ago; have lost sight of them. Elizabeth, the second daughter of old Willis Huggins, married, first, a Mr. Lupo; Lupo died childless, and his widow married John Hill, for whom she had two children—a son, Charles, and a daughter, Adaline, when the mother died. Charles Hill is on Bear Swamp. Adaline married a Mr. McCormic, of Cotton Valley; know nothing further of them. Polly, the youngest daughter of old Willis Huggins, never married, and is dead. There are other Huggins in the county, of whom the writer knows but little. The Huggins family and their connections are extensive, and especially the descendants of old John. The old house he lived in and raised his family stands yet, near Huggins' Bridge; it is a unique old building, weather-boarded with shingles—was very old and dilapidated. The other Huggins alluded to above are sons, and, perhaps, daughters, of the late Neill C. Huggins (I think that was his name); he married a daughter of old Squire Neill Carmichael, near Carmichael's Bridge, on Little Pee Dee; he has long since died, either in the war or soon after, from wounds received in the war or from exposure; he left a good large family; was a coming man, doing well; his sons, as known to the writer, are D. A. Huggins, Neill Huggins and Judson Huggins, who are among our citizens; whether the mother is dead or alive, is unknown to the writer.

HAYES.—The next family to be here noticed is the Hayes family, of Kirby Township. The first of this family in this county were James Hayes, John Hayes, William Hayes and Ebben. Of these, Ebben did not remain here, but emigrated West; nothing further is known of him. They all came from Virginia, and were of English descent. The other three married and settled in this county. This family came here during or before the Revolutionary War. Don't know who any of these old Hayes married. James Hayes had four sons, whose names were Levi H. Hayes, William Hayes, John G. Hayes and Mills Hayes. The first, William Hayes, had three sons, Ebben, Dwight and Henry Hayes. Ebben Hayes, known to many living, was a local Methodist preacher, and represented his county in the State Legislature after the war and during the Reconstruction period; he was twice elected, served two terms or four sessions of the Legislature, and died at an advanced age a few years ago. Dwight Hayes, a brother of Ebben, became a Baptist preacher of some note; he died many years ago. Henry Hayes grew up and married Miss Marina Dew, a daughter of old Christopher Dew; his wife was a sister of his brother Ebben's wife; he died comparatively young, leaving a widow and several children, who with their children and grand-children are now among us. We have thus traced the sons of the three brothers (leaving Ebben out, who went West), James Hayes, William Hayes and John Hayes. Of old James Hayes' children, Levi H. Hayes married a Miss Whittington, and by her had seven sons, James N., Levi G., Benjamin F., Erastus W., Hamilton R., A. G. and Robert H. Hayes. Levi H. Hayes had two daughters, if no more. One became the wife of Joel Meggs, who, perhaps, raised a considerable family; only two sons, William H. and John L. Meggs, are known to the writer; and a daughter, who married Dr. N. C. McLeod. Another daughter of Levi H. Hayes, named Ann Elizabeth, married John A. Dew, who died and left his widow childless; she still lives. Of the sons of Levi H. Hayes, James N. and Erastus W., are dead, but left families. Levi G. Hayes married a Miss Jackson, and went West many years ago. A. G. Hayes married, also, a Miss Jackson, sister to his brother L. G. Hayes' wife. A. G. Hayes, called G. Hayes, died or was killed in the war. Erastus W. Hayes married a Miss George; think he died in the war. James N. died some time before the war. B. F. Hayes married a Miss Dew, daughter of Wilson Dew; has only one child, a son, our good fellow-citizen, Rich Hayes. Hamilton R. Hayes married a Miss Harper; has four sons, Charles W., James Adger, Humbert and Hamilton R. Hayes, Jr; and six daughters, names not known. One married W. H. Meggs; one married Rich Hayes; one married Tracy Fore; one married Andrew Tart; one married a Napier; one married Wilson Berry; and one is unmarried. Of his sons, Charles W. married a Miss Hill; James Adger married a Miss Napier; Hamilton R., Jr., and Humbert are unmarried. William Hayes, a son of old James, married some one, but do not know to whom; he has been dead many years; and of John G. Hayes and Mills Hayes the writer knows nothing. The late Ebben Hayes married a daughter of old Christopher Dew, as before related; he had seven sons and several daughters; the sons were Jessee H., Ebben, Wilson, Joseph D., Nicholas W. and John David; these, with their sisters, are all married, have children and grand-children, and are among our many good citizens. Old John Hayes, one of the first comers, married a Miss Berry, an aunt of Cross Roads

Henry, and raised a family; his sons were Newton, Coburn, John C. and David S. Hayes. Of Coburn, nothing is known. Newton married a Miss Clark, and had a family of sons and daughters, but of them nothing is known. Newton Hayes died some twenty years ago, over eighty years of age. John C. Hayes married a Widow Lindsay, whose maiden name was Mary Ann Stubbs, an excellent woman she was; by this marriage he had five sons, who lived to be grown—Lewis E., Henry C., James S., Thomas C. and John C.; the latter was born one month after the death of his father; these are all now living, and among our best citizens. Of the daughters of John C. Hayes, Sarah Jane first married an Adams, of Marlborough, who died in a year after the marriage, leaving her with one child, a daughter, named Dora, who is now the wife of Jasper C. George, and who has now five sons. The Widow Adams afterwards married the late James DuPre; she still survives. Another daughter of John C. Hayes—Ann Eliza, I think, was her name—married Philip B. Meekins; they went to North Carolina; know nothing more of them. Another daughter, Mary Ellen, married Elihu Berry; by this marriage were born one son, named Elihu Lide Berry, and another son, Thomas, both of whom are single; and four daughters, Telatha, Emma, Lucy and Leilah; of whom Telatha married J. W. Davis, went West, and died, leaving twin daughters, whom her mother now has, and is raising. Emma Berry married Montcalm Dow Atkins; they have now two children. Another daughter of John C. Hayes married Charles Miles; they moved to North Carolina. Another daughter married Sydney E. Jackson; they now live at Dillon, and have seven or eight children, two daughters grown. Jackson is a good citizen and doing well. Another daughter, Addie, married James Greenwood; had one child, and died; the child then died; Greenwood is a widower of ten or fifteen years; he inherited the entire estate of his wife, is a business man and is doing well. Of the sons of John C. Hayes, Lewis E. married a widow (name forgotten). Henry C. Hayes married a Miss Legette, daughter of the late James B. Legette; they have a family, don't know how much. Thomas C. Hayes is yet unmarried. John C. Hayes, Jr., married, first, a Miss Stubbs, of Sumter; she died a few months ago, leaving five or six children, one quite an infant; he married a few days ago, the second time, Miss Rebecca Fore, daughter of the late Willis Fore. David S. Hayes, the youngest son of old John Hayes, married, rather late in life, a Miss Fladger, daughter of old Hugh Fladger; by this marriage two daughters were born; one died unmarried, at about twenty years of age. The other, named Ida, is the wife of John B. Moore, of Latta; they are doing very well, and have some children; don't know how many, a daughter grown. David S. Hayes died some twenty years ago, and left a good landed estate to his daughter, Mrs. Moore. The information the writer obtained as to the old Hayes did not extend to the females; but was confined exclusively to the males. The writer knows from other sources that old John Hayes had one daughter, at least, named Mary; she became the wife of old man Isham Watson, and in turn became the progenitress of most of the Watsons in the county, and their connections, hereinbefore mentioned. I will close this notice of the Hayes family with the relation of an incident in that family, as told to the writer some years ago by old Aunt Fama Tart, who was, in many respects, the most remarkable woman with whom he ever met; old Aunt Fama was a grand-daughter of James Hayes. She related that during the Revolutionary War in Virginia, her grand-uncle, William Hayes, was drafted to go into the war; that his wife was a large and portly woman, and had considerable beard upon her upper lip; that when the time came for her husband, William Hayes, to report to his company to go into camp, she donned his clothes, cut off her hair in man's style, and went and reported to the officer as William Hayes; she was accepted, went into camp, and for several days performed all the duties of a soldier in camp life, until such time as she thought her husband had gotten out of the reach of the officials, when she disclosed her sex to the officer in charge. She was discharged from service, made her way back home, and in the progress of time got a hearing from her husband in South Carolina, where he had fled, and she then made her way to him. From this narrative, the writer infers that James Hayes, an older brother, had previously came to South Carolina, and that William fled from Virginia to South Carolina, to join his older brother, James, there; and as soon as the wife, left in Virginia, ascertained that he had made good his escape and had reached his brother, James, that she then put off to join him. According to the account we have of the family, this heroine of a wife was the mother of the late Ebben Hayes, and the grand-mother of all his children and also of Henry Hayes' children.

DEW.—Another family may be noticed here—the Dew family, once pretty extensive, but not so much so now. The two old Dews, of whom the writer has any knowledge, were Christopher and Absalom. The writer has heard of one old John Dew, but what became of him or of his family, if he had one, he knows not. Cross Roads Henry Berry bought his land more than sixty years ago, and he seems to have disappeared from the county. Old Christopher Dew seems to have been a man of some note in his day; he bought and owned a vast barony of lands on the Great Pee Dee River and in and out of the "Slashes;" he lived on the Pocosin, and died there, 18th December, 1827. The late Bryant Lane married his youngest daughter, Henrietta, that day, whilst her father lay a corpse in the house. This remarkable coincidence was related to the writer, many years ago, by old Bryant Lane himself; hence the precise date is remembered and here stated. Old Christopher was a prosperous man; he married a Miss Berry, daughter of the first old Andrew Berry, who was in the settlement at "Sandy Bluff," about 1735, as hereinbefore stated. That it may be better known, old Christopher's wife was the aunt of Cross Roads Henry Berry; they raised a family of three sons and five daughters, as known to the writer; the sons were Wilson, Christopher and Abraham Dew; the daughters were Marina, Nancy, Mary (Polly), Charity and Henrietta. Wilson Dew married his cousin, a daughter of old Stephen Berry, and sister of Cross Roads Henry Berry; he raised a family; only one son is known, Christopher T. Dew, called "Little Chris," who married some one not known to the writer; had a family of several sons and, perhaps, daughters; he moved to Horry many years ago, with his family; was alive a year or so ago—an old man, eighty or more. Wilson Dew had daughters, how many is not known. One married her first cousin, the first wife of the late Captain S. D. Lane; she died childless, some forty years ago; and in November, 1865, he married again, Miss Flora Bethea, a daughter of the late Rev. S. J. Bethea. Captain Lane died childless, 5th July, 1899, and his widow, Flora, died a month or so ago. Another daughter of Wilson Dew married B. F. Hayes, as has been already stated herein; they have only one child, a son, Rich Hayes; I think another daughter married the late Samuel Berry; if so, it is already noticed herein in or among the Berry family. Christopher Dew, Jr., son of old man Christopher, married a Miss Jones, sister of Bryant Jones, which has already been noticed in or among the Jones family. Abraham Dew, the third son of old Christopher, lived to a good old age in a state of single blessedness. Of the daughters of old Christopher, Marina and Nancy have already been noted herein, in or among the Hayes family. Charity married a Mr. Wise, and he died, leaving her with several children, James C., Finklea G. and Thomas Aquilla; and, perhaps, some daughters—one, I know, a Mrs. Wetherford, and, I believe, another, the wife of John G. Kirby. James C. Wise died a few years back, at an old age, eighty years or more, leaving a large family. Finklea G. Wise lives in Wahee, a very old man; don't know to whom he married—think his wife is dead; he raised some family. A. G. Wise, of Wahee, a son of his, is one of the best citizens of that township, a very reliable man every way; he has a family of several children, sons and daughters, grown; they are quite respectable. Thomas Aquilla Wise was idiotic; he had some property, and Finklea G. Wise was appointed by the Court a committee to look after him and his property; Aquilla died some years ago. Another daughter of old Christopher Dew, Mary (Polly), marrie Jesse Perritt; she died childless, years ago, as has already been noticed in or among the Perritt family. The youngest daughter of old Christopher, Henrietta, married Bryant Lane, as above stated, the day of her father's death; they made a good living, raised a family of four sons—Stephen D., Joseph, Robert L. and Bryant. Stephen D. Lane married, first, his cousin, Miss Dew, daughter of Wilson Dew; she died childless, and he married again, Miss Flora Bethea, as above stated; he was a first-class, good citizen. Joseph Lane was killed in the war, or was wounded and died. Robert L. Lane, now of Dillon, another first-class good citizen, married Miss R. C. Gaddy, daughter of the late Hardy Gaddy; by this marriage six or seven children have been born, mostly sons, none of whom are known to the writer, except the oldest, Verner, who was one of the late volunteers in the 2d South Carolina Regiment for the Spanish War. His uncle, Stephen D. Lane, willed to Verner his home place, which, I suppose, Verner will soon occupy, with a Miss Somebody as a helpmate. Bryant Lane, Jr., was an idiot, and died a few months ago, at his brother's, R. L. Lane, who was committee for him and his property. The daughters of Bryant Lane and wife were four—Miss Kesiah, now an old maid, Mary (called Polly), Anne and Flora Ellen Lane. Hartwell C. Dew, one of our best citizens, married, first, Mary (Polly), and had by her six or seven children—Preston L., John L., Duncan M. and Joseph H. Dew, and two daughters, Roberta and Dora. Preston L. Dew married Miss Eugenia Allen, daughter of Rev. Joel Allen; they moved to Greenwood some years ago, having several children. John L. Dew, now of Latta, married a Miss Cottingham, daughter of Daniel Cottingham, and has one child, a son; is at Latta, merchant and postmaster. Duncan M. Dew married, first, a Miss Thornton; she had one child, and died, afterwards the child died; and he married, a second time, a Miss Chappel; don't know where from; they reside at Latta, and have some children; he is one of the leading merchants at Latta—a man of fine character, wholly reliable and trustworthy. Joseph H. Dew, as will be seen elsewhere in this book, is a graduate of Furman University, and, I believe, of the Baptist Seminary at Louisville, Ky.; is a preacher of reputation in the Baptist denomination; married some lady foreign to this county; stands well among his people; don't know where he is. Miss Roberta Dew married Wylie Berry; they reside at Latta; have one child, a daughter; they are doing fairly well. Dora Dew married H. E. K. Smith, on Buck Swamp; he is a successful farmer, doing well; have some children, don't know how many. Hartwell C. Dew lost his first wife, Mary (Polly), and he married again to Anne Lane, a sister of his first wife; by her has had several children—Mollie, Isla, Julian, Lawton, Janie, Harvey and another son, name not known; his second wife, Anne, died; he survives, and has not again married. Hartwell C. Dew is one of our plain, honest and successful men; has amassed a good property, is well advanced in life—I suppose, over seventy years old. His daughter, Mollie, by the last wife, married a Dr. Baker, from Georgia, and resides there. Isla married Rev. Mr. Crumpler, who died in a year or two, leaving her a widow, with one child. Janie married a Mr. Kinard, of Newberry; they reside in that county. Julian, Lawton, Harvey and Lawrence, are all unmarried, and still remain under the parental roof. Flora Ellen Lane, the youngest daughter of Bryant Lane and wife, married James R. Watson; they now reside in Dillon, and have already been noticed in or among the Watson family. The other old Dew, mentioned in the beginning of this notice of the Dew family, was Absalom Dew. Whether he was brother to old Christopher Dew or not, is not known to the writer—think, however, that he was; he also married a Miss Berry, daughter of the first old Andrew, of the "Sandy Bluff" settlement, and sister to the wife of old Christopher, and aunt of Cross Roads Henry Berry. Never knew or heard of but two of his children, sons, named William and Alexander. William Dew married a Miss Coleman, sister to the Rev. John D. Coleman, well known in this county as a Baptist minister; by this marriage there were three sons, Leonard M., Hartwell C. and John, and two daughters, Ann Eliza and Martha. Of the sons of William Dew, the oldest, Leonard M., married a Miss Miles, a daughter of John M. Miles; by this marriage, three sons, Calvin (called Cad), Frank and Dennis, and, perhaps, a daughter, were born, when the father died, and left his widow and children; she being what is usually called a smart woman, raised her children creditably; they moved some years ago to North Carolina. Calvin married Mary Jane Brown, daughter of the late William M. Brown; she died within a year or two, and left no child; Calvin himself died a few months ago. Know nothing of the other two boys, Frank and Dennis. Hartwell C. Dew has already been noticed above herein. John Dew, the youngest son of old William, went off into the war, and has never been heard of since. Ann Eliza Dew married Mr. John Atkinson, below Marion, and had one child, Thomas Atkinson, when she died. Thomas Atkinson married a daughter of the late Stephen A. Hairgrove, and is now one of our good citizens. Martha Dew married another Atkinson, below Marion, and by him she had a son, W. B. Atkinson, when Atkinson died, and left her a widow; she still survives and has not remarried; her son, W. B. Atkinson, resides with her on the old William Dew homestead, and is one of our most enterprising and successful citizens; he married a Miss Gaddy, daughter of Samuel T. Gaddy, and has a considerable family; think they have already been noticed in or among the Gaddy family. This closes the notice of the Dew family, an old and respectable family of the county. Much more might be said of some of them, but space will not permit; enough has been said to enable future generations to trace their ancestry.

NICHOLSON.—The next family to be noticed is the Nicholson family. The first of the name known in the county was John M. Nicholson; he came direct, as I think, from Scotland; don't know how it was that he came to South Carolina, but think he came with some of the old Sinclairs. He was a blacksmith; whether he learned that trade in Scotland or after he came to this country, is not known; he was a large, strong and muscular man, unpretentious, made no display, personally or otherwise; honest and upright in his dealings with others, jealous of his own rights, while he accorded to every man the same rights which he claimed for himself; was not querulous, but would not be imposed upon; was of equable temperament, until he was aroused, then an antagonist might look out; physically he was a powerful man. He married, I think, a Miss Sinclair, and had and raised, as known to the writer, three sons, Archibald, Duncan and Walter Nicholson—may have had other sons; these are all that the writer ever knew. He had one daughter, Nancy; she married Mr. Elly Greenwood, a second wife of his; they have some family. Old man Nicholson may have had other daughters. Archie Nicholson, now in the Mullins region, married a Miss Martin, daughter of Matthew Martin, and by her has several children, and is doing well—a good, industrious and law-abiding citizen. Duncan Nicholson married a Miss Edwards, daughter of Captain L. M. Edwards, and by her has several children; he, likewise, is an industrious, progressive and prosperous citizen; such men constitute the bone and sinew of the country, and its hope for the future. Walter Nicholson is unmarried, but, like his brothers, is attentive to his business—keeps it before him, and is perfectly reliable in every respect.

JACKSON.—The Jackson family will next be noticed. This family is and has been very extensive in name and in its connections in the county. The first old Jackson was from Virginia, his name was Edward; said to have been a very small man in size—somewhat like the late Dr. James C. Mullins; he settled on Catfish; his wife was a Miss Manning, of Virginia, or it may be that Miss Mannning was the wife of his son, Edward; he raised a considerable family of sons and, perhaps, daughters; of the latter, the writer knows nothing; the sons were, Edward, Jr., William, John, Reuben, Owen and Ervin Jackson. I cannot trace all these different sons *seriatim,* for the want of information, but will do so as far as I can. Edward, Jr., the oldest son, married, if not a Miss Manning, some other lady—I think, though, a Manning—and had and raised a considerable family of sons, and, perhaps, daughters; the sons were, as known to the writer, William R., Edward M. and Warren R. Jackson. William R. Jackson married a Miss Hayes, daughter of John Hayes, and a sister of old man Isham Watson's wife; he raised a considerable family—one son, William R., and other sons, whose names are not remembered; some daughters also, only one of whom is remembered, Mary, who became the wife of the late Stephen A. Hairgrove, and they raised a considerable family of sons and daughters. Only one son survives, Thomas H. Hairgrove, now of Wahee. One daughter married Thomas Atkinson, who has some family—I think, two daughters. Miss Huldah Hairgrove also survives; she has never married. Think all the sons of William R. Jackson, Sr., went West. William R. Jackson, Jr., went to the Mexican War; I saw him after his return; he then went West. William R. Jackson, Sr., died more than sixty years ago; old man Isham Watson administered on his estate. Their wives were sisters. Edward M. Jackson, son of Edward, Jr., and his brother, Warren R. Jackson, married sisters, Ellen Adams and Anne Adams, daughters of old Elias Adams, whose wife was a sister of old Thomas Harllee. Misses Ellen and Anne Adams were first cousins of the late General W. W. Harllee. Edward M. and Warren R. Jackson both raised quite respectable families. Edward M. moved West many years ago, and carried his whole family—though some of them, perhaps, two or three, were married; two of his sons became Baptist preachers. Warren R. Jackson raised sons, Anderson W., James R., Jefferson A. and Sydney E. Jackson, and one boy killed accidentally by another boy, and, I think, two daughters, Agenora and Missouri; another daughter, Amelia, died when a girl. Anderson W. Jackson married a Miss Flowers; he became a Methodist itinerant preacher, traveled for some years within the South Carolina Conference, finally superannuated on account of eyes failing, and, I think, now lives in Williamsburg County; he had and raised two or three sons and, perhaps, one daughter—all of whom, I think, are married. He had one son, Preston B., who became, also, a Methodist preacher, and attained much distinction as such in the Conference; he married a lady in Darlington, and after traveling for several years, was transferred to California; I can follow him no further. James R. Jackson married a Greenville lady; was waylaid one night on the road from Marion and shot within a mile or so of his home; he died from the wounds in a week or so. It was pretty well understood who was the assassin, but no proof could be made. Jefferson A. Jackson married and had a family; he became a Baptist preacher of some note, and moved off to Texas, and in some town there had charge of a church for several years, and stood high in his calling; he died there some five or six years ago; don't know about his family. Sydney E. Jackson married a Miss Hayes, daughter of the late John C. Hayes; has seven or eight children—two daughters grown; he left his excellent farm on Catfish some five or six years ago, and moved to Dillon, because of better school facilities there; he is a carpenter by trade, and it is supposed that as Dillon is a growing and progressive town he is doing well at his trade; the income from it, together with the rents of his farm, enables him to support his large family. The oldest daughter of Warren R. Jackson, Agenora A., married the late Colonel John J. George; the fruits of the marriage were seven children, four sons and three daughters. One son died when about arriving at manhood; the other sons are Jasper C. George, John J. George and William Warren George. Jasper C. George married Dora Adams, a grand-daughter of the late John C. Hayes; they have five sons. The oldest, Percy, is grown and now at Clemson College. Jasper C. George is one of our most energetic, persevering citizens; is doing well, and making money—a good farmer. John J. George, named for his father, married, first, a Miss Bethea, daughter of E. Bethea; she died childless; then he married a Miss Rogers, daughter of Philip B. Rogers; is raising a family, a farmer, and is doing well. William Warren George married a Miss Ellen Gaddy, daughter of John Gaddy; he is and ever has been a merchant, now at Latta, S. C.; a man of indomitable pluck and enterprise; has failed once or twice, and was apparently down to stay down; but not so, he rises and comes again; has done more for Latta than any man that has been in it, according to his means, in building it up and booming the town—such a man cannot be kept down; he has no children. The daughters of Colonel J. J. George and wife were three. Mary Ann married Michael Finnegan; they have several children, one or two married; Michael Finnegan is one of our best and most progressive citizens, doing well, and raising a nice family; such men tell upon the prosperity of the country. Della George, another daughter of Colonel J. J. George and wife, married John Haselden; they have a family, two sons and two daughters; they have moved to Horry, and are said to be doing well. Aurelia George, the youngest daughter, married Henry Berry, a widower; they have no children; Berry is a good citizen. Colonel J. J. George died soon after the war, having lost a leg in the last battle at Bentonville, above Fayetteville, N. C., just before General Joe Johnston's surrender; he left his wife, Agenora, with seven little children, and no property except a little farm, perhaps, 200 acres poor land; she was an *extra* smart woman; they went to work, she soon began to gain; they made ample support and some money; she raised her family in credit, and they are all doing well; she died two or three years ago; she lost one son, Henry. Missouri Jackson, youngest daughter of Warren R. Jackson, married Frank Dew; they went to North Carolina, where she now resides, Frank being dead; she has six or seven children, some of them grown; know nothing further of them. Warren R. Jackson died in 1857, leaving his wife, Anne, with her several small children; his estate was involved, and much litigation ensued both in the Circuit and Appeal Courts, she finally was successful, and saved the estate from utter wreck and ruin. The writer knoweth whereof he speaks, being mixed up in it as her attorney from beginning to end. Of the sons of Edward Jackson, Sr., William married a Miss Manning, also settled on Catfish, and raised a family; don't know how many—two sons only were known to the writer, Reuben and John M. Jackson. Of Reuben and his family, little is known; he is dead; don't know what has become of his family. John M. Jackson married a Miss Miles, a daughter of old David Miles and sister of the late Francis A. Miles; he settled on his father's, William Jackson, homestead, and lived and died there; he raised one son, Frank M., and three or four daughters; his wife died; he lived for several years a widower, and died. His son, Frank, married a Miss Miles, his first cousin, a daughter of Charles Miles, Sr. The daughters of John M. Jackson, after the death of their father, moved off, perhaps, to Georgia. Frank M. Jackson then took possession of the old homestead and lived on it for several years, then sold it and moved into North Carolina, and thus he has been lost sight of. Of John Jackson, son of Edward, Sr., nothing is known as to what became of him. Reuben married some one and settled on Maple; raised a family, of whom the writer knows nothing, except two sons of his, James and John Jackson. James Jackson married a Miss Herring, and raised a family of sons and daughters. Of his sons, Arthur and John became notorious during the war. James Jackson and his brother John were killed, just after the close of the war, on account of their sons, and especially Arthur and John, by parties in revenge. The writer has ever thought that these two old men, James and John Jackson, were wrongfully killed; but it was done at a time when human life was cheap, and in very troublesome times. Another brother of old James and John Jackson was Henry Jackson. The three brothers married three sisters, Misses Herring, sisters of old Whittington Hamilton's wife, and Whittington, Jr., married a daughter of Henry Jackson; she was a first cousin to him. While not much can be said in favor of this branch of the Jackson family, yet there are worse men than these three old brothers. Old Edward Jackson, Sr., had a son, Owen Jackson, who married Dilla McKenzie, a daughter of Robert McKenzie; he lived upon and owned the lands where Missouri R. Hamer and Philip B. Rogers now live and own; he was a simple-minded old man, worked hard, was strictly honest and law-abiding, and strictly attended to his own affairs; he raised a considerable family, mostly daughters, and two sons only known. Hugh P. Price's wife is one of the daughters, and, like her father, stays at home and mind's her own business; she has no children. One son, William Jackson, called "Fire-coal Bill," married a daughter of old man William Hamilton, and who has already been mentioned herein, in or among the Hamilton family. Another son, Ervin M. Jackson, married Sarah Ann McKenzie, who died a few years back, leaving an only child, a son, Thomas Jackson, who has already been noticed herein, in or among the McKenzie family. Old man Owen Jackson may have had another son, if so it has escaped the memory of the writer; and as to his other daughters, the writer has lost sight of them. Ervin Jackson, the youngest son of old Edward, Sr., married a Miss Watson, on Hayes Swamp, near the North Carolina line; they settled near the father, old Mark Watson, and by industry and frugality amassed a good property, and raised quite a respectable family. Owen Jackson, Jr., a son or a grand-son of old Ervin, married a sister of the late Duncan Murchison; he died a few years ago; made a considerable property, raised a very respectable family of sons and daughters, some of whom are among the leading men of Marlborough County. One son is known to the writer, John M. Jackson, as a leading merchant and business man in Bennettsville. They reflect credit upon the Jackson name. There is also a John R. Jackson, grand-son of old Ervin, now a leading man in the community of his ancestors. There may be others of the name in some one or other of the many branches of the Jackson family not mentioned, but they are not known, or, rather, their genealogy is not known, and hence not especially mentioned.

GALLOWAY.—The Galloways may here be mentioned, four of them. They are importations from Marlborough, and our county would not be hurt by many more such importations— James T., William, Samuel T. and Joseph Galloway are their names. James T. Galloway married Miss Louisa Bethea, daughter of Levi and Mary Ann Bethea, just after the war, and has been in this county ever since his marriage; he has a considerable family, has succeeded well in life. Has one son, Henry, married, don't know to whom—I think, a Miss Barrentine, of Marlborough. One daughter married to Mr. Maxcy McCown, of Florence County. His other children are with him; he is one of our most substantial citizens. William Galloway, a later importation, a brother of James T., has bought land in upper Marion. A comparison of his place with what it was fifteen years ago will show that he is a farmer right; he is a hustling man; know nothing of his immediate family, and the same may be said of Samuel T. and Joseph Galloway, a late importation, who have bought land on Catfish, near Ellerbe's Crossing, and are moving ahead, first class men and excellent citizens; know nothing of their immediate families. Samuel T. Galloway married Johny Carmichael, and Joseph married a daughter of Elmore Allen, of Marlborough County. I knew their father and mother, James Galloway and Rebecca, his wife; she was a Townsend, daughter of old Jabish Townsend, and sister of the late Meekin Townsend, of Marlborough.

SHERWOOD.—The Sherwoods will next be noticed. The first Sherwood known in the county was John Sherwood, an old man, more than sixty years ago; he was a great church man and exceedingly pious; he had two or three sons and one daughter. Of the sons, nothing is known, except as to James. James Sherwood married Miss Martha (Patsy) Bethea, a daughter of William Bethea, near Harlleesville; by the marriage three sons were born and raised—Cade, Postell and John. Cade Sherwood owns the old homestead of his grand-father, John Sherwood. James Sherwood died and left his widow with her children small; the widow married again—do not remember to whom. Cade and Postell grew up, and Cade bought the old homestead of his grand-father, and married a Miss Legette, of Marlborough, daughter of James S. Legette. Cade Sherwood has one of the best plantations in upper Marion, an excellent manager and farmer; everything about his house and premises denotes comfort and convenience not excelled by any one in the county. Postell Sherwood, of Mullins, married his first cousin, Miss Lou Scarborough, daughter of the late Rev. Lewis Scarborough, many years an itinerant preacher in the South Carolina Conference, and sister of the Hon. R. B. Scarborough, of Conway. Postell is doing well; has a small family, two daughters, but has not succeeded like his brother, Cade Sherwood. John Sherwood is unmarried.

ALFORD.—The late Neill, James L. and Lodwick B. Alford, brothers, were importations from North Carolina, and were quite an acquisition to the moral, social and material prosperity of the county—men of high character, and contributed much to the upbuilding of the county; would be glad to have many more similar importations. Neill Alford married a Miss McPherson, settled on the Big Reedy Creek, near where the Reedy Creek Presbyterian Church now stands; by his marriage he had and raised a large family of five sons and ten daughters; William McD., Henry, Robert, John and Walter L. Alford. William McD. Alford married a Miss McLean, of North Carolina, and has raised a large family of sons and daughters, five of each sex; the sons are McLean (called Mack), Yancy, Robert, Plummer and William. Mack and Yancy only are married; don't know to whom. Yancy Alford is a practicing physician in Sumter County. One of Wm. McD. Alford's sons is a practicing dental surgeon; think his name is Plummer or Robert. None of his daughters are married; one of them, Miss Ella, I believe was a teacher for some time in the Columbia Female College. Wm. McD. Alford has performed his duty in the relations of life, and one specially—that is, he has educated his children well, and exceedingly so, for a man of his somewhat limited means and the number of his children; he and family are among our best people—a man of high character, indomitable will and energetic; no task too heavy, and no difficulty insurmountable; the words "fail" or "I can't," are not in his vocabulary. The people of his county appreciating his many good qualities have made him their Representative in the State Legislature. He is, as it were, relegated to the rear, because for the last ten years he has not been in line with the dominant party in the State—many of our best men are in the same category. W. McD. Alford is one of our leading and most progressive farmers. Henry Alford, a brother, married in North Carolina, and resides about Floral College, in Robeson County. Robert Alford, another brother, died about 1868; he was a promising young man. John and Walter S. Alford have never married, though both are old enough to enter upon that, to them, untried relation in life. Of the ten daughters of old man Neill Alford, two are yet unmarried and may be called "old maids." Two of the married ones, Mrs. McLucas and Mrs. DuBose, are dead; Mrs. McLucas childless; don't know as to Mrs. DuBose. Three died unmarried. Of the married ones, three are living—Mrs. Currie, Mrs. James Berry and Mrs. Benjamin McKibben. Of Mrs. James Berry's family, they have already been noticed in or among the Berry family. James L. Alford married a Miss McPhaul or McFail; by the marriage, twelve children were born, six sons and six daughters. Of the sons, two are dead; those living are Daniel M., Frierson, Neill and Manton. Daniel M. Alford married a Miss Walter; they reside at Dillon; have a family, one daughter grown; don't know as to others of his family. Frierson Alford married a daughter of Dr. William J. David; resides in upper Marion, and is one of our good citizens; has a family, some grown children. Neill Alford, a quiet and inoffensive man, married a Miss Stackhouse, daughter of the late Colonel E. T. Stackhouse; they have a considerable family, some grown; don't know how many grown or otherwise; they reside at Marion. Manton Alford married an Alabama lady, and resides in upper Marion—one of our most respectable and worthy citizens. Of James L. Alford's six daughters, only one survives, Dian or Dianna, who married Dr. McLean, in upper Marion; they have one daughter, the wife of Clarence McLaurin; are said to be doing well. Not one of her five sisters ever married. Loderick B. Alford, brother of Neill and James L., also came from North Carolina, with his brothers, but did not remain long, he went to Tennessee, and married there a Miss Hall; after some years he returned with his family to upper Marion, and died there along in the fifties. He raised a considerable family—the names of only two of them are remembered. Althea, his oldest child, who married, first, James P. McInnis, who died and left her a widow; she afterwards became the second wife of Colonel Levi Legette, and still survives; think she had one child by McInnis, a daughter, who married W. D. Carmichael, now one of the citizens of the county below Marion. The late Warren L. Alford married, and raised a considerable family; the names of only two of his children are known to the writer. Dock Alford married a Miss Harrelson, daughter of the late John E. Harrelson, and has a family of sons and, perhaps, daughters, names unknown. A daughter of Warren L. Alford, named Della, has never married; she may be classed now as an old maid. Warren L. Alford, a peaceable, quiet and harmless man, died a few years past; his family are four or five miles below Marion, on the Galivant's Ferry road.

GREENWOOD.—Of this family, William and Frank Greenwood were known to the writer, sixty years ago. He once saw their mother, old Mrs. Greenwood. William Greenwood married a sister of Cross Roads Henry Berry; only two children of this marriage were known to the writer—there may have been others—Dawson Greenwood and a daughter, whose name, I believe, was Mary. Dawson married an illegitimate daughter of old John Manning, on Buck Swamp; think they went West or elsewhere. The daughter, Mary (or other name), became the wife of the late David R. Owens; by him she had and raised two sons, Stephen G. and Leonard R., and two daughters. Of the sons, Stephen G. married a Miss Godbold, daughter of Ervin Godbold; had two sons, one of them dead. Stephen G.

Owens was elected Clerk of the Court in 1872, and filled that position for four years; the upheaval in 1876 defeated him for re-election. He was a very competent man, but became a lunatic some years afterwards, and died in the Asylum. Leonard R. Owens married a Miss Wall, and has considerable family at Marion—names not known, except oldest son, Paul, who is said to be very bright; one daughter grown. Leonard Owens is a very competent business man; was postmaster for four years under the Harrison administration, and four years a deputy under D. McIntyre, during Cleveland's second term; was again appointed by McKinley, and served two or three years, when he got into some trouble and was removed from office. He seems to be under a cloud—yet resides in Marion. Don't know whether his mother is dead or alive. Of the two daughters of Mrs. David R. Owens, one married George Wall, brother of L. R. Owens' wife. They live at Marion, and have a family, about whom nothing is known. Don't know what became of the other daughter of David R. Owens. Frank Greenwood died a few years ago, a very old man; he raised some family; was a harmless, inoffensive and good citizen; don't know who his wife was; he had three sons and one daughter; the sons are Elly B., James and Donaldson. Elly married, first, a Miss Platt, daughter of Daniel A. Platt; by her he had no children; she died, and he married again, a Miss Nicholson, who has already been mentioned in or among the Nicholson family; he has by this marriage some family, don't know how much; James Greenwood married Miss Addie Hayes, youngest daughter of the late John C. Hayes, who has already been mentioned in or among the Hayes family; his wife died, then her child died, and he became heir to her property; he has not remarried; is a first-rate business man, and resides at Latta. Donaldson Greenwood has never married; is harmless and inoffensive, a good young (old) man. The daughter, Amanda Greenwood, married Henry Berry, a widower; she had some children, don't know how many, when she died. Berry has married, the third time, Miss Aurelia George; no children by this marriage.

McINNIS.—The McInnis family, in the Carolina neighborhood, will next be noticed. Of this family, the first known was Duncan McInnis, who was a most excellent man and worthy citizen. He is thought to have been a Scotchman, though, perhaps, born in this country. He married some Scotch lady, settled in the Carolina neighborhood, raised a considerable family, four sons and four or five daughters; the sons were Neill, John L., Miles and another, name not remembered. The two latter emigrated to Texas some years ago, together with John L. McInnis. John L. married in Texas, a Texas lady, and some years after returned to this State, and now occupies and owns the old homestead of his father; he had two sons born in Texas, William and one, name unknown. William McInnis has a family; married his cousin, a Miss McDonald, and has, perhaps, two or three children; is a first class man, of high character, good habits, and has proper ideas of life; if misfortune should overtake him, he would still be a man. His brother, younger than himself, unmarried. Neill McInnis died a few years ago; he left a family, unknown to the writer; he was a most excellent man and worthy citizen, and will be much missed not only by his family, but by his community. Miles McInnis and another brother are in Texas. Of the daughters of Duncan McInnis, two of them married McLaurins, whether in Marion or Marlborough County, is unknown; they both have families, number and names unknown. One daughter married our respected fellow-citizen, A. J. McDonald; they have children grown and married, and, perhaps, grand-children, but for want of information can say nothing about them. Another daughter married one James McDonald, I think, of Marlborough; they seem to be doing well. Another daughter is yet unmarried. There was, a way back in the forties or fifties, one James P. McInnis, who married Miss Althea Alford, daughter of Lodwick B. Alford, who has already been mentioned in or among the Alfords; he did not live long after marriage; seemed to be an energetic and pushing man. Whether he was any relation of the "Carolina" McInnises or not, is unknown to the writer. Another McInnis (Miles), who has been dead many years, lived in upper Marion; he married a Miss Townsend, a sister of old man Light Townsend, a well known citizen of Marlborough County.

Old Miles McInnis was a harmless and inoffensive man; raised a considerable family, of whom nothing is now known. Don't know whether he was related to the "Carolina" McInnises or not; but Miles seems to be a family name; as John L. McInnis has a brother by that name, I infer that old Miles. McInnis, of whom I am now writing, was of the same family—perhaps, a brother of old Duncan McInnis. Old man Miles McInnis has been dead many years; he was not a man of much energy, though full of native Scotch honesty.

STAFFORD.—The first Stafford in the county known to the writer was the late Malcolm Stafford; don't know anything of his parentage or whence he came; he was a Scotchman, a man of more than ordinary intelligence, better educated than most men of his day, a Christian gentleman, and a very useful man in his neighborhood; was much missed therein after his death, which, I think, occurred some time in the fifties. He married Miss Jeanette Campbell, daughter of old man Duncan Campbell, on north side of Little Pee Dee, in what is now called Carmichael Township; he settled on the south side of that river, near where Stafford's Bridge now stands; he raised a considerable family—three sons, James Harvey, Duncan C. and Neill E., and three daughters. Of the sons, not one of them ever married. James Harvey Stafford died a few months ago, I suppose, near seventy years of age; he was one of our best citizens, accumulated a large property, had a fine plantation, upon which he built a palatial residence, and had everything about him necessary for comfort and the enjoyment of life, except a wife and children. He had $5,000 stock in the Dillon factory; a large stockholder also in the Bank of Dillon, and president of the same. He lost, some years ago, by the failure of the Bank of Hanover, in Wilmington, N. C., $3,000, and his maiden sister, Laura, lost therein $10,000; they were very prosperous. Captain James H. Stafford was no ordinary man. The following is from the pen of Captain A. T. Harllee, in reference to Captain Stafford: "He was a man of superior intelligence, and traveled much in his time. In 1856, he, with a number of other young men from the State, went to the then Territory of Kansas, and was engaged in what was called the pro-slavery war, in which old John Brown, afterwards hung at Harper's Ferry, Va., Jim Lane and other Abolitionists were conspicuous figures. Matters becoming somewhat settled at the theatre of war, Captain Stafford betook himself away out on the frontier of the territory on the Big Blue River, 200 miles from the settlement, and pre-empted a claim of 160 acres of land; but the winters were too severe, and after remaining a year, he returned to his home in South Carolina. At the breaking out of the war he raised a company with John W. Harllee as First Lieutenant, Duncan Murphy, Second Lieutenant, and William Manning as Brevet Second Lieutenant. The two latter were killed in Virginia, and Lieutenant Harllee was permanently disabled for field service by a wound in the knee. His company saw much service in Virginia in Jenkins' famous brigade. Since the war he lived most of his time on his old home place; but having purchased and built a fine residence on his plantation on the North Carolina State line, at 'Lone Home,' he resided there till his death, a few weeks ago, his sister, Laura, living with him." He was postmaster at "Lone Home." Captain J. H. Stafford was an extensive farmer, and succeeded well in his vocation. He was elected, without seeking it, a County Commissioner in 1880, served very acceptably one term, and never after sought any office. Duncan C. Stafford, the second son, was killed in the trenches by a sharpshooter, in 1863; he was Second Lieutenant in Captain A. T. Harllee's company of the 8th Regiment. He was an excellent young man, of fine character and very promising. Neill E. Stafford, the youngest son, lives at the old homestead, near Dillon; he is a graduate of Davidson College, is a well informed man, went into the war at fifteen years of age and was a gallant soldier; has never married, lives a bachelor's life. Of the daughters of Malcolm Stafford, the eldest, Delitha, married the late William R. Stackhouse, near Dillon; by this marriage, three daughters and one son were born. The eldest daughter is yet unmarried. Another daughter, Fannie, married Stonewall Watson; she has five children, three daughters and two sons. Another daughter married H. B. Floyd, near Campbell's Bridge; they have a young family. The son, Duncan Stackhouse, married a Miss Williams, daughter of J. B. Williams, of Nichols, S. C. Evaline Stafford, daughter of old Malcolm Stafford, married D. J. McKay; by this marriage, six daughters were born and raised; four of these daughters married, one of whom is dead; don't know to whom these daughters married. The two youngest daughters of D. J. McKay and wife are single, and live with their parents. Miss Laura Stafford, another daughter of Malcolm Stafford, has never married; she lived with her brother, James H., until his death, a few weeks ago, and still resides there, in a state of single blessedness. Old man Malcolm Stafford was a surveyor, and did much in that line. The writer has seen many of his plats, which were characterized by accuracy and neatness; has also seen wills and deeds drawn by him; in these respects he was a very useful man.

BLUE.—William Blue, first of the name in upper Marion, on north side of Little Pee Dee and Shoe Heel Creek; he was the original grantee of the lands on which he and his descendants have ever since lived. William Blue had only two sons, Alexander and Daniel, and several daughters. Daniel Blue married a Miss McArthur, and raised a large family, all girls but one, William Blue, who was killed in battle in Virginia, in Captain J. H. Stafford's company of 1st Regiment South Carolina, Hagood's Brigade, early in the war. Of the daughters of Daniel Blue, Mary married Duncan N. McCall, who was a gallant soldier of the Confederacy, and now resides on part of the Daniel Blue homestead, and has two children, both girls—one of whom is the wife of Albert M. Baker, a live and progressive farmer of that section of the county. Another daughter, Sarah, married Milton McPhaul, of North Carolina; he and his wife are both dead; their children have moved to Georgia. The youngest daughter, Nancy, married a Mr. Miran, of North Carolina; he died soon after their marriage, and she lives on the old homestead, with her three sisters, Martha Ann, Flora and Catharine—all of them now well advanced in years. Alexander Blue, the younger of the two brothers, was one of the staunchest citizens of the county; he was from early manhood to his death one of the ruling elders in Ashpole Presbyterian Church, just across the State line from where he lived, and he rarely ever missed a service at that church; he was beloved and respected by all who knew him. He married Ann Alford, a daughter of Major Sion Alford, a prominent citizen of Robeson County, N. C., when a young man; two children were the issue of the marriage, daughters. The eldest, Mary Ann, just after the war, married Captain A. C. Sinclair, who was the surviving commander of Fairlee's old company of Orr's Rifles, and they now reside on the Alexander Blue homestead, and have a family of five grown up children. The youngest daughter, Bettie, married Nathaniel McNair, of North Carolina, who died in 1894, leaving her with one child, a daughter, married to Edwin Smith, a lawyer of Red Springs, N. C., where he, his wife and Mrs. McNair now reside. One of the daughters of old William Blue and a sister of Daniel and Alexander Blue, married Daniel McDuffie; by this marriage only one child was born, a son, named William McDuffie, who was a very promising young man; he graduated at Davidson College with distinction, and died soon after graduation, in 1860. Many in the Hofwyl Academy neighborhood will remember William McDuffie, as a teacher in that academy for two or more sessions, about 1855 or 1856—may be 1854. He was a close student, bent on education—his close application to study may have shortened his days. The writer's older children went to school to him at Hofwyl. Another daughter of old William Blue married a Mr. Campbell, and had one daughter, but she, too, died young. His other daughters never married, but lived to be very old ladies; all are now dead. The name of Blue, so far as this family is concerned, is already or about to become extinct in the county.

BAKER.—The Baker family, in North Marion, will next be noticed. Squire Neill Baker, the first known in that section, was a sturdy Scotchman and an excellent citizen of the northern section of the county; he married Polly McArthur, and left many descendants in his section. One of his grand-sons, A. M. Baker, hereinbefore mentioned as a prosperous and progressive man, owns the old homestead. One of his sons, Edmund Baker, married a Miss McGist; he died without issue. Another son, James Baker, married a Miss Bracy, and moved to North Carolina, where he died, and left a family of several children. An older son, John D. Baker, married Miss Lovedy McPriest, and died, leaving her with two sons—Albert M. Baker, above spoken of, and Neill A. Baker. The widow, Lovedy Baker, lives with her son, Neill A. Baker, in Georgia. Old man Neill Baker had but two daughters. The oldest married William McKay, of North Carolina, and moved to Mississippi, where his wife died. The other daughter, Jeannette, married, just at the close of the war, Captain Gilbert W. McKay, who was at one time Captain of Fairlee's old company, and who may be remembered by many who now live in the town of Marion, as he lived there when he went into the war. Both are now dead, leaving two children surviving—John W. McKay, who lives at McCall, S. C., and Mary, who married John Millsaps, and moved to Georgia, where they now reside.

McPriest.—Alexander McPriest, a good citizen and staunch old Scotchman, lived in the same section of the county; he married a Miss McKellar, raised a large family of children, all girls, but one, named Peter E. McPriest, who served through the war, but is now dead. One daughter married John D. Baker, as already mentioned. Another married William Braddy Lester, who also served through the war in Orr's Rifles; he and his wife are both living. Two other daughters, Katie and Mary Ann, never married, and are living on their portion of their father's old homestead.

McKellar.—Peter McKellar was among the first settlers of this section of the county. He raised a large family, some of whom moved away, but many of their descendants still remain and own portions of the old McKellar lands. A. McKellar Trawick and his brother, William, grand-sons of Archie McKellar and great-great-grand-sons of the original Peter McKellar, now own one of the finest plantations in Carmichael Township, adjoining the plantations of Captain A. C. Sinclair, Captain A. T. Harllee and R. P. Hamer, Jr., the latter owning a portion of the McKellar lands, and Captain D. J. McKay another portion of the same. Archie McKellar, a grand-son of old Peter, married a Miss McCormick, of North Carolina, and raised a large family of daughters, and two sons, Peter and John, both of whom were killed in battle in Virginia early in the war. All the daughters died single, but one, Elmyra, who married David Trawick, who was also killed, leaving her with the two sons above mentioned, "Mack" and William, with whom she lives; neither of them are married. Captain D. J. McKay, as noted above, lives on the John McKellar homestead, near "Lone Home," in this section; he has been and still is one of the most progressive of the many progressive farmers of his section of the county; by industry and perseverance he has amassed a comfortable living, and is one of the substantial and wealthy farmers of the county. He volunteered in the commencement of the war, and was First Lieutenant of Co. D, 25th S. C. Regiment, McKerrall's old company, and served to the close of the war; he was severely wounded and still suffers at times from his old wounds.

McKAY.—Daniel McKay, the grand-father of Captain D. J. McKay, came to this county direct from Scotland, at what time is not known; he had and raised two sons, John and Archie. John McKay married Katie Alford, a daughter of Major Sion Alford, of North Carolina, by whom he had and raised three sons, Captain G. W. McKay, Alford McKay, who died just as he attained manhood, and D. J. McKay, and three daughters, Flora Ann, Bettie and Clarkey. Of the sons, G. W. McKay married a Miss Baker, as already related, and he and wife are both dead, as herein stated. Captain D. J. McKay, just after the close of the war, married Miss Evaline Stafford, daughter of Malcolm Stafford, as herein already stated in or among the Stafford family. D. J. McKay is an Elder in the Ashpole Presbyterian Church, a regular attendant; he has, from early manhood, been an enthusiastic Mason, and has several times been Master of the lodges of which he was a member. Of the daughters of John McKay, Flora Ann, the eldest, married Colonel John A. Rowland, of Lumberton, N. C., whose eldest son, Hon. Alfred Rowland, was a Representative in Congress for two terms, from the Sixth Congressional District of North Carolina, and declined a re-election on account of his health, and died soon after the expiration of his term. Bettie McKay, daughter of John McKay, married Dr. John K. Alford, of North Carolina, and had one son; and after the death of her husband, moved with her son to Texas, where she died; her son is now a prominent lawyer of the "Lone Star State." Clarkey, the youngest daughter, married Henry Alford, of Selkirk, S. C., a son of the late Neill Alford; they moved to North Carolina, where they raised a family, two sons and three daughters; the sons are successful business men at Maxton, N. C., and Henry Alford's wife has been dead several years, which leaves Captain D. J. McKay the only survivor of John McKay's children. Archie McKay, brother of John, married a daughter of John Drake, of Robeson County, N. C. Archie McKay was the father of the late Hector T. McKay, who married a sister of Hon. James McRae, as his first wife; and James McRae, for his first wife, married a sister of Hector T. McKay; another sister of H. T. McKay married R. B. Braddy, who died, leaving one child, a daughter, who married a Mr, Morrison, of North Carolina. Hector T. McKay married, as a second wife, the widow of Dr. McKinnon. John J. McKay and his sister, Janie (don't know whether by the first or second marriage), are the only surviving children of Hector T. McKay, and live on his old homestead. Hector T. McKay was one of the first men of the county; well informed, of good habits, industrious and frugal, kind-hearted and liberal minded, thought for himself, and allowed the same privilege to others; he was a man of well-rounded character every way; never aspired to political preferment, was elected and served one term as County Commissioner without seeking it; he was an exemplary citizen. Would like to dwell more on his many good qualities, but space will not permit.

McCORMICK.—The McCormick family and history of Little Rock will next be noticed, and is from the pen of Captain A. T. Harllee: "John McCormick, better known to every one in his day as 'Little Mack,' was another old settler of the upper section of the township, on Shoe Heel Creek and the North Carolina State line, and lived in the immediate section of the Blues, Bakers, McKellars and McArthurs; he was a jolly old Scotchman and everybody admired him; he married a daughter of Duncan McEachern, on Wilkinson Swamp, in North Carolina, and raised a family of five sons, but no daughters. His two eldest sons, Neill and Allen, married in Anson County, N. C., and moved there and have lived there ever since, raising large families. His sons, Malcolm and Archie, died when young men. Duncan E. McCormick was the youngest of his sons; he married and lived all his life in Marion County; he was well known all over the county, having held the office of Tax Collector and various other stations of a public character; he was a good business man, and started out in life as a clerk in the store of Colonel Thomas Harllee, at old Harlleesville, which is now Little Rock; he afterwards taught school, and was one of the pioneers in business at what is now called Little Rock. The business of all that section before was done at the bridge, near where R. P. Hamer, Sr., now lives, and the postoffice was Harlleesville, and had been since the days of Thomas Harllee, Sr., who was the original owner of most of the lands around there for several miles. Duncan E., with Tristram B. Walters, bought some lots from Enoch J. Meekins, not far from the church and school house, which had been given the public by Thomas Harllee, Sr., for church and school purposes; and they built on the lands they bought dwellings, storehouse and a large hotel building, and thus launched the town of Little Rock, named it after a rock that protrudes above the ground some three or four feet, and weighs, perhaps, 500 pounds, and now stands in the fork of the roads, one leading to Mars Bluff and the other to Marion *via* Dillon. They went to work and got the postoffice removed there, and the name changed from Harlleesville to Little Rock. No opposition developing to the removal or change of names, as some parties who had procured a lot close at hand started a grog ship; and those who would have protested under other conditions and circumstances, were glad of the change of name; the grog shop, however, was short-lived, and there has never been one there since. It must not be inferred that Duncan E. was favorable to or a promoter of the grog-shop, for he was not, and was and always remained until his death a strictly temperate and moral man. Little Rock boomed for a while. At one time there were eight or ten stores in full blast and a large amount of business was done there. J. W. Dillon commenced business at that point and accumulated much of his large fortune there; he remained there until the railroad was projected and the town of Dillon established, and he removed all his business to that point. Duncan E. McCormick first married Martha Beckwith, and raised a family of three sons and two daughters. Mary, the eldest, married John McGirt, of Robeson County, N. C.; they have a large family of sons and daughters. Flora married John C. Hargrove, son of Asa Hargrove; he first moved to North Carolina, and then to Mississippi, where they now live, and have several sons and daughters, all grown. Duncan E. had three sons, John, Philip and General (nick-name), all of whom were gallant soldiers of the Confederacy, and after the war all of them removed to Texas, where they are good citizens. Duncan E. McCormick's second marriage was to Harriet Walters, the widow of William Walters; she was the daughter of one Ridgell, and in her marriage with William Walters had two daughters and one son. The eldest daughter, Bettie, married Daniel W. Alford, and they live at Dillon, S. C., and have two daughters and one son. The youngest daughter, Willie (Walters), married R. A. Brunson, after the war, and had two daughters and one son; she is now dead. Augustus J. Walters, the son, married Sallie, the daughter of Alfred Edino; they now live at Forreston, Clarendon County, S. C., and have two sons and one daughter, all grown—the latter married. In his second marriage, Duncan E. had one son and three daughters. The son, A. P. McCormick, was a brilliant young man, was a lawyer and died soon after his admission to the bar. His eldest daughter (by the second marriage), Georgianna, married Duncan McLaurin, one of Dillon's most prominent and progressive citizens; he was the first settler in the new town, was its first Postmaster, and on the organization of the town was its first Mayor or Intendant; he owns three fine plantations; one near the town of Dillon, one on the east side of Little Pee Dee, in Carmichael Township, and one above Little Rock, which includes the old William Walters homestead; he is a large stockholder in the Dillon Tobacco Warehouse, in the Dillon Bank, oil mill and the new cotton factory; he has three children, two sons and one daughter, all of whom are living with him. The other two daughters of Duncan E. McCormick, Ada and Ellen, the youngest children, and were twins. Ellen died when about grown. Ada married W. Boone White, and they live in Forreston, in Clarendon County, S. C. "Little Mack McCormick," so-called, I suppose, to distinguish him from some other larger John McCormick, was a capital man and of unique character; he loved whiskey and sometimes drank too much, perfectly harmless when drinking, and at such times was very religious, and talked religion a great deal. On one occasion, in the fall of 1839, the writer chanced to spend the night together with "Little Mack" and his wife at old man Gilbert McEachern's on Hayes Swamp. "Little Mack" married the sister of old Gilbert, who at the time had a lot of hard cider on hand. It was on Saturday night. During the afternoon and evening the cider was passed around pretty frequently, and "Little Mack" got pretty tight. The writer in those days did not drink cider or anything stronger—besides, I went there to see Miss Margaret Ann, a daughter of old man Gilbert, and a nice girl she was, too—hence I did not join in the cider drinking. At a late hour we all retired. Before day the next morning (Sunday), I was awaked by "Little Mack," who slept in a room adjacent to mine, singing aloud so as to be heard through the whole house, the following familiar lines:

> "Sweet is the day of sacred rest,
> No mortal care shall seize my breast;
> O may my heart in tune be found
> Like David's harp of solemn sound," &c.

He did not stop at singing one verse, but kept on until the whole hymn was sung, and aroused the whole house—to which he gave a lecture on Sabbath observance. Another instance of his religious zeal when "in his cups" is related as follows: Away back in the thirties, there was a circuit preacher on this circuit by the name of Mahoney. At one of his revival meetings or a camp meeting, which were very common in that day, "Little Mack" professed religion. Some years afterward, Mahoney paid a visit to his people about Harlleesville, and had an appointment to preach at Liberty Chapel, as it was then called. Mahoney was very popular when he was on the circuit, and consequently a great many went to hear and to see him, and among them was "Little Mack"—he went pretty tight. On meeting Mahoney, he grabbed his hand and said, "O, Brother Mahoney; I am so glad to see you. I never will forget you, for you were the one that converted my soul." To which Mahoney replied, "It looks like some of my bungling work; if God had converted your soul, you would not have been here to-day drunk." Notwithstanding this stinging reply of Mahoney, "Little Mack" was not nonplussed in the least, but insisted that his conversion was genuine, and Brother Mahoney was the instrument. There were worse men than "Little Mack," if he did drink; he has been dead fifty years or more—*requiescat in pace.*

Another family of McCormicks will next be noticed. Neill McCormick, known as Squire Neill, was the elder brother of "Little Mack," and lived in the fork of Hays and Persimmon Swamps, adjoining the McKellars and the McArthurs; his old homestead is now owned by D. J. McKay; he married Katie McDonald, a direct descendant of Flora McDonald, of Revolutionary fame, and her grand-daughter, Bettie McCormick, married another descendant of the same heroine, Hugh A. McDonald, who now lives at Dillon, S. C. Squire Neill had eight sons and one daughter. His elder sons, Daniel, Joe and John, went West—the first to Mississippi, the two latter to Texas, where they all married and raised families. Randall and Wylie died soon after reaching manhood, and the three others, James, Thomas and Frank, were all killed in battle in Virginia. James and Thomas were in Fairlee's old company, Orr's Rifles; Frank was in Captain Stafford's company. Thomas and Frank were both killed in the second battle of Manassas, at about the same time, and James was killed at Gaines' Mill. The latter married Drusilla McCormick, of North Carolina, and left a family of two sons and four daughters. The eldest, Warren Alford McCormick, married a Miss Wise, and moved to Marlborough, where they now live. The other married Virgie Legette, the great-grand-daughter of old James McArthur, and lives on his old home place. One of the daughters, Flora Amanda, married T. R. McLellan, who is dead; but she, with a large family of sons and daughters, survives. Laura, another daughter, married Henry Barnes, of North Carolina. Another married Richard Atkinson, of North Carolina, and they live at McColl, S. C.; and the youngest, as noted above, married Captain Hugh A. McDonald, of Cumberland County, N. C.; he was a gallant soldier of the Confederacy; they now live at Dillon, S. C., and have a large family of children. The one daughter of Squire Neill McCormick, Manila, married Neill McEachern, and they left two daughters and three sons. One of the daughters, Manila, married Charles Altman, and they, with a grown up family of five children, live in Horry County. The other daughter, Flora, married James McKellar, both of whom are dead, and left several children—the youngest son, Peter McKellar, being a prosperous merchant at Bennettsville, S. C., where he married a niece of Hon. Joshua H. Hudson. Of the three sons of Neill McEachern, William died just as he was grown. Edmund Q. served through the war, and died soon after. John C. McEachern is still living; he, too, was one of the heroes who served from the beginning to the end in the cause which was lost; he was a private in Fairlee's company, and bears the honorable marks of service on his person; soon after the war he married Jennie, a daughter of "Hatter" John Carmichael, and they have raised a family of four sons and two daughters, and he and his family live on his fine farm in the fork of Little Pee Dee and Hayes Swamp. The widow of Squire Neill McCormick lived to a very great age, and died on his homestead since the war. Neill McEachern after the death of his wife, Manila, again married, Sallie McCall, of North Carolina, by whom he raised a family of four sons and two daughters. Neill Duncan, the eldest, married Margaret McDuffie, daughter of Neill McDuffie, and has a family of four daughters; he lives at McColl, S. C. Robert Bruce, the next son, married Amarantha, daughter of A. S. Buie, and has a family of one son and three daughters; they live near Hamer, S. C. Peter G. and Edmund Bishop McEachern, the two youngest sons, live on their fine plantation, near Hamer, and their mother and two sisters live with them; neither of them have married; they are up-to-date, progressive farmers, and it is said of them that no matter how high the price of cotton may rule, they always keep a lot for a better price. The writer heard a candidate who visited these McEacherns say that he saw eleven fat Chester hogs there that would average 400 pounds each, besides a number of smaller ones—that was some three years ago; they owe no one anything; they have much more to sell than to buy.

McARTHUR.—James McArthur was one of the original settlers on the north side of Hays Swamp and on the North Carolina State line; he married a Miss Campbell and raised a family of three sons and four daughters. The eldest daughter, Effie, married Gadi Braswell, and her only son, Richard H. Braswell, now owns and lives upon a part of the old McArthur lands or homestead, just across the State line. Mary, another daughter, married Richard J. Millsaps, and moved to another part of the McArthur lands or homestead in North Carolina; they had one daughter, Mary Jane, who married T. J. Legette, and she now lives at Rowland, N. C. Her four daughters, the eldest, Louise, married Joseph A. McEachern, and she died, I think, childless. The next oldest married Robe Bond; the third to James A. McCormick, and the fourth and youngest to W. A. Ivey, who lives at Dillon, S. C.—all of them owning part of the McArthur lands. The other two daughters, Katie and Jennie, never married, and both of them died at advanced ages since the war. Alexander, John and James were his three sons. The two former lived to be old men and never married, and died since the war; both of them were too old for service in the army, but were patriotic citizens and contributed all in their power to the success of the cause that was lost. James, the youngest son, married Sarah McDonald, daughter of Neill McDonald, in the "old Fork," which is known in that region as such, being the territory in the fork of Shoe Heel Creek and Wilkinson Swamp and Little Pee Dee River; they had one child, a daughter, Ella, who married George R. Campbell, of North Carolina, and they live on their father's old homestead, or a part of it; Mr. Campbell is a good farmer and a good citizen. James McArthur went to the front in the beginning of the war, in Captain Stafford's company; was sent to the hospital, sick, at Culpeper C. H., and was never heard from after being sent from his company, and it is supposed that he died there, and is one of the many unknown dead whose remains repose in the soil of old Virginia. His widow, in 1873, married M. M. Watson, of North Carolina, who was a gallant soldier in the Confederate army, and lost a leg in the service; he was one of our most respected adopted citizens at his death, and his widow died soon after; they left two sons and one daughter, and they live on another part of the old McArthur homestead, and are progressive and industrious young men.

McIntyre.—Dougald, Daniel, Duncan and Archie McIntyre, four brothers, came from Scotland to Marion County in the early part of the nineteenth century—say from 1815 to 1820; all of them grown young men. Dougald, the eldest, married in Scotland; his wife was Lilly Campbell; they settled on the place where they lived and died, and where their daughters, Jennette and Lilly, now reside; they raised a family of twelve children, six sons and six daughters—the two eldest of whom, Elizabeth and John B., were born in Scotland; the sons were John B., Dougald C., Joseph, Duncan E., James and William Wallace McIntyre—none of them are now living; the daughters were Elizabeth, Jennette, Nancy, Margaret, Lilly and Mary. John B., the eldest son, was a tailor by trade; moved to North Carolina; he married Civil Legette, and lived until after the war, when he acquired the farm near Hamer, where he remained until his death; he raised six children—three sons and three daughters; the sons were John A., Cousar and Dougald; and the daughters were Sarah, Mary and Margaret. John A. lives in North Carolina, and is unmarried. Dougald married Lilly Faulk, of Selkirk, and lives in North Carolina. Cousar married Fannie Willis, and moved to Georgia. Sarah, the eldest daughter of John B., married John W. McMillan. Mary married John W. McLean, and is still a resident of the neighborhood. Margaret is unmarried, and lives with her brother, Dougald, in North Carolina. Dougald C., second son of old Dougald, moved to Robeson County, N. C., when quite a young man, and remained there during his life; he was a leading spirit in many benevolent and public enterprises in his county, and for a long time filled the office of School Commissioner and also that of Magistrate; his widow and several children and many grand-children survive him, and are among the most highly respected people of Robeson County. Joseph, the third son of old Dougald, was an energetic and active farmer; at the outbreak of the war he volunteered and went to the front, where he remained until the surrender; he married Emaline Carmichael, a daughter of Sheriff Archie Carmichael, and settled on the place near Hamer, where they lived and where they both died, leaving a family of seven children—three sons and four daughters; the sons are Duncan, Archie and Leighton; the daughters are Nettie, Lizzie, Isla and Blanche, and have all, with one exception, removed elsewhere. Duncan went to Texas. Archie married Katie McLellan, daughter of Timothy R. McLellan, and settled on a place adjoining that of his aunt. Leighton is an invalid, and lives with his sister. Nettie, the eldest daughter, married J. Edgar Bass; they live in Florida; this couple when they married weighed over five hundred pounds avoirdupois. Lizzie, Isla and Blanche are single, and live in Dillon, with their invalid brother, Leighton. Duncan E., the fourth son of old Dougald, was a Presbyterian minister; he was pastor of the Presbyterian Church at Helena, Ark., when the war commenced; he returned to his old home, and in order that his brother, James, who was the business manager and dependence of his widowed mother, might remain with her and his sisters, he went to the front as a substitute for his brother, James, and died while in service. James, the fifth son of old Dougald, was a man of some sterling qualities, was noted for his kindness of heart, and his affectionate care for those dependent upon him; he lived with his mother until after the war, when his younger brother, Wallace, succeeded him; he married Mrs. Rebecca McCormick, a daughter of Woodward Manning, and removed to his late residence on Buck Swamp; his widow and one son survive him; the son's name is W. M. McIntyre. William Wallace, the sixth son of old Dougald, the youngest of the six brothers, was an active and progressive farmer; he lived with his mother and sisters, managing the farm, and also owned the place near Hamer, now the property of Frank Edens; he served through the war in Co. I, Tenth Regiment, S. C. V. The daughters of old Dougald McIntyre, Elizabeth, Jennette, Nancy and Lilly, never married. Elizabeth and Nancy are dead. Jennette and Lilly are living on the old homestead. Margaret married A. C. McKenzie, and lives in North Carolina. Daniel McIntyre, one of the four brothers from Scotland, was a farmer; he settled on a place adjacent to that of his brother, Dougald, where he lived and died; he married Mary Carmichael, a daughter of "Commodore" Dougald Carmichael, and had three sons—Dougald W., John C. and Duncan A. McIntyre—none of whom are now living. Dougald W. was a farmer and surveyor; he was twice married; first, to Margaret McArthur, of North Carolina; she died, leaving three children—one son, Palmer, and two daughters, Celestia and Rosanna; both of whom are married and live in North Carolina. His second wife was Katie Roberts; she died, leaving six children—one son, Donald, and five daughters, Margaret, Kittie, Delia, Lilly and Cora; all are single, and with their elder brother, Palmer, and live on the homestead of their father. John C., second son of Daniel McIntyre, was by occupation a farmer; at the breaking out of the war he enlisted in the Confederate army and went to the front; he was severely wounded in battle, from which he never entirely recovered; he married Sarah Ann Carmichael, a daughter of Captain Neill M. Carmichael, and settled on the old homestead of his Grandfather Carmichael, on Pee Dee, where he lived for several years; afterwards moved to the home of his father, whose failing health required the care and attention he and his kind-hearted wife could give him; his father died soon after, leaving to him the place, but he survived his father but a short while; his wife, also, is dead; they had five children, two sons and three daughters; the sons are Jefferson D. and Daniel Frank; the daughters are Loretta, Mary Catling and Orella. Jefferson is an energetic and progressive farmer; he lives on his farm, near Hamer; he married Louise Carmichael, a daughter of Archie M. Carmichael. Daniel, Frank and his eldest sister, Loretta, are single, and live on the homestead of their father. Mary Cutting married G. Raymond Berry, and they live at Dillon, S. C. G. Raymond Berry is now the County Superintendent of Education. Orella married Peter Stewart, of North Carolina, and they live on their farm, near Carmichael. Duncan A., third son of Daniel McIntyre, was a man of some education and business attainments; he was engaged in teaching school at the outbreak of the war; he enlisted in the Confederate army and served through the war; after the war he accepted a clerkship with S. A. Durham & Co., of Marion, where he remained several years; he married Anne Legette, a daughter of Dr. A. S. Legette, of Centenary, and removed to Centenary, but died soon after, leaving one son, Daniel McIntyre. Duncan and Archie, brothers of Dougald and Daniel McIntyre. Duncan was a Presbyterian preacher; he died unmarried, while still a young man. Archie married Miss Effie McCollum, of North Carolina—I believe, an aunt of the late Brown McCollum—and settled on land adjoining his brother, Daniel; and after having four or five children, sold his land, 175 acres, to the writer, in 1836, for $225, and moved to Alabama. Mary McIntyre, daughter of old Dougald, married Joseph W. Williamson, and they settled on their homestead, near Kentyre Church, where they lived, and where they both died in the prime of life, leaving a family of seven children, several of whom were quite small. In connection with the McIntyres of Carmichael Township, another family of the same name in the county will here be noticed—I mean the McIntyres of the town of Marion. Archie McIntyre was the first known of this family—don't know where he came from or anything of his parentage; he was, doubtless, a Scotchman; he was a tailor by trade—this in former times was a lucrative trade; he married Miss Sophia Howard, of West Marion, daughter of old man Richard Howard, of that section, who was both wealthy and prominent in his day. Archie McIntyre settled in Marion, and lived there all his life; by his marriage he had seven sons and three daughters, that were raised; the sons were Richard, Robert C., Duncan, Archie, George A., Joseph and Douglas; the daughters were Matilda, Rebecca and Sallie. Of the sons, Richard married Miss McColl, and settled in West Marion; he had one son, named Richard (may have had other children); Richard, Sr., died, while yet young, and his widow married Rev. D. E. Frierson, a Presbyterian minister of some note, and went to Anderson

County. Richard McIntyre, Jr., grew up and married a Miss McPherson, daughter of Robert McPherson, of West Marion; he had some family, don't know how many or of what sex; he died a few years ago, and left his widow and family on the homestead, and they are still there. Think Richard (senior) was a graduate of the South Carolina College, and a young man of promise. Robert Charles, the second son, was also a graduate of the South Carolina College; he married, first, a Miss Murdoch, of Marlborough County; she died in a few years, childless, when he married, a second time, a sister of his first wife. These Murdoch girls had two brothers, who both died young, unmarried; hence the fine plantation of their father, near "Beauty Spot," in Marlborough, fell to Mrs. McIntyre; they moved up there and raised a considerable family of sons and daughters, all of whom are now grown. The mother died, and Robert Charles and his family surviving, reside thereon. Robert Charles McIntyre was quite a literary man, was a Magistrate for some years in Marion, soon after the close of the war; he was very capable and filled that position very acceptably. Duncan McIntyre, the third son of Archie McIntyre, married, first, Miss Rosa Evans, a daughter of General William Evans; she died, childless, after a year or so, and he married again, the widow of John C. McClannaghan, whose maiden name was Betts, a daughter of Rev. Charles Betts, of grateful memory; they have no offspring, and live in West Marion or Florence County. In the early part of the war, Duncan McIntyre raised a company as Captain, which formed a part of the Eighth South Carolina Regiment, and gallantly went through the war; he also went to the South Carolina College, but think his educational course in that institution was interrupted by the war; he, though, is a well informed man. Archibald McIntyre, the fourth son of Archie McIntyre, Sr., grew up, and married Miss Martha Betts, another daughter of Rev. Charles Betts, about the commencement of the war; Archie, notwithstanding his recent marriage, volunteered in the first company (Captain M. B. Stanley's) that left Marion for Morris Island, near Charleston, the 4th January, 1861. After the capture of Fort Sumter by the Confederate forces, the company was reorganized, and W. P.

Shooter, who was First Lieutenant in the original company, was elected Captain, in which Archie, Jr., was a member; they went to Virginia, and in some of the early battles in that frontier State was fatally wounded and died—a more gallant soldier was not in the Confederate army. Dr. A. McIntyre, now in the town of Marion, a prominent practicing physician, was born, I think, a short time after his father's death; the widow married, a second time, Dr. E. B. Smith, an able physician, and a most excellent farmer, below Marion, who has a family of sons and, perhaps, daughters; one or two of Dr. Smith's sons are practicing physicians. George A. McIntyre, the fifth son of Archie, Sr., was a young man at the beginning of the war, was also a Lieutenant in Captain Stanley's, afterwards Captain Shooter's company; volunteered and went to the front, and remained in the service till he lost his arm; he became Captain of the company after the promotion of Captain Shooter to a Lieutenant Colonelcy. After Captain G. A. McIntyre became disabled for active service by the loss of an arm, he was appointed enrolling officer and assigned to Marion, and continued to perform the duties of that position to the end of the war. Soon after the war, Captain McIntyre married Miss Emma Young, daughter of Major Johnson B. Young, and settled on a part of his mother's fine plantation, on the west side of Catfish, and has succeeded well in his calling. At one time since the redemption of the State from carpet-bag and scallawag rule, in 1876, Captain McIntyre was appointed County Treasurer, which position he honestly and faithfully filled for three or four years, when he resigned, or declined a further appointment; since which time he has been in retirement upon his excellent farm, and may be truthfully said to be one of our best citizens; he has raised a considerable family, mostly or all girls. One married W. C. Foxworth, who lives near him, and I think, another one is also married, but to whom is not remembered. Captain McIntyre is a model man and is what is termed the noblest work of God, "an honest man." Joseph McIntyre, the sixth son of Archie, Sr., went into the war and was a gallant soldier; married Miss Mary Mullins, oldest daughter of the late Colonel W. S. Mullins; they first settled over Catfish, on a part of the late Daniel F. Berry's lands, where he farmed for several years with as much success as might be expected on such a place; after a while there was a division of the large body of the Mullins lands, near Mullins, and the old Mullins homestead was allotted to Mrs. McIntyre, to which they moved and now own, and are doing fairly well; they have several children, how many or of what sex is unknown. Douglas McIntyre, the seventh and youngest son of Archie, Sr., is a prominent and leading merchant of Marion, and has been for several years; he married, first, Miss Jennie Moody, a daughter of E. J. Moody; by the marriage three children were born, as I think, two daughters and one son, or *vice versa;* his first wife dying, he married a Miss Fore, daughter of the late Daniel Fore, by whom he has some children, all small. His oldest daughter, Jennie, by his first marriage, married Robert Proctor, and they have gone West. Douglas McIntyre, in addition to his large mercantile interest, has a large farm nearby town, which he successfully runs; he is full of energy and enterprise and a model citizen; he was honored some few years ago by his fellow-citizens with a seat in the Representative branch of the State Legislature, which position he filled with credit to himself and satisfaction to his people. Archie McIntyre, Sr., had three daughters. The eldest, Matilda, married Ezra M. Davis, of West Marion, a well-to-do man; they raised a considerable family, but the writer does not know enough of them or about them to say more. Rebecca, the second daughter, married Rev. J. E. Dunlap, a brave and daring soldier of the Confederacy, in which he obtained the title of Colonel, and was and is a preacher of the Presbyterian Church—an able preacher he is; they raised a family of several children, sons and daughters; his wife died some years ago, and Colonel Dunlap has had the misfortune to lose, by death, two or three of his grown and promising children. Some years ago, Colonel Dunlap resigned his pastorate of the Presbyterian Church in Marion, and moved to Williamsburg County, and has charge of two or more churches in that county; he has not remarried, is yet a widower; his children are all grown. Colonel Dunlap is a large-hearted man, brave as "Julius Cæsar;" thinks for himself, and generally thinks right—no deceit in his make-up; a friend to the poor and a warm sympathiser with the distressed—a friend indeed. Sallie McIntyre, the third and youngest daughter of Archie, Sr., a charming lady, married Dr. D. F. Miles, our present and efficient Clerk of the Court, personally a very popular man; has just been elected to the third term; has been honored twice with a seat in the State Legislature; he has a farm some four or five miles from Marion; they have had five children—three daughters and two sons; the daughters are Sophia, Mary and Lillian—all married. Sophia married Charles E. Evans; they have three or four children. Mary married Lanneau Stackhouse; they have, perhaps, two children. Lillian married a Mr. Owens, first name not remembered; they all reside in Marion, and are good women. Dr. Miles and his wife, Sallie, had two sons, Frank and Lanneau. Frank, just at manhood, sickened and died, in 1899; so they have but one son left, *spes gregis,* who is a lad—hope he will live and help keep up and perpetuate the name. Archie McIntyre, Sr., though he began life as a tailor, managed well and accumulated a large property, and left it unencumbered for his widow and children; several of his children were small when he died, but the widow was a good manager also, and kept the estate free from debt, and at her death transmitted the same to them unencumbered. Archie McIntyre, Sr., though a tailor, like Andrew Johnson, of Tennessee, and who became President of the United States, was no ordinary man; he and his wife, Sophia, raised a family of high standing in every way. Of such a parentage their children and grand-children ought to be proud.

McKINLY.—John McKinly and his wife, who was Catharine McNish, and their children, Daniel, Duncan and Neill, Mary and Jennette, came from Scotland, and settled on the homestead, where they lived and died, and later where their children, Neill and Jennette, lived and died. Daniel, the oldest, was twenty-one years old when they landed, and Neill, the youngest, was six. Daniel married a Miss McCormic, of North Carolina, and settled on the place adjacent to the homestead of his father, where he lived and died; he applied himself to his chosen occupation with energy and perseverance, was a farmer on the intensive system of farming, and attained considerable success;

he had only one child, a son, Duncan C. McKinly; he was likewise a farmer, and settled on his fine farm near Kentyre Church; he married Sarah Gaddy, a daughter of William Gaddy; they had four children, two sons and two daughters; the sons are William D. and John D.; the daughters are Leonora and Mary. William D. removed elsewhere. John D. married Florence McKenzie, a daughter of David J. McKenzie; they live in Dillon. Mary is dead. Leonora married Hugh McLean, and they moved to Florida. Duncan C. McKinly, the father, is dead. Duncan. the son of old John, engaged in commercial pursuits and moved to Mississippi, where he accumulated a large property, but never married, and is dead. Neill McKinly never married, nor did his sister, Jennette; they lived and died on the homestead of their father, John McKinly. Duncan C. ultimately got all the property of his Uncle Duncan, of Mississippi, all his father's, and all his Uncle Neill's and Aunt Jennette's; but it seemed not to do him or his family any good—only whilst it was going; he died poor. Mary, the oldest daughter of old John McKinly, died unmarried, soon after attaining to womanhood.

McLELLAN.—Alexander McLellan and his brother, Malcolm, came to this country from Scotland, in the close of the eighteenth century, and settled on the lands on which some of their descendants now live and own. Alexander was married in Scotland, to Mary McKinnon, and lived there for some time after his marriage, and several children were born to them there, who died in infancy; one, a lad, named John, died after he settled here; he resided on the place recently the home of J. W. Williamson, where Daniel Walker Campbell now lives, and he died there in 1838 or 1839; he devoted himself to farming and stock raising, accumulating considerable wealth; of his children who reached maturity, there were four sons, Daniel, Duncan, Archie K. and Colin; and one daughter, Flora. Daniel lived on the homestead of his father; never married and died in 1860. Duncan lived on a farm adjacent to his brother and a part of his father's old homestead; he never married, and died in 1872. The plantation where Duncan lived has been divided—a part owned by R. P. Hamer, Sr., another part by R. P. Hamer, Jr., and still another part by Neill McDuffie, and on which he now resides. Archie K. McLellan married Miss Harriet Rogers, a daughter of Timothy Rogers, 4th December, 1833 (where Dr. J. F. Bethea now resides). The writer attended the wedding; there were more people there than he ever saw convened on such an occasion—the cavalcade that accompanied the groom was over one hundred. He settled on lands adjoining his brothers, Daniel and Duncan, and near his father's homestead, and resided there for many years, and then removed to North Carolina, remaining there till after the death of his brother, Duncan, and inheriting the homestead tract of his brother, he returned to South Carolina, and lived until his death, in 1887; he raised a large family of children—nine sons and five daughter; the sons were Malcolm, Alexander, Timothy R., Daniel, John B., Archie K., Jr., F. Tristram, Duncan and Robert. Malcolm moved to Pollard, Ala., when quite a youth; was married there to Miss Celia Jernagen, and lived and died there. Alexander was a brave and gallant soldier in a North Carolina regiment; he was captured and died in prison. He married, during the war, Miss Roxanna Gaddy, but left no children. Timothy R. married Flora Amanda McCormick, daughter of James Hunt McCormick; he resided near the old homestead of his father until his death, in 1897; his widow and eight children, four sons and four daughters, survive him. Daniel lived with his father until his death, and remained there until the old homestead was broken up and sold for division; he married Miss Sallie Legette, of North Carolina, in 1888; after her death, in 1892, he removed to North Carolina, where he now lives. John B., on attaining his majority, went to Benton, Ala., where he remained during his life; he was a man of splendid ability, and was elected to an important office of public trust, which he filled for many years; he was married to Miss Patty Blackshear, of Alabama, who, with three daughters, survive him. Archie K., Jr., lives in North Carolint, and is unmarried. F. Tristram is at present writing the very efficient Auditor of Marion County, to which he was elected in 1896, and again in 1898, and resides at Marion C. H.; he married, in 1899, Miss Harrelson, of this county. Duncan formerly lived in this county, but removed to North Carolina; he has been twice married; first, to Miss Hannah Wiggins, and then to a Miss Willis; his first wife left two children, a son and a daughter. The son, John Robert, was adopted by his Uncle Tristram, and is the Assistant Auditor of the county; he is a bright and intelligent youth. The daughters of Archie K., Sr., were Sarah, Margaret, Mary Ann, Flora and Moranza. Margaret married Allen Seely, and moved to North Carolina. Mary Ann married Archie Stewart, and also moved to North Carolina. The other daughters, Sarah, Flora and Moranza, are all unmarried, and live with their brother, Archie K., Jr., in North Carolina. Flora, the daughter of old Alexander McLellan, married Dougald B. Carmichael; they both lived on the place they settled upon, and died there; it is now owned and occupied by their youngest son, Malcolm C. Carmichael; she died at an advanced age, in 1877, her husband having died, in 1857, at the age of seventy-eight; the fruits of their marriage were two daughters, Mary Ann and Catharine, and five sons, Alexander A., Duncan C., Daniel, John L. and Malcolm C. Mary Ann, the oldest daughter (and, I believe, the oldest child), married Neill McDuffie; both are still living,* in far advanced age; they and their numerous family will be further noticed among the McDuffie family, *sequeus*. The daughter, Catharine, married Neill B. McQueen; she lived only a short time, and died; it is not known whether she left any offspring. The five sons all volunteered in the early part of the war; three of them, Alexander A., Daniel and John L., were killed or died in the service; the other two remained in service to the end, and returned home; Duncan C. and Malcolm C. still live, and are energetic and progressive farmers; have fine lands and are successful. Duncan C. Carmichael (familiarly called "Red Duncan"), married, first, Miss Sallie McKinnon, of North Carolina; she died, leaving two children—one son, Dougald A., and one daughter, Charlotte. Dougald A. went to Georgia, where he still lives. Charlotte married Neill J. Carmichael; he married, the second time, Lemantha Walters, of North Carolina; she has four children, none of whom are grown. Malcolm C. Carmichael, fifth son of Dougald B. and

---

*She (Mary Ann McDuffie) died a short time ago; her husband, Neill McDuffie, yet survives, eighty-three years of age, 15th March, 1901.

Flora, married Miss Amanda Carmichael, daughter of "Hatter John;" they have eight children—four sons, Albert E., John L., Neill C. and Walter; four daughters, Flora C., Ann Murphy, Martha and Mary. Albert E. and Neill C. moved to Mississippi, where they are prosperously engaged in the turpentine business. John L. died when about eight years old. Walter, the youngest son, is still at school. Flora C., the eldest daughter, married S. A. McQueen, of North Carolina; they live at Red Springs, N. C. Ann Murphy married Alexander McLellan, and they live at Dillon. Martha and Mary are still single, and are with their parents. Dougald B. Carmichael, the husband and father, was a very quiet, peaceable man, of lymphatic temperament and a man of remarkable equanimity; he was a blacksmith by trade—a good trade in those days; he did a great deal of work in the shop, whilst his wife, Flora, looked after the house department and somewhat after the farm; and after his death she looked after it all, except the blacksmith shop; Mrs. Carmichael was no ordinary woman; she had mind enough to grasp anything and everything in the affairs of life; a woman of fine physique, her mental qualities were of a superior order; of sanguine temperament, a cheerful disposition, of boundless ambition, and had the energy to back it up; made her hospitable home the seat of comfort; method and order were displayed in all the household affairs; she took the troubles of the war, the death of her daughter, Catharine, and husband, the loss of three sons in the struggles of war, philosophically, and with heroic courage set to work to repair the losses in property and means as far as she could, and help and render comfortable her surviving children; she succeeded well in so doing, and left them not only in homes of their own, but also left them her virtuous example, which is worth more than gold and silver. Colin McLellan, the youngest son and youngest child of old Alexander McLellan, married Rebecca Bethea, oldest daughter of "Buck Swamp" William Bethea; he settled on the place where he lived and died, in 1858; he was a successful farmer; he raised a family of four children, two sons and two daughters; the sons were William and Daniel; the two daughters were Mary and Flora. The sons were Confederate soldiers and served through the war in Captain Fulmore's company, Fifty-first Regiment, North Carolina Volunteers. Daniel died at the old home, in 1868, when quite a young man. William moved to North Carolina, and married Victoria McCormick, a daughter of James McCormick; he settled on lands inherited from his father in North Carolina, and was a successful farmer; but in a personal difficulty with an employee, Thomas Gilchrist, he was shot and killed, in 1872. Mary, the eldest daughter, married Carl Faulk, and moved to North Carolina, and died a few years ago. Flora married Richard Faulk, and resided for several years on her father's old homestead, on Buck Swamp, but removed to North Carolina a few years ago, where she now lives.

There was and is another family of McLellans in the county. The first of them known to the writer was Rev. Archie McLellan, and a blacksmith; he lived on the south side of Catfish, on Pigeon Bay; he was a local Methodist preacher; had a small farm, which he cultivated; he was a good man—the "salt of the earth;" he married a Miss Buie; had and raised a considerable family of several sons and daughters; he had also two orphan nephews, sons of a deceased brother, whom he raised—their names were John and Angus McLellan. Just before the war, the old gentleman sold his place on Pigeon Bay, and moved off to Britton's Neck, and bought another place, where he lived and died some time after the war; by his removal the writer lost sight of his family. Two sons, Peter and Enos, are remembered, and only two daughters are remembered—one named Elizabeth, the other name not remembered, but she married a Mr. Moore. His two oldest children, Elizabeth and Peter, together with his nephews, John and Angus, went to school to the writer in 1840, sixty years ago. Peter McLellan was also a blacksmith; he married a Miss Lane, a daughter of the late James C. Lane, and lived and followed his trade for some years at Little Rock, S. C.; he died and left some family; of them, however, nothing is known. Enos, another son, married a Miss Myers, of West Marion, and now lives at Dillon, a widower—his wife having died some years ago; he has not remarried; he has four or five daughters, some of whom are grown; he is a poor man, but a man of fine character, strict integrity and a hard worker. Elizabeth, the oldest child, has never married. Mrs. Moore was made a widow, about the time of General Lee's surrender, by the atrocious murder of her husband, at Little Rock. Moore was a good soldier of the Confederacy, was at home at the time, near Little Rock, on furlough, with a broken arm in a sling—fresh from a battle, in which his arm had been broken by a Minie ball or piece of shell; he went up to Little Rock, one afternoon, where he met with some parties who had imbibed spirits other than the patriotic spirit of the times, and they charged him with being a spy for the deserters of Maple Swamp notoriety, which he denied most vigorously—yet they shot and broke his other arm; he fell, and they walked up to him and cut his throat, dragged him off a few steps, and partially buried him in the jamb of a fence. His distressed wife, after the garrison came to Marion, went to the commandant for redress; they said they had no jurisdiction in the matter, but they advised her to go to the civil authorities and get a warrant for the arrest of the parties accused; she accordingly did so, and the warrant was lodged with the Sheriff; but no arrests were made, for reasons of State policy—that is, the authorities high in official life did not countenance prosecutions for murder committed during the war or just after the surrender—because, if the door was opened to such prosecutions, it would work both ways and would involve many of our best citizens; hence the warrant in question was never executed. It was, nevertheless, an inexcusable murder; the parties charged are all now dead, and have been for several years. I could specify more particularly as to the policy of the State, and as to the offense and the parties charged, but these things are already known. The widow remained in the neighborhood for two or three years and disappeared—at least, so far as is known to the writer. A girl raised by the late Samuel Stevenson (called Bettie Stevenson), and who married a Mr. Dozier, son of the late Dr. T. J. Dozier, of Britton's Neck, was the daughter of Mr. Moore, the man murdered—whether by a former marriage or by the McLellan marriage, the writer knoweth not. Old Archie McLellan, the preacher and blacksmith, was a Scotchman, and, perhaps, related to the McLellans, of Carmichael Township; he was an upright and just man.

SINCLAIR.—Archie Sinclair was a resident of Harlleesville Township, above Little Rock; he came from Scotland, in 1820, and settled on the place where he lived and died; his youngest daughter, Mary, now owning and living on his old homestead, and one of his grand-sons, A. M. McColl, living with her. (A. M. McColl died a few days ago, unmarried). He married, in Scotland, Catharine McGilvray, and they raised five sons and three daughters. The eldest son, John C., was born in Scotland, and when he attained manhood here, was married to the Widow Jennette McLucas; he died in 1852. Duncan removed to Georgia, and married and died there, leaving a family of grown-up children. Captain Daniel C. was the third son; he served throughout the war in cavalry; was one of the best farmers in the county, and a pioneer in the development of the now famous Contrary Swamp section of Carmichael Township; he accumulated by his farming operations a handsome property; he never married, and died in 1882. The fourth son, Captain A. C. Sinclair, has already been mentioned in or among the Blue family. The fifth son, Malcolm, was a soldier in the Confederate army, in Fairlee's company, Orr's Rifles, and died in the hospital in Charlottesville, Va. His eldest daughter, Nancy, married John L. McCall, Esq., of Marlborough, and they had a large family. Colonel C. S. McCall, of Bennettsville, is the eldest; he is one of the most successful men in the Pee Dee section of the State; conducts the largest mercantile business in this section, and owns several large plantations in Marlborough, which he, with his next oldest brother, T. Dickson McColl, manage very successfully; he has been, since 1876, three times elected State Senator from Marlborough, and on account of his manifold business connections, declined further service in the Senate; he has been frequently mentioned and solicited to become Governor of the State; he has never married. His other brothers, J. G. B. McColl and A. M. McColl (both now dead), own and successfully conduct the famous "Contrary Swamp" plantation, formerly owned by their uncle, Captain D. C. Sinclair; neither of them have ever married. The youngest son, John, is blind, but is a remarkably bright young man and a fine musician; he and his mother live near Bennettsville. Since the death of Squire McCall, their eldest daughter married John A. Pate, and they live in Bamberg, S. C. The second daughter, Pocahontas, married a Mr. Roper, and lives in Williamsburg County. The third daughter, Kate, married Hon. H. H. Newton, and lives in Bennettsville. The youngest daughter, Sallie, married Joe Edens, and lives near Clio, S. C. The second daughter of old Archie Sinclair, Sallie, never married, and died in 1869. The youngest daughter, Mary Sinclair, as elsewhere herein mentioned, never married, and lives on the old Archie Sinclair homestead. There are but few of this family, but what there are of them seem to prosper in everything except in the matrimonial field—they don't marry much.

McDuffie.—Alexander McDuffie, with his brothers, Duncan, George and Daniel, were the sons of Archie McDuffie, who came from Scotland, and settled on the Raft Swamp, in North Carolina, and died there, his sons and two daughters removing to this county after his death. Alexander, the eldest, settling on what is now known as the old "McDuffie place," on Little Pee Dee, where the Rev. J. H. Moody now lives; he married Jennette McQueen, and had seven sons and two daughters. Mary, the eldest daughter, married Daniel Fore, on Spring Branch, who has already been noticed in or among the Fore family. The eldest daughter of Daniel and Mary Fore married Douglas McIntyre, who has already been mentioned in or among the McIntyres. Margaret, the other daughter of Alexander McDuffie, married Edward D. Carmichael, a son of "Hatter John," and had one child, a daughter, also named Margaret, and she lives with her aunts, Nancy and Katie Carmichael, on the old homestead of "Hatter John" Carmichael. Hon. A. Q. McDuffie was the oldest son, he was a lawyer, a graduate of Davidson College, and before he read law taught school for several years. The writer went to school to him at Pine Hill Academy, during the year 1844. He settled and lived and died at Marion Court House, and was for a long time the partner of General W. W. Harllee, and in their day had the finest practice of any firm at that bar; he married the widow of Dr. James R. McQueen, who was the daughter of Captain Singletary, one of the old landmarks of Marion; by this marriage three children were born, a son, named Alexander, who died when two or three years old, and two daughters, Lizzie and Jennie; both are yet living, and unmarried. Lizzie, the eldest, is or was the finest female scholar in her day in the town of Marion; she graduated at Due West Female College in one year after matriculation, and was then elected one of its professors; she accepted the position and held it for one year, and on account of her failing health, resigned and came home. Jennette was also well educated, and after their father's death, 31st March, 1889, they both engaged in teaching, which they continued at intervals till after their mother's death; they own a plantation in Woodberry Township; don't think they reside on it, but rent it out; when last heard of, they were in Hampton or Colleton County, both teaching school; they are unmarried. "A. Q." McDuffie, as he was familiarly called by everybody, was for eight or ten years before his being stricken with paralysis, and of which he died, after living two or three years, Master in Equity for Marion County. Just after the war, in 1866, under Andrew Johnson's proclamation, during Governor B. F. Perry's administration of the State government, at one election held throughout the State for Senators and Representatives in the Legislature, "A. Q." McDuffie was elected Senator for or from Marion District, and served one session of the Legislature—which election and all the legislation of that session of the Legislature was made void by the Reconstruction Acts of Congress—his senatorship was vacated or set aside. "A. Q." McDuffie, being a very diffident man, was not an effective public speaker, but he was a good office lawyer and a safe adviser. Neill McDuffie was the second son of Alexander; he is the oldest citizen now living in Carmichael Township, now nearing eighty-three, but is hale and healthy, and remarkably active for a man of his age; he was too old for active service in the war, but he volunteered and was a Lieutenant in the reserves, and saw much service about Georgetown and Charleston, S. C., and Savannah, Ga. He married, in early life, Mary Ann, the oldest daughter of Dougald B. Carmichael, and they have raised six sons and six daughters; the sons are Alexander, Dallas, George, John, Daniel and Dougald. George and John are dead, all the others are living with their father and mother. Dougald, being a skillful first class mechanic, is much of his time away. The other three are industrious, persevering young men, and are farmers; they run a store of general merchandise at Hamer, in connection with their farming operations; they are all unmarried. The six daughters are Katie, Nancy, Flora, Margaret, Martha and Sallie. Margaret married Neill Duncan McEachern; they have four daughters, all nearly grown, and live at McColl, S. C. Sallie died when about grown; the other four are unmarried, and live with their father. Of the next sons of old Alexander McDuffie, John and George, the latter a physician, went West, and both are dead; neither of them were married. Alexander, the next son, died at his home, when about grown. Daniel, the next one, was a brave and gallant soldier in Captain A. T. Harllee's company of the Eighth South Carolina Regiment; he was Second Sergeant of the company; he was mortally wounded 2d July, 1863, at the battle of Gettysburg, and died the next morning. Duncan McDuffie was the youngest son of old Alexander, graduated at Oglethorpe College, in Georgia; he is a Presbyterian preacher, and now lives in Florence County, S. C., and has been School Commissioner of that county; he married Margaret Clark, a daughter of Malcolm Clark, and they raised a family of four sons and two daughters, all grown; his first wife died, and he has married again in Florence County. Alexander McDuffie had two sisters, who lived with him. The eldest, Margaret, married John Murphy, and had three sons, viz: Archie, Edward J. and Malcolm. The two latter died while young. Edward J. Murphy was a graduate of some college in Virginia, and was a young man of more than ordinary ability and promise. Archie Murphy married Nancy Carmichael, daughter of Duncan Carmichael, and sister of Dugald B.; he was a hatter by trade, and settled on Little Pee Dee, Enos Moody now owning the place and living upon it; he died there; they had three sons, John, Duncan and Dr. Neill C. Murphy—all of them were in the Confederate army; John was in Captain W. D. Carmichael's company of the Eighth Regiment; Duncan was Second Lieutenant in Captain Stafford's company, and was killed in battle in Virginia; Dr. Neill C. Murphy was Assistant Surgeon of the Tenth Regiment. Dr. Murphy married, since the war, Mary, the daughter of the late George W. Reaves, and he lived and died at Marion Court House, 4th September, 1886; his widow survives him and lives at his old home, near Marion; they raised three sons and two daughters. The elder daughter married a Mr. McMillan, and, I think, they live in Clarendon County. Edward Murphy, one of the sons, is a popular teacher of the county. Nancy, the other sister of old Alexander McDuffie, married Malcolm Carmichael, and removed to Alabama soon after their marriage; they raised a large family of children, many of them wealthy and prominent citizens of that State, one of them having been a Judge of the Courts there. Duncan McDuffie, brother of old Alexander, married Mary Carmichael, sister of Sheriff Archie and "Hatter" John; they had four sons, viz: Archie B., who never married, was a prominent commission merchant in Wilmington, N. C., and is now dead. Neill C. was Sheriff of the county before the war, and without disparaging other Sheriffs, will say he was one of the best Sheriffs Marion has ever had. He raised a company as Captain and went into the Twenty-third Regiment, and served through the war. In January, 1865, was again elected Sheriff, and after a protest against his election was decided in his favor, he went into the office again in April, 1865; he held the office for two years, when he resigned. The office was not worth much at that time, under bayonet rule; his reasons for resigning, as he told the writer, were, that if he held on, he would have to hurt his sureties or let his family suffer, hence the resignation. He married, first, Miss Lizzie Ford, daughter of Elias B. Ford, and after her death he married her sister, Miss Fannie; he raised a family of children, sons and daughters. One of the daughters married Prof. Kenedy, of Clinton, S. C. Another married Dr. William A. Oliver, who was a few years ago a Representative in the Legislature from Marion County, a fine physician and a good farmer; he was the pioneer in tobacco culture in Hillsboro Township; he is now dead. Another of Neill C.'s daughters married Shepherd Oliver, of Robeson County, N. C., and he has several times represented his county in the Legislature of that State. Another of his daughters married Johnson Gilchrist; they live at Gilchrist Bridge, on

Little Pee Dee; they have some children. Another daughter, Madge, married a Mr. Herring, of North Carolina. Of N. C. McDuffie's sons, one, Julius, is a Baptist preacher in North Carolina. Another son, D. K. McDuffie, who lives at Mullins, an excellent man every way, and successful business man at that place, married Miss Maggie Haselden, daughter of the late Cyrus B. Haselden; they have two children, a daughter and a son, not grown. Two other sons of Neill C., twins, Watson and Ellerbe,* have removed elsewhere—think they are both married. And still another son, the youngest, named for his father, Neill C., is also married, and lives in Williamsburg County, S. C. Duncan D. McDuffie, the third son of Duncan, his father, married Miss Penelope Ford, another daughter of Elias B. Ford, and is now living on his father's old homestead, in the "Fork," between Buck Swamp and Little Pee Dee; he has raised a family of several children. One son, Duncan, in El Paso, Tex. Another son, name not remembered—Jasper, I believe—died a young man. Another son, Emerson, the leading machinist in this part of the State, and owning and running an iron foundry and machine works at Marion. Duncan D. McDuffie served throughout the war, and was a Lieutenant in the Tenth South Carolina Regiment, in Manigault's Brigade, of the Western army. D. D. McDuffie is one of our best citizens and a leading man in his neighborhood; he has some daughters, to the writer unknown; think he has educated his daughters well. George Alexander, another son of Duncan, moved to Horry County, and married a Miss Alford there, but moved back to the old homestead and died there. Nancy, the only daughter of Duncan, married Isham H. Watson, who was once the Coroner of the county and a good citizen; he and his first wife are both dead—she died of small-pox, 16th January, 1864; he married again, Miss Mary Nichols, who has no children; he had two sons, George Elmore and Duncan J. Watson, and one daughter, now the wife of J. D. Montgomery. These have already been mentioned in or among the Watson family. George, the third brother of old Alexander, died

---

*Ellerbe McDuffie was killed, by the blowing up of a steam saw mill recently in Williamsburg County, a prosperous young man. His remains were brought to Mullins and buried there, near his father.

while a young man; he was a hatter by trade, and never married. Daniel, the youngest of the four brothers, married a Miss Blue, and they left a son, William. These have already been noticed in or among the Blue family.

CAMPBELL.—Edward Campbell was the first of the family of that name that settled north of Little Pee Dee. He came from Scotland with a family of children, and settled near where Hamer station, on the Florence Railroad, is located; the land on which he lived is now owned by Neill McDuffie. He was a sturdy old Scotchman; his wife was Mary McLellan, and others of her name and quite a colony came across the ocean with old Edward—some of them settling in Cumberland and Robeson Counties, N. C., others settled in Marion County, S. C. Old Edward, after living here many years, went West, and all his family went with him except his son, Duncan Campbell, who had married and settled on Little Pee Dee, where his son, Daniel, now lives. Duncan Campbell was another old settler on the east side of Little Pee Dee, south of Hayes Swamp; he came from Scotland with his father, Edward, and owned a large body of land; he married Margaret McEachern, and they raised a family of three sons and five daughters. Edward and Neill both died long before the war. Edward married Martha J. McCollum, daughter of Dougald McCollum, of North Carolina, and they had one child, Flora Margaret, who married George J. Bethea, of Buck Swamp, near Latta, where they now live, and have raised a large family of children. Neill Campbell never married. The youngest son, Daniel, is among the oldest and staunchest citizens of that community, and lives on the old homestead where he was born and raised, and where his father lived and died. It is a notable fact that may be here noted, that throughout Carmichael Township there are but four men who live upon and own the homesteads of their fathers, who were the original settlers of said homesteads, and who are owning and living upon the same, viz: Daniel Campbell, Malcolm C. Carmichael, Daniel M. Carmichael and Captain A. T. Harllee, although much of the lands in the township are owned by and lived upon by the descendants of the original settlers. Daniel Campbell served throughout the war in the company of his nephew, Captain J. H. Stafford, and was a true and brave soldier, undergoing many hardships from which he is still a sufferer; before the war, he married Eliza, the eldest daughter of "Hatter" John Carmichael (the name by which that old Scotchman loved to be called), and has raised a large family of sons and daughters, two of the latter being married to industrious and worthy citizens of North Carolina; the two youngest, with his two youngest sons, Neill Murdoch and Oscar, living with him; his two eldest sons, Duncan M. and John Edward, both died several years ago. Another son, Daniel Walker, married the eldest daughter of Joseph W. Williamson; they live near Kentyre Church, he being one of the Ruling Elders; he is also an earnest Mason of the lodge at Dillon, also a Knight of Phythias of the lodge there, a School Trustee of the township, and a sturdy, staunch and progressive citizen. Another son, William Simeon, is largely engaged in the manufacture and shipping of shingles to the northern markets; he, too, is a worthy young man and up-to-date citizen; he was quite recently married to Miss Sue Campbell, the youngest daughter of Hugh Campbell, formerly a citizen of Cumberland County, N. C., but for many years past a citizen of this county. Old Duncan Campbell raised five daughters. The eldest married Malcolm Stafford, as already noticed in or among the Stafford family. Another daughter, Mary, married Leonard Walters, and removed to Alabama, and raised a large family, her sons being among the wealthiest men about Montgomery, Ala. Christian, another daughter, married A. S. Buie, who, in his lifetime, was a peaceable, industrious and Christian gentleman; they had three daughters. The eldest, Louisa, married Gilbert Butler; both are dead. The next, Margaret, married Calvin C. Carmichael, and are living. Nancy married Robert Monroe, of North Carolina; both are dead. Margaret, the youngest, died when about grown, from yellow fever, which she contracted from going with her father to Charleston, in the month of August, with a drove of sheep and turkeys; several of the negroes who went with him also contracted the disease, and some of them died; Duncan Campbell himself took the fever and died also; he left a large estate unencumbered for his widow and children. There are other families of the name of Campbell in the township in no way related to each other. Duncan Campbell was the original settler in that region; he was a unique character. It was told of him, that once he was drawn to serve on the jury at Marion, twenty-five miles away; that on Sunday night, while at the supper table, he said to his wife that she must be up before day and get him breakfast before he started to Marion. He still sat at the table talking about the trip to Marion; that he must be there by 10 o'clock; that he must have his breakfast early, and so forth; at last he said to his wife, "Peggy," as he called her, "if you will get it, I will eat it now—it will be in me and I can get up and start when I please."

There are other families of Campbells in the county. Campbell is a very populous name. Such as I know and know of will now be mentioned. The family of the Campbells that formerly lived (and some of them may be there now), about Campbell's Bridge, were old Peter Campbell, who came from Scotland, about 1800, and settled on the east side of Little Pee Dee, near where Campbell's Bridge now is; don't know who his wife was; he had and raised six sons—Alexander, Archie, Duncan, James, Hugh and David—who are all long since dead. Alexander Campbell lived on the east side of Little Pee Dee; don't know who his wife was; he had one son, John J. Campbell, who married a daughter of John D. McRae, in Marlborough; he disappeared or was lost sight of after the war; his father was a jolly old Scotchman, was a farmer, who had some property, but was not considered rich, yet he lived at his own home and had plenty to live on; he died many years ago—think John J. was his only child. Archie Campbell lived on the west side of the river, not far from Campbell's Bridge; he married a Miss Paul; he raised four sons, John P., Peter, William P. and Alexander. John P. and one of his sisters, Sarah Ann, I believe, together with his brother, Peter, lived on the old homestead together before and during the war; neither of whom ever married, and all died since the war. Alexander married and had a family, and lived just below Campbell's Bridge; don't know who he married or how many children he had, nor what has become of them. William R., the most active and most prominent one of the sons of old Archie, married a sister of Wm. S. Campbell, who lived and died near Ebenezer Church and Temperance Hill; they had one son only, who died with typhoid fever, about 1855, after being down with it for four months, the only child. Wm. P. Campbell was Deputy Sheriff for Neill C. McDuffie during his term of office, from 1857 to 1861, and was very effective as Deputy, and was also very popular personally; he was elected, in January, 1861, as successor to McDuffie. Under the then Constitution of the State (Constitution of 1790), a Sheriff was not re-eligible to election to a succeeding term of four years—hence McDuffie could not succeed himself. Wm. P. Campbell went into office, in April, 1861, just as the war was commencing. It was a trying time to a Sheriff, but Campbell, nevertheless, discharged his duty faithfully and satisfactorily until the fall of 1863, when he was killed, near the home of his birth, one night just after dark, and when he was actually in the discharge of a public duty, by the leader of a gang of Maple Swamp deserters. He was in his buggy, and there were two buggies along in a path that led through a thick woods, from one road to another; two of the company were carrying a light before them or on each side (a very unwise act to have the light, as it enabled the assassin to pick his man, the Sheriff); when his buggy passed, the assassin stepped in the road behind him and shot him in the back; Campbell did not fall out of the vehicle, but he was dead, and his brother, Peter, got up into the buggy with him and held him therein till they got to the house, two or three hundred yards off. He had gotten an order, as Sheriff, from the authorities, either civil or military, to arrest those Maple Swamp deserters, so as to send them to the army; he obeyed the order, as he did all orders, and gathered some men to go with him up there to hunt for and to arrest them—don't remember who all the men were that were with him; Captain Samuel T. Page was one of them, and who yet lives and can tell about it, although in his eighty-third year. Thus an efficient officer and a good man was assassinated in the dark. The county was then without a Sheriff; Isham H. Watson was then Coroner and by operation of law became Sheriff and conducted the office until the next general election for Sheriff came on, in January, 1865, when

Neill C. McDuffie was again elected, and went into office, in April, 1865, as hereinbefore stated. Campbell's widow, childless, went to her people, and died a few years after the war. There are many yet living who gratefully remember Wm. P. Campbell. In the early fifties, the Campbell brothers went into a mercantile business at Campbell's Bridge, under the firm name of A. Campbell & Co. The business was not successful, and they failed about 1855; it was managed mainly by Alexander; they were harassed for a few years by creditors in the Courts, but managed some way to save their homes. Hugh Campbell, one of the six brothers, married Miss Absala Bethea, daughter of Buck Swamp William Bethea, and settled at and owned the land at Campbell's Bridge—the bridge was so called because the Campbells lived around it, and owned all the lands round about. Hugh Campbelll settled and lived and died where his grand-son, William Hugh Breeden, with his mother, now lives; he in a short while died, leaving his widow and one child, a daughter, Adaline. The widow continued to reside there, and raised her daughter; she also prospered and was well-to-do. Adaline married, about 1848, John A. Breeden, a native of Marlborough County, and first cousin of J. B. Breeden and his brothers, Joseph and others. John A. Breeden was in some respects a remarkable man, of very quick and acute perceptions; his habits were not good, yet he managed well and kept his property; he lived on the place with his mother-in-law till her death; after which he remained there till his death, some fifteen or twenty years ago; he raised a family of three daughters and one son, William H. Breeden. The oldest daughter, Mollie, married Wesley Stackhouse; they have a considerable family, sons and daughters, some of whom are grown; they live at Dillon. The second daughter, Jackey, married Frank Edens; they live in North Carolina, and have eight or ten children, some of them grown—a first class family and are well-to-do. The third daughter, Absala, named for her grand-mother, but called "Appey," married Faulk Floyd, of Robeson County, N. C., who was Sheriff of that county at the time of the marriage; they live in Robeson, and have only one child, a daughter, Pearl. The son, William H. Breeden, a capital citizen, married Miss Victoria Godbold, daughter of the late Asa Godbold, Jr.; they reside with his mother, Adaline, who yet lives, at the old homestead of Hugh Campbell, his grand-father. William H. Breeden has no children; is a very quiet man and well informed on most subjects. The name Breeden is likely to become extinct in the county. James Campbell, son of old Peter, married in North Carolina, and moved to that State. Duncan Campbell, another son of old Peter, married and settled just above Campbell's Bridge, on the west side of the river; don't know who he married; he had and raised two children, a son, named Hugh, and a daughter, Mary Ann. Mary Ann married Hugh Dove, near Campbell's Bridge, and, I think, had two or three children; her husband, Hugh Dove, was killed, about 1855, by her brother, Hugh Campbell—a wilful and premeditated murder. Hugh Campbell fled from the country and has not been heard of since. David Campbell, another son of old Peter, married some lady in North Carolina, and went to that State and died there; know nothing further of him.

Another family of Campbells to be next noticed are those living in the Ebenezer and Temperance Hill community. The first known of this family was William S. Campbell, who was one of our best and most respected citizens—unpretending, no display, but gave close attention to his business, and treated that of others with "masterly inactivity;" he married,
and raised three daughters and two sons, John C. and Samuel. The eldest daughter, Flora, married Stephen L. Lane, who was killed in the last battle fought during the war, at Smithfield, in North Carolina; they had and raised a family of sons and daughters; the widow managed well after the death of her husband; took care of the property and perhaps added to it; she died some few years ago; she had a son, named William, and a daughter, that became the second wife of Meredith Watson. Another daughter married our fellow-citizen, now at Marion, W. J. B. Campbell, and who is merchandizing there; she, perhaps, had other children, unknown to the writer. Another daughter of old Wm. S. Campbell, married John E. Perritt, whose family has already been noticed in or among the Perritt family. And still another, the third daughter, I think, her name was Mary, married David Perritt, a nephew of John

E. Perritt; he died soon and left her a widow; don't know if she had any child or children. John C. Campbell, the older son, married Miss Amelia Tart, a daughter of old James Tart, who lived and died just above E. J. Moody's mill, now owned by Governor Ellerbe's estate. By this marriage nine sons were born and two daughters; the sons were Byron, Preston, Valcour, Samuel, Frank, W. J. Beauregard, Thomas LeGrande and another whose name is not remembered. Of the sons, Valcour, Frank and Thomas are dead—died unmarried; Byron went to Texas; Preston married some one to the writer unknown; also the same of Samuel; W. J. Beauregard married his first cousin, the daughter of Stephen Lane and Flora, his wife, above mentioned. W. J. Beauregard Campbell owns the old homestead, or the greater part of it, situate just below Ebenezer Church, eight miles above Marion; don't know if he has any children. LeGrande is yet single, and is also merchandising at Marion. Of the two daughters of John C. Campbell, Roberta and Romine, one of them died unmarried, but grown and very handsome; the other married Samuel Lane and lives near by. Samuel Campbell, the younger son of old William S., married, first, a Miss Fore, and has already been noticed in or among the Fore family; she had one daughter, who married Herod W. Allen, and is dead. Samuel Campbell married, a second time, a Miss Hays, daughter of Levi H. Hays, and sister of W. B. Hays, of Hillsboro Township; by this marriage three daughters were born to them, names unknown. One married James Lane; they have some family, how much is not known. Another daughter married Thomas A. Lamb; they had four or five children, two or three years ago, when they left here and went to Florida, where they are now. The other daughter married some one and went off; don't know what has become of her. Samuel Campbell's widow still survives, and is on the old homestead. John C. Campbell and his wife are both dead. Old William S. Campbell was no ordinary man; quiet and unassuming, thought right and acted right; prudent and seldom made mistakes; neither of his sons were equal to him; he made a good property and transmitted it by will to his children unencumbered.

There are other Campbells in the county, but the writer

knows nothing about them. There is a family near Hamer, Hugh Campbell,; think he came from North Carolina; have been told that he has six sons and two daughters. The elder daughter married John B. McEachern, near Hamer, a very substantial man and a good farmer; they have one or two children. The younger daughter, Sue, a charming girl, has lately married William Simeon Campbell, a son of Daniel Campbell, who has already been mentioned herein. Hugh Campbell has six sons, but the writer knows only two of them by name—John, I think, the oldest, and James, perhaps, the youngest, who was recently telegraph operator and depot agent at Sellers, on the Florence Railroad, for some time, now at Elrod, on the same road.

BUTLER.—The Butler family will next be noticed. They live on Hays Swamp and Little Pee Dee, and they are the descendants of old Isham Butler, who was one of the first settlers of that region of the county; he was the father of Stephen and Isham Butler of later times, and had six daughters. Annie, the oldest, never married, but lived and died at the homestead of her brother, Isham. Laney married her cousin, Dempsy Butler, and they have one son, Alfred W. Butler, who has a large family of grown-up children, and lives on the plantation formerly owned by Neill McDuffie, near Stafford's Bridge. Patience, the third daughter, married Green Watson, and moved to Alabama. Polly married Stephen Moody, and moved to Tennessee. Zilla married Reuben Paul, and he and she both died before the war, without issue. The youngest, Susan, died unmarried, when about eighteen years old. Stephen Butler was the oldest son of old Isham, and he and his brother, Isham, lived near each other; J. W. Dillon & Son own the old homestead of Isham, and R. P. Hamer, Jr., a part of that of Stephen, which was sold a few years ago for division; the descendants of Stephen live on the other parts of his old homestead. Stephen Butler married Katie McEachern, and had three sons, Gilbert, Silas and Thomas, all of them good soldiers—Gilbert and Thomas in Captain Stafford's company, and Silas in Captain W. D. Carmichael's company, Eighth Regiment. Silas came home on sick furlough, and died in one week after reaching home. Gilbert married, first, before the war, Louisa, the eldest daughter of A. S. Buie; they are both dead, and left three children, all grown. The youngest daughter is a deaf-mute, but was well educated at the Cedar Springs Institute, and is a young woman of remarkable intelligence; she lives with her brother, in North Carolina. Thomas Butler, the youngest son, married Mary, the daughter of Cade B. Rogers; both of them are dead, but left a family of four daughters and two sons, who are living on a portion of the old Stephen Butler homestead. Of the four daughters of Stephen Butler, the eldest, Jennie, married William Blue, before the war; he was killed in battle in Virginia, in Captain Stafford's company, and his widow survives and lives at McColl, S. C. Clarissa, the next oldest daughter, married Allen Stephens, and both of them are dead, but their sons, Stephen, Gilbert, Allen, Preston and Silas, are all living near each other, in the Bermuda section of Carmichael Township, and are amongst the foremost citizens of their section; all of them married and are raising large families of children, and all of them progressive farmers and first class citizens. Charity, the third daughter, married Washington W. Norman, generally known as "Colonel Norman," by reason of his being the best fisherman on Little Pee Dee, and is one of the sturdy citizens of the section; they live on a portion of the old Stephen Butler homestead; they have three grown daughters living with them; they had two sons, but both were drowned in Little Pee Dee, while bathing near their home, several years ago—one of them nine and the other eleven years old. "Colonel Norman" is a good farmer, and a kind and hospitable citizen. Miss Flora A. Butler was another daughter, older than Charity, and owned and lived and died a few years ago, on the old homestead, where her father lived and died. Isham Butler, the brother of Stephen, had but one child, a daughter, Mary, who married Nathan McCormick, her cousin, and he was a gallant soldier of Fairlee's company, in the war; both of them are living, and have six sons and three daughters, all of them grown. Nathan Butler, son of old Isham, was another of the first settlers; he had four sons. Dempsy, the eldest, married his cousin, Laney; Solomon married Polly Brasswell and had no children; Samuel married Milly Brasswell, and went to Georgia; James, the youngest, married the Widow Jane Davis—all of them are dead. Laney, the wife of Dempsy, according to the census return of her son, Alfred, in 1890, was 110 years old; she, too, is now dead. As to the age of Laney, as above, the writer has something to say. Dempsy Butler, her husband, was killed by a man by the name of McCormick, in 1859. I was a Magistrate at the time, and was sent for to hold an inquest; I went and held it; it was right on the North Carolina State line, and as the line was shown to me by those present, the killing was about five feet in South Carolina; he was killed by a stab with a knife, in the abdomen. Dempsy Butler, from appearance (I had seen him often before he was killed), was about forty-five years of age; his wife, Laney, was also present, and would judge her to be younger, not older. According to this she could not have been, in 1890, more than seventy-five or seventy-six—there must be some mistake about her age, sure. Nathan also had five daughters. The eldest, Viney, married Benjamin Locke, and had a large family of children, one of whom is our good citizen, William Locke, who lives on a part of the old McDuffie homestead, on Little Pee Dee. Willie, a daughter, married John McCormick, who had several children, all of them dead but Charles, who lives at McColl, S. C., and Nathan, who still lives in that section. Sallie married Philip Rouse, and Ada married William Abbott. Geriah, the youngest, never married. All of them are dead, but have left numerous descendants living here and in the West. The writer knew Benjamin Locke back in the thirties; he was the greatest rail-splitter he ever knew; have often said and now think he split rails enough to make a fence half around the county; he split rails for that whole section, and it mattered not how far he was from home at work in his chosen avocation, he would go home every night—he would brave any weather to get home; he was a hard working, honest and harmless man.

Recurring again to the Haseldens. The writer has learned that the progenitor of Major James Haselden and his brothers, John and William, was William Haselden; he lived and owned the place where Dr. D. F. Miles now owns and farms; he had, in addition to the sons already herein mentioned, four daughters. The eldest married a Mr. Cox, who had only one child, a daughter, Sarah; her father and mother both died and left her; she was raised by some of her people, grew up, and married Asa Godbold, about 1828. His family and hers have already been noticed herein. Another daughter, Anne, I believe, was her name, married, first, a Mr. Brown, of Marlborough; he died in a short time, childless, and the widow married Cyrus Bacot, of Darlington County; they lived together some years, and Bacot died, and left her with considerable property, and by her will (she had no children), she gave some of it, said to be $2,000, to her nephew, Cyrus Bacot Haselden, who was named for her husband—which has already been mentioned herein. The third daughter of old William Haselden married Stephen G. Godbold, who only raised one child, a daughter, who married Francis A. Miles; they had and raised three sons and two daughters, as already noticed herein. The fourth daughter of old William Haselden died or disappeared; no account of her is obtainable. The Haseldens, as a family, seem to be short-lived, as has already been stated.

Moody.—The Moody family will next be noticed. Robert Moody and Barfield Moody, two brothers, were only known to the writer as one branch of the family. Another branch of the family is headed by the Rev. Tapley Moody, and there is still another branch whose head in this county is not known to the writer; James A. Moody, of Marion, belongs to this branch. These branches are all collaterally related to each other. All collateral relations have a common ancestor somewhere, either proximate or remote; Robert Moody married Elizabeth Smith, daughter of Samuel Smith, Sr.; he lived and died just below Temperance Hill, on the road to Marion; she was a sister of Samuel, Jr., as he was called, back in the twenties, who lived and died on Buck Swamp; to this marriage were born several sons and daughters; the sons were Hugh, Richard, Salathiel and Charles; can't give the names of all the daughters—as remembered, they were Milly, Celia, Smithy, Evaline and another one or two—have just learned that one was named Mary. Hugh Moody married Miss   and raised one son and several daughters. The son was named John

Thomas, who married his first cousin, Sarah Ann Moody, daughter of Richard Moody; they had and raised a family—two sons, David and Robert, and several daughters, number and names not known. His son, David Moody, married a daughter of Peter Parley McCormic, and lives at Dillon. Robert married a daughter of Thomas Sawyer. Hugh Moody, the grand-father, has one daughter that married William Hamilton, as a second wife, and has several children; Hugh was a farmer, and was a local Methodist preacher; also a Magistrate for a number of years, and was a useful man in his community; his influence was for good, always in favor of right and justice; he died some twenty years ago or more. Richard Moody, the next younger brother, married Miss Harriet Edwards, daughter of Rev. David S. Edwards, and had and raised four sons and four daughters; the sons were Thomas D., Richard J., Hugh and Barfield; the daughters were Martha, Sarah Ann, Helen and Sophia. Of the sons, Thomas D. married a daughter of Needham Perrit; had only one child, and she is grown and married. Richard J. Moody married a daughter of Reuben B. Jackson, and has a family, already mentioned in or among the Jackson family. Hugh Moody, Jr., married Miss Massey Smith, a daughter of the late William H. Smith, of Buck Swamp; they have a family, how large or small is unknown. Barfield Moody, Jr., married a daughter of Bennett Perritt, and has some family. Of the daughters of Richard Moody, Sr., Martha, the oldest, married William McKenzie, of the Maple Swamp region; they have a family, how many is not known. Sarah Ann married John Thomas Moody, as above stated. The daughter, Sophia, married John H. Ellen, of the Dothan section, who is one of the most progressive farmers in the county; they have three children, a son in Wofford College; don't know the sex of the other two children. The daughter, Helen, is unmarried. The third son of Robert Moody, Salathiel, married in March, 1843, the Widow Jane Bass, up on Catfish; she was the widow of Bryant Bass, hereinbefore mentioned; they had only two children, a son, who was idiotic and died before maturity, and a daughter, Josephine, who married Mack Martin, who has already been noticed in or among the Martin family. Charles, the fourth and youngest son of Robert Moody, married a Miss Monroe, of North Carolina, and settled and lived and died on a part of the homestead of his grand-father, Samuel Smith, Sr.; they raised a family of three sons and one daughter; the mother died many years ago. The daughter married Milton Watson, already spoken of in or among the Watson family; he soon died, childless; the widow went back to her father, and remained with him until his death, a few years ago, and still remains there with her brothers—all of whom are unmarried, and names not remembered. Of the daughters of Robert Moody, Mary, the oldest, married a Mr. Edwards, who died soon and left her with one child, a daughter, who grew up and became the first wife of Meredith Watson; she soon died, and left two children, a son, who was imbecile and weak and soon died; the daughter married and has some family, unknown to the writer. Robert Moody's daughter, Celia, married William Bryan, in Robeson County, N. C., where they resided till both died; as to their family, the writer only knows of a son, Quincy Bryant or Bryan, who came back to this county, and married his first cousin, Miss Lizzie A. Moody, a daughter of the late Joshua T. Moody. Quincy Bryant is one of our most worthy citizens, and resides six miles below Marion; they have a family of several children, sons and daughters—a son, named Marvin, who is now a promising young man; a daughter grown, and I think, married; know nothing of the other members of the family. Milley, another daughter, married Joseph D. Bass, who has already been noticed herein in or among the Bass family. Smithy, another daughter, married Evander Brigman, of Marlborough, who has raised a considerable family; one of her sons, an energetic and prosperous man, now lives at Dillon; I think Mrs. Brigman yet lives; if so, she is the sole survivor of the children of Robert Moody. Another daughter, the youngest, Evaline, married Joshua T. Moody; in the latter part of his life he resided on his farm, near Ariel, nine miles below Marion; they raised only two children, Lizzie and James A. Lizzie married her cousin, M. Q. Bryant, as above stated. James A. is unmarried, though twice old enough; is and has been for several years past merchandizing at Marion; he conducts his business on a safe plan, buys and sells only for cash, is close and hoards his money; if he makes but little, he holds on to that little with tenacity; think he and Mrs. Bryant, his sister, still hold on to their father's lands, near Arial. Robert Moody died more than sixty years ago; he made a good property, and his widow and children held on to it to the old lady's death, just before the war; their land on Buck Swamp was valuable; had about fifty negroes. The lands are now owned by Mrs. Lucy Godbold, wife of Willie A. Godbold, and is much more valuable now than when in the hands of the old lady Moody. Barfield Moody, a brother of Robert, whether older or younger is not known, was a very prominent man in this county from 1830 to 1860, when he died; he was very popular before the people, though sometimes beaten; he was elected twice as Representative of the county in the Legislature. After the death of General Wheeler, in 1859, he was elected Clerk of the Court; but on account of his failing health, he could not perform the duties thereof in person, and he deputed his young son, Thomas C., and placed him in as deputy, who discharged the duties of the office until the death of his father, 7th April, 1860. Barfield Moody was a Magistrate for many years, and he did not run that office as it is run in these latter days, for the money that was in it, but mostly as an arbiter among his neighbors as to their civil rights and a pacificator in their quarrels and fights—making peace many times and hindering prosecutions in the criminal courts—which is regarded as one of the first and best qualifications of a Magistrate; he was also a good surveyor, and was called to its practice often. The writer, in his extensive land law practice in the county, has had occasion to see and scrutinize his work as a surveyor; his plats were neat and mathematically correct, in most instances. He was a useful citizen in many ways, did a great deal of surveying for poor people without charge, and in suits before him as a Magistrate would often charge no costs, and especially in cases compromised or settled. Barfield Moody married Miss Sallie Crawford, a sister of James Crawford, who lived at Spring Branch, four miles above Marion—she was only a half-sister; they had and raised five sons and four daughters; the sons were William H., Evander J., Robert B., Thomas C. and Albert C.; William H. and Robert B. are dead. Of these sons, William

H. married a Miss Lamb, of Marlborough. Afterwards the Lamb family moved into Marion, having bought the late Crawford plantation, four miles above Marion, and they all lived and died there, except those who went West. The Lamb name is now extinct in the county. Barfield Moody settled on the north side of Catfish, opposite Watson's, and William H., after a while, settled on a part of the Lamb plantation, where his widow now resides. William H. and his wife had and raised several sons and daughters; the sons were Sandy, Clarence, James C., Bartow, Rhett and Theodore; the daughters were Lucy and Sue. Of the sons, Sandy went to Kershaw County, and there married; know nothing further of him. Clarence died a few years ago, unmarried. Rhett emigrated to parts unknown. James C. is unmarried, though twice old enough; he was County Auditor for several years, and now has some State employment; he is a competent man for any business position. Bartow married, a few years ago, a Miss Cottingham; they may have some family. Theodore died just as he was arriving at manhood. Miss Lucy married a Mr. McIntyre, of North Carolina; both are dead, and left two children, a son and a daughter, who stay with their grand-parents in North Carolina. Miss Sue married Joseph Bruce, of Marlborough; suppose they have some family, how many is unknown. William H. Moody died, maybe twenty years ago; he was a good citizen. Before the war he first held a Captain's commission in the Berry's Cross Roads militia company, and as hereinbefore stated, the contest for the Captaincy of said company, in 1840 or 1841, was spirited and hot, but Moody was elected by thirteen votes. Afterward, when Major James R. Bethea was elected Colonel of the regiment, the Majorship of the upper battalion became vacant, and William Moody was elected Major of the upper battalion, which position he held with credit to himself for several years; he never aspired to any other position. Evander J. Moody, the second son of Barfield Moody, grew up, and first married Miss Florence Smith, a daughter of Samuel Smith, of Buck Swamp; she had one child, a daughter, named Florence, and died. Florence, the child, was raised by her Grand-mother Smith while she lived, and after the death of her grand-mother she went back to her father, who in the meantime had married again, to the Widow Lester (twice a widow, her maiden name was Jane Tart), and remained with him until 17th May, 1871, when she married Dr. J. C. Mullins (a second wife); by this marriage three sons and one daughter were born—Randolph, Frank and Woods; the daughter is also named Florence, and is approaching womanhood. Frank Mullins died a young man, unmarried. Randolph has emigrated to Greenville, and is in the drug business. Woods and Florence, Jr., are with their mother, at Marion. Dr. J. C. Mullins died about three years ago. By E. J. Moody's second marriage, he had and raised two sons, Thomas E. and Cornelius G. Thomas E. grew up and married a Miss Little, daughter of Rev. Lewis H. Little; he gave promise of being an energetic and progressive man, but suddenly died soon after his marriage, childless; his widow remained for a year or two with E. J. Moody's family, and then returned to her own people. Cornelius G. never married; he was a very steady, level-headed, straightforward young man, and gave promise of success and good citizenship; but, alas! he took sick and died some three or four years ago. The two daughters of E. J. Moody, by his last marriage, were Virginia and Maggie. Virginia married Douglas McIntyre, of Marion, and has already been noticed herein in or among the McIntyre family. Maggie married Dr. D. I. Watson, now of Southport, N. C., and has already been noticed in or among the Watson family; they have several children. E. J. Moody has been and is yet a large-hearted man, hospitable to a fault; has been a man of affairs, farming and merchandizing all his life, and during his long life (he is now seventy-five years of age) he has given away at his table and house enough to make a small fortune; his wife, Jane, was one of the noblest of women; she died several years ago, after which her husband kept house with his son, Cornelius (called Neill), for a while, and then broke up, and E. J. Moody since that time has been staying with children (surviving) and other relatives; he has an income sufficient for his support; he has done his part in developing the resources and bringing up the county to its present high position, and has nothing now to do but to ruminate on the past and to prepare for his approaching end. Robert B. Moody, the third son of Barfield, grew up and early volunteered for service in the Confederate army, rose to a Lieutenantcy therein, and continued to the end of the war; he went first in Captain Stanley's company, and on its reorganization left it and went into Captain Finklea's company as Lieutenant, which composed part of the Twenty-third Regiment, South Carolina Volunteers. After the war he married Miss Delilah Wyche, of Virginia, who came down into this county to teach school; upon his marriage he repaired with his wife to her home in Virginia (Greenfield or Westfield), where he settled and lived for many years; he had but one child, a daughter, who grew up, and after her mother's death married her first cousin, Dr. Robert A. Bass, of Latta, S. C., and who now resides at Latta, and has three or four children; her father, after some time, married again, a widow lady, with one child, a daughter; they went to Richmond, Va., where, in 1891, they were keeping a large hotel—whether it belonged to his wife or whether it was rented, the writer knoweth not, but rather thinks it belonged to his wife. The writer spent one day and night with them very pleasantly, in the summer of 1891; when he went to leave, he asked for his bill, and "Bob," as we used to call him, said it was nothing; he insisted upon paying it, but he and his wife absolutely refused it. They showed me much attention while in Richmond, got a carriage with two horses and took me with his wife over the city to various places of interest and among them the "White House of the Confederacy," where the lamented Winnie Davis, the daughter of the Confederacy, was born. We went into every room in the house, and Mrs. Moody pointed out the room in which Winnie was born—a sacred spot to every Southerner. The house was then unoccupied; the key to it was obtained from its keeper, a colored man. It is in a very eligible spot, not far from the Capitol. I suppose it has been much adorned and beautified since that time. Some four or five years after that time, "Bob" came out here to see his friends and relatives, and was sick and died at Latta, with a cancer on his lip, and he was buried here in the land of his birth. Peace be to his ashes. He had no child by the last wife. Thomas C. Moody, the fourth son of Barfield Moody, was in the Clerk's office as his father's deputy, at his father's death, in April, 1860—when, as a matter of course, he had to retire. Asa Godbold, the then Ordinary, became Clerk until a successor to the dead Clerk was elected and qualified; this was then existing law. An election for Clerk was ordered by the proper authorities to be held in June following. At this election the young deputy was a candidate for the office against five others, every one of whom was much more competent than "Tom," as he was called, and is so called yet; he was then twenty-three years of age, with but little education, no experience in such matters, a verdant, green, country youth—could not write legibly—yet led the ticket at the election by seventy votes. One of his supporters in that election was the writer. It was thought by many that, on account of his youth and inexperience, he would not be able to properly perform the duties of the office. This is said, not in disparagement of Mr Moody, but it is said to his credit, as the sequel will show. He qualified and took charge of the office and held it till the next regular election, when he was again elected, and held the second term until he was ousted by reconstruction. As time rolled along, he improved, and became a very efficient Clerk and performed its duties satisfactorily. As an evidence of his inefficiency on account of his lack of experience, I will relate an incident of what occurred in Court shortly after Mr. Moody went into office—I think, the October term, 1860. The Clerk, as required by law, made up the dockets for the Court. Judge Whitner presided; and in calling the cases on the docket the Judge mistook the letter "C" for "G," which made quite a difference in the name or word. Some member of the bar spoke to the Judge and corrected the call. The Judge looked at it more critically and said, "I would never call that a 'C.'" He then spoke to the Clerk, and said to him, "Come up here, you are a young Clerk, and let me show you how to make a 'C.'" The Clerk, of course, went up to the Judge and the Judge took up his pen, and made a "C" for the Clerk's guidance. This is also related to the credit of Mr. Moody. "Tom" was again a candidate for Clerk, in 1872, and was elected, but the then powers that be counted every Democratic candidate (and all were elected) out. "Tom" kept improving as time advanced, and after the redemption of the State in 1876, he was elected to the lower House of the State Legislature (don't remember what year); he served a term in that house, and in 1884 was nominated and elected Senator from the county in the Legislature; he served four years, was again nominated and again elected to the Senate, in 1888, and served a second term, till 1892. The upheaval in the State that year relegated every man to the rear that did not chime in with the views of B. R. Tillman. During Mr. Moody's first term in the Senate, or just before, he married Miss Eliza Ellerbe, a daughter of Captain W. S. Ellerbe, and sister to the late Governor Ellerbe; they had no children, and she died in 1896 or 1897; he did not marry till late in life, and he has not remarried; and lives a life of retirement and "splendid leisure," he having acquired a competency to live on; he is now sixty-four years of age. T. C. Moody is a kind-hearted man and very considerate of the poor, and after he went out of the Clerk's office kept many a poor fellow from going to jail by going on his bond for his appearance at Court; his sympathies were not hard to arouse in favor of the distressed. Could say much more favorable to Mr. Moody, but space will not permit. Albert C. Moody, the fifth and youngest son of old Barfield Moody, grew up just in time for the war; he volunteered, went into the service early in the war and remained to the last; when he came home from the army he went to Lumberton, N. C., and there married a daughter of Sheriff King, and remained there until King's death. King was murdered, as it was said, by the Lowry gang—a gang which terrorized Robeson County for several years after the war, robbing and killing many of the citizens. The State troops were called out to suppress them, but they were of little avail. Sheriff King was a wealthy man and reputed to have plenty of money—which, no doubt, was the inducement to his murder. Albert, with his wife, came from there to this county, and settled about six miles above Marion, on the road leading to Buck Swamp Bridge; has raised a considerable family of sons and daughters, some of them grown—a daughter, who married a Mr. Hunter; he lost a grown son by death a few years ago. Albert is a farmer, and though not very progressive, yet manages to support his family. Barfield Moody had four daughters, Sarah Ann, Lucy, Julia and Lizzie.

The eldest, Sarah Ann, a very accomplished lady, married John Crawford, of Alabama, a relative of hers through her mother; soon after the marriage they went to Alabama; she had one child, a son, named Albert, familiarly called here "Dock;" she died, and Albert, or "Dock," was raised by his people in Alabama and by those here—especially the latter part of his raising; he was intelligent and promising; he merchandised a while at Marion, but did not succeed well; he was appointed County Auditor. It was soon discovered that he was incompetent, his habits not good, and finally he was removed or resigned his office, and was sent to the Asylum for treatment; after staying in the Asylum for some months, he was discharged and sent home; he was unmarried; he left for Georgia or Alabama and died in Georgia—doubtless a victim of the drink habit. A lesson for all young men who are cognizant of his case. The third daughter of old Barfield Moody, Lucy, married Captain James W. Bass; a good woman she was, but she has already been noticed in or among the Bass family. Julia, the fourth daughter, married William P. Deer, just at the beginning of the war; he volunteered and went through the war; the fruits of the marriage were two daughters, Blanche and Lula. Blanche married Henry Berry, and lives upon the Deer homestead; they have two or three children, all small. Lula married her first cousin, C. G. Bass; they have only one child, and have already been noticed in or among the Bass family. Wm. P. Deer left or disappeared some fifteen or twenty years ago, and he has not been heard of since, as the writer has been informed lately by his sister, Mrs. William Watson. Mrs. Lucy Bass and Mrs. Deer are both dead. The second daughter of Barfield Moody (omitted in the order of births), Lizzie, married Major W. D. Lamb, then a citizen of the county; they had and raised seven sons, names not remembered; their mother died some years ago; the boys grew up and one by one they emigrated to Florida; and finally the father went and soon after died in Florida. The sons are all there. Major Lamb was a character, but space will not permit a further notice of him.

Rev. Tapley Moody, an old man sixty or seventy years ago, was the head of another branch of the Moody family in this county. Old "Tap," as he was called, was an excellent man, a Christian gentleman, a local Methodist preacher, and a man of no ordinary ability—if he had been educated, he, doubtless, would have been a power. The writer has heard him preach many times—he was a strong preacher. In some parts of a sermon he became truly eloquent; the confidence the people had in his piety gave effect to his sermon. He was greatly beloved by all, whether in the church or out of it—was universally popular; married more couples than any other man of his day or since his time—was sent for far and near to marry people. He was a poor man, and had and raised a large family of sons and daughters—he raised them right and respectably; don't know that I can name all of his sons; they were, as now remembered, John H., Stephen, Daniel, Tapley, Wesley and James R. Ervin; may have been another one or two, and some daughters—three or four; don't know who his wife was, but think she was a Miss Herring. All the sons were good men and made good citizens; think they are all dead. John H., the oldest, married Miss Elizabeth Mace, already mentioned in or among the Mace family. Stephen married Miss Obeda Butler, a daughter of Elias Butler, in the Gaddy neighborhood; they had and raised a family, don't know how many—know but one, Enos Moody, a capital citizen of Carmichael Township, near Dillion; he has a family, not known of; his mother, Obeda, still lives. The name, in that family of Butlers, I think, is extinct. Daniel Moody married the Widow Mary Edwards, a daughter of the "Widow Betsy Moody," on Buck Swamp; think they are both dead. Tapley married some one not known; so did Wesley. James R. Ervin married, first, a widow, whose maiden name was Mary Crawford, a niece of Cross Roads Henry Berry's wife; she died; think she left two children; he married again, a Miss Finklea, daughter of the late Willis Finklea, and had some family, how many not known; he is dead. Of the daughters of old Tapley Moody, one married the late Jessee Hays, of Reaves Township; she had one child, a daughter, who married some one unknown. Jessee Hays was a good citizen; he and his wife are both dead; don't know anything of the other daughters of old Tapley Moody, who was a Mason, and died in 1843; was at his funeral

(Masonic) ; he was buried on the plantation of Wm. D Roberts, on Buck Swamp.

Another branch of the Moody family was represented by three brothers, Josiah, John W. and Joshua T. Moody. They were related to all the foregoing Moodys, but what it is, is not known. Josiah Moody went to school at Pine Hill, in 1842 and 1844—the writer went to school there at the same time; he was a genial young man and full of the spice of life; he was then grown; he afterwards married the Widow Polly Platt, widow of old Daniel Platt, who lived just below Latta; she had six or seven children. In 1854, he and Hugh Haselden built a large hotel at Marion, as Moody & Haselden; the hotel was near the depot, and is remembered by many now living. It was intended for a railroad house—was built just as the railroad was finished, but did not run long; they sold it to Philip P. Bethea. Of course, a barroom was appended to it. Bethea and Gilbert W. McKay ran it till about the beginning of the war, when they sold it to Woodward Manning. It is not necessary to trace its history any further. John W. Moody emigrated with his family, or as many of them as would go, to Texas; know nothing further of him. John W. Moody, when quite young, went to clerking for Wyatt Fuller, at Allen's Bridge; and such was his aptitude for business that Fuller kept him until his (Fuller's) death, which, I think, occurred in the last of the forties or early fifties, and for the last two or three years of Fuller's life, he being unable to attend to it, the whole business was run by John W. Moody, and apparently with success. Moody was well up to such business and was trustworthy. In the meantime, he married Miss Shooter, the only daughter of Benjamin Shooter. After Fuller's death and his affairs wound up, Moody's wife having died in the meantime, he, I think, went to Texas also—he disappeared, and have heard that he was dead; don't know if he had any children. Joshua T. Moody, the youngest brother, was well known in this county; he was also a genial gentleman, large-hearted and liberal to a fault; he would make any personal sacrifice to accommodate a friend; honest and honorable in all his dealings, full of life and buoyancy, and of gushing hospitality; he merchandized a while, run a barroom a while, and finally bought a part of the John J. Collins land, near Ariel, and for several of the last years of his life he farmed on it, and succeeded very well; he married Miss Evaline Moody, a relative, as herein already stated; they had two children, Lizzie and James A. Lizzie married McQuincy Bryant, as already stated, and has a family. James A. Moody has not married; he is a worthy son of a noble father and mother, both of whom are dead—the father died first; the place, as I suppose, belongs to James A. and his sister, Mrs. Bryant. There was another Moody, named Jessee, who belonged, as said, to this branch of the Moody family; he was an excitable and over-religious man, an exhorter in the Methodist Church; his hair curled as much as I ever saw; the old man would shout when he felt like it, and I heard one of the clerical brethren once say of him, that when old Jessee got happy in church, that his hair was so kinky that it would lift him off the floor; suppose he's dead.

HARLLEE.—The name, Harllee, is a change in the orthography, retaining nearly the same pronunciation as the original name, *Harley*, which the ancestor of the Harllees bore. These descended from a younger branch of the house, which was represented by Robert Harley, Earl of Oxford, during the reign of Queen Anne. The younger brother, Peter Harley, the ancestor of the present Harllees, espoused the cause of the exiled house of Stewart, and was among those active in attempting to restore the *"Pretender"* to the throne of England. A price was put on his head as a penalty of this prominence in the Jacobin cause, and he was compelled to remain concealed until his kinsmen obtained for him a pardon from the government; but, probably at the suggestion of the Earl of Oxford himself, who was anxious to sever all connection with one of the unpopular party, the condition of the pardon was that Peter Harley should change his name. He agreed to alter the spelling of the name, but to retain the sound as nearly as possible— so thenceforth he became Peter Harllee. Through the patronage of his then powerful kinsman he obtained an appointment in the navy for his only son, Peter, who was subsequently promoted to the Captaincy of a British man-of-war. Peter remained in this position until his sixtieth year, when, owing to his failing health and on account of a wound, he resigned his commission, retired on his pension and settled in Virginia, then a British colony about the year 1758. He had remained a bachelor until this time, but the following year, when sixty-one years old, he married Ann Leake, of Goochland County, Va., a maiden lady, forty-five years old; the result of this marriage was four children—Ellen, Jane, John and Thomas. Ellen married William Adams, for whom Adamsville, in Marlborough County, is named; Jane married Thomas Cottingham; John died in youth; Thomas, the youngest, was just sixteen years old at the surrender of Cornwallis, at Yorktown, 1781. His father having a contract with the commissary of Washington's army to supply beeves, sent his sons, with some negro slaves, in charge of a herd of cattle to Yorktown; they reached there on the eve of Cornwallis' surrender. The boy witnessed, and in after years often related the circumstances to his children. The son was too young to serve in the army, and the father too old, being then over eighty years of age. Peter Harllee died soon after the close of the war, leaving his family impoverished, not only through the loss of his British pension, but because that portion of Virginia had suffered devastation at the hands of both armies. Thomas moved with his mother and sisters to South Carolina. He often related to his children, that, being very poor, he engaged in manual labor beyond his strength to obtain money to forward a claim to the British government for the renewal and the arrears of pension due to his father. This claim, made through our Minister to Great Britain, was refused, the authorities asserting that Captain Peter Harllee had been a *rebel,* and had aided the colonies in their revolt, and had thus forfeited all claims upon Great Britain. Finding himself without other resources than those of youth, health and energy, he literally became the architect of his own fortunes. He had settled on Little Pee Dee River, where R. P. Hamer, Sr., now lives. Agriculture being in its infancy in that section, offered little hopes of livelihood; but having considerable mechanical skill, he engaged in boat and flat making and found it very profitable. By this means he laid the foundation of the large property which he possessed at his death. He sold his flats to the rice planters, and loaded his pole-boats with merchandise for his store on Little Pee Dee. This was the only store between Marion Court House and Cheraw. He engaged largely in farming and stock-raising, and entered all the lands for several miles around him on both sides of the river. With an education so limited that when he came to South Carolina, he could only read and write, his ambition stimulated him to educate himself. Being too poor to buy candles, often, after a hard day's work, he studied for hours by a fire of blazing lightwood; thus he acquired the rudiments of knowledge and made sufficient progress in mathematics to begin surveying, and did much of this work; was employed by the State to survey several districts in the eastern part of the State for a large map of the State. This map is still extant and very accurate. He was aided in this work by his eldest son, John, who became one of the best surveyors in the State. He continued to enter and buy land as he accumulated the funds to do so, paid for it in coin weighed by avoirdupois, as was then customary. He prospered in everything in which he engaged. He often told his children that he attributed the blessings of Providence upon his undertakings to his life-long respect, affection and devotion for his aged mother, who continued to live with him until her death in 1810, at the advanced age of ninety-six years; she had retained the most extraordinary vigor of mind and body. When Marion was first organized as a district, Thomas Harllee represented it in the Legislature; he was for many years Clerk of the Court for Marion District, having in his office a poor boy from Lumberton, N. C., as assistant, E. B. Wheeler, who succeeded his benefactor as Clerk, and held the office continuously until his death in 1859. Thomas Harllee, when young, married a girl of Scotch parentage, named Elizabeth Stuart; her father, David Stuart, emigrated from Scotland and settled in Richmond County, N. C. He, with his two sons, David and Hardy, fought through the Revolutionary War under General Marion. David Stuart, Sr., died about the close of the war, but his two sons survived him; neither of those sons left descendants. David Stuart, Jr., was taken prisoner by the British, and was one of the few who survived the terrible incarcerations in the British prison ships in

Charleston harbor. In this connection it may be mentioned that in the lower part of Barnwell, Hampton and Orangeburg Counties, there is a large family of Harleys, between whom and the Harllees of the Pee Dee section is a very striking resemblance—so marked is this resemblance, that at one time before the war, when Dr. Robert Harllee represented Marion County in the State Senate, and Dr. Robert Harley represented Barnwell in the same body, the presiding officer of the Senate frequently mistook the one for the other. There were born to Thomas Harllee and wife ten children—John Anne, Elizabeth, David S., Peter, Robert, Thomas, Harriet, William W. and Lucretia; the last died in childhood; the others all attained to manhood and womanhood—some of them living to advanced ages, rearing large families of children; but all of them are now dead—General W. W. Harllee, the youngest, being the last one to die—he died in 1897, at the age of eighty-five years. The oldest son, Major John Harllee, was a well known man throughout the Pee Dee section; he was a man of fine mind and splendid intellect. In his youth he was appointed a Lieutenant in the United States army; he saw much service with the Indians and with General Jackson against the British at New Orleans. While stationed on the frontier, which was then Louisiana, he became involved in a personal difficulty with a fellow-Lieutenant, and the latter challenged him to mortal combat—duelling in those days, especially among army officers, was very common. Lieutenant David E. Twiggs, afterwards a Major General of the United States army, and who distinguished himself in the war with Mexico, was the second of Lieutenant Harllee in the affair. They fought with rifles at forty paces; Lieutenant Harllee threw away his shot at a sapling in the opposite direction from his challenger. After the latter had fired, he taunted Lieutenant Harllee with being afraid to shoot at him, and demanded another shot, which was accorded him, and at the word fire, the rifles cracked and the challenger fell dead—shot through the hips. Soon after this affair of honor, which he ever after deplored, Lieutenant Harllee resigned from the army and returned to his home, where he engaged in surveying and teaching school, until he became an old man. He was an expert and very correct surveyor, but did not work at that employment constantly. He was an excellent and pains-taking teacher, but did that work also spasmodically. During his long vacations his visits to his brothers' and sisters' families, where he spent these intervals, were welcome events to the children of the families, especially his quaint and original expressions and narrations of his varied career, all of which were enjoyed by everybody, and can never be forgotten by those who knew him. In early life he was a keen sportsman, but as age grew upon him he could only indulge in fishing, which seemed to be a ruling passion; this and reading were his only occupations in his last years. His literary talents led him to read everything; he could quote pages and pages from his favorite poets, and had rare poetic gifts himself—he, indeed, had in himself the elements of a grand and original character. He was never married, and spent his last years in comfort at the home of his niece, Mrs. Elizabeth McRae, at Argyle, N. C., where he died at the age of eighty-nine years.

Colonel David Stuart Harllee was the second son. His father settled him near him on lands now owned by M. R. and E. R. Hamer. He was Sheriff of the county, while he lived there, but soon sold out his lands and moved to Cheraw, S. C., where for a long period he was a leading merchant of the town. He finally sold out his mercantile business, bought a large plantation in Marlborough County, moved and lived there till he died. He was admitted to the bar late in life, at the age of fifty-one years—he and the writer were both admitted in the same class; he became a good lawyer. He married Harriet Barnes, of Robeson County, N. C., and they raised a family of three sons and four daughters. The eldest son, Major James J. Harllee, was a lawyer; he began the practice of his profession at Marion Court House, but soon gave up the law to devote his entire attention to his large farming interest, near town. He married the only daughter of A. L. Scarborough. Just before the civil war, he sold out his land and moved to Arkansas; he owned a large number of slaves, and he carried them with him to Arkansas. He was a successful planter until the breaking out of the civil war. He fought through the war in the cavalry, and after the surrender the government, through the Freedman's Bureau, seized several hundred bales of cotton belonging to him. After a long controversy, he gained back his cotton, and on the day he succeeded in his suit for his cotton, he mounted his horse, in the town of Arkadelphia, to return to his home, a few miles distant, but his horse becoming frightened became unmanageable, threw him and killed him. He was married before leaving South Carolina, but left no children. Dr. William F. Harllee, was the second son. He first married a Miss Medley, in Anson County, N. C., and after her death, a Miss McRae, daughter of General McRae, of Newberne, N. C. He raised several children, and died several years ago. He was an Assistant Surgeon in the Confederate army during the entire war. The youngest son of Colonel D. S. Harllee is Thomas Henry Harllee, Sr., who lives at Florence, S. C. He married Margaret McColl, daughter of William McColl, near Florence, S. C.; they have raised a family of three sons and four daughters, all of whom are now living. Two of his sons, Thomas H., Jr., and David S., are popular conductors on the Atlantic Coast Line Railroad. The eldest daughter of Colonel D. S. Harllee, Elizabeth, married, first, Dr. Neill McNair, of Robeson County, N. C.; they had one son, Harllee McNair, who entered the Confederate service, and was stationed at Wilmington, N. C., where he died early in the war. After the death of Dr. McNair, his widow married Alex. McRae, of Wilmington, N. C.; they lived at Argyle, their country home, until the death of Mr. McRae. Mrs. McRae now lives in Wilmington, N. C., with her stepdaughter, Mrs. Emily Payne; she is quite an intellectual woman; most of her time is given to missionary work for the Presbyterian Church in the mountains of North Carolina. The second daughter of Colonel D. S. Harllee, Mary Ann, married B. H. Covington, of Richmond County, N. C.; they raised a family of several sons and one daughter. One of the sons, Rev. J. E. Covington, is an able minister of the Baptist Church, and lives in the upper part of South Carolina. Another son, Frank F. Covington, of Marion, S. C., is the efficient stenographer of the Fourth Circuit, and is Chief Clerk in the enrolling department of the General Assembly; he married Miss Nora Aycock, of Wedgefield, S. C., and has a family of four children. The youngest son, Benjamin Harllee Covington, married a Miss Cox, and lives in Marlborough, on his grand-father's plantation. The daughter, Hallie, married Mr. William Lawson, an Englishman, who is now a prominent merchant in Birmingham, Ala. The third daughter of Colonel D. S. Harllee, Julia, married Colonel John N. McCall, of Mars Bluff, S. C. After the war they removed to Statesville, N. C., where Colonel McCall died, and where his widow still lives. They raised a large family of children. Colonel McCall represented the County of Marion in the Legislature before the war; he was a large planter and owned a great many slaves. On the same night that Julia was married, Ellen, her youngest sister, was married at the residence of their brother, James J. Harllee, at Marion, to Robert F. Graham, who was then a young lawyer of fine talent and large practice, associated with General W. W. Harllee; he had graduated with high honors at the South Carolina College; he entered the army and was Colonel of the Twenty-first Regiment. After the surrender, he allied himself with the Republican party in the State, and was one of the leaders from 1868 until his death, which occurred from yellow fever, in Charleston, in 1874; he was Judge of the First Circuit at the time of his death. He had several sons and daughters. His widow married Dr. Muckenfuss, and they reside at Summerville, S. C. Colonel Thomas Harllee was the third son of Thomas Harllee, Sr. He inherited the old homestead, where he continued the mercantile business near the river for a long time, and conducted the large farm. He sold out his possessions to John A. McRae and John B. McDaniel, of Clio, S. C., and they afterwards sold to Elias Townsend, who in turn sold to R. C. Hamer. R. C. Hamer gave it to his son, Robert P. Hamer, Jr., who now lives upon it, on the very spot where Thomas Harllee first settled and built. Colonel Thomas Harllee was a very popular man and was beloved by all who knew him; he represented the county in the Legislature in the olden times. Later in life, after selling out Harlleesville, he removed to Charleston, where he did business as a commission merchant until his death, in 1855; he never married. The fourth son of Thomas Harllee, Sr., was Captain Peter Harllee, who inherited the plantation on

A HISTORY OF MARION COUNTY.   349

the east side of the river from Harlleesville, where he lived and died, and where his son, Captain Andrew T. Harllee, now lives. This is the only land, out of the vast possessions originally entered and owned by Thomas Harllee, Sr., now owned and lived upon by his descendants. Captain Peter Harllee married, in 1830, Ann Fulmore, of Robeson County, N. C.; they raised a family of four sons and four daughters; Captain Peter Harllee died in 1860. All four of his sons being in the army, the widow successfully conducted the farms with the slaves, and raised and furnished large quantities of provisions for the soldiers, until her death, in 1863. The oldest son, Captain Robert Z. Harllee, married Susan A. Munnerlyn, daughter of Thomas M. Munnerlyn; they had four sons and two daughters. The eldest son, Thomas M. Harllee, lives in St. Louis, Mo.; he won the prize in New Orleans for being the most rapid typewriter in the United States. John W. Harllee is Captain of a steamer running out of Georgetown, S. C. Peter Zack, the third son, is the superintendent of an oil mill at Gibson, N. C.; and the youngest son, Robert E., of one at Darlington, S. C. The eldest daughter, Sallie, married Edwin J. Wall, and they have a large family of children; they live in Georgetown, S. C. The youngest daughter, Anne, married Joseph O. Wilson, who owns and runs a steamer out of Georgetown, where they live. Captain Robert Z. Harllee served throughout the war in Bragg's army, and was Captain of Company D, of the Tenth South Carolina Regiment, Manigault's brigade. He commanded the regiment at the battle of Atlanta, on July 28th, 1864, and was severely wounded in that battle; he also commanded the regiment in the series of battles through North Carolina just before the close of the war, and surrendered at Greensboro. He preserved the regimental flag by hiding it under his saddle blanket, and it escaped capture. He died at the residence of his brother, Captain Andrew T. Harllee, on the 17th April, 1900; his wife died in 1896. Captain Andrew T. Harllee, when quite a youth, went with a number of young men from the State to Kansas Territory, in 1855; he remained there for a year, fighting under Atchison, Stringfellow and other pro-slavery leaders, against old John Brown (Ossauwatomie), afterwards hung at Harper's Ferry, Jim Lane and others of the Abolition party—hence he was no stranger to the whistling of bullets from Sharp's rifles (Beecher's Bible), when the civil war began. After the failure of Kansas to be made a slave State, he returned to his native State, but soon after got an appointment, through his patron, Thomas A. Hendricks, in the Interior Department, in Washington, and held this position until South Carolina seceded, when he resigned and returned to Charleston, where he was appointed Assistant Quartermaster on the staff of Governor Pickens, with the rank of Captain; discharged the duties of this office until the fall of Fort Sumter, when he resigned to raise Company I, of the Eighth Regiment, South Carolina. He went with that company to Virginia, and fought through the first battle of Manassas with a rifle. After that battle, Lieutenant R. H. Rogers having resigned, he was promoted to fill the vacancy, and on the reorganization of the company he was elected Captain, and served as such till the surrender. He was several times wounded—twice severely; first at the capture of Harper's Ferry, on Maryland Heights, through both thighs, and then at Gettysburg, in the right thigh again. After the surrender he went to Florida, remained there for three years, and then returned to his home, where he has resided ever since; he is a farmer and a bachelor; he has held many places of public trust—was a Trial Justice from 1876 to 1886, was a delegate to the National Democratic Convention in 1884, is commander of Camp Harllee of Confederate Veterans at Dillon, S. C. John W. Harllee was the third son of Peter Harllee. He was First Lieutenant of Captain Stafford's company of Hagood's brigade, and was a good officer. He was wounded twice—the last time he was permanently disabled by a resection of the knee joint, at the battle of the Wilderness, and his was the first successful operation of the kind performed in Lee's army, as the medical record shows; being disabled for active service, he performed the duties of enrolling officer until the close of the war, having been promoted to Captain. After the war he removed to Florida, and married there Mary Ellen Curry; his wife died after the birth of his fourth son, and he never married again; he accumulated a handsome fortune in the mercantile business, and died in 1887, of yellow fever; he left four sons—the eldest, John, is a wholesale and retail hardware merchant in Havana, Cuba. His next two sons, Horace E. and Andrew C., are merchants and fruit and truck farmers in Manatee County, Fla., at the town Palmetto. His youngest son, William C., left West Point Military Academy when half through his course, and went to the Philippines as a private in the Thirty-third United States Volunteer Infantry. After two months' service there he was promoted to Lieutenant in the United States Marine corps, and he is now with his command en route for China, and was promoted to First Lieutenant, 23d July, 1900. Peter Stuart Harllee is the fourth and youngest son of Peter Harllee. He joined the army of the Confederacy at fifteen years of age, and served until the surrender in his brother, Captain A. T. Harllee's company, of the Eighth Regiment; he was in many of the battles in which the company engaged, but escaped without injury. After the war, he remained at home with his sisters until the return of Captain A. T. Harllee from Florida, when he went, first, to Texas, and then to Florida; he married, in Florida, Miss Alice Bullock, and they have several children; he is a large stock and fruit and vegetable grower, and has fine possessions along the Matinee River, in Tampa, and the interior of the State. Ann Eliza was the oldest daughter; she was a lady of remarkable intelligence; died in 1895. Amelia is the second daughter; she lives with her brother, Andrew, at the old place where they were born—she and her brother being joint owners of the old homestead. Agnes, the third daughter, married Captain W. D. Carmichael, and they live three miles west of Harlleesville; they have six sons and four daughters, nearly all of whom are grown. Their eldest son, William D., graduated with distinction at the University of North Carolina, in 1897, and he is now the Principal of the Durham High School, where he has been teaching since his graduation; he married, in 1899, Margaret Mae Robert McCaull, daughter of Colonel John A. McCaull, of New York city; he is a young man of fine talent. Captain Carmichael has one daughter, Jessie, married to Walter Tatum, one of the leading merchants of McColl, S. C. The youngest daughter of Captain Peter Harllee, Bettie, was a very accomplished and superior young lady, a favorite with everybody; she died just after reaching womanhood, in 1882. Dr. Robert Harllee was the fifth son of old Thomas Harllee; he graduated in medicine and settled at Marion Court House, and while he practiced there his profession, he had a very extensive practice all over the county. He married, first, Miss Ann Gurly, a daughter of Joseph Gurly; she died in a short time, childless; he afterwards married Mrs. Amelia Howard, widow of Charles Howard, of West Marion—her maiden name was Cannon, a daughter of old Major Cannon, of Darlington; she had two children, a daughter, Melvina, and a son, Richard G. Howard, when she married Dr. Harllee; he (Dr. Harllee) raised a family of four sons and three daughters. His eldest son, Robert Armstrong, was a good soldier in the Eighth South Carolina Regiment; he died in camp, near Manassas, in 1861, of pneumonia. The next oldest son, Walter C., is a commercial traveler; he lives in Florence, S. C. The third son, Harry T., is a farmer; he lives near Florence; he married a Miss McCall, and they have a family of grown children. The youngest son of Dr. Harllee, Arthur, is a lawyer; he lives in New Mexico, and is unmarried. The second daughter, Sallie, just after the war, married Dr. J. F. Pearce, and they have one son, Robert H., who is now associated with his father in business. Dr. and Mrs. Pearce had one daughter, Anne, who married a Mellichamp, of Charleston, and they now live in Atlanta, Ga. After the death of his first wife, Dr. Pearce married her sister, Louisa, and they live on a part of Dr. Dr. Harllee's homestead. Dr. Pearce is well known throughout the State. He and his son are progressive and successful farmers as well as eminent physicians. Dr. Pearce represented his county (Marion) once in the Legislature, and declined re-election. Hattie, the youngest daughter of Dr. Harllee, married Hon. Marsden Bellamy, of Wilmington, N. C., where they reside, and have a large family of children. Dr. Harllee was an exceedingly popular man; he was several times a Representative in the lower House and for two terms a Senator before the war; he died after the war, at the age of sixty-five. General W. W. Harllee was the sixth and youngest son of Thomas Harllee, Sr.; he read law with Chancellor Dargan, of

Darlington, and began the practice of his profession at Marion Court House. He volunteered for service in the Florida War with the Indians, and commanded a battalion from South Carolina in that war; he was Brigadier and Major General of the militia long before the war. He represented his county in the Legislature twice before the war, and since the war was elected Senator, and served one term, and while Senator was elected President *pro tem.* of the Senate; he was President of the Wilmington and Manchester Railroad for five years, from its organization to its completion; it was due to his untiring efforts that the road was built; he was delegate to the Secession Convention of the State, in 1860, and was Lieutenant-Governor at the beginning of the war; he was the commander of the "Harllee Legion," that was stationed near Georgetown. When a young man, he married Miss Martha Shakelford, of Charleston; they raised three sons and three daughters. Edward Porcher, his eldest son, was a brilliant young man; he was a gallant officer on the staff of Generals Kershaw and Kennedy. He was admitted to the bar, but preferred journalism to law, and until a short time before his death was on the editorial staff of the New Orleans *Picayune;* he fell a victim to overwork, had softening of the brain as a result, and died, unmarried, in the prime of life. Charles Stuart, the second son of General Harllee, was also in the army, and did gallant service. He removed to Texas after the war; married there and died, leaving three children, who, with their mother, live in Texas now. James, the youngest son, also went to Texas, married, and is living there now. Florence and Lizzie, the two oldest daughters, have never married; they are teachers, and live at Florence, with their mother; the city was named for the eldest daughter, Florence, it having been esatblished at the time of the building of the Wilmington and Manchester Railroad, of which her father was then President. The third and youngest daughter, Mattie, married Frank Coachman, of Georgetown, and they have a large family of children, who live with their father, at Plantersville, S. C., since the death of their mother. Their eldest daughter, Helen, married Mr. LaBruce, a large rice planter of that section. The three daughters of Thomas Harllee, Sr., were Annie, Elizabeth and

Harriet. Annie married John McNeill, and settled on the east side of Little Pee Dee River, on Hays Swamp, but they soon moved to Wilcox County, Ala.; they raised a large family of children, some of whom are now prominent in their State. Mrs. McNeill lived to be eighty years of age. Elizabeth, the next oldest, married Parker Bethea, and they lived and died near where they first settled, near what is now called Mineral Springs; they raised two sons and four daughters. Their eldest son, Harllee, married Elizabeth Roberts, a daughter of Reddin Roberts, on Buck Swamp; they moved to Florida, and died there. One of their daughters married her first cousin, W. D. B. Hays, a good citizen and farmer; they live on Buck Swamp. The other children live in Florida. Benjamin Parker Bethea, their youngest son, was an officer from the beginning to the end of the war, and was a gallant and brave soldier. After the war, he married a Miss Woolvin, of Pender County, N. C., below Wilmington, to which place he removed and now resides, and is a successful farmer; his products are principally peanuts; he has a family of group-up children. The eldest daughter of Parker Bethea and wife, Elizabeth, married a Mr. Henderson, of North Carolina, and they had one son, Robert, who was a good soldier; he and his mother are both dead. The second daughter, Harriet, married Jesse Rogers, and both of them are dead. Their sons, David S. and Albert, are successful farmers of the county. The third daughter, Laura, married, late in life, Mr. Thompson Allen, of Marlborough County; and the youngest daughter, Maria, married a Mr. Harris, and they moved to North Carolina. Harriet, the youngest daughter of Thomas Harllee, Sr., married George I. W. McCall, of Darlington, and they raised a family of three daughters. Hannah Jane, the youngest, has never married. Rebecca and Caroline both married gentlemen by the name of Saunders, of Sumter County, and they have numerous descendants living in Sumter and Darlington Counties, many of whom are prominent in business and social circles in those counties.

The foregoing notice of the Harllee family was furnished to the writer by Captain A. T. Harllee, which has been copied herein, *in extenso verbatim et liberatim*, except in a few instances in the phraseology has been changed, and a few omissions and additions made, at the expense of space. It is a history of which the family may be proud as also the county.

WOODBERRY.—Two brothers, Richard and Jonah Woodberry, came to Britton's Neck from Socastee, in the early part of the eighteenth century; where they came from to Socastee is not known, but it is supposed they came from Wales or elsewhere in England. Richard Woodberry settled in what is now called Woodberry Township, and married Miss Lizzie Balloone, on Black River; they raised two sons, Richard and William. Richard Woodberry, Jr., married Miss Desda Davis, and they had and raised two sons and two daughters; the sons were John and George W.; the daughters were Mrs. Benjamin Gause and Mrs. John Gause. The three daughters of old Richard, Sr., were Margaret, who married Dr. Thomas Britton; she died childless; another daughter, Fannie married Samuel Wilson, and she died childless; another daughter (name not known), married Rev. Jeremiah Norman, of North Carolina; they had and raised Mrs. John Woodberry (first wife), Mrs. James Jenkins and Samuel Norman. The latter grew up and went to Horry, and married a Miss Beaty, sister of Colonel James Beaty, of Conway, who, before her death, in 1882, was universally called "Old Aunt Norman." She kept a public house; was born in 1791—a remarkable woman; she had and raised a family, mostly daughters, and one son, who was a doctor—his name not remembered; married and died some years ago. The husband of "Old Aunt Norman" died many years before she died; she was a hustler in business; kept a good house—the writer knows whereof he speaks. John Woodberry, son of Richard, Jr., married, first, his cousin, Miss Norman (Mary), and they had and raised sons, Franklin, William, Norman, Benjamin Gause; and daughters, Eloise and Martha; know nothing of any of these children, except Benjamin Gause Woodberry; he is now in Britton's Neck; he married, first, a widow lady; she had one child, a daughter, who married a few years ago, and is among us now. Benjamin Gause Woodberry married, a second time, a Miss Brown, in Britton's Neck, and they live down there,

John Woodberry married, a second time, Miss Ann Gregg, daughter of our late venerable R. J. Gregg; she had two sons, John and Waddy; I think Waddy is dead. John Woodberry, the son, married a niece of Mrs. Sturges, at Florence, and lives in Florence County; he is a genial gentleman and has a good deal of the "get up" in him, which will count for him in days to come. George Washington Woodberry married a Miss Brown, sister of the late T. F. Brown, and had and raised three sons and three daughters; the sons are Travis Foster, James and Edward; the daughters are Dora, Mary and Julia. Julia went to school at Hofwyl Academy, in 1857—a charming girl, about grown; she married some one; I have lost sight of her; can trace the others no further. General William Woodberry, the brother of Richard, Jr., a very noted and prominent man in his day, was born 10th January, 1788, and died 31st January, 1851; he married, first, Miss Hannah Davis; they had four children, all dying quite young; his second wife was Miss Sarah Johnson, of Horry; by this marriage four sons and four daughters were born, all of whom, except one daughter, married and raised families. General Woodberry's sons were Richard, William, Evander McIver and Joseph Alston. Richard Woodberry, the third, married Miss Joanna Balloone; had two children, both died in infancy. William married twice; had three children by the first wife and five by the last; his oldest son, Richard, 4th, married a Miss Britton; a daughter, Venetia, married a Mr. Pope; another daughter, Agnes, married a Mr. McIlveen; William, a son, married a Miss Cannon; another son, Benjamin Gause, married a Miss Hucks; another son, Harrison, also married a Miss Hucks; another, Joseph A., also married a Miss Hucks, and a daughter, Martha, married Arthur Hucks (the Hucks seemed to be popular with the Woodberrys); they all have families, about whom I know nothing. Evander McIver Woodberry married a Miss Scott; they had two children. Joseph A. also married a Miss Scott, and had three sons and two daughters. General Woodberry's oldest daughter, Elizabeth Ann, married William H. Johnson; they had three sons and five daughters. Another daughter, Mary, married Rollen Kimball; they had two sons and one daughter. Margaret F., the youngest daughter, married the late Hugh R. Johnson, who lived and died near Nichols, S. C.; they had and raised five sons and two daughters; the sons are Whiteford F., Richard Olin, Samuel A., William Woodberry and Edward Evander. Whiteford married Miss Ella Page, daughter of the Widow Pinckney C. Page, near Carmichael's Bridge, on Little Pee Dee; they have some children. Whiteford is the only one of the five sons married. The daughters of Margaret F. are Sallie and Maggie May. Sallie married E. T. Huggins; they have considerable family, some grown. Maggie May married Thomas J. Capet, of Marlborough; they have a young family. General William Woodberry was a very popular man in his day; he filled several important positions of honor, profit and trust, and filled all with credit to himself and came out with unstained official integrity; he was Brigadier General of the militia, and was several times elected to the lower House of the Legislature; he was Sheriff of the county from April, 1833, to April, 1837; he was hospitable to a fault, kind-hearted and liberal, especially to the poor; he was full of wit and humor, and could tell a story with great zest; a great hand to perpetrate a joke and to play innocent tricks on people. The writer has heard of many of them—one as to how he made the Methodist preacher bail the canoe with his fine beaver hat, as the General was putting him across the river; another, how he accidentally (purposely) turned over the canoe, in putting the venerable and reverend James Jenkins across the river, and luckily saved the old man from drowning; another of his adventures with an old gobbler, when a boy, with a red coat on; wherever he went he drew a crowd around him by his wit and humorous stories, which he could tell with the greatest glee, to the great amusement of the listeners; with all his wit, humor and innocent frivolity, he was a man of great good sense; he was a man of wealth, and managed his farm and financial affairs with great success; his home was ever crowded, and his table substantially supplied, and was free; he left no son his equal; his daughter, the youngest, Mrs. Margaret F. Johnson, approaches nearer to her father and inherited more of his humorous fun, and perhaps more of his towering intellect, than any other of his children; and I don't mean, by thus saying, to disparage her other sisters, whom I have never seen, or any other member of the family. As already stated, the first Woodberrys in the county were Richard and Jonah; as to Jonah, he disappeared or emigrated to other parts; nothing further is known of him or his posterity, if he had any. They had a sister, who married General Wade Hampton, of Revolutionary fame, the grand-father of our present General Hampton. The name Hampton will ever be remembered in South Carolina with grateful recollection and pride.

STACKHOUSE.—John Stackhouse, the progenitor of the Stackhouse family in the county, came here from Virginia, before the Revolutionary War; he married a widow, whose maiden name was Bethea, a sister of old Buck Swamp John Bethea; they had and raised two sons, John and William; don't know if there were any daughters. William, I believe, at any rate, one of them, emigrated to other parts; the other, John, remained in the county; he was the grand-father of our fellow-citizen, T. F. Stackhouse; don't know to whom he married—he did marry, however, and had and raised five sons and one daughter; the sons were Herod, Isaac, John, Hugh and Tristram; the daughter's name not remembered. Herod Stackhouse, a very public-spirited man, a good man and a successful farmer, married Miss Nancy Roper; they had and raised two sons, Lysias and Wesley, and one daughter, Mary Ann. Lysias married Miss Mary Gaddy, daughter of old Ithamer Gaddy, and who has been noticed in or among the Gaddy family. Wesley Stackhouse, the second son of Herod, was a most excellent man and citizen, a good business man, well qualified by education and training; married the Widow Lucretia Meekins, whose maiden name was Bethea, a sister of the late Samuel J. Bethea; she had no children by her first marriage; by her marriage with Wesley Stackhouse, two daughters were born and raised, Martha and Nannie, and one son, Wesley, now of Dillon, S. C. His daughter, Martha, married Lieutenant William Manning, who was killed at the second battle of Manassas, 29th August, 1862; by him she had one child, a daughter, who, I think, was born after her father's death, and was named for him, "Willie;" her mother soon after married her cousin, H. Milton Stackhouse, now of Marlborough, and its late Senator in the State Legislature, and a first class man every way; they have had and raised four sons and one daughter; the sons are R. E. Stackhouse, now a first class preacher in the South Carolina Conference of the Methodist Church; Wade, a first class physician, and is married to a Miss Steed, daughter of the late W. H. Steed, of upper Marion; George F., who is a Paymaster in the United States navy, in the Philippines, and who married Miss Texia Young, of Marion, S. C.; and another son, whose name is not known, and who, I presume, is yet with his parents, and one daughter (name not known), who married Mr. J. C. Dunbar, who is now a member of the Legislature from Marlborough County. Miss Willie Manning, the daughter by her first husband, was well educated in the best schools in the South, and a highly accomplished lady, is unmarried, and makes teaching a business, and is somewhere in the State following her vocation, and has been thus engaged ever since her graduation. Nannie, the second daughter of Wesley Stackhouse, married Knox Clark, late Clerk of the Court and County Treasurer—a man of nerve and force, and the power to say *no*, which many men cannot or do not say—a sober, progressive man; he died in the prime of life, in September, 1888, and left Nannie a widow, with some children, three sons and four daughters—the youngest not two years old. Nannie Clark, the widow, survived her husband only a few years; she died, and left all her children unmarried, except Mrs. Brown. Wesley Stackhouse, the only son of his father, Wesley, grew up and married Miss Mollie Breeden, daughter of the late John A. Breeden; they live at Dillon, and have a family of seven or eight children, some of them grown. Unfortunately, Wesley's habits were not good; he dissipated a great deal, and did nothing for several years—spent his inheritance and came down pretty low; but for the last eight or ten years he has abstained—is now and has been for that time a sober man, and is trying to rebuild his lost fortune, in which it is hoped he will succeed; he now has a heavy load to carry. He has a nice and very interesting family. His father died Christmas day, 1864. Mary Ann Stackhouse, the only daughter of old Herod, married Evander R. Bethea, a very successful farmer; they had and raised one son, Jasper, and three daughters, Josephine, Carrie and Nannie. The son grew up, and after some years went to Texas, where he married and where he now lives; he has no children. The eldest daughter, Josephine, married her cousin, William B. Stackhouse, who was a very progressive man and farmer, and was at one time elected as County Commissioner, and served one term very acceptably; he died some years after, leaving Josephine and four or five children surviving, mostly girls. The oldest, Miss Cora, is well educated, and is one of the teachers in the Latta Graded School. The widow is doing well on her fine farm. The second daughter, Carrie, married Joseph J. Bethea, who resides and merchandizes at Latta; he has also a good farm near by; he is a very successful man in affairs; they have no children. The third daughter, Nannie, married Rev. Samuel J. Bethea, who is a regular itinerant Methodist preacher in the South Carolina Conference—stands fair; they have but one child, a son, Samuel J. Isaac Stackhouse, the brother of old Herod, also married another daughter of old man John Roper, a sister of old Herod's wife; he, as well as old Herod, resided on his fine place, below Harlleesville, on Little Pee Dee, all his lifetime. This pair was more prolific than Herod and his wife; they had and raised six sons and one daughter; the sons were Masten C., Eli T., William R., Tristram F., Milton and Robert B.; the daughter's name not remembered. The oldest son, Masten C. Stackhouse, married Mary Ann Rogers, a daughter of William Rogers. Masten C. Stackhouse was a very quiet man, a farmer, and managed well; they had and raised a considerable family of sons and daughters; the sons are Mark, John R., William B. and I. P. Stackhouse, as remembered; one daughter, Janie, one Florence, and one Charlotte, the other name not known. Mark or Marcus was the first graduate of Wofford College from Marion County; he graduated in 1871; he married Miss Mary Lester, an excellent woman, stepdaughter of E. J. Moody; they have three sons grown, named Walter, Edward and Robert, all unmarried. Don't know who John R. Stackhouse married; he lives and is doing business at Mullins. William B. married Josephine Bethea, and has already been mentioned. I. P. Stackhouse married his first cousin, a Miss Rogers, daughter of Philip B. Rogers; they have children, don't know how many; he lives near Moody's Mill, six miles above Marion—is a farmer, and one of the registers of voters in Marion County. One of the daughters, Janie, married Dempsy Lewis, in the "Fork," now of Mullins; he is an excellent manager of his farm, and is now also merchandizing at Mullins; they have ten children, eight of them boys and two girls—they have five grown children. One of the daughters of Masten C. Stackhouse married a Mr. Edens; another one married her first cousin, William Rogers; they live at Mullins; one married Fet Bethea; one married a Mr. Pipkin, in Marlborough, and one is unmarried; there may be others. E. T. Stackhouse, the second son of Isaac, was born 27th March, 1824; his birthday was the same as the writer's—six years younger; he grew up and married Elizabeth Ann Fore, a daughter of the late Thomas Fore; they raised three sons and five daughters. Of the sons, James Stackhouse is the oldest; he married a Miss McAlister, of North Carolina; they have a considerable family, sons and daughters—two sons grown. One, Lanneau, married Miss Mary Miles, daughter of Dr. D. F. Miles, Clerk of the Court; they have some two or three children. The other grown son, Lacy, not married; other children small. James Stackhouse runs a livery stable (sale and feed); in early life he tried merchandizing and hotel business, but failed; he then went into the livery business, and has succeeded well—this business suits him; he is emphatically a horseman; he now represents the county in the State Senate. The second son, William Stackhouse, at Dillon, married a daughter of B. F. Davis, just below Marion; they have some children, don't know how many—they are small; he, too, is in the livery business, and seems to be doing well; he is a capital citizen, and will doubtless succeed. The third and youngest son, Walter F. Stackhouse, is a graduate of Wofford College, in the class of 1895; has studied law and is associated with W. J. Montgomery, his brother-in-law, in its practice, at Marion; he married, a few months ago, a lady of Greenwood, and lives at Marion; he is United States Commissioner at Marion; a man of business, and is quite promising. Of the daughters of Colonel E. T. Stackhouse, the eldest, Mary, married James H. Berry, and has already been noticed among the Berrys. Another daughter, Mattie, married Houston Manning, and has already been noticed among the Mannings. Another, called "Duck" (though not her name), married Neill Alford, who has already been noticed in or among the Alfords. Another, Anna, married W. J. Montgomery, Esq., of Marion; they have several children, one or two grown—mostly girls. Mr. Montgomery graduated at Wofford College, in 1875; came home and studied law with General Harllee, was admitted to the bar and practiced some few years with that veteran of the law; they dissolved partnership, and Mr. Montgomery set up for himself; he has succeeded admirably, has become a fine lawyer and made money; is President of the Merchants and Farmers Savings Bank of Marion, and has been ever since its organization, ten or twelve years ago—the bank has prospered under his administration of its affairs; he has been Mayor of the town, Representative of the county in the Legislature, and also a delegate from the county to the Constitutional Convention of the State, in 1895; he is a man of affairs, and succeeds at all; deserves the more credit, as he was raised as poor as anybody. Much more might be said of him, but space will not allow it. Another and youngest daughter of Colonel Stackhouse, called "Pet" (not her real name), married T. C. Covington, his second wife; they have some children, small yet. Mr. Covington is a high-minded, honorable gentleman, of fine address, and magnetic; he merchandized for a while, but did not succeed well; is now farming in the "Free State" section—it remains to be seen how he will succeed in the farming role.

Colonel E. T. Stackhouse deserves more than a passing notice. He was raised on a farm and received only a common school education. After he was married, he settled on the place where he ever after lived; he was a farmer, a good and very successful one—farmed on the intensive system; his farm was like a garden—all his house and farm arrangements were complete and adapted to comfort and convenience; his farm was a model one. When the war commenced, he raised a company of which he was made Captain; his company formed part of the Eighth South Carolina Regiment; he went through the war to Appomattox, and came out Lieutenant Colonel of the regiment. He was twice elected to the Legislature of the State. When the "Farmers Alliance" began to boom, Colonel Stackhouse went into it with all his might—it seemed to be in accord with his chosen occupation, and operated for the benefit of the farmer and its votaries. He became President of the State Alliance and held that position for one or two terms. Whatever may have been the purpose and intentions of the founders of the Alliance, it was popular and flourished for a time; but the politicians got hold of it and worked it for their benefit, made it a stepping-stone to office and killed it, much to the regret of those honest people who had gone into it to better their condition as farmers. Under its influence and auspices, Colonel Stackhouse became a candidate for Congress, in 1890, and was overwhelmingly elected; he took his seat in that body, in December, 1891, and died suddenly, in Washington, 14th June, 1892. Between the meeting of Congress, first Monday in December, 1891, and his death, in June following, his good wife died. The complete reversal of the habits of his life, together with his ambition to get into the routine of business as done in Congress, so as to be able to do something for his people, was too much for him, for one of his age— he being sixty-eight years old in March preceding his death. A young man may change or reverse his habits with impunity, but an old man dare not do it. It is highly probable that, if Colonel Stackhouse had remained at home on his farm, he might have been living to-day. He was a model citizen and a model farmer. William Roper Stackhouse, the third son of Isaac, died a few weeks ago, a retiring and unassuming man, a good farmer and successful man; he married a Miss Stafford, daughter of Malcolm Stafford, and has already been noticed in or among the Stafford family. Tristram F. Stackhouse, the fourth son of Isaac, one of our very best citizens, married Miss Mary Ann Bethea, a daughter of the late old man, Cade Bethea; he settled on the place near where he was born, now near the town of Dillon; they had and raised three sons, Tristram Bascom, Adolphus and Lawrence. The oldest son, T. Bascom Stackhouse, is a graduate of Wofford College, in the class of 1880; he married a Miss Hamer, daughter of Robert P. Hamer, Sr., and settled near his father, between Harlleesville and Dillon; has a large farm there and is succeeding well thereon, although he gives it but little of his personal attention; he is Cashier of the Bank of Dillon, which requires most of his time; he is a first class business man every way—is up-to-date in almost every branch of commercial and financial life; he has only one child, a daughter, I think. Adolphus Stackhouse, a younger brother, married Miss Lucy Thompson, a daughter of the late Lemuel S. Thompson; they first settled near Harlleesville, and after a few years he sold out and moved to Sumter County, know nothing as to their family—think he has been in the Legislature from Sumter and in the Constitutional Convention in 1895; it is said his wife is a most excellent lady, and the same may be said of him as a man. Lawrence, the youngest son of T. F. Stackhouse, is unmarried—unfortunately he is afflicted with epilepsy; everything possible has been done for him, but to no avail; suppose he is twenty-four or twenty-five years old, lives with his father. T. F. Stackhouse lost his wife some years ago; he has not remarried; his niece and her husband, Masten Gasque, with their family, live with him and keep house for him and also runs his farm. T. F. Stackhouse is a modest, unassuming man and a capital citizen; he has a large and splendid farm, and is well fixed for living; he has been twice consecutively elected to the lower House of the General Assembly, and is now serving a second term—a man of good judgment and fine sense. If our county was filled up with such men there would be little use for courts or lawyers. H. Milton Stackhouse, the fifth son of Isaac, has already been incidentally mentioned above with his wife, who was a daughter of Wesley Stackhouse, of the Herod branch of the family. Robert B., the sixth son of Isaac, was a promising young man; sickened and died soon after coming out of the war—a young man of promise. Hugh Stackhouse, a younger brother of old Herod and Isaac, was drowned in Little Pee Dee River, about 1837 or 1838; was unmarried—a young man. The circumstances were these: there had been a tremendous freshet in Little Pee Dee, and it floated the planks off each end of Stafford's Bridge, and as soon as the freshet went down low enough, A. Q. McDuffie, who lived near by, and then a young man, together with Hugh Stackhouse, and a negro man, took a canoe and went down the river hunting up the planks, so as to bring them back and put them on the bridge again; in going down the river, their canoe struck or got into a whirl in the river, which (the river being very full) was strong, so much so as to turn the canoe over. McDuffie was a good swimmer; Stackhouse could swim but little, and the negro could not swim at all. Stackhouse soon sank; McDuffie, seeing it, managed to sustain himself in the whirl, till Stackhouse rose to the top, when McDuffie made for him and caught hold of him; Stackhouse, like all drowning men, had no sense, tried to cling around McDuffie's neck; the latter knew that would not do—that both would be drowned together; he tore loose from Stackhouse and the latter sank again. McDuffie waited till he rose the second time, and caught him again, with the same result as at first. McDuffie freed himself from him, Stackhouse sank again, and he was seen no more. The negro, who could not swim at all, managed to get hold of an overhanging bough of a tree and saved himself. McDuffie, several times in his life, told this to the writer; said he could have saved Stackhouse, if he could have gotten him to have acted otherwise; said he hollered to Stackhouse with all his might, not to cling around his neck, but Stackhouse would not heed him, hence he tore loose from him and saved himself. The question was, shall both drown or only Stackhouse?

The Stackhouse family is extensive and numerous in itself and its connections; yet there are as few "dead-beats" in it as, perhaps, in any family in the county. They are self-sustaining, all bread-winners. Old Herod and old Isaac were working men and had right ideas of life, and, above all, were God-fearing men—did all they could for the church and the cause of their Maker. From the twenties to the forties, inclusive, there were annually camp meetings at or near Harlleesville, and they two were among the strongest advocates and supporters of those meetings, and their daily life and intercourse with their neighbors showed the same spirit and was in strict accord with their professions. It reminds the writer of the language of the Psalmist, David, where he said, "I was young, but now

I am old, yet have I not seen the righteous forsaken, nor his seed begging bread." Of the two brothers of Herod and Isaac, to wit: John and Tristram, John either died or went elsewhere; Tristram Stackhouse became a Methodist preacher of the South Carolina Conference in 1830, a young single man, and died on Cypress Circuit, Colleton County or Orangeburg, in 1831.

WAYNE.—This family, though the name is now extinct in Marion County, yet its descendants are numerous, and its connection extensive—hence it is now herein noticed. Francis Asbury Wayne, the first one known in this county (born in 1787 and died in 1870), was the second son of William Wayne, who was a first cousin of General Anthony Wayne, was brought up with the General in the latter's family. William was a brave Revolutionary soldier, and after the war (Revolutionary), moved to Georgetown S. C., where he lived and died, about 1820. It is recorded in Asbury's journal (which I have not now before me), that William Wayne was the only Methodist at Georgetown, when the Bishop first visited that place. He married Esther Trezevant (a Huguenot), and I suppose a sister of Judge Lewis Trezevant, who was elected a Judge, 10th February, 1800, and died 15th February, 1808 (vol. I., Statutes at Large, page 439), and both he and his wife were buried *under* the Methodist Church at Georgetown, S. C.—a wide marble slab now covering both their graves. Other children of William Wayne were progenitors of Mrs. Eleanor Gregg, widow of the late Wesley W. Gregg, of Marion, the Mellichamps, of Sumter, a family of Elliotts and Daniel G. Wayne, and the Von Kolnitzs, of Charleston. Francis Asbury Wayne came to this county from Georgetown, and married, first, the widow of old Nathan Evans and mother of the late General William Evans; she was a sister of the late William Rogers, of Dothan; the fruit of this marriage was an only daughter, Martha, who married Alexander Murdoch, of Marlborough, and became the mother of the two wives of Robert Charles McIntyre, which has already been noticed in or among the McIntyres, and of two sons, John and Kenneth, both of whom died young and unmarried. The first wife dying, F.

A. Wayne married, a second time, Miss Elizabeth Marjory Legette, daughter of Jessee Legette, Sr., a sister of Captain David Legette, Jessee, Jr., and Ebenezer, and of Mrs. Ann Snow and Jane Legette; there was another sister, Theresa Ann, who married a Palmer. By this marriage they had and raised six daughters and three sons. Of the daughters, the eldest, Jane Trezevant, married Jeremiah Sessions, of Horry; they had and raised two sons. Lawrence Trezevant, who married a Miss Smith, daughter of the late William H. Smith, by his first wife, Miss Helen Bass, and by this marriage were born six or seven children, sons and daughters. This wife died, and he married again, I think, a Miss Campbell. Of the children of Lawrence T. Sessions, the writer does not know their names, though some of them are young men grown, except the youngest, Clyde, who was an infant when his mother died, and he was taken and raised by his cousin, J. J. Bethea, of Latta; he is now nearly grown. Laurens Trezevant Sessions is a capital man, good citizen and a good farmer. The other son was Percy Sessions, who became a dental surgeon, and settled in Williamsburg County. Caroline Anna Wayne, the next oldest daughter, married the late John Wilcox, of Marion; she had two children for him, John and George—don't know which was the older; she died, and afterwards her son, George, died. John Wilcox, now of Marion, is her only surviving child; he married Miss Leila Smith, daughter of the late J. Albert Smith; they have four or five children, all boys. John Wilcox is one of the most efficient business men we have; he has been well trained, first as clerk for the Sheriff, I think, about eleven years; then as Sheriff of the county for two years; then as Deputy Clerk of the Court for two years; then as Clerk of the Court for ten years. In all these varied positions he acquitted himself with credit, and to the entire satisfaction of his people; in each and all these places of trust he maintained the utmost official integrity, and when he was beaten, in 1892, for re-election to the Clerk's office, it was not because of any charges made against his competency or official integrity, but solely because he would not, or did not, wear the badge of Tillmanism; fortunately for the county, the people got another good man in his place in the person of our present efficient and gentlemanly Clerk, Dr. D. F. Miles. The next daughter of old man Wayne, Elizabeth, married Wyatt Fuller; by this marriage three children were born—two sons, Frank and George, and one daughter; Fuller and his wife are both dead. Of the sons, Frank was merchandizing in Florence, the last the writer knew of him; he married a Miss Collins. George Fuller either went off or died—disappeared as to the writer. The daughter, Sallie Fuller, married Daniel J. Oliver, now of Marion, Magistrate and merchant; they have several children. The eldest, a son, L. Wyatt Oliver, married Miss Alice Jones, daughter of the late Fred. D. Jones, of Marion; he runs a farm and some mercantile business; think they have one or two children. The eldest daughter of D. J. Oliver and wife, Mary, married Quincy Berry, and lives near Berry's Cross Roads; they have no child. There are four Mary Berrys in the Cross Roads community, and they are distinguished from each other by the names, "Mary Elihu," "Mary Burke," "Mary Neill" and "Mary Quince." D. J. Oliver has another son grown and married, whose name is not remembered, and other younger children. The next daughter, Sarah Wayne, married Dr. O. J. Bond; they had several children, sons and daughters; they removed to Chester County some years ago—think both are dead; their sons were Bernard, James and Harper Bond. Of these, James graduated in the Citadel Academy some years ago, and stood so well that he was elected one of its professors—suppose he is there yet. Of the others, the writer knows nothing. The next daughter of old man Wayne was Catharine Maria, who married Rev. Osgood A. Chreitzberg; he died childless; she went West, perhaps to Florida, and married some one, know not whom. Mary Adelaide, the youngest daughter of old man Wayne, first married her first cousin, Dr. Armand C. Legette, who afterwards became a Methodist preacher of the South Carolina Conference; he traveled here a few years and was transferred to the Florida Conference, where he died in a short time, and his widow married another minister, named Younge; he died, and she has recently married another preacher of the same Florida Conference, whose name is not known; how many children, if any, she has, is not known. The writer can say this of her: when she was a single lady, she was the most elastic and agile untrained woman he ever saw; she could walk along by the side of a horse of ordinary height, and lay her hand upon his withers and spring from the ground into the saddle—he saw her perform this feat once, and it seems she is expert in catching Methodist preachers. Of the sons of old man F. A. Wayne, Gabriel I., the eldest, married, first, a Widow Britt; by the marriage was born and raised one child, a daughter, Julia, who married, first, George C. Bethea; they lived together several years, when he died, childless; the widow married again, a Methodist preacher, then belonging to the Florida Conference, by the name of Nathan Wiggins, but now of the South Carolina Conference; they have two children, as I am informed. Gabriel I. Wayne's first wife died, and he married a second time, and lives now in Florence County; he is a farmer. The old gentleman, Francis Asbury Wayne, settled, lived and died near Marion Court House, near or on the place now owned by J. M. Johnson, Esq. Intellectually he was far above the ordinary; he was in some respects an oddity—truthful and honest.

LEGETTE.—There were three old Legettes, of whom the writer has knowledge—David, Jesse and Abner Legette. Old David Legette married, I do not know to whom, but he had and raised three children, Colonel Levi Legette, Abner Legette, Jr., and Mrs. General Wheeler. Colonel Levi Legette married, first, a Miss Evans, sister of Thomas Evans, Sr., and half-sister of General William Evans; the fruits of this marriage were three or four sons and three daughters; don't know the names of all the sons or what has become of them. One son was named Morgan, who it was said was a very promising young man; he was very muscular and athletic; he volunteered early in the war and went into the Confederate service; during the war he was killed in some one of the battles in Virginia, or died from disease contracted in service. Another son, Levi, grew up and married some one, and may be in the county now, but is unknown; he may have had other sons. Colonel Levi Legette had and raised three daughters, Anna, Mary and Melvina. Anna married, first, Ebben Rogers, of the Dothan community; he settled below Marion, and was killed in October, 1855, by a man named Harrelson, as already mentioned herein. By this marriage, two children were born, a son, named Ebben, and a daughter, name not remembered, and who is the wife of Addison J. Snipes, below Marion. Ebben went off to parts unknown. Snipes and wife have a family, how many is not known, and perhaps grand-children; one of Snipes' daughters married A. P. Johnson, of Horry. The Widow Anna Rogers married again to Jessee Rogers, a first cousin of her first husband; no fruit of this marriage; both are dead. Mary, the second daughter of Colonel Legette, married Mr. Edward C. Collins; they had and raised several sons and two daughters; don't know the names of either sons or daughters, except one son, Lawrence, who is clerk for the dispensary at Florence. One of the daughters married Frank Fuller; they reside in Florence. Think the other daughter is dead. Melvina, the youngest daughter, married William Loyd; they have a family, of how many is unknown; think they have two sons, names unknown; they live below Marion, and are said to be doing well. After the death of Colonel Legette's first wife, he married the widow of James P. McInnis, of upper Marion, whose maiden name was Althea Alford, a daughter of Lodwick B. Alford; they had no children; Colonel Legette died in 1871, at the age of seventy-six years; his widow still survives. Colonel Legette was a man of marked individuality—there was but one Levi Legette; he was a good surveyor and did a great deal of work in that line; had a fair education for his day; was a farmer, and represented his county in the lower House of the Legislature for one term. Abner Legette, Jr., a brother of Colonel Levi, was one of nature's men; he was rough and outspoken, a man of great personal independence; don't know of his family, if he had any; have not seen him in many years— he has disappeared, by death or removal. The only daughter of old David Legette, Clara L., married General E. B. Wheeler, as well known in his day as perhaps any man in the county; he was Clerk of the Court for thirty years consecutively; he died in 1859—he was no ordinary man; the fruit of the marriage was an only son, who became Dr. James Hamilton Wheeler. He married Miss Sarah Jane Cherry, a daughter of Dr. Cherry, of Spring Branch; the fruits of the marriage were two sons, our present fellow-citizen, Ed. B. Wheeler, and Liston C. Wheeler, of Marion. Their father died when his two sons were quite small; his widow, their mother, still survives, and lives at Marion; she is a most amiable woman. The widow of General Wheeler died some years ago, leaving her money and little property to her two grand-sons, E. B. and Liston C. Wheeler, to whom she was passionately devoted in her latter days. Ed. B. Wheeler married Miss Effa Blue, daughter of the late Colonel John G. Blue, of Marion; two or three children are the fruits of the marriage; they reside in Marion. Liston C. Wheeler married Miss Carrie Boyd, daughter of the late Rev. J. Marion Boyd, who some years ago was the Presiding Elder of this, the Marion District, and who thereafter died suddenly on the Spartanburg District, a very able preacher; the fruit of this marriage is an only child, I believe, a son; they reside in Marion.

Old Jesse Legette, Sr., had three sons, as known to the writer; don't know who his wife was; the three sons were Jessee, Jr., Ebenezer and David; he also had four daughters, Elizabeth, Marjory, Ann, Jane and Theresa Anna. Of the sons of Jesse, Sr., Jesse and Ebenezer were Methodist preachers, traveling for several years; don't know to whom they married, but they did marry; and Ebenezer, after location in the Conference, settled in Marion, and merchandized for a while, when he died; Jesse, Jr., his brother, died also; know nothing of the family of either. Rev. David Legette (called Captain David), the next or third son in the order named, married a Miss Richardson, daughter of John Richardson ("King John") and sister of the late William F. Richardson, and settled on the place now known as Legette's Mill, ten or twelve miles below Marion, where he lived and died; the fruits of this marriage were two sons, Hannibal and Kossuth, and three daughters. Of the sons, the eldest, Hannibal, a very promising young man, volunteered in the early part of the war and entered the Confederate service—I think he was a Lieutenant—and was killed or fatally wounded and died early in the war; he was a brave man, and his memory should be and doubtless is cherished by all who knew him. Kossuth Legette, the younger son, grew up and settled on part of his father's plantation, on the west side of the mill, on the road leading from Marion to Britton's Ferry, on Great Pee Dee; he married rather late in life a daughter of Allen Gibson; they are raising a family—all young; he is one of the progressive farmers of that section of the county, and is succeeding well—a quiet and law-abiding citizen. Of the daughters of Captain David Legette, the eldest, Amelia, married James Hamilton Evans, who died a few years ago, childless; the widow lived at Marion since his death, and owns still a house and lot on Godbold street; an orphan girl, Lizzie Bond, whom she raised, lately married a Mr. Douglas, of Fairfield County, and Mrs. Evans has gone with her into that county. A second daughter of Captain David Legette (name not known) married Rev. Wm. B. Baker, of the South Carolina Conference; they have a family, how many and their sex and size unknown. Rev. Baker is said to be a very good man and an effective preacher. The third daughter of Captain D. Legette married A. R. Oliver, now a member of the Board of Registration of Voters; he is a successful farmer and an excellent citizen; the fruits of the marriage are several sons and daughters; don't know the names of all of them. His daughter, Eveline, married L. M. Gasque, of Marion; she died, leaving one child, and he married another one, Lizzie, who is now his wife. He has another daughter, named May, who is grown and unmarried—there may be others; he has several sons, some of them grown; one, named Haskell; has one son, Eugene, in the South Carolina College; another son, Robert, gone out West; another, named Langdon. Of the daughters of old Jessie Legette, Sr., the eldest, Elizabeth Marjoray, married Francis A. Wayne, and she and her family have already been noticed in or among the Wayne family. Another daughter of Jessie Legette, sr., named Ann, married a man by the name of Snow, of the low country; he died and left her with two children, a daughter and a son; the daughter was named Ida, don't remember the son's name—he was younger; they lived in Marion, in the early 70's, in the house afterwards owned and occupied by the writer, who purchased it in 1874; Mrs. Snow moved out of it just before the writer went in; don't know what became of them—saw Miss Ida in Marion some few years after. Jane, the third daughter of Jessie Legette, Sr., married her first cousin, Ashley S. Legette, who lately died (Ashley), over eighty years of age. Dr. Ashley Legette and wife, Jane, had and raised five sons—Dr. Arman C., Major Ringold, Virgil, William and Woodson, and two daughters, Theresa A. and Elizabeth. Of the sons, Dr. Arman C. Legette married his first cousin, Mary Adelaide Wayne, who has already been noticed in or among the Wayne family. The other sons of Dr. Ashley, the writer does not know whether they are married or single. Of the daughters, Theresa Ann married, first, Duncan McIntyre, who lived but a short time; he left her with one child, a son, who has already been mentioned herein in or among the McIntyres; she afterwards married Mr. T. J. Ledingham, who now live in the Legette neighborhood, and are bringing up a family; know but little about Mr. Ledingham—he has been a Magistrate for several years, and seems to be an intelligent gentleman. The daughter, Elizabeth, married a Mr. Vaught, about whom the writer knows nothing, nor of his family, or his or their whereabouts. The writer has seen a young lady, said to be his daughter, a pretty girl. Dr. Ashley S. Legette had a brother, Nelson Legette, who, I think, died many years ago—whether married or unmarried, the writer knows not. The father of Dr. Ashley and Nelson was Abner Legette, Sr., brother of old David and Jesse, Sr.

There are some Legettes in Wahee Township. Their father was John Legette, called Jack Legette—whether they are of kin to the other Legettes below, is not known. The Legette family is one of the old families of the county, and have ever been men at the front as citizens. Captain David Legette was no ordinary man—was above the ordinary—a man of great energy and perseverance; he was a local preacher in the Methodist connection; he was also a dental surgeon. The Legette family have always stood well in the county. Legette Township was named thus for the Legette family. Recurring back to Captain D. Legette's children—one was overlooked, a daughter, who married J. Clement Davis; they have five children. Mr. Davis is one of our best and most progressive citizens.

GASQUE.—The Gasque family will next be noticed. Samuel

Gasque, the first known, settled opposite Marion, over Catfish, before the Revolutionary War. He had five sons, Archie, Samuel, Henry, John and Absalom, and one daughter, Nancy; the mother of these was a Dozier. Archie and Samuel went West. Archie has not been heard from or what become of him. Samuel raised a family, one son of whom, named Samuel, died a few years ago, in Louisiana, unmarried, and had an estate, at the time of his death, worth ten or twelve thousand dollars, which was divisible among his first cousins, many of whom or all of them were of this county. W. B. Gasque, Mastin Gasque, Charles F. Godbold and others in the same degree of relationship, shared in the division, and got $400 each net, clear of expenses. The deceased had been or was County Judge in Louisiana. Henry Gasque married three times; first, Miss Mourning Brown, and by her had Henry, Elly, Elizabeth and Rebecca; his second wife was Nancy Brown, and had two children—Nancy, who married Drury Thomas, and Edith, who married a Mr. Brown. His third wife was Milley Bryant, and by her had ten children, viz: sons, Love, William B., Alfred, Wilson, Addison and Mastin; daughters, Nellie, who married a Mr. Brown in North Carolina, and is dead; Olive, who married a Mr. Hucks, in Horry; and Martha, who married a Mr. Frye, and went to Horry County; they all have families. John Gasque married a Miss Crawford, and had three sons and two daughters; the sons were James C., Samuel and John, all dead, and none of their descendants are in the county. Of the two daughters, Caroline, the mother of Rev. Sumter Gasque, now of the Western North Carolina Conference, she married a Mr. Foxworth, who died about the first of the war, *a felo de se;* Mrs. Mary Harrel, of Marion, was the result of the marriage, who has several children—sons, James, Joe, Frank and Fred, and three daughters, one of whom lately married Robert Boyd Jones, of Marion. These are descendants of old John Gasque. His daughter, Mrs. Foxworth, still survives, eighty-two years of age, and lives with her daughter, Mrs. Harrel, at Marion. Another daughter of old John Gasque, Ann, was the mother of the late Jessie C. Rowell's wife. Mrs. Rowell is an excellent woman, the "salt of the earth;" she has a large family of sons and daughters. These are descendants of old John Gasque.

Absalom Gasque, the old Court crier before the war, was married twice; first, a Miss Dozier, by whom he had sons, James W., Archie, John D. and Henry A., and daughters, Celia, who became the wife of ____ Atkinson; Olive, who became the wife of Ebbie Atkinson; Polly, who became the wife of Benj. Richardson; Ann, who became the wife of David J. Rowell, and Sarah, who became the wife of John Tyler. Absalom's second wife was a Miss Davis, and had Susan, the wife of Val. Dozier Ervin, killed at Cold Harbor, Va., in 1864. Samuel married Cade Thomas' daughter, and lives in Britton's Neck. James W. moved to Georgetown. John D. died suddenly, the day of the bombardment of Fort Sumter, 12th April, 1861. Henry A. married a Miss Collins, and had two children, daughters. Francis married Calvin Lee; the other, Sallie, is yet unmarried. The father, Henry A. Gasque, Court caller for years, like his father, Absalom; he was a capital man and law-abiding citizen. Archie Gasque married Miss Ann Rowell; they had eight boys, David A., Marion, Arny M., Wesley E., Samuel, McB. R., Franklin J., Archie B., and five daughters. Monetta died in 1862. Jennette married John Jones, and lives at McColl, S. C. Susan married Starr Shelly, on Terrel's Bay, and have a family. Idella married Fletcher Stalvey, and have a family. Mary married David Dozier, and died—burned to death, in 1890, leaving four children. Marion Gasque was killed at Drewry's Bluff, Va., in 1864. Samuel died in prison at Elmira, N. Y. Marion married a Miss Davis, and left three children—the wives of Willis Baxly, Evander Perritt and Charles B. Martin. David A. moved to Beaufort, and raised a family; now dead. Arny M. married the Widow Devon, whose maiden name was Phillips, and has five children. Eugenia married Thadeus Mace. Philip, Boyd M. and Emma unmarried; and Moses Mace married Lena Gasque. Wesley Gasque married twice—first, Miss Williamson, and had seven children, Hannibal L., Troy, Elmore; of the daughters, Mattie married Joseph Fowler, Emmile, Julia and Bettie are unmarried; the sons are all married. His second wife was Ann Watson; they have no children; Wesley died in 1899. William B. Rowell Gasque married his cousin, Sallie Gasque, and has six children, five daughters and one son, Cicero. Florence married R. H. Begham; she died and left two children. Nannie married a Mr. Matthews, near Effingham, and has one child. Walker died at eighteen years of age. Cora and one son, Cicero, are unmarried. Franklin J. (called Dock) married Mary McMillan, and left children, all girls—Claudia, Flossy and Mary. Dock, the father, died in 1895. Archie B. married a Miss Atkinson, and left no children; he died in 1875. Henry Gasque married Miss Harriet Porter; they had thirteen children, and raised twelve—six sons and six daughters. Of the daughters, Jane married John A. Hatchel, of Florence County; Mary married Arthur Hutchinson, of Florence County; Martha Ann married, first, Benjamin Hatchell, and then James Farley; she has two sons at Dillon (Farleys) in business there; Rebecca married Jessie Atkinson, they have a family of children; Kitty married Samuel Lane, and is in Horry; Charlotte married Frank Lane, and is also in Horry—both have families; and Virginia, who is unmarried, stays with her brother, Eli. Henry and Elly Gasque were brave Confederate soldiers, and both died in the war. Eli H. married, first, a Miss Shaw, in Mississippi; her father, Merdock Shaw, went from Marion County; they had ten children, sons and daughters; the sons were Lonney M., Henry E., Boyd R., Charles W., John O., Joseph H., Andrew Stokes and Henry Little; the daughters were Hattie and Edna. Hattie married a Mr. Twining, of Wilmington, N. C., and has seven children, all small. Lonney M. married, first, a Miss Oliver, and secondly, his first wife's sister, as already mentioned among the Legettes. Henry E. married Miss Nannie Gregg, of Marion; they have two or three children (small), one son, Andrew Stokes, died when young. The other sons of E. H. Gasque are all unmarried. E. H. Gasque married, a second time, Miss Sallie Foxworth, daughter of the late William C. Foxworth; the fruits of this marriage are two sons and two daughters—Herbert and Carroll, Rena and Lucy (small). David Gasque married Miss Anna Smith, daughter of the late John M. Smith, and has, I think, four girls; the eldest has just graduated with distinction in Knoxville, Tenn. David has been in Columbia for years in the railroad service. Wesley married, don't know who; he has a family, a son in South Carolina College; he is a farmer and is doing well; he resides in Florence County. Bond Gasque married a Miss Rogers, daughter of Nathan Rogers; has two boys; lives at Mullins. William B. Gasque married, first, a daughter of "Corn-making Willis Finklea;" he had by her two children, a son, Alfred, and a daughter, who married a Mr. Brady, and they moved to Kansas. William B. Gasque married, a second time, a Miss Clark, daughter of Kenneth Clark, and by her had George K., Robert, James and Sallie, now the wife of W. B. R. Gasque; also, Mrs. Jefferson Braswell and Mrs. Mitchel Lane. Addison L. Gasque married a Miss Frye, who has a number of children, and lives in the Gapway section, a farmer, and is doing fairly well. Alfred Gasque (son of old Henry) married a daughter of Kenneth Clark, and died in two weeks after marriage. Wilson Gasque (son of old Henry) married a daughter of Malcolm Clarke; he died in prison during the war; he left one son, R. K. Gasque. Love Gasque, another son of old Henry, married Miss Susan Rogers, a daughter of old Timothy Rogers, and soon after moved to Mississippi. Mastin Gasque, another son of old Henry, married a daughter of Daniel Fore and a niece of T. F. Stackhouse; he has seven or eight children, and lives with T. F. Stackhouse and conducts his farm; he is a local Methodist preacher and an excellent man; his eldest son, Randolph, died a year or two ago, at El Paso, Texas; some others of his children grown. Randolph left a wife in Marion County, with two children. The Gasque family and its connections are very numerous and extensive, and quite respectable. Eli H. has merchandised all his life except during the war; he is at Marion, doing a large business and is well known throughout the county—a very public-spirited man and indomitable in energy and perseverance; hard to down, and when down will rise again—no such thing as holding him down. The Gasques, as a family, did their full share in the war. I forgot to note, in its proper order, the only daughter of the first old Samuel Gasque, which I now mention: Nancy Gasque, sister of old Henry, John and Absalom; she married Thomas Godbold (called "Tom Cat"), and raised a large family, mostly sons, who have already been noticed in or among the Godbold family. Many people called her Aunt "Nancy Cats"—she was an extraordinary woman; her husband died in 1836 or '7; several of her children were then small; she, however, braved all difficulties, raised her children respectably and made property, and at her death, in 1863, left a large property in lands and slaves; she ran a public house in Marion for thirty or forty years with great success—her table was ever loaded with the substantials of life and well prepared. Major Elly Gasque, son of old Henry by his first wife, married, first, a Miss Brown; by her he had no children; he married, a second time, the Widow Montgomery, mother of J. D. and W. J. Montgomery; by her he had and left two sons, Elly A. and Henry I. Gasque. Elly A. is a first class dental surgeon, unmarried. Henry I. married Miss Jennie Evans, daughter of Sheriff W. T. Evans; she died some four of five years ago, leaving a son and a daughter, quite small; Henry I. has not remarried.

BROWN.—The Brown family will next be noticed. The first Brown known was John Brown, "Cut-face," as he was called; came from Columbus County, N. C., and settled below or east of Marion; don't know to whom he married; he had and raised six sons, Richard (Dick), Joshua, Thomas, John, Stephen and William, and two daughters. Mollie married a Mr. Fowler, the father of the late Jessie Fowler, and Patsey married a Mr. Campbell, who went West or disappeared. Richard Brown married a Miss Beach, and had two sons and two daughters; the sons were Lewis and Joseph; the daughters were Pattie and Fannie. Lewis married, first, a Miss Elliott and next a Miss James, and had twenty-one children; nine grew up and were named Charlotte, Ann, Mary (first set); W. J., Rebecca and Lewis (second set); Henrietta, Temperance and Frances (third set). Charlotte married James Carter, who was the father of our John Carter (horse trader). The father was killed in the war, and his son, John, was also in the war, but came out unhurt, and lately a volunteer in the Spanish war, Second Regiment; he deserves the plaudits and well done of his countrymen. Ann Brown married Frank Capps, and was the mother of David Capps. Mary Brown married Wilson James, and had a number of daughters and one son, Preston, who was killed in the war. William J. Brown, two miles below Marion, and a most excellent citizen, married Miss Mary Pace, and has six living children (names unknown). Lewis Brown, Jr., married Miss Rachel Flowers, and had no children; was killed in the war. Henrietta married Love Flowers; had three children, now living (name and sex unknown). Temperance Brown married Baker Lewis, and has four sons and two daughters living. Frances married John Drew; they live in Horry County. Joshua Brown, son of the first old John, married a Miss Brown, and moved to Horry, and has a number of children and grand-children in this county. Thomas Brown, second son of first old John, married a Miss Brown. Most of this family of Browns have emigrated to other parts. John Brown, Jr., the third son of old John, moved to Georgetown, married and raised a family, and died there. Stephen, the fifth son of old John, married a Miss Whitner, of North Carolina, and had and raised two children, "Hon. John Brown," and daughter, Jane, who married Henry Waller, who was killed in the war; he left a family of three children. "Hon. John" lives about two miles below Mullins, I suppose, on his father's old homestead; he has attained to some notoriety by his unique character, quaint sayings, and by numbers of quaint and spicy letters which he has had published in *"The Marion Star"* for the last thirty years. Any one who takes the "Hon. John" to be a fool, is badly sold; he has talent for wit and humor that few have, and if "Hon. John" had been educated and had turned his powers at wit and humor in the proper channel, he might now be classed with Zeb. Vance and other distinguished wits of the age; but, alas! John—"Hon. John"—is limited to a narrow sphere around Mullins and his native county. "Hon. John" married a Miss Rogers, "Pat," and has raised several sons, who are a credit to "Hon. John," and form a part of our good citizenship. I know only two or three of them—Allison H., at Latta, Edward W., of Marion, and Charles V., late of Latta. "Hon. John's" environments in early life, I suppose, were not the best; it rarely happens that a man rises above his environments, and the society in which he is brought up to manhood, and the active realities of life. William, the sixth son of old first John, married a Miss Whitter or Whittier; he was the father of William A. Brown, on Sister Bay, and a number of other boys, who were all killed in the war, or died from disease or wounds. Joseph Brown married a Miss Richardson, in Britton's Neck, and had a son, James, killed in the war, and Evander, Pinckney, Washington and Lex, and two daughters, Ann and Julia. Ann married Mr. Benjamin G. Woodberry. Julia married Charles Pace; they had, or have, Charles, Joseph and Mrs. A. P. Hucks, Mrs. Richard McRae and Mrs. Sydney Richardson, when Pace died, and she married M. H. Collins (Hook); they have no children. The Brown family and connections, it may be inferred from above statements, suffered greatly in the war, by fatalities—as much or more, perhaps, than any other family in the county, in proportion to their numbers. Brown is a very popular name throughout the United States, Marion County included. It may be here stated or re-stated, that old Henry Gasque's first and second wives were Browns; Miss Edith Gasque married a Mr. Brown; Miss Nellie Gasque married a Mr. Brown, of North Carolina; Major Elly Gasque's first wife was a Miss Brown; George W. Reaves' second wife was a Miss Brown. To what particular families of the Browns these wives and husbands belonged, does not appear. Perhaps the present Brown families, when they shall have read this sketch, can assign each to his or her particular branch of the Brown family.

Another family of Browns, not related to the preceding Browns, will now be noticed, to wit: the family to which the Hon. W. A. Brown belongs. Jeremiah Brown, the great-grand-father of Hon. W. A. Brown, married a Miss Jolly—the same family that is or was related to the McIntyres of Marion; they had four sons, Jerry, James, William and John S.—the last named was in Fanning's army and was massacred by the Mexicans, about 1835 or '6, at the Alamo. There were two daughters—Rebecca, who married John Graham, and Annie, who married another John Graham, relative of the other. The son, James Brown, was the grand-father of Hon. W. A. Brown; he was born in West Marion, near Mars Bluff; he married Miss Julia Davis, a sister of Jackey Davis and aunt of Wm. J. Davis; they had only two children, a daughter, Harriet, who married G. W. Woodberry, and an infant son, the late Travis Foster Brown, who was born July, 1822, and died December, 1894. Travis Foster Brown married Miss Martha

Caroline Baker, the youngest daughter of William and Annis Baker—were very young when they married; they had and raised five children, John O., William A. and James T. Brown, and two daughters, Susan A. and Julia M. Susan A. married Captain T. E. Stanley; Julia married J. E. Stevenson; John O. married Miss Louisa Brunson, of Darlington; William A. married Miss Eliza Clarke, daughter of the late R. K. Clarke; James T. married Miss Louise DuRant—all are living except Julia, who died in 1885. J. O. Brown was delicate from childhood; he joined the Confederate Army when eighteen years old, Neill C. McDuffie's Company L, 21st Regiment, Graham, Col., in 1861; served in same company under the young and gallant Captain Hannibal Legette, and after his death, under Captain W. B. Baker, and was captured at Fort Fisher, imprisoned at Point Lookout, and remained there two months before Lee's surrender. The father, T. F. Brown, was in Colonel Cash's regiment, Captain W. S. Ellerbe's company, while it was in service. T. F. Brown having lost his wife, never more married, but devoted himself to the raising and education of his children; he was a widower for about forty years; he and his sister, Mrs. G. W. Woodberry, were raised orphans by their uncle and aunt, Jacky Davis and Susie Davis, who were as good and kind to them as if they had been their own children. T. F. Brown began life a poor boy; he at first clerked for John Henry, at Marion, for $5 per month, but soon rose and was depended on everywhere. When he married, he gave up clerking and engaged in farming on a small scale, near Tabernacle Church; he was soon able to buy a larger farm and moved to it, where he spent the balance of his life; by industry and good judgment he was successful, and at the breaking out of the war was considered to be in good circumstances; so decided was he, that he never hesitated, but did the right as by intuition; he was a life long and consistent member of the Methodist Church. The grand-parents of Hon. W. A. Brown, on his mother's side, were William and Annis Baker; his grand-mother's maiden name was Phillips; she first married a Giles, son of Colonel Hugh Giles, of Revolutionary fame; by this marriage she had only one child, Hugh Giles, Jr., when he died, and she then married William Baker; by this latter marriage were born Mary, who married Gause Sweet; Eliza, who married Nathan Evans; Susan, who married Alexander Owens; Jennette, who died quite young, and Martha Caroline, who married T. F. Brown; and sons, James, who married a Miss Taylor, and who is the mother of our fellow-citizens, Joseph A., W. W. Baker and James Baker, of Marion; their mother still survives. Old Mrs. Annis Baker was an extraordinary woman; her husband having died and left her many years before her death, she managed with unusual success a large landed estate and many negroes, and also a considerable amount of money, and accumulated much more property before her death, and superintended the whole in person; would not employ an overseer—she overseed for herself—lived to a great age, active and energetic to the last; she divided her property among her grand-children; she was, indeed, a most remarkable woman; she had and raised another son, William J. Baker, who lived and died a bachelor.

GILCHRIST.—The family of Gilchrist will next be noticed. This family is not very extensive, neither in name nor its connections in Marion County; yet its respectability and prominence require that it shall have some notice, though it be short. The progenitor of the family in this county was Dr. Daniel Gilchrist, a dental surgeon, from Richmond or Robeson County, N. C. The writer recollects seeing Dr. Gilchrist when a boy, in 1831. The writer was going to school at Red Bank, N. C., that year, and Dr. Gilchrist came along the road during a recess in the school, on horseback, with a pair of saddle-bags under him, in which his dental instruments were stored or packed—there was no such a thing as a buggy in that day. Two of the grown young men, Archie Baker, afterwards a Presbyterian minister, and Daniel McNeill, knew Dr. Gilchrist; he recognized them, stopped, and they talked a while with him, and among other things he said he was going down South to see if he could not find work to do down there. I suppose he had just graduated in dental surgery; he was then a young single man. Whilst they were talking to him, the smaller boys in school, of whom I was one, gathered up around them to hear what was said, &c. The next I knew of Dr. Gilchrist, I think, about 1840, he was settled and living at what formerly was called Newsom's Bridge, afterwards and now called Gilchrist's Bridge, on Little Pee Lee. Dr. Gilchrist had evidently found work to do down South, for he had married a Miss Johnson, of Horry County, had bought the old Newsom place and was living upon it; by his marriage he had and raised a family of four sons and three daughters; the sons were Archie, D. E., Charles B. and Johnson; the daughters were and are Virginia, Georgia and Ida. Of the sons, Archie married Miss Augusta Bethea, a daughter of Captain Elisha C. Bethea, and raised a family of three sons and three daughters; the sons are Eugene B., Archie Hill and Claudius; the daughters are Bessie, Alice and Mary. Eugene B. married some one to the writer unknown, and has, perhaps, one child; the other sons not grown. Of the daughters, Bessie and Alice are grown and unmarried; Mary is not grown. Archie Gilchrist, the father, settled at Mullins soon after the war, and was engaged in mercantile and turpentine pursuits for years, also had a farm near by; he died some time in the last of the 80's. D. E. Gilchrist, called "Van," has never married; he was agent for many years for the Atlantic Coast Line Railroad Company, at Nichols; but when it was made a telegraph station, he had to resign his position to make room for an operator; he went back to his old home, and is there with his brother, Charles, who also has never married, and his two maiden sisters, Miss Georgia and Miss Ida. Johnson Gilchrist, the youngest son of Dr. Gilchrist, married Miss Bettie McDuffie, daughter of the late ex-Sheriff; they have two or three children; they also live on the parental homestead. Who is "boss" there is not exactly clear. The daughter, eldest, Virginia, of Dr. Gilchrist, a highly accomplished lady, married Dr. J. W. Singletary, of Marion, who was also a well educated and genteel gentleman and a fine physician; owing to incompatibility in their views of life, they did not agree and upon suit brought in the Court for divorce, it was granted; three sons were the offspring of the marriage; one of them died in boyhood; the other two, Archie G. and Joseph W., were raised. Archie G. Singletary is a graduate of the Citadel Academy, and after graduation went to Louisiana and taught as principal of a high school there, at $1,500 a year, for several years; has studied law and, I think, is now practicing; he is fine-looking and a polished gentleman—very much like his father. His brother, Joseph W. Singletary, is also in Louisiana, in the saw mill business, and it is said is making money, and stands fair; their mother has gone out there and lives, I think, with Archie. The father, Dr. J. W. Singletary, died a few years ago, and is buried in the cemetery, beside his father and mother; his sister, Mrs. A. Q. McDuffie, has died since, and is also buried there. D. E. Gilchrist is a man of talent and one of the best informed men we have; he is now advancing in years, and if he had performed or fulfilled his mission in society and had not frittered away his powers, he might have attained to the highest positions in the State, and most certainly in his county; and this much is said with no view to disparage him. Dr. Daniel Gilchrist was a very intelligent man and successful in his business every way; he married some property, which he greatly improved; he was one of the many good importations from the Old North State. In politics he was a Whig, and, therefore, did not succeed in his political aspirations. He died just at or after the close of the war, also his wife; his sons, all that were old enough, were good soldiers in the war for Southern independence, and went down only when the cause, for which they fought and suffered four years of hardship and privations, went down.

EASTERLING.—The Easterling family in Marion County is an importation from Marlborough—a very extensive and respectable family in that county. James Easterling married a Miss Manship, a sister of Rev. Charles Manship, of Marlborough, and came down into Marion and first settled near what was then called Bethea's Cross Roads, in the early part of the nineteenth century. After some years, he sold his lands in the vicinity of Bethea's Cross Roads, now the Widow Ann Manning's, and moved on a place on the north side of Catfish, and just at the lower end of Catfish Bay, where he lived the remainder of his life; he raised a considerable family of sons and daughters; his sons were Enos, Silas and, I think, John, Tristram, Henry and James F., and several daughters, whose names are not all remembered. Of the sons, Enos and Silas, and John, if there was a John, migrated West soon after they grew up, and never returned except on a visit. Tristram married, January 4th, 1844, Miss Jane Bethea, youngest sister of Squire Samuel J. Bethea. The writer was one of "his best men" on the occasion. He settled near by his mother-in-law, on lands belonging to his wife; some years afterwards he bought the land, near Harlleesville, where John H. Hamer now lives and owns; in a few years he sold his Harlleesville place and moved to Mississippi; he remained in Mississippi some years—his oldest daughter, Martha, married there—when he moved back to Marlborough, and lived near Bennettsville. Whilst there, his wife, Jane, was killed. She was drawing water at the well; the well-sweep broke and fell on her head, fracturing the skull, of which she died in a day or two. Tristram Easterling had and raised a considerable family, sons and daughters. Of the sons I know nothing. His second daughter, Lucretia A., married William Platt, who died some fifteen years ago; Lucretia took her six children and went to Texas, where she and her children are doing well; children all married respectably and well. "A rolling stone does not gather much moss," so with Tristram Easterling; he was ever moving—is alive yet in his eighty-third year, and is in Texas. Henry Easterling, the next son of old "Jimmy," married Miss Rhoda Crawford, daughter of Willis G. Crawford, of the "Free State" section; by this marriage three sons were born and raised, Willis C., Thomas C. and Frank, and two daughters, Ella and Florence. Willis C. Easterling married a Miss Legette, daughter of James B. Legette, of "Free State," and lives now upon the Daniel Platt place; they have five daughters (one married) and two sons. Willis C. is an excellent man, kind-hearted, a straight-forward, honest citizen, and prominent in his community. Thomas C. Easterling, when a young single man, went to Florida, and married a lady of that State; is now Sheriff of his county and has been for two or three previous terms and is doing well; suppose he has a family. Frank, the youngest son, a very estimable man, married Miss Maggie Watson; they have two boys, Rupert and Henry (small); Frank is a capital man and doing fairly well. Of the daughters of Henry Easterling, Ella married Leroy Bethea, son of the late Captain D. W. Bethea; they have several children, some of them may be grown; they live in Marlborough. Florence, the younger daughter, married Robert McPherson, of West Marion, now in Florence County, and had one child, a boy. McPherson Easterling is a capital and progressive citizen of that county. Henry Easterling was a very excellent man, full of good hard sense, sober and industrious, and was making a good living, when he went into the war; he was killed in Virginia, in 1864—it was said he was literally cut in two by a shell or piece of shell; he was greatly missed not only by his family but by his community. James F. Easterling, the youngest son of old "Jimmy," never married; he went into the war early, and was killed during the same. Of the daughters of "Jimmy," one married a Fletcher—John Fletcher, I believe, of Marlborough. Another daughter, Celia, married the late Matthew Watson, who has already been noticed in or among the Watson family. The youngest daughter, Sallie, a very pretty girl, went to Alabama with one of her brothers, Enos or Silas, and married in that State, near a town called Benton, on the Alabama River, a man by the name of Melton. The writer passed through Benton on a stage in 1854, and on inquiry, heard of her four miles away, and was told she was doing well and had four children. Think old "Jimmy" had another daughter or two, but it is not remembered what became of her or them. Old "Jimmy" was a model citizen, very social in his disposition, a farmer, lived at home, and lived as well, perhaps, as any man in the State; he raised from his nursery fruit trees, apples, pears, peaches, &c., very extensively, and sold them; he had a fine vineyard and grew all kind of grapes, made wine and sold it; also a fine apple and peach orchard, from which he made cider and brandy, and sold that, and yet with all these drinkables about him, all his sons together with himself were sober, temperate men.

LANE.—The Lane family, with its many connections, will now be noticed. They all came from old Osborne Lane, on Buck Swamp. He was here, and a man grown, with, perhaps, a family, in the Revolutionary War, and was a Tory; he died in 1840. Bishop Gregg, in his history, page 359, says: "Nothing of importance occurred until they reached 'Hulin's Mill.'" Note—"This was the site of the mill owned by the late Joseph

Bass, ten or twelve miles above Marion Court House." "Here they surprised two notorious Tories, John Deer and Osborne Lane. The latter was shot in attempting to make his escape into Catfish Swamp, and got off with a broken arm. Deer was overtaken as he reached the swamp, and killed. It was on this occasion, or shortly before, that Caleb Williams, a desperate marauder, noted especially for house burning, was taken by Kolb's party and hung. After proceeding further, capturing other guilty parties, and punishing or discharging them on promise of good behavior, Colonel Kolb returned home and dismissed his party, feeling secure for a time at least in the thought that the Tories had been overawed, and would not soon renew their depredations. In this, however, he was most sadly deceived," &c. The division line between Whig and Tory as made during the Revolution, and kept up for many years afterward, should be forever obliterated—in fact, our late Confederate War knocked that line into smithereens; some of the best soldiers we had in the army from Marion County were descendants of Tories; were it necessary to do so, numbers of them could be named, hence it is no longer an opprobrium to be called a Tory or the descendant of a Tory. Many of the descendants of this very Osborne Lane, mentioned by Bishop Gregg above, were and are among our best people, and were among the best soldiers in the Southern army. Many of the old Tories, and perhaps a majority of them, were Tories from conviction, and thought it would be treason—the highest crime known to the law—to take up arms against the king and his government; that by so doing, in the event of the king's success, that they would all be hanged as rebels. They were honest in it. The consequence was, they were under the ban of the local provincial government. They were compelled to take a stand, and forced to leave their homes and families, and lie out in the woods and swamps, or be carried into a war, the end of which might make them amenable to all the penalties of high treason; and being thus compelled to lie out, they could not pursue their several vocations in life for the support of themselves and families. In these circumstances, they were forced to steal and plunder or starve themselves and families. They became thieves, marauders, from compulsion, from high necessity, and not from choice. There was no moral turpitude in it, because they were forced to it by the powers that be. So it was in our war from 1861 to 1865. It is true, that many were Tories, not from conviction but from a desire to be in a position to live upon the labor of others; were rogues at heart, and only wanted an opportunity to exercise and gratify their thievish inclinations. With all such, the writer nor any honest man sympathizes—they became thieves and marauders from choice. Osborne Lane lived here till 1840, an honest, good citizen, and had the respect of all who knew him.

Osborne Lane often told the story afterwards: That when he was shot by Colonel Kolb's party, he got off into the swamp with his broken arm; that he crawled into a hollow log and lay there whilst they were hunting him, and after a while they came and sat down on the log into which he had secreted himself; that he was so agitated and so much frightened that he was afraid they would hear his heart beat. If Osborne Lane was like his sons, he, although a Tory from conviction, was no marauder from choice. We have not any people within our bounds more honest and law-abiding than the descendants of Osborne Lane, nor did the Confederacy have any better soldiers or truer patriots in its armies than the descendants of old Osborne. The many Lanes, Smiths and, more than all, the late John Blackman (Jack), went into the Southern army and stood shoulder to shoulder with the descendants of the Whigs of the Revolution, and do not deserve to be taunted with the Toryism of their ancestors. "Jack" Blackman, as we called him, was a grand-son by his mother of old Osborne Lane, and a grand-son by his father of the Blackman (Tory), whom Colonel Maurice Murphy tied up and gave him fifty lashes, and this was repeated several times, because Blackman said and stuck to it to the last, that he was for King George (Gregg's History, p. 354). If Toryism in the Revolution was odious, and still odious, then the late Jack Blackman was doubly odious—for he had it on both sides. The whole South might be challenged to produce a parallel to Jack Blackman for unquestioned patriotism and cool courage. He volunteered in the Southern cause at the age of fifty-nine; he went into the army in Virginia, and after staying in service, was discharged on account of his age.

He knocked around the camp for three or four days, with a discharge in his pocket. In the meantime, a battle occurred. Jack went back to his company, took his gun and went into the fight, was shot through the abdomen, the ball passing out at the rear—it happened not to cut any of his intestines, and Jack survived it; he lay in the hospital for two or three months, and then returned home. I will say nothing of his future services in the war. Here is a descendant of Tories on both sides. Was he odious? Blot out the line between the Whigs and Tories of the Revolution and never mention it again. Jack Blackman lived to be ninety years of age; in many respects, he was the noblest man of his day. I think this has already been mentioned herein, but it is so appropriate to the purpose just here, with the Lane family, that I cannot forbear repeating. Jack Blackman ought to have a monument erected to his memory—it is already erected in the hearts of all who knew him and knew of him.

Osborne Lane married a Miss Crawford, a sister of old James Crawford, of Spring Branch—I suppose, older than her brother. The Crawfords were quite respectable in that day and have continued to be so down to the present time. The fruits of the marriage, as known, were eight sons, John, Thomas, Alexander, James, Robert, David, Stephen and William, and two daughters, Kesiah and Elizabeth. Of the daughters, one, Elizabeth, married old John Blackman, a son of the old Tory John, that Colonel Murphy tied and whipped; by this marriage were three children born and raised, as known to the writer—Stephen Blackman and John, called Jack; the name of the daughter was Elizabeth, or Betsey; when an old maid, she became the second wife of Rev. John D. Coleman, below Marion; both are dead; don't know whether she left any children or not. Stephen Blackman married some one, to the writer not known; he died many years ago, and left a son, William, called Billy Blackman, and is now a middle-aged man and lives somewhere in the Latta neighborhood; married, and has a family. John (Jack) Blackman married a Miss Bird, a sister of the late Hugh and Joe Bird, of the Toby's Creek section; by her he raised two sons, Joseph A. and Hamilton, who, like their father, were good soldiers in the war. Hamilton was killed about Charleston, S. C. Joe died since the war, leaving several children; his widow married again, Robert C. Rogers, of Wahee Township; know nothing of Joseph A. Blackman's children, suppose some or all of them are grown. John (Jack) Blackman was married a second time, late in life, to Caroline Mears, and by her had and raised one or two sons—one, named John, is as much like old John as it is possible for a young man to favor an old man; these sons are in the Mullins section. Old John (Jack) died in 1895, in June, and was ninety years of age in December before he died, as brave and patriotic as any man that ever lived in the county, and as honest as the days were long. The other daughter, Kesiah, of old Osborne Lane, married old Samuel Smith (three junior), of Buck Swamp; the results of the marriage were two sons, John L. and Stephen Smith, born, respectively, in 1811 and 1813, when she died; and old man Samuel, Jr., married a second time, Miss Sallie Hays, daughter of old Ben Hays, of Hillsboro Township (now), and who has already been noticed herein among the Hays family. Two better citizens than John L. Smith and Stephen Smith are hard to find anywhere. John L. Smith became a Methodist traveling preacher, and after traveling three or four years, married a Miss Wannamaker, of Orangeburg County, and located, but continued to preach in a local position up to a short time before his death; he was an exemplary, pious, Christian gentleman. John L. Smith settled in the Fork, on Buck Swamp, and accumulated a good property, which he left unincumbered to his widow by a second marriage and his children; he raised five sons and three daughters; his sons were Daniel Asbury, Marcus L., Jacob W., John A. and Wilbur F. Smith, each and every one of whom, except, perhaps, Wilbur and Albert, who was too young, went into the war early and remained in it to the end. Marcus L. was badly wounded, and carries the evidence of it in his person every day since. Daniel Asbury came out of the war as a Captain; married, after the war, Miss Alice Bethea, a daughter of Captain E. C. Bethea; by the marriage four sons were born and raised, of whom Dr. Maxcy Smith, the eldest, now at Page's Mill, is one and the only one in the State. The other three, with their mother, are in Birmingham, Ala., all doing well. Dr. Maxcy Smith married an Alabama lady, and has three or four children (small). Daniel Asbury Smith died some years ago. Marcus L. Smith married Miss Mary Smith, a daughter of Reddin W. Smith, east of Marion; they have some children; don't know how many; has one or two married daughters. Jacob W. Smith, the third son, married Miss Fannie Nichols, who has already been noticed in or among the Nichols family. John Albert Smith, the fourth son, married a widow, Jennie Smith, of Mississippi; had and raised three daughters and one son, Henry Smith, now at Mullins, and has a family (small). The three daughters are married—the eldest to John Wilcox, of Marion, already mentioned among the Wayne family. Another daughter married Dennis Berry, of Marion; they have some children, how many is unknown. The youngest daughter, Laura, married Chalmers Rogers, of Mullins, and resides there. John Albert Smith was first appointed County Auditor, which place he held with success for three or four years, when he was elected Clerk of the Court in 1880, as successor to R. K. Clark; he held that office for two years, when he died, and was succeeded by John Wilcox, as hereinbefore stated. The three daughters of John L. Smith were Anna M., Jane and Hettie. Anna M. married Philip W. Bethea; by the marriage, three sons and three daughters have been raised—George C., L. Asbury and Pickett; the daughters are Bettie, Nannie and Lilian. George married Julia Wayne, the only daughter of Gabriel I. Wayne; they had no offspring, and he died a few years ago. L. Asbury never married, and died two years ago. Pickett Bethea, the third son, married a daughter of Captain R. H. Rogers, of the Gaddy's Mill section; they have, perhaps, two or three children (small); Pickett is a graduate of Wofford College, and has successfully followed teaching ever since his graduation—has been teaching in the same school in Darlington County for four or five years, which evidences his popularity as a teacher. Bettie, the eldest daughter, married David E. Allen, and has already been noticed among the Watson or Allen family. Nannie and Lilian recently married two Mr. Williams, brothers, saw mill men; may have a child each. The second daughter of John L. Smith, Jane, became the second wife of Dr. John J. Bethea, of Mullins; by this marriage, two sons,

26

Lawrence and Julian, and one daughter, Minnie, were born. Lawrence Bethea married a lady in Mississippi, first, and by her had three or four children—a son grown, named John; a daughter, Ruth, who married a Mr. West, from Augusta, Ga., and who is now at Mullins, merchandising; and one daughter, Pearl, who died before maturity. The first wife died, and Lawrence married a Miss Rogers, daughter of David S. Rogers, of the "Free State" section; he is farming. Julian M. Bethea, the second son of Dr. John J. Bethea, married a lady in Mississippi; has only one child, a daughter; he is merchandising at Mullins. Hettie Smith, the youngest daughter of John L. Smith, married Pinckney C. Page, who was killed in the war or died of disease, and left three children, who has already been noticed herein or among the Page family. Wilbur F. Smith, the youngest son of John L. Smith, graduated at Wofford College, in 1875, and soon afterwards emigrated to Mississippi, where he still remains; I suppose he has a family. Minnie Bethea, the daughter of Dr. John J. Bethea, married Robert M. Daniel, son of W. H. Daniel, of Mullins; she died in two or three years after marriage, childless. Stephen Smith, brother of John L. and a grand-son of old Osborne Lane, married Polly Huggins, a daughter of old John Huggins, of Huggins Bridge, on Little Pee Dee; by this marriage seven sons and four daughters were born and raised; the sons were George W., Ebenezer, B. Gause, S. Elmore, S. W. Smith, J. Emory (all gallant soldiers in the war), and another killed on the railroad, near Florence, during the war; these, together with their sisters, have already been mentioned in or among the Huggins family, the Martin family and the Harrelson family. Of the sons of old Osborne Lane, it is not known which of the eight was the older—I think, however, John, who was a very old man in 1840 (the year old man Osborne died). John Lane had but one son, John G. Lane; don't know who his mother was; John G. Lane married, I think, a Miss Johnson; they had but one child, a daughter; don't know what became of her; John G. Lane died years ago, was an excellent man and good citizen. The next son of old Osborne, Thomas, and whom the writer never saw, married and settled, lived and died on a place near Sellers Depot, on the "Short Cut" Railroad, now owned by B. B. Sellers and Mrs. Lucy B. Watson. Thomas Lane had and raised one son only, Bryant Lane, who married, in 1827, Miss Henrietta Dew; when his father died is not known. Since writing the above, the writer has learned that Thomas Lane had another son, named Frederic, who married and settled within 100 feet of where the depot at Sellers now stands; that he afterwards emigrated to Alabama; that his descendants are there now; that some of Frederic's family came out here a few years ago, to visit their relatives, and that subsequently the late Captain Stephen D. Lane went to Alabama to see his relatives in that State; that Frederic's family and descendants are doing well. Thomas Lane may have had a daughter or daughters—if so, where she or they are is unknown. Bryant Lane's family have already been noticed in or among the Dew families, to which the reader is referred. Alexander Lane, the third son of Osborne, I think, married a Miss Blackman (in this I may be mistaken); he lived and died on upper Buck Swamp, below Latta, and near where his father lived and died. Alexander Lane had and raised a numerous family of sons and daughters, only a few of whom are known to the writer. Samuel Lane, the oldest son, as I suppose, now a very old man, married, first, Sarah Coward, a daughter of Wilson Coward, who owned the lands whereon Dillon now is situated, and by her had six or seven children, two of whom only were sons, William B. and _____ Lane. One of these emigrated to Texas some years ago, having a family (increasing) when he left. Joseph Lane, another son of old Alexander, married twice (don't know to whom), and had several sons; those known are Alexander, William and Elisha—there are, perhaps, other sons and daughters; he died some years ago; was an honest, hard-working man, a good soldier in the war. Osborne Lane, another son of Alexander, married a Christmas, and lives near Mallory, on Little Reedy Creek; he has several sons, the names of whom are unknown; he is an honest, hard-working man and a good citizen. Another son of Alexander married a Miss Hensey, and has several sons—has removed to Florence County, and it is said is well to do. Another son of old Alexander, Robert Lane, married a Miss Rogers, and has a family, about whom the writer knows nothing. Another son of old

Alexander, Leonard, was killed in the war. They were all good soldiers in the Confederate war. James C. Lane, I think, the youngest son of old Osborne, was a most excellent man and a good citizen; he married a Miss Lee, daughter of old John Lee, on the north side of Buck Swamp, and settled on Catfish, just opposite Latta; he had and raised four sons, James C., Jr., Crawford, John O. and Stephen L. Lane, and four daughters, Hapsey, Sarah Anne, Orphea and Priscilla. Of the sons, James C., Jr., married a daughter of old William Bryant, a sister of the late John M. Bryant; he had and raised one son, David, and one daughter. The son married some one to the writer unknown; he has a large family of sons and daughters, several grown; he lives in Kirby Township. The daughter married Peter McLellan, and had several children; Peter and she (Rebecca, I think, was her name), are both dead; don't know what has become of the children—suppose they are all grown. Crawford Lane, second son of James C., Sr., married a Miss Perritt, daughter of David Perritt, and settled down on the Maiden Down and Ten Mile Bays; he raised a large family of sons and daughters; the names of two sons only are known—Addison and James. Addison married a daughter of John M. Bryant, and has several sons, two of whom are married, and several daughters, some grown. James Lane, son of Crawford Lane, married a daughter of the late Samuel Campbell, and has a family, how many are not known. Stephen L. Lane, the youngest son of James C., Sr., married Miss Flora Campbell, a daughter of the late William S. Campbell; he was killed in the last battle of the war, just before Johnston's surrender, after having gone through the whole war; he left his widow, Flora, and several sons and daughters, none of them personally known to the writer; one son is named William, and one daughter became the second wife of Merideth Watson. There are several other children. Another son of James C. Lane, Sr., was John O. Lane; he married a Miss Sweat, daughter of old George Sweat; they had and raised a family, none of them known to the writer—both are dead. Of the daughters of James C., Sr., Hapsey married the late James Porter; they had and raised a large family of sons and daughters, none of whom are known to the writer, except Robert P. Porter, in

Marion; he married a Miss Johnson, and has a family of several children, none grown. The second daughter of old James C., Sr., Sarah Ann, married a Mr. Jones, who either died or left the country, leaving her one child, a daughter—what has become of the daughter is unknown; Mrs. Jones is long since dead. The third daughter of James C. Lane, Sr., Orphea, married a Mr. Turbeville; they had and raised a family, and have grand-children, but none of them are known. The youngest daughter of James, Sr., Priscilla, married "Sandy" Norton, who was killed or died in the war; they had and raised three sons, Woodberry, Houston and Holland Norton, who are now among us and good citizens—especially Houston Norton, of Latta; there may have been daughters—if any, they are unknown to the writer. Another son of old Osborne Lane, William, married, don't know to whom, and from whom are many descendants in the county. Think Rev. William and James Lane and the late Henry J. Lane are or were descendants of old William; there are other descendants of this old man, but they are unknown to the writer. Of the three other sons of old Osborne Lane, Robert moved to Barnwell; David moved to Union, and Stephen went to Georgia in the long past, and no tidings from them.

BETHEA.—The Bethea family will next be noticed. This very large and extensive family, both in name and in its vast network of connections, all sprang from one common stock, John Bethea, who emigrated from England to Virginia, at what precise time is not known, but supposed to be in the latter part of the seventeenth or early part of the eighteenth century. The name was originally spelled Berthier, and is supposed to be of French origin. The writer has been furnished, by Philip Y. Bethea, of Marion, with a family tree, and chart of the family from old "English John" up to date—at least, so far as Marion County is concerned, and I suppose generally, so far as can be ascertained. This chart only gives the names of males, no females—for the reason that they generally lost their identity by marriage; yet the females transmit the blood just as much as the males do—hence the writer will hereinafter notice the females as well as the males, in every instance where they are known. Old "English John" had two sons, John and Tristram. John settled in Nansemond County, Virginia, and Tristram settled on Cape Fear River, in North Carolina, as is supposed, in the early part of the eighteenth century. John, the second, had two sons, John, third, and William. John, third, emigrated to South Carolina, about the middle of the eighteenth century, or a little later, and settled on Buck Swamp, about two miles above the present town of Latta. His brother, William, about the same time, came to South Carolina (or they may have come together), and settled on Sweat Swamp, three or four miles above Harlleesville. These were the progenitors of all the Betheas and their numerous connections in Marion County, and, I suppose, throughout the Western States. Hereinafter these two families will be referred to as the "Buck Swamp family or set," and the "Sweat Swamp family or set." The wife of "Buck Swamp John" was Absala Parker, hence their youngest son was named "Parker." "Buck Swamp John" settled on the plantation now owned by one of his descendants, John C. Bethea, of Dillon; he was a prosperous man—took up and owned at the time of his death, in 1821, six or eight thousand acres of land around him and in near by parts, the most of which is now owned by some one or another of his descendants; he farmed and raised stock, drove it to Charleston; had and raised large orchards, raised fruit; made cider and brandy, and sold it, in his day, without let or hindrance; he accumulated a large estate for his day and time, which he gave almost entirely to his five sons, William, James, Philip, Elisha and Parker—giving nothing, comparatively, to his four daughters, Sallie, Pattie, Mollie and Absala (I think, was the name of the latter). Sallie married Levi Odom, of Revolutionary fame; two of them, Absala and Mollie, married a Mr. Owens; and Pattie married another Mr. Owens. None of them except Pattie have descendants in this State—as Sallie and Absala died childless, and Mollie and her Mr. Owens emigrated to Natchez, Miss. The five sons all settled, lived and died in Marion County. William, the eldest, married, first, a Miss Crawford; had one child, a son, John C. Bethea; his second wife was Mary (Polly) Sheckelford; the fruits of the marriage were five sons, Levi, Willam S., Frank, George J.

A HISTORY OF MARION COUNTY. 897

and Evander S. Bethea; the daughters were Rebecca, Absala, Mary, Catharine and Sarah Ann. Levi married Miss Mary Ann Bethea, a daughter of John Bethea, of the "Sweat Swamp set," and had two sons, Henry L. (who died in youth), and George, and four daughters, Sophia, Hannah Jane, Louisa and Charlotte. Of these, Sophia married William H. Smith, on Buck Swamp, and had and raised sons, Samuel O. Smith, Wm. B., Henry E. K. and John B. Smith, and two daughters, the wife of B. S. Ellis (first cousins), and Hamilton Edwards' wife. Hannah Jane Bethea married John C. Bass, and died childless. Louisa Bethea married James F. Galloway, and has a family of two sons, Henry and James, and four daughters, Sallie, Rebecca, Mary and Rachel. Charlotte Bethea married John E. Henry, who lives on the old William Bethea homestead, and has already been noticed in or among the Henry family. George Bethea, son of Levi, married a Miss Campbell, daughter of the late Edward Campbell, and has five sons, Edwin, Henry, Gary, Robert and Chalmers. Think Edwin lately married a Miss Smith, daughter of Marcus L. Smith. William S. Bethea, second son of William Bethea by his Sheckelford wife, married Miss Sarah Ann DeBerry, of Marlborough; by her he had two children, a daughter, Missouri, and a son, William Henry. Missouri became the first wife of John H. Hamer; she died, leaving one child, a son, Missouri Robert Hamer, who has already been noticed in or among the Hamer family. The son, William Henry Bethea, married, first, a Miss Wilson, of Wilmington, N. C., and by her he had two daughters, Adaline and Ella, both single, and two sons, Wilson and Henry (twins); Henry died in 1899; Wilson survives, and is unmarried. William Henry's first wife died, and he married, a second time, Miss Ellie Sherwood; she has one son, Evander S., a boy nearly grown. William Henry Bethea died in 1891 or 1892, *a felo de se*. Frank Bethea married, late in life, Miss Rebecca Manning, daughter of Woodward Manning; had one child, a son; father and son (an infant) both died the same year; the widow, Rebecca, married twice after that, and has already been mentioned among the Manning family. George J. Bethea married Miss Irena Page, daughter of Captain William Page; they had and raised two sons, William

A. and John D., and several daughters, Amanda, Ellen, Mary, Kittie and Belle. William A. married a Miss Floyd and moved to North Carolina. John D. married Miss Sallie Manning, daughter of Woodward Manning. Of the daughters, Amanda married William B. Ellen; Kittie married Joseph Watson, her first cousin; don't know who the others married. William A. has a son, named Jasper, and John D. has a son, named Herbert. Evander S. Bethea, the youngest son of old Buck Swamp William, never married. The oldest son of Buck Swamp William, by his Crawford wife, was named John C., born in 1798, and died January, 1863; married, first, a Widow Irby, whose maiden name was Allison; she had one child, a daughter, Elizabeth, when he married her, who grew up and married Henry Rogers, of Marlborough; they raised a large family of sons and daughters, and among the daughters is Henrietta, who is now the widow of the late Governor W. H. Ellerbe; by his marriage with the Widow Irby, he had and raised one son, Edwin Allison, when she died; and he afterwards married Sarah Ann Davis, and by her had and raised one son, John C., now of Dillon. Edwin A. married Ann Eliza Godbold, youngest daughter of Asa Godbold, Sr.; they live at Latta, and have a family of several sons and daughters; the sons are Asa, John C., Edwin and Reed Walker, and several daughters. One daughter married to W. C. McMillan, and is in Columbia, S. C. Asa has gone West; others all here. John C. Bethea, of Dillon, married Miss Hettie Bethea, daughter of W. W. Bethea, of Mississippi, and of the "Sweat Swamp family;" they have two sons, Horace and John C., and five daughters, all small. Of the sons of Buck Swamp William, there was one noticeable peculiarity—they all, except old John C., drank liquor excessively, and when intoxicated or drinking were perfectly quiet and harmless—much more so than when sober, except, perhaps, Evander S.; they were all capital men, energetic and progressive citizens. Of the daughters of old William Bethea (Buck Swamp), Rebecca married Colin McLellan, who has already been noticed in or among the McLellans. Absala married Hugh Campbell, already mentioned in or among the Campbells. Mary married William W. Bethea, of the "Sweat Swamp set," who will be noticed further on.

Catharine married Averitt N. Nance, of North Carolina, and raised one son, Daniel, and several daughters. Sarah Ann married a Mr. Folk, of North Carolina, and raised a family of two sons and two daughters, names unknown. All the sons and daughters of Buck Swamp William are dead; he himself died 13th June, 1840. James Bethea, the second son of old "Buck Swamp John," married Miss Margaret Cockrane, a daughter of Thomas Cockrane, of Marlborough County, and settled in the fork of Big and Little Reedy Creeks; they had and raised to be grown twelve children, five sons and seven daughters; the sons were Thomas C., Samuel J., John R., David and Claudius; the daughters were Nancy, Deborah, Sallie, Rachel, Lucinda, Lucretia and Jane. Thomas C. married Miss Miranza Rogers, a daughter of old Timothy Rogers, and emigrated to Mississippi. Samuel J. married Miss Mary Rogers, another daughter of old Timothy Rogers; he was a local Methodist preacher for more than forty years, a man of high character and a most excellent citizen; he died in 1877; he married, a second time, Miss Elizabeth Bass, daughter of old man Joseph R. Bass; by his first marriage he had and raised to be grown eleven children—sons, James, Andrew J. and David N.; daughters, Sarah, Margaret, Harriet, Flora J., Louisa, Lucinda, Charlotte and Cattie; and by his last wife, one son, Samuel J., Jr. Of the sons, James died unmarried, just on arriving at manhood. Andrew J. was a practicing physician, and married Anna Maria Allen, daughter of Rev. Joel Allen, settled in the "Free State" section, and died in 1881, leaving his widow and five children—all now grown— three sons, Herbert, Percy and Andrew, and two daughters, Mrs. Rev. Pearce Kilgo, who has five children, and Mrs. William T. Bethea, who has three children, sons, James Earle, William Thaddeus, Jr., and Philip Osborne. The next son of Rev. S. J. Bethea, David N., who died last week, married, first, Anna J. Sellers, daughter of the writer, and settled in the "Free State" section; they had eight children, three of whom are dead, also the mother; of the eight, five were sons and three daughters; the sons were William T., Samuel Stoll, David A., Swinton Legare and Andrew Pearce; the daughters were Cattie May, Lillian and Anna Laval. Of these, Samuel Stoll,

David A. and Cattie May are dead—died before majority. William Thaddeus married his cousin, Georgia Bethea, as above stated and children as above stated; he is railroad agent at Dillon and has been for more than ten years, and Mayor of the town for three years. By the second marriage of Rev. S. J. Bethea, he had one son, Samuel J., Jr., who is and has been for ten years or more a traveling Methodist preacher in the South Carolina Conference; he married Miss Nannie Bethea, of the "Sweat Swamp" family, and have only one child, a son, Samuel J., Jr. Of the daughters of Rev. S. J. Bethea, three, Lucinda, Cattie and Charlotte, all grown young ladies, died unmarried. Sarah married James Moore, of Marlborough County; they had only one child, a son, James B. Moore, of Latta; the father died when James B. was an infant; the widow never married again, and died a few years ago. The son, James B. Moore, married Miss Mollie Godbold, daughter of Asa Godbold, Jr.; they have three children living, two sons, Clancy and LaCoste, and a daughter, Lorena (small). Margaret, the next daughter of Rev. S. J. Bethea, married John W. Tart; they had and raised three sons, James, John and Andrew; the father and mother are both dead. James went to Savannah, married a Miss Fuller, of Waycross, Ga., and when last heard of was said to be doing well. John married a Miss Bethea, daughter of Elisha Bethea, Jr., of Latta; they have some family, how many and of what sex is not known. Andrew Tart married a Miss Hays, daughter of Hamilton R. Hays, and lives near Kirby's Cross Roads; suppose they have some family, how many and of what sex is unknown. Of the daughters of John W. Tart and wife, two or three of them died unmarried, after maturity. One married Samuel O. Smith, of Buck Swamp; they have a large family. Their oldest, a son, Stephen Lane Smith, lives at Latta, and lately married a Miss Edwards, a daughter of Austin Edwards. Another daughter married C. C. Gaillard, and has three children—a daughter, Maggie, and a son, Luther, and another name unknown; they now live at Dillon; their children are grown. Another daughter married James Johnson, a nephew of Chancellor W. D. Johnson, called "Black Jim," to distinguish him from J. W. Johnson, Esq., another nephew and son-in-law of the Chancellor; they live at Fair Bluff, N. C.; they have some children, how many and of what sex is unknown. Another and youngest daughter of John W. Tart and his wife, Margaret, married Solon Lewis, of Latta; she died some months ago, and left two children, a daughter and a son, I think. The next daughter of Rev. S. J. Bethea, Harriet, and the only survivor of his eleven first children, has never married, and is sixty-one or two years old. Flora, the next daughter, married the late Stephen D. Lane; both are dead, and died childless. Louisa, the next daughter, married Newton Owens, of North Carolina; they moved to Texas several years ago; she is dead, leaving several children, sons and daughters—perhaps, all grown. John R. Bethea, the third son of old James Bethea, married Miss Harriet Bass, daughter of old Joseph R. Bass. I think this family has been already noticed in or among the Bass family. The fourth son of old James Bethea, David, died a young man, unmarried, in 1843. Claudius Bethea, the fifth and youngest son of old James Bethea, married, late in life, Miss Mary Ann Miles, daughter of Charles Miles, of the "Free State" section; he and his wife are both dead, childless. Of the daughters of old James Bethea, the eldest, Nancy, married Salathel Moody, an older brother of old Barfield Moody; they had several children, sons and daughters, some grown, when they broke up and moved West. Deborah, the second daughter, married James Spears, a very successful man in Marlborough; they had and raised a large family—two sons, Andrew J. and Edwin A., and six or seven daughters; they have descendants, grand-sons, in Marion County now, in the persons of Dr. J. H. David and Frank B. David,* enterprising, progressive men, with their families. They have many descendants in Marlborough County. The two sons, Andrew J. and Edwin A., died childless; Edwin married. Lucinda, the fifth daughter of old James Bethea, married Colonel Wilie Bridges, of Marlborough, and emigrated West. Sallie, the third daughter, married Willis Crawford, from whom sprang several sons and two daughters; the sons were James, Hardy, Thomas C., Willis, William and Gibson G. Crawford, now of Latta; the daughters were Rhoda and Margaret. Of the sons, James died when about grown,

---

*Frank B. David died recently.

unmarried. Hardy married a Miss Platt, and went West. Thomas C. married twice, is well known in the county; married, the last time, a Miss McPherson, in West Marion, and has resided there for more than thirty years; his wife died a short time ago, childless; he is a most excellent man and a good citizen.* Willis Crawford was a physician; married a lady in Charleston, and was soon after accidentally killed in a fox drive by his own gun—verifying the adage, "That more people are killed or hurt at play than at work." William died, a single man, after having gone through the war and came out unhurt. G. G. Crawford married Miss Kate Bethea, daughter of Colonel James R. Bethea; they had and raised two sons, James C. and Samuel B., and two daughters, Jessie and Mary; his wife is dead; he has not remarried. James G. has lately married a Miss Evans, of Society Hill. Jessie married, two or three years ago, William Ellis Bethea; no offspring. Samuel B. and Mary are yet single. The oldest daughter of Willis and Sallie Crawford, Rhoda, married Henry Easterling, and has already been noticed among the Easterlings. Margaret, the youngest daughter, never married, and is dead. Rachel, the fourth daughter of old James Bethea, married Enoch Meekins, of Marlborough; he, however, settled and lived many years near Harlleesville, and raised a considerable family of sons and daughters, and finally moved to North Carolina, where he and his wife both died; don't know enough about his children to trace them. He had one son, Philip B., who married a Miss Hays, daughter of John C. Hays; they also moved to North Carolina, and are lost sight of. One daughter married John R. Carmichael; he died, and left two sons, Alexander and McCoy, and one daughter, Johny; the mother still lives. Another daughter married James McGirt; they went to North Carolina. Lucretia, the sixth daughter, first married Aaron Meekins, of Marlborough, brother of Enoch, who had married Rachel; Aaron Meekins lived but a short time, and died childless; the widow afterwards married Wesley Stackhouse, who has already been noticed among the Stackhouse family. Jane, the youngest daughter, married Tristram Easterling, who has already been noticed in or among the Easterling family. Philip Be-

*Thomas C. Crawford has recently died.

thea, the third son of old "Buck Swamp John," married, in 1801, Rachel Cochrane, daughter of old Thomas Cochrane, of Marlborough, and sister of his brother James' wife. (As to Thomas Cochrane—he was a Vermonter, ran away from his parents in Vermont when a mere lad, and married a Miss Council, and settled on Great Pee Dee, just above the mouth of Crooked Creek; raised a family; married three times; the two Bethea's wives above mentioned were daughters of the first wife, together with another daughter, Polly, who became the wife of old John Hamer, and the progenitress of the large family of that name in Marlborough and Marion, and a son, named Robert; he amassed a large property and lived to a great age.) Philip Bethea settled on Catfish, where he lived and died in 1865; they raised to be grown two sons, Elisha C. and James R., and three daughters, Clarissa, Margaret and Martha Ann. Of the sons, Elisha C. married Martha Ann Walters, daughter of Jeremiah Walters, of upper Marion; Captain Elisha C. was a very successful man as a farmer and well to do in life; they had eleven sons and four daughters; the sons were Philip W., John J., Robert C., James A., Elisha, Picket, Morgan, George, William W., Clarence and Julius N.; the daughters were Elizabeth Ann, Wilmina R., Augusta B. and Alice. Of the sons of Elisha C., Philip W. married Miss Anna Smith, a daughter of Rev. John L. Smith, of the "Fork" section, and settled where he now lives; his family has been noted among the Lane family. The second son of Captain Elisha C. Bethea is Dr. John J. Bethea, at Mullins; has been practicing medicine since 1852; he married, first, Miss Mary Bethea, a daughter of Tristram Bethea, of Floral College, one of the "Cape Fear set;" she had one child, a daughter, Emma, who grew up and married Dr. William Harrel, who moved to Georgia some years ago, and had when they left six daughters and no son. Dr. John J. Bethea married, a second time, Miss Jane Smith, a daughter of Rev. John L. Smith, and sister of his Brother Philip's wife. Owing to some trouble growing out of the war, Dr. John had to leave the county and State for fear of the Federal garrison stationed at Marion in 1865 to 1868; he went to Mississippi, and his family soon followed after him, and he stayed in that State some fifteen or twenty years, when he came back, and has been in this county ever since. His family have been noticed in tracing the Lane family. Robert C. Bethea, the third son of Captain Elisha C., married, some time before the war, a Miss Legette, daughter of John C. Legette, of West Marion; before the war, he removed to Mississippi; they had some little family before leaving this county—know nothing more of them; he was also a physician, and in his adopted home he became a local Methodist preacher. James A. Bethea, the fourth son of Captain Elisha C., was a bright young man; volunteered in the early part of the war, was a Lieutenant or rose to a Lieutenancy in Co. E, Twenty-third Regiment, S. C. V., and remained in the war to the end, a gallant soldier. After the war he went to Mississippi; and from there went to a law school at Lebanon, Tenn.; returned to Mississippi, was admitted to the bar, but soon after took sick and died—a worthy and promising young man; he never married. Elisha Bethea, Jr., the fifth son of Captain Elisha C., married, on the 9th March, 1861—the writer officiating at the nuptials—to Miss Sallie Ellis, daughter of the Widow Ginsy Ellis. He also volunteered and went into the army, and remained in it till he was disabled for field service, when he came home, and for some time his friends supposed he would not survive the wounds, but he did and has been going on crutches ever since—the wound being in his hip; he yet lives, and is near Latta, an energetic and successful man, a farmer. He had by his first wife several sons and daughters. His oldest living son, William Ellis, is now merchandising at Latta, and has been twice married—first, a Georgia lady, who had three sons, Charles, Robert and Dallas, and one daughter, Florence, and died; he married, a second time, Miss Jessie Crawford; she has no children. Arthur, his second son, has lately married a Miss Hays, of Hillsboro Township, a daughter of William B. Hays; he teaches school. Morgan, his third son, is a young man, unmarried; he teaches school. Of his daughters by his first marriage, one, Mattie, married John J. George, who died childless. Another, Carrie, married John Tart; they have five children (small). Another, Augusta, is unmarried. Another, Nellie, married Tristram Hamilton; she has two children, Bertha and Sallie (small). Elisha Bethea, Jr., had another son, Benjamin, and one named Elisha; both died in youth. Elisha Bethea's first wife, Sallie, died; he married again, her sister, Mary Ann, who at the time of her marriage was the Widow Thomas; by this second marriage he has one son, named Power, who is now in Wofford College, and a daughter, named Eva, and perhaps others (small). Pickett Bethea, the sixth son of Captain Elisha C., married Miss Carrie Honour, daughter of Rev. John H. Honour, of Charleston, about the first of the war; by this marriage two sons were born, Walker and Pickett. Walker died when a child. Pickett K. grew up and became a doctor, and married a Miss Davis, of North Carolina, and has removed to Socastee, in Horry County, and is there practicing medicine, and is said to be doing well. His father, Pickett, volunteered early in the war, and was a Lieutenant in Captain McKerall's company, in 25th Regiment; he was killed in one of the battles in Virginia, in 1863. His widow married again to J. W. Saintclair, a school teacher; they removed West; she had several children for him, and died. Morgan, the seventh son of Captain Elisha C., volunteered early in the war; he sickened and died at home while on a furlough; he was unmarried. George, the eighth son, was killed, when about thirteen or fourteen years of age, by what was called a "flying mare"—another verification of the adage "that more people are killed or hurt at play than at work." William W. Bethea, the ninth son of Captain Elisha C., now living in West Marion, married Miss Sallie Morrison, a daughter of Rev. Mr. Morrison, a Presbyterian minister, of Anson County, N. C., a very estimable and accomplished lady; the fruits of this marriage are four sons, Morrison, Theodore, Oscar and James. Of these, Morrison is married to a lady of Clinton (name unknown), and has two sons, Curtis and Eugene; there may be a daughter or two (all small). William W. Bethea may have daughters, the writer does not know. One of the sons, Theodore (I believe) is a graduate of the Citadel Academy of Charleston—said to have graduated with distinction. Clarence, the tenth son of Captain Elisha C., died when a small boy. Julius N., the eleventh son of Captain Elisha C., married, first, Miss Anna Shrewsberry, daughter of the late Edward C. Shrewsberry, of the "Free State" section. An incident of their marriage may be here related: They were married at a school house near by her father's, in the woods on a road not much frequented, by the Rev. Joel Allen, on Christmas day, in 1871; he gave them a certificate of their marriage Only one person was present at the nuptials besides themselves and the officiating clergyman; and at their special instance and request, the marriage was to be kept secret until the 19th day of April following, it being Julius' birth-day and the day of his arrival at the age of twenty-one years. Julius carried his wife back to her home, half a mile away, and left her there; he went to his father's, and said nothing until the appointed time, 19th April, 1872, when he told his father and mother about it, and went to her father's, and their marriage was satisfactorily established to her parents, and he took her and carried her to his father's. A sufficient reason, satisfactory to them, may have existed for their marriage and subsequent secrecy, but it does not accord with the writer's views of propriety, nor with the conduct of 999 out of 1,000. His bride was a very intellectual and well cultivated lady—far more so than many in that region; the fruits of the marriage were three sons, Herbert, Ernest and Adger, and one or two daughters, one named Mattie May—suppose they are all grown. Anna, his first wife, died, and he married, a second time, Miss Carrie Sessions, daughter of John D. Sessions, of Marion; they reside now at Mullins; children of the last marriage, if any, are small—names, number and sex unknown. Of the daughters of Captain Elisha C. Bethea, the eldest, Elizabeth Ann, married John B. Bethea, of the "Sweat Swamp" family; her mother was a half Bethea of the same set; he had previously gone to Mississippi, and came back to her home in Marion County and married; the bridal trip was to be to Mississippi. She had some negroes, which her father had given her, and they with their little baggage were taken along for the trip. This was before the war, about 1856. When the bridal party arrived at Marion to take the train, the groom put the bride on board, and stepped back to see to getting on the negroes—a woman and some children, and whilst thus engaged the train pulled off and left him; of course, he ran after it and tried to stop it, but failed in his almost frantic efforts. His bride went on to Florence (then a small village) and stopped over for the night; the groom spent the night in Marion and went over the next day and joined his wife. I will leave the reader to imagine whether there was intense disappointment or not, and whether there was any cursing done by the groom. The bridal party went to Mississippi and settled there—I think, in Smith County. John B. was a very energetic and persevering man, a farmer; he went into the war, and in 1863, he died of disease, and left his wife and four sons, Augustus B., William, Sumter and John—the latter born after his father's death, all then small. After John B.'s death, Captain Elisha C. went out to Mississippi and brought the widow and her children to this county. The widow settled on a place given her by her father, and went to work to raise and educate her sons; in this she succeeded well. She was no ordinary woman; well educated herself and of fine literary taste, and to this added her fine business qualifications and her success, placed her in the front rank among women. Much more might be said to her credit, but space will not permit a further extended notice. Her sons grew up and one by one they went to Birmingham, Ala., and she finally followed and, I think, yet lives. The second daughter of Captain Elisha C., Wilmina Rachel, has never married, and is now in the sixtieth year of her age. The third daughter, Augusta B., married A. E. Gilchrist, of Mullins, and has already been noticed herein among the Gilchrist family. Alice, the fourth and youngest daughter of Captain Elisha C., married D. Asbury Smith, who has already been noticed among the Lane family. She, too, has gone to Birmingham, Ala., where three of her four sons reside.

According to the chart of the Bethea family in all its branches, including the Nansemond County, Va., Betheas, the Cape Fear, N. C., Betheas, the "Buck Swamp set," and the "Sweat Swamp set," Captain Elisha C. Bethea "takes the cake" for having and raising the greatest number of sons, eleven; while Dr. J. F. Bethea stands next, with eight. Not much danger of extinction. Colonel James R. Bethea, the second and youngest son of old man Philip Bethea, who has been mentioned in several places herein before in connection with other matters, married, rather late in life (thirty-four or thirty-five years old), to Miss Mary McLeod, of Marlborough, one of the best and most devotedly pious women I ever met; and should any of her children turn out badly in the future, it cannot be charged to any fault in the mother's training, either by precept or example; they had and raised (Jessie, the oldest, was near grown when he died) six sons and three daughters; the sons were Jessie, James D., Philip Y., Elisha, D. McLeod and Robert Lucien; the daughters were Kate, Clara and M. Isabella. Of the sons, Jessie died when about grown. James D., the second son, married Miss Flora Fore, daughter of the late Stephen Fore; she is dead. Of James D.'s family, mention has already been made in or among the Fore family. Philip Y., the third son, now in Marion, a first class business man; has been County Auditor, and is now and has been for ten or more years cashier of the Bank of Marion; married Miss Florence Johnson, of Charleston, a distant relative of his—his father and Florence's grand-mother, Sallie Strobel, were first cousins; they have had six sons (one, Philip Y., dead), Eugene, Arthur, Johnson, Stewart, Philip Y. and Markley, and three daughters, Eloise, Edith and Mary McLeod—none of whom are married. Eugene, the eldest, is in the Philippines or China, in the United States army, an officer, a promising young man, and may rise to greater distinction. The other children are all at home—Eloise and Arthur are grown. Philip Y. has a very interesting family; his wife is a superior woman, and well fitted by education and early training to raise a family. Elisha, the fourth son of Colonel J. R. Bethea, was quite a promising young man, but the fates decreed that he should not live, and he died when twenty-five or six years of age, unmarried. D. McLeod Bethea, the fifth son of Colonel J. R. Bethea, a first class man, an excellent and successful farmer, married Miss Florence Fore, daughter of the late Stephen Fore, and who, with his family, have already been mentioned herein in or among the Fore family. Robert Lucien, the sixth son of Colonel Bethea, has married twice; first, a Miss Shaw, of Bishopville; by her he had one child, a daughter, Leona, who is now nearly grown. The first wife died, and he married, a second time, to Miss Rosa Carnes, of Bishopville, and by her has some three or four children; names and sex unknown; they are yet children. Robert Lucien lives in Bishopville, and runs a hotel.* Of the daughters of Colonel J. R. Bethea, the eldest, Kate, married Gibson G. Crawford; both of whom and their family have already been noticed herein among the Betheas above. The second daughter of Colonel Bethea, Clara, married Holland Manning, who lives on her patrimony, and are doing well—in fact, Clara is an extra smart and sensible woman; they have two children, daughters, both children, Mary Belle and Hope. Holland Manning was a widower with five children, three of whom are married; he has a place of his own in extreme upper Marion, which he rents. Colonel James R. Bethea died in 1878, at sixty-nine years of age, and his widow, Mary, some years afterward. The youngest daughter, Isabella, or Belle, has never married; she has a good farm, which she rents; she also teaches school, and when not thus engaged she stays with her sister, Clara Manning.

Colonel James R. Bethea, when young, imbibed a military spirit, and manifested a strong ambition to attain to high honors in the militia of the State. Starting as a private in his local beat company (Cross Roads), he soon obtained a Lieutenancy; and from that to the Captaincy of the company; and from that to Major of the upper battalion; and by seniority soon became Lieutenant Colonel of the regiment; and from that by election to the Colonelcy of the Thirty-second Regiment, which position he held at the time of his marriage, in March, 1844, and continued to hold that position for three or four years afterward—and in the meantime declined to be a candidate for Brigadier General, to which place he could have been elected, perhaps, without opposition. He was an efficient officer, and was popular as such. It was very expensive, and as he had a growing family he wisely chose to abandon the further pursuit of military honors (empty as they were), and devote his means to the support and education of his fast-growing family. He resigned his commission as Colonel, and Elly Godbold or John J. George was elected in his place. They both were successive Colonels, but do not remember which of the two were first elected. Afterwards Colonel Bethea was elected as a Representative from the district in the State Legislature (1848 to 1850).

*He is now at Dillon in the same business.

Of the daughters of Philip Bethea, a son of old "Buck Swamp John," Clarissa, the eldest, never married, and died in 1861, at the age of fifty-eight. The second daughter, Margaret, married Willis Finklea, called Arter Willis; in a short while Finklea moved to Alabama; there they had several children, five of whom were raised. Willis Finklea was a drinking man and treated his wife badly, so much so that she could not stand it; they separated, and her father, in 1841, went to Alabama, Monroe County, in a wagon, and brought her and her five children back to Marion County; Finklea soon after died; her children were raised mainly by her father; there were two sons, James C. and William; the daughters were Lucinda, Sallie and Margaret Agnes. James C. Finklea is now one of our fellow-citizens, known as Captain Finklea, in Wahee Township, and, in fact, all over the county. Captain Finklea volunteered in Captain C. J. Fladger's Company E, 23d South Carolina Regiment, in the Confederate War; went off as a Sergeant in that company. Captain Fladger in a few months resigned, and Harris Covington, First Lieutenant, became Captain, the other Lieutenants went up, and Captain Finklea was elected Third Lieutenant, made vacant. Some time after Covington resigned, and the company was reorganized by orders from the proper authorities, and Captain Finklea was elected Captain of the company, and served gallantly until the latter part of 1864—having fought through all the campaigns from Virginia to Mississippi. At that time Captain Finklea was the senior Captain in the regiment, when by the casualties of war the Major's office became vacant, and according to rules of promotion, Captain Finklea was entitled to the place; but a Junior Captain was promoted, by appointment, not by election, to the Majoralty over him; when Captain Finklea resigned and came home, and did not return to the service. It was said he was a good and brave Captain; that his men all loved and respected him, but he was not popular with the higher officers, because he always associated with his men and not with them. Captain Finklea is known as a modest, retiring man; not self-asserting. Had the vacancy for Major been left to his company, he would have gotten the vote of every man; he sympathized with his men, fared as they fared, and assumed no superiority over them on account of his position. As an evidence of Captain Finklea's popularity, when he was first elected County Commissioner, a few years ago (he was twice elected), he received every vote at Berry's Cross Roads, something over 200. He is a man of good sense, a good and safe manager of his farm and home affairs, unostentatious and unassuming, rather avoids company—unfortunately, of late years, his habits are not good. After the war he went, first, to Alabama and then to Texas, where he married a Miss Kyle; she had one child for him, a son, who died in infancy, and the mother died; he then came back to South Carolina, and married the widow of Dr. William H. Godbold, a most excellent and cultured woman; by her he had one son, named for his first wife, a very promising boy, but he died at the age of four or five years. William Finklea, the youngest brother, died when about grown. Lucinda, the oldest daughter, married John T. Kinney, of Marlborough, and emigrated to Texas, where they raised a family; both are dead, and nothing is known further of them. Sallie, the second daughter, married Cyrus B. Haselden; they had and raised five children, two sons, John and Frank, and three daughters, Lucy, Maggie and Fannie. Cyrus B. Haselden and wife, Sallie, and family, have already been noticed in or among the Haseldens. Margaret Agnes, the youngest daughter of Willis Finklea and wife, Margaret, never married, and died of cancer on the breast, at the age of forty, in March, 1882. A noble girl she was. Martha Ann Bethea, the third and youngest daughter of old man Philip Bethea, married W. W. Sellers, the writer, 10th January, 1847, and died 2d February, 1893; they had seven children, four sons, John C., William W., Benjamin Morgan and Philip B.; of these, Benjamin Morgan died a little under two years of age; three daughters, Anna Jane, Rachel C. and Mary O. Of the sons, John C. is a graduate of the South Carolina College, studied law, was admitted to the bar in 1870, was elected to the Legislature in 1870, practiced law only one year, and retired on the farm where he now lives; his first wife was Miss Maggie E. Mace, daughter of the late John Mace; she had seven children, three sons, Benjamin B., John M. and Wallace Duncan; of these, John M. died under one year old; there were four daughters, Lucy B., Annie R., Maggie Leila and Maggie Ellen (called Pearl). Benjamin B. Sellers is a graduate of Wofford College; married Miss Norma Watson, youngest daughter of the late William Watson; they have two children, Harry and Margaret Ellen; he is farming. Wallace Duncan's education is not completed. Of the daughters, Lucy B. is a graduate of the Columbia Female College; she married D. Maxcy Watson; they have no children. Annie R. went to the Female College for more than a year, but did not graduate; is unmarried. Maggie Leila is near grown, is going to school. Maggie E., called Pearl, was only three days old when her mother died; her Aunt Rachel Norton took her and has so far raised her; she is near thirteen years of age. W. W. Sellers, Jr., married Miss Harriet J. McPherson, daughter of C. Ervin McPherson, of West Marion; they have had seven or eight children, only three of whom are living—two daughters, Rachel Elise and Etta; the son is Marvin McSwain—none of them grown. W. W. Sellers, Jr., is one of the Chiefs in the present State Constabulary, and has been for several years; he resides at Latta. Philip B. Sellers is a graduate of Wofford College; studied law and was admitted to the bar in 1884 (May); he married Miss M. Sue DuBois, daughter of J. T. DuBois, of Marion, in December, 1886; they have five children, three sons, John DuBois, Philip Bruce and William Maynard, and two daughters, Agnes Leona and Mildred Eugenia—all children, none grown; he resides at Dillon, and is actively engaged in the practice of his chosen profession, with apparent success. Of the daughters of the writer and his wife, Anna Jane, the eldest daughter married her cousin, D. N. Bethea; he and Anna Jane and their family have been already noticed in the same connection, Betheas. The second daughter of W. W. Sellers and wife married Hon. James Norton, of Mullins; they had but two children, sons, Evan Lewis and William Fitzroy. Evan Lewis, the eldest, died when four or five years of age. William Fitzroy grew up to manhood; first went to Wofford College, and after two years spent there, he went to the law department of the South Carolina College for two years, graduated in law, and *ipso facto* became a lawyer—he does not practice, however; he married Miss Florence Smith, daughter of B. Gause Smith, at Mullins; they reside at Mullins, and have no children. Mary O. Sellers, youngest daughter of W. W. Sellers, married Thomas N. Godbold, a son of Dr. W. H. Godbold; they have only three children living, Thomas Carroll, Anna and Bessie. Thomas N. Godbold is in the railroad service, on the "Plant System" between Charleston and Savannah. This family has already been noticed in or among the Goldbold family. Recurring back a few lines: John C. Sellers, after living about ten years a widower, married, a second time, to Miss Jaquiline Oliver, of North Carolina, 2d February, 1898— a most excellent woman; they have had two children, boys, who are both dead. Elisha Bethea, fourth son of old "Buck Swamp John," known as old Colonel Elisha, never married. It is said of him that he was a very handsome man in his young days; he was born in 1787, and was Captain of a company in the war of 1812-14; he was better educated than any of his brothers—in fact, better than most men of his day. His father left him a fine property, his homestead and a large number of negroes; few men of that time had such a prospect. He was very popular and had more natural politeness than any Bethea I ever saw. But, alas! the demon of intemperance ruined him; he died poor in 1854, at the age of sixty-seven years. After the war of 1812, he became Colonel of the militia. He was true to his friends and true to his country. It seemed to be his delight to make others pleasant, happy and comfortable even at the expense of his own convenience. This was the man after he became poor, which proved it to be natural with him. His bearing and appearance in poverty and old age was that of a nobleman, of a cavalier. Parker Bethea, the youngest son of old "Buck Swamp John," was born in 1790, and was given his mother's maiden name, Parker; he settled opposite the head of Catfish, at the Cross Roads on the Marlborough line, twenty-two miles above Marion, and died there, St. John the Evangelist Day, 27th December, 1867; he married Elizabeth Harllee, daughter of old Thomas Harllee; they raised two sons, Harllee and Benjamin Parker, and four or five daughters. Harllee had one son, Reddin, and Benj. P. had one named Charles. Harllee moved to Florida many years ago; his wife was a Miss Roberts—Benj. P.'s wife was a Miss Woolvin; he moved just after the war to Pender or Onslow County, N. C., thirty miles on the coast above Wilmington. These families have already been noticed in or among the Roberts family and the Harllee family.

One more remark about these old Betheas, sons of "Buck Swamp John." They all loved liquor and, except old Philip, drank it to excess, till after middle life, when they tapered off, and by the time of old age became perfectly abstemious, and this was specially the case with William, James and Parker. They were all good men and excellent citizens, and did much in starting the development of the resources of the county. The first gin house built in the county was built by old "Buck Swamp John;" it stood on what has ever since been called the "Gin House Branch," near the Cross Roads, at John C. Bethea's plantation; a good part of that gin house is still in use. After the death of old "Buck Swamp John," in 1821, the plantation fell to old Colonel Elisha, and he in his financial extremities years afterwards sold the gin house to Cross Roads Henry Berry; he pulled it down and hauled it to Berry's Cross Roads, and it stands there now, the property of James Berry, between his (James Berry's) dwelling and the storehouse. It has been there, to the writer's knowledge, more than sixty years.

Of the grand-sons of old "English John," John settled on Buck Swamp, as already stated, and William settled on Sweat Swamp; he married, and had four sons, John, Goodman, Philip and Jessie. Of these, John, the man who, after the Revolution, hung the Tory, Snowden, married, and he had and raised four sons, William, Tristram, John and Cade—the latter, no doubt, is remembered by many now living in upper Marion and elsewhere in the county. Goodman Bethea married and had two sons, Philip and Jessie. Philip, the brother of Goodman, never married, or if he did, he had no children. Jessie, the fourth son of old "Sweat Swamp William," had Hugh Goodman, William, Henry and Tristram. According to the Bethea chart none of these latter five had any posterity. Supposed they emigrated to parts unknown or died in youth. William, the grand-son of "Sweat Swamp William," had seven sons, John, Tristram, Philip, Jessie, William, Thomas C. and Cade. Of these latter, John, William, Thomas C. and Cade had no offspring. Cade is in upper Marion now an old man.* Of the other three, Tristram had one son, named William; Philip had four sons, Jessie, William, Tristram and Philip—these last four seem to have had no offspring. Jessie, the great-grand-son of old "Sweat Swamp William," had five sons, John, William, Charles, Farquehard and Holden; their mother was a Miss Bethune; she had some daughters, one the wife (now dead) of Patrick Finagan. By the Bethea chart now lying before me, none of these five latter Betheas have any offspring, but the writer knows to the contrary. John has twelve or thirteen children, boys and girls. Holden married Miss Alice Rogers, daughter of Jessie Rogers, and has some children. The Bethune wife of Jessie Bethea had a daughter other than Mrs. Finagan, who was the wife of the late Edward C. Shrewsberry. Tristram, the grand-son of old "Sweat Swamp William," married and had one son, Philip, who was a lawyer, but did not practice much here, and soon went to Alabama, and his father soon after moved himself there; father and son have been lost sight of—suppose both are long since dead. John, another grand-son of "Sweat Swamp William," married Miss Hannah Walker; by the marriage four sons, William W., Alfred W., David W. and John B., were had and raised, and five daughters, Sophia, Mary Ann, Charlotte, Sallie and Hannah. Of the sons, William W. married, first, Mary Bethea, a granddaughter of "Buck Swamp John;" they had three sons, John F., Dallas and William; don't know of any daughters by William W.'s first marriage; he married, a second time, Miss Mary Platt, a daughter of old Daniel Platt; by his (Platt's) second marriage with Polly Lane, a daughter of old James C. Lane, who was a son of old Osborne Lane, I know of but two children; by William W. Bethea's second marriage, two daughters—Hettie, the wife of John C. Bethea, of Dillon, who has already been mentioned; the other daughter married a Mr. Floyd, a son of Judge Floyd, of Alabama or Mississippi. J. F. Bethea (our Dr. Frank Bethea) married his first cousin, Hannah Jane, daughter and only child of Dr. Alfred W. Bethea; by this marriage eight sons, Alfred, Preston L., Tristram, William, Frank, Charles, Archie and Victor, and, I think, three

---

*Died recently.

daughters, Flora and two others whose names are not known, have been born. Alfred (I think) died about the time of his majority. Preston L. married a Miss Weatherby, daughter of Colon W. Weatherby, of Bennettsville, and resides at Dillon. Tristram married a Miss McRae, daughter of Hon. James McRae, of Albriton, in extreme upper Marion; he resides at Dillon. Frank married a Miss Smith, of Alabama or Georgia, and is now a resident of one of those States. William recently married a Miss McLeod, of Robeson County, N. C. The other three sons are yet with their father, Dr. Frank, I suppose, not grown. Of the daughters of Dr. J. F. Bethea, the eldest, Flora, married Tristram Thompson; she was a most excellent lady, loved and respected by all who knew her. The Doctor's two other daughters are minors and still with him. Dr. J. F. Bethea is a successful man every way; as a farmer, he is a man of affairs, a turpentine and saw mill man, is merchandizing at Dillon, he and his sons (don't know how many or which), under the firm name of J. F. Bethea & Co.; he has once represented the county in the State Legislature. Dallas Bethea, brother of Dr. J. F. Bethea, is in Mississippi; he has three sons, William, Preston and Franklin. Alfred W., another great-grand-son of "Sweat Swamp William," married Flora Bethea, a daughter of Tristram Bethea, of Floral College, who was one of the "Cape Fear set," and by her had only one child, a daughter, Hannah Jane, who married Dr. J. F. Bethea, with the results above stated. Dr. Alfred W. Bethea was no ordinary man; he was eminent as a physician, a good farmer, a well-informed man and of sound practical sense and judgment; he was a member of the Secession Convention of 1860; he was waylaid, shot and killed by the deserters in the last months of the war, much regretted by all who knew him; he lived where Dr. J. F. Bethea now lives; the widow, who survived him, is now dead. David W. Bethea, another great-grand-son of "Sweat Swamp William," married, first, Miss Sarah Jane Manning, daughter of Mealy Manning, of Marlborough; by her he had two sons, LeRoy and David W., they are both married. LeRoy has two sons, Henry and Leon—these have already been mentioned in or among the Mannings and Easterlings, to which reference is made. David W., Jr., has lately married, I think, a Miss

Townsend, of North Carolina; gives promise of becoming a useful man—is already so; if like his mother he cannot be otherwise, as she was one of the best of women. D. W. Bethea, Sr., represented the county one time in the Legislature, 1860-1862; he was a good citizen; he married, a second time, a Miss Brunson, of Darlington, who yet survives; no offspring. John B. Bethea (the youngest), another great-grand-son of "Sweat Swamp William," married Elizabeth A. Bethea, a daughter of Captain Elisha C., of the "Buck Swamp set;" they had four sons, as already mentioned among the "Buck Swamp set," to which reference is made. Of the daughters of John Bethea, the grand-son of "Sweat Swamp William," as given herein above, Sophia, the eldest, married Robert B. Platt, and in a few weeks or months after her marriage she was accidentally burned to death, and, of course, died childless. Mary Ann, the second daughter, married Levi Bethea, of the "Buck Swamp set," and has already been herein noticed in the "Buck Swamp set," to which reference is made. Charlotte and Sallie, the third and fourth daughters, both married the same evening—Charlotte to Zack Fulmore and Sallie to Dr. John K. Alford, both of North Carolina, where they thereafter lived and died; know but little of the family of either. Hannah, the fifth and youngest daughter, married Alexander Fulmore, of North Carolina; they moved to Alabama; know nothing of them. Cade Bethea, the youngest grand-son of old "William of Sweat Swamp," through his son, John, married Kittie Bethea, a sister of "Floral College Tristram," and a great-grand-daughter of Tristram, the son of "English John," who settled on Cape Fear River, N. C.—her father being Jessee and her grand-father was Jessee, whose father was Tristram, the settler on Cape Fear, whose father was old "English John." This I get from the chart now lying before me. Cade Bethea and Kittie had and raised five sons and three daughters; the sons were John W., Evander R., William C., Calvin and Henry; the daughters were Caroline, Harriet and Mary Ann. Cade Bethea settled on Sweat Swamp, north side, just opposite the mouth of Beaver Dam, on the south side, where he lived and died; I think the place now belongs to Hon. D. W. McLaurin. There was but one Cade Bethea in regard to character; he was an incessant talker, and in his latter days was always on the go, around among his kinsfolk and friends; was a great complainer and murmurer, and to hear him tell it, he was going to come to nothing—going to perish to death. An illustration of his character in this regard may be here related: On one occasion, his nephew, Creek Jessie Bethea, went to see his Uncle Cade, in the month of July or August; the old gentleman was in his piazza —it was a very hot day; the old man was complaining and murmuring as usual, that his crop was a complete failure, that he was not going to make anything, and he and his family would all perish in a pile. After a while, Jessie, his nephew, proposed that they would go out and look around his crop; the old man did not want to go; said he did not want to see it—it made him sick to look at it; they, however, went, and after looking around and seeing it all, Jessie remarked to him, "Well, Uncle Cade, your crop is ruined—you won't make anything. I thought my crop was hurt pretty badly, but not near as bad as yours; I declare you will not make bread and you will have to go to the poor house." The old man Cade replied, "You are a liar, sir; my crop is as good as yours, and I am not going to the poor house either." This is not all that was said, but is the pith of it, and shows pretty clearly what the old man was in this respect. Jessie knew him, and said what he did just to bring the old man out, and to hush up his complaints. John W. Bethea, the eldest son of old man Cade, married a Miss McLaurin; they had and raised four sons, Jessie, Laurin, Festus and Alonzo, and one daughter, at least, who became the second wife of Robert A. Brunson; they moved to North Carolina. Jessee, the oldest son of John W., married an Alabama lady; he died four or five years ago, at Dillon, and left his widow, two sons, Jessie and John, and two small daughters, Bessie and Lucile. John W. Bethea and wife are both dead. Evander R. Bethea, the second son of old Cade, married Mary Ann Stackhouse, and had one son, Jasper, and three daughters, Josephine, Carrie and Nannie, all of whom have already been noticed in or among the Stackhouse family. Laurin Bethea, the second son of John W. Bethea, married a Miss McLaurin, as I think; he is a farmer, and lives on Buck Swamp; know nothing of his family. "Fet" Bethea, the third son, married a Miss Stackhouse, daughter of the late Mastin C. Stackhouse; he died, leaving his widow with some children—the youngest of whom, a little girl, was taken by Rev. S. J. Bethea and wife, and they are raising it. Alonzo Bethea, the youngest son of John W. Bethea, is lost sight of; don't know whether he is living or dead, or whether he married or not—think, however, that he has emigrated to other parts, or is dead. Wm. C. Bethea, the third son of old man Cade Bethea, married Miss Virzilla Mace, a daughter of Moses and Drusilla Mace; they had two sons, Henry and John D., I think; they and their children have already been mentioned in or among the Mace family, to which reference is made. Calvin C. Bethea, the fourth son of old man Cade, married Miss Caroline Bethea, a daughter of "Creek Jessie;" they had one child, a son, named Jessie; the father, Calvin, was subject to epileptic fits, and on one occasion, while crossing a branch on Sweat Swamp, as supposed, an epileptic fit struck him and he fell in the water and was drowned; some years after his death, his widow, with her son, went to Texas; the son is grown, and the report is that they are doing well in that far off State. Henry, the fifth and youngest son of old man Cade Bethea, never married; he was killed or died in the war. Of the daughters of old Cade Bethea, the eldest, Caroline, a highly accomplished lady, as it was said, married James DuPre, of Marlborough County; she died childless, in about a year after her marriage. Harriet, the second daughter, married James McLaurin, of North Carolina; a few years back, they bought land on Buck Swamp and moved to it; think they are both dead—know nothing of their family. Mary Ann, the youngest daughter, married T. F. Stackhouse, and is dead, leaving him surviving; they have already been noticed in or among the Stackhouse family, to which reference is made. Not one of old man Cade Bethea's immediate family now survives.

Of the "Cape Fear set," Tristram, a son of old "English John," settled on Cape Fear River, N. C.; he had sons, James, Jessee, Elisha and William. Of these, Jessee, had Jessee, Simeon, David and Jessee (it seems two sons were named Jessee); Simeon had Reddick, Jessee, William and Philip; and Jessee, the elder, had Thomas, Tristram and John—this Tristram was the "Floral College" Tristram; and Jessee, the younger, had

John, Tristram, David and Jessee; and this latter Tristram had Jessee and Noah. William, the son of old Tristram, the "Cape Fear" settler, had John and William. Of these latter, John had William, John L., Jessee, David and Alexander; and William had David, John and Philip. The "Floral College" Tristram had Jessee, Daniel, Tristram, John and Thomas. Of these latter, all of them died without offspring. The eldest of these, Jessee, was well known in Marion; he was a graduate of the South Carolina College; studied law, settled in Marion to practice his profession, was a partner of the writer, as Sellers & Bethea, for several years; left Marion, abandoned the practice, never married, and died; he was a good lawyer, but too modest and diffident to enter into the "rough and tumble" of the Court House—he was a good office lawyer; after leaving Marion, he went to Marlborough and died there. This disposes of the "Cape Fear set" of Betheas—at least, as far as known.

Referring, again, to the "Sweat Swamp" set—old William had four sons, John, Goodman, Philip and Jessee—I think, all these have been noticed except, perhaps, Goodman. Goodman had two sons, Philip and Jessee, and the latter, Philip, had Goodman, William and Philip. Of the grand-daughters of "Sweat Swamp" William, Elizabeth married Jeremiah Walters, and raised a large family. Sarah married Timothy Rogers, a nephew of "Buck Swamp" John, and raised a large family. Pattie married John Braddy, and was the mother of the Braddys and their descendants, as have been and are now known in the county.

The writer may have inadvertently omitted some of this numerous and extensive family as laid down on the chart kindly furnished him, but do not think I have. From the original stock, "Old English John," it runs down to and includes the seventh and in one instance the eighth generation among the males bearing the name, and it is not improbable that among the females (if they had been given and traced), it would extend to and include the ninth and tenth generations, as it is a well known fact, that females generally marry younger than males, and consequently propagate faster than through the male line. If every family had a chart or tree like this, it would be an acquisition to the history of our people. It is a fact, that many of our people are shamefully ignorant as to their ancestry. It is a fact, that the writer has found in his inquiries on the subject among the people of Marion County, a few instances where the party inquired of did not know, and could not tell, who his grand-father was, and to his great surprise he has found it of men otherwise intelligent, and well posted in other matters. A chart, like that of the Betheas, in every family would forever dissipate such ignorance, and would enable every man to tell, at a word, whether he descended by natural and generic processes from his own species, or evoluted from a tadpole or a monkey. The Bethea chart is so constructed as to be indefinitely extended *ad infinitum* to the remotest generations.

McMILLAN.—The McMillan families will now be noticed. First, the family in the Mullins region. The first known were John, Malcolm and Neill V. MacMillan, three brothers. Neill V. lives in the Mullins region, and has a family of sons and daughters. One of his daughters married, last week, to Mack Harrelson, of Buck Swamp. Neill V. McMillan is a farmer, a law-abiding man, and a quiet, inoffensive citizen; don't know to whom he married or how many children he has. Malcolm McMillan married a Miss Williamson, daughter of John Williamson; by this marriage were born and raised three sons, John, Neill and Malcolm. Of these, John married Mary Williamson, of Marion County. Neill married Rebecca Brown, of Clarendon County. And Malcolm married Elizabeth Williamson, of Marion County; by this marriage were born and raised three daughters and four sons. Of the daughters, Sarah, the eldest, married J. Robert Reaves; Mary married J. F. Gasque, and Alice married Pendleton G. Ayres—these all have families, greater or small, some of whom are now among our present promising young men and women, and are of energetic and progressive parents. Of the sons, John married Miss Sarah McIntyre, daughter of John B. McIntyre, and grand-daughter of old Dougald McIntyre, who has already been noticed herein; they have several children, some grown and married—one daughter, any way, married to Mayrant A. Falk. Neill married Eunice Davis, of West Marion, now Florence County; and

Malcolm, Jr., married Miss Keith, and has a family. The early progenitors of these McMillans were a family of McMillans and Pattersons, who emigrated from Scotland before the Revolutionary War, and settled near Philadelphus Church, or where Philadelphus Church now is, in Robeson County, N. C. Of the sons of old McMillan, Hector married Barbara Patterson, and Malcolm married Flora Patterson, both settled near their parents. There were several daughters. One married a McNeill; one married a Crawford; one married John McMillan (I suppose, a brother of Hector and Malcolm); another married a Mr. Blue; and another married a Mr. Buchanan—some of these children were born in Scotland and some in America. Malcolm, the progenitor of the family about Mullins, was born in Scotland, and was three years old when the family emigrated to America, and lived to be ninety years of age when he died. This old Malcolm, as already stated, married Flora Patterson, and to them were born four sons and four daughters; the names of the sons were Neill, Daniel, John and Malcolm. Neill was a school-teacher, and married Sarah Wilson, of Horry. Daniel, John and Malcolm emigrated West. The daughters were Jane, Mary, Margaret and Flora. Don't know who Jane married; Mary married Alfred Biggs; Margaret married Archie Smith; Flora married Hugh Lammond—the latter went to Georgia or Alabama. Neill McMillan, as before stated, married Sarah Wilson, daughter of Samuel Wilson, of Horry County, and were the grand-father and mother of Malcolm, Neill and John, now prosperous citizens of the Mullins community. There is a numerous connection of them in this county and Horry, and Robeson County, N. C., and many, doubtless, in the West.

Another family of MacMillans are at Marion Court House. The first known of this family was old John McMillan, a sturdy Scotchman, born, as I think, in this country, but his ancestry not very remote came from Scotland. Old John married a Miss Avant, of a Marion family, and came and settled in Marion in the latter thirties or early forties; he was Postmaster for some years and ran a drug business. In those early times the drug business was not what it is now—one or two stick baskets would have held his stock, and his was as large as most of the stocks of the kind then kept in the country towns of the State. He had and raised to be grown two sons, Sydney E. and William Cicero, and three daughters,   Sarah and Elizabeth. Of the sons, Sydney E. married, first, a Miss Palmer, a daughter of the then late Hon. David Palmer; by this marriage, one son, John C. McMillan, was born, when the mother died; the child, now Dr. J. C. McMillan, was taken and raised by his grand-parents, the McMillans. Sydney E. McMillan, the father, married, a second time, a Miss Sherwood, of Wilmington, N. C., a most excellent lady; the fruits of this second marriage are several sons and daughters, names of all not remembered. A son, S. A. McMillan, called "Lex," is one of the leading merchants at Latta; he married Miss Sue Rogers, the eldest daughter of Hon. Lot B. Rogers; they have two children. Another son, whose name is Frank, married a Miss Smith, daughter of Hon. J. W. Smith, at Latta. The eldest daughter of Major S. E. McMillan, Mary, married to W. M. Monroe, one of the most successful merchants now at Marion; they have six or seven children, all boys. Major S. E. McMillan has several other sons (one Robert) and daughters. Some of them grown and some not; those grown are unmarried, names not remembered—the grown children, especially the girls, are nice and worthy; they cannot well be otherwise, after being raised and trained by such a mother as theirs. Major S. E. McMillan was Major of the militia before the war, and commanded a company in the 10th South Carolina Regiment, as Captain. It is needless to say to those who know him, that there is but one S. E. McMillan in this section of the country. W. C. McMillan, the second son of old man John, married twice; first, a Miss Cameron, daughter of the late Hector Cameron, of West Marion; by her he had one child; the mother and child both died. After a time, W. C. McMillan married Miss Mattie Porter, daughter of Rev. John A. Porter, of the South Carolina Conference; by this marriage they had and raised ten children, five sons and five daughters; the sons are William C., John P., Sydney, Walter and Edwin; the daughters are Emma, Sue, Belle, Louise and Mary. Of the latter, the eldest, Emma, who was a charming young lady, sickened and died in blooming young womanhood. The next daughter,

Sue, married Samuel A. Blackwell, a young merchant of Marion; they have one or two children. The other three girls are unmarried—two of them not grown. Of the sons of W. C. McMillan, the eldest, W. C. McMillan, Jr., married Miss Sallie Bethea, a daughter of Edwin A. Bethea, now of Latta; W. C. McMillan, Jr., is and has been in Columbia for several years, in the drug business, and is said to be doing well; he is well qualified by training and education for that business; he graduated in a college of pharmacy in Philadelphia, some years ago, and was the only graduate of such a school in the county whilst he was here; they have two children. John P., Sydney and the other sons of W. C. McMillan, Sr., are all unmarried, and remain with their mother or are off in some business—they may be said to be "hustlers." The father, W. C. McMillan, Sr., died some years ago; he was a successful man in business, looked closely after his affairs, and left a good estate unencumbered; he ran for years a successful drug business, together with a farm. Recurring again to Major S. E. McMillan's family: The son by his Palmer wife, John C., grew up and was mainly educated by his uncle, W. C. McMillan, Sr.; he studied medicine and graduated in a medical college some years ago, and settled down in his native town to the practice of his chosen profession, in which he succeeds well; he married Miss Mattie Robson, daughter of Major Robson, of Charleston, a most estimable lady—think they have two children, a son and a daughter. Of the daughters of old John McMillan, the eldest married James Potter, of Georgetown, who died a few months back, at the advanced age of eighty-seven years; by the Potter marriage three children were born and raised. The eldest, Eugenia, is now the wife of J. T. DuBois, of Marion, who have several daughters, M. Sue, Kate, Sallie, Etta, Meta and Hattie. Of these, M. Sue is the wife of P. B. Sellers, Esq., at Dillon. Kate married C. S. Herring, of Dillon, a young business man; they have two sons (small), John and Charles. J. T. DuBois and wife have only one son, William J., who is at Laurinburg, N. C., in the bakery business. The other daughters of DuBois are unmarried. The other daughter of the Potter marriage married Willie Sheckelford, who is dead; they had several children; the widow and children when last heard of were in Horry or at McColl. Evander Potter, the only son of the Potter marriage, married a Miss Wolling; they have three or four children; the father died at Marion a few months ago; children small. The second daughter of old John McMillan, Sarah, never married. Elizabeth, the third and youngest daughter, married Robert Gregg, of West Marion; they had and raised one son, W. C. Gregg, who is now in the machine shops of Emerson McDuffie at Marion, and it is said is a fine machinist or workman; he is married, and lives with his mother in Marion; they have no children.

MILLER.—The Miller family, in North Marion, were formerly a large and noted family. Old man William Miller, whose wife was a Herring, was a stout, athletic man, and noted for his great strength and physical power. They had and raised several sons, John, William, Jessee, Edmund, George and Hezekiah, all of powerful physique, and one daughter, I knew—there may have been other daughters. The writer knew the parties named well in his youth, but for the last fifty years has known but little of them, and the subsequent generations of the family are not known to him. The one best and longest known was the second son of old William, named William, called "Gunger Bill Miller;" he was an excellent citizen, attended to his own business, farming, kept out of debt, and made a comfortable living; he lived on the North Carolina State line, close to a large white pond, suppose three or four miles in circumference, and called "No Man's Friend;" he married, first, a Miss Abbott, and by her had three children, two sons, John and Henry, and a daughter, Mary; don't know what became of Mary. John had epileptic fits, and died of them when a young man grown. Henry, now one of the good citizens in that part of the county, grew up and married a Miss Ward, and has several children, sons and daughters; he has a son, William, who married a Miss Townsend. "Gunger Bill Miller" lost his Abbott wife, and married, a second time, the widow of Isham Philips, and by her had two sons, David and Robert, both grown, yet single, and live on their father's homestead, industrious and steady young men, and bid fair to emulate their father in good citizenship. Jessee Miller, the third son, was a good citizen, but do not know to whom he married; he raised a family of sons and daughters; know nothing of them, except that one of his daughters married Duncan Gaddy, near Gaddy's Mills. Edmund Miller, the fourth son of old William, married a Miss Gilchrist, as I remember it, and had but two daughters, one named Diana, the name of the other forgotten. George Miller, the fifth son, married a Miss Snow, and had three sons, George, Hezekiah and Allen; had two daughters—one married David Rowell, the other daughter still single. Hezekiah married and has one son, Edward, and one daughter. Edward married a Miss Barnes; the daughter is single. Allen Miller married Miss Effa Martin, daughter of Rev. Norman Martin, and raised three sons, Robert H., William and Alexander Carson. Robert H. married a Miss Thompson, and has two sons and five daughters. William married a Miss Mack Pipkin, and has two sons. Alexander Carson married a Miss Bemna Benton McGirt (a relative of the writer's children), a daughter of Joe McGirt and wife; they have eight children. Hezekiah Miller, the sixth and youngest son, married a Miss Hill; they have three sons living and some daughters. It is said this latter family have not turned out well. These older Millers were raised in a day when the muster-field bully was the most noted man in the community—talked of most, was honored and feared more, much more, than those who did not aspire to bullyship. These Millers, all except John and "Gunger Bill," partook more or less of the spirit of the times, and were ambitious of the honors that wreathed the brow of the muster-field bully. These were the times of which Judge Longstreet wrote in his "Georgia Scenes," to which the reader is referred, if he desires to call to mind the vivid pictures drawn by that able author. In those times, the scenes pictured by Judge Longstreet as occurring in Georgia were comon everywhere, and especially so in the South. Those scenes were drawn by a master in the art. The writer will not attempt to draw one—they are much easier to be imagined than to be described. John Miller and "Gunger Bill" were not ambitious for such honors—their minds and energies ran in a less barbarous and more civilized and praiseworthy channel. Jessee and Edmund were the bullies of the family; George and Hezekiah were not so much so. Jessee and Edmund were giants in size and strength; George and Hezekiah were of medium size or a little over medium, but were very agile. About 1830 or 1831, on a muster day, then at Carmichael's Bridge, on Little Pee Dee, the Millers and the Barfields and perhaps others got into a row and a general fight. In the *melee*, Thompson Barfield, a small man, weighing not over 120 pounds, but active as a cat and fierce as a tiger, cut Edmund Miller across the abdomen a gash four or five inches long, and also one of his intestines; his intestines came out, and he caught them in his hands and walked some twenty-five or thirty yards to a place where he could lie down. Dr. Robert Harllee, at Marion Court House, was then the only physician in the county east of the Great Pee Dee River; he was sent for and came; he sewed up the intestine and put all back in proper place, and then sewed up the outside wound, and in due time Miller got well and strong as ever. Such occurrences were common in that day. They were usually, however, only fisticuffs—no deadly weapons, and I suppose the knife was used on this occasion because of the great disparity in size of the two men. A somewhat similar row occurred just across the State line, in North Carolina, some years afterwards, between the Millers and Gaddys—which was the foundation of the suit between the Millers and W. H. Grice, a Magistrate at the time, who at the instance of old James Gaddy, issued a warrant for the arrest of the Millers, and under which they were arrested and lodged in jail in Marion and kept there for some time—the arrest was for an offence committed in North Carolina. The suit was brought (I believe, two of them,) to recover damages for the arrest and imprisonment. The case or cases are reported, I believe, in 2 Rich. Law, or in Strobhart's Law, 1 vol.—I have not the books before me. Those old Millers are long since dead, and it is hoped and believed the younger and present generation of those families are an improvement upon their ancestors in this regard. John and "Gunger Bill" are excepted.

SPENCER.—This family, bearing the name, is not very extensive, but may in time become so. John F. Spencer (late) came from Greenville District, I think, in 1845, then an old-young man—at least thirty years of age; he was a dancing master and a most excellent violinist, an adept in the art; he dressed well and made a fine appearance; he captivated and married a Miss Godbold, then only thirteen years of age, a young girl going to school in Marion; she was the daughter of old Stephen Godbold, in Wahee; the marriage created some flutter in the family, as also in the community at the time (an elopement); the marriage was, however, an accomplished fact, and could not be undone—the *status quo* could not be restored. Old man Stephen Godbold did not long survive the marriage, and his lands, where she now lives, with a number of negroes and other property, fell into the hands of his daughter, Mrs. Spencer. As the law then stood, the whole personal property of a married woman, upon her marriage, vested in the husband, and his marital rights attached as soon as it went into his possession; in this case, however, his wife had no property of her own at the time of the marriage—it was only in prospect upon her father's death; her friends invoked the power of the Court of Equity for her protection, and had the whole property settled upon her, through a trustee, appointed by the Court, and which effectually prevented the marital rights from attaching. The Court of Equity was ever ready to exercise its jurisdiction in this regard, for the protection of married women as to their property. This ancient and cherished jurisdiction of the Court is not now necessary to be invoked. The Constitutions, both of 1868 and 1895, emancipated married women as to their property, and it is effectually protected and cannot be taken for her husband's debts, although by him contracted for the support and education of the family, except by her consent. J. F. Spencer and wife had and raised eleven children to be grown—five sons and six daughters; the sons are John, William, Thomas, Henry and Nathan; of the daughters, one died unmarried, when about grown; the other five are all married—don't know to whom, except one, who married a Mr. Sessoms; it is said they are all doing well. The sons are all married, except the two youngest, Henry and Nathan, very promising young men. John, the eldest son, married a daughter of old man George Turbeville, near by, and has a considerable family—one son, named John, now grown and unmarried; don't know who the other two sons, William and Thomas Spencer, married. J. F. Spencer became and was a good citizen; he lived to a great age, more than eighty years old when he died; for the last several years of his life he was paralyzed and helpless as a baby; Mrs. Spencer survives, and is and has been all the way through life a most excellent lady, a good mother and a good manager of her affairs and of her family; is deserving of all honor and great credit for so doing; she was the only surviving child of old Stephen Godbold, by his last marriage. An elder sister of her was unfortunately killed in a runaway on the road, in the early forties, when returning in a carriage from Carolina Female College, in Anson County, N. C., to her home. Dr. William H. Godbold was driving the carriage, and his niece, Miss Desda Gibson, was also in the carriage, but escaped with only slight bruises, and afterwards became the wife of C. C. Law, of Darlington.

WILLIAMSON.—The first of this name came from London, England, some time before the Revolutionary War. His name was Joseph Williamson, was a merchant either in or near Georgetown, and married the Widow Jordan—her maiden name was Mary Jenkins; to them were born two sons, Joseph and John. Joseph died when young. John married Martha Owens, and eight children were born to them, five sons and three daughters; the sons were Joseph, John and William D.; the other sons died when quite young, so did the daughters, except one, Elizabeth O. Joseph Williamson married Emma Wise, the daughter of Moses Wise. John Williamson married Frances Philips. William D. Williamson married Prudence Nance. Elizabeth O. Williamson married Levi Gerald, the grand-son of Samuel Gerald, a noted Whig in the time of the Revolutionary War, and of whom it is said the Tories sawed his legs to the bone or to the marrow, to make him tell where his money was. To Joseph Williamson and Emma Wise were born ten children, seven sons and three daughters, named as follows: Martha A., John J., Emma J., Joseph M., Solomon M., David R., Robert L. and Samuel W.—the other two having died young. To John Williamson and Frances Philips were born eleven children, four sons and seven daughters, named as follows: Martha Ann, Elizabeth S., Sarah E., Leonora S., Hanna F., John B., Bright J., Mary, Annie, Annis and Joseph W. To Elizabeth O. Williamson and Levi Gerald were born six children, four girls and two boys, as follows: Martha Ann, Kate E., John L., Samuel W., Catharine and Sarah. To William D. Williamson and Prudence Nance were born eight children—one son, Daniel J., who was killed in the war, and seven daughters: Martha A. R., Sarah Ann, Susannah, Elizabeth Annie, Prudence Anne; two others died in infancy. Martha A. Williamson, daughter of Joseph and Emma Wise, married Thomas W. Ayres. John J. Williamson married Mary E. Baker, daughter of William B. Baker, Sr., and to them were born two sons, named W. Lawrence and John J., Jr. Emma J. Williamson married Allen Griffin. Joseph M. Williamson married Elizabeth Annie Williamson, his cousin, and to them were born three sons and one daughter, named as follows: William J., Gustavus A. and Sydney G.; the daughter, Artimissia M. Solomon M. Williamson married Zilpha Collins, daughter of John J. Collins, and to them were born two sons, John C. and Ferdinand Williamson. David R. Williamson married Jane A. Collins, daughter of William Collins, and to them were born three children, one son and two daughters, named as follows: Alice, David C. and Adra. Robert L. and Samuel W. Williamson were killed in the war at Fort Fisher, N. C.; Solomon M., David R. and Daniel J. Williamson were also killed in the war. Martha Ann Williamson, daughter of John Williamson and Frances Philips, married J. H. Thompson; they had no children. Elizabeth S. Williamson married Malcolm McMillan, as already stated among the McMillan family. Sarah E. Williamson married W. A. Brown, of the Sister Bays. Hannah F. Williamson married John L. Gerald. John B. Williamson married Martha Coleman, daughter of James Coleman; to them were born seven children, all dead, but one daughter. Mary Williamson married John McMillan. Annie Williamson married W. E. Gasque. Annis Williamson married N. D. Coary. Joseph W. Williamson married Mary Kate McIntyre; to them were born eight children; these have already been mentioned among the McIntyres (don't know sex or names). Leonard S. and Bright J. Williamson were killed in the war. Martha A. R. Williamson, daughter of William D. Williamson and Prudence Nance, married David J. Owens, son of old Solomon Owens. Sarah Ann Williamson married John D. Jordan. Daniel J. Williamson married Trecia Fowler, daughter of the late Jessee Fowler, and they had six children, three sons and three daughters, named as follows: Martha P., Elizabeth, Susan, William D., Jr., Jessee and Charley. Susannah Williamson married Daniel M. Carmichael. Elizabeth Anne Williamson married Joseph M. Wilsiamson. Prudence Anne Williamson married H. G. Harrelson. W. Lawrence Williamson married a Georgia lady (don't know her name); they had a family, number and sex unknown. John J., Jr., died unmarried. William J. Williamson married L. M. Tululah Elvington, daughter of John E. Elvington, and to them have been born twelve children, five sons and seven daughters, as follows: Modanza, Sidi, Eulah, Willie, Overton, Ryan, Marcellus, Cristie, Lolah, Walter, Velna (baby), dead. Gustavus A. Williamson married Francois Belk, daughter of Rev. Julius Belk, and to them have been born six children, three sons and three daughters (don't know their names). Sydney G. Williamson married Mary A. Oliver, daughter of the Hon. A. C. Oliver, of North Carolina; they have eleven children, nine sons and two daughters, named Junius, Rembert, Bertha, Wilborn, Lonnie, Monroe, Grover, Ambrose, Layton, Luna and Charlie. Artemissia U. Williamson married J. Emory Smith, near Mullins; they have a family, number and name unknown. John C. Williamson married a Miss Johnson, and have eight children, mostly boys. Don't know who Ferdinand Williamson married. David C. Williamson married a Miss Watson; William D. Williamson, Jr., married Martha Martin; Charlie Williamson married Miss Celia Martin; Jessee Williamson married a Miss James; Martha Williamson married H. G. Collins; Elizabeth Williamson married Robert Brown; Susan Williamson married David H. Shelly. The last nine or ten mentioned above all have families, but the number, sex and names are unknown, and the writer has no convenient means of ascertaining; they are all young, and have not as yet attained to manhood or womanhood. The Williamson family is large in name and extensive in its connections—is and ever has been a respectable name in the county.

WALL.—This family, extensive in name and its connections, can be traced no farther back than to Wright Wall, the grandfather of ex-Sheriff William A. Wall. Wright Wall married a Miss Rice; the fruits of the marriage were six sons, viz: John, James, Washington, Hugh G., Isaiah and Lawson. Of these, John emigrated West, James never married. Washington married a Miss Vaught, they had children: Columbus, George, Peter, Martha, Amanda, Sarah, Elizabeth and Gabriella. Of these, Columbus married in Horry and resides there now. George Wall married Mary Owens, daughter of the late David Owens; they have three children, girls. Peter Wall married in Horry; don't know to whom—he and his wife separated, and what has become of them is unknown. Martha married a Mr. Cox, in Horry; nothing further is known of them. Amanda married Barney Collins, son of the late Sheriff, Robert Collins; it is said they have several children, and are at McColl. Sarah married Henry Shaw; by him she had some children, don't know how many; Shaw died, and the widow afterwards married William R. Hux, a widower, with several children, in Horry; don't think the two families agreed; Hux lived on the Dog Bluff Road, leading to Conway. The writer, during his long practice in Horry, passed the house of Mr. Hux, and on one occasion stayed with him a night. His first wife was then sick, and soon after died; he had then one or two children grown. Some year or so after his marriage to Mrs. Shaw, it was observed by the writer, in passing, that Mr. Hux had built another dwelling house near by his residence, and had put his first children in it, which of itself was evidence of disagreement, and on inquiry was informed that disagreement was the cause. Some time afterwards they separated, and she went up to Marion to her sister, Mrs. L. R. Owens, who lived near the writer. Mrs. Hux sent for me to go over there, she wanted to see me. The writer went and had a talk with her, heard her statement of her troubles, and gave her such advice as he thought proper under the circumstances. Was informed some days afterwards by Mr. Owens, that Hux came there the next evening after I was there; that they compromised their difficulties; that Mrs. Hux went home with him the next day; heard no more of the trouble; Hux soon after sickened and died; don't know what has become of her or her children. Afterwards heard that one of her sons by her first marriage was in the Citadel Academy in Charleston, and was very smart; don't know whether he graduated or not, or what has become of him or the other children. Elizabeth married a Mr. Cox, in Horry. Gabriella married L. R. Owens, of Marion; they have a number of children—two, perhaps, grown—all born and raised in Marion. Owens was a very competent business man; was in the postoffice at Marion for years—twice under appointment, and served one term (four years) as assistant; he eventually got out of the office, became a lunatic and was sent to the Asylum, where he now is. His older brother, S. G. Owens, died in the Asylum some years ago, who was also a very competent business man—served one term, from 1872 to 1876, as Clerk of the Court, was a very efficient Clerk. There seems, however, to be a "crazy streak" in the family. Since L. R. Owens has been sent to the Asylum, Mrs. Owens and her children have moved to Augusta, Ga.; she left an elegant home in Marion—I think, unsold. Hugh G. Wall, Sr., married, first, a Miss Davis, and by her had three children, to wit: Hugh G., Jr., Albert and Sarah; he married, a second time, a Miss Eagerton, and had children, to wit: Henry (killed in the war), Marion, Edwin, Furman, William B.; and daughters, Elizabeth, Eliza, Laura and Simpson. Hugh G. Wall, Jr., has had two wives; the first, a Miss Wall (a cousin), and by her had one child, a daughter, who grew up and married T. C. White—they have some children; by the second wife, a Mrs. Richardson (widow), *nee* Watson; by her he has several children, sons and daughters, names unknown—one daughter married, to whom is not known. Albert Wall married a Miss Wall (a cousin), they have no offspring, but are doing well. Sarah married Ben Davis; they have two sons and two daughters, all married. George Davis married a Miss Richardson. Jefferson Davis married a Miss Davis; they have some children. Anne Davis married Nicholas Davis; they have children. Maude Davis

Married Ervin Richardson, Jr.; they have offspring. Marion Wall married a Miss Baker; they have two sons and two daughters. Edwin Wall married a Miss Harllee, daughter of Captain Robert Harllee; they have a family, number and names unknown. Furman Wall married a Miss Mace, daughter of John M. Mace. Furman is dead; left his wife a widow with three or four children. William B. Wall married a Miss Altman; they have three or four children. Elizabeth Wall married J. F. Gasque; they have two or three children; they moved to Savannah, Ga. Eliza Wall married F. M. Philips, in the "Friendship" neighborhood; he is dead, and left four or five children. Laura Wall married A. V. Rowell, and had four children; she is dead. Simpson Wall married Robert Rowell, they have a family. Isaiah Wall married, first, a Miss Keith, and had two children; the wife and both children dead; he married, a second time, to a Miss Gasque, a daughter of old John Gasque—the latter was quite a character. It is said of old John that he had a case in Court, and George W. Dargan (afterwards Chancellor) was his lawyer. The other side put up some witness on the stand, who swore pretty strongly against old man Gasque, and when he had concluded his testimony, the witness was turned over to Gasque's lawyer for cross-examination; and as Dargan rose from his seat, old man Gasque spoke out aloud and said: "Tangle him, Dargan, tangle him." To this second marriage ten children were born, nine sons and one daughter; of the sons, six are dead; there were two named James—the first thus named died, and another born after his death was also named James, and he died; the other dead ones were Chapman, Samuel, Isaiah and Lawson D. Wall—the latter died in January, 1901, leaving only one child, a son, named Marion; the surviving sons are William A., Julius and Pressly. William A. Wall married Miss Ellen Keever, had six children, four sons and two daughters, one son dead; the surviving sons are H. Witherspoon, William A., Jr., and Victor S.; the daughters are Wilmar and Mary Ellen. Wilmar is grown, and one son nearly so. William A. Wall has been for years quite a prominent man in the county—first a Deputy Sheriff for several years, and finally was elected Sheriff in 1888—made a good Sheriff, served his full term; but the tidal wave, politically speaking, in 1892, put him out; he was succeeded by W. T. Evans, who held the position for two terms, when he was sucseeded by B. R. Mullins, the present Sheriff, and in his practical judgment he has made ex-Sheriff Wall his chief clerk and deputy. One peculiar trait of ex-Sheriff Wall was and is his reticence and detective power—you never know what his business was till you see it executed, and always successful in making arrests without trouble, and was always successful in detecting crime and ferreting out criminals. Julius Wall married a Miss Saunders; they have one child only, a son (small). Pressly Wall married a Miss Byrd, daughter of Dr. Byrd, near Scranton, where they now live; they have five children, three sons and two daughters (small). Lawson D. Wall, Jr., married a Miss Flowers, and had an only son, Marion; the father died 1st January, 1901, as before stated. Amanda, the only daughter of Isaiah Wall, married J. J. Richardson; they have no children. Lawson Wall, Sr., son of old Wright Wall, never married. The Wall family, as a whole, were and are good, honest people, inoffensive and quiet citizens, law-abiding, seldom or never in the Courts—and especially in the criminal Courts; trustworthy in every respect.

McEACHERN.—Some of this name have been incidentally mentioned already, but none of the family now to be noticed—I mean, the family near Hamer, on the "Short-cut" Railroad. Neill McEachern emigrated from Scotland with his then family to Marion County, S. C., in the first part of the nineteenth century; he married, in Scotland, Miss Effa McKellar; they had four sons, Duncan, Daniel, Gilbert and John, and two daughters, Sallie and Elizabeth—I think four of his children were born in Scotland. The father, Neill McEachern, was a sturdy old Scotchman, industrious, economical, energetic and persevering; was honest, and accumulated property. Duncan married, lived and died in Marlborough; he married Mary Ann McGill, and is yet living; he settled on Hay's Swamp, one of the best agricultural sections of the county; they had and raised four sons, Neill, Joseph, John B. and Duncan, and four daughters. Neill, the eldest son, never married, is an old bachelor. Joseph, the second son, married a Miss Legette; they had one son, named Benjamin; his wife died, he is now a widower, and is merchandising at Rowland, N. C., and it is said doing a fair business. John B., the third son, married a Miss Campbell, and has two children (small); he lives on the old homestead, with his mother and maiden sister, Margaret, who has never married; John B. is an excellent man, a good farmer, and is succeeding well. Duncan, the youngest and fourth son, is a practicing physician; some two or three years after his graduation he emigrated to Georgia, where he married a Miss Grimes, and has two children; it is said he is succeeding well in his profession. Effa, the second daughter of old Daniel, married Richard Braswell, of North Carolina, just across the State line; they have two daughters only, Mary and Isla. Mary is married to Thompson Williams, of North Carolina. Isla is yet single. Richard Braswell is doing well. Louise, the third daughter, married William D. Carmichael, the youngest son of old Sheriff Archie Carmichael. There are four W. D. Carmichaels in the county—hence I have to identify this one by his father, old Sheriff Carmichael. W. D. Carmichael resides at Marion; he is a mechanic, and runs a bicycle shop, with E. H. Byers as a partner, and he and wife run a public boarding house in Marion and have much patronage; they have three children, two daughters and one son; the daughters are Nina and Edna. Nina is grown and is now in school at Red Springs, N. C.; Edna is near grown; the son is named Daniel Archie, for his two grand-fathers, is a lad; the children are all very promising, and are being raised right—their mother, Mrs. Carmichael, is one of the many good women and an excellent manager of affairs. The writer knows whereof he speaks, as he boarded in their house for about five years. Miss Sallie McEachern married John R. Jackson, who is one of the many progressive farmers of that section of the county; they have two small children, a boy and a girl.

Another family of McEachern, no relation to these mentioned above, may be here noticed—the family of Neill McEachern, whom I knew more than sixty years ago; he was twice married—one of his wives was a Miss McColl; he had several sons and some daughters; the sons are Peter, Edward, John, Edmund, William (dead), Neill and Robert; a daughter named

Manilla, and Flora Catharine—the latter married James McKellar; the youngest daughter by the last wife not married. The sons, Peter and Edward, live, together with their mother and two maiden sisters, in the Hay's Swamp section, and are well to do—think they have already been noticed herein, and need not be repeated; their father, I suppose, is dead—he was a man with a family more than sixty years ago; of the other sons the writer knows nothing.

CARMICHAEL.—This large and respectable family live mostly on the north side of Little Pee Dee River. They are a Scotch people, as their name implies—honest and frugal, industrious, practical and trustworthy every way, ambitious seemingly only to establish and to preserve an unsullied character. This family originated in and came from Scotland in the latter half of the eighteenth century. There were three or four of them, first settlers, whether brothers or relatives does not clearly appear, but it is supposed they were, at least, in some degree, related to each other. Whether they came together or at different times, does not appear, but they settled in close proximity to each other. Neill Carmichael was one of them; he married Miss Christian Carmichael, a daughter of one of the emigrants —whether he and his wife were cousins, does not appear; they had three sons, Archie, John and Daniel. Archie, known as Sheriff Carmichael, was born in 1797, and lived to the advanced age of eighty-six years, and was universally loved and respected, venerable for his years and his high Christian character; he was twice elected Sheriff of the district, which office then as now was for four years; a man then could only be elected and hold the office in alternate quadreniums. Carmichael's first quadrennium was from April, 1841, to April, 1845. During his first term in the Sheriff's office there was great monetary depression—the mass of the people were in debt. Money could not be raised, property had but little value, and consequently there was great distress among the people. Fortunately for the debtor class, they had a kind-hearted man in the Sheriff's office, and he would not force collections by levy and sale of their property in such time of general distress; some of the creditor portion, money sharks, who had executions in his office, had the Sheriff ruled for not forcing the collection of their demands, and the result was that the rules were made absolute, and the Sheriff had to go to jail; he became a martyr to his kindness of heart, to his leniency in office. He was in jail for about twenty months, in 1842 and 1843; he and his family occupied the apartments in the jail provided for the jailor's family. He moved his books, papers, &c., into the jail, and there attended to the business of his office just as though he had remained in his office in the court house; collected money and paid it out—he was, to all intents and purposes, still Sheriff, except as to his personal liberty; he did not put his foot on the ground during his incarceration. His oldest son, A. B. Carmichael, was born in jail. The creditor party were not hurt, they ultimately got their money, and have gone into oblivion with it, while Sheriff Carmichael multiplied his friends and had the consciousness of having discharged his duty, and palliated the distresses of his people without injury to any, and lived for many years in grateful remembrance by his fellow-citizens; and though now dead, will continue to live in the hearts of people for all time to come. The people manifested their appreciation of his martyrdom by triumphantly electing him Sheriff again at the next alternate election for Sheriff, notwithstanding the combined opposition of the money sharks of the county, and served another term from April, 1849, to April, 1853. For six terms of that office it may be said that it was Godbold in and Carmichael out, Carmichael in and Godbold out. The sixth term, instead of Carmichael, it was his nephew, N. C. McDuffie. Carmichael did not run again on account of his age, and the office was turned over to his popular and efficient nephew. Archie Carmichael, in his younger days, was elected Captain of the militia, an office then much sought, and which place he filled with acceptability and much to his credit—hence he acquired the honorary title of Captain Carmichael. Much more might well be said of Captain Carmichael, but space will not permit. His private character was unsullied, was without spot or blemish; he was in every way a Christian gentleman. The three sons of old Neill Carmichael were Archie, John and Tailor Daniel. Captain Archie married, first, a Miss Murphy, and by her had three children, Archie B., Mrs.

Joseph McIntyre and Mrs. John E. Perritt; his second wife was Miss Margaret McLeod, who still survives, and by her had two sons, Neill J. and William D. Carmichael. A. B. Carmichael married Miss Lizzie Gaddy, daughter of the late Henry Gaddy; by this marriage there were two sons born and raised, to wit: Clyde and Gaddy. Clyde married Albert Edward's daughter; Gaddy Carmichael is yet unmarried. Emaline Carmichael married Joseph McIntyre, deceased; to this marriage were born and raised seven children. The eldest, Nettie, married J. Edgar Bass; they went to Georgia. Of the other six children, Archie married a daughter of Timothy R. McLellan, and Blanche married Henry Farley, of Dillon, the other four, Lizzie, Duncan, Isla and Layton, are unmarried; their father and mother are both dead. These may have already been mentioned in or among the McIntyres and McLellans. Mrs. John E. Perritt has no children. Neill J. Carmichael, oldest son of Sheriff Carmichael by his second marriage, married a daughter of Duncan C. Carmichael, called "Red Duncan," and by her has ten children, the eldest of whom is grown; the others less, down to the youngest, perhaps a baby. William D., the youngest son of Sheriff Carmichael, married Miss Louise McEachern, daughter of Daniel McEachern, and live at Marion; they have three children, Nina, Edna and Daniel Archie. These have already been noticed in or among the McEacherns. John Carmichael, a jolly Scotchman, called "Hatter John," the next brother of Sheriff Carmichael, married, also, a Miss Murphy; to them were born some eight or ten children. Edward D. Carmichael, an excellent man and good citizen, married a Miss Carmichael, daughter of Daniel W. Carmichael, of the Fork section, and by her had several children, only two of whom are known to the writer, to wit: R. J. Carmichael, a graduate of the United States Military Academy at West Point, N. Y., now a Lieutenant in the regular army of the United States, and Thaddeus Carmichael, a graduate of the Citadel Academy, in Charleston, S. C., and who is a promising young man. Of the other children of "Hatter John," James married Martha Campbell, daughter of the late John J. Campbell. Eliza married Daniel Campbell; Jennette married John C. McEachern; Amanda married Malcolm C. Carmichael; Caroline married

Joseph Murphy; Martha married David S. Edwards, of the Fork section; Nancy and Catharine are unmarried. Of these, it is supposed they all have families of children, more or less numerous, though not known to the writer. Martha, who married David S. Edwards, has several children grown and, be it said to their credit, that their children are being educated—at least, a son, G. E. Edwards, is a graduate of Wofford College, is quite a promising young man, is engaged in teaching, very popular, and is preparing for the ministry and, as is supposed, will apply to the next South Carolina Conference to enter upon the duties of his chosen profession in the Methodist Church, South. Mr. D. S. Edwards has, also, two daughters, graduates of Rock Hill, very smart and promising to be useful as well as ornamental to society; I think, one or both of them is now engaged in teaching. What a contrast between them and their ancestors of fifty and a hundred years ago! Daniel, called "Tailor Daniel," the youngest brother of Sheriff Carmichael, never married—don't know what became of him, but suppose he has long since died. Of the daughters of old Neill, sisters of Sheriff Archie, Mary married Duncan McDuffie, who settled in the "Fork;" they raised a family of four sons—A. B., Neil C., D. D. and George Alexander, and one daughter, the first wife of Isham H. Watson, and who have already been noticed in or among the McDuffie and Watson families. Nancy Carmichael married John Carmichael, of Cumberland County, N. C., and Catharine married Captain Neill M. Carmichael; whose father, Duncan, came from Scotland, and married a Miss Monroe, and had six sons, Neill M., John, Malcolm, Duncan, William and Archie. Of these, Duncan married a Miss McRae; the wives of John and Malcolm are unknown; William married a Miss McRae; Archie married Sarah Harrelson. Duncan Carmichael had sons, William D., Archie, Mack and John R., and daughters, Mary and Flora. Mary married Duncan Murchison, and for him she had two sons, William and John D., who are now young men in the town of Marion; William is a Representative from the county in the lower House of the General Assembly; both are unmarried. The other daughter of Duncan Carmichael, Flora, is unmarried. Of William Carmichael's (brother of Duncan) family nothing is known.

Of Duncan Carmichael's sons, William D. married a Miss Harllee, daughter of Captain Peter Harllee, and has a considerable family—one son, I think, named William, very promising, a graduate of the North Carolina University at Chapel Hill; he acquired distinction, and is now and has been since his graduation principal of the High School in Durham, N. C. William D. Carmichael was a Captain in the late war, and was badly wounded in the jaw and tongue, which affects his speech; he was a gallant soldier, and is a progressive and successful farmer in upper Marion; he has other children grown, unknown to the writer. John R. Carmichael, brother of Captain W. D., married a Miss Meekins, daughter of E. J. Meekins, of the Harlleesville section, and had three children, one daughter and two sons. The daughter, Johny, married Samuel Galloway, a farmer, and has some family, how many is unknown; Coy Carmichael, a young man and unmarried, and Alexander, who is married, and now lives in Atlanta, Ga. Their father died when his children were quite young. Archie Carmichael married a Miss Harrelson, and had John, Monroe, Albert J., William and Joel, and girls, Mary, Nancy, Civil, Lou, Hettie, Lilly Mack and Ellen—the latter married Albert Rogers; she is dead, left no offspring. John married some one unknown, also Monroe. Joel married Hattie McLellan, daughter of Timothy R. McLellan, and has a family, Mary married a Carmichael, and has some family. Lou married Jefferson McIntyre. Albert J., William, Nancy, Lilly Mack, Civil and Hettie, are all unmarried. Captain Neill M. Carmichael, another of the six sons of old Duncan, married Miss Catharine Carmichael, a sister of Sheriff Archie, and raised a family of eight sons and three daughters. The eldest daughter married John C. McIntyre, mentioned elsewhere herein; their son, David, married Catharine Carmichael, daughter of Malcolm Carmichael, and have no children. Calvin C., son of Captain Neill M., married Margaret C. Buie, and they have no children. Duncan D. married Julia M. Wright, of Marlborough County; they have five children. None of the rest of Captain Neill M.'s children ever married. Daniel M., one of the younger sons, and his two maiden sisters, Mary and Margaret, live on and own the homestead where Captain Neill M. lived and died.

Daniel M. is a prosperous farmer and merchant, and a large and successful tobacco grower. Gilbert, the youngest son, was a partner of Daniel M. in their various business enterprises, and was a man of fine judgment; he was County Commissioner for one term, just previous to his death, in 1894. Another son, Alexander, died in 1877. All of them were gallant soldiers in the Confederate war, except Gilbert, who was too young to go. The eldest, Franklin, and the youngest (except Gilbert), Evander, were killed at the same time by a shell at Petersburg, Va., in 1864.

An instance of the devotion and patriotism of our Southern women will not be out of place here. About the last year of the war, an agent of the government was through the country buying up corn, meat, &c., for the soldiers. Captain Neill M. sold him, for Confederate money, as much as he had to spare; and at dinner the agent asked Mrs. Carmichael if she had any sons in the army, and she promptly answered, "Yes, seven of them—all but that little fellow there," pointing to Gilbert, "and I wish he was old enough, I would have him there, too." Instances of like kind were not uncommon among Southern matrons.

Another Duncan Carmichael came from Scotland, and settled in upper Marion; he married a Miss Carmichael, and had three sons and three daughters; the sons were Dougald B., Neill C. and Daniel; the daughters were Mary (Polly), Christian and Nancy. Dougald B. married Flora McLellan, and raised a considerable family, who have already been mentioned in or among the McLellan family. Neill C. married the widow of Edward Campbell, whose maiden name was Martha Jane McCollum, who had three sons, Dougald, Chalmers and Lanier B. Carmichael. The latter was a fine looking man and full of promise, but died unmarried, two or three years ago, after a short illness. The two former, Dougald and Chalmers, went West, and, I suppose, are married. They had four daughters. Catharine married Richard McColl; they have a family. Matilda married William McCollum, and Ida became the wife of William McQueen, in North Carolina. Viola, the youngest, is single. Neill C. Carmichael, called "Cut-face Neill," from severe cuts in his face made by some of the Millers, when a young man, in a fight with them, died many years ago; his widow, Martha Jane, being a thorough business woman, kept right on making money and raising and educating her children; she died within the last year; as already stated, she was the widow of Edward Campbell; by him she had one daughter, who became the wife of George J. Bethea, on Buck Swamp, and has already been noticed in or among the Betheas. The other brother, Daniel, died, a medical student in Charleston, unmarried. The daughters of old Duncan were, as stated above, Polly, who never married and lived to the age of ninety-three years; Christian was the first wife of George W. Reaves, as stated already in or among the Reaves family. Nancy married Archibald Murphy, and had three sons—John, who married in North Carolina; Duncan Murphy was killed in the war, and was a Lieutenant in Captain J. H. Stafford's company; the third son was Dr. N. C. Murphy, who married a Miss Reaves, and who died in Marion, in autumn of 1886, and left three sons and two daughters—all of whom have already been noticed in or among the Reaves or Watson family. Dougald Carmichael came from Scotland, and settled in Marion County, on north side of Little Pee Dee; don't know to whom he married, but he had sons: Major Daniel, Squire Neill, Michael, Malcolm and Archie. Daniel married Agnes Campbell, had one son, John C., and five daughters. John C. is unmarried. Squire Neill married a Miss McColl, and settled on south side of Little Pee Dee, near Carmichael's Bridge; they had and raised a considerable family, three sons, Daniel W., Dougald and Neill, also three or four daughters. Daniel W. married a Miss Edwards, daughter of Samuel W. Edwards, on Buck Swamp, settled in the "Fork," and is still there; they had Luther, Oliver, Gilbert, Samuel, Maston Neill and Baker Carmichael, and daughters. Anne married Edward D. Carmichael; Martha married Austin Edwards; Jennie married a Sinclair; Rebecca married an Edwards; Susan married Asbury Jackson; Fannie married a Rogers. Luther Carmichael married a Miss Martin; Gilbert married, also, a Miss Martin; Oliver married a Miss Carmichael; Samuel married Miss Harrelson; Maston and Baker married sisters, names unknown; Neill went West, married and had four children; his wife is dead. Don't know what became of Dougald and Neill, younger sons of Squire Neill. Squire Neill was a Magistrate in his day, also a surveyor, and was a useful man. Michael Carmichael married and settled on north side of Little Pee Dee, opposite Carmichael's Bridge; don't know to whom he married; he had a family, not, however, known to the writer. Malcolm, another brother, married and settled on Bell Swamp, on north side of the river, but know nothing of his family; and the same of his brother, Archie.

Another family of Carmichaels, on Buck Swamp and Maiden Down, is also to be noticed among this large connection—whether related to those above mentioned, is not certainly known, but suppose they are, and had a common ancestor in Scotland, whence they came. I allude to old Squire Dougald, a prosperous and capital man in the section named. Squire Dougald Carmichael married Martha Carmichael, and had four sons, James, Alexander, Angus and Daniel, and five daughters, Flora, Margaret, Nancy, Mary and Sarah. Angus married Miss Pencie Lewis; died and left his widow and one child, a daughter, who grew up and married John W. Norton; she had one child, a daughter, named Iva; when she was six or eight years old, was caught on the band wheel of a gin and killed. Alexander Carmichael married a Miss Geve, in North Carolina, and by her had six children, three boys and three girls; the boys were Albert, John and Solon; the girls were Susan, Nettie and Augusta. Albert never married; he is in Florence. John died when young, unmarried. Solon is in Horry County. Susan married Calvin Morgan, and resides in Florence. Nettie and Augusta died unmarried. Daniel Carmichael married a Miss Williamson, and had a number of children, and among them was William D. and Gilbert Carmichael, of the Ariel section. William D. married a Miss McInnis, of upper Marion, and has a family. Gilbert married a Miss White, and also has a family. James Carmichael married the Widow Woodward, *nee* Jordan, and died, leaving one child, our rising B. M. Carmichael, who married, first, Miss Murray, daughter of Rev. John W. Murray; she had one child, mother and child both died; and he married a second time, Miss Maggie Williams, and has a family coming up. Polly Carmichael never married. Flora married W. L. Lewis, who has already been mentioned among the Lewis family. Margaret married David W. Edwards, and has three children, E. C. Edwards, late County School Superintendent, and Melvin Edwards—both of whom are married, have families and doing well; Mrs. Edwards is dead; her daughter married one of the Rogers, in that region, and they are prospering and have a family. Sarah Carmichael married Daniel Lewis, of Horry, ex-Sheriff, an excellent man and first class citizen.

BAKER.—This old and respectable family had its origin, so far as Marion County is concerned, as stated by Bishop Gregg (p. 75): "Soon after (1735), a family of Bakers came from Newbern, N. C., to Pee Dee. One of this name married a daughter of Nathan Evans. William Baker was prominent in the Revolution, and marked for his devotion to the cause of liberty." From the above extract, it seems they came here as a family—the head of it not being named. One of the name married a daughter of Nathan Evans. Whether it was William, that became "prominent in the Revolution" or another, does not appear; but from tradition we glean the fact that the grand-father of Long Billy Baker and the late William J. Baker, was named William, and, I suppose, he is the "prominent" William spoken of by Bishop Gregg; and if he is not, the one that "married a daughter of Nathan Evans," it is not known to whom he did marry, nor do we know how many children he had, except two sons, William and John. Tradition informs us that William Baker was the great-grand-father of Mrs. Wm. J. Davis, B. F. Davis and J. Preston Davis—but whether he was William Baker, Sr., or William Baker, Jr., does not appear. We are further informed by tradition that the grand-father (maternal) of Mrs. W. J. Davis was Joshua Avant, who married Miss Catharine Baker. William and John Baker are the proximate progenitors of the family, as now known. This William Baker married the Widow Hugh Giles, whose maiden name was Annis Philips; by this marriage there were two sons, James Baker and William J. Baker—the latter was called "Fat Billy;" he never married.

I will relate an incident that occurred a few years before the death of "Fat Billy," in the Court. On Monday morning of the Court, there were several jurymen excused or wanting to be excused from serving on the jury during that term—some on account of the recent confinement of their wives, and some on account of the daily expectation of confinement. Of these applications there were an unusual number—so much so that it attracted the attention of Mr. Baker, who had been drawn and summoned to attend as a juryman for that term, and was sitting in the jury seats near by the writer. Mr. Baker beckoned to me to go to him; I went, and he said to me he never heard so many applications to be excused from service on account of the expected confinement of their wives; and added, "he wanted to be excused himself, and thought he might be;" and looking down upon his front, said, "from appearances, it looked like he might be confined himself before the week ended, and he did not want to be in Court, when that event happened." He was a capital man and a first class citizen.

James Baker, the elder brother, married a Miss Taylor, the half-sister of Major David J. Taylor; by their marriage three sons, William W., Joseph A. and James M., were born and raised, and two daughters. Of the two daughters, one married Robert Monroe; they have no offspring. The other daughter married Benjamin Baker, and they have five children. Of the sons, William W. married, first, Miss Martha Tennent, and by her had seven children (two of them are dead); there are now three sons and two daughters; the sons are James Oscar, John Tennent and Warren Caldwell. The two oldest have gone West; the youngest, Warren Caldwell, grown but unmarried, remains with his father. The two daughters, Mary and Lillian, unmarried. William W. married, a second time (his first wife dying), the Widow China, her maiden name was Gordon, and by the second marriage they have one son, named David Gordon. Joseph A. Baker, the second son of James Baker, married, first, Mary J. Graham, daughter of James Graham; they had two sons, James G. and Joseph Mary. James G. Baker married Anne Monroe, daughter of Dr. F. M. Monroe; they have four children, daughters, all small. Joseph Mary married Anne Gaddy, daughter of the late James M. Gaddy; they have three children, two sons and a daughter. The first wife dying, Joseph A. Baker married a second wife, Anna M.

Graham, and have two children—one a son, Marion Taylor Baker, who married a Miss Wrightson, of Spartanburg, and a daughter, Mary R. Baker, unmarried—she is a physician, and located at Rock Hill, S. C. James R. Baker, the third son of James Baker, Sr., married Miss Mary Monroe, a daughter of Major David Monroe; they had six children, all boys—one is dead, five now living; the mother is dead, and the father has not remarried; he lives in Marion. These three sons of James Baker, Sr., are all progressive farmers, doing well, and among them own a large landed property, and are first class citizens. William Baker, as hereinbefore stated, married the Widow Giles, whose maiden name was Annis Philips; to this marriage were born a daughter, Mary, who married Gospero Sweet—they removed West; and another daughter, Eliza, who married Nathan Evans; another daughter, Susan, who married Alexander Owens; another daughter, Jennette, who died quite young; and another, Mattie, who married T. F. Brown, and the two sons above mentioned, James and William J. The father, William Baker, died when his children were quite young; Mrs. Annis Baker lived to a very old age, and was a very remarkable woman; the death of her husband did not seem to affect her success in life and business in the least—she was an excellent manager of affairs and of money, raised her children quite respectably, and continued to accumulate property and amassed a large fortune, which she distributed herself during her life. John Baker, brother of William, above mentioned, married Katie Evans, and by their marriage two children were born and raised, William B. and Polly. William B. married Addie Lenora Davis, a sister of Wm. J. Davis; Polly married Hugh Giles. To William B. Baker, called "Long Billy," and wife, Addie Lenora, were born nine children, they raised eight; their names were Mary Elizabeth, James D., W. B., Jr., J. E., Benjamin B., Susana C., Rebecca and Thomas D. The eldest daughter married John J. Williamson; they had two children, William L. and John J.; the father, John J. Williamson, died, and left these two children. James D. never married. William B., Jr., married Lou Legette, daughter of Captain David Legette; they had nine children, raised six, named Gertrude, Hannibal, Mattie, Carry, Pauline and Boyd. John E. Baker married

Elwood Davis, daughter of Dr. W. M. Davis; they had six children, named Brockinton, John, Mary, Lenora, Neill and Herbert. Benjamin B. Baker married Jennette Baker, daughter of James and Rebecca Baker; they had six children, raised five, named Robert, Alex. T., Leola, Rebecca and Benjamin B., Jr. Miss Susan Baker never married. Rebecca Baker married F. M. Wall; they had seven children, raised four, named Estelle, Beaty, Nevada and Willoughby. Thomas D. Baker married Mattie Snipes, daughter of Wilson Snipes; they had seven children, named Adger, Eloise, Lizzie, Imo, Mattie, Cary Lenora and Thomas Wilson. William B. Baker, Sr., was a most excellent man, always cheerful and pleasant, kind-hearted and obliging, took the world easy, made the best of all circumstances in life—and did not fret as to that which he could not control; honest, straight and liberal to a fault. Peace be to his ashes—his many virtues are a rich heritage to his posterity.

DAVIS.—The name Davis is very common, and is met up with in almost every section of the country. In Marion County, it is very numerous in name and in its connections. The first appearance of it here was about 1735, in Britton's Neck, where a colony from England came and settled about Old Neck (now) Methodist Church. This was four years before John Wesley made the move in England, as the basis of the Methodist Church in the present day, both in Europe and America. One of that colony was a Davis—what the given name was, is unknown. Bishop Gregg, in his history (page 69), says: "One of these (settlements) was in Britton's Neck, twenty miles below Moss Bluff and forty miles above Georgetown. It was composed of the families of Britton, Graves, Fladger, Davis, Tyler, Giles and others. They came directly from England, as one colony, and being members of the Established Church, one of their first acts was to erect a house for the worship of God. Their minister, Dr. Robert Hunter, came with them, and is supposed to have died there. He was succeeded by the Rev. Mr. Allison." In a note to the above extract, the Bishop further says: "This building was of black cypress, with a brick foundation, and is still to be seen (1859), or was a few years since, in a good state of preservation, on the road leading from

Port's Ferry to Potatoe Ferry, on Little Pee Dee. About the year 1780, the congregation having been long without a minister, and doubtless much broken up by the troublous times of the Revolution, united with the Methodists, and the building passed into the hands of the latter, by whom it has since been retained. Charles Wesley is said to have once preached in it."
In the extract above, the name Davis appears, and it is to be presumed that he is the progenitor of the Davis family now below Marion, or a great part of that extensive family. The writer has made every effort possible to trace the family from him down to the present generation, but has not been able to do so; but will present such facts as he has been able to find and obtain. First from William J. Davis and wife, Susan B. Davis—the latter was a Miss Davis before her marriage, no relation to her husband (if any, it is very remote). William J. Davis' grand-parents (maternal) were Baker and Evans; his paternal grand-parents were Harry Davis and McCants. His father was named John Davis, called "Jacky Davis;" married Miss Susannah Baker; he had four children, two sons, Eli or Elihu and William J., and two daughters, Laura or Louisa, who married William B. Baker, and Susan, married John B. Sheckelford. William J. Davis married Susan Brownfield Davis. Nothing is said of Elihu Davis, brother of William J. Davis. Mrs. William J. Davis' grand-father was Joseph Davis, who married Anne Keene, and had eleven children, viz: Daniel, Benjamin S., William, Joseph and A. G. Davis, sons; the daughters were Maria, Mary, Eliza, Christianna, Susan and Rachel. Daniel died, leaving no child living. Benjamin S. Davis, the father of Mrs. W. J. Davis, married Miss Julia Avant; they had six children—three sons, Keene, B. F. and J. Preston Davis; the two latter are now leading and prominent citizens of Marion; and three daughters—Catharine, Susan Brownfield and Julia F. Avant Davis. Of these sons, Keene Davis died unmarried, when quite a young man. B. F. Davis married, first, Miss Ella Jenkins, the only daughter and child of the late James Jenkins, and they had: sons, James, C. L., Fontaine, Benjamin F. (dead), Claudius (dead), Robert L. and Marvin Warren; and daughters, Lizzie, Sallie, Mary, Emma (dead) and Julia. James C., the eldest son of B. F.

Davis, married a Miss Oliver, daughter of A. R. Oliver, and has a coming family. L. Fontaine Davis, the second son, married a Miss Stevenson, daughter of the late James N. Stevenson, and has four children, three girls and a boy. Robert L. married Kate McIntyre, daughter of Captain G. A. McIntyre, and has one son. Marvin Warren married a Miss Hodges, of Abbeville. Lizzie is unmarried. Sallie married Jessee G. Holliday, lives in Marion, and have a coming family.* One daughter, Mary, married William Stackhouse, of Dillon; they have three children, two daughters and one son. Emma, a promising young lady, died a year or two ago; Julia, the youngest daughter, is unmarried. B. F. Davis is a prosperous man, an excellent citizen; has represented his county in the lower House of the General Assembly, and has the confidence of all who know him. B. F. Davis' first wife dying, he married, a second time, Miss Corinna McCormic, of upper Marion, and by her has one son, a lad, named Henry Grady. J. Preston Davis resides and merchandises at Marion, with his son, Cantey, and they are doing a fair business; he also has a farm below Marion; married a Miss Cantey, of Clarendon or Kershaw County, and has three sons, Cantey, Joseph and Keene. Of these, Cantey married a Miss Oliver, of Clarendon County, and has three children, two girls and a boy. Joseph Davis married a Miss Hodges, of Abbeville, and has three children, two boys and one girl. Miss Cora, the eldest daughter, is unmarried; the son, Keene, is also unmarried. Mary married Harold Brunson, of Florence. Mineola married Dr. Thomas P. Baily, of Georgetown, now professor in the University of Chicago; they have two boys. Eva married Albert Guery, and has one daughter. J. Preston Davis has the confidence of his fellow-citizens; he was elected some years ago County Treasurer for the county, and served acceptably one or two terms; was also elected a Representative of the county in the State Legislature, and was faithful to the trust reposed in him by his people. Abram, or A. G. Davis, brother of Benjamin, married (name not known), and had three sons, A. G., Dr. William M. and Joseph Davis. Don't know who A. G. Davis, Jr., married; he moved to North Carolina, some years ago. Dr. William M. Davis

---

*Sallie, J. G. Holliday's wife, recently died.

married a Miss Belin, of West Marion, now Florence, and lives in Florence County. Before the formation of Florence County, Dr. Wm. M. Davis represented Marion County one term in the State Legislature; he has a family; Joseph Davis married Miss Ervinia Richardson, oldest daughter of the late William F. Richardson, and by her had two children, a son, William G. Davis,* and a daughter, Addie Davis; when the father died, his widow married Rev. J. B. Campbell, of the South Carolina Conference, and of whom more will be said later on. Joseph Davis, the grand-father of Mrs. Wm. J. Davis, B. F. Davis and others, it seems, had two other sons, William and Joseph, but as to them and their posterity, if any, the writer has no further information. The grand-father, Joseph, had, also, daughters: Martha, who married Tristram Thomas, of Marlborough; Mary also married James Thomas, of Marlborough (had no children); Susan married James Lyles, of North Carolina; Anna Maria married Hugh Fladger; Eliza married Joseph or James Johnson, the father of the late Dr. William R. Johnson; and Rachel married James Newson (had no children). Benjamin S. Davis, the father of Mrs. W. J. Davis, B. F. Davis and others, had three daughters: Catharine Davis, who married, first, John Collins, and he died and the widow married Hugh James Floyd, of Horry; Mrs. William J. Davis and Julia F. Miss Julia F. is unmarried, and from her (Julia F.) the writer has had much of the above account of her family. Harry Davis, the grand-father of Wm. J. Davis, it seems, had three sons—maybe four; they were James, Jackey, Harry and David Davis. Of Jackey's posterity and old Joseph's we have already spoken; now I will notice that of James, brother of Jackey; he married some one unknown, and had a son, named Theodore Gourdin Davis, who married and lived on the Godfrey's Ferry Road in Britton's Neck. The sons of Theodore Gourdin Davis were Edward William, Theodore G. and Nicholas Calvin. Edward William Davis lives in Florence County, and is quite a respectable citizen. Harry Davis, Jr., married and had sons, Dr. Oliver, Jackson, James C. and Ervin Davis (don't know that these are stated in the order of their ages).

---

*William G. Davis died in 1900, leaving his widow and three or four children.

Jackson Davis married and had three sons, viz: Foster, Stephen and Abraham Davis. James Davis emigrated to Georgia. Ervin never married (dead). Oliver Davis married Eugenia Richardson, and had six children—three sons, Orion, Shep. U. and Richelieu, and three daughters, May, Sarah and Lorine. Of the daughters, May and Sarah died unmarried; Lorine married James Porter, of Georgetown. Of the sons, Orion and Richelieu went to Georgia. Shep. U. Davis married, first, Miss Maggie McWhite, and by this marriage four children were born—one son, Alva, and three girls (all small); the wife died, and he married, a second time, Miss Mamie Smith, of North Carolina. S. U. Davis is no ordinary man; only a few years ago he commenced life with nothing comparatively, but by diligence and strict attention to business and good management, he has accumulated a comfortable living; yet comparatively young, he may by continued good management acquire large wealth; he is a man of high moral character; in 1898, he was elected as a Representative of the county in the lower House of the General Assembly, and declined re-election in 1900; a worthy, exemplary, good citizen and Christian gentleman.

Another branch of this large and numerous family remains to be noticed—that of David Davis. He was one of the old Davis', a brother of Harry, Sr., or Harry, Jr., Jackey and James. David Davis had two sons, and may be others; the sons were Frank and Henry. Frank married, first, Miss Argent Gerald, and by her had Marion Davis and Sarah Ann. Marion Davis married some lady to the writer unknown; he died, and left several children, none of them known, except Mrs. Sturgis, now residing in Florence; she first married a Mr. Timmons, who died and left her a widow, with one or two children—one I know, Miss Annie Timmons; the widow married the late Morgan W. Sturgis, and he died, leaving his widow and one or two children; Mrs. Sturgis and daughter, Annie, are running the American Hotel, in Florence, which I understand they have bought and paid for, and are doing well in their hotel business. Sarah Ann, the daughter of Frank Davis, married, in July, 1847, John C. Bethea, Sr.; they had one son, John C., Jr.; his father died when John C., Jr., was about two years old, leaving him a good property; the mother never again married; she died, 9th April, 1893, at the age of seventy-five years; she was a remarkable woman in many respects, of fine sense, and managed the large property left to her and her son with much success; her son, John C., Jr., married, and has a family of seven children, resides at Dillon, and has already been noticed in or among the Betheas. Frank Davis married, a second time, the Widow Brown, the mother of the late T. F. Brown, whose maiden name was Julia Davis; by her, it seems, there were no children; his Brown wife dying, he married, a third wife, who was a Miss Port, and by her he had one son, Joseph P. Davis, who never married, though he lived to middle life or past it, and died at Port's Ferry, on the Great Pee Dee—which took its name from the Port family. Henry Davis, the other son of David Davis, and brother of Frank, married twice; don't know who his first wife was; she was killed in the blowing up of the steamer Richland, Captain Brock, in or about 1848, she had no child or offspring; Henry Davis married, a second time, a Miss Bostick, of West Marion, now in Florence County; by the Bostick wife, he had six sons. The eldest, John C. Davis, married a daughter of William J. Davis; he died some year or two ago, his widow surviving, with five children, daughters. Henry, the next son, married a Miss Sistrunk; they have no children. The next son, David, married a Miss Harrel; he is dead, leaving his widow and two children. Preston, the next son, married a Miss Harnagor, and has five or six children. Wardlaw, the next son, married a daughter of William J. Davis; they have three children; the youngest son, Joseph, is unmarried, is a physician and is in Georgia or Florida. Henry Davis, Sr., the father, is also dead, and I think his widow is dead, too.

Henry Davis was elected as a Whig to the Legislature, in 1840. The political contest that year, between the Democrats and Whigs, was very heated and bitter, not only in Marion District, but throughout the entire country. It was the Van Buren and Harrison campaign, and may be designated as "the coon-skin, log cabin and hard cider" campaign. The Whig party was successful, and Wm. Henry Harrison was triumphantly elected President of the United States. The contest was very exciting in Marion District—each party had its candidates. The Democratic candidates were, for the Senate, Addison L. Scarborough, and for the House, John C. Bethea, Hugh Godbold and William T. Wilson. The Whig candidates were, for the House, David Palmer, Henry Davis and Dr. Daniel Gilchrist; and for the Senate, Benjamin Gause. The result was Gause was elected Senator by eighteen votes; David Palmer, Henry Davis and John C. Bethea were elected as members of the House. Of the six candidates for the House, there were not fifty votes between the highest and the lowest vote. John C. Bethea was the only Democrat elected. In 1842, Henry Davis, Joseph Jolly and another were elected without opposition. The "coon-skin, log cabin and hard cider" fever had abated. President Harrison died in a month after his inauguration, and John Tyler was President, and he very much dampened the ardor of the Whig party.

Daniel Davis, a brother of Jacky Davis, was the father of Randall, William, George and James Davis. George Davis had sons, Hugh, John R., Benjamin and James. William Davis had two sons, John and Wiliam. Randall Davis married, first, a Miss Avant, and by her had two children, Henry and Sarah; the Avant wife dying, he married a Miss Lucas, and by her had several children. His son, Henry, married a Miss Wiggins, first, and by her had five children; his second wife was a Miss Lucas, and by her has one child, a daughter. Sarah, the sister of Henry, married Ira Avant, and has two children, boys (small); think she and her husband have separated. Hugh Davis married Miss Annie White, daughter of the late Wesley White; Hugh is dead; he left four children, Hugh G., Julius and David, three sons, and one daughter, named Orilla. John R. Davis married a Miss Shaw; he died, and left several children, names unknown. William Davis married, and had two sons, John and William. Know nothing of James Davis, brother of Randall, nor of the sons of William Davis—have heard they were killed or died in the war; these all live or did live in Wahee Township. The Davis name and family are very numerous and extensive in its connections, and have ever been prominent and respectable.

Recurring again to the family of William J. Davis: He had

and raised nine children; six of them are married and three single. Ella married Wm. G. Davis; he died last year, 1900, and left three or four children; they are at Marion. Richard F. married Miss Mary Louise Godbold, daughter of Dr. Wm. H. Godbold; they have two sons (small). Ida May Davis married John C. Davis (dead), as above stated. William Preston Davis married Miss Cornelia Raysor, daughter of Rev. Dr. Raysor. Viola Davis married B. F. W. Davis, now living at Waycross, Ga. C. Keene Davis married Laura Brockinton, daughter of the late Dr. John Brockinton, of Kingstree. The three single children are George Pierce, Jennie and Gary Davis.

STANLEY.—Captain M. B. Stanley and his brother, Thomas E. Stanley, are importations from Darlington County. Captain M. B. Stanley was a volunteer in the Mexican War as a private soldier, was in many of the battles and came out unscathed. After the Mexican War, he came to Marion County, where he has since lived; he married Mary Jane Godbold, daughter of the late Asa Godbold, Sr., and settled where he now lives, below Marion, on the Big Reedy Creek, east of Legette's Mill. At the breaking out of the late war between the States, he was elected Captain of the first company from Marion County, composed of its best men, and left for Charleston harbor 4th January, 1861, and his company was mustered into the 1st South Carolina Regiment (Maxcy Gregg, Colonel), and was stationed on Morris Island, and participated in the first battle of the war, which eventuated in the capture and surrender of Fort Sumter, in Charleston harbor, commanded by Major Anderson, on 12th and 13th of April, 1861. This act marked the beginning of the four years' war which followed—the bloodiest war on record. Soon after that action, owing to the terms of enlistment of the company, it was reorganized for service in Virginia or for the Confederacy, and a revolunteering for the war. The greater part of the company revolunteered and formed a new company, and the distinguished Wm. P. Shooter was elected its Captain. The new company went to Virginia, and saw hard service during the remainder of the war. Captain M. B. Stanley did not enter the new company, but was an active partisan in other branches of the service throughout the bloody struggle. As before stated, he had married and settled; he had and raised a family of three children—two sons, Elbert B. and William Edward, one daughter, named Charlotte. The eldest son, Elbert, married, first, a Miss Nesbit, by whom he had five children (small); the Nesbit wife dying, he married Miss Melvina Gregg, daughter of the late O. S. Gregg, of West Marion, by whom he has one child. William Edward married the only daughter of Robert Godbold, and has two children, both girls (small). Charlotte, the only daughter of Captain M. B. Stanley, married J. J. Richardson; they have five children (small). Captain Thomas E. Stanley, the younger brother of Captain M. B. Stanley, came into the county just before the war, as a clerk for C. Graham; he volunteered in the first company from Marion, and continued in the service till the close of the war; was a gallant soldier, a very genial and good citizen; he married, after the war, a Miss Brown, daughter of the late T. F. Brown, and settled on Tyrrel's Bay, on his wife's patrimony, and has an excellent farm; they have had and raised two sons and four daughters, names unknown; two of the daughters are married—one to James Godbold, and the other to a Mr. Owens; the other two daughters are single—said to be smart. Captain T. E. Stanley is a very intelligent man, harmless, honest and a good, patriotic citizen.

HARRELS IN BRITTON'S NECK.—Samuel Harrel is eighty-two years of age; his father was Levi Harrel, from North Carolina; came here in 1806; married Elizabeth Jones; his grand-father was Ephraim Harrel, who married an Indian woman, on Roanoke River, in North Carolina, and moved to Fort Clairborne, Ala., and died there. Samuel Harrel first married Anna Isgat; they had four children, all dead, but one daughter, named Frances Maurice, who is the wife of James G. Altman. Samuel Harrel's second wife was a Miss Fountain; by her he had one son, George W. Harrel, who lives in Florence County.

ALTMAN.—James D. Altman is a son of Thomas Altman, who married Elizabeth Dozier; had three sons and two daughters; the sons were William, John and James D. Altman.

William and John both died in the war; one of disease, the other from wounds received—he died at home. James D. Altman was also in the war, in Captain Crawford's company. Thomas Altman had three brothers, Stephen, William and Jack. Stephen Altman lived on "Big Sister" Bay, five miles east of Marion; was a quiet and inoffensive citizen; he married a daughter of Rev. Moses Coleman, and raised some family, don't know how many—one son, Preston, and one daughter, and perhaps other children. Of old William and Jack Altman and their families, the writer knows nothing. James D. married a daughter of Samuel Harrel; they have twelve children, all daughters, but three; one daughter dead; they have twenty-one grand-children; five daughters married—one to John West; one to Alexander McKethan, in North Carolina; one to Alva Todd, in Horry; one to John W. Davis; and one to Benjamin James, in Williamsburg. The oldest son of James D. Altman, Benjamin E., married a Miss Foxworth; the other two sons not married.

WHALEY.—John H. Whaley married Susan Carter; they had ten children, six sons and four daughters. Two of the sons were lost by the casualties of war. F. D. Whaley dead; left wife and one child. Three of John H. Whaley's sons are now living, to wit: H. J., D. B. and W. Manly. H. J. Whaley married twice; first wife was Miss M. F. Altman, who had nine children; his second wife was Miss Ella Guyton, children none; he has three daughters married—one married Rev. J. D. Harrelson; one married W. H. Thompson, and the other married Rev. H. D. Jones. D. B. Whaley married Miss Ida Davis; they have seven children, five girls and two boys, names unknown. W. Manly Whaley married Miss Frances Regan, daughter of the late Charley F. Regan; they have three children (small).

RICHARDSON.—This large family in name and its connections, so far as Marion County is concerned, had its origin in the names of William Richardson and John Richardson, who came from Roanoke, Va., just after the Revolutionary War; they were brothers—William was much older than John. William was old enough to go into the war, and, as tradition informs, served throughout the war four years in place of his father and three years for himself. John was too young to go into the war. The two brothers, soon after the war, came to South Carolina, married and settled in Marion County, and from these two sprang the large family and its connections now existing and remaining in the county—many having emigrated to other parts. Old William married (don't know who), and had sons, Hardy, John, Hopkins and William, and two daughters, Polly and Alice; he married, a second time, Nancy Roberts, and by her had sons, Richard, Jackson, Thomas and Henry, and three daughters, Martha, Nancy and Betsey. John M. Richardson, now living, eighty-four years of age (and my informant was the son of William, Jr., who was the youngest son of William, Sr., by his first marriage). Hardy, the oldest son of William, Sr., married a Miss Davis, and went West. John, the second son, married Sallie Johnson, and by her he had Benjamin, John, Washington, James and Ebby, and daughters, Betsy, Sarah Ann and Catharine. Benjamin married a Miss Gasque, and had Graves, James, Preston and Sydney Richardson. Graves married, first, a Miss Altman, then a Miss Dill, and then a Miss Smith. James married a Miss Britton, and has a family, how many is not known. John died young. Washington married in Georgetown, and lived and died there. James never married, and died in the war. Ebby married a Miss Atkinson, and had two children; he died in the war. Henry married a Miss Davis, and moved to Mississippi. Hopkins and Richard never married. William Richardson, Jr., married Leasy Martin, a sister of old "Cuff Mose" Martin (well known in his day). "Cuff Mose" Martin was quite a character. It was said of him that he never wore any shoes or hat, but wore a cloth cap, which his wife spun, wove and made for him. This was his garb when the writer saw him last, in 1860; he lived then on the west side of Little Pee Dee, near the river swamp, on the Galivant's Ferry road. The writer, with several others, were on our way to the Horry Court, and passing Mr. Martin's house, close to the road, the old man was out in his yard. We stopped, and the old gentleman came to his bars at the road, and we had some talk with him, principally about his bees and bee-gums. There was a line of bee-gums on each side of the path from his bars to the edge of his yard—forming a little lane or street from the bars to his house; he said there were a hundred gums there, and said that he had a hundred other gums back of his house (a little cabin), on the side of the river swamp. Those bees and bee-gums were his chief crop; he saved his honey and sold it. I suppose the old gentleman, in his apparent poverty, was a happier man than any of our crowd. He was then (1860) an old man and died some years afterward, at the age of ninety-one years. He was a true man, and as independent in his action and modes of life as King Edward VII. of England. I could relate other incidents in his life, illustrative of his unique character, but want of space will not permit. They had two children, sons, John M. and William. The Martin wife died, and William, Jr., as distinguished from the first old William, married a second wife, a Miss Richardson; by her he had sons, Matthew, Hopkins, James, Ervin, Arna and Hampton; he then married Miss Chinnis, and by her had two children, one boy and one girl. The boy, Edward, died. John M. Richardson married Polly Drew, and had three boys, William, Hamilton and Peter; the Drew wife died, and then he married Caroline Cribb, and by her had three sons, Lee, Hampton and English. William, son of John M., died in the war. Hamilton married a Miss Deck, and moved to Horry. Peter married Milly Richardson, daughter of Ervin Richardson, and by her had Walter, Eddy, Byrd, Coy and twin brothers, Troy and Corde. Lee died, four years ago, unmarried. Hampton married a Miss Richardson, and has two sons (small). English married Miss Alice Cribb; has no children. Matthew married Miss Sallie Johnson, and had one son, Marion, who died in the war. William married his cousin, daughter of John M. Richardson; he has Jessee, Ervin and Franklin, and Ann Eliza, Susannah Lee, Eugenia and Lena. Hopkins, when a young single man, was thrown by a horse and killed. James, brother of Matthew, married Miss Rebecca Cribb, and had sons, William, Avery, Arny and others, names unknown. Ervin Richardson married Ann Pace, and by her had Cornelius, Henry, Preston and Allen; first wife dying, he married, a second wife, Miss Boatwright, and by her had a son, Boyd—no daughters. Avery married a Miss Pace, and by her had John Calhoun, Robert, Sydney, Bradley and Sumter. John Calhoun married a Miss Foxworth, and has children. Robert Richardson married Miss Alice Sanders, and has two children (small). Sydney married Miss Nannie Carter; they have no children. Bradley married Miss Patsy Baxley; they have two children (small). Sumter is grown and unmarried. Hampton Richardson married, first, a Miss Atkinson, and has some children (unknown); his second wife was a Miss Godbold, daughter of Vincent Godbold; had two children, one named Cicero; his third wife was Victoria Smith, and they have several children (names and number unknown); the third wife dying, he married, a fourth one, Nancy Richardson; they have no children. John Richardson, the younger brother of old William, called "King John," married a Miss Fladger, the sister of old Hugh Fladger, and sister of General Thomas Godbold's wife; they had and raised four sons, Valentine, James J., William F. and Andrew Jackson Richardson, and three daughters, Charlotte, Martha and another. Charlotte married Jessee Legette; Martha married David Legette, and the other married Nelson Legette. Valentine Richardson married a Miss White and moved to Georgia. James J. Richardson became a Methodist traveling preacher; he married in North Carolina. The South Carolina Conference then extended into North Carolina, and included Lincolnton, Fayetteville and Wilmington. He died in 1833—I think, at Lincolnton, N. C.—engaged in his ministerial duties. William F. Richardson, born in 1806, married Miss Elizabeth Palmer, a daughter of David Palmer, then a prominent man in his community and county; they had and raised daughters, Ervinia, Augusta Alice, Mary and Emma, and one son, James J. Richardson. Ervinia, the eldest, married, first, Joseph Davis, and by him she had two children, the late William G. Davis, and a daughter, Addie Davis; Joseph Davis died, and she afterwards married Rev. J. B. Campbell, of the South Carolina Conference, and by him she had two sons, Rev. J. A. Campbell and John S. The former is a traveling Methodist preacher, is married and has a growing family. James S. Campbell is unmarried, and is a druggist. Mrs. J. B. Campbell has five daughters, four of whom are married and one single. The second daughter of William F. Richardson, Augusta, married James Godbold, and settled on the old homestead of Wm. F. Richardson; they have five children—two sons, Wade and Warren, and three daughters (names forgotten); these sons and daughters are all grown and unmarried—they are smart and promising. Alice, the third daughter of W. F. Richardson, married John H. Hamer, of Harlleesville; she is dead; she had and left surviving her five children, to wit: Edward R., Mary C., Tristram, Ovianna and John H. Of these, Edward R. married Miss Julia Berry, daughter of James Berry, now lives at Dillon, and has five or six children (small). Mary C. married Neill Berry, and has three children (small). Orianna married Lawrence Manning; they have no children. Tristram, a doctor, is unmarried, and has emigrated to Texas. John H., Jr., is grown and unmarried—a dentist. Mary, the fourth daughter of W. F. Richardson, married John O. Willson, D. D., of the South Carolina Conference, and after having one child, Bessie, she died. Bessie grew up and married Captain Donaldson, of the United States army, a son of T. Q. Donaldson, of Greenville, S. C. Emma, the fifth and youngest daughter of W. F. Richardson, married Hon J. M. Johnson, now serving his thirteenth year as Solicitor of the Fourth Judicial Circuit of South Carolina, and who resides at Marion; they have seven children, Flora, John M., Jr., Palmer, Louise, Robert, Richardson and Alice; the four first named are grown and promising young people. J. J. Richardson, the only son of W. F. Richardson, married Miss Charlotte Stanley, who has already been noticed among the Stanleys; they have five children. Of the two old Richardson brothers, William and John (King John), the latter was the more prosperous, the former was the more prolific in his progeny. William F. Richardson, son of "King John," was a most excellent man, a solid, good citizen, of high character and remarkable for his fine sense. The writer knew him well; we served in *ante-bellum* days together on the Board of Commissioners of the Poor for the county, two or three terms; he died at the age of fifty-seven, in 1863, universally loved and respected. Much more might truthfully be said of him, and his many fine traits of character, but want of space forbids. Andrew Jackson Richardson, brother of William F., married a Miss Palmer, half-sister of William F.'s wife; he moved to Georgetown many years ago, and died in that old town. The writer saw his widow a few days ago.

STEVENSON.—The great-grand-father of J. Edwin Stevenson, Benjamin Stevenson, came from Virginit, and was a soldier in the Revolutionary War under General Greene. He settled in Horry County, on the Lake Swamp (don't know to whom he married); he had two children, a daughter and a son; the son was named Benjamin; the girl died. Benjamin, Jr., married three times—first, a Miss Booth, who was the mother of the late Samuel M. Stevenson; his second wife was a Miss Anderson; she had one son, William, and two daughters, Anne and Margaret. Anne married Daniel Oliver, and was the mother of A. R. and D. J. Oliver, and another son, named Samuel. Margaret not known. A. R. Oliver married a Miss Legette, and has already been noticed in or among the Legettes. Daniel J. Oliver married Miss Sallie Fuller, daughter of the late Wyatt Fuller, and has several children, a son, L. Wyatt Oliver, and another name unknown; they also have a daughter, Mary, who married Quincy Berry—the latter have no children. L. Wyatt Oliver married Miss Alice Jones; they have one or two children (small). Don't know what became of William Stevenson. Benjamin, Jr.'s, third wife was Martha McCracken, and by her he had two sons, James Norton and Benjamin Purefoy Stevenson. The latter, if living, in in Horry County. Samuel M. Stevenson, the son by the first wife, many years ago moved to Marion County, after marrying a Miss Sarvis, a sister of the late Cornelius Sarvis, of Horry; he lived and died where W. W. Baker now lives; had no child, was successful in life, was a very intelligent man, good citizen and, above all, an exemplary Christian gentleman. James N. Stevenson married, first, a Miss Hughes, of Horry; by her he had one child, a son, J. Edwin Stevenson; his wife died; he came to Marion and merchandised there till the war, with seeming success; he married, a second time, the Widow Gause, relict of the Hon. Benjamin Gause; her maiden name was

Susan Gregg, youngest daughter of the late R. J. Gregg, who was Tax Collector for Marion District for thirty years, and well known to every one in his day as an honest, straightforward, Christian gentleman and faithful official; the Widow Benjamin Gause had one child, a son, Benjamin, by her marriage with Gause, who now lives in Bennettsville. Benjamin Gause, Sr., was quite a prominent man in his day, well-to-do, and was twice elected to the State Senate, served with ability two terms, and was universally loved and respected by all who knew him. James N. Stevenson married his widow, and by her had and raised eight children, four sons and four daughters, to wit: Robert, Samuel, James N. and Charles W., and daughters, Mary, Anne, Mattie and Susan. Of these, Mary, Susan and Charley are married—Mary to L. Fontaine Davis, and has five children; Susan married Dixon Gregg, and has no child; Charles W. married a Miss Gray, and has one child; Robert, Samuel and James N. are unmarried; Anne and Mattie are also unmarried; they live on the Gause homestead. J. Edwin Stevenson, son by James N.'s first marriage, married, first, Miss Julia Brown, daughter of the late T. Foster Brown; by this marriage five children were born, and I think all raised, and perhaps all married, but one daughter—to whom is unknown, except one son, married a daughter of Captain G. A. McIntyre; the Brown wife dying, J. Edwin Stevenson married, a second time, Miss Mattie Godbold, oldest daughter of the late Dr. William H. Godbold; by her he had some four or five children, three of whom survive; the Godbold wife died, and he married Mary, daughter of Sheriff Lewis, of Horry, and has removed to that county, and is merchandising; is an energetic, progressive man, of good habits and of high character, as was his father, James Norton Stevenson.

CRAVEN.—Of this family the writer has not been able to learn anything prior to William H. Craven, our present fellow-citizen, in Britton's Neck. William H. Craven married a Miss Richardson, and has had ten children (one dead), as follows: Julius Edward (a deaf mute), Preston, Lane, Henry, Charles and Boyd, Gertrude, Lula and Claude. Julius married Anne Wall; Preston married a Miss Shelby; Gertrude married

George Broadhurst—she is a widow; the other six children are single, and remain with their parents. William H. Craven is an industrious, energetic and good citizen, quiet and inoffensive, lives by his farm, is upright in his dealings and a good neighbor.

THOMPSON.—John C. Thompson married a Miss Edwards, daughter of Rev. David S. Edwards, on Buck Swamp; he had three sons, Chapman, Jefferson and Howard. The two former are dead; the latter, Howard, married twice—have not been able to find out to whom, nor as to their children, if any. John C. Thompson is dead; he was prominent in his neighborhood and a useful, good citizen. Jesse Thompson, brother of John C., is an excellent man in the Gapway section; he married, first, Martha Williamson; no child by this marriage; he married, a second time, a Miss Carter, and they have no offspring. There were two other brothers, Stephen and William; they moved to Horry.

KIRTON.—William Kirton came from Ireland to this country before the Revolutionary War, and married a Miss Avant, and had two sons, John and William. John never married; William married a Widow Williams, *nee* Avant; they had two sons, Thomas and Philip, and one daughter, Elizabeth. Thomas Kirton married and went to Horry County. Philip married Miss Olivia Gasque, and had four sons, Thomas, Henry, Philip and Samuel, and three daughters, Elizabeth, Mary and Olivia. Thomas married a Miss Jones, and went to Horry, and was killed by Jeptha Jones, on the Great Pee Dee River. Henry Kirton married the Widow Sinoth, *nee* Hannah Philips; they had an only son, Thomas H. Kirton, our worthy fellow-citizen, now near Tyrrel's Bay, in lower Marion, and he married, first, a Widow McQueen, *nee* Gerald, who had two McQueen daughters—none by her marriage with Kirton; one of these McQueen daughters is married, but to whom is unknown; the other one still resides with Kirton; the McQueen wife having died, he married, a second time, Miss Catharine N. Floyd; they have no child. What became of Philip Kirton, brother of Henry, the writer knows not. The other brother,

Samuel, I think, married a Miss Gasque, sister of the late James C. Gasque, went to Georgetown and died there. Of the sisters of Henry Kirton, Elizabeth, Mary and Olivia, the writer has no information. Thomas H. Kirton was a gallant soldier in the Confederate War, and is a whole-souled man and an honorable citizen.

PHILIPS.—John Philips came from England long before the Revolutionary War, and settled in this county, below Marion, and married Miss Margaret Linton, also from England, and by her had an only son, John, called "Jockey John." "Jockey John" Philips married a Miss Kirton, and by her had sons, William L., Thomes, Jockey, Isaac, John and Zack, and daughter. Annis Philips married Hugh Giles, son of Colonel Hugh Giles, of Revolutionary fame, and by him had one son, the late Hugh Giles—about whom something has already been said, and who may again be noticed among the Giles family. Another daughter, Elizabeth, married a Rice, and moved to Tennessee. William L. Philips married Nancy Owens, and they had sons, John, William, David and Palmer, and daughters, Rebecca, Jane, Anna and Hannah—the latter was the mother of Thomas H. Kirton. John married a Miss Dansey; they had no children. William married a Miss Rice; they had no children. David Philips married a Miss Owens; they had no children. Palmer Philips married a Miss Graham; they had one daughter, and moved to Horry. Jockey Philips moved West. Isaac married a Miss Eagarton, and had one son, Isaac, and daughters, Anna, Frances and Elsey. Anna married David Gibson. Frances married John Williams. Elsy married William Collins. John moved West. Isaac, Jr., married Miss Julia Davis, and had two daughters, Mrs. John A. Atkinson and Mrs. Anna M. Gasque. Thomas Philips married a Miss Avant, and had one son, William, who married a Miss Marce, and had one son, named Isaac. Zack married a Miss Lewis, and had one son, Zack, and two daughters, Elizabeth and Celia. Zack Philips, Jr., married a Miss Rice, and had four sons, William L., Francis Marion, Hugh G. and J. Benjamin Philips. William L. Philips died in the war and Hugh G. was killed in the war. Francis Marion Philips married Clarissa

Wall, and had Francis Marion, Jr., Percival and McGee, sons, and Julia, Issora, Vernull, Delta and another, name unknown, daughters. J. Benjamin Philips married a Miss White, daughter of the late Wesley White, and had five children, three sons, William, Chalmers and Remington, and two daughters, Cora and Martha Fleetwood. Francis Marion Philips and J. Benjamin Philips were good men, of high character and much respected; they are both dead. Elizabeth Philips, daughter of Zack Philips, Sr., married Richard Collins, and Celia married Addington James; have no information as to their posterity, if they had any.

OWENS.—Rev. David Owens, first of the name known in the county, was the founder of Tyrrel's Bay and Gapway Baptist Churches—perhaps the two oldest Baptist Churches in the county. He was married twice—first, to Mary Palmer, by whom he had David, Nancy, Martha and Elizabeth; and his second wife was the Widow Martha Williamson, *nee* Jenkins, and by her he had one son, Solomon. David married some one, but had no children. Nancy married William L. Philips (which see among the Philips). Martha married John Williamson. Elizabeth married "Gold-headed" Richard Edwards. Solomon married, first, Catharine Gerald; they had and raised Alexander, David, Joseph, Elizabeth and Catharine. Alexander married Susan Baker, first; they had five daughters and three sons; the sons were Albert, Alexander and William J. Albert Owens was killed at Gettysburg, was color-bearer, and had, at the time he was shot, both the State and Confederate flags stuck in his belt—a gallant youth. Alexander Owens, Jr., married a Miss Harrel, and had five or six children. One of his sons, David, married a daughter of Captain T. E. Stanley. Willie J. Owens married a Miss Eaddy, of West Marion; he died a year or two ago, leaving a family of several children, neither the number or sex is known; had a son, Lamar, who married Lillian Miles, daughter of Dr. D. F. Miles, and live at Marion. David Owens, son of old Solomon, had a son, Daniel, who married a Miss Fowler; had some family, but has left the country. Joseph W. Owens married a Miss Lambert, and is dead, but left several children—three sons and three daughters—sons, Daniel, David and Solomon. David married a Miss Collins; Leonora married a Mr. Springs, of Georgetown; Dora married a Mr. Collins; Solmon and Maggie are yet unmarried. Solomon Owens, Sr., married, a second time, Rachel Brown; by her he had one son, E. B. Owens, who married Miss Ida Mullins, sister of the late Colonel W. S. Mullins; by her he had several children; moved some years ago to Georgia. Solomon Owens, Sr., married, a third time, Miss Annie Flowers; by her he had no children; he was a prominent citizen in his day.

There are other Owens in the county, about whom the writer knows but little; but he has gathered some facts, as herein presented. Shadrack Owens, an old man years ago, perhaps seventy-five or a hundred, had three sons, Elisha, Elijah and "Shiver Bill." Elisha's family moved to Georgetown County. Elijah had Avant Owens, of political campaign notoriety, Robert and Gourdin; Elijah also had three or four daughters (names unknown). Avant Owens had Memminger, Gause and Dock, and some daughters (names unknown). Robert Owens married a Miss Shelly, and had several sons (names not known). Gourdin Owens married a Miss Shelly, also, and had one son, named Wesley, and moved to Horry. "Shiver Bill" married a Miss Ammons, and had two sons, William and Ezekiel, and several daughters. William married a Miss Smith, and had sons and daughters unknown. Ezekiel married a Miss Holden, and has a family unknown. Gause Owens married a Miss Price, and has a family unknown. Memminger married a Miss Dozier, and has no children. Dock K. married a Miss Atkinson, and has a family (unknown).

There are some other Owens in upper Marion, and some of them may have already been noticed incidentally—I allude to the late David R. Owens, father of the late S. G. Owens, and Leonard R. Owens, late Postmaster at Marion. David R. Owens had a brother, Newett Owens, one of the most industrious and hard-working men I ever knew; he died in middle life, of typhoid fever, and left a large family, who have not turned out well. There was, fifty years ago or more, two other Owens, some relation to David R. and Newett, named "Wattie and Neddie;" they had families; but who their immediate ancestors were is unknown, or what became of their families. There is another set of Owens originally in the "Fork" section; the old progenitor of this family was named Shadrach Owens—not the "Shadrach" spoken of above. Old Shadrach was an old man, seventy years ago—was exceedingly superstitious, afraid of ghosts and spirits, a working man, however, and harmless—raised a large family; the names of two of his sons only are remembered, Reddin and Lot. Reddin married and settled in Hillsboro, and died two or three years ago, at the age of ninety-four, and left many children, grand-children and great-grand-children. Lot married a Miss Huggins, and died without children. Reddin and Lot were quite respectable men and good citizens. Don't know anything further of old Shadrach's posterity.

ROWELL.—The Rowell family and its connections are large, respectable and influential and has been prominent ever since Marion became a district or county. The first of the name, as well as can be ascertained, was Jacob Rowell, the grand-father of the present old gentleman, Valentine Rowell, over eighty years of age, near Centenary and Tyrrel's Bay Churches. Jacob Rowell was twice married; his first wife's name unknown; his second wife was a Miss Palmer, or Polson; they had two sons, William and David. William went West. David, the father of old man Val. Rowell, married Rebecca Philips, and raised six girls and four boys; the boys were Jacob, William L., David and Valentine. Jacob never married. William L. married Miss Eliza Landing, and had Benjamin, Richard, William and Jacob, who died in childhood; he had daughters, Stacy Ann, Elizabeth, Mary Jane, Sarah, Agnes and Rebecca. Richard was killed, how or by whom is not stated. Benjamin never married. William married, and went to Georgia. Stacy Ann married Benjamin Rogers, had no children. Elizabeth married Green Williams, and died childless. Mary Jane married Wesley Richardson; she has a family of seven or eight children (unknown). Sarah married Stephen Brown, and has ten or twelve children. Agnes married Tony Watson, and has ten or eleven children, all sons but two. Rebecca married Thomas Altman, and has six or seven children. David Rowell married Ann Gasque, daughter of old Absalom Gasque; they had thirteen children—sons, James, Albert, William, Alpheus, Jessee, Hugh G. and Julius, and daughters, Eliza, Rebecca, Susan, Emaline, Sallie and Dora. James married Fannie Gainey, and had two children, a daughter and a son, Oliver; the latter is married and has four or five children. Albert and William both died in the war or were killed. Alpheus died when young. Jessee married Mary Gasque, daughter of Ann Gasque; they had sons, Samuel, Paul, John, Thomas and Herbert, and daughters, Ann Eliza, Carrie and Eva. Samuel married Miss Julia Atkinson, and has four children (small). Paul married a Miss Rogers, and has two children (small). None of the other children of Jessee Rowell are married. He died suddenly at Marion, some four or five years ago; he was jailor for several years, and was a capital and reliable amn. Hugh G. Rowell married a Miss Lovell, and has a large family (unknown). Julius Rowell married Ann Glisson; she had seven children and died; Julius married again, Miss Lizzie Boatwright; no child by the second marriage. Eliza, the eldest daughter of David Rowell, married John Dozier; they had twelve children (names unknown), but all of them are married, but to whom not known. Rebecca, the second daughter of David Rowell, married James Shelly; they have a large family (names unknown); some of them are married. Susan, the third daughter, married Reuben Shelly; they have a family unknown. Emaline, the fourth daughter, married a Mr. Floyd, in Horry County. Sallie, the fifth daughter, married a Mr. Edwards, in Florence County. Dora, the sixth and youngest daughter, married Levin Rogers; he is dead; his widow survives, with five children. Valentine Rowell, eighty-two years of age, son of David Rowell, Sr., married Mary Collins, daughter of William Collins; they have five children, four sons and one daughter—the sons are William David, Alexander Valentine, Robert Charles and Joseph; the daughter is Alice Rebecca. William David, the eldest son, married Miss Annis Dozier; they have four children, three sons and one daughter; the sons are Claudius, William and Benjamin; the daughter, named Mary, married Boyd Shelly; no offspring. Alexander Valentine married Miss Laura Wall;

they have four children, Willie, Arthur and Maxcy, sons, and one daughter, Mamie. Robert Charles married Miss Simpson Wall; they have eight children, two sons and six daughters, none of them married. Joseph married Miss Sallie Keever; they have ten children, six sons and four daughters; the sons are Joseph, Keever, Archie, Bruce, Grady and David Oscar; the daughters are Alice, Ellen, Eva and Clara—none married. Old man Valentine Rowell's only daughter, Alice, is unmarried, and lives with her parents. Major William B. Rowell, quite prominent in his day, was the son of Valentine Rowell, and was born 28th March, 1800; his father, Valentine Rowell, married Miss Ann Baker, who became the mother of Major W. B. Rowell, and another son, whose name is unknown. Valentine Rowell was also prominent in his day; he represented his county (Marion) several times in the Legislature, as will be seen in the list of Representatives hereto appended. Valentine Rowell, though only a lad in the Revolution, was with General Marion in the latter part of the war. Major W. B. Rowell had a fair education, though not collegiate; he married twice; first, to Elizabeth Avant, a daughter of Thomas Avant and wife, a Miss Baker; Major Rowell and his first wife were first cousins; by the marriage he had only one child, Ann Elizabeth; the Avant wife dying, he married, a second time, Miss Martha Brantley, by whom he had one child, a daughter, Martha Eliza; she grew up and married Dr. C. D. Rowell, her cousin. Ann Elizabeth, daughter by his first marriage, married Major D. J. Taylor; she had one child only, a daughter, and died leaving the child only two weeks old; it was raised by her grand-father and his Brantley wife, and became the wife of Captain Huett, by whom she had one child, a son, now our fellow-citizen, William L. Huett, late County Supervisor. Captain Huett was killed in the Confederate War; his widow has since married J. T. Jones, of the Nichols community. Major Rowell's daughter, by his second marriage, Martha Eliza, married Dr. C. D. Rowell, a grand-nephew of Major Wm. B. Rowell; the fruits of this marriage were five sons and three daughters; the sons are W. B., R. W. D., Melvin L., C. Thomas and Percival E. Rowell; the daughters were Mary A., Linnie I. and Mattie E.; of these, Mary A., C. Thomas and

Percival E. are dead. W. B. Rowell, Jr., is in Florence, married. R. W. D. Rowell is at Bamberg. Melvin L. is at Lewiedale. Lennie I. is Mrs. Hook, and lives in Lexington; and Mattie E. is Mrs. Crawford, and lives at Chester. Dr. C. D. Rowell and wife are both dead; he raised and was Captain of a company in the war. Afterwards a Methodist preacher in the South Carolina Conference, and died in that relation; his father was named Cornelius, and was a nephew of Major W. B. Rowell. Major W. B. Rowell was no ordinary man—a South Carolina gentleman of the old type; never was beaten for any position to which he aspired; served four terms, eight years, in the Legislature; of a high and unspotted character, faithful to all trusts committed to him, was liberal to all worthy enterprises in State or in church, and at home dispensed unbounded hospitality; was a great friend of the church—his house was the home of the preachers; he was devotedly pious—the "salt of the earth," lived it in his every day life. He died May 22d, 1880, eighty years old. In politics he was a Democrat of the Calhoun school, and I may say the idol of his people—loved by everybody. There were and are some Rowells above Campbell's Bridge, whether related to those below Marion is not known. There were two old Rowells up there, name not known. One of them had sons, James V., Jeremiah, John and David. James V. died or was killed in the war, left children; others were all in the war. Jeremiah is up there now, is quite respectable, and has a respectable family.

GILES.—The late Hugh Giles was the son or grand-son (the latter, I think,) of Colonel Hugh Giles, who played a conspicuous part as Colonel of a regiment in the war of the Revolution. He married Polly Baker, sister of "Long Billy Baker;" they had ten children, and raised seven of them—their names are Catharine and Rebecca (the latter died when about three years old); Sarah and Edward died when quite young. William H., the oldest son, was killed in the fight around Atlanta, Ga., 28th July, 1864; he belonged to the 10th South Carolina Regiment, and was a Lieutenant of his company. Abram J. Giles was also a member of the 10th South Carolina Regiment, and was captured at the fight of Missionary Ridge, and imprisoned at

Rock Island for eighteen months and seven days. John B. Giles was a member of same regiment, and died in hospital at Rome, Ga., in May, 1863. Robert B. also belonged to same regiment and company, and survived the war. The other two daughters were named Jeannette and Eliza Franconia. Catharine married Joseph A. Taylor; they had five children—their names are Hugh G., Charlotte J., Joseph A., Edward E. and Archie. Abraham married Julia Flowers, daughter of Jeremiah John Flowers; they had seven children, raised six—their names were Mary Eliza, Jennette Elizabeth, Hugh, John B., Julia Daisey, Sarah Annis and James Robert. Robert never married. Franconia married John B. Richardson—one child was born to them; after the death of Franconia, he married his wife's sister, Jennette. Hugh Giles, like his distinguished ancestors, was or had the elements of true manhood in his make-up—was quiet, inoffensive and law-abiding, generous and kind-hearted.

COLEMAN.—Griffin Coleman, the grand-father of our present fellow-citizen, Griffin B. Coleman, married a Miss Dozier, and had and raised four sons, to wit: Griffin, John D., Jacob and James. Griffin, Jr., married Betsy Whaley, and had three sons, Amos, Griffin and Daniel. Amos married a Miss Floyd, and had six children. Griffin, Jr., Jr., married a Miss Boatwright, and has eight children. Daniel, son of Amos, died unmarried. John D. Coleman first married a Miss Baxley, and by her he had seven sons and one daughter; the sons were Isaac M., Willian J., Griffin B., John W., David, Joseph and Daniel, and one daughter, Mary Ann, who married David Shelly. Isaac M. married Martha Waller, and had William, Augustus, Mary, Donnella and Bettie. His son, William, first married a Miss Richardson, and by her had one son, Pressly; the first wife dying, he married, a second time, a Miss Jones, and they have six children, Fontaine, Howard, Iris, Nina, Eula and Eugenia. Augustus married Catharine Floyd, and had two children, girls, Mattie and Lena; Thomas H. Kirton took the latter and is raising her. Isaac M. Coleman married, a second time, Miss Anna Jones, and had by her two sons, Gary and Cantey (small). William J., the second son of John D., married Miss Nancy

Shelly, and by her had one son, Wesley, who married a Miss Avant. Griffin B. Coleman, third son of John D., married Celia Baxley; they have three living children—one son, John W., and two daughters, Mary Ann and Emma R. Emma R. married C. R. Moore; they have eight children, five girls and three boys. One daughter, Margaret Parham, married Robert Eagerton, and have one child (small). John W., fourth son of John D. Coleman, married twice, and died in Alabama. David, the fifth son of John D. Coleman, married Miss Angelina Smith; he and his wife died, and left five children, all grown and married; their names are Julius, Cornelius, Dora, Willie and John. Julius married Miss Virginia Pearce; no offspring. Cornelius married Alma Pearce; they have four children (small). Dora died childless. Willie married Miss Mamie Cook, and has one child (small). John married Miss Ida Shelly, and has two children (small). Joseph, the sixth son of Rev. John D. Coleman, married Mary Drew, and has one child, Mattie, who married Quincy Ballard, who has four children (small). Daniel, the youngest and seventh son of Rev. John D. Coleman, married Hannah Drew, and they have four sons and four daughters; the sons are John D., Willie, Major and Pressly; the daughters are Mary Ann, Anna, Alice and Charlotte. John D., Jr., married Miss Mary Allen, daughter of D. S. Allen, and has three children (small). Willie, Major and Pressly are single. Of the daughters of Daniel Coleman, Mary Ann married D. S. Allen, and has four children (small). Anne married Harllee Baxley (now dead), and left three children (small). Alice married Willie Baxley, and has two children (small). Charlotte married John Hatchel, and has one child (small). Rev. John D. Coleman married, a second time, Miss Polly Sasser, and by her had one son, Joel S. Coleman; he is in North Carolina; his second wife dying, he married, a third time, Miss Elizabeth Blackman, and by her had seven children, four sons and three daughters; the sons were J. P. Coleman, E. J., Dayton and Frank; the daughters were Anna M., Martha J. and Sarah. Of these, Martha Jane, Sarah, Dayton and Frank, are dead, never married. J. P. Coleman married Miss Beda Rogers, and moved to Columbia. E. J. Coleman married, first, a Miss James, who died, leaving four children, two of whom are married. Cora married a Lane, and has two children (small). John married Miss Sue Lane, and has two children (small). Lide is single. E. J. Coleman married, a second time, Miss Jane Flowers; they have seven children (small), in Columbia. Anna Maria married Hugh Brown, and had nine children, all dead but two (small). Jacob Coleman, the third son of Griffin, Sr., married Miss Caroline Tart, a daughter of old Mrs. Fama Tart; they had many children, mostly daughters; had two sons, Griffin and Enos. Enos is in Marlborough County, and Griffin is, or was, in Texas when last heard of. The family has scattered, and has been lost sight of. James Coleman, the fourth and youngest son of Griffin, Sr., married Miss Leah Baxly; they had three sons and four daughters; the sons are Williamson, Jessee and Griffin. Williamson died, leaving no issue. Jessee married Laura Godbold, daughter of Vincent Godbold; they have a family, number and sex unknown. Griffin married Miss Mary Smith, first, and had two sons and two daughters. One of the daughters married Willie Dozier and has three children (small). Griffin married, second time, Lizzie Bryant; they have seven children living, three sons and four daughters (small).

There is another family of Colemans in the county that may be here noticed—whether related to those above mentioned or not, is not known to the writer. Old John Coleman lived about four miles east of Marion; don't know who his wife was; he raised three sons, Moses, John and Edward. Of these, Moses married Miss Elizabeth Flowers, sister of Love Flowers, and by her had and raised two sons and five or six daughters; the sons were Sampson and Elly; the daughters' names unknown. Of the daughters, one married Stephen Attman, a very worthy man, on Sister Bay; Attman is dead; left two sons, Preston and Davis, who are married and have families. Another married Wilson Snipes and they had and raised several sons and daughters, to wit: Addison, Willie, Wilson and others, who will be noticed hereinafter. Another married Bethel Rogers, who has a large family, quite respectable. Another married Edward Rogers, who has a son, Coleman Rogers, and he married Sallie Ewart, and has a coming family. Another married William Martin, and had a considerable family—three sons, W. P. and

Daniel Martin, enterprising citizens of Mullins, and another, Charles B., and daughter. One daughter married Joseph M. Price, nephew of the writer; they have five or six children. Sampson Coleman married a Miss Huggins, daughter of Rev. John (Jack) C. Huggins; had no offspring. Elly Coleman married a Miss White, and had one son, the late W. D. Coleman, and Mrs. Chesley D. Jones. W. D. Coleman married a Miss White, niece of Colonel E. T. Stackhouse; they have three sons—J. T. Coleman, now a professor in the Citadel Academy, Charleston; another, Edward, single, and another not grown, name not known. John and Edward Coleman, brothers of old Moses, never married. Moses Coleman was a local Methodist preacher, a man of high character, a useful man in his day, and a man in whom every one had unbounded confidence.

NORTON.—The first of this family came from England to New England, at a very remote period in the past, about the first of the seventeenth century; that his name was John; that he or one of his descendants, named John, afterwards came down to Virginia and settled near what is now Alexandria, Va. This Virginia John had five sons, all of whom were soldiers in the Revolutionary War; one of them, James, served in Washington's guard as a Sergeant; another one of them was taken prisoner and died in a prison ship, in Charleston harbor, in 1780 or 1781. Their names were William, James, John, David and Solomon. After the Revolution, the old man and two of his sons, James and John, went to Kentucky; two others of them came to South Carolina—one, William, went to Georgetown, and the other went to Beaufort. William, the Georgetown one, went from Georgetown up into what was then called Kingston, now Horry, and took up large bodies of land. One grant that the writer has seen for 3,300 acres, below what is now called Green Sea, on the Iron Springs Swamp, just above its confluence with Lake Swamp. William Norton married a Widow Miller, maiden name not known, and she had at the time of their marriage four children—two sons, Nathaniel and Elias Miller, and two daughters, Rebecca and Martha. Nathaniel Miller gave the land to and was one of the founders of the present Miller Church. The deed for it was made to

Bishop Asbury, and is said to be now in the possession of Rev. Simeon Campbell. The two Millers lived and died near by, and are buried near where Valentine Martin lives. Of the two Miller sisters, one, Martha, married old Moses Wise, and the other, Rebecca, married old William Bryant. William Norton married the Widow Miller, as above stated, and had by her two sons, William and James, and three daughters, Ruth, Martha and Mary. William, Jr., married and settled where Green Sea, in Horry, now is, and was a prominent man down there, and built and was one of the chief founders of a Methodist church there, then called Norton's Cross Roads, and it was then known as Norton's Church. This was about the first of 1800. William Norton had two sons, John W. and James, and several daughters. One of the daughters, Ruth, married Benj. Sellers, who moved to Mississippi. John W. and James both joined the South Carolina Conference. John W. located, and his family are in Georgia. James was quite prominent as a preacher; he died in 1825, and is buried in Columbia, Washington Street Church. James Norton, the other brother, settled in Marion District, near his half-brothers, the two Millers, on Maiden Down. This James Norton was the grand-father of the present Hon. James Norton, of Mullins; he had two daughters, one of whom, Martha, married John Roberts; the other, Mary, married Gadi Campbell. James, Sr., had three sisters, Ruth, Martha and Mary. Ruth married Joel Lewis; Martha married Norton Roberts, grand-father of the late Colonel John Roberts; and Mary married a Flood. James Norton, Sr., married, first, Jerusha Reaves, and had one son, William, and three daughters, Sarah, Nancy and Martha; his second wife was a Honeycut, and he had by her Mary, Solomon and John. Solomon married, had one son, named John, and died, and his widow married Jack Woods, who overseed for General Evans, back in the 40's or 50's, for several years. William Norton, son of James, Sr., married Anna Roland, of Camden; by her he had Jerusha, Sarah Ann, Mary, Nancy and Olive, daughters; James and Henry, sons. Jerusha married Anthony Meares. Sarah Ann married William Bryant, of Horry. Mary married Evans Bryant. Nancy married Leonard Cribb. Olive married Lewis Huggins. James married a Miss Moody, went to

Alabama and died. Henry married Nancy Carmichael, daughter of Squire Dougald Carmichael, on Maiden Down and Buck Swamp; they had Catharine, Colin Murchison, Milton, Virginia and Sarah. Catharine married S. G. Porter. Colin Murchison went to Mississippi. Melton married Miss Relda Proctor, and has a family—a son grown, Lonney, and a daughter grown, Bessie, and other children. Virginia married R. J. Rogers, and has a large family—a son, Henry, grown, and a daughter, Mary, grown, and other children. Sarah married M. M. Bird; they have a family of children, two grown, Claudius and Mary. John Norton married twice; first, Nancy Huggins, daughter of Willis Huggins; by this marriage he had John W., Mary Elizabeth and Caroline; he married, second time, the widow of Angus Carmichael, whose maiden name was Pensy Lewis; by this marriage he had Evan, James, Eliza, Martha and Margaret. His son, John W., married, first, Susannah Carmichael daughter of his second wife, Pensy, by her first husband, Angus Carmichael; his wife died, leaving one child, a daughter, named Ires, who, when seven or eight years of age, was killed in a cotton gin; John W. Norton married, a second time, the Widow Carmichael, *nee* Jordan; by this marriage he had only one child, a daughter, Minnie, who died when about grown—her mother having died before she did; John W. married, a third wife, Sarah Ivey, and by her he had four children, two sons and two daughters (small); he is now seventy years of age or more; he was always a modest and retiring sort of man. Away back in the 50's, he went to Mississippi and enlisted in the regular army of the United States, Second United States Cavalry Regiment, of which Algernon Sydney Johnson was Colonel; Robert E. Lee, Lieutenant Colonel; E. Kirby Smith, Major, and Earle Van Dorn, Senior Captain. J. W. Norton was in Van Dorn's company, and was promoted to the rank of Quartermaster Sergeant. All these officers became, in the Confederate army, distinguished and highly distinguished Generals. J. W. Norton served five years in this regiment, and at the end of his service he was given a three months furlough to visit his home; at the end of which he went to his regiment, with a view to re-enlist; but just at this time Secession occurred; his Second Regiment of Cavalry was broken up—its officers being all Southern men—and he came back to South Carolina, volunteered in Captain W. P. Shooter's company, went to Virginia, and remained in the Confederate Army till its surrender at the end of the war. He was wounded twice in battles with the Indians while in the United States service, and again slightly while in the Confederate service. He did not marry till late in life, and after the Confederate War; since which he has married three times, as above stated. With the prestige of this five years' previous service with and under officers so distinguished, he might have gotten some soft place in the Confederate service, but for his modesty and unpretentious disposition. Mary Elizabeth, the eldest daughter of John Norton, married Aaron Oliver, of Robeson County, N. C., where she ever afterwards lived and died; she raised quite a large family in that State. Caroline, the second daughter of John Norton, married Lewis Huggins, and raised a large family; they emigrated to Georgia a few years ago, and are there now. Of the children of John Norton by his second marriage, Eliza, the eldest daughter, married Gilbert D. Johnson, a nephew of the late Hugh R. Johnson; they live near the old Norton homestead, and have no children. The third and youngest daughter, Margaret, married Valentine Martin; they have had twelve children—lost two; six are grown, Don, Lilly, Pensy, Maggie, Kate and May; and of this six, Pensy married Hampton Rogers, two or three days ago; the other five are not grown. Mattie, the second daughter of old John Norton, married D. Latta Townsend, of North Carolina; they have a large family, some of them grown; they emigrated to Georgia some years ago, and are now in that State. Of the sons of old man John Norton by his second marriage, Evan, the eldest, after the war, married Miss Ella Powell, moved to Conway, and is yet there; he has five children—three sons and two daughters; the sons are J. O., James and John Clarence; the daughters are Ella Wood (called Daisey) and Mabel. Of the sons, J. O. (called Van) is a graduate of Wofford College, in the class of 1895; he is unmarried, and is an employee in the Census Department in Washington. James went to Wofford, but did not graduate, and is now taking his third course in a medical college. John Clarence is now a student in Clemson College. Of the two daughters, Ella Wood (Daisey) married a Mr. Crouch, Clerk of the Court for Saluda County, resides in that place, and has one child. Mabel, the youngest, is grown. The father, Evan Norton, is a fine physician, of high moral character, well posted and a man of great good sense; has never sought or held any public position except that of County Auditor for Horry, but has declined all such, when offered to him. James, the youngest brother of Dr. Evan Norton, married, 18th May, 1870, Rachel Cochrane Sellers, the daughter of the writer, and located at Mullins, near where he was born and raised, and merchandised for several years; he had two children, boys, Evan Lewis and William Fitzroy. The oldest, Evan Lewis, died when between four and five years of age. William Fitzroy, the younger, grew up, and after spending a year or two in Wofford College, he entered the South Carolina College law department, and graduated therein, but has never practiced; he married, in 1896, Miss Florence Smith, eldest daughter of B. Gause Smith, of Mullins; he runs a farm and a tobacco warehouse—the future must determine his success or failure.

The career of Hon. James Norton merits more than mere personal mention. Raised on a farm, as it were, between the plow-handles, and opportunities for education being limited, he went into the war as a private at the age of seventeen, and fought it through to the end; wounded several times before 1864; was thought to be mortally wounded, being shot through one of his lungs; he was furloughed to go home, as soon as he was able to travel; after getting, as he and his friends thought, about well of his wound, he returned to his command in Virginia, and was soon captured and carried to Point Lookout, and kept there till July, 1865, when he was turned out of prison and came home. Not being physically able to do hard work, he engaged in turpentine and mercantile pursuits at Mullins. He married, in May, 1870, as before stated, and in the fall of that year was nominated and elected School Commissioner for the county. Served a term, two years, was again nominated and elected for a second term; but he, with all other officials elected that fall (1872), were counted out by the negro scalawag and carpet-bag election officials. In 1886, he was a candidate for

Representative of the county in the Legislature, was elected at the head of his ticket, and served during the term for which he had been elected. In 1890, he was again nominated and elected at the head of his ticket for another term, which he served with credit to himself and satisfactory to his constituents. In the meantime, the late Governor Ellerbe had been elected Comptroller General of the State, and he appointed Hon. James Norton as chief Clerk, which place he filled with entire satisfaction to his chief and to the public for two terms of that office; and owing to Ellerbe's bad health during his two terms, Norton practically ran the Comptroller's office; he did it with such signal ability and success, that he was triumphantly nominated and elected, at the expiration of Ellerbe's second term, as Ellerbe's successor. He then held the office as Comptroller General for his term, two years, and was then re-elected for another term without opposition, and Ellerbe, at the election in 1896, was elected Governor. In May following, Joseph H. Earle, one of our United States Senators, died, and Governor Ellerbe appointed John L. McLaurin United States Senator, in place of Earle—which necessarily vacated McLaurin's seat in the United States House of Representatives for this, the 6th Congressional District of South Carolina—whereupon James Norton became a candidate to fill the unexpired term of McLaurin, and after a spirited campaign, Norton was elected, and again elected in 1898, and served with credit to himself in the Fifty-fifth and sixth Congresses. It does not become the writer to say much, as he is the father-in-law of Norton, and, therefore, he states only facts; but will add that Norton is no ordinary man, otherwise he could not have accomplished so much.

LEWIS.—This family were from Ireland, and settled in Virginia. A son of this family, named William, came to South Carolina before the Revolution; he married Miss Mourning Vampelt, a Hollander. Tradition informs us that her father and she came from Holland together, leaving his family in Holland; they came, as it seems, prospecting, and got down into South Carolina, where they met up with William Lewis, and soon an attachment (mutual) sprang up between the two young people, and they got married; whereupon old man Vampelt went back to Holland for his family, and was never afterwards heard of. William Lewis settled in Horry County; they had and raised seven sons and two daughters; the sons were William, James, Isaac, Hardy, Joel, Jonathan and Patrick; the girls were Polly and Zilpha. Of these, Polly married Averitt Nichols, of Columbus County, N. C., and was the mother of the late venerable Averitt Nichols, of Nichols, S. C. The other daughter, Zilpha, married William Gerald, of Horry. Of the sons, Hardy, Joel and Jonathan settled in Marion County— Hardy on Little Pee Dee, below Gilchrist's Bridge, Joel and Jonathan higher up the river, on the south side, near where Miller's Church now stands; and James at Allen's Bridge. Hardy Lewis married Dicey Floyd; they had and raised two sons, William L. and Joel W. P. Lewis, and four daughters—Betsy, who never married; Mourning, Margaret, Lizzie and another, the wife of James D. Smith. Mourning married W. H. Grice; Margaret married John Price; Lizzie married Henry Price. Of the sons of Hardy Lewis, William L. marired Flora Carmichael, daughter of Squire Dougald, on Maiden Down and Buck Swamp; they had sons, Angus, Allen C. and W. A. D. Marion Lewis; and daughters, Catharine, Mary and Flora. Of the sons, Angus was killed in the war. Allen C. married, first, a daughter of Hiram Lee; by this marriage he had one son, Herbert, now in Wofford College, and Capers, and three daughters, grown. The Lee wife dying, he married a daughter of George W. Smith, and by her has some small children. W. A. D. Marion Lewis, called Dougald, married a Miss Bullock in North Carolina, and lives on part of the old homestead; has a family, sex and number unknown. Catharine married Randal McDaniel, and moved to Darlington. Mary married Randal Barnes; has no offspring. Flora married in North Carolina, and died without issue. Joel W. P. Lewis, the youngest son of old Hardy, married a Miss Cox; had two sons, Solon A. and Dio. The latter lately married a daughter of Duncan Nicholson. Solon A. Lewis, now at Latta, married a Miss Tart, youngest daughter of the late John W. Tart; she died a year or so ago, leaving two children (small), both daughters. J. W. P. Lewis has three single daughters; he died a year or so ago. Jonathan Lewis, brother of old Hardy, married, first,

Susannah Porter, of Columbus County, N. C.; by her he had two children, one son, Evan, and one daughter, Pennsy or Pennsylvania; his second wife was Feraba Strickland, and by her he had two sons, William S. and Joel. Of the children by the first marriage, Evan Lewis married Miss Margaret Cribb, and by the marriage had two sons, Jonathan and Dempsy, and two daughters, Carrie and Adaline, called Addie. Of the daughters, Carrie Lewis married Dr. F. M. Monroe, of the Latta section; by this marriage several children were born. Addie, the younger daughter, married Oliver Williams, of North Carolina; they have two sons. Of the sons of Evan Lewis, the eldest, Jonathan, has never married—a young man about fifty years of age, of good habits and morals, a well-to-do, good citizen and reliable every way. Why he has not married and made some good woman happy, is a mystery, which, perhaps, will never be solved! Dempsy Lewis, the younger brother, married in early life, Miss Eliza Jane Stackhouse, daughter of the late Mastin C. Stackhouse; they have ten children, eight sons and two daughters; the sons are Taylor, Leon, Marvin, Victor—these are grown; four others, Odell, Rupert, Evan and Ernest—these are not grown; the two daughters, Maggie and Addie, near grown—not one of the ten children married; he is a good man and substantial citizen. William S. Lewis, by old Jonathan's second marriage, married Miss Rhoda Mace (both now dead); they had five children, Sarah, W. Evan, Anne, Joel J. and J. Wesley. Sarah married Robert Edwards; had two sons, Sandy and George; the father is dead. The two sons went to Arkansas; Sandy is dead; George is in Texarkana, and is Sheriff of that county or the one in which that city is located, and is well to do. W. Evan is on the old homestead, married a Miss Avant, and has some family (young); is a good citizen. Anne married, first, Marion Avant; by whom she had one son, Willie, who grew up to manhood and died—a very promising young man; his mother, the widow, married again John A. Wilson, of Wilmington, N. C., and is, as it is said, doing well. Joel and Wesley went West; Joel is said to be doing well in New Orleans. Pennsy, the only daughter of old Jonathan Lewis, and full sister of Evan Lewis, married, first, Angus Carmichael, and by him she had one child, a daughter, who grew up and married John W. Norton, as hereinbefore stated in or among the Norton family; Pennsy, the widow, then married John Norton, the father of Hon. James Norton, and who has already been noticed among the Norton family. Evan Lewis was a capital man and good citizen—a useful man in his day; was a good surveyor—plats, made by him, are now to be seen often, and bear the scrutiny of the Courts. He was opposed to the Confederate War, but had the good sense to keep his mouth shut, and to "stand to one side and let the procession pass by." Joel Lewis, the brother of old Jonathan, and one of the seven brothers, married Ruth Norton, grand-aunt of Hon. James Norton; they moved to Mississippi, about 1818; and thence, years afterwards, to Texas. This ascertained from recent correspondence with Mrs. Minerva Lewis Jones, the youngest and only surviving child of old Joel and his wife, Ruth, and who resides at Gonzales, Gonzales County, Texas. Joel Lewis, the youngest son of old Jonathan, by his second marriage, married a Miss Flowers, after he went to Mississippi; can follow him no farther.

FOWLER.—The first Fowler known in the county was William Fowler, who came from North Carolina, about the date of 1800. He married a daughter of George Brown, and lived near Gapway; he had some daughters and one son, Jessee. Jessee married a sister of Harrison Lambert; they had several children. Martha married Daniel Williamson. Patience married a Mr. Keith, and had one child; Keith died, and the widow then married Levi Edwards. Sarah married a Mr. Tolar, and both died. Mary Fowler never married. The oldest son, Furman Fowler, married a Miss White, and raised a family unknown to the writer. Joseph Fowler married, first, a Miss Brown and had a family, how many not known—they are grown; his Brown wife died, and he married again, a daughter of Stephen R. Collins, and had several children by her. Stephen Fowler married a Miss Collins, daughter of William Collins and a sister of Valentine Rowell's wife, and has a family of sons and daughters, the oldest son grown. Major Fowler married, first, a daughter of Bethel Rogers, of the upper Fork section; she died at her first accouchement—the child, however, lived; his second wife was a daughter of Daniel Snipes, and she has three or four children. His first child, Maggie, married Daniel Owens, and she has considerable family, number and sex unknown. This family of Fowlers are good people. Few better men, if any, can be found than old man Jesse Fowler was—of the strictest integrity, scrupulously honest in all his dealings with his fellow-men, industrious and frugal; though not a rich man, yet he acquired by honest endeavor a comfortable living; was true to his church, his God and his country; his good influence will tell upon his children and his community for years to come.

SHOOTER.—The first of this family in Marion County was old Benjamin Shooter and his wife, Mary; her maiden name is unknown. They came from Virginia or North Carolina, about 1790. They had and raised three children or more— one son, Benjamin, Jr., and two daughters, names unknown. One of the daughters married old Thomas Rogers, and the other married the late Captain John Rogers, of the Fork section. Captain John Rogers, a capital citizen, had and raised a considerable family; the sons were Bethel, Ferdinand, Tristram B. and John W. Rogers; the names of the daughters are unknown, also the number. One became the wife of George W. Reaves, already mentioned herein among the Reaves; another was the wife of Matthew Martin, and another was the wife of the late Aaron Martin. These latter have already been noticed in or among the Martin family. There may have been other daughters of Captain John Rogers. Know nothing of old Thomas Rogers' family. Of the sons of Captain John Rogers, the eldest, Bethel, married a daughter of Rev. Moses Coleman; he has raised a considerable family, who are now among us, and energetic and respectable people. Ferdinand Rogers married a daughter of Samuel Edwards, and has raised several children, who are now among us and respectable citizens. Tristram B. Rogers was a capital man; he married a daughter of Joseph B. Hays; he had and raised a large family. One of his sons, J. Marion Rogers, is a graduate of Wofford College, and a minister in the South Carolina Conference of the Methodist Church. Another son, Herbert, is a graduate of the Citadel Academy, Charleston, and is said to be very bright and promising. T. B. Rogers had other sons and daughters, who are among us and are coming people. John W. Rogers, another son of old Captain John, married a daughter of old William Hays; he died some years ago, and left a promising family of sons and daughters, all doing well. W. R. Rogers, a merchant at Marion, is one of them, and is succeeding well. Benjamin Shooter, Jr., married a daughter of George Ford, as hereinbefore stated among the Ford family, and settled in the "Fork" section, on the place now belonging to Dempsy Lewis; he had and raised a family of eight sons, to wit: Berry A., George E., W. Pinckney, William, Benjamin Franklin, Evander C., John Milton and Albert H.; and one daughter, Martha, who married John W. Moody, and had one child, a daughter, and died. Of the sons, Berry A. married a Miss Campbell (I think), and had and raised a family. George E. Shooter was a doctor, and married, first, Miss Caroline Ford, a daughter of Major Jessee Ford; and had by her several children, when she died, and he married again, a Miss Harrelson, and by her had children also—how many not known—when the father died. Dr. Shooter was no ordinary man—he had one failing which, perhaps, shortened his days; I know nothing of his family. W. Pinckney Shooter was the first graduate from Marion County (1859) in the Citadel Academy; after graduation, he studied law at Marion with George M. Fairlee, and was admitted to the bar just as the war commenced; he was talented and brilliant; he volunteered and was elected First Lieutenant in the first company that went from Marion. The company left Marion 4th January, 1861, and went to Morris Island, Charleston, and formed a part of the First Regiment under the command of Colonel (afterwards General) Maxcy Gregg, and participated in the capture of Fort Sumter, in April (12th and 13th), 1861. After the fall of Fort Sumter, there was a revolunteering of the company for the war and for the Confederacy, and W. P. Shooter was elected its Captain, and went with his company to Virginia. He was a brave and gallant officer, and rose from Captain to Lieutenant Colonel of the Regiment, when he was killed at Spottsylvania

C. H., in May, 1864; he never married. B. Frank (killed 6th May) and Evander C. (killed 12th May, 1864), two of his brothers lost their lives in the series of battles fought that month between Grant and Lee's armies. William N. Shooter, I think, married a Miss Campbell, also; they have a family, about whom nothing is known. John Milton married in North Carolina. Albert H. Shooter, the youngest son of Benjamin, Jr., married Miss Josephine Roberts, a daughter of the late James Roberts, and has a coming family—how many and their sex, is not known; he is one of our good citizens. Of the eight sons, three were killed in the war, and two have died since the war; the survivors are William, John Milton and Albert H. As a family they were intellectual and of acute perceptions, brave almost to rashness, and full of pluck and energy. John Milton and Albert were too young to go into the war. Old Aunt Mary Shooter, as she was familiarly called sixty-five years ago, the grand-mother of these soldier boys, lived to a great age—over ninety years.

CAMPBELL (OF MAIDEN DOWN).—The progenitor of this family was named James. He came from Virginia in the eighteenth century, married and had five sons, John, James, Jr., Jerre, Gadi and Theophilus; and one daughter, Nancy Ann, who became the wife of old John Huggins, of Huggins' Bridge, on Little Pee Dee, and who has already been noticed herein among the Huggins family; and Mary, who married Willis Huggins, cousin of old John, and Elizabeth, who never married. James Campbell, Jr., married Miss Molsey (Mary) Barnes, and had Ebby and James, and three daughters. One of the latter died unmarried. James (second), Jr., married Chloe Rogers, and had one son, Frank; his wife died; he married no more; is now dead. Frank married a Miss Jones, daughter of Ebby Jones, and is now a young citizen and promises well. Ebby Campbell married Charlotte Lane, and has six children—three sons, Spencer, George and another, name unknown; one daughter married Leonard Lewis, and has a family (small); another daughter married some one unknown; think the other daughter is single. Jerre Campbell married Miss Patience Scott, daughter of old Pharoah Scott, in the

Tabernacle section, in Hillsboro; they had two sons and four daughters; the sons are Kenneth and Eli. One daughter married Willis Rogers, and had Simeon, Hampton and others. Eli Campbell married Miss Josephine Huggins, and had one child, a daughter, who married Percy Harrelson, and has one or two children (small). One daughter of Jerre married Lawrence Sessions; she had three or four children, and died. Two of Jerre's daughters are unmarried. Kenneth Campbell married a Miss Harrelson, and has two daughters, unmarried. Gadi Campbell married Mary Norton, sister of John Norton and aunt of Hon. James Norton; they had four sons, Warren W., Charles Fletcher, Theophilus and Benjamin F., and three daughters, Martha, Emaline and Elizabeth. Of the daughters, Martha married James Dudney, and had and raised several children, all grown, about whom little is known; Emaline Campbell married the late Thomas A. Proctor, and had several children. Of the daughters of Thomas A. Proctor, the eldest married Thomas Cottingham, and had one or two children; she died several years ago. Another daughter, Mary Proctor, married Major Bird, and had one child, and died. Relda Proctor married Milton Norton, and has a family (coming). Sarah married a Mr. Williams, and has a large family; they are in Hampton County; and Miss Fannie Proctor is unmarried. Elizabeth Campbell married R. B. Game, and they had and raised a considerable family. Of the daughters of R. B. Game and wife, Hattie married a Mr. Hunter; they are in Florence County. Mary Game married Samuel Rogers; they have quite a family; they live in Columbia. Roberta Game married Albert Rogers; have a family (small). Georgia Game married a Mr. Chreitzberg; they had two children, a son and a daughter, Robert and Lula (small). Chrietzberg dying, the widow married Daniel Martin, of Mullins; no children by her Martin marriage. Lila Game is unmarried. Of the sons of Gadi Campbell, Warren W. died a young single man, just as he was preparing to enter as a minister in the South Carolina Conference (Methodist). Charles Fletcher Campbell, son of Gadi, never married; he joined the South Carolina Conference in 1859, and died in 1860, at the age of twenty-seven. Benjamin F. Campbell, son of Gadi, never married; he died or was killed in the war. Theophilas Campbell, son of Gadi, married Emma Huggins; he is dead; left his widow, two sons and four daughters. Of the daughters, Louisa married a Mr. Proctor; he died and left her with two children; she is in Washington—whether married again, the writer knows not. Dora, the next daughter, married T. W. Sellers, the nephew of the writer; she died, and left two children, daughters (small). Etta, the next daughter, is also in Washington, D. C.; said to be married, but to whom is not known. Maggie, the youngest, is unmarried, perhaps not grown. Of the two sons, Iverson and Capers, they are with their mother; neither one of them is grown. Theophilus Campbell, son of James, Sr., and brother of Gadi Campbell, married Miranda Cribb; had several children, emigrated to Mississippi. Of the sons of Thomas A. Proctor, Marion, the oldest, married a Miss Shuler, of Orangeburg County, and has a large family; don't know their names. George Proctor married a Miss McCoy, and has one or two children (small). Thomas, a son, went to Alabama. Robert married Jennie McIntyre, and has gone to Georgia. Of the sons of Robert B. Game, Simpson married a daughter of Huger Godbold, and has quite a family. Morgan Game went to Anderson County, and married there. Joseph Bethea Game, the youngest son, is grown; he married in North Carolina; has a family; he belongs to the South Georgia Conference, and is now stationed in Brunswick, Ga.—is said to be a fine preacher; he is well educated, well equipped for his profession. R. B. Game's Campbell wife died, and he married, a second time, Miss Lizzie Fladger, daughter of Captain C. J. Fladger, and by her has one daughter, Minnie, who is said to be very smart and intellectual. John Campbell, brother of Gadi, Jeremiah, &c., married some one not now remembered, but had no offspring.

ATKINSON.—This family, or rather the Widow Atkinson, came from Sampson County, N. C., with her children, about the last of the eighteenth century, and settled near where Miller's Church now stands. She had three sons, Jessee and two others, names not ascertainable, and one daughter, if no more; she married Nat, or Elias Miller, one of whom was the founder of Miller's Church, and for whom that church was named, and is still called and known by that name. It has already been mentioned in or among the Norton family. The eldest son of the widow (if not the oldest), the one named Jessee, married a Miss Bryant, first, and to that marriage were born and raised four children, three sons and one daughter; the sons were Jessee, Ebby and Hugh; the daughter was Sarah Ann, and she became the wife of Vincent Godbold, and had and raised six or eight daughters and one son, Eli Godbold, now in Horry. Old Jessee Atkinson's second wife was Miss Margaret Cave, and by her had eight children, to wit: Charlotte, Elizabeth, Eliza Ann, Annis, Jane, William J., John W. and Thomas. Of these, Charlotte married a Mr. Welsh; had no children. Elizabeth married William Woodward, and had one daughter, named Charlotte. They all, if alive, are in Richmond County, N. C. Eliza Ann, the third daughter, died unmarried. Annis, the fourth daughter, married Stephen H. Price, of the Maple Swamp section, and brother to one Hugh P. Price, now in that section; they had four children, two boys and two girls. Stephen H. Price died, leaving those children all small. The eldest, Jessee, has a family, in Horry. The youngest boy died young. The oldest girl died unmarried. The younger one married Mr. Gause Owens, and has a growing family. Jane, the fifth daughter, married Joseph Stevens; he is dead—left three children, two sons, Benjamin and Hamilton, and one girl—all married Ammonses. William J. Atkinson, oldest son of old Jessee by his second marriage, married Martha Jane Harrelson, daughter of old Hugh H. Harrelson; died and left three children, Hugh J., George, and a daughter—the latter married an Ammons. George married a Miss Berry, daughter of Bright W. Berry, near the Reedy Creek Springs, in upper Marion; has some children, don't know sex or number. Don't know to whom Hugh J. married. John W. Atkinson, now of Marion, the second son of old Jessee by his second marriage, married, first, Miss Eliza Dew, daughter of old William Dew, of upper Marion, near Catfish Baptist Church, and by her had one child, a son, Thomas J., when the wife, Eliza, died. Thomas J. grew up and married a daughter of Squire Stephen A. Hairgrove, and now resides in the Catfish neighborhood; he has two daughters, Viola and Lilla, who are the idols of their Aunt

Huldah Hairgrove, an old maiden lady of fifty years or more. Thomas Atkinson, the youngest son of old Jessee or Jessee, Jr., by his second marriage (Cave), married Martha Dew, the youngest daughter of old William Dew, above mentioned; they had one child, a son, William B. Atkinson, who grew up and married a Miss Gaddy, daughter of Samuel T. Gaddy, near Gaddy's Mills; he lives on the old William Dew homestead, with his mother. William B. Atkinson is an excellent manager of affairs, a good farmer and prosperous; he has seven or eight children, some of them grown, names unknown. His father, Thomas Atkinson, died when he was quite a child; he was and is the only child of his mother, who yet lives—rather an extra woman, of fine sense. John W. Atkinson's wife dying, he married the Widow Beaty, *nee* Hemingway, mother of Rev. L. F. Beaty, of the South Carolina Conference, a strong preacher; by this second marriage John W. Atkinson has no children. Ebby Atkinson, third son of Jessee, Sr., son of the old widow from Sampson County, N. C., married Olive Gasque, daughter of old Absalom Gasque, the old court crier, who was calling the Court away back in 1840, and how long before is unknown; he continued to call the Court while he lived, and after his death it descended, not by inheritance but by appointment, to his son, Henry A. Gasque, and he held it to 1890 or 1891, when the "Tillman boom" lifted him out—reform downwards. Old man Ebby Atkinson and wife raised quite a family, mostly girls, one son, Ebby, who married a daughter of the late J. C. Thompson; they have children. One daughter, Celia Ann, married Eli Godbold, who moved to Horry County; they had several children, mostly sons, the three oldest known—Christopher Columbus, Ebby and William Eli—and others not known. Ebby Atkinson had another daughter, Mary, who married a Lovel— and one married a Richardson—think her name was Minnie. Know nothing further of old man Ebby's family or descendants. Hugh Atkinson, a brother of old Ebby, married a Miss Goldbold, lived to an old age and died childless. The Atkinsons, as a family, are honest and straight, retiring and unpretending; live at home and harmless. The old widow from Sampson County, N. C., had two other sons, whose names are not remembered. The Atkinsons of Georgetown are said to be relatives of these in Marion, but what relation is unknown. One of the Georgetown Atkinsons was Circuit Solicitor some twenty-five or thirty years ago; he may be a descendant of one of the widow's sons. Ex-Governor Atkinson of Georgia may also be a descendant of one of the widow's sons—who can tell? The name is spelled in the same way. Her two sons went somewhere. Jessee only remained here.

FLADGER.—Since noting the families of Evans, Godbold, Haselden and Richardsons herein, the writer has obtained information that enables him to connect branches of the above named families with the Fladgers—a name now extinct in the county, except one female, now forty years of age, Sallie Maria Fladger, daughter of the late Captain Charles J. Fladger, by his second marriage with the Widow William S. Bethea. That female will hardly ever marry; and if she does, will, perhaps, change her name from Fladger to some other name—so that, it is the remotest possibility that the name will continue much longer in the county, once prominent. About 1735, one of the first settlements was made by a colony, direct from England, in Britton's Neck, and one of these colonists was a Fladger (Gregg's History, page 69), and from him the name and its connections have come down to the present time. The writer is indebted to Mrs. Major S. A. Durham, a descendant of this old colonist Fladger, for the missing link. Hugh Fladger was his name (a name in the family ever since); to whom he married is unknown—he may have married in England and brought his wife with him; he had a son, named Henry Fladger, who married a Miss Keene, daughter of Brockingham Keene, and Keene's wife was a Miss Horry, a sister of Colonel Horry. Henry Fladger had a son, named Hugh Fladger (our old Hugh, whom the writer has often seen), and two daughters—Sarah, who married General Thomas Godbold, and another, name not known, who married John Richardson (called "King John.") Henry Fladger was active in the Revolution, was under General Francis Marion, and was killed by the Tories during that momentous struggle. The above sketch being read in connection with the Godbold, Evans, Haselden and King John Richardson's family, it will be seen that these families and their descendants are all related to each other collaterally—their common ancestor being Henry Fladger, son of old Hugh, the colonist to Britton's Neck from England, about 1735. Fladger blood runs through all their veins.

SMITH.—The name Smith is almost universal. It is found, I suppose, wherever the English language is spoken. It may fairly be assumed that all the Smiths had somewhere, at some remote period, a common ancestor—that is, an original stock whence they all sprang. To find it, the writer thinks is impossible, and he will not undertake to do so—does not know that he can do so, so far as Marion County is concerned, but will approach as near to it as he can. The first of which the writer knows or has any information concerning was John Smith, who settled upon and lived near the place now known as E. J. Moody's Mill, long before the Revolution—during the Revolution it was known as Tart's Mill. When it was built or by whom, is not known. It may have been built by John Smith or by Enos Tart. Enos Tart's mother was the sister or daughter of John Smith. This old John Smith had a family of sons and daughters, but how many of each is not known; from the best information obtainable this old John Smith had sons, named John, Samuel and James, and may be others; can't say as to any daughters, but am pretty sure that old Enos Tart's mother was his daughter rather than his sister. John Smith, Jr., as is supposed, lived before and after the Revolutionary War, between the two (lower) Reedy Creeks, west of Gapway Baptist Church and east of Marion Court House. It is told of him that he was well-to-do, and that during the war he buried considerable money (specie) near the Little Reedy Creek. This John Smith, it is supposed and believed, was either the grand-father or the father of Hugh Godbold Smith, John Smith, Willis G. Smith, Leonard Smith, Ebby Smith and two or three daughters. One daughter married a Malloy, and moved to Horry. Another married James Tart, who had a considerable family, all of whom are dead, except one son, the youngest, C. Murchison Tart, in Columbus County, N. C. Of these sons, John and Ebby Smith moved to Alabama about 1820 or 1825. Willis G. Smith married a Miss Beverly, and raised a family; don't know how many. One daughter married G. W. Smithey, who had and raised two children, a son, J. W. G. Smithey, and the wife of John Smithey—"One-eyed John." The son, J. W. G. Smithey, married a Miss Malloy, of Conway; lives now in Marion, and has an interesting and promising family, some of them grown. Leonard Smith married a Miss Foxworth; his male descendants were John, David and Jerry; don't know who they married or what has become of them or their posterity, if they had any. Old man Willis G. Smith was quite a character—there was only one Willis G. Smith; he never wore any socks—at least, the writer never saw him with any; saw him frequently, and often in cold, bitter weather, at Marion, without any socks—he was emphatically "Sockless Willis;" he was very profane, and in the habit of frequently using words not suited to a Sunday School, and about 1846, when the project of building the Wilmington and Manchester Railroad was being discussed at Marion, General Evans, General Wheeler and others were telling old man Willis about how it was to be constructed, how it was to be propelled, how many people it could carry, and how fast it could run, or its rate of speed, &c., old man Willis would swear most bitterly that they were all liars; that such a thing could not be and they knew it could not be; that they were just gassing and trying to fool him, &c.—this done with the most vehement expletives. I think the old man lived to see the road completed to Marion. They tried to get him to take a trip on it, but he persistently refused, and never would risk himself on it. If the old gentleman could wake up now, and see the gilded flying palace cars running fifty miles an hour, half a dozen coaches filled with passengers, all eating and sleeping while thus flying over and through the country, he would be astounded, sure enough—he would look on it with awe and incredulity, and regard it as supernatural or miraculous. The other brother, Hugh Godbold Smith, married a Miss Wheeler, sister of General E. B. Wheeler; by this marriage several children were born and raised—four sons, Redding, Edward, John G. and Hugh H. Smith; and one daughter, Margaret Smith. Redding W. Smith married, first, a Miss Brown, whose mother was a Godbold; his children were Dr. Edward B.,

Zack, Mary E. and Sally H. Smith. Of these daughters, Mary E. married Captain A. H. Ford; they raised a family, the number and sex unknown—some or all are grown. They first moved to Anderson County, and after remaining there for several years, they with their family emigrated to Texas, where they now reside. The other daughter, Sally H., married M. L. Smith, of Buck Swamp; they raised a family, some of whom are married and have families. Of the two sons, Zack, the younger one, was a Lieutenant in Captain Shooter's company, 1st Regiment (Gregg's), and died unmarried, from wounds received in battle at Hagerstown, Md. The elder son, Dr. E. B. Smith, married, after the war, Mrs. Pattie McIntyre, *nee* Betts, widow of Lieutenant Archie McIntyre, who was killed in September, 1862, at Sharpsburg, Md.—a brave and generous young officer; she was a daughter of the Rev. Charles Betts, of the South Carolina Conference, a strong preacher in his day. She had a son by McIntyre, Archie McIntyre, named for his father, now an excellent physician and prominent citizen of the town of Marion; by this marriage four children were born and raised, to wit: three sons and one daughter—Charles B. Smith, in Philadelphia; Dr. Zack Smith, who married Miss Lilly Clark, daughter of the late R. K. Clark; and Richard Smith, who married Miss Isla Ellerbe, daughter of Colonel E. B. Ellerbe. The daughter, Miss Anna Smith, is unmarried; the mother died a few years ago; the doctor has not remarried. Dr. E. B. Smith deserves more than a passing notice; he graduated in the medical college in Charleston, in 1860, with first distinction; was Assistant Surgeon in the army during the Civil War; he was, some years ago, elected to the lower House of the General Assembly without canvassing the county—he declined to canvass, stayed at home while others canvassed the voters; he is a very intelligent and well-posted man, up-to-date in every way, and one of our best citizens. He is a model and progressive farmer—his farm is a large one for these times and for this county, yet it seems to be cultivated like a garden—in first class condition; all the appointments about it seem to be arranged for convenience and success; he is great for experiments, and, I suppose, has made more experiments with the application and use of fertilizers than any experimental station in the State. Redding W. Smith, the father of Dr. E. B. Smith, married a second time, and by that marriage had a son, Stonewall Jackson Smith, a druggist at Mullins. John G. Smith married a Miss Jordan, and his sons are John, Elly and Ellison H. Smith, and three daughters; the sons are all doing well, and are substantial citizens. Elly Smith married, first, Miss Kate Brown, daughter of old C. B. Brown, of Marion, and had two sons, Tillman and LeGrande; the Brown wife died, and he married, a second time, a daughter of Daniel Snipes; know nothing as to his family by the last marriage. Know nothing of John and Ellison H. Smith's family, nor of the three daughters of John G. Smith. Margaret Smith, a daughter of Hugh Godbold Smith, married Stephen T. Collins; they are both dead, and their children live in the Gapway neighborhood, of whom the writer knows but little and that little will be deferred to the Collins family, when he comes to notice them. Hugh H. Smith married a Miss Shelly, and had one son and three or four daughters. Edward Smith married a Miss Collins, and by her had Redding (called Little Redding), Keene Davis, Ham E. G. and George Smith. This Redding was the father of Edgar, Lide, Dr. Frank and Edward Smith, all in the Mullins region; "Little Redding's" first wife was a Miss Spivey, daughter of Isaac Spivey, in the Bear Swamp and Holmesville section; the Spivey wife died, and he lately married the daughter of Jerry Lambert; "Little Redding" is a prosperous and well-to-do citizen. Of the others of Edward Smith's children and grand-children by Little Redding the writer can say nothing, for the want of information; he knows Dr. French Smith, at Mullins, a young single man, and is well spoken of as a physician, and no doubt but that he will do well.

James Smith, one of the sons of old John Smith, will represent another branch of the Smith family as it now exists in the county. Old man Hugh Smith, remembered by many now living, who lived and died some years ago at or near Temperance Hill, eight miles above Marion, on the road leading to Campbell's Bridge, on Little Pee Dee River, was a son of James Smith, and through him a grand-son of old John; don't know who old man Hugh Smith's mother or grand-mother was; old

Hugh married Miss Chloe Perritt, a sister of old man David Perritt; by their marriage they had five sons, Elly, Hugh G., Hardy, Willis and Joseph, and daughters, Sarah Ann (Mrs. James V. Rowell), Betsy (Mrs. James Lee), Sallie (Mrs. Wm. Turbeville), and Ailsey (Mrs. McLean), in Texas. Of these daughters, they all, perhaps, have children and grand-children, mostly unknown to the writer. Of the sons, Elly married in Mississippi; he was killed by a railroad train running over him, some fifteen or twenty years ago, at Marion; he left one son, who lives in Mississippi. Willis Smith married Miss Adaline Powers, and had six sons, Elly, Augustus, Mitchell Andrew (dead), Robert, Foster and Hugh, and two daughters, Harriett and Elmira. Augustus Smith married Hettie Perritt, and has five children (small). Foster Smith married a Miss Rogers, and has one child, a son. Hugh G. Smith married a Miss Turbeville, and had one daughter, who married Lemuel Turbeville; she is now dead, leaving several children. Joseph Smith married Miss Jane Page, daughter of the late John S. Page, and after living together some few years, they were divorced (during existence of the divorce law); they had no children. Hardy Smith married Ann Turbeville, and had Willis, Guery and several other children; he lives in the Gaddy's Mill section. Mrs. James Lee had Calvin, Willis and Elly, and daughters, Telatha (Mrs. McCrackin) and Lizzie (Mrs. George Turbeville). Mrs. Turbeville has only one son, Joseph, who married a daughter of Jerry Rowell, near Campbell's Bridge. Mrs. James V. Rowell had two sons, William and Volentine, and one daughter, Silsy, who married a Mr. Bailey. The writer's information as to this branch of the Smith family is somewhat meagre; and can say no more concerning it.

Another branch of the Smith family in the county is derived from old John Smith, a common ancestor, through his son, Samuel Smith, who lived and died on the road from Marion Court House to Buck Swamp Bridge, just below Temperance Hill—think he died in 1843, a very old man, between eighty and ninety years of age; he accumulated a large property for his day and time—lands, slaves and money; in his day, channels of investment were restricted almost exclusively to lands and negroes; old man Samuel lived close, managed well, and hence he accumulated much. It was said of him (and I suppose it was true) that he never used any of the produce of his farm until it was a year old—always looking for a famine; he made on his farm what he and his family lived on—spent nothing. It was further said of him that he never spent any silver or gold, but hoarded it—that when he died he had a barrel full of silver interspersed with gold; whether this was true or not, is not certainly known, but such is the traditional reputation. Don't know to whom he married—he, however, did marry, and had and raised a family of three children, two daughters and a son. Of the daughters, one (name not known) became the wife of old Captain William Page, and the other, Elizabeth (called Betsey), married Robert Moody. Old Captain William Page had and raised a large family, who have already been noticed herein among the Page family. Robert Moody lived and died on south side of Buck Swamp, opposite the bridge; he left his widow, Betsey, and a large family of children, who have already been mentioned herein among the Moody family and others, with whom connected. The son, Samuel (called Samuel Smith, Jr., while his father lived), married, first, a daughter of old Osborne Lane, hereinbefore mentioned; he settled on Buck Swamp, near where Mrs. Sophia Thompson, *nee* Sophia Bethea, now lives. By the Lane wife, Samuel Smith, Jr., as then called, had and raised two sons, John L. and Stephen. I think these have already been mentioned among the Lanes, and perhaps among the Huggins. As to the latter, John L. Smith became a member of the South Carolina Conference of the Methodist Church, as it then was (1834 or 5), and after traveling some three or four years, married a Miss Wannamaker, of Orangeburg, and located and settled on the north side of Buck Swamp, opposite his father's, where he lived, raised sons and daughters, and died there, after marrying a second wife, the Widow Henry; he died in 1878; he raised five sons, Daniel Asbury, Marcus L., Jacob W., John Albert and Wilbur F., and three daughters, Anna M., Mary J. and Hettie. I think these have all been noticed herein among the Lanes, the Betheas, the Nichols and the Pages. John Albert married a Widow Smith, *nee* Collins, in Mississippi, and afterwards came back here, was elected Clerk of the Court in

1880, and died before his time expired, leaving three daughters and a son. Henry, the latter, has a family and lives at Mullins. One of the daughters became the wife of John Wilcox, at Marion, and has a coming family. Another daughter became the wife of Dennis Berry, and has five children, daughters (small); and another, Laura, became the wife of Chalmers Rogers, at Mullins, and has two children. The widow, Jennie Smith, has not remarried, and lives with her daughter, Laura, at Mullins. Wilbur F. Smith, youngest son, after graduation in Wofford College, went to Mississippi, yet remains there, has a family. These latter have been mentioned here, because not among the Lanes, Betheas, Nichols and Pages. Stephen Smith, the other son by Samuel, Jr.'s, first marriage, married Polly Huggins, the (only) daughter of old John Huggins, and I think he and his children have already been mentioned among the Lanes and Huggins. Lest it may not have been done, I will say, Stephen Smith had sons, Ebby, George W., B. Gause, S. Elmore, S. Whiteford, J. Emory, and another named, as I think, Augustus, who was killed on or by a train, near Florence, during the war—he was a mere boy, and was among the reserves, on his way to service or returning from it, when the accident that terminated his life happened. Stephen Smith had and raised four daughters—one the wife of the late Mitchel Martin; another the wife of George Rogers, at Mullins; and two others, who married Nances. One of the Nances died or was killed in the war, and his widow afterwards married John C. Harrelson. These have alrady been mentioned among Huggins, Martins and Rogers. Samuel Smith, Jr., as he then was called, lost his Lane wife, and he married, a second wife, Sallie Hays, daughter of Benjamin Hays, of (now) Hillsboro Township, and by her had two sons, William H. and Samuel Smith, whom we will hereinafter designate as Junior and his father as Senior, and daughters, Mrs. Elizabeth Allen, Mrs. Mary Roberts, Mrs. Ginsey Ellis and Mrs. Florence Moody, the first wife of E. J. Moody. All these, I think, have already been mentioned among the Hays, Allens, Roberts, Betheas and Moodys. Samuel Smith, the father, was an enterprising and successful farmer, a good manager of his affairs and accumulated a large property, which he left to his children, what he had not previously given them—a large property entirely unencumbered, and which they and their descendants yet retain, notwithstanding the ravages of the war. This family of Smiths, as a whole, are industrious, energetic, frugal, honest, law-abiding and trustworthy citizens.

There is another family of Smiths, below Marion, which I understand is in no way related to those hereinabove noticed— I refer to the late William B. Smith and his family. He, as it is said, came when young from North Carolina, and settled below Reedy Creek Baptist Church, on an apparently poor place; he was called "Horse-swapping Billy Smith"—he was a great horse trader, and in that respect his mantle has fallen upon his sons, Nat. P. and Henry. "Nat Smith" don't stop at horses and mules, but he descends to oxen, and, I suppose, to all domestic quadrupeds and, maybe, to domestic bipeds, such as chickens, turkeys and geese. William B. Smith, away back in the 50's, carried the mail on horseback from Marion to Bennettsville, by way of Catfish, Reedy Creek, Harlleesville, Selkirk, Brownesville and Clio to Bennettsville, and back the same route, once a week—at which time the writer was postmaster at Reedy Creek; he went up one day and came back the next; sometimes one of his boys, James or Nat, would carry it. The writer remembers on one occasion, the old gentleman went up; his horse sickened and died at Bennettsville, and the next day Mr. Smith came back, walking and carrying the mail bags on his shoulders, and went on to Marion that evening. I suppose he was then fifty years of age, and the distance traveled on his zig-zag route was at least sixty miles. One of the men of the present day, much younger than Mr. Smith, would not think of such a trip. Mr. Smith had much of the "get up" in him, and whatever he undertook to do, he did it, and if he failed it was no fault of his; he was accustomed to labor and hardship, hence it did not hurt him. He lived to be over ninety years of age, and died only a few years ago, much respected. Don't know who his wife was; he raised a considerable family—four sons, if not more, James, Nathaniel P., William B. and Henry, and maybe others—these are all the writer remembers; don't know anything of his daughters, if he had any. James married Miss Anne Grantham, daughter of Owen Grantham, of North Carolina; by the marriage three daughters were born, Elizabeth, Kittie and Jimmy. Jimmy, I think, was born after the death of her father, who was killed by his wife's cousin, Bright Grantham, just after the war closed; he left his widow and, it may be said, three little children, all girls; the widow scuffled with the privations of the times incident to the war and reconstruction, and raised her daughters in credit and respectably. The eldest, Bettie, married a Mr. Smith—Charles, I believe, is his name; they have raised a family, several of them grown. The second daughter, Kittie, married W. S. Foxworth, now a leading and prosperous merchant in Marion, a capital man in many ways; they have three or four children, none grown. Jimmy, the youngest daughter, married Filmore Whitehearte, who is dead and left his widow with five or six children, all small. Nathaniel P. Smith married a Miss Foxworth, sister of W. S. Foxworth, of Marion; by this marriage several sons and daughters have been born. Two daughters married, don't know to whom. The oldest son, Harvey, sickened and died, a young man just entering life, a year or so ago. His other children are with him. William B., Jr., is one of the citizens below Marion; he married and has a family. Gilmore Smith, of Dillon, and the efficient marshal of that town, is a son of W. B. Smith, Jr.; married, I think, a Miss Stalvy, and has a coming family; he is an excellent man and officer, and is much respected. C. W. Smith, below Marion, is another son; has a family, about which nothing is known; he is also a good citizen. Henry, the youngest son, married a Miss Dozier, a daughter of the late Tully Dozier, and sister of J. T. Dozier, the present County Supervisor; she died a few years ago, and left, I think, two or three children (small). Henry has not remarried; he and his brother "Nat" are each running a livery stable in Marion, and are successful men.

There are some other Smiths in the Mullins section of the county, and is supposed to be no relation to the other Smiths of that community. John Smith, of Clay Hill, and George Smith, are referred to; they descended from our old Moses Smith, who is said to have been a very excellent man; he was a preacher (Methodist), and the reputation of him is, that he practiced in his own life what he preached to others; he was the grand-father of John and George, now of that community. The old man, Moses, had three sons, Isaiah, Daniel and James. What became of Isaiah and Daniel is not known to the writer. James married Celia Lewis, daughter of old Hardy Lewis; they had three sons, John, Daniel and George, and may have had daughters—know nothing of any. John Smith (which is said to be no name) and George are both good, honest, hard-working men, unpretentious; they are farmers—John in particular; he has an excellent place at Clay Hill, and the writer heard him once say that he could grow anything on his place common to that region, except mortgages—it would not grow them; and from that expression, it may be inferred what sort of man and farmer he is. "He lives at home and boards at the same place." Know nothing of their immediate families. John Smith is as independent in his circumstances as is Vanderbilt, and, I presume, a much happier man.

The late John M. Smith, of Marion, was the son of a Methodist preacher—I think from Marlborough County; he was a tailor by trade; he married a daughter of James H. Pearce, and sister of Dr. James F. Pearce, of West Marion—an excellent lady she was; they raised a nice family of three sons, Robert J., Colin and A. Jackson, and two daughters, Mollie and Anna. Of the daughters, Mollie never married. Anna became the wife of David Gasque, brother of E. H. Gasque, of Marion; they live in Columbia, and have for years; they have a family. Of the sons, I think, Robert J. is dead—was an upright business man, moved off somewhere. Colin and Jackson are in high railroad positions—Colin in Columbia and A. Jackson in Knoxville, Tenn, and has his mother with him; they have been in railroad positions ever since they were grown, and Colin is now a middle-aged man. John M. Smith, the father, was the first railroad agent at Marion, 1854; he remained in that position for many years—was honest, straight and harmless, and one of the neatest and most cleanly men I ever saw; he would wear a pair of linen pants in the summer all the week and handle freight every day, and at the end of the week the iron prints would not be out of his pants. He lived and died in Marion, at the age of seventy-two or seventy-three, on the 3d February, 1893, without an enemy.

There is another Smith in Britton's Neck, of what family is unknown. The writer only knows of him—has seen him at Marion. I allude to Scotch Smith; he is an energetic and capital man and good citizen.

FLOWERS.—This family sprang from Henry Flowers, who came from England, about the middle of the eighteenth century. He married Patsy Savage, and settled and lived where ex-Sheriff W. T. Evans now lives; he took up and owned large bodies of land around him, many thousands of acres; he had and raised a large family; the sons were Archie, John, Henry, William, James, Jacob and Bennett; the daughters were Mollie, Betsy, Nancy, Sallie and Olive, or Olivia. Of the sons, the writer can get no definite information, except as to Bennett, the youngest son of old Henry, who married Miss Annie Payne, and had and raised two sons, Ervin Huger and John J., and three daughters, Annis, Olivia and Annie. Of the sons, Ervin Huger married Elizabeth Keeffe, and had one daughter, Telatha, when the father died, and his widow married Matthew Martin, and had several children for him. Telatha grew up and married the late D. S. Henry, and by him had one son, John E. Henry, our present energetic and progressive fellow-citizen on Buck Swamp, who has already been noticed herein among the Henrys. The widow, Telatha Henry, afterwards married Rev. John L. Smith, on Buck Swamp; from this marriage there was no offspring; Mr. Smith died and left her a widow, and she is now seventy-two years of age, and lives with her son, John E. Henry. Of the other son of Bennett Flowers, John J., the writer knows nothing or but little; he infers that he was the immediate or remote progenitor of our present fellow-citizen at Marion, John H. Flowers, who married, about 1859 or 1860, Miss Anne Flowers, his cousin, at Marion; she died childless, some years ago; her husband still survives. Annis, the eldest daughter of Bennett Flowers, married Solomon Owens, who soon died and left her a widow; she died childless some years after, at a very advanced age. Olivia, the second daughter of Bennett Flowers, married General Elly Godbold, and by the marriage six children were raised, three sons, Huger, Zack and David, and three daughters, Ann, Cherry and Maggie. Huger

Godbold, the eldest son, married a Miss White, daughter of old man Stephen White; they had and raised, I think, three sons and three or four daughters, who have already been noticed among the Godbolds. Zack Godbold married a Miss Gregg, and had six or seven children, three sons and three or four daughters; his wife died, and he married again, and moved off. Of his sons, our excellent and enterprising fellow-citizen, D. E. Godbold, one of the leading merchants now at Mullins, is the oldest; he married a Miss Young, daughter of the late Major J. B. Young, and has some family (small); he is Mayor of the town of Mullins, at this writing, is much respected and a very efficient officer. Of his sisters, I think they are all dead, except Miss Susy, the youngest, who is with him, quite an accomplished lady and an efficient business woman. Zack Godbold raised a company for the Confederate Army, and went into the war as Captain, and was a brave and efficient officer. David Godbold, the youngest son of General Elly Godbold and his wife, Olivia, went into the Confederate Army, and was killed in battle or died of disease—a promising young man. Of the daughters of General Godbold and wife, Ann, the eldest, married Alexander Gregg, of West Marion, who was murdered by some negroes, on the morning of the election, 7th November, 1876—perhaps the most memorable election ever held in South Carolina. Four or five of the negroes were tried for his murder, and one (Jack Burgoyne) was convicted for it by a negro jury, sentenced to be hanged, and was hanged. The writer was Solicitor at the time, and knows whereof he writes. Mr. Gregg was an excellent and well-to-do citizen, a harmless and inoffensive man. Those were troublous times. The widow, Ann Gregg, still survives; she has some three or four children, all grown. Cherry, the second daughter of General Godbold and wife, married Robert Gregg, of West Marion, who died some years after marriage, childless; his widow married then J. Maston Gaddy; they had no offspring, Gaddy died, and she died soon after. Maggie, the youngest daughter of General Godbold and wife, died at about eighteen years of age, unmarried.

Henry Flowers, one of the seven sons of old Henry, the first comer, was the father of the late Love Flowers, below Marion;

don't know who the wife of Henry, Jr., was, nor is it known whether he had other sons than Love nor whether he had any daughters. Love Flowers, born in 1790, lived to be eighty-four years old, and died in 1874; he married twice; his first wife was Elizabeth Brown; there were two sons by this marriage, William and John. William married Caroline Brown, daughter of Richard Brown; he died about two years ago, in Horry County, leaving a number of children. John married Elizabeth Dozier, a sister of J. Tulley Dozier; John died about three years ago. Love Flowers' first wife dying, he married Martha Baxley, a daughter of Barny Baxley; by this marriage he had twenty-two children, all of whom died in infancy, except James J., Henry, Williamson, Barny, A. Love, Bennett, Nathan, Joel, Elly, Everett, Samuel S., Lucy Ann and Rachel. It seems that thirteen of the twenty-two were raised. James J. Flowers never married; he died in 1865. Henry Flowers married Sarah Ann James, a daughter of Henry James; he died in prison, in Elmira, N. Y., 1864; he left a number of children. Williamson Flowers married, first, Elizabeth Marlow; by her he had a number of children; this wife died, and then he married Mrs. Martha Parker; they have no children; live below Marion Court House. Barny A. Flowers married, first, Ann Lambert, daughter of James Lambert; no children; she died, and he married, a second wife, Mrs. Ann James, widow of Henry L. James; they have five children (small). Love A. Flowers married Henrietta Brown, daughter of Lewis Brown, and had a large family; he was killed by lightning, below Marion, in 1872. Bennett Flowers married Miss Mary James, daughter of Henry James; had one child, and died of disease in the Western Confederate Army during the war. Nathan Flowers married Miss Ann Marlow; no children; he died in prison at Rock Island, Ill., about the close of the war. Joel Flowers never married; he died in prison at Elmira, N. Y., during the war. Elly Flowers married Miss Minnetta Brown, daughter of William Brown; they had one child; they live on the old homestead of his father, on Reedy Creek, below Marion. Everitt Flowers married Margaret A. James, daughter of Henry L. James; they have five children (small), and live at Dillon. Samuel S. Flowers married Susan Best, daughter of Captain John J. Best, of Horry; they had several children; moved to Texas eight years ago; the last heard from them, his wife was dead and he was in Keaney, Nebraska. Lucy Ann Flowers married J. Tully Dozier; they have a number of children, among whom is our present County Supervisor, J. T. Dozier, Jr. J. T. Dozier, Sr., is dead; the widow is living with her son, J. T., Jr. Rachel Flowers first married Lewis Brown, Jr.; they had one child, and her husband died during the war; after the war, the widow married J. C. Price; they have a large family, now in Horry. Old Love Flowers, a patriarch, had eleven sons in the war, including the two by his first wife, William and John; all his sons went to the war, except Everett and Samuel S.—the two latter were too young. Few men contributed so many to the lost cause. The first Methodist Church or meeting house built in the county was built (I suppose, of logs,) by old Henry Flowers, and was located near the house of ex-Sheriff Evans, about 1783 to 1790. Bishop Asbury's Journal speaks of it, which I have not now before me, but to which I refer. Asbury and Whatcoat, in passing through the country on their way to Charleston, stopped at Flowers' house, and preached under the oak now standing in ex-Sheriff Evans' yard, and with such success as to induce Mr. Flowers to build a meeting house, in which the Bishop afterwards preached in his annual travels. Flowers and his family became members of his church and others also, and it is said that old "Jimmy Jenkins," afterward and for many years a distinguished preacher of that denomination, joined the church at that place, which was for many years thereafter called "Flowers' Meeting House." Flowers and his seven sons and five daughters, together with their families—for several of them had, doubtless, married by that time—were enough of themselves to form and keep up a respectable church of their own without the accession of others to it, and it may be reasonably supposed that others joined and worshipped there. The last vestige of the large body of land owned there by old Henry Flowers, was bought by the Commissioners of the Poor for the county, in 1860, from John H. Flowers and wife, Anne, for a county poor farm and house, and it was located and erected there in 1860. The writer was, at the time, Chairman and Treasurer of the board—made the trade for the land (ninety-seven acres, I think), drew the deed, had it executed, paid the purchase price to the grantors, $970, had the buildings constructed, and established it as a home and farm for the poor, and, I believe, it is kept up and used for that purpose to the present time. The deed is recorded, and if the original deed is examined, it will be seen to be in my handwriting. The wisdom of the scheme has been vindicated by over forty years' continued use. Have not seen it for fifteen or twenty years; don't know how it is managed now.

MULLINS.—This family is an importation from North Carolina, and a good importation it is—would like to have several others such. The first of the name in this county was the late Colonel William S. Mullins, followed a few years later by his brother, the late Dr. James C. Mullins, and from these two brothers came all by that name now in the county. Their parents were Fayetteville, N. C., people—names not known. It is said their father was a merchant in Fayetteville, and did not succeed in making a fortune for his children—only enough to educate them—three sons, William S., James C. and Henry; one daughter, as known to the writer, Ida, who became the wife of E. B. Owens, of this county, and another daughter, who became the wife of a Mr. McNeill, who finally settled in Horry. It seems that the greatest ambition of their father was to educate his children (a very laudable ambition). His son, William S., after graduation in the University of North Carolina, and after admission to the bar of North Carolina, came to Marion County, and married a Miss Hodges, daughter of the late Dr. Samuel Hodges, of the Little Pee Dee and Gapway section; by his marriage he acquired a large property in lands and negroes; and having a competency thus acquired, and the exigencies of the family and the large estate which had fallen in by the death of Dr. Hodges, and of his only son, William H., who died unmarried, he did not pursue the profession of law, for which he was peculiarly and eminently fitted, but devoted himself to his farm and family, to which may be added politics or state craft, and he was much better adapted to the latter than to farming. Colonel Mullins was first introduced to the public of Marion County in the memorable contest between Co-operation and Secession, or Separate State action, in 1851. The contest was exciting and bitter—every nerve was strained and every legitimate means used by each party. The county was carried by the Co-operation party by only thirty-five majority, and the success of the party in Marion County was attributed mainly to the eloquent appeals to the fears of the people by Colonel Mullins; he was a natural born orator, and having a mind well stored with general knowledge of affairs, and especially with the knowledge of governmental science, his stump speeches were overwhelmingly effective. The State was also carried my a safe majority for Co-operation, and thus prevented, for the time, the final issue between the North and the South. The Secession party believed then, as it is most generally believed now, if the State had then (1851) seceded, there would have been no attempt on the part of the Federal Government to coerce the seceding State or States, as the case might be; that the fanaticism of the North had not been worked up to the point of war as it was in the next nine or ten years, and the South would have been allowed to depart in peace. Whether that would or would not have been better for us, need not and cannot be discussed here. Thus was Colonel Mullins introduced to the people (publicly) of Marion, and initiated into South Carolina politics; he filled a large place in the confidence of the people, it may be said, to the end of his useful life. In 1852, there was a general election for Senators and Representatives in the Legislature, and the contest in that election was about as lively as it had been the year before—each party had its candidates. The result was that Dr. Harllee (Secession) was elected Senator by 171 majority, and Dr. W. R. Johnson (Secession) and W. S. Mullins and Colonel W. W. Durant (Co-operation) were elected members of the lower Houses by small majorities. Colonel Mullins was then successively elected to the lower House from that time to 1868, when Reconstruction put him out, with all other Democratic white people. Colonel Mullins at once took a high stand in the Legislature—a strong and successful debater, was one of the then several leaders in that body. During his career as a member of that body he was run for Speaker against (now) Judge C. H. Simonton, and was beaten only by three votes. There were strong men then in that body—such men as James Simmons, B. F. Perry, C. H. Simonton and many others. To be Speaker of that House was no little honor or attainment. William S. Mullins was no ordinary man—hence so much space (much needed) in this book is devoted to him. He was brilliant, quick and always ready, and had a reputation as orator and legislator of which his adopted people and his family, descendants may justly be proud. Colonel Mullins was President of the Wilmington and Manchester Railroad Company for one or two years; he was also elected Senator to the Legislature in 1872, but was counted out, as all other Democrats elected that year were by the Radical election officials then in power. As already stated, he married Miss Hodges, and they raised to be grown six sons, William L., Frank, Charles, Edward, Henry and Guerry, and three daughters, Mary, Lizzie and Julia. Of the sons, Frank and Charles died young men and unmarried. William L. is yet unmarried. Edward married a Miss Shaffer, lives in Marion and, I think, has two daughters, not grown; he was so unfortunate as to be accidentally shot on Thanksgiving Day, a few years ago, by which he became paralyzed and lost both his eyes. Henry married a Miss Norwood, daughter of Geo. A. Norwood, of Greenville, and is one of the leading merchants of Marion; has two or three children (small); he was a graduate of the South Carolina College; studied law and entered upon its practice with flattering prospects of success, but after two or three years abandoned it altogether, engaged in merchandising, and is now following it, in partnership with his brother-in-law, Samuel A. Norwood, at Marion—apparently doing a large business. Guerry Mullins, the youngest son of Colonel Mullins, married, first, Maggie McKerall, daughter of the late W. J. McKerall, Esq., who died childless, in about a year after marriage; he married, a second time, Miss Emily Price, daughter of the late Dr. D. S. Price, of Marion; think he has by her one or two children (small); he is engaged in buying cotton at Marion. The eldest daughter, Mary, married Joseph McIntyre, of Marion; they live at Mullins, and own and cultivate the old homestead of her father, W. S. Mullins; they have several children, some of them grown, names unknown to the writer. Lizzie, the second daughter, married Dr. Archie McIntyre, of

Marion, within the last year; they live in Marion. Julia, the youngest daughter, is unmarried. Dr. James C. Mullins, the second importation from North Carolina, after graduating in medicine, came to South Carolina for the practice of his profession, about 1851, and located first near Parnassus, in Marlborough County; he married there Miss Artemissia DeBerry, a daughter of old Henry DeBerry; he moved to Marion just before the war, and settled in the town for the practice of his chosen profession, and at once obtained a good and lucrative practice; he had three children, sons, Benjamin R., Henry and Johnson; he went to the war as an army surgeon, and remained therein till the end at Appomattox; his wife, Artemissia, died during the war—I think, in 1863 or 1864; he came home from the war, and remained a widow until 17th May, 1871, when he married again, Miss Florence Moody, daughter of E. J. Moody; by this marriage he had three sons, R. Randolph, Frank K. and Charles Woods, and one daughter, Florence. Of these, Frank died unmarried, a young man. Randolph and Wood are both single. Of the children of his first wife, Henry, a very promising young man, died in Bennettsville, where he was engaged in a profitable business, some ten or more years ago. B. R. Mullins, his oldest son by first marriage, married a daughter of Dr. Dixon Evans, of Marion, and has several children; he is a capital business man and is now Sheriff of the county, and promises well in that important position. Johnson, the youngest son by his first marriage, went West some years ago. R. Randolph, the oldest son by the second marriage, is in business (druggist) in Greenville. The Doctor died some five or six years ago; his widow, with her two youngest children, Woods and Florence, live in Marion. Dr. Mullins was an excellent physician; up to a short time before his death, he did an immense practice and had the confidence of the entire community; for the last year or two of his life, there seemed to be a failure of his mind—his mental powers gave way. Colonel W. S. Mullins and Dr. J. C. Mullins, it was said, had a brother, named Henry, who was more talented than either of his brothers; he went into the war as Captain of a company in a North Carolina Regiment, and was killed in battle in Virginia. The Mullins were loyal to their section.

GREGG.—Robert J. Gregg, formerly of West Marion, and one of the numerous and respectable family by that name, came over on the east side in 1818, and married a Miss Evans, a daughter of old Nathan Evans, and sister of the late Thomas Evans, Sr., and ever after lived and died, in 1874, in the town of Marion; he had and raised two sons, William Wesley and Robert Evans Gregg, and several daughters. Of the daughters, one, Serena, became the wife of William C. Foxworth, who raised a family, now among us as fellow-citizens. Another, Ann, married John Woodberry, of West Marion, and she raised, I think, two sons (names not remembered). Another married the late William J. Dickson; she had and raised quite a family—four sons, James J., Bonna (both dead, unmarried), Wesley and Maxcy, our present County Auditor. Wesley married in Darlington and resides there. Maxcy is unmarried (he and a maiden sister live together); and, I think, four daughters. The eldest, Ida, married Dr. D. S. Price, and is now a widow, with some children. Two other daughters married George C. Walsh, and he and the latter wife have gone West. Of the two sons of old man R. J. Gregg, William Wesley married a Miss Wayne, of Georgetown; they had a family of the three sons—William, who was killed in the war, Wesley and Robert James; and three daughters, Nannette, who married a Mr. Carter, and have gone elsewhere, and Anna and Lizzie—the two latter are unmarried. Our fellow-citizen, Wesley L. Gregg, married a Miss Bell, of Columbia, an excellent lady; they have, I think, three sons (names unknown), all grown, and one daughter, whose name, I think, is Belle. None of the sons of Wesley nor the daughters are married. Wesley is a cotton buyer of Marion. Robert James Gregg, the younger brother of Wesley, married a lady, I think, of Wilmington, N. C., her maiden name not known; they have a considerable family; sex and number not known, some of them are grown; he is merchandising at Marion. The father, William Wesley Gregg, was killed or died of disease in the war; his widow still survives and is now well advanced in years—an excellent old lady. Robert Evans Gregg, the younger son of old R. J. Gregg, married a Miss Shaw, sister of the late Judge Shaw; they had several children, don't know how many. A son, Robert E., Jr., who married a Miss Miller, in Marion; he died last year—don't know whether he left any child or not. Another son, Thomas, who is unmarried and lives at Dillon, superintends the Emerson Hotel in that town, and is a worthy young man. Another son, who died some four or five years ago, not grown. The eldest daughter, Nannie, married Henry E. Gasque; she is a very smart woman—they have one or two children; and another daughter, Lena, grown and unmarried. If there are other children, they are unknown to the writer. Robert Evans Gregg died two or three years ago, at about seventy-five years of age; was an industrious and harmless man, honest to the core. The old man, Robert J. Gregg, the progenitor of all the Greggs herein mentioned, was one of the best of men—"the salt of the earth;" he was Tax Collector for the county in *ante-bellum* days for more than thirty years—was first elected in 1838, and was elected every two years consecutively thereafter till the war. The Tax Collector in those days took the tax returns, which the Auditor now does, and then collected the taxes, and made his returns to and paid over the moneys collected to the Treasurer of the Lower Division, in Charleston. And the old gentleman, often before the day of railroads, walked to Charleston and carried his returns and money, paid it over to the Treasurer, and bring home a clear receipt. On one occasion, he and General William Evans were in Charleston together—old man Gregg a foot and the General in a sulky; they both left Charleston on the same morning, a three days' travel from home. Sometimes one would be ahead on the road and sometimes the other, and so they had it, and on the evening of the third day, old man Gregg arrived in Marion about half an hour ahead of the General. This was fifty years ago or more. Great improvements have been made since that time—the facilities for travel and communication with Charleston and with the world generally have been greatly multiplied; but while these great improvements have been made, the morals of the county has greatly deteriorated. No Tax Collector or County Treasurer would now dare take such a trip with his thousands of money in his pocket; he would be killed and robbed on the road, as was Treasurer Copes a few years ago, in Orangeburg County. No doubt, old Uncle "Jimmy Gregg" felt as safe on the road then as he did at home—if he had felt otherwise, he would not have ventured the trip. During the long service of old "Uncle Jimmy Gregg," as he was affectionately and familiarly called in that office, there were never any shortages, as now-a-days—not the least breath of suspicion of wrong-doing, be it said to his credit in memory of him. It is a legacy to his descendants to be prized higher than wealth, more precious and lasting than gold. Wealth may take to itself wings and fly away, but character never. R. J. Gregg was one of the extensive family of Greggs in West Marion, but to which branch of that family the writer knows not.

COLLINS.—Of this scattered and extensive family the writer has not been able to gather sufficient data from which to connect them and to trace their genealogy satisfactorily. The first now known of them were two brothers, a hundred or more years ago—the two brothers were Thomas and Jonah. Thomas was the progenitor of the Collins about Maiden Down and Mullins. The writer saw old man Thomas seventy years ago; he lived and died on Maiden Down and Martin Swamp, right at the junction of the latter with the former; he was then past middle life, and, I think, was a Justice of Peace or Magistrate away back in the 30's—a prominent man in his day; he had a family, but do not know who his wife was; he was the great-grand-father of the late Sheriff Robert Collins. He had a son, named Thomas (and perhaps others), who was the father of John, Solomon and Samuel, and probably four daughters. Solomon and John married sisters—the sisters of old Captain John Rogers, of the "Fork" section; and their father, Thomas Collins, Jr., married, for a second or third wife, another sister; thus it appears that the father's wife and the wives of his two sons, Solomon and John, were sisters—and if they all had offspring by the respective marriages, it would be difficult to tell what relation the children would be to each other. John Collins, the grand-son of old Thomas, was the father of the late Sheriff Robert Collins, and of his brothers, the late Stephen T. Collins and Samuel Collins; John may have had other sons and, perhaps, daughters, not known to the writer. Don't know who Samuel Collins married; or anything of the children (if he had any) of Solomon Collins. There are two very respectable, good citizens now in the Mullins section, by the name of John and Owen Collins—they, perhaps, are sons of Solomon Collins or Samuel; they both have families. Owen has a son, married, who is called "Romney"—that his true name is Deuteronomy, a name taken from the Pentateuch, one of the five books of Moses. Stephen T. Collins, brother of Sheriff Collins (older), married Miss Margaret Smith, daughter of Hugh Godbold Smith; he raised a family, how many and of what sex is not known; he had a son, Hugh Collins, living on the road to Mullins just above Gapway Church, who seems to be doing well, and has a family; he also had a daughter, who married E. B. Owens, already noticed among the Owens family. Stephen T. Collins may have had other children but they are not known to the writer; he was deputy for his brother, Robert, while Sheriff, and was very efficient; he died a few years ago. Robert Collins, the Sheriff, married a Miss Powell, of North Carolina, and had and raised a family of three sons and, perhaps, daughters. Of the three sons, Barney, the eldest, married a Miss Wall, sister of George Wall, of Marion; they have a family, already mentioned among the Walls. John, the next son, died a young man, at Marion, whilst his father was Sheriff. Sydney, the youngest son, married some one to the writer unknown, and has gone out of sight—don't know what has become of him. Sheriff Collins, the father, died some years ago. The writer will here relate the circumstances under which he became Sheriff: In May, 1867, during the Reconstruction period, Neill C. McDuffie, who was then Sheriff, resigned the office, and the fact of his resignation was not known in Marion to the public for two weeks, when it became known in the following manner: The writer one day received a letter from Governor James L. Orr, announcing the fact, and saying that if we could get some man who could take the "iron-clad oath," that was suited to the office, that he thought he could get General Canby to appoint him, and urged that we attend to it at once, lest General Canby might appoint some objectionable negro or some carpet-bagger. I immediately showed the letter to Hon. A. Q. McDuffie, Judge Wilcox and others. It was agreed among us that Robert Collins was the man—that he was fit for the office, having been a deputy for several years, and that he could take the required oath, as it was known to us that he was opposed to the war. I saw Mr. Collins that evening and opened the matter to him; he said he could take the oath and would accept the office if he could give the required bond, and asked me to wait a reply to the Governor until the next day, when he would let me know whether he would accept or not. The next day he saw me and said he could give the bond and would accept the position. I immediately replied accordingly to the Governor, and in a few days the appointment came from General Canby through the Governor; and thus Robert Collins was made and became Sheriff of the county. At the first general election after the Constitution of 1868, Collins was a candidate for Sheriff, and was elected for four years more, and served until his term expired; he made an excellent Sheriff, and especially in those troublesome times, but was not "Radical" enough to get the nomination of the dominant party for a second term. Daniel F. Berry received the Radical nomination, and General Elly Godbold, the Democratic nomination, in 1872. The latter was elected, but was counted out, and Berry was counted in, as was the case with all others at that election. Of the two brothers, old Collins, Thomas and Jonah, the latter became the progenitor of the Collins below Marion and the Pee Dee Island Collins; don't know much about them. There were two or three brothers, descendants of old Jonah, to wit: William, James and Jonah—these were either sons of old Jonah or grand-sons. William Collins was the father of Mrs. Valentine Rowell; he may have had other daughters and sons, of whom nothing is known. James Collins was the mediate or immediate progenitor of Benjamin Collins, of the Pee Dee Islands; he may have had other descendants. The late Shadrach Collins, of Pee Dee Islands, the great fisherman—the man that in late years supplied the Marion market with Little Pee Dee bream and other fish, belonged to this branch of the Collins family. Shadrach acquired the distinction or *sobriquet* of being president of the ugly club; he was not a handsome man, but a genial, good-natured one; always pleasant and in a good humor; ambitious only to live and to let live, did not want much of this world's goods. In the contest for the presidency of the ugly club, some twenty-five or thirty years ago, Shadrach was beaten by a man by the name of Powell, of West Marion; but Powell did not live long, and upon his demise Shadrach came in without opposition, and enjoyed his honors till his death, a few years ago. Under an unseemly exterior was a kind, good heart; he thought no evil and did none, and was respected by all who knew him.

Another family of Collins, not related, as I am informed, to those mentioned above, is that of the late John J. Collins, of the Ariel section; know nothing of his ancestry or where he came from; he was, before the war, a very substantial man and citizen; lived on a very poor place, yet he amassed a considerable fortune—did so mainly by raising young negroes. He was married, I think, three times—married, first, a Miss Wheeler, sister of General E. B. Wheeler; she had one son, John E., and perhaps other children. John E. Collins married a Miss Davis, sister of B. F. and J. P. Davis, of Marion. John E. Collins had some children, about whom nothing is known; he died, and his widow married a Mr. Floyd in Horry; the Wheeler wife died, and old man John J. Collins maried a Miss Howard, aunt of Colonel R. G. Howard, of West Marion; by the Howard wife he had sons, J. Burt and Edward Collins, and may be others, and a daughter, who married McRae, the father of our late County Supervisor, John A. McRae; she also had another son, Malcolm D. McRae, and daughters unknown to the writer. Edward C. Collins married a Miss Legette, daughter of Colonel Levi Legette, and by her had five or six sons and two daughters. One of the daughters married Frank Fuller, and resides at Florence. Think the other daughter died unmarried. One of the sons (Woodson) died in youth; the other sons are scattered—some in this county and some in Florence. Mrs. Collins, the mother, died, and her husband, Ed. C. Collins, went to Florida. J. Burt Collins married Miss Prudence Harrelson, daughter of old Hugh H. Harrelson, on the Buck Swamp, near Ariel; he was killed or died in the war; his widow survived him, and two daughters; the widow married again to A. P. Johnson; and the daughters married—one a Mr. Vaught and the other James Turbeville. The war and its results seemed to baffle and to paralyze the efforts of old man John J. Collins; he could not adapt himself to the changed conditions and did not survive the war long—he died in June, 1871, broken in spirit and in fortune; a good citizen in his day. This account of the Collins families may not be correct in some particulars, but it is given according to my knowledge and information—it is not satisfactory to the writer, but is inserted as it is.

WIGGINS, OF WAHEE.—The writer has not been able to obtain the genealogy of this family any further back than to old Micajah Wiggins, the father of the late Baker Wiggins. Old Micajah married (don't know who), and had and raised sons, Elias, Daniel, Micajah, Jr., Stephen, Benjamin and Baker, and one daughter, who married the late Thomas Shaw, and raised a family, who will be noticed further on. Baker Wiggins married Judah Foxworth, a daughter (I think) of old Job Foxworth—if not a daughter, a descendant; they raised three sons and two daughters, to wit: Charles, Henry Houston and Francis Marion, and Virginia and Martha Ann. Charles died unmarried. Henry Houston married Miss Florence Johnson, a daughter of the late William Johnson, of Wahee; they have seven children—one son, Harman, grown, the others not grown. Francis Marion, a merchant at Marion, unmarried, but ought to be. Of the daughters, Virginia married Corde Whiteheart; they have four children; reside at Florence. Martha Ann married Yancy Thomas, not long since, of whom nothing further is known. Baker Wiggins, the immediate progenitor of the above, was a first-rate man and excellent citizen; unfortunately for him, he had no early opportunities for education; he could not write his name, yet he was genteel and very courtly in his bearing and manners; in these respects he was excelled by but few; he was a well-rounded man and reliable in his dealings with his fellow-man. Elias Wiggins, brother of Baker, married, and had a family, how many is unknown—one son, Jasper Wiggins, and two daughters, Eliza and Susan. The son is unmarried. Of the daughters, Eliza married Joseph Powers; they have one or two children. The other daughter, Susan, is unmarried. Daniel Wiggins died, unmarried. Micajah, Jr., married a Miss Tanner, and removed to Georgetown. Stephen Wiggins married Elizabeth Powell; they had a daughter, who married Jerry Holden, a capital man and good citizen, in Wahee Township. Another daughter in Florida or Georgia—Susan (I think) ; don't know whether she is married or not. Benjamin Wiggins disappeared in the war—may have been killed.

There were in the early part of the nineteenth century some other Wiggins on the Pee Dee, who gave name to the "Wiggins Landing," on Great Pee Dee; they figured and were prominent previous to 1820. They are referred to as relatives of old Mason Lee, in his (Lee's) will, which gave rise to the celebrated will case of Mason Lee, as found in one of McCord's (second volume, I believe) Reports. Lee was a Marlborough man, and one of the most remarkable men I ever read of. He was wealthy, and gave all his property to the two States of South Carolina and Tennessee. He was never married. If he had died without a will, the Wiggins would have inherited his property. He had two illegitimate sons, twins; one of them he acknowledged to be his, the other he would not acknowledge, and gave as a reason that in crossing a staked and ridered fence, that one of the boys went over the rider and the other went under it. He stated in his will that he did not want any of the Wiggins to have any of his property, and authorized his executors to employ the best counsel in the State to defend his will against the Wiggins from the lower Courts to the highest Court. He further said that he would have given his property to the Penniwells, his two bastard sons, or the one he acknowledged, but he was afraid they did not have sense enough to successfuly contend with the Wiggins; and, therefore, he gave his property to the two States of South Carolina and Tennessee, who might be able to cope with the Wiggins. The will was attacked by the Wiggins, and it was carried by appeal from the Court of Ordinary to the Court of Appeals; the will was sustained, and the Wiggins were worsted. One of them was named Baker, and from that fact and the circumstances of their living near Wiggins' Landing, near the present location of the Wiggins family hereinabove mentioned, the writer draws the inference that the now existing family of Wiggins on Great Pee Dee are of the same stock as those related to old Mason Lee, and against whom old Mason had such strong aversion—this is only conjecture.

There are some other Wiggins in the county, in the Gaddy Mill section. Many now living knew old man Charles Wiggins; his first wife was a Miss Johnson, of Black River; his second wife was Molly Britt, of North Carolina; they are both dead. The first wife had three sons, John M., Henry and C. Wesley Wiggins. John M. married Aby Butler, has a family, of how many is not known; he has a son, Marion Wiggins, of Dillon, who married a Miss Grantham; has five children (small). Henry Wiggins married and had a son, named Charles, and lives at Dillon. The son married, and had two children; the mother died, and he married, a second time, the Widow Price, whose maiden name was Pauline Watson, daughter of the late William Watson; no offspring. Henry went West. C. Wesley married a McCormic, and settled in the Cotton Valley section of the county; he was doing well when last heard of by the writer—have not seen him for years. The old gentleman was a jolly old soul; he was jailer at Marion in the early 70's; his second wife had no children.

SHAW.—The first Shaw known in the county was William Shaw, born in March, 1759, and died in February, 1863, at the age of 103 years and eleven months to a day, as his son, the late John D. Shaw, told the writer—a case of remarkable longevity. The writer saw and talked with the old gentleman at Marion Court House, in 1859 or 1860, and he said he was 100 years old; could get about then with much agility—much more so than most men at the age of seventy years. In connection with old William Shaw, I will quote from Bishop Gregg's History, pp. 403 and 404, and note: "Another name which has no place in history and is now unknown in the region where he lived, deserves, in one respect at least, the first place in the annals of the Pee Dee, if not in the story of the Revolution throughout the thirteen colonies. Jacob Brawler gave his own life and the lives of twenty-two sons to the cause of liberty in Carolina. He removed from Tar River, North Carolina, to Liberty Precinct, and settled on Catfish, sixteen miles below the present village of Marion. He was married twice, and had large families by both wives, of whom all were sons, except one daughter. After the fall of Charleston, some of his sons were drafted; but the old man said there should be no division among them—that if one went all should go, and that he would accompany them. Twenty-four (three) in all, they embarked in the strife, and almost incredible to relate, but one of the sons returned to tell the tale of their slaughter. Overwhelmed by the calamity, the frantic wife and mother went off, not knowing whither, in search of her loved ones, but only to return, after a fruitless search, a broken-hearted mourner. She was eventually put upon the parish and lived to old age. The surviving son, who was of weak mind and body, died a few years after, and the name became extinct in Marion." In a note to the foregoing passage the Bishop says: "This account, which may appear almost incredible, was related to the author by the late Hugh Godbold, of Marion, and confirmed in every particular by William Shaw, a humble but worthy and respectable man who was of age at the time, lived in the same neighborhood and knew the family of Brawler well. Mr. Shaw was born in March, 1759, and in the spring of 1859, when the author spent the night with him at the house of Mr. Godbold, was possessed of astonishing vigor of body and mind for one of his years. Neither his sight nor hearing was very seriously impaired. He sat up to a late hour, listening with unabated interest to a conversation about the early days of the Pee Dee, taking part himself, and was as cheerful as a man in his prime. He said a red oak was then living, which stood in Brawler's yard. Brawler was poor, but ingenious. He adopted the following method of catching bears: Driving sharp nails, pointing downward, in a bee-gum, he baited it at the bottom (with honey), having secured it well. The bear putting his head down, would be caught beyond the possibility of extrication. William Shaw had passed his hundredth year when the author saw him for the first and last time, and considering his activity was one of the most remarkable cases of longevity on record."

The writer has made these lengthy quotations for the purpose, first, of showing to posterity the almost unparalleled case of longevity of one of our old citizens, William Shaw, and, secondly, to perpetuate the name and fame of old Jacob Brawler and family—a name that should ever be dear to the people of Marion County. Bishop Gregg's History has long been out of print, and is now read only by very few; but by giving it a place in this book, written for Marion County, the name and fame of Jacob Brawler and family may be preserved in the county for another hundred and fifty years—*esto perpetua.*

William Shaw married some one to the writer unknown; has tried to ascertain her maiden name, but has not been able to do so; he raised three sons and may be others, as well as daughters—one daughter, Ann; the sons were John D. Shaw, who died a few years ago, at the age of eighty-nine, and Thomas Shaw, who married and died some years ago, leaving four sons, Edward Baker, Daniel, Armstrong and Henry, and perhaps daughters. Henry was a soldier in the Confederate War; he married a Miss Wall, daughter of Washington Wall, and sister of George Wall, of Marion; they lived together several years, and had several children, when he died and left his widow and children surviving; the widow married again, a Mr. Hux, of Horry (see the Wall family). John D. Shaw, the oldest son of old William Shaw, married a Miss Davis, and had one son, our capital citizen, Stewart T. Shaw, and one daughter, Ann, and may be other children. Stewart T. Shaw married a Miss Altman, daughter of William Altman, and has a family, not grown. Stewart Shaw, like his father, John D. Shaw, is a most excellent man and a substantial, good citizen. His sister, Ann Shaw, married a Davis, and has a family, unknown to the writer. Thomas Shaw married a Miss Wiggins, sister of the late Baker Wiggins; they had four sons. Edward Shaw, killed in the war. Baker Shaw, who married Betsey Tanner; he is dead, and left five children, four girls and one son, named Thomas. Daniel Shaw married a Miss Foxworth, and has five sons, Willie, Clarence, Charley, Joseph and Evander. The two latter are married. Joseph married a Miss Boatwright, daughter of Foster Boatwright. Evander married a Miss Shaw. The other sons are unmarried, and live with their parents. Armstrong Shaw, the youngest son of Thomas Shaw, married Miss Maria Lucas, and has but one child, a daughter, named Julia, who lately married McRoy Dozier, who is clerking for W. S. Foxworth, at Marion, a promising young man. Old William Shaw had one daughter, Ann, who married Robeson Tanner, and became the grand-mother of Mrs. James T.

Dozier. The writer has learned that John D. Shaw married twice, but who, except the Davis wife, is not known, or whether there was any progeny by that marriage is not known.

DOZIER.—Of this family but little information has been obtained, yet it is a name long and favorably known in Marion. It is a French name, and came to South Carolina among the Huguenots (as is supposed). The first of the name as now known in the county was the great-grand-father of James Tully Dozier, the present County Supervisor of Marion County. His name was James Tully Dozier, a name which seems to have been continued in each succeeding generation to the present. Old James Tully had a son, James Tully, and he in turn had three sons, James Tully, John F. and Henry. Henry Dozier was very deaf; he and his brother, James Tully, are both dead; John F. still survives. To whom the three brothers, James Tully, John F. and Henry, married, is unknown to the writer. The late James Tully Dozier left a son, James Tully (now County Supervisor), who has been for years a very efficient deputy Sheriff, and, I suppose, knows not only all the public roads in the county, but all the neighorhood roads, and even many of the footpaths; he knows almost every man in the county above twenty-five years of age, and notwithstanding his extensive knowledge in these respects, he could not tell me much of the genealogy of his family—from which this lesson may be learned, viz: that no man can be an adept at everything. As already stated, he is now our County Supervisor; has not been long in office, but promises to make an efficient officer; he married Miss Iris Grice, a daughter of the late Sheriff, A. E. Grice, well remembered by many; he has two small boys, names not remembered; he had a sister, who married Henry W. Smith, now a liveryman in Marion; she died a few years ago, and left some three or four children. There is one David Dozier, a good citizen of the county, of the same Dozier family, but to which branch of the family he belongs, is not known to the writer. There were in former times other Doziers in Marion. I think one of our first Sheriffs and first Clerks of the Court were Doziers. A public street, one of the oldest streets in the town of Marion, was named and is now called

Dozier street; they were prominent in that day. There were other Doziers, I suppose of the same family, here in the early part of the last century. One, A. W. Dozier, represented us in Congress in the early days of the republic; he was a lawyer of ability and a man of high character; he lived in Georgetown or Williamsburg—a brother or uncle of our highly esteemed late fellow-citizen, Dr. T. J. Dozier, whose family are now in Britton's Neck and much respected. I think I rightfully infer that all these Doziers in Marion, Georgetown and Williamsburg had a common ancestor among the Huguenot stock, and are all collaterally related, either proximately or remotely. We had a young Dozier here, a lawyer, since the war, who lived and practiced law in Marion for two or three years, who manifested ability; he left, however, and went to California, and in a few years became a Circuit Judge in that great State, with a salary of $3,500 or $4,000 annually—no mean position, in honor or emoluments.

FOXWORTH AND BOATWRIGHT—Of this family, the writer is wanting in definite information which he has made efforts to obtain, but has not been able to do so. There were two old men here years ago, Stephen and Job Foxworth, and he presumes that most or all of the name now in the county are descendants of these two old men—in this, however, he may be mistaken. William C. Foxworth, on west side of Catfish, was a descendant of one of them; he was an exceptionally good man, was always on the side of right; he married Miss Serena Gregg, oldest daughter of R. J. Gregg. Old "Uncle Jimmy," as he was called, died a few years ago, leaving his wife, four sons, and two daughters—Edward, William Capers, George and Thomas, as I remember them, and the two daughters were Sallie and Lucy. Of the sons, Edward is single. William Capers married a daughter of Captain G. A. McIntyre, and has a family of some children, and is one of our good citizens. George married a Miss Watson, a niece of Major H. B. Cook's wife, in Horry. Thomas, I suppose, is not married. The eldest daughter, Sallie, married E. H. Gasque, and has already been noticed in or among the Gasque family. Lucy, the younger daughter, married a Mr. Hutaff, who died and left her with

two children, and then she died; don't know what became of
the children. William S. Foxworth is a descendant of one of
the old Foxworths, don't know which; think his father was
named Charley J.—in this, however, I may be mistaken. William S. Foxworth is a leading merchant of Marion; commenced there with nothing, comparatively, twenty-five or
thirty years ago, and by strict attention to business and good
management has succeeded well, has accumulated a large property and may be regarded as one of the heavy men, financially,
in the town of Marion; he married Miss Kittie Smith, a granddaughter of "Horse-Swapping Billy Smith," an excellent woman, and is raising a family—has three or four children. W.
S. Foxworth is no ordinary man; he is W. S. Foxworth—does
not pretend to be any one else; a strictly religious man, and by
precept and example tries to influence others in the same line—
he is a good and useful man; if we had more men like him the
county would be bettered. There is one Benjamin Foxworth
in Wahee, a quiet, hard-working and inoffensive citizen, a descendant of one of the old Foxworths; he married the Widow
Annis McWhite; has two children, a son, Truman, and a
daughter (name unknown). Truman married a Miss Godbold, daughter of Huger Godbold; they have some children.
The daughter married some one about Mullins; don't know
who, and has a family. There is, or was, a Jack Foxworth,
near Marion, some years ago; he married a Miss Johnson or
Meares; raised some family, don't know how many or what
has become of them, or whether Jack is dead or alive. Jack
was harmless, not ambitious of wealth or honors—he was contented to be Jack and Jack alone. Mrs. Goddard, now at
Marion, is a sister of Jack. I suppose they are descendants of
one of the old Foxworths, Stephen or Job. There was, before
the war, two Foxworths, William (called "Little Billy") and
James. William, I think, died and left a widow and, perhaps,
children. James moved off elsewhere; he lived, one year or
two, before the war, in the "Free State" section, on a place
afterward owned by the writer. As well as remembered, he
moved to Sumter County. These two latter, "Little Billy" and
James, were, as is supposed, descendants of one of the old Foxworths named herein. I think the late Ervin Godbold's wife

was a Foxworth, likewise a descendant of one of the old Foxworths; she died before Ervin, and left several children, one of whom married the late S. G. Owens, once Clerk of the Court in Marion. Another one, Thomas Godbold, is in Wahee, who, I think, lives on and runs the farm of S. G. Miles. I omitted to state in connection with the late William C. Foxworth, that he had a sister, who was the wife of Thomas W. Boatwright, a most excellent, good woman; she had only two children, daughters. One married Frank Dill, in Wahee; they have a family, don't know how many. One daughter of Frank Dill married Augustus Smith, of Mullins, a thriving, promising young man. The other daughter of Mrs. Boatwright married Hon. S. W. Smith, of Mullins, whose family, only two children, a son and a daughter, have already been mentioned among the Smiths or Huggins families. Frank Dill and S. W. Smith, the husband of these two Boatwright girls, are first class men and leading citizens of their respective communities. Frank Dill, of Wahee, is a son of the late Bright Dill, of Britton's Neck, who was, I think, an importation from Abbeville County, and a good importation it was—would like to have many more such; he was none other than a Christian gentleman. In connection herewith, the Boatwrights may be noticed. Thomas W. Boatwright, as above stated, married Miss Foxworth, sister of the late W. C. Foxworth; he was a harmless, inoffensive man—if he ever harmed any one, it was himself, yet he had energy and push about him; his wife was a most excellent lady; they had but two children, daughters, who were well raised, with right ideas of life, have made good housewives, and have raised and are raising nice families—the virtues of the parents are inherited by the children and shape their course in life. Don't know anything of the ancestry of T. W. Boatwright, or of any other Boatwright in the county; there are other Boatwrights in the county, or have been—Foster, John and Eli Boatwright, but of the families of either the writer knows nothing, nor what relation they are to each other, if any, is not known; they are humble and peaceable citizens, content with their own and live houestly. There may be other Boatwrights with their connections in the county, not known to the writer.

A HISTORY OF MARION COUNTY. 525

WHITE AND MONROE.—The genealogy of this family was obtained from W. M. Monroe, of Marion, whose mother was a Miss White. He says the first known to him was his great-grand-father, Joseph White, who came from England; but when, he does not state; he married Judith Gainey; they had five children—four sons, Silas, Matthew, Benjamin and Stephen, and one daughter, Elizabeth. Silas married Elizabeth Avant, and had two sons, John and Andrew, and two daughters, Charlotte and Elizabeth; he married, a second time, Eliza Rowell, sister of Major Wm. B. Rowell, and had three sons, Joseph, William and Whitby; he married, the third time, the Widow Fladger, widow of old Charles Fladger; they had no children; he (Silas) was the grand-father of all the Whites living in the Centenary neighborhood, below Marion. Matthew White never married; he died a young man. Stephen White married Mary Fore, daughter of Richard Fore, and a sister of old Joel Fore, whose family has already been mentioned herein; they had six children—two sons, Nelson and James, and four daughters, Fanetta, Angeline, Mary and Rhoda. James married Ann Eliza Stackhouse, daughter of Isaac Stackhouse, and sister of Colonel E. T. Stackhouse; they had one child only, a daughter, Martha; he died soon after marriage; the widow married Daniel Fore, who has already been mentioned herein among the Fores and Stackhouses, as also her daughter, Martha. Nelson White married Frances Finklea, and had six children—two sons, James and Stephen, and four daughters, Mary, Eugenia, Sallie and Alice. Can trace them no further. Fanetta, the eldest daughter of Stephen White, married David Monroe; they had eight children—five sons and three daughters; the sons, Robert, William M., David, Walter and Thomas; the daughters were Sallie, Mary and Maggie. Of the sons, Robert married a Miss Baker, and has a family. William M., one of the leading merchants at Marion, married Miss Mary McMillan, a daughter of Major S. E. McMillan; they have a family of six or seven children, all boys. Don't know who David married, if married at all. Walter S. Monroe married a Miss McCall, of Bennettsville, sister of Colonel C. S. McCall, and died; don't know whether with or without issue. Thomas Monroe married Miss Rhoda Gaddy, daughter of the late James M. Gaddy; they have some children, how many or of what sex is unknown. Of the Monroe daughters, Miss Sallie is unmarried. Mary and Maggie both married— one to James T. Baker, and is dead, leaving five or six children, all sons; they live at Marion. The other daughter married a Mr. Summerset, and, I think, is dead. While writing about the Monroes, it is proper to mention (and it may have been mentioned herein already) that Major David Monroe was one of the many good importations from North Carolina; he had been married twice before his marriage to Miss Fanetta White; first, to a Miss Mace (and may have already been noticed among the Mace and Godbold families); by the Mace wife he had one child, a daughter; her mother died and left her an infant; she grew up and married a Mr. King, of Fayetteville, N. C.; did well, and, I suppose, has children and grand-children in the old North State; Major Monroe's second wife was a Widow Haselden, whose maiden name was Elizabeth Godbold; by his marriage with the Widow Haselden he had two sons, James and Francis Marion. James, I don't think married; he was Colonel of a regiment in the Western Army of the Confederate States, and was killed or died with disease or wounds. Francis Marion Monroe married Miss Carrie Lewis, daughter of the late Ebben Lewis; lives near Latta, and has long been a prominent physician of the county and of the Latta community; he has a nice family—five daughters and two sons. His eldest son, Clement, died a young man, quite promising, while a student in the South Carolina College. The younger son, McKay, or McCoy, is now a young man about grown. One daughter, Anna, married James G. Baker, now of Spring Branch; they have some children, how many or of what sex is unknown. The other daughters are all unmarried. Angeline, the second daughter of old Stephen White, married Joseph Hunter, I think, of Darlington; they had three sons, Stephen, James and William, and a daughter, Mary. Of the sons, one married Miss Costaricca Jones, daughter of the late Fred D. Jones, of Marion—think they have already been mentioned herein among the Jones or Watsons; he died a few years ago, and left Costa. a widow, with six children. Don't know of the other Hunter children. Mary, the third daughter of old man

Stephen White, married Huger Godbold; they had seven children—four sons, Julius, Elly, Waties and Robert, and three daughters, Maggie, Alice and Leila. Of the sons, Waties is the only one now living in the county; he married a Miss Rogers, daughter of Joseph Rogers, of Wahee; I think they have two children. His youngest son, Robert, married Lizzie Jones, daughter of Allen Jones, of Mullins; he was in railroad employ and was killed on the railroad, and left her a widow, with one child, a daughter. Of the daughters of Huger Godbold, one married a Mr. Gause, another married Truman Foxworth, and one not married. Rhoda, the youngest daughter of old Stephen White, married, first, James Graham; he soon died, and then she married Stephen Smith; he died, and she is now a childless widow. Benjamin White, the youngest son of old Joseph White, married Hannah Gerald; they had born to them six children—three sons, Hugh, Evander and James, and three daughters, Ann Eliza, Mary and Fannie. Of the sons, Hugh never married. Evander married Jane Fort; he was killed in the war. James married Maggie Lucas; they had three children; he died from wounds received in the war. Of the daughters, Ann Eliza and Fannie never married. Mary married William Haselden, near Mars Bluff; he died a few years ago, and she is the only one of her father's children now living; she has three sons and one daughter living with her. Benjamin White and wife lived to be very old; he was paralyzed and she was blind; they were living near Darlington, when a cyclone passed through there some years ago—the house was blown down and they were both instantly killed. Elizabeth White, the only daughter of old Joseph White, and sister of Stephen White, married Henry Foxworth; they had six children—three sons, Eli, Job and Wesley, and three daughters, Matilda, Judith and Elizabeth. Eli married Eliza Foxworth; Job married Carolin Gasque, and Wesley married Ann Woodward. Silas White has a number of grand-children living down below Marion, bearing the name of White, but my information is too meagre to trace them *seriatim*. Stephen White has only two grand-sons bearing the name. There was an excellent man and good citizen in Wahee Township, who died a few years ago, by the name of Wesley White, who raised a family, mostly daughters, and one son, James White; he was said to be a cousin (first) of old man Stephen White, but how or in what way does not appear; he married Sallie Mace. Think this family has already been noticed herein among the Mace family.

SNIPES.—The first Snipes of this family came from England, some time before the Revolution, and was a Baptist preacher; his wife was a Miss Cox, from Ireland; they settled near Tyrrel Bay Church, now the Gibson estate; there is a creek on the Gibson estate, now known by the name of Snipes Branch or Creek. These Snipes sold their lands and moved up on Little Reedy Creek (below Marion), near the Reedy Creek Baptist Church, and some of the Snipes family have ever since owned these lands. This Baptist divine, whose name was Daniel, had a son by the name of Joseph (it is not stated whether he had other sons or not), who it was destined should become famous in after times—this was the Captain (afterwards Colonel) Snipes, who was a terror to the Tories of the Revolution, and who, in turn, so much terrorized him, as related in General Horry and Mason L. Weems' Life of Marion, whose account of it will be transcribed herein, and thus is perpetuated to the credit of the Snipes family. It is not stated to whom Captain Snipes married; he had five sons and two daughters; the sons were James, Daniel, Nelson, Thomas and William; the daughters were Jane and Mary.

Genealogy of James Snipes—He married a Miss Baxley, by whom he had one son, David, and three daughters, Martha, Telatha and Mary. David Snipes, the son, married a Miss Drew, and died without issue. Martha married Henry Squires, of Horry County, to whom were born four sons and one daughter. Telatha and Mary Snipes never married, and hence no issue.

Genealogy of Nelson Snipes—He emigrated to North Carolina, and from him descended a numerous progeny; they are in the old North State.

Genealogy of Thomas Snipes—He married Patty Brown, to whom were born four sons, David, Thomas, Joe and John, and four daughters, Emaline, Amelia, Mary and Caledonia.

David and Joe died without issue. Thomas married Miss Matilda Stanly, to whom were born six sons and one daughter, Robert, William, Charles, Wade Hampton, Doctor and Barnes; the daughter was named Rosa. Robert Snipes married Miss Minnie Stephens, to whom was born one child, Mattie. William Snipes married Miss Lizzie Haselden, of Williamsburg County; they have one child, Bessie Louisa. The other four boys are not married. The daughter, Rosa Snipes, married William Haselden, of Williamsburg County, to whom was born one child, Patsy. John Snipes, son of Thomas Snipes, married a Miss White, of this county; they moved to McColl's Station, where they now reside. Emaline Snipes married Benjamin Ammons. Amelia Snipes married John Carter. Mary Snipes married a Mr. Brown. Caledonia Snipes married Hamilton Capps. This ends the genealogy of Thomas Snipes' family down to the present time. William Snipes, brother of Thomas, Jimmie, Daniel and Nelson, married Polly Venters, of Williamsburg County; have no issue. Daniel Snipes, brother of these, and the progenitor of the late Wilson Snipes, well known to the present generation, and the most prominent branch of the Snipes family of to-day, married Polly Marlow, to whom were born nine sons and one daughter; the sons were Wilson, Daniel, James, Charley, Michael, Perry, Allen, Richard and Thomas; the daughter was Julia Ann. Wilson Snipes, I suppose, was the eldest of the nine sons, and was unquestionably the most prominent—a most excellent man and good citizen every way; an honest, hard-working man, of much larger heart than his purse—the poor of his neighborhood, although he was not rich, missed him when he died; he was a very illiterate man, could not read or write—had no education except what he got from observation; in his talk, he murdered up the King's English at a terrible rate, yet he could always express himself so as to be understood. He always "called a spade a spade," and so of everything else he talked about—he never hesitated to speak his mind about anything, without regard to which way it cut. There was but one Wilson Snipes, and long will he be remembered for good by all who knew him. Notwithstanding his ignorance of letters, he was a zealous supporter of schools; he gave his children, or the most of them, a good common school education, such as the best schools of the county afforded; he built and furnished a school house with the best apparatus of the times, at or near Reedy Creek Baptist Church, and was one of the prime movers in originating and erecting Mount Olivet Methodist Church, on the east side of Big Reedy Creek, where he and his wife now lie buried. Some amusing incidents are told of old man Wilson, and one or two of them will not be out of place here. In his early days—in fact, almost to old age—he was very profane, even in common conversation; so much so, that he would swear unconsciously. In his latter days, he reformed, joined the Methodist Church, professed religion and, of course, quit swearing, and every one who knew him believed in the genuineness of his conversion. On one occasion some minister went to Mount Olivet to preach. Before the preaching commenced, he looked around in the "amen corner," saw Brother Snipes at his place in the corner, and beckoned to him to come to him; Snipes got up and went to the preacher, who asked if there was any one there who could lead in prayer in conclusion of the services. Wilson looked round over the congregation, and turning to the preacher, says, "No, not a d—d one." On another occasion, his pastor went to old man Wilson's house, as I suppose, on a pastoral visit, and while sitting in the piazza, concluded he would examine the old gentleman somewhat as to the condition of his soul and prospects for heaven, &c.; among other things he asked him if he enjoyed religion, when old man Wilson replied, "D—d if I don't." Whereupon the pastor spoke reprimandingly to him about using such language, and old Wilson replied, "I was not conscious of it." Such was the force of habit, that old man Wilson could not quit all at once; every one who knew Wilson Snipes believed fully in his piety. He married Mary Elizabeth Coleman, a daughter of Rev. Moses Coleman; to the marriage were born four sons and four daughters; the sons are Addison Jonathan, Wilson, Calhoun and Augustus Beauregard; the daughters are Julia, Serena Adelaide, Mary Elizabeth (for her mother) and Mattie Carrie. Addison Jonathan married Miss Louisa Rogers, a grand-daughter of Colonel Levi Legette; to whom have been born five sons and three daughters, Evan, William, Blakely, Edwin and Carl;

daughters, Lilly, Anne and Louisa. None of the sons are married. Lilly married A. P. Johnson, of Horry County. Wilson Snipes, Jr., married Miss Minnie Caroline Timmons, of Williamsburg County, to whom were born four sons and four daughters; daughters, Ethel Millissa, Mary Lucretia, Willie Maude and Edith Ximena; the sons are Winfred Hubert, Bertie Fay, Ralph Vincent and Wyatt Ense. Only one of this family being married—Mary Lucretia, to Rollin Kemball Johnson, of Williamsburg County; they have one child, Brighty Evelyn. Wilson Snipes, Jr., has been school teacher and farmer for a quarter of a century; and two of his daughters, Ethel and Mary, are prominent teachers. Calhoun Snipes, brother of Wilson, Jr., married Miss Maria Shelly; they have three sons, Rufus, Clyde and Monroe; daughters, Viola and Mabell—none married. Augustus Beauregard Snipes married a Miss Ward; they have no issue. Julia Snipes married Henry Grantham, of Horry County. Serena Adalaide married Jerry H. Lambert; had one child, a daughter, and died; the daughter has lately married Redden Smith, called "Little Reddin." Mary Elizabeth, no issue, dead. Mattie Carrie Snipes married Thomas Baker, of this county. Daniel Snipes, brother of the late Wilson Snipes, and the only survivor of the nine brothers, like the others of them, went into the war—he was a Sergeant in his company; was captured by the Federals, and sent to Elmira prison, in New York, where, as he said, he was nearly perished to death; had to rest several times from weakness while walking through the city of New York, on his way home; he was shipped from New York to Savannah, where he landed and walked from there home; he yet lives, near Mullins. Daniel Snipes married Miss Elizabeth Loyd, to whom have been born eight sons and two daughters; the sons are John, Thomas, Robert Charles, Henry Rufus, Joe Hooker, Daniel Preston, Benjamin Franklin and Archie Gilchrist. Of these, John Snipes died in Hawkinsville, Ga., brought home and buried in the Mullins cemetery. Thomas Snipes, second son of Daniel, married Miss Louisa Castles, of Chester County, and is now at Janesville, N. C., a telegraph operator. Robert Charles Snipes married Miss May Waller. Henry Rufus Snipes married Miss Janie Roberts, issue one daughter, Janie Ethel. Joe Hooker Snipes married Miss Rosa Belle Coleman, of Florence County; no issue. Daniel Preston Snipes married Miss Hester Hausea, of Florence County; issue one daughter, Jessie Pearl. Benjamin Franklin and Archie Gilchrist Snipes are unmarried. Of the two daughters of Daniel Snipes, names not given, one married Elly D. Smith, below Marion; know nothing of their family. James Snipes, brother of Wilson and Daniel Snipes, was killed in the battle of Franklin, Tenn. A young lady of this county, now married, has his photo and a small quantity of gold, which he gave her on his departure for the war. He was a volunteer, and stayed in the war until he was killed; he seemed to have a presentiment of his death—he said just before the battle to his comrades, "Well, boys, it is hard to fight through this war to near its close, and then be killed." Poor fellow! he has his reward, if nothing more—he has the gratitude and veneration of his countrymen. Michael Snipes and Richard, two other brothers of old Wilson, died in Richmond, either of disease or wounds, and are buried in Hollywood Cemetery. Richard had married Miss Charity Ikenor, to whom were born two sons, Edward and Christopher. Edward married a Miss Porter. Chesley Snipes, another brother of Wilson and Daniel, died in the war, at Georgetown; he was brought home and buried. Perry Snipes, another brother, died in the war; he had married a Miss Avant, and had one child, a son, Major Snipes. Thomas Snipes, another brother, emigrated to Texas, and from there went into the war, and was killed in battle or died of disease or wounds; his sons are now said to be prominent bankers in Seattle, Washington (State). Allen Snipes, another brother of Wilson and Daniel, died in Charleston, in the war; he was brought to Florence, and buried there, by his brother Daniel. Thus it will be seen that of the nine Snipes brothers who went into the war, only two of them survived the struggle and lived to get home, Wilson and Daniel. Daniel Snipes is now the only survivor, an excellent man and good citizen, and deserves more than a passing notice. They were poor men, had not much to fight for, yet nine brothers of them went into the war, and seven of them never returned. But few such instances occurred. There is another reason why this notice of them should be extended—that is, on account of their grand-father, Captain Joe Snipes, of the Revolution, and I will give it in the language of the author of the Life of General Marion (Brigadier General Horry and Rev. Mason L. Weems, pp. 197-202). I insert it in full, that it may be transmitted to the people of his own county—that the Life of Marion is out of print, and, if not, is not generally read as this book will be: "Captain Snipes, who made such a figure in the wars of Marion, was a Carolinian of uncommon strength and courage, both of which he exerted with great good will against the British and Tories—from principle partly, and partly from revenge. But though a choice soldier he was no philosopher. He did not consider that to fight for duty, people must love it; that to love it, they must understand it; that to understand it, they must possess letters and religion; that the British and Tories, poor fellows! possessing neither of these, were not to have been expected to act any other than the savage and thievish part they did act; and, therefore, no more to be hated for it than the cats are for teasing the canary birds. But Captain Snipes had no time for investigations of this sort. Knowledge by intuition was all that he cared for; and having it, by instinct, that an Englishman ought never to fight against liberty, nor an American against his own country, he looked on them, to use his own phrase, as a 'pack of d———n—d rascals, whom it was doing God's service to kill wherever he could find them. But Snipes was not the aggressor. He kept in very decently, till the enemy began to let out, as they did in plundering, burning and hanging the poor Whigs, and then, indeed, like a consuming fire, his smothered hate broke forth.

" 'That hate which hurled to Pluto's gloomy reign
The souls of royal slaves untimely slain.'

"Afraid, in fair fight, to meet that sword which had so often shivered their friends, they determined to take him, as the Philistines did Samson, by surprise; and having learned from their spies that he was at home, they came upon him in force about midnight. His complete destruction, both of life and property, was their horrid aim. Happily, his driver or black overseer overheard their approach, and flying to his master with terror-struck looks, cried out, 'Run! run! massa, run! de enemy 'pon you.' Snipes, stark naked save his shirt, darted out as swift as his legs could carry him. 'But where shall I run, Cudjo—into the barn?' 'Oh, no, massa! dey burn de barn, dat sure ting.' 'Well, where shall I run, then?' 'Take de bush, massa! take de brier-bush.' Within fifty yards of the house was a clump of briers, so thick set that one would have thought a frightened cat would scarcely have squeezed herself into it from hot pursuing dogs. But what will not fear enable a man to do? Captain Snipes, big as he was, slipped into it with the facility of a weasel through the chinks of a chicken coop; but lost every thread and thrumb of his shirt; and moreover got his hide so scratched and torn by the briers, that the blood trickled from him fast as gravy from a fat green goose. Scarcely had he gained his hiding-place before the Tories, with horrid oaths, burst into his house, with their guns cocked, ready to shoot him. But oh, death to their hopes! he was gone; the nest was there, and warm, but the bird had flown! Then seizing poor Cudjo by the throat, they bawled out, 'You d—d rascal, where's your master?' He told them he did not know. 'You lie! you black son of a b—h! you lie.' But he still asserted that he knew nothing of his master. Suspecting that he must be in some or other of his houses, they set fire to them all—to his dwelling house, his kitchen, his stables, and even his negro cabins—watching all the while with their muskets ready to shoot him as he ran out. From their nearness to his lurking place, the heat of his burning houses was so intense as to parch his skin into blisters; but it was death to stir, for he would certainly have been seen. Not having made the discovery they so much wished, they again seized Cudjo, and with their cocked pieces at his breast, swore if he did not instantly tell them where his master was, they would put him to death. He still declared he did not know where he was. Then they clapped a halter round his neck and told him to 'Down on his knees and say his prayers at once, for he had but two minutes to live!' He replied, that he 'Did not want to say his prayers now, for he was no thief, and had always been a true slave to his master.' This fine sentiment of the poor black was entirely lost on our malignant whites; who, throwing the end of the halter over the limb of an oak, tucked him up as though he had been a mad dog. He hung till he was nearly dead, when one of them called out, 'D—n him, cut him down, I'll be bound he'll tell us now.' Cudjo was accordingly cut down; and as soon as a little recovered, questioned again about his master; but he still declared he knew nothing of him. He was then hoisted a second time, and a second time, when nearly dead, cut down and questioned as before, but still asserted his ignorance. The same inhuman part was acted on him a third time, but with no better success, for the brave fellow still continued faithful to his master, who squatted and trembled in his place of torment, his briar bush, and saw and heard all that was passing.

"Persuaded now that Cudjo really knew nothing of his master, they gave up the shameful contest and went off, leaving him half dead on the ground but covered with glory. It is not easy to conceive a situation more severely torturing than this of Captain Snipes. His house, with all his furniture, his kitchen, his barn and rice stacks, his stables, with several fine horses, and his negro houses, all wrapped in flames; himself scorched and blistered with furious heat, yet not daring to stir, his retreat well known to a poor slave; and that slave alone, in the hands of an enraged banditti with their muskets at his breast, imprecating the most horrid curses on themselves, if they did not instantly murder him, unless he disclosed the secret! What had he to expect of this poor slave, but that he would sink under the dreadful trial and to save himself, would sacrifice his master. But Snipes was safe. To discover his hiding place, death stared his slave in the face, but happily his slave possessed for him that 'love which is stronger than death.' Captain Snipes and his man Cudjo had been brought up from childhood together; and the father of our hero being a professor of Christianity, a Baptist preacher, whose main excellence is 'to teach little children to love one another,' had taken pains to inspire his son with love towards his little slave. Nor did that love pass unrequited. For Cudjo used every day to follow his young master to school, carrying his basket for him, prattling as he went; and smiling would remind him of the coming Saturday, and what fine fishing and hunting they would have that day. Many a time had they wrestled and slept side by side on the green, and thence springing up again with renovated strength, set out in full march for some favorite fruit tree, or some cooling pond, there to swin and gambol in the refreshing flood. And when the time of dinner came, Cudjo was not scornfully left to sigh and to gnaw his nails alone, but would play and sing about the door till his young master was done, and then he was sure to receive a good platefull for himself. Love thus early engrafted on his heart grew up with daily increasing strength to manhood, when Snipes by the death of his father became master of the estate, made Cudjo his driver or overseer, and thus riveted on his honest bosom that sacred friendship which, as we have seen, enabled him to triumph in one of the severest trials that human nature was ever put to. The above is a solemn fact, and the wise will lay it to heart."

WILCOX.—This family has only been mentioned in part, among the Waynes and perhaps Smiths. John Wilcox, the progenitor of the family, was one of the many valuable importations from North Carolina. He came to Marion in 1837, at the age of twenty-four; he married a Miss Wayne, as already noticed, and to which reference is made; after the death of the Wayne wife, he married a Miss Clark, of Clarendon County, who still survives, and to the marriage five sons were born and raised, Clark A., James C., Henry M., Edward T. and P. A. Wilcox, now in Florence. Of these, Clark A. married Miss Minnie Moore, of Bennettsville, daughter of John S. Moore; they have several children, number and sex not known; he merchandized in his native town for several years, and though well trained in mercantile life he did not succeed in business—failed a few years ago, and is now one of the Knights of the "Grip;" his family still resides in Marion. James C., the second son by the Clark marriage, grew up, was very promising; graduated in medicine, settled for practice in Darlington, and at once entered into a large practice; married some lady in Darlington, to the writer unknown; was Mayor of the town for one or two terms, very efficient; and at his early demise had not only acquired a good reputation but had made some money; he died early in his career and left his widow with some children, number, names and sex not known. Henry Wilcox, the third son by the Clark marriage, is a graduate of Wofford College in the class of 1880; after graduation he went to Darlington and engaged in business there—I think, a drug store; he married in Darlington, to whom not known; don't know how his business in Darlington terminated, but some eight or ten years ago, he returned to Marion, and opened up a hardware business, a rather large establishment for the place; since which time he has been thus engaged with seemingly fair prospects of success; he has a family of children, how many or of what sex is unknown. Edward T. Wilcox, the present Mayor of the town (and, I think, he has been Mayor once or twice before) and a very efficient one, married a Miss Buck, daughter of the late Hon. W. L. Buck, of Horry; she died a year or two ago, and left him two or three children—a most estimable lady she was; he has not remarried; he ran a furniture business for several years in the town with seeming success, but sold that out, and went into the flour mill business; his establishment is near the depot, and promises success—Ed. is not wanting in enterprise and energy; as Mayor of the town he is doing much for its improvement, as any one can see, who has known the town for some years past. P. A. Wilcox, the fifth and youngest son of Judge Wilcox, is yet a single man; he graduated in the South Carolina College, studied law with C. A. Woods, Esq., of Marion; after admission to the bar, he went to Florence as a partner of his preceptor to practice; in a few years the partnership was dissolved and he practiced for a while by himself. Old Judge Wilcox (he was Probate Judge for many years) was a unique character in many respects—there was but one Judge Wilcox. The writer could relate or dilate upon many of his traits of character, but want of space will not permit.

YOUNG.—This name, now extinct in Marion County, was once prominent. Johnson B. Young, I think, another of the many good importations from North Carolina, was the head of the name in Marion; he came here in his youth, perhaps from 1838 to 1840. He and John Wilcox were for many years, and up to the war, partners in a large mercantile business. Johnson

B. Young married a Miss Whilden, of Charleston; they had and raised three sons and four daughters; the sons were Frank, J. Blake and "Hal" (don't know the name); the daughters were Emma, Willie, Celeste and Julia. Of the sons, Frank married Miss Murchison, of Wilmington, N. C.; he merchandised in Marion several years, with R. J. Blackwell as a partner; he sold out his interest to G. A. Norwood, and the business continued three or four years under the name of R. J. Blackwell & Co., when Norwood in turn was bought out, and since that time it has continued by Blackwell alone. Frank Young removed to Birmingham, Ala., and there engaged in some business, don't know what; he died four or five years ago in that city, childless; his remains were brought to Marion for interment. J. Blake Young merchandised two or three years with T. Leon Bass as a partner, at Latta; the business was not successful, and he, Young, emigrated to Texas; was unmarried when he left—know nothing further of him. "Hal," the other son, I think, married a Miss Stevenson, daughter of J. E. Stevenson; he has moved to Florence, has a family, and is said to be doing well. Of the daughters of Major J. B. Young, the eldest, Emma, married Captain G. A. McIntyre, and has already been noticed among the McIntyres. The next oldest daughter, Willie, has never married. The third daughter, Celeste, married R. J. Blackwell, a leading and successful merchant at Marion; they have a family of children of both sexes, the number and names unknown—the elder ones near grown. Major Young died some years ago, a worthy man and good citizen, and much respected. I inadvertently overlooked the youngest daughter of Major Young, Miss Julia; she married D. E. Godbold, now of Mullins, and a leading merchant there; they have three or four children, all small, already noticed among the Godbolds.

JOHNSON.—This is a very populous name everywhere. There are two or three families of that name in Marion County, but I do not know enough of them to trace them or their connections back to the original. The late Dr. William R. Johnson, a leading and prominent man in his day, was born in this county, I think; his father was named Joseph, and lived in Wahee in 1843; suppose there were other children—one A. G.

Johnson, and another. Dr. Johnson's mother was a Miss Davis, I think, a sister of B. F. Davis' father, whose name, I think, was Benjamin; Dr. Johnson settled and,practiced medicine at Marion, was a very successful and popular physician, and a perfect gentleman in his deportment; he married a Miss Gregg, a sister of J. Eli Gregg, and raised three sons, Ed W., Hezekiah and Keene, and several daughters, names unknown. Edward W. Johnson was a graduate of the South Carolina College, studied law, was admitted to the bar, never practiced but little, went to farming; was elected Sheriff in 1880, and again in 1884, served both terms, and retired from office. Florence County was established in 1888, and in 1889 he was elected Sheriff of that county, and served the balance of that term, three years, as Sheriff of that county, when he retired from office, and in a few years died, unmarried; he was an excellent man, a good citizen and made a good Sheriff in both counties. Hezekiah Johnson is also a graduate of the South Carolina College; married a Miss McCall, in Marlborough, settled on a farm near his father, at Mars Bluff; has raised a family, number, name and sex unknown; like his father, is an excellent man and good citizen. Keene Johnson has never married; lives on his farm near the old homestead. Keene seems to be a family name among the Davises. A hundred years ago or more, there was a family by the name of Keene; and one of the old Davises married a Miss Keene (as a family the name is now extinct in the county); hence the name among the Davises and their descendants, one of whom is Keene Johnson. A. G. Johnson, youngest brother of Dr. W. R. Johnson, went to Marlborough, and married, I think, first, a Miss Thomas; had one child, a daughter; his wife died, and he married again, don't know who, and married, a third time, a Miss Henagan, daughter of Governor B. K. Henagan; know nothing of his children. The daughter of the first wife married Hon. H. H. Norton, of Bennettsville; she soon died. Dr. Johnson had another brother, whose name is not known, but was the father of the late William ("Bill") Johnson, of Wahee, and three other sons, Joseph, Thomas and David; of these sons, they all had families, of whom nothing is known—think they are all dead, except, perhaps, David, in Britton's Neck. Dr. W. R. Johnson was no ordinary man—a born leader, and, with all, was very popular, shrewd and sagacious; he represented the county in the House and Senate; was also a member of the Secession Convention in December, 1860; he commanded respect in whatever position he was placed—a high-toned gentleman and of the strictest integrity.

In former times there was another family of Johnsons in the Temperance Hill and Buck Swamp region, of prominence and standing, but by death and emigration they have dwindled to only a few. Old Enos Tart's wife, "Susannah," was a daughter of one of these old Johnsons. The mother of old John and Absalom Turbeville was another daughter, and, doubtless, there were others of that generation, but the writer has not been able to get them in any traceable shape. The late Samuel, Carey and David Johnson were descendants, also Hardy and Zeno, and, perhaps others, all from the same stock. These descendants, as known to the writer, are and were good, honest men, respectable citizens all of them. Samuel Johnson, whose wife was a Turbeville and still survives, was a most excellent citizen, died childless. Carey and David had families, more or less large; also Hardy and Zeno. David Johnson left, I think, two children, who are now among us. One of his daughters, Anne, married Milton F. Price, a nephew of the writer; they have a family of five or six children, only one son among them, Connerly, by name, a grown young man, steady and level-headed, a promising boy.

Seventy years ago there was another Johnson, suppose not connected with any of the above named Johnsons, whose name was Lewis Johnson. He lived then and owned the place afterwards owned and occupied by old Dew Rogers, on the north side of Bear Swamp, below Gaddy's Mill, on the road leading to Fair Bluff, N. C.; he was well-to-do, and then an old man; he had an only son, Allen, who married a Miss Elvington, sister of old Jessee Elvington; he settled and lived on the road to Fair Bluff, lower down the swamp, opposite or rather below Page's Mill (then called Ford's Mill), and on Cowpen Swamp —place now owned by Isaac Spivey or estate of the late Joseph N. Page. The son, Allen Johnson, had also an only child, a son, named Alexander, with whom the writer went to school, in 1832—Alexander was then grown; the next year, I think, in 1833, Alexander married a Miss Thompson, daughter of "Moccasin-jawed" William Thompson, three or four miles below Lumberton, N. C. There was something peculiarly romantic in the incidents to that marriage, which from their character are worth relating at this late day. Old man Thompson was a well-to-do man, of more than ordinary intelligence, but very unique; had an angular character—some of the angles were very acute, others were obtuse, more generally acute. Young Johnson had been paying attentions to his daughter, Mary, for some time, and the old gentleman, suspecting that matters between the young couple were about to come to a focus, kept out of Johnson's way, to prevent Johnson asking for her—or, rather, the old man's consent to their marriage. It was said old man Thompson, having several daughters, never consented to any of their marriages. Johnson went two or three times, intending to ask for her, but never could meet up with the old man, who managed to elude him. He asked the mother, who readily consented—it was a very good match for her daughter, and the old lady had sense enough to see it. At last Johnson met up with the old man one morning early—as he was making off to avoid Johnson, but the young man anticipated him, and met him as he was going off. Very unexpectedly to the old man, Johnson "popped" the question to him. The old gentleman replied, "I cannot consent to it, but you and Mary can do as you please." This satisfied Johnson—thinking, although he did not consent to it, yet that he would not oppose the marriage. The old man pretended to be in a hurry and left him. A time was appointed for the marriage. Johnson lived in Marion, some eighteen or twenty miles from Thompson. On the morning appointed for the marriage, at breakfast, old man Thompson said Mary should not marry Johnson—that he intended to take Mary and carry her off, if he had to tie her to carry her. The old lady and Mary, knowing the old man so well, suspected some sort of trouble with him about it, and they had everything ready to spirit Mary away, with her *trousseau*, clothing, &c. Mary got up and left the table. The old man said he would go and get a line to tie her with, and went out—ostensibly to get it. The old lady followed Mary, and got a negro to take her to the Widow Pitman's, who lived on the road that Johnson would travel in coming. Mrs. Pitman, I think, was a sister of Mrs. Thompson (I suppose Mrs. Pitman had been posted before). The negro carried Mary to Mrs. Pitman's, and Mrs. P. sent her into a bay not far off on the road, and put one of her own negroes on the road near the bay to cutting wood—this negro was let into the secret, and instructed to tell Johnson, as he passed, where Mary was. Johnson did come that afternoon, with some few friends, and among them Major Benjamin Lee, who was a Magistrate, brought along to perform, as he supposed, the ceremony at old man Thompson's house. When Johnson and his party approached the negro cutting wood, the latter stopped him and told him where Mary was, and conducted him to her; she came out of the bay, and Johnson took her in his gig (no buggies in that day), and they drove up to her Aunt Pitman's, and Squire Lee married them, and the party then rode back to Lee's (the White House), some twelve or fifteen miles, and there stayed all night. Next day Johnson carried his wife home, and they had a big infare, as it was called—to which the writer was invited and which he attended, and has personal knowledge of much of what has been written of this marriage. They lived there together. Johnson's father and mother having died, he sold out and went West, after having three or four children; heard nothing from them since. Alexander Johnson was at least five or six years older than the writer. I am very sure there are none now living (1901) that ever saw old Lewis Johnson, and may be none that remember his son, Allen. The episode above written only impresses a lesson, long since learned by observant minds—that is, that when two young people, of opposite sexes, get it well into their heads to get married, the opposition of parents don't amount to much. It is about as easy to stop Pee Dee River from running as to prevent them, and especially when they have the mother on their side. Nothing will here be said of the lawyer Johnsons in Marion; they are well known in the county and their names will herein be transmitted to succeeding generations among the list of lawyers practicing in the Courts of Marion since 1800, when the first Court was held in the county.

There are other old families and names in the county, which have not been specifically mentioned herein, for the want of knowledge or information concerning them—they are not omitted designedly. For instance, the Baxleys, the Drews, the Britton's Neck Watsons, the Williams, the Holdens, the Wallers and others. Of these, so far as known, they are all good people, honest, law-abiding and harmless—never heard of any one of them being in the criminal courts of the county. There are others in the county not mentioned herein, to wit: the Calders, the Turners, the Cooks, the Barrentines and the Sweats. They are an humble, obscure and honest people; made good soldiers in the war; associate only with themselves, content to be humble and obscure, but are doing their part in the general make-up of the county, and contribute their share to its general prosperity; and to these may be added the Christmas families. Many not specifically named herein are incidentally brought forward, in connection with those named. It is generally the case that females lose their name and identity upon their marriage, taking the name of the husbands, yet they transmit the blood, if not the name, and in many cases purer and more surely than do the males. In these pages I have traced the genealogy of families through the female line as well as the male, whenever I could; and in so doing, many not specially named are included in those connections.

In reference to the conduct of our soldiers in the Confederate War, the writer has said but little, for the reason that it would take up too much space—it would take more books than one to tell of all the gallant deeds and exploits of each soldier; moreover, where all were good soldiers and all did their duty so well, it would be invidious to tell those of one and not of all. As a whole, our soldiers did their duty, and where any did not, it is an exception, and does not affect the general rule. Besides, it will be seen by examining the copy of the Marion County rolls, herein published, who did their duty and who failed—that is, in a great measure. Hence, in speaking of any particular soldier, it is only in a general way, so as not to disparage others equally good and brave.

SELLERS.—This family, to which the writer belongs, came

from about Tarboro, N. C., about 1750. They were of Scotch, Irish and English descent. My great-grand-father, William Sellers, headed the family; he settled in Columbus or Brunswick County, N. C., on what was called the "Seven Creeks;" he had and raised six or seven sons—Elisha, Joel, Matthew, Henry, Benjamin and Sion—of these, my grand-father, Benjamin, was born about 1740; grew up and married a Miss Bryant, by whom he had five children—of these my father, Jordan, was the eldest, and the only one raised to be grown. My father was born 16th February, 1763, and died 9th September, 1838, at the age of seventy-five years, in this (Marion) County. My grand-father, Benjamin, married, a second time, don't remember to whom; by this marriage he raised four children—three sons, Wright, Luke and Levin, and one daughter, Rhoda; my father was half-brother to these. Rhoda married Jonathan Rothwell, on Cape Fear River, Bladen County, N. C. Rothwell was a very successful man, and accumulated a large property. The writer has seen some of the descendants of Rothwell since the war—they were good people and well educated. Wright Sellers, the oldest son by the second marriage, married a Miss Duncan, of Horry or Columbus County, and settled and lived on the Iron Springs Swamp, near what is now called "Green Sea," in Horry. My grand-father, Benjamin, had in the meantime moved to that section, owned and had taken up much land in that community, and died there in April, 1817, at the age of seventy-seven years. My uncle, Wright Sellers, had and raised one son, Benjamin D., and six or seven daughters. The Sellers and Nortons built the first church at Green Sea, then called "Norton's Church," between the years 1801 and 1807. My grand-father was a Methodist preacher, and was ordained by Bishop Asbury in 1801 (see Asbury's Journal, 3 vol., p. 9). The Nortons and Sellers kept that church up or were the most prominent members in it until 1826, when they sold out and went to Alabama. Luke Sellers, the second son of my grand-father by his second marriage, married, don't know who, and had one son, Jacob, and died. Jacob grew up and married, and also went West. Levin Sellers, the youngest son of my grand-father, grew up and became a Methodist preacher, joined the Conference in 1806 or 1807, and was sent first to Edisto Circuit (now Orangeburg), and the next year to Cypress Circuit, where he died in August of that year. My father, Jordan Sellers, went there and got his horse, clothing, saddle-bags, books, &c. The Methodist preachers in that day traveled on horseback and carried their clothes, books, &c., in saddle-bags—not so with the preachers in 1901. My father, the only child raised of the first marriage of my grand-father, at the age of eighteen years joined the Continental Army of the Revolution, under the command of General Nathaniel Greene, and was in the battle at Eutaw Springs, S. C., 8th September, 1781, and served to the end of the war. The results of that battle turned the tide of success of the British arms in South Carolina, and with the fall of Yorktown, Va., a month or two afterwards, under Washington, forced the evacuation of Charleston in 1782, and finally forced George III. to acknowledge the independence of the United States of America early in 1783. At the age of twenty-six, in 1789, my father married Miss Elizabeth Hunchy, a Dutch lady; by her he had one child, a daughter, Mary; the wife was an invalid, bed-ridden from the birth of Mary, for twenty-four or twenty-five years, when she died; Mary grew up, and married James W. Edwards, and in 1819 moved to Montgomery County, Ala., then a frontier region; Edwards raised seven or eight children; amassed large property, and he and wife both died, and are buried about four miles below Montgomery, Ala. The writer was in the graveyard in 1854, and saw their tomb-stones, and while there learned that the children were all dead, except two, Dr. Charles Edwards, of Prattville, Ala., and one daughter, Amanda, who was the wife of a Methodist preacher, a presiding elder (name forgotten). In 1817, my father married again, my mother, Mary Osborne—he being fifty-four years of age and she twenty years; I was the oldest child, born 27th March, 1818; they raised to be grown three sons—the writer, James O. and Bryant J., and two daughters, Susan and Civil. I am the only survivor of the five. My brother, James O., went to Alabama, married there a Miss Willis, and had and raised one son, James Jordan, and four daughters. James O. was killed in a skirmish in Hood's Army, 28th October, 1864. Bryant J. went into the army in a Marlborough company of cavalry, Peter L. Breeden, Captain; he died of typhoid fever, 13th August, 1863, at McPhersonville, S. C.; I brought him home and buried him at Dothan, in this county; he left two sons, James F. and Thomas W. James F. married Miss Chloe Rogers, daughter of Johnson Rogers, in the Mullins section; he died in 1889; left four sons and one daughter, now in that community. Thomas W. Sellers married Dora Campbell, daughter of Theophilus Campbell, of the Mullins section; she died four or five years ago, and left two children, girls; the father has not remarried. Of the daughters, Susan married James J. Rogers, brother of Johnson Rogers; he died last October, childless, and Susan died 17th May, 1901. My sister, Civil, maried Ruffin Price, of North Carolina; he left her with two children, boys, Milton F. and Joseph M., both now citizens of Mullins, both married and have coming families. I married Miss Martha A. Bethea, daughter of Philip Bethea, as already stated herein among the Betheas; we raised six children, three sons and three daughters, John C., W. W., Jr., and Philip B.; of the daughters, Anna Jane, Rachel and Mary, all married, as will be found among the Maces, Betheas, Nortons, McMillans, DuBois and Godbolds. Of the five brothers of my grand-father, Benjamin Sellers, they scattered, and they and their posterity may be found in North Carolina, South Carolina, Tennessee, Alabama, Mississippi, Texas and perhaps other States. My mother's father, Joseph Osborne, was an Englishman—came here as a British soldier in the Revolution; was taken a prisoner by the Americans, and, though exchanged, refused to return to England; married in Sampson County, N. C., to Miss Civil Foley (Irish people), and by her had four children, of whom my mother was the eldest—born in 1797, and died 12th February, 1868; had only one son, Charles Osborne, who died years ago, childless. Hope I will be pardoned for having said so much about my own family, but knowing so much about them, I could not well say less.

The Negro.

The negro was introduced into the province of Carolina almost coeval with its first settlement in 1670. The first shipment was made by Sir John Yeamans, in 1671. He was an

Englishman, who went to Barbadoes and there procured a small colony to go with him to Carolina. Large grants of land had been obtained by him from the Proprietors in Carolina. And from Barbadoes, he not only carried his small colony, but also a number of negro slaves. These were the first negroes in South Carolina. How or by whom they were carried from Africa to Barbadoes, does not appear (Ramsay's History of South Carolina, pp. 2 to 18). The colony of the year before was under William Sayle as Governor, who died soon after his arrival, and was succeeded by Joseph West, 28th August, 1671; and he was succeeded by Sir John Yeamans, 26th December, 1671. He held till 13th August, 1674. Negroes had been previously imported into Virginia. Thus was established the nucleus of slavery in South Carolina, and the germ for our present negro population in the State. Whether wise or unwise, yet remains to be determined. "There is a Providence that shapes our ends, rough-hew them as we may." They are here and, I suppose, her to stay—not as slaves to the cupidity of man, but as human beings entitled to the benefits to be derived from the laws and usages of humanity. He came here a barbarian, a savage—could not speak or understand our language, knew not how to work—in fact, knew nothing except what his animal instincts and propensities taught him; he knew nothing except by intuition—nothing except to gratify his animal propensities, and to supply his natural wants. He knew nothing of civilization and its concomitant and consequent pleasures and enjoyments, and as for a God, that rules and governs all worlds and is everywhere and at all times present, disposing of the destinies of all men and all worlds, the negro had never heard. His two hundred years of hardship and slavery has been greatly for his benefit. It has transformed him from a barbarian to a civilized and christianized man. He has not only learned to speak our language, but to read and write it; he has not only learned to make and use all the arts of civilized life, but has learned to appreciate them. The thick darkness that beclouded his mind as to a true and living God, that created and upholds and continues all terrestrial things for man's benefit, has been dispelled. His mind has been enlightened, and he feels and knows that he is accountable to that Great

Being for all his actions—that there are rewards and punishments in the future. The great struggle in the South from 1861 to 1865, involving his continuous state of servitude or his freedom, terminated in his favor, and he was set at liberty, and the powers that then were conferred upon him all the rights and privileges of citizenship, civil and political—whether he was fitted for the political privileges conferred upon him has been and still is a disputed question. I, for one, did not, nor do I yet, think he is fitted for the due and proper exercise of that high privilege. There are a few, compared with the whole, that might be trusted with the ballot in this free country, and, I think further, that it ought to be intrusted to them gradually, as they may develop a fitness for it, and thus in the progress of time all may attain to that high privilege. The negro, as a race of people, is unlike every other race. He lives for the present, while the Mongolian lives in the past, and the Caucassian or European lives in the future or for the future. The negro is improvident, as a general rule; he looks only to the present, and if he has enough, however simple it may be, for the present, he is satisfied—his wants are few and they are easily supplied; hence he is the best laborer that the South can have—his place as such cannot easily be filled. He is contented with his status and condition, wants employment only to supply present and pressing needs—is easily satisfied; not aspiring, since the days of carpet-baggery and scalawagism—and they were to blame, not the negro, and were not as trustworthy as the negro; they stole it by thousands, the negroes only by littles. They are mostly gone—left for the country's good, and to save their mean carcasses; the negro is still here and, I trust, for all time to come. He does not seek, nor does he expect, social recognition—they gang to themselves, and would not be contented otherwise; they have a contempt for the white man who puts himself on a level with them. As a race, they are cowardly—at least, as to the white man. They are somewhat brutal among themselves, and especially to their children. The negro can live on less than any one among us—his wants are few. There are few or no strikes in the South—the negro don't strike; the agricultural people of South Carolina and of the South will never suffer from a strike as long as they employ negro labor. The negro has a monopoly of that class of labor, and the agriculturalists have a monopoly of its employment—the one monopoly is entirely dependent upon the other, and so long as that relation subsists and is maintained, there will be no friction, but harmony and good feeling will be maintained. Destroy that relation, and bring the white labor—a laborer that is hard to satisfy, that is ever looking out for the future, and seeking avenues to better his condition and fortunes, constantly demanding social recognition for himself and family—there would soon be friction and trouble, no end to it; and we of the South would soon be involved in a strike, such as now pervading other parts of the country, where corporate wealth and corporate greed abound. Agriculture would languish, and every thing dependent upon it would be wrecked. The means of supplying the natural wants of man and beast would be cut off, and bloodshed and revolution might follow in the wake, and finish up the sad catastrophe of our now happy country. If the negro is wisely utilized, our section of the country will be spared the direful calamity.

The conduct of the negro during our late unpleasantness, from 1861 to 1865, is without a parallel. There were then, say, six millions of slaves (negroes) in the Southern Confederacy. The section was drained of its effective men—every effective man from the Potomac to the Rio Grande was required to be and was at the front. The old and ineffective men and boys were alone left at home with the women and children, as their only protection, surrounded with these six millions of negroes. Did the negroes rise in mass, and massacre these old men, boys, women and children, which they could have done at any time in 1864 and '65? and which any other race of people, similarly circumstanced, upon the face of the globe, seeing their opportunity, would have availed themselves of, and instituted a general butchery throughout the length and breadth of the Confederacy. Nothing to hinder them. No; instead thereof, the negro was loyal, truly loyal, to his master and his family, and also to his section of the country. He labored upon the farm, raised provision crops for the support of themselves, their masters' families, and to support and maintain our vast armies in the war. But for them, our armies would have had to disband and give up the cause for which they had gone to war and for which they were fighting—there was no other source of supply. The negro knew all this; that the war was being waged on his account, and upon its result depended his freedom, or his continued state of slavery; yet, knowing all this, he chose, under the providence of God, to be loyal to his master and to his master's cause. It is without a parallel, and I may say miraculous. Had he chosen to take advantage of the situation and to strike for freedom, the results, *horibile dictu*, would have been indescribable, and horrifying beyond toleration. I will turn from its contemplation and let the reader do the further imagining. We owe the negro a debt of gratitude immeasurable, and which can never be paid. He is now our only and best laborer—he is emphatically "a hewer of wood and a drawer of water," and it is probable he ever will be. We should utilize him, but treat him justly and fairly, aid him in every way we can to better his condition, and elevate him to a plane of self-respect in his status and position in society. We are due him this much, at least, as some sort of reward for his loyalty to us, in a time and in a crisis when we most needed it, and where it was the very *sine qua non* of our existence. There are those among us who are advocating the policy of applying the taxes paid by white people to the public education of the white children of the State, and the taxes paid by the negro to the public education of the negro—the latter a mere bagatelle What base ingratitude does such a proposition evince! It is to be hoped such a policy will never be adopted in the South, and especially in South Carolina. It would be rank repudiation of the debt of gratitude we owe them—it would be publishing ourselves to the world as a set of ingrates. The white people now control the policy of the State, and I hope ever will—but do not bring upon us such moral degradation as such a policy would betoken and entail. We claimed to be a civilized and christianized people—if so, we cannot favor and adopt such a policy.

Towns of the County.

There was no town in the county previous to 1800. The Act of 1798, establishing a Judicial District in what was then called Liberty County or Precinct, by the name of Marion District, and providing for the location of a court house and jail therein by the first January, 1800, was the first step towards the building of a town. The court house and jail (comparatively rude structures) were built, and the nucleus of a town planted. A county seat is always followed by an aggregation of people (necessarily so) at said county seat, more or less numerous and pretentious according to circumstances, environments and prospects of trade, &c. Who the first settlers were is not known, and is not now ascertainable. The writer has heard old "Aunt Nancy Godbold" say that she and family moved there in 1812, and built a good large house (for that day), about where the Marion Bank stands, a boarding house or hotel, and lived in it and kept it as such; she was there and keeping it as such in 1843. The writer boarded with her there one week, attending Court as a juryman—the first and last time he ever was juryman. The old house stood there until after the war. The leading merchants there have been Thomas Evans, W. H. Grice, Ebby Legette, Durant & Wilcox, Wilcox & Young, T. W. Godbold, McDonald & Crawford, M. Iseman, I. Iseman (called Lightfoot), C. Graham, E. H. Gasque, J. N. Stevenson, R. H. Reaves, Moody & Smith, Durham & Stanley, S. A. Durham & Co., W. C. McMillan, druggist. These bring us down to the present day merchants—all of whom are well known, and of whom there are now many.

MARION.—Marion grew very slowly. In 1838, when the writer first saw it, it was a mere hamlet. The native oak saplings were then growing in the public square, to which persons going to town then hitched their horses. More business is done there now, in the fall and spring, in one week than was done there in 1838 in a whole year. In 1838, the population was perhaps 150 or 200, not more. It remained a little court house town for a period of fifty-five years. The first impetus given to the town of Marion was by the building the Wilmington and Manchester Railroad, which was not completed to that point until 1854. Marion then began to move up, business and trade were increased; its population increased, and some life and activity prevailed—a spirit of enterprise and improvement began to show itself, not only in the town but in the county generally. This upward movement was, however, soon checked by the war, and after the war and its devastations it was further retarded by the horrors of Reconstruction and the rule of the "Carpet-bagger." The war and subsequent conditions and agencies held back the town and county—little progress made for fifteen years, say, till 1876 and '7. Since 1876, Marion grew slowly, mostly by the natural increase of its population. Bar-rooms were numerous, and tolerated until 1883, when the town, at an election held for the purpose, voted it "dry" by a majority of twenty-five; soon afterwards, by an amendment to its charter, the Legislature passed an Act by which liquor was forbidden to be sold there for twenty years. The town remained dry, except an occasional "blind tiger," until the dispensary was planted in its midst. This great "moral institution" seems, for the present, to be the policy of the State, in reference to the sale of liquor within it—how long it is to remain the State's policy, we can't tell. The little morality there is in it can hardly be seen with a microscope. Take the profit feature out of it, and it would not last three months. To say it was established to promote good morals would be a libel on truth, bold hypocrisy. I think Marion was first incorporated in 1854 (I have not the Act before me). The improvements since 1876 have been gradual, up to a few years back, when a new imputus was given her, and she is now on a boom; her population is about 2,000. Instead of bar-rooms, we have two flourishing banks, a cotton factory, an oil mill, an iron foundry and machine shops, the largest and best in the eastern part of the State; two large tobacco warehouses, with pack houses, and a stemmery of tobacco; and this is not all, the old wooden shanties for dwellings and stores are being replaced by large and commodious buildings for dwellings—some of wood and some of brick have gone up and are going up; also the same as to stores, and other buildings; there are also five or six livery stables and five or six drug stores, and from two or three places of business, stores, in 1840, small establishments, they now number at least thirty, with large stocks of goods of every variety, and every one seems to be busy and doing a fair business. From three to five hundred men and women now find employment there daily in the different channels of trade and business—where formerly there were many unemployed, loafers about town, mostly bar-room patrons, and, I might say, vagabonds—now employed and prosperous. In 1840, there was but one church in town—the old Methodist Church; now there are four good church buildings, commodious, viz: the Methodist, Baptist, Presbyterian and Episcopal, all well attended, and each with its minister, and two of them with parsonages. The Methodist have also a Presiding Elder's parsonage with its glebe. There are also three or four colored church buildings, commodious and substantial; each has its minister, and their churches are well attended. And above all and as its climax, they have a large and commodious town hall of brick, with all necessary furniture, two stories high—the lower one for the meetings of the town coucil, and for a town market, and guard rooms. They also have a fine and commodious brick building, two stories high, for their graded school, and one of the best graded schools in the State. These last are a great credit to the liberality and public spirit of the town. To one living in 1840, and leaving at that time and coming back there now, would hardly know the place. The old town has waked up. The people who are there now are a progressive and large-hearted people, *esto perpetua.*

NICHOLS AND MULLINS.—The construction of the Wilmington and Manchester Railroad, completed in 1854, and the establishment of depots at those respective places, formed a nucleus for a town at each point. At first, and for years afterwards, these places were mere hamlets. There gathered near them a few families and some few business men; several houses were built here and there around the depots, without any seeming regard to an ultimate town, but with an eye only to their then personal convenience. Thus they were and thus remained until after the war. At both places, after the war, churches were built—a Methodist and a Baptist Church at each, and perhaps a colored church or two at each. A while after the war, Nichols seemed, as between the two places, to take the lead. The lands above the railroad belonging to the estate of the late Harman Floyd were sold, and with a view to the building up a town, were sold near the depot in convenient lots. The purchasers began to build, and did build several very good dwellings and storehouses upon their respective purchases. The turpentine business there was pretty extensive and profitable, and under these influences Nichols took on a little boom for a while, and seemed to outstrip its neighbor, Mullins, in business enterprise and business prospects; but in a few years the turpentine began to fag, and finally in a measure played out, and with it Nichols came to a stand-still. Recently, however, the cultivation of tobacco for market has found its way into the country around it and in upper Horry, just across the river, which has given Nichols an impetus, and she is again looking up and is forging her way to the front. A. B. Nichols, a good and successful business man and a man of large means, has erected a commodious warehouse there for the handling and sale of tobacco, and the quantity sold there is having its effect upon the town, and she is looking up. The population, I suppose, is 200 or more. There are three or four stores, owned and managed by A. B. Nichols, John H. Stroud and C. R. Ford—there may be others. The section of country around Nichols is not as agricultural as it is around Mullins and other sections of the county. Mullins is situated in one of the many good sections of the county for agricultural purposes, and in that respect has the advantage of Nichols. For a while she ran a turpentine business, but not to the extent that Nichols did, and she abandoned it earlier. There was not much emigration to either, but more to Mullins than Nichols. I think, by the census of 1890, Mullins had a population of 282. In one respect, Mullins has outstripped all other towns in the county, Marion not excepted, and that is in establishing and keeping up her Sunday schools, in both her churches. They were living, moving institutions years ago, and the interest in them does not seem to abate, either in the attendance or in mastering the lessons. No other public Sunday meeting, however important, such as a district conference or an association, is allowed to side-track the Sunday schools. It has been so for years—the interest in them does not seem to abate in the least. The moral influences at Mullins, which are very good, may be attributed in great part to those Sunday schools, which have been in existence for a generation, and it tells upon the town and surrounding country. In addition to this, they have and keep up, and have for years, a school—the peer of any school in the county—don't know whether it is what is called a graded school or not, but it is deeply rooted in the minds of the people of the town, and is much to their credit. What is now booming Mullins is the tobacco trade—it has only been a few years that tobacco has been cultivated in the county. The Mullins region early saw its opportunity, and embarked largely in its culture and production, and in that regard is far ahead of any section of the county. The consequence is that Mullins sells more tobacco than any market in the State. She sold last year, 1900, over 4,000,000 pounds, and bids fair to become the Danville of South Carolina. She has three large and well equipped tobacco warehouses, a number of pack houses, and four large and well equipped tobacco stemmeries (one of brick), and employs, of men, women and children, four or five hundred hands. It has given Mullins an impetus not dreamed of ten years ago. People are emigrating to Mullins from all parts, houses (dwellings) are not to be had. From 1890 to 1900, as shown by the census, the population increased from 282 to over 800; and now, 1901, it is over 1,000. The town is spreading; large and handsome houses, dwellings, stores, &c., are going up all around (some of brick); a spirit of enterprise and "expansion" is engendered and developing fast, and bids fair to equal, if not surpass, in wealth and population in the near future her near neighbor (might say mother), Marion; she has a bank, through which her finances pass and are transacted, and is also doing a good business, launched and based on the capital of her own people. The spirit that animates the town actuates and permeates the whole surrounding country. A new and active life manifests itself everywhere. Much more might be said of this thriving town, but want of space will not permit.

LATTA AND DILLON.—These towns, yet in their youth, owe their origin to the building of the Florence (Short Cut) Railroad. The road was completed up to those points, seven miles apart, in 1888, depots located, and a nucleus of a town planted, and at once persons began to build and to come in and dwell there. W. W. George built, as I think, the first storehouse, a large and commodious one, at Latta, and also built a large dwelling, now occupied by J. W. Smith, and the store is occupied by S. A. McMillan. Soon others began to come in and build, until the town has attained to its present proportions. It is a thriving, progressive and enterprising place. Three churches for the white people have been built—Methodist, Baptist and Presbyterian—and each has its minister and are well attended. They have also constructed a school building, large and convenient, and have established a first class graded school, which is kept running from year to year by first class teachers. There are two or three colored churches, of moderate pretensions, gone up. The town has ample church facilities, as also schools. The graded school established, of course, includes the colored population, and they share in its benefits. This arrangement is required by law in the graded schools of the State. The white and colored, each, has its school house—the races are thus kept separate. Latta has caught the tobacco fever, which is epidemic in all northeastern South Carolina. They have two large and well equipped tobacco warehouses, together with pack houses, also a tobacco stemmery, and have launched into the tobacco trade, and are competing with other tobacco centres in the county; and the prices paid this year (1901) will doubtless stimulate its production, perhaps, for years to come. They have also some banking facilities—I think, a branch of the Merchant and Farmers Savings Bank of Marion, conducted by Mr. Austin Manning, a very competent young man, which affords sufficient money facilities for the business of the town. The leading merchants and business men of the place are S. A. McMillan, J. J. Bethea, D. M. Dew and John L. Dew, and recently a large wholesale and retail supply store has been launched by E. B. Berry and Lonzo Smith, which seems to be doing a large business and promises much in the future; and last, but not least, is W. W. George, a regular hustler, who has done more in the way of building than any one else, apparently with but little money, and carries on a large mercantile business all the time. Such an one deserves more than a passing notice. To enumerate: He first built the large and commodious store building now occupied by S. A. McMillan; a large ten-room dwelling, now occupied by J. W. Smith; next a store house on the corner next the railroad, afterward occupied by Young & Bass; next the Farley store, a large two-story building; next a two-story building storehouse, in the branch (formerly) near the livery stables; next a fine and pretentious two-story dwelling, in Northeast Latta, in which he now lives; next a large tobacco warehouse and pack house, in East Latta; and last, but not least, a large two-story brick storehouse in East Latta. He has done all this within the last thirteen years—began with nothing, and has never seemed to have much money, and in the meantime made a trip to Mexico. He is a prodigy. Latta is a live little railroad town. It has a population of 467, by the census of 1900. It has good surroundings, a good agricultural country, and no reason can now be seen why it should not continue to grow and prosper. It is incorporated.

Dillon was started about the same time, 1888, and under the same or similar influences, about one mile from Little Pee Dee, and about seven miles from the North Carolina State line. The growth and prosperity of Dillon have been somewhat phenomenal, for a railroad town in a sparsely settled country, backed up by only agricultural products. I think Duncan McLaurin was first to settle there, a level-headed, progressive man; he was soon followed by others. The founders of that town had an eye to the future of the place. It is well and sensibly laid out; the streets are wide and at right angles to and with each other, and in this respect is the Philadelphia of the county. The location was uninviting—it was comparatively in a pond. The writer waded through the site of Dillon, sixty-one years ago, several times in the water from ankle to half-leg deep, along a little winding footpath, leading from about Dothan Church to Stafford's Bridge, on Little Pee Dee. It is now well drained and apparently high and dry. The town presents gentle undulations of hill and dale, and is pleasant to look upon or to travel on. Dillon had a large territory, and the best agricultural section of the county to draw from. Its trade extends over Little Pee Dee to the North Carolina line and into that State. It absorbs the whole Little Rock section and about to the Marlborough line, including the whole of Harlleesville Township, also Carmichaels, Manning and Hillsboro, and down into Reaves Township to the lower end of the Fork. Its territory covers the best portion of the county, and within that territory are many men of large means. When all this is considered, it can be seen why and how Dillon has outstripped Latta, and, I may say, all other towns of the county; she is only thirteen years old. By the census of 1900, she had within the corporate limits of the town 1,015 population, and including her suburbs, which take in the cotton factory people, she has at least 1,500. While Latta has a good country around it, it is not near so extensive as that of Dillon, nor are there so many moneyed men in it. Dillon has three churches for whites, Methodist, Baptist and Presbyterian. The Baptist Church is of brick, large, commodious, and well finished and furnished. She has had for eight or ten years a large cotton seed oil mill which has been very successful; its stock paying annually twenty-five per cent. or more. Has had for several years a fine and large brick structure as a graded school building, in which is kept from year to year a first class school, under the supervision of a first class man as Superintendent, with a corps of able teachers. There is also a $150,000 cotton factory, built by local capital, and is now running successfully, and in a few years more its capacity will be doubled by additions. Also, an Electric and Water Power Company, with what capital is unknown. Likewise a bank founded entirely on local capital, of sufficient strength to run the finances of the growing town and its varied business interests. There are also two large and well equipped tobacco warehouses, one of brick, together with pack houses sufficient to handle the staple of the surrounding country, and in the near future will have a stemmery. There are two or three colored churches in the town. All the churches, white and colored, have a minister, and are well attended. The colored people share in the benefits of the graded school. There are shipped from Dillon annually for the last few years from 10,000 to 15,000 bales of cotton, and the shipments are increasing every year, besides large shipments of tobacco. It is said to be the strongest station on the "Short-cut" Road, except, perhaps, Fayetteville, N. C., and it will surpass Fayetteville in a few years more. It will be remembered that Fayetteville is over

100 years old, and for fifty years or more of the nineteenth century Fayetteville had a monopoly of trade for many miles around, extending down into South Carolina. As another evidence of the growth and prosperity of Dillon, the postoffice there has lately been raised from a fourth class office to a third class, or Presidential office. There are many large two-story brick buildings going up, and ere long the wooden structures will give place to brick ones. The wooden dwellings are well built, present a good appearance, are commodious and comfortable, and but for fires (occasional), would be as safe and convenient as brick dwellings. Everything about Dillon indicates life and a spirit of progress. She is looking forward to become the county seat of a new county, of which she is deserving, in the event a new county is ever or in the near future established. Dillon, if she continues to grow and progress, is destined to become a city of no mean proportions. May it be realized. Don't know how many mercantile establishments there are in Dillon. Some of the leading merchants of the town are J. W. Dillon & Son, Dr. J. F. Bethea & Co., J. H. David & Bro., A. J. C. Cottingham, T. S. Richburg, E. L. Moore & Co., Huger & Co., supply store, wholesale and retail, J. C. Dunbar, J. H. Hursey, I. I. Foss and others not known. Corps of cotton buyers and corps of tobacco buyers every season.

Little Rock, four miles above, as before stated, has been absorbed by Dillon. It never was much more than a cross-roads hamlet, though there were three or four business houses there. It was incorporated some years ago, as I understood at the time, mainly for the purpose of heading off the illicit liquor traffic, which it did pretty effectually. It is in a sober, quiet community, and there are three churches there, Methodist, Baptist and Presbyterian.

HAMER AND SELLERS.—Hamer and Sellers are stations on the Florence Railroad. The first was named for R. P. Hamer, Jr., who resides there and owns the adjacent lands. It is on the east side of Little Pee Dee, in Carmichael Township, in the midst of a thriving section of the county, and large shipments of cotton and other farm products are sent from that point, and much guano is shipped to the station for the surrounding farmers. There is one store and a ginnery, both operated by R. P. Hamer, Jr., who is one of the most extensive farmers in the county. A few years ago, he was planting 900 acres in cotton. Sellers was named for John C. Sellers, who lives there, and operates the adjoining lands as a farm. It also is in the midst of a prosperous and progressive section of the county. There are three stores, operated by J. K. Page, J. D. Haselden and E. J. Garrison—the last an industrious colored man, who is prospering. Many of the lots in the town are owned by colored people, who form a large part of the population. This is an important shipping point.

The Denominational Churches.

All denominations are tolerated here; there are, however, only four denominations now obtaining in the county, to wit: the Methodist, the Baptist, the Presbyterian and Episcopal—their numerical strength are as in the above named order. The Methodist are the most numerous, and the Episcipalians are but few, only one church of that denomination in the county, the Church of the Advent, located at Marion, and that is weak. The oldest church in the county is the "Old Neck" Methodist Church, twenty-three miles below Marion, built in 1735, by the first settlers in that region, as an Episcopal Church, or the Church of England. It has already been mentioned herein. It was used as an Episcopal Church until some time after the Revolutionary War, when by some arrangement agreed upon, it was used by both the Episcopalians and Methodists together, and after a while it fell into the hands of the Methodists as sole owners, who have rebuilt it and used it ever since. About the same time, 1735, the settlers at Sandy Bluff, on the Great Pee Dee, just above where the railroad crosses that river, built another Episcopal Church, of which Wm. Turbeville was the minister, as hereinbefore stated. No vestige of that church remains. According to the best information (traditional) the writer has been able to obtain, the next church built in the county was the Tyrrel's Bay Baptist Church, I think, about 1750 to 1760; by whom or what particular persons, I have not been able to learn. I suppose the Rev. Daniel Snipes, the father of Captain Joe Snipes, who settled in that neighborhood, was one of its founders, and, perhaps, was its first pastor. This is only a conjecture. That church still subsists and is prominent among the churches of that denomination to this day. Not long after Tyrrel's Bay was established, the Gapway Baptist Church was built; don't know by whom. Tyrrel's Bay and Gapway are, no doubt, the two oldest churches in the county, except the "Old Neck" Methodist Church, as hereinbefore stated. It will be remembered that at the time of the erection of Tyrrel's Bay and Gapway Baptist Churches, there was not a Methodist Church in America. There were no Methodist Churches in American until Bishop Asbury came here, in 1771, and none in South Carolina until after the Revolution, when Bishop Asbury (not a Bishop then) first visited the State, in 1783 or 1784. The first South Carolina Conference was held in Charleston, in 1785.

Bishop Asbury came from England to America in 1771, landed in New York, and from that time till the Revolution traveled only in the Eastern and Middle States, perhaps as low down as Baltimore. When the Revolution broke out, Asbury, fresh from England, was opposed to the Revolution, and he had to lie low, and, I think, part of the time in the latter part of the war, had to be in hiding for his personal safety. After the Revolution he extended his travels and came to South Carolina and to Georgia, and founded churches and schools wherever there was an opening, and continued to come through here as long as he lived. He died in Fredericksburg, Va., in 1816, on his way to a General Conference in Baltimore. I have not the "Life of Asbury" nor his journals before me, but have read them, and I make this statement from memory, and which, I think, is in the main correct. The first Methodist Church built in Marion County, according to tradition, was "Flowers Meeting House," already herein mentioned among the Flowers family; built of logs, as I suppose, on one of Asbury's trips through the country on his way to Charleston, after the Revolutionary War. About the same time another Methodist Church was founded by Asbury, just above Little Rock, about half mile on the Rockingham Road. When Herod Stackhouse died, in 1846, a class leader and steward of the then Little Rock Church (Liberty Chapel), the writer was informed that the class leadership of that church, Liberty Chapel, had been in the Stackhouse family for sixty years—which would throw it back to 1786. This was stated in his obituary, which was written by the writer hereof. I suppose, Flower's Church and Liberty Chapel at that time, 1786, were the only Methodist Churches in the county.

Another church of olden time was the "Saw Mill" Baptist Church, located on the east side of what is now called Gaddy's Mill; don't know when it was built, but it was an old, rickety, dilapidated building in 1831 or '2. The writer attended an association there in one of those years, and there and then first saw Rev. Joel Allen and his brother, Thompson Allen, who yet survives, eighty-eight years old, and lives in the Brownsville community, in Marlborough. Thompson was the older, and then about grown; Joel, the younger, was a large lad. I remember how they were dressed—they each had on a well-made suit of grey jeans, tinged with red. No young man there on that occasion was better dressed than they were; their mother spun and wove the jeans. Our mothers, in that day, spun and wove and made all the clothing for her family, and the most of the mothers prided themselves and vied with each other as to who should make the nicest cloth, and especially jeans for dress or Sunday wear. This old church soon decayed, and was afterwards replaced by the present Baptist Church, "Piney Grove," located on the south side of Bear Swamp, near where Captain R. H. Rogers now lives. It was at that association that the writer saw old man "Zaw Ford," who lived near by, and owned the mills there located. Old man "Zaw Ford" was the grand-father of the late Elias B. Ford, and, I suppose, was the son or grand-son of the James Ford mentioned by Dr. Ramsay, in his History of South Carolina (page 302), as dying about 1804, at the age of one hunderd years. The Ford family in the county is very ancient—I suppose, coeval with its first settlement. Bear Swamp Church (Baptist) is an old church, but cannot say when nor by whom it was founded. The Catfish Baptist Church is also an old church, founded, I think, about 1802, by old man Henry Berry, uncle of Cross Roads Henry.

The Presbyterians, the third in point of numbers, are mostly the Scotch and their descendants in the county. Their ancestors came here in the long past, and brought with them the ideas, doctrines and proclivities of the Presbyterian Church of Scotland. Sixty-five and seventy-five years ago, they had a church, then old and dilapidated, just across the Little Pee Dee, at Campbell's Bridge, which, I think, was then the only Presbyterian Church in what is now called Carmichael Township. The old Carmichaels, Campbells and McIntyres were the chief men and worshipped there. Since that time other and more commodious church buildings have been located and constructed in the Scotch settlement and in other portions of the county, to wit: Pee Dee, Kintyre, Dumbarton, Little Rock, Reedy Creek, Carolina, Marion, Mullins, Latta and Dillon—each with its minister. The Presbyterians have no church in the county below Marion Court House and the Wilmington, Columbia and Augusta Railroad. Though the Presbyterians are not very numerous in the county, yet their membership is quite respectable, and include many of our best people.

As already stated, there were no Methodists or Methodist Churches in the county till after the Revolution. Bishop Asbury and Whatcoat planted the seeds of Methodism in the county—the seeds germinated, sprang up and grew rapidly, and as a church we are having the harvest. Methodist Churches now dot the whole county—there is scarcely a neighborhood in which there is not a Methodist Church. Not saying anything of its doctrines as contradistinguished from other denominations, the writer attributes its success to their Church polity, mainly its itinerancy. The Methodist Church is an aggressive Church—more so than any other denomination among us. It goes, as it were, into the highways and byways, everywhere carrying the gospel to all people, the high and the low, the rich and poor alike. Another cause of its success is the rotation of its ministers. Formerly two years was the limit of a preacher's pastorate of the same church—it has been latterly extended to four years, though they may be moved short of that period, and is very often the case. If a preacher is unacceptable, he is soon sent somewhere else, where he may be more acceptable, and consequently more successful. If a preacher is strong and acceptable at any particular church or circuit, it matters not how much so, he cannot remain on any particular work more than four years—he is sent to some other work, that others may share somewhat in the benefits of his ministry, and thus do as much good as possible to others, to as many as possible, to extend his useful influence to the greater number. Another cardinal characteristic of the Methodist Church (though not written) is that the preacher goes, without question, to wherever he is sent, and the membership accepts whoever is sent to them. If a mistake is made in this, it is soon remedied by their rotatory system.

The Baptist, in the county, are strong, and though not so numerous as the Methodist, yet they are respectable in numbers; their churches are to be found in every section of the county. Their church polity is not so cumbrous as that of the Methodist—they are more democratic. Every Baptist Church is independent of any other. There is no appeal from its decisions to a higher tribunal—it is final; not so with the Methodist and Presbyterian. They each have their higher courts. The Baptists, Methodists and Presbyterians are liberal to each other, sometimes exchange pulpits, and sometimes hold union services, and manifest a true Christian spirit, though each holds to its distinctive views and doctrines. I will say, however, that the Constitution of the United States was a death-blow to a State denomination. The country is wide enough for all, and enough for all to do in their respective spheres, in restraining men from sin and in promoting the glory of God.

CLERKS OF THE COURT FROM 1800 TO 1900, INCLUSIVE, FOR MARION DISTRICT, NOW COUNTY.

John Dozier, 1800.
Samuel Cooper, 1804.
John McRae, 1808.
Thomas Harllee, 1810, and continued to 1826.
E. B. Wheeler, by successive elections from 1828 to his death, 24th September, 1859.
Barfield Moody, from November, 1859, to his death, 7th April, 1860; when Asa Godbold, as Ordinary, by operation of law, became Clerk, until June, 1860; when T. C. Moody was

elected, 1860, who held the office two terms, when Reconstruction put him out.

W. W. Braddy, from 1868 to 1872.
S. G. Owens, from 1872 to 1876.
R. K. Clarke, from 1876 to 1880.
J. Albert Smith, 1880, to his death, in 1882; when John Wilcox, Jr., was elected to fill the unexpired term to 1884.
John Wilcox, Jr., 1884 to 1888.
John Wilcox, Jr., 1888 to 1892.
D. F. Miles, 1892 to 1896.
D. F. Miles, 1896 to 1900.
D. F. Miles, 1900 to 1904. He is the present Clerk.

Sheriffs for Marion District and County from 1800 to 1900, Inclusive.

Leonard Dozier, 1800 to 1804.
Richard Godfrey, 1804 to 1805.
Samuel S. Savage, 1805 to 1808.
Thomas Godbold, 1808 to 1811.
Enos Tart, 1812 to 1816.
Henry Davis, 1817 to 1821.
Enos Tart, 1821 to 1825.
D. S. Harllee, 1825 to 1829.
Samuel Bigham, 1829 to 1833.
William Woodberry, 1833 to 1837.
Elly Godbold, 1837 to 1841.
A. Carmichael, 1841 to 1845.
Elly Godbold, 1845 to 1849.
A. Carmichael, 1849 to 1853.
Elly Godbold, 1853 to 1857.
N. C. McDuffie, 1857 to 1861.
W. P. Campbell, 1861 to 1863, when he was killed. I. H. Watson was Coroner, and filled out balance of the term to 1865.
N. C. McDuffie, 1865 to 1869. He resigned in May, 1867, and General Canby (Reconstruction) appointed R. Collins to 1868.
R. Collins, 1868 to 1872.
Daniel F. Berry, 1872 to 1876.

A. E. Grice, 1876 to 1880. He died in 1878, and John Wilcox was elected to fill the unexpired term.

E. W. Johnson, 1880 to 1884.

E. W. Johnson, 1884 to 1888.

Wm. A. Wall, 1888 to 1892.

W. T. Evans, 1892 to 1896.

W. T. Evans, 1896 to 1900.

B. R. Mullins, 1900 to 1904, now Sheriff.

REPRESENTATIVES IN THE STATE LEGISLATURE FROM LIBERTY COUNTY AND MARION DISTRICT AND MARION COUNTY.

James McPherson, Thomas Wicham, 1792.

John Baxter, Gavin Witherspoon, 1794.

John McRee, Thomas Wicham, 1795.

John Ford, Lewis Harrelson, 1798.

Philip Bethea, James Ervin, 1800.

James Ervin, Thomas Harllee, 1802.

Thomas Harllee, James Ervin, 1804.

Thomas Harllee, James Ervin, 1806.

Thomas Harllee, John Gibson, 1808.

Alexander Gregg, Daniel Platt, Gospero Sweet, 1810.

Charley D. Daniels, Valentine Rowell, Henry C. Legette, 1812.

Valentine Rowell, Alexander Gregg, Chesley D. Daniel, 1814.

Chesley D. Daniel, Valentine Rowell, Alexander Gregg, 1816.

Enos Tart, Alexander Gregg, Valentine Rowell, 1818.

Nimrod Davis, Jessee Ford, 1820.

Evander R. McIver, Valentine Rowell, 1822.

William Woodberry, John Gregg, 1824.

John Gregg, William Woodberry, 1826.

Wilson Hemingway, W. H. Grice, 1828.

William Woodberry, Thomas Evans, 1830.

Robert Harllee, William B. Rowell, 1832.

Robert Harllee, John McGrams, 1834.

Ferdinand S. Gibson, W. W. Harllee, 1836.

Barfield Moody, William Evans, 1838.

David Palmer, Henry Davis, John C. Bethea, 1840.

Henry Davis, Joseph Jolly, C. J. Crawford, 1842.
John C. Bethea, C. J. Crawford, Barfield Moody, 1844.
C. J. Crawford, William Evans, W. W. Harllee, 1846.
William Evans, James Haselden, James R. Bethea, 1848.
George J. Myers, D. J. McDonald, William B. Rowell, 1850.
William S. Mullins, W. W. Durant, William R. Johnson, 1852.
William S. Mullins, William R. Johnson, William B. Rowell, 1854.
William S. Mullins, John N. McColl, Levi Legette, 1856.
R. G. Howard, Nathan Evans, William S. Mullins, 1858.
R. G. Howard, William S. Mullins, David W. Bethea, 1860.
William S. Mullins, R. F. Graham, E. T. Stackhouse, 1862.
E. T. Stackhouse, William S. Mullins, R. F. Graham, 1864.
William S. Mullins, E. T. Stackhouse, R. F. Graham, 1866.
W. S. Collins, B. A. Thompson, Ebben Hays, E. M. Stoeber, 1868.
Joel Allen, F. A. Miles, T. R. Bass, John C. Sellers, 1870.
B. A. Thompson, Ebben Hays, E. H. Gourdin, John W. Johnson, 1872.
W. A. Hayne, W. D. Johnson, A. H. Howard, R. G. Howard, 1874.
John G. Blue, James McRae, R. H. Rogers, J. P. Davis, 1876.
R. H. Rogers, W. M. Davis, John G. Blue, T. C. Moody, 1878.
John M. Johnson, William A. Brown, A. A. Myers, J. G. Blue, 1880.
B. F. Davis, W. J. Montgomery, J. F. Pierce, J. W. Smith, 1882.
J. G. Haselden, J. G. Blue, W. McD. Alford, W. A. Brown, 1884.
D. F. Miles, L. S. Bigham, James Norton, J. F. Bethea, 1886.
E. D. Carmichael, R. G. Howard, D. F. Miles, E. B. Smith, 1888.
D. McIntyre, D. W. McLaurin, James Norton, 1890.
W. A. Oliver, D. W. McLaurin, L. B. Rogers, 1892.
D. W. McLaurin, J. E. Ellerbe, J. D. Haselden, 1894.
D. W. McLaurin, L. M. Gasque, J. D. Haselden, 1896.

W. J. Montgomery, T. F. Stackhouse, S. U. Davis, 1898.
J. E. Jarnigan, Wm. Murchison, T. F. Stackhouse, 1900.

Senators from 1800 to 1900, Marion County.

Thomas, J. Wickham, 1800.
Leonard Dozier, 1804.
Thomas Godbold, 1808.
Thomas Godbold, 1812.
Thomas Godbold, 1816.
Alexander Gregg, 1820.
Enos Tart, 1824.
John Gregg, 1828.
Thomas Evans, 1832.
Thomas Evans, 1836.
Benjamin Gause, 1840.
B. K. Henagan, 1844.
Benjamin Gause, 1848.
Robert Harllee, 1852.

Robert Harllee, 1856.
William R. Johnson, 1860.
Robert Harllee, 1864.
Henry E. Hayne, 1868.
C. C. Smith, 1872.
R. G. Howard, 1876.
W. W. Harllee, 1880.
  (President of the Senate.)
T. C. Moody, 1884.
T. C. Moody, 1888.
William A. Brown, 1892.
William A. Brown, 1896.
James Stackhouse, 1900.

Ordinaries and Probate Judges from 1800 to 1900.

Asa Godbold, 1860.
John Wilcox (Prob. J.), 1868.
James Graham, 1872.
John Wilcox, '74, till death, '91.
John D. McLucas, 1892.
P. B. Hamer, 1898.

Hugh Giles, 1800.
Samuel Cooper, 1802.
J. J. McRee, 1803.
Thomas Harllee, 1810.
Edward B. Wheeler, 1826.

Proprietary Governors of the Province of South Carolina from 1670 to 1719.

William Sayle, commissioned in England, 26th July, 1669; Joseph West, 28th August, 1671; Sir John Yeamans, 26th December, 1671; Joseph West (second time), 13th August, 1674; Joseph Morton, 26th September, 1682; Joseph West (third time), 6th September, 1684; Sir Richard Kirle (time unknown); Colonel Robert Quarry (time unknown); Joseph Morton (second time), 1685. James Colleton, 1686; Seth Sothel, 1690; Philip Ludwell, 1692; Thomas Smith, 1693; Joseph Blake, 1694; John Archdale, 1695; Joseph Blake (second time), 1696; James Moore, 1700; Sir Nathaniel Johnson, 1703; Edward Tyute, December, 1709; Robert Gibbes, 1710; Charles Craven, 1712; Robert Daniel, 1716; Robert Johnson, 1717, deposed in 1719.

In 1719, there was a bloodless revolution, by which the government was changed from Proprietary to Regal government. Pending which, Robert Johnson was deposed and James Moore was elected by a convention of the people as Governor, and for a year or more was recognized as such. The Royal Governors were as follows: Sir Francis Nicholson, from 1721 to 1725; Arthur Middleton, 1725 to 1730; Robert Johnson, 1730 to 1735; Thomas Broughton, 1735 to 1737; William Bull, 1737 to 1743; James Glen, 1743 to 1756; William Henry Littleton, 1756 to 1760; William Bull, 1760 to 1761; Thomas Boone, 1762 to 1763; William Bull, 1763 to 1766; Lord Charles Gevillo Montague, 1766 to 1769; William Bull, 1769 to 1775; Lord William Campbell, from June, 1775 to September, 1775.

Under the temporary Constitution of 1776, there were two Presidents, John Rutledge and Rawlins Lowndes.

Under the Constitution of 1778, to the Constitution of 1790, there were six Governors, John Rutledge, 1779 to 1782; John Matthews, 1782 to 1783, inclusive; Benjamin Guerard, 1783 to 1785; William Moultrie, 1785 to 1787; Thomas Pinckney, 1787 to 1789; Charles Pinckney, 1789 to 1790, inclusive.

Under the Constitution of 1790, and up to the Constitution of 1865: Charles Pinckney, 1791; A. Vanderhorst, 1793; William Moultrie, 1795; Edward Rutledge, 1798; John Drayton, 1800; James B. Richardson, 1802; Paul Hamilton, 1804; Charles Pinckney, 1806; John Drayton, 1808; Hugh Middleton, 1810 to 1812; Joseph Alston, 1812 to 1814; David R. Williams, 1814 to 1816; Andrew Pickens, 1816 to 1818; John Geddes, 1818 to 1820; Thomas Burnett, 1820 to 1822; John L. Wilson, 1822 to 1824; Richard J. Manning, 1824 to 1826; John Taylor, 1826 to 1828; Stephen D. Miller, 1828 to 1830; James Hamilton, 1830 to 1832; Robert Y. Hayne, 1832 to 1834; George McDuffie, 1834 to 1836; Pierce M. Butler, 1836 to 1838; Patrick Noble, 1838—died and B. K. Henagan, Lt. Gov., to 1840; John P. Richardson, 1840 to 1842; J. H. Hammond, 1842 to 1844; William Aiken, 1844 to 1846; David Johnson,

1846 to 1848; Whitemarsh B. Seabrook, 1848 to 1850; John A. Means, 1850 to 1852; John L. Manning, 1852 to 1854; James H. Adams, 1854 to 1856; R. F. W. Alston, 1856 to 1858; William H. Gist, 1858 to 1860; Francis W. Pickens, 1860 to 1862; Milledge L. Bonham, 1862 to 1864; A. G. Magrath, 1864 to 1866; B. F. Perry, by Andrew Johnson, President, 1866 to 1867; James L. Orr, 1867 to 1868.

Under the Constitution of 1868: Robert K. Scott (two terms), 1868 to 1872; F. J. Moses, Jr., 1872 to 1874; Daniel H. Chamberlain, 1874 to 1876; Wade Hampton (two terms), 1876 to 1880; Johnson Hagood, 1880 to 1882; Hugh S. Thompson (two terms), 1882 to 1884—resigning during second term to accept Assistant Secretary of the Treasury of the United States, John C. Shephard, Lieut. Gov., filled place to 1886; John Peter Richardson (two terms), 1886 to 1890; Benjamin R. Tillman, 1890 to 1894; John Gary Evans, 1894 to 1896; W. H. Ellerbe (two terms), 1896 to 1900—Ellerbe dying, M. B. McSweeney, Lieut. Gov., to 1900; M. B. McSweeney, 1900 to 1903, present Governor.

LAWYERS PRACTICING AT MARION FROM 1800 TO 1900.

Herriot.
Madan.
Rothmahlor.
A. Myers.
Pringle.
S. Wilds, Jr. (Judge).
Keating L. Simmons.
Croft.
William Falconer.
Grant.
James Ervin.
Daniel J. Stevens.
Richardson (Judge).
C. Mayrant.
Charley Daniels.
J. R. Ervin.
Carr & Taylor.
Evans (Judge).

Davis & Gourdin.
E. Gee.
King.
Gillespie.
Levy.
Gillespie & Melichamp.
Kollock.
Mathis.
E. B. Simmons.
B. F. Dunkin (Ch'n. and C. J.).
Verdries.
Hemingway.
Robbins.
Muldrow.
Wilkins.
Coit.
Dargan, G. W. (Chan.).
Ferdon.

Holt.
Philip Bethea.
F. W. Arnold.
Thomas H. Edwards.
Graham.
F. J. Moses (Chief Justice).
Smith (Judge).
Bentham & Duncan.
C. W. Dudley.
John McQueen.
DeSaussure.
Youngblood.
A. McIver (Solicitor).
Fleming.
John A. Pouncy.
North & Couchman.
R. Munro (Judge).
A. W. Dozier.
J. E. David.
W. W. Harllee.
J. L. Pettigru (At. Gen.).
Wilson.
Blakeny.
E. A. Law.
Thompson.
Sims, A. D.
Henry Bailey (At. Gen.).
Julius A. Dargan.
John A. Inglis (Chan.).
Ervin (Erasmus).
Ervin (Samuel).
Johnson, W. D. (Chan.).
Thornwell, Charles A.
Evans, C. D.
Evans, Thos. (U. S. Dis. At.).
Grice, A. E.
Hanna, W. J. (Solicitor).
McIver, Henry (C. J.).
Townsend, C. P. (Judge).

Townsend, S. J.
Hudson, J. H. (Judge).
Newton, H. H. (Solicitor).
McDuffie, A. Q.
Sellers, W. W. (Solicitor).
Shaw, A. J. (Judge).
Warley, F. F.
Inglis, W. C.
Blue, John G.
McKerall, W. J.
McColl, D. D. (Solicitor).
Johnson, J. M. (Solicitor).
Walsh, J. T.
Hamer, L. M.
Mullins, Henry.
Kelley, John A.
Graham, R. F. (Judge).
Sellers, John C.
Smith, C. C.
Montgomery, W. J.
Woods, C. A.
Evans, Junius H.
Bryant, F. D.
Stackhouse, W. F.
Johnson, W. D., Jr.
Johnson, J. W.
Sellers, P. B.
Bethea, J. T.
McLucas, John D.
Miller, C. W.
Mathison, Donald.
Mullins, W. S.
LaBorde, John B.
Boylston, R. B.
Harllee, James J.
McCall, John N.
Singletary, William J.
Spain, A. C.
Hamer, P. B.

Macfarlan, Robert.
Boyd, R. W.

Edwards, B. W.
Dozier.

VOLUNTEERS IN CONFEDERATE ARMY.

Company L, 21st Regiment Infantry S. C. Volunteers, in the Confederate States Provisional Army, from Marion County:

McDuffie, Neill C., Captain. Transferred to Quartermaster Department, 1862. Died 1881.

Legette, Hannibal, Captain. Wounded Walthall Junction. Promoted from First Lieutenant, 1862. Died at home, 1864.

Baker, William B., Captain. Promoted from Second Lieutenant, 1864. Captured.

Woodberry, William D., First Lieutenant. Captured. Died since the war.

Sweet, Ebenezer L., Second Lieutenant. Resigned. Living.

Gibson, Albert, Second Lieutenant. Wounded Morris Island. Captured, imprisoned at Elmira. Promoted from Second Sergeant. Dead.

Williamson, Robert L., First Sergeant. Killed at Fort Fisher.

Gasque, A. M., First Sergeant. Promoted from Corporal. Wounded at Morris Island. Living.

Collins, Wm. T., Sergeant. Wounded Walthall Junction. Killed at Petersburg.

Huggins, Christopher, Sergeant. Wounded Morris Island. Promoted from ranks. Killed at Fort Fisher.

Reaves, Robt. H., Orderly Sergeant. Promoted from ranks. Killed at Walthall Junction or Fort Fisher.

Williamson, Leonard, Fourth Sergeant. Killed at Morris Island, 1863.

Coleman, Samson J., Corporal. Died 1880.

Baker, Wm. W., Corporal. Surrendered North Carolina, 1865. Living.

Lane, Joseph V., Corporal. Killed at Gaines Mill.

Sawyer, James A., Corporal.

Carmichael, Franklin, Corporal.

White, Augustus K., Corporal. Promoted from ranks.

A HISTORY OF MARION COUNTY. 573

Wounded Morris Island, July 10, 1863. Died Charleston, July, 1863.

Privates.

Ammons, W. Edward. Surrendered in North Carolina. Living.

Ammons, H. Calhoun. Discharged January, 1863.

Ayers, William D. Died Walthall Junction, May 1, 1864.

Ayers, Joseph. Died Walthall Junction, May 7, 1864.

Ayers, Thomas. Discharged Wilmington Hospital, 1865. Living.

Avant, Jordan. Discharged January, 1863. Died since war.

Anderson, James R. Died at Hospital.

Baily, Lias. Discharged sick, 1863.

Baily, Wesley. Living.

Baily, Mathew. Living.

Baker, John E. Wounded at Drewry's Bluff. Surrendered in North Carolina, 1865. Living.

Baker, Benjamin B. Surrended in North Carolina, 1865 Living.

Bird, Hugh G. Died in Virginia, 1864.

Bethea, Edwin A. Discharged January, 1863. Living.

Brown, William. Surrendered in North Carolina, 1865. Living.

Brown, John O. Surrendered Point Lookout, 1865. Living.

Beaty, Thomas.

Campbell, Mike C. Killed at Battery Wagner, September, 1863.

Clark, Robt. C. Killed at Fort Fisher, January 15, 1865.

Cooper, Ralph. Living.

Criddle, James R. Discharged July, 1862.

Collins, John W. Died of disease at Petersburg, 1863.

Collins, David C. Wounded at Walthall Junction, May 7, 1864. Died of wounds, May 13, 1864.

Collins, Joel B. Killed on Darbytown Road, July, 1864.

Collins, Shadrach. Discharged January 26, 1863. Living.

Collins, Richard. Died in Union Prison at Elmira, February, 1865.

Carmichael, Archibald B. Surrendered in North Carolina, 1865. Living.

Carmichael, Evander. Killed on Darbytown Road, 1864.

Carmichael, Franklin. Killed on Darbytown Road, July, 1864.

Carmichael, Archie. Surrendered in North Carolina, 1865. Living.

Carmichael, Judson D. Died in Union Prison at Elmira, 1865.

Carmichael, Daniel M. Surrendered in North Carolina, 1865.

Carmichael, J. B.

Cole, E.

Cohen, Isaac. Wounded at Morris Island, 1863. Living.

Carter, John. Surrendered in North Carolina, 1865. Wounded at Petersburg.

Franklin, Deas. Transferred to Abney's Battalion, 1863.

Dennis, George W.

Edwards, Richard W. Transferred to Stanley's Battery, 1863.

Evans, N. J.

Flowers, Elly. Discharged January 26, 1863. Living.

Flowers, William. Discharged August 1, 1862.

Fowler, James F. Wounded at Battery Wagner, 1863.

Frierson, J. M. Transferred to Co. "B."

Gardner, Daniel. Killed at Petersburg.

Gerald, John. Surrendered in North Carolina, 1865. Living.

Gasque, J. Maston. Imprisoned at Elmira, where he was discharged, 1865. Living.

Gasque, Samuel O. Died in Union Prison at Elmira, 1865.

Gasque, Wesley E. Wounded Drewry's Bluff, May, 1864. Living.

Gasque, William B. R. Wounded ten times—The Crater, by shell; Davis' farm, six times in succession; Sharpsburg, skull fractured; Virginia, in left leg; Virginia by shell—disabled. Living.

Gasque, Henry. Died at Charleston, September 26, '62.

Gibson, Robt. W. Died in Union Prison at Elmira, 1864.

Gibson, Oscar E. Wounded at Fort Fisher, January 15, 1865. Died June, 1866.

A HISTORY OF MARION COUNTY. 575

Gibson, John S. Died in Union Prison, Point Lookout, May, 1865.
Godbold, Huger. Living.
Godbold, Thomas. Dead.
Hair, James. Discharged August 1, 1862.
Huggins, S. Lewis. Living.
Huggins, Wesley. Killed at Fort Fisher, January 15, 1865.
Huggins, William D. Killed, 1864.
Harrelson, John L. Killed Morris Island, July 10, 1863.
Huggins, William. Surrendered at Castle Thunder, 1865. Living.
Harrelson, Timothy. Killed at Walthall Junction, May 7, 1864.
Harrelson, Benjamin. Surrendered in North Carolina, 1865. Living.
Haywood, John W. Transferred to Co. "A."
Haywood, James.
Herring, Pinckney L. Surrendered in North Carolina, 1865. Living.
Harrell, Ephraim. Surrendered in North Carolina, 1865. Living.
Jones, Frederic D. Dead.
Jones, James A. Died in Union Prison at Elmira, 1865.
Jordan, William. Surrendered in North Carolina, 1865. Living.
James, William P. Discharged January 26, 1863. Living.
Jacobs, M. A German. Surrendered, 1865, in North Carolina. Living.
Legette, Henry C. Died at Wilmington, 1864.
Legette, Levi. Discharged, 1862. Living.
Lane, Robert L. Wounded in Virginia, 1864. Surrendered in North Carolina, 1865. Living.
Lambert, Robt. Surrendered in North Carolina, 1865. Died since war.
Martin, Mac F. Living.
McCall, Barney. Discharged. Living.
Matthews, Samuel P. Transferred to 5th Cavalry, September, 1863.
Miller, Chas. W. Discharged, 1862. Dead.

Oliver, Alexander R. Discharged January 26, 1863. Living.

Powell, William. Died since war.

Potter, James. Discharged, 1862. Living.

Porter, James. Discharged, 1862. Dead.

Porter, S. Goss. Surrendered in North Carolina, 1865. Living.

Pitman, David G. Discharged January 26, 1863.

Richardson, Stephen. Discharged Elmira, 1865. Wounded at Drewry's Bluff. Living.

Richardson, John. Transferred to Co. I, 1862.

Richardson, Thomas. Died at Columbia, 1862.

Rogers, John W. Wounded, 1864. Surrendered in North Carolina, 1865. Died since war.

Rogers, Owen M. Killed Darbytown Road, 1864.

Rogers, Cary. Died Petersburg, 1864.

Rogers, Fred G. Transferred to 4th Cavalry. Living.

Rogers, Bethel. Living.

Rogers, T. Living.

Rowell, Valentine. Living.

Rowell, William. Killed at Walthall Junction, May 7, 1864.

Robertson, L. D.

Sawyer, John. Transferred, 1863.

Sawyer, Thomas. Surrendered in North Carolina, 1865. Living.

Shelley, Joseph G. Living.

Snipes, Moses. Dead.

Summerford, Wm. Wounded at Morris Island, July, 1863. Living.

Shackleford, John B. Discharged, 1862. Living.

Shaw, Benjamin A. Died at Point Lookout, 1863.

Smith, Enoch. Died at Morris Island, April 23, 1863.

Thompson, Jas. T. Discharged, 1863. Living.

Tedder, Daniel M. Discharged, 1863. Living.

Townsend, Francis M. Discharged, 1863. Living.

Thomas, Samuel B. Living.

Tyler, Richard. Dead.

Webb, John. Killed at Morris Island, July 10, '63.

Wise, J. M. Discharged August 1, 1862.

Williamson, Bright J. Died at Point Lookout, 1863.
Williamson, Joseph M. Discharged August 1, 1862. Living.
Williamson, David R. Died at Wilmington, 1863.
Williamson, Sol. M. Killed at Swift Creek, May 9, '64.
Williamson, Samuel W. Wounded at Fort Fisher, January 15, 1865. Died at sea, January, 1865.
Worrel, James. Wounded at Battery Wagner, 1863. Living.

Roll of Company "H," of Orr's Regiment of Rifles, South Carolina Volunteers, in the Confederate States Provisional Army:

Fairlee, George M., Captain, Richmond, N. C. Died Guinea Station, June, 1862.

Henegan, J. Hamilton, Captain, Marlboro. Promoted from First Lieutenant, June, 1862. Killed Gaines Mill, June, 1862.

McKay, Gilbert W., Captain, Marion. Wounded near Richmond. Promoted from Lieutenant, 1862.

Brown, J. Graham, First Lieutenant, Marion. Promoted from First Sergeant, June, 1862. Killed at Gaines Mill, June, 1862.

Braddy, Robt., Lieutenant, Marion. Resigned June 1, 1862.

Tolar, John H., Second Lieutenant, Marion. Promoted from Sergeant, July, '62. Killed at Plank Road, April, 1864.

Mace, Gregg, Lieutenant, Marion. Promoted from ranks, June, 1862. Killed at Fredericksburg, June, 1862.

Rogers, Hugh G. Lieutenant, Marion. Promoted from ranks, 1862. Killed at Petersburg, October, 1864.

Sinclair, Archibald C., Lieutenant, Marion. Wounded at Petersburg, 1864. Promoted from ranks, December, 1862. Living.

Moody, John H., Lieutenant, Marion. Wounded North Anna, 1864. Promoted from ranks, 1865.

Salmon, Samuel J., First Sergeant, Marion. Promoted, June, 1862. Killed in Second Battle of Manassas, July, 1862.

Smith, Neill, First Sergeant, Marion. Promoted from First Corporal, June, 1862. Killed Gaines Mill.

Foxworth, Charley, Sergeant, Marion. Promoted from ranks, 1862.

Collins, John E., Sergeant, Marion. Promoted from ranks, 1862. Killed at Horse Shoe, May, 1864.

Goff, Azariah, Sergeant, Marion. Promoted from ranks, 1865.

Hall, Mark, Sergeant, Marion. Transferred, 1862.

Legette, Morgan, Corporal, Marion. Killed at Gaines Mill, June, '62.

Hinds, Rester, Corporal, Marion. Transferred March, 1862.

McInnis, John L., Corporal, Marion.

Gaddy, Levi, Corporal, Marion. Wounded at Fredericksburg, 1862. Died at Fredericksburg, 1863.

Privates.

Alford, Douglass, Marion. Died at home, 1865.

Alford, Malcolm. Killed at South Anna, June, 1864.

Alford, Daniel W. Wounded Wilderness, 1864. Limb amputated, 1875.

Alford, W. Warren, Marion.

Alford, Moses, Marion. Transferred March, 1862.

Ammons, John T., Marion. Wounded Richmond, June, 1863.

Baker, Neill, Marion. Died of wounds at home, May, 1864.

Bradshaw, John, Marion. Died at hospital, October, 1862.

Bryant, Evan, North Carolina. Died at hospital, 1862.

Bryant, Solomon, North Carolina. Killed at Wilderness, April, '63.

Bryant, Bethel, North Carolina.

Blackman, John, Marion. Transferred to Cavalry, 1863.

Bethea, Redden, Marion. Wounded at Petersburg, April, 1865.

Bethea, Philip, Marion. Died since war.

Baily, Benj., Marion. Died since war.

Butler, William, Marion.

Campbell, James, Marion. Killed in battle, June, 1864.

Cusaik, Joseph, Marion.

Clark, John, Marion. Wounded Horse Shoe, May, 1864. Captured.

Connor, Wilson, Marion. Wounded Second Manassas.

Cox, Hugh, Marion. Wounded South Anna.
Cobb, Thomas, Marion. Wounded Fredericksburg, 1862.
Collins, Perry, Marion.
Davis, William, Marion. Died in camp, 1862.
Dew, John A., Marion. Died since war.
Dunsford, Asa, Marion. Transferred, 1862.
Davis, Arthur, Marion. Killed at Ox Hill, 1862.
Emanuel, Frank, Marion. Transferred, 1862.
Evans, Nelson, Marion. Killed at Horse Shoe, May, 1864.
Evans, Solon, Marion. Wounded at Petersburg, April, 1865.
Finklea, William, Marion. Died since war.
Finklea, Hardy, Marion.
Finklea, Alfred, Marion.
Finklea, Hugh. Died at home, 1862.
Fladger, Hugh, Marion. Died in Virginia, 1862.
Graner, John, Marion. Killed at Horse Shoe, May, 1864.
Graves, George, Marion. Killed on train.
Grice, George, Marion. Discharged by Medical Board, 1862.
Gaines, John, Marion. Transferred, 1862.
Gilbert, William, Marion. Killed at Turnpike, April, 1864.
Goff, James, Marion. Killed at Horse Shoe, May, 1864.
Goff, Henry, Marion.
Gray, J., Marion.
Gasque, Thomas, Marion. Died in prison.
Hindes, Alexander, Marion. Wounded Gaines Mill.
Hale, Samuel, Marlboro. Died since war.
Hamilton, Edward, Marion.
Home, William, Marion. Killed near Richmond, July, 1864.
Hodge, Charles, Marion. Died in hospital, 1863.
Hazleton, Hugh, Marion. Died since war.
James, Robert, Marion. Killed at Gaines Mill.
Jones, Wesley, Marion. Died at Danville, 1862.
Jones, Evander, Marion.
James, Preston, Marion. Killed at Gaines Mill.
Jackson, Andrew K., Marion.
Kelly, Daniel, Marion.
Lister, William B., Marion. Wounded at North Anna.
Lane, David, Marion. Died at hospital, 1864.

Lowrance, Lawrence, Marion. Died at home, 1861.
Legette, John, Marion.
McCormac, James, Marion. Killed at Gaines Mill.
McCormac, Thomas, Marion. Killed at Second Manassas.
McCormac, Nathaniel, Marion.
McCall, William, Marlboro. Transferred, 1862.
McDaniel, James, Marion. Died at Sullivan's Island, February, 1862.
McDaniel, Preston, Marion. Died at Richmond, 1862.
McDaniel, Daniel, Marion. Wounded at North Anna, 1864.
McEachern, John, Marion.
McInnis, Norman, Marion. Killed at Riddle's Shop, May, 1864.
McInnis, Neill, Marion. Wounded at Fredericksburg, December, 1862.
McIntyre, Joseph, Marion. Company Commissary.
McIntyre, Duncan, Marion. Died at Richmond, 1862.
Moody, Robt. B., Marion. Died at hospital, 1862.
Meggs, William, Marion. Died since war.
McKellar, Peter, Marion. Killed in Pennsylvania, 1864.
Martin, James, Marion.
O'Neill, John, Charleston.
Oakley, Robt. N., Marion. Died since war.
Peabody, Charles, Marlboro. Died in hospital, 1864.
Pond, Foster, Marion.
Ramsey, Richard, Marion. Killed at Ox Hill, August, 1862.
Roberts, Roger R., Marion. Wounded near Richmond.
Richardson, Thomas, Marion.
Rogers, William, Marion. Killed at Fredericksburg, December, 1862.
Rogers, Joseph B., Marion. Died in Virginia, 1862.
Rogers, Eben, Marion. Died in Virginia, 1862.
Rogers, Jessee, Marion.
Rogers, Thomas, Marion.
Rogers, Anson, Marion. Captured, 1862.
Rogers, L., Marion.
Rogers, Williams, Marion. Discharged by Medical Board, 1862.
Rogers, William, Marion. Transferred, 1862.

Rogers, Joseph, Marion. Died at Sullivan's Island, '62.
Russ, Zack, Marion.
Russ, John, Marion.
Salmon, Joseph, Marion. Wounded at Fredericksburg.
Sinclair, Malcom G., Marion. Died at Charlottesville, August, 1862.
Sanders, Peter, Marion. Wounded at Gaines Mill.
Steen, James, Marion. Wounded at Horse Shoe and captured.
Shaw, Baker, Marion. Promoted, 1862.
Shaw, Daniel, Marion. Promoted, 1862.
Sessions, Wesley W., Marion.
Sassar, Benjamin, Marion. Killed at Horse Shoe, 1864.
Squires, Thomas, Marion. Transferred, 1862.
Turner, John, Marion. Died in Virginia, 1862.
Taylor, William, Marion. Transferred, 1862.
Thomas, Joseph, Marion. Killed at South Anna, 1864.
Taylor, George, Marion. Transferred, 1862.
Wiggins, Calvin, Marion. Wounded at Petersburg, 1865.
Wiggins, Calvin, Marion. Killed at Gaines Mill, 1862.
Wiggins, Baker, Marion. Killed near Richmond, 1864.
Walter, William B., Marion.
Walter, John R., Marion.
Wayne, David, Marion. Died in Virginia, 1862.
Wright, Daniel, Marion.
Whaley, George, Marion. Killed at Horse Shoe, 1864.
Whittington, Moses, Marion. Died since war.
Walter, Augustus J., Marion.

Roll of Company F, Fourth Regiment Cavalry, South Carolina Volunteers, in the Confederate States Provisional Army:

Monroe, D., Captain, Marion. Resigned. Dead.
Godbold, Huger, Captain, Marion. Resigned and served in ranks. Living.
Hewett, W. C., Captain, Marion. Promoted from First Lieutenant. Wounded Hawes' Shop. Died of wounds in prison, Washington, 1863.
Evans, W. B., Captain, Marion. Promoted from Third and First Lieutenant to Captaincy. Wounded at Cold Harbor. Living.

Gilchrist, A. E., Lieutenant, Marion. Captured. Died July, 1885.

Reaves, J. L., Lieutenant, Marion. Wounded Hawes Shop. Died of wounds in prison, Washington, 1863.

Pitman, H. M., Orderly Sergeant, Marion. Killed at Hawes Shop, 1863.

Owens, E. B., Sergeant, Marion. Wounded Hawes Shop. Died since war.

Collins, E. C., Sergeant, Marion. Living.

White, W. S., Sergeant, Marion. Died July, 1885.

Williamson, D. V., Sergeant, Marion. Died in Virginia, 1863.

Wall, W. B., First Corporal, Marion. Died Union Prison, Point Lookout, 1863.

Smith, A. J., Corporal, Marion.

Harllee, David, Corporal, Williamsburg. Killed since war.

Stackhouse, M., Corporal, Marion. Living.

Privates.

Ammons, M., Marion. Living.
Alford, W., Marion. Living.
Alford, J., Marion. Living.
Anderson, H. J., Georgetown. Died, 1875.
Boatwright, T., Georgetown. Killed at Trevillian Station.
Baily, R., Georgetown. Killed at Hawes Shop.
Baily, D., Georgetown. Living.
Baily, Ervin, Georgetown. Died January, 1884.
Brown, D., Georgetown. Killed at Trevillian Station.
Brown, Stephen, Georgetown. Living.
Brown, Solomon, Georgetown. Living.
Brown, Asa, Georgetown. Died in Union Prison at Elmira.
Brown, J. C., Georgetown. Living.
Brown, Ransom, Georgetown. Wounded Hawes Shop. Died of wounds, at Jackson, Va., June 28, 1863.

Baxley, Riley, Williamsburg.

Baxley, William, Williamsburg. Died in Virginia, 1863.

Benson, Jacob, Williamsburg. Died in Virgina, 1862.

Blackman, John, Marion. Wounded Reams Station. Dead.

Blackman, H. G., Marion. Died in Union Prison, Point Lookout, 1863.

Coleman, J. P., Marion. Wounded Hawes Shop. Living.
Coleman, I. M., Marion. Living.
Cook, James C., Marion. Died, 1882.
Clark, Angus J. C., Marion. Killed Hawes Shop.
Collins, S. T., Marion. Living.
Collins, H. G., Marion. Living.
Cox, N. D., Marion. Wounded Hawes Shop. Died of wounds, Jackson, Va., 1863.
Carter, James, Marion. Killed at Cold Harbor, June, 1863.
Coleman, D. W., Marion. Discharged for disability. Dead.
Collins, R., Marion. Killed at Trevillian Staion, 1863.
Davis, J. R., Marion. Living.
Dillard, J. H., Marion. Living.
Egerton, C. B., Marion. Living.
Eaddy, Henry, Marion. Living.
Foxworth, B. F., Marion. Living.
Foxworth, Charles, Marion. Killed Hawes Shop.
Foxworth, T., Marion. Died Pocotaligo, 1862.
Foxworth, S., Marion. Died 1880.
Flowers, J. A., Marion. Died Point Lookout, 1863.
Flowers, Henry, Marion. Killed Trevillian Station.
Flowers, J. H., Marion. Living.
Gilchrist, D. E., Marion. Was acting Orderly at close of war in command of company.
Godbold, Z., Marion. Was Captain Co. "D," 10th Infantry, but served as private.
Goud, S., Georgetown.
Garrett, W., Georgetown.
Griffin, James, Marion. Died in Virginia.
Griffin, Stephen, Marion. Died in Virginia.
Hunter, J., Marion. Killed at Gaines Mill.
Hampton, G. W., Marion.
Hampton, W., Marion.
Haselden, J. G., Marion. Dead.
Haselden, H. G., Marion. Died Point Lookout.
Hinds, J. D., Marion. Living.
Hinds, R., Marion. Living.
Howard, R., Marion. Living.
Hays, L. B., Marion. Died at home, 1864.

Hays, Wilson, Marion. Died 1880.
Harrelson, Jessee, Marion. Discharged 1863. Living.
Huggins, R., Marion. Living.
James, H. L., Marion. Died 1874.
Johnson, P., Georgetown. Living.
Jones, William, Marion. Died 1872.
King, Simeon, Georgetown. Living.
Kinton, Stephen, Clarendon. Living.
Lucas, Jessee, Marion. Living.
Legette, J. G., Marion. Died 1880.
Legette, J. B., Marion. Died 1872.
Martin, William, Marion. Living.
McCall, John, Marion. Died 1880.
Newton, James W., Williamsburg. Living.
Parker, E., Marion. Killed at Hawes Shop.
Page, W., Marion. Living.
Price, Alonzo, Marion. Discharged for disability.
Pitman, David, Marion. Died at Richmond, 1864, on his way home.
Rogers, E., Marion. Living.
Rogers, R. R., Marion. Living.
Rogers, B., Marion. Living.
Rogers, F. G., Marion. Living.
Rowell, R. F., Marion. Killed 1874.
Reeves, Chas. J. W., Marion. Killed Trevillian Station.
Robinson, L. D., Williamsburg. Died, 1872.
Smith, James, Marion. Killed at home, 1865.
Smith, N. P., Marion. Living.
Smith, Eli, Marion. Living.
Smith, J. G., Marion. Living.
Smith, R., Marion. Wounded at Cold Harbor.
Smith, W. B., Marion.
Smith, Edward, Marion. Died 1880.
Smith, Wesley, Marion. Living.
Smith, John, Marion. Died 1878.
Smith, E., Marion. Died 1872.
Smith, S., Marion. Living.
Stephenson, A. E., Marion. Living.
Stone, William, Marion. Died 1878.

Stacks, Evander, Marion. Died 1880.
Tanner, Tom, Marion. Living.
Weatherford, W. T., Marion. Wounded Black River, S. C. Living.
Wall, H., Marion. Living.
Wall, Jim, Georgetown. Died 1878.
Walker, A., Georgetown. Died at Georgetown, S. C., 1862.
Wells, G. H., Tennessee. Dead.
Wiggins, H., Georgetown. Killed at Hawes Shop.
Wilder, A. J., Georgetown. Died 1880.
Williamson, D. J.
White, W. S.

Roll of Company E, Gregg's First Regiment, South Carolina Volunteers, in the Confederate States Provisional Army:

Shooter, Washington P., Captain, August, 1861. Promoted Lieutenant Colonel, April or May, '64. Killed May 12, '64. Graduate of Charleston Citadel.

McIntyre, George A., First Lieutenant. Captain April, 1864. Resigned. Wounded at Chancellorsville, May 3, 1863. Left arm amputated.

McIntyre, Archibald, Second Lieutenant. Killed September 11, 1862.

Smith, Zach, Third Lieutenant. Died from wounds received at Hagerstown, Md., July, 1863.

Smith, Christopher, First Sergeant. Transferred July, '62. Cadet of Charleston Citadel. Dead.

Smith, David A., Second Sergeant. Elected Second Lieutenant September, '62. Promoted Captain. Cadet Charleston Citadel. Surrendered April, '65. Dead.

Gregg, William W., Third Sergeant. Killed June 27, 1862. Color-bearer of regiment.

Shooter, Evander C., Fourth Sergeant. Elected Second Lieutenant, May 4, 1864. Killed May 12, 1864.

McClenaghan, George S., Fifth Sergeant. Promoted First Sergeant, May 4, 1864. Surrendered April 9, '65.

Oliver, Samuel L., First Corporal. Promoted Second Lieutenant, May, 1864, for gallantry. Transferred by promotion, May, '64.

Keith, David L., Second Corporal. Promoted Second Sergeant, May 4, 1864. Surrendered April 9, '65.

Wayne, Francis A., Third Corporal. Transferred, January, '64. Clergyman.

Reaves, Charles W., Corporal. Killed July 1st, 1863, Gettysburg.

Privates.

Altman, John. Promoted for bravery to Corporal, October, 1862. Died June or July, '63.

Baker, Joseph A. Surrendered April 9, '65.

Baker, Thomas. Left sick on the march to Manassas, never heard from afterwards.

Barfield, Harllee. Transferred January, 1864.

Baxter, David. Killed January, 1865.

Baxter, George W.

Basin, David, August 1, 1861. Died December, 1861.

Bedford, John, August 1, 1861. Killed at Chancellorsville, May 3, 1863.

Boatright, Foster, August 1, 1861.

Capps, William W., August 1, 1861.

Carmichael, Daniel, August 1, 1861. Discharged May or June, 1862, on account of age, and physical weakness.

Crawford, Henry L., August 1, 1861. Killed August 29, 1862.

Crawford, Thomas C., January, 1864. Wounded at Petersburg; carried to Point Lookout Prison.

Cribb, Dempsey, August 26, 1861. Killed August 29, 1862.

Cribb, Geo. Talley, August 1, 1861. Discharged or retired, time unknown. Lost leg at Fredericksburg, Va. Living.

Cribb, W. Thomas, August 26, 1861. Wounded several times. Surrendered April 9, '65.

Deens, Stephen R., August 1, 1861. Died.

Deer, William P., January, 1864. Surrendered April 9, 1865.

Durant, William L., February, 1864. Promoted Corporal, 1864. Surrendered April 9, 1865.

Edwards, Levi H., August 26, 1861.

Elmore, William J., August 1, 1861. Died July, 1862.

Elvington, David, August 1, 1861. Killed July 24, 1864.

Elvington, John, August 1, 1861. Died July or August, 1862.
Elvington, Owen, August 1, 1861. Died, time unknown.
Elvington, Nathan, August 1, 1861. Killed July 28, 1864.
Flowers, James J., August 1, 1861. Died July, 1862.
Ford, Chas. P., August 1, 1861. Died September, 1863, in Fort Delaware.
Ford, Geo. W., August 1, 1861. Died September, 1863, in prison.
Ford, Hardee, August 1, 1861. Wounded June, 1862. Returned to company, '64. Surrendered April, 9, 1865.
Ford, H. Pinckney, August 1, 1861. Wounded at Chancellorsville, May 3, 1863. Discharged January, '64. Living.
Goodyear, John Emory, August 1, 1861. Killed at Second Manassas.
Hays, David Pinckney, August 1, 1861. Promoted Sergeant, October, 1864. Surrendered April, 9, 1865.
Hays, Jessee, August 1, 1861. Killed May 3, 1863, at Chancellorsville.
Hays, W. Dwight, August 1, 1861. Surrendered April 9, 1865.
Hill, James, August 1, 1861. Transferred January, '63.
Millen, John, August 1, 1861. Surrendered April, '65.
McCormac, Simeon P., January, 1864. Died June, 1864.
Nobles, John N., August 1, 1861. Surrendered April, 1865.
Norton, Evan, August 26, 1861. Promoted Sergeant May 4, 1864, First Lieutenant September 10, '64. Surrendered April, 1865. Wounded.
Norton, James, August 1, 1861. Promoted Corporal, September, 1864. Wounded at Fredericksburg, Va. Badly wounded 16 August, 1864. Imprisoned at Point Lookout near close of war, and remained there till July, 1865. Living.
Norton, John W., Sharpshooter, August 1, 1861. Served five years in Second Cavalry U. S. Army. Transferred 1860, joined C. S. A.; captured 1865. Prisoner.
Oliver, Alexander R., January, 1864. Recruit. Surrendered, 1865.
Owens, Albert P., August 1, 1861. Died August 1, 1863.
Powell, Jessee, August 1, 1861. Died in prison, time unknown.

Price, William, August 1, 1861. Died August or September, 1862.

Ray, John, January, 1864. Killed August 16, 1864.

Roberts, Benj. Franklin, August 26, 1861. Died May 12, 1864.

Roberts, Pinckney J., August 1, 1861. Wounded several times—once in mouth. Surrendered April, 1865.

Rogers, Allen. Transferred from 8th Regiment. Surrendered April, 1865.

Rogers, Ervin. Transferred from 8th Regiment. Surrendered April, 1865.

Rogers, Dennis, August 1, 1861. Escaped from Point Lookout; and killed a few days after in battle—July 24, '64.

Rogers, J. Dew, August 26, '61. Surrendered April, '65.

Rogers, James, August 1, 1861. Killed July 24, 1864.

Rushing, Archibald, March, 1862. Discharged June, 1862.

Rushing, Henry, August 1, 1861. Lost left arm at Fredericksburg, December 13, 1862. Discharged May, 1863.

Rushing, William, August 1, 1861. Killed at Fredericksburg, December 13, 1862.

Sanderson, Solomon, August 1, 1861. Surrendered April, 1865.

Scott, Andrew, August 1, 1861. Surrendered April, 1865.

Scott, Aquilla, March, 1862. Discharged February, 1863, from wounds.

Hodges, John, August 1, 1861. Killed May 12, 1864.

Huggins, Jasper A., August 1, 1861. Thigh broken May 3, 1863, at Chancellorsville. Died July, 1863.

Huggins, Christopher C., August, 1862.

Ivey, Berry, August 1, 1861. Thigh broken August 16, 1864. Died September, 1864.

James, Simpson T., August 1, 1861. Died August, 1862.

James, Joseph, January, 1861. Promoted Corporal October, 1864. Surrendered April 9, '65.

James, William, August 1, 1861. Killed August 29, 1862.

Johnson, William, August 1, 1861. Died July, 1862.

Keelyn, John G., August 1, 1861. Disabled by gun-shot wound left hand. Discharged November, '64.

Keith, Evander, January, 1862. Died July, 1862. Furnished five sons for war.

Keith, Eli, August 1, 1861.
Keith, James, January, 1862. Died January, 1865.
Keith, Jessee, October, 1864. Surrendered April 9, 1865. Youngest son.
Kirton, Thomas H., August 1, 1861. Promoted Corporal, 1864.
Leach, Duncan N., August 1, 1861. Died June, 1864.
Leach, Jas. Madison, August 1, 1861. Surrendered April 9, 1865.
Leach, John, August 26, 1861. Badly wounded. Promoted Sergeant, 1864. Surrendered.
Lane, David, August 1, 1861.
Lane, Lemuel, August 1, 1861. Died April, 1864.
Lewis, Allen C., August 1, 1861. Wounded severely at Gettysburg, Pa. Surrendered April 9, 1865.
Lewis, Angus, August 1, 1861. Wounded July 3, 1863. Died July 17, 1863.
Lewis, Hardee, August 1, 1861. Killed May 12, 1864.
Lewis, John. Unknown. Thigh broken August 16, 1864. Died August, 1864.
Lockey, Benjamin B., August 1, 1861. Died in prison, 1864.
Lovet, Levin, August 1, 1861. Discharged February, 1862.
Moody, Curtis, August 1, 1861. Died July, 1862.
Moody, Calvin C., January, 1864. Killed May 12, 1864.
Moody, Oliver, August 1, 1861. Died October 12, 1862, from wounds received at Sharpsburg.
Scott, John W., January, 1864. Surrendered April, '65.
Shooter, Chas. F., January, 1862. Promoted Sergeant May 4, 1864. Killed May 6, 1864.
Shooter, William N., August 1, 1861. Surrendered April, 1865.
Snipes, Allen, August 1, 1861. Died November, 1864.
Stephens, John, August 1, 1861. Killed May 6, 1864.
Taylor, Aquilla, August 1, 1861. Killed May 6, 1864.
Taylor, David, August 1, 1861. Killed May 6, 1864.
Taylor, Joseph, October, 1861. Killed August 29, 1862.
Thomas, Cade, August 1, 1861. Surrendered April, '65. Wagon driver.
Thomas, David, August 1, 1861. Surrendered April, 1865.

Thomas, James, August 1, 1861. Surrendered April, 1863.

Thomas, Samuel W., August 1, 1861. Killed July 1, 1863, Gettysburg.

Turbeville, Solomon, August 1, 1861. Died. Left too sick to travel at Frederick City, Md. Never heard from again.

Walsh, Henry, August 1, 1861. Died July, 1862.

White, William, August 1, 1861. Died September, 1862.

White, Nelson J., January, 1864. Surrendered April, 1865.

Woodward, William J., August 1, 1861. Surrendered April, 1865.

Watson, David E., March, 1862. Discharged 1863.

Barfield, Henry, January, 1862. Died June, 1862.

Campbell, Erasmus D., January, 1862. Surrendered April, 1865.

Campbell, John J., May, 1861. Surrendered April, 1865.

Smith, Benj. Gause, October 26, 1864. Surrendered April, 1865.

Roll of Company I, Eighth Regiment Infantry, South Carolina Volunteers, in the Confederate States Provisional Army, from Marion County:

Stackhouse, E. Thomas, Captain. Transferred Captain Co. L. Dead.

Harllee, Andrew T., Captain. Wounded at Maryland Heights, Gettysburg, Beans Station. Promoted Second Lieutenant 1861. Captain May 13, 1862. Surrendered Greensboro. Living.

Cook, Henry B., First Lieutenant. Wounded First Manassus. Resigned 1862. Living.

Ross, J. Newton, First Lieutenant. Wounded Sharpsburg. Killed at Deep Bottom, July 28, 1864.

Rogers, Robert H., Second Lieutenant. Resigned 1862.

Carmichael, William D., Second Lieutenant. Wounded at Malvern Hill, Petersburg, Gettysburg, Deep Bottom. Surrendered Greensboro. Living.

Stafford, Duncan C., Second Lieutenant. Killed at Petersburg, 1864.

Cameron, Alexander W., Second Lieutenant. Died at home, 1863.

Cusack, George W., Second Lieutenant. Wounded at Cold Harbor. Lost a leg. Surrendered at Greensboro. Living.

McClenaghan, Honorine H., First Sergeant. Surrendered at Greensboro. Died since war.

Harllee, Peter S., First Sergeant. Surrendered at Greensboro. Died since war.

Pearce, James F., Second Sergeant. Surrendered at Greensboro. Living.

Ayers, Enoch S., Third Sergeant. Living.

McDuffie, Daniel Q., Second Sergeant. Killed at Gettysburg.

Harllee, R. Armstrong, Fourth Sergeant. Died at Manassas 1862.

Gregg, A. Stuart, Fourth Sergeant. Living.

Jenkins, Robert W., Fifth Sergeant. Transferred to Cavalry. Living.

Woodrow, John E., First Corporal. Died in Virginia.

Huggins, George W., First Corporal. Surrendered at Greensboro. Living.

Harrelson, Joel, Second Corporal. Surrendered at Greensboro. Living.

Sparkman, Levi, Third Corporal. Died in Virginia.

Cusack, Samuel C., Third Corporal. Wounded Sharpsburg. Surrendered at Greensboro. Living.

DeBerry, Edmund, Fourth Corporal. Living.

Robbins, John B., Fourth Corporal. Killed at Gettysburg.

Fenagan, James, Fifth Corporal. Wounded Maryland Heights. Surrendered at Greensboro. Died since war.

Rogers, Ebenezer, Fifth Corporal. Killed at Gettysburg.

Carmichael, Alexander, Sixth Corporal. Killed at Maryland Heights.

Privates.

Brigman, Archibald. Died in Virginia.
Butler, John A. Died in Virginia in 1861.
Butler, Silas W. Died at home, 1861.
Bigham, W. Harvey.
Bullock, Joel. Living.
Benton, George W. Killed at Manassas.
Baker, John. Died in Virginia.

Cox, George B. Transferred to Cavalry.
Cribb, Levi.
Collins, Edward H. Died in Virginia, 1861.
Crawford, Hardy B. Transferred to Cavalry.
Cottingham, Stewart. Detached as Corporal Guard, 1861. Transferred 1st Infantry and killed.
Cottingham, Thomas F. Wounded Cold Harbor. Surrendered at Greensboro. Died since war.
Cohen, David. Transferred 21st Infantry. Living.
Cohen, Isaac.
Dove, John W. Killed in Virginia.
Dove, Hugh G. Killed at Manassas.
Ellen, Elijah J. Died in Virginia.
Elvington, Dennis. Died in Virginia, 1861.
Fryer, Andrew J. Transferred to Cavalry. Living.
Freeman, Joseph. Killed at Spottsylvania.
Gaddy, Richard M. Transferred to Cavalry. Living.
Gaddy, William D. Died in Virginia, 1861.
Gregg, Thomas C. Transferred to Artillery.
Harralson, M. Jackson. Killed at Cold Harbor.
Harralson, E. Preston.
Herring, Ed B. Surrendered at Greensboro. Living.
Hinton, Jessee W. Died in Virginia, 1861.
Jones, Jessee. Died in Virginia, 1861.
James, Robert. Discharged.
Lloyd, Henry, Alabama. Died in Virginia, 1861.
Llewellyn, B. Frank. Transferred to Cavalry.
Mace, James C. Died in Virginia.
Meekins, Philip B. Transferred to Cavalry. Died since war.
Morgan, W. Colin. Killed at Malvern Hill.
Miller, William H. Discharged, Virginia, 1862. Dead.
Myers, John E. Died in Virginia.
Moody, John B. Discharged, Virginia, 1862. Living.
Murphy, John C. Dead.
McCall, L. Allsbrooks. Transferred to Cavalry. Living.
McRae, James. Living.
Owens, David R. Killed in Virginia, '63.
Owens, Shadrach S. Killed at Cold Harbor.

Sparkman, George R. Died in Virginia.
Snipes, Michael. Killed at Cedar Creek.
Smalley, Isaiah. Died in Virginia.
Turner, John C. Killed at Cedar Creek.
Watson, John R. Killed at Malvern Hill.
Watson, Quinn. Killed at Savage Station.
Woodrow, William J.
Whitner, Joseph N. Transferred to Cavalry.
Woodberry, William D. Transferred to 21st Infantry.

Roll of Company H, Eighth Regiment Infantry, South Carolina Volunteers, in the Confederate States Provisional Army:

Singletary, R. L., Captain, Marion. Resigned May, 1862.

McIntyre, Duncan, Captain, Marion. Promoted from First Lieutenant, May, 1862. Wounded December 13, 1862, July 21, 1864. Living.

Myers, G. Matthew, First Lieutenant. Promoted from Third Sergeant May, 1862. Killed at Gettysburg.

Brunson, J. Boyd, Second Lieutenant. Resigned May, 1862.

Culpepper, George, Second Lieutenant. Promoted from ranks, 1862. Resigned December, '62.

McPherson, C. Ervin, Second Lieutenant. Promoted from Third Sergeant to Second Junior Lieutenant, for gallantry at Beans Station, East Tennessee. Dead.

Gregg, Walter, Jr., Second Lieutenant. Resigned May, 1862.

Cooper, Robert D., Second Lieutenant. Promoted from Second Sergeant May, 1862. Wounded at Wilderness.

Gregg, Smiley A., First Sergeant, Marion. Discharged December 14, 1861.

Gregg, McFadden, First Sergeant, Marion. Promoted from Corporal. Killed at Knoxville.

Moore, Blaney, First Sergeant, Marion. Died in Union Prison, Camp Chase.

Gregg, John W., Second Sergeant. Surrendered with General Johnson.

Matthews, Frank, Second Sergeant, Marion.

Hughes, George W., Third Sergeant, Marion. Promoted from Second Corporal. Wounded at Cedar Run. Surrendered with General Johnson.

Godbold, David, Third Sergeant, Marion. Promoted from Corporal. Died at Charlottesville.

Folston, George, Third Sergeant, Marion. Promoted from Corporal. Discharged under age.

Stone, W. C. P., Third Sergeant, Marion. Killed at Spottsylvania.

Armfield, A. L., Corporal, Marion.

McWhite, E., Corporal, Marion.

Privates.

Altman, J. Died at Bull Run.

Bartley, J. G. Discharged, 1862.

Bartley, Charles. Killed at Gettysburg.

Bartley, Edward. Surrendered with General Johnson.

Bartley, Henry, Marion.

Bellflowers, H., Marion. Died at hospital, 1862.

Braydon, J. J., Marion. Wounded at Spottsylvania. Surrendered General Johnson.

Bailey, John, Marion. Discharged, 1862.

Broach, G. W., Marion. Died in hospital, 1861.

Cain, S. G., Marion. Discharged, 1861.

Cain, K. S., Marion. Died at Bull Run, 1861.

Cain, J. J., Marion. Died in hospital, 1862.

Cain, Rix M., Marion. Discharged, 1862.

Cain, Church, Marion. Discharged, 1862.

Cain, J. Coon, Marion. Discharged, 1861.

Cain, J. H., Marion. Discharged, 1862.

Cox, J. T., Marion. Discharged, 1861.

Cooper, Brunson, Marion. Surrendered with General Johnson.

Cooper, Witherspoon, Marion. Surrendered with General Johnson.

Christman, Jarrott, Marion. Died at Charlottesville, 1862.

Davis, J. G., Marion. Surrendered at Navy Yard.

Deas, Simon, Marion. Surrendered with General Johnson.

Eagerton, Henry, Marion. Surrendered with General Johnson.

Finklea, John, Marion. Surrendered with General Johnson.

Flowers, W. D., Marion. Discharged, 1862.

A HISTORY OF MARION COUNTY. 595

Guy, J. H., Marion. Surrendered with General Johnson.
Graham, John M., Marion. Discharged 1862, under age.
Hampton, Thomas, Marion. Killed at Gettysburg.
Hampton, George, Marion. Surrendered with General Johnson.
Hutchison, George, Marion. Unaccounted for after Gettysburg.
Hutchison, W. C., Marion. Died at Culpeper, 1861.
Hutchison, Samuel, Marion. Wounded at Wilderness. Discharged, disabled.
Hunter, Dawson, Marion. Discharged, 1862.
Harral, Ephraim, Marion. Died in Virginia, 1861.
Harral, N. W., Marion. Died in Virginia, 1863.
Harral, W. T., Marion. Killed at Maryland Heights.
Hyman, Benjamin, Marion. Discharged, 1862.
Hyman, C. E., Marion. Died in Virginia, 1861.
Hughes, R. S., Marion. Surrendered with General Johnson.
Holland, J. S., Marion. Killed at Cedar Run.
Holland, George, Marion. Surrendered with General Johnson.
Hodges, Barney, Marion. Wounded at Chattanooga.
Kennedy, Alfred, Marion. Discharged, 1862.
Kennedy, Andrew, Marion. Discharged, 1862.
Kersey, E., Marion. Discharged, 1861.
Lewellyn, Jessee B., Marion. Discharged, 1862.
Leach, Julius, Marion. Killed Gettysburg.
McKissick, A. G., Marion. Discharged, 1862, under age.
McKissick, Murchison, Marion.
Myers, William, Marion. Died in Virginia, 1863.
McWhite, A. A., Marion. Killed at Maryland Heights.
Myers, A. A., Marion. Surrendered with General Johnson.
Pearce, R. H., Marion. Discharged, 1862.
Prosser, Michael, Marion.
Rogers, Cambyses, Marion. Wounded at Camp Chase. Surrendered with General Johnson.
Rogers, Millington, Marion.
Ray, A., Marion. Surrendered with General Johnson.
Stephenson, Andrew, Marion. Discharged, 1861.

Stone, F. F., Marion. Died Bull Run, 1861.
Stone, W. C. P., Marion.
Williams, Henry, Marion. Killed at Manassas, 1861.
Williams, Thomas, Marion. Died at Bull Run, 1861.
Williams, R. L., Marion. Died at Bull Run, 1861.
Williams, S. B., Marion. Discharged, under age.
Weatherford, W. S., Marion. Discharged, 1861.
Weatherford, Ben, Marion.

Roll of Company I, First Regiment Infantry (Hagood's), S. C. Volunteers, in the Confederate States Provisional Army, from Marion County:

Stafford, James H., Captain. Wounded at Spottsylvania, May 6, 1864. Resigned March, 1865, continuous bad health. Dead.

Harllee, John W., First Lieutenant. Wounded Wilderness, May 4, 1864. Incapable of active service after wound. Dead.

Manning, William L., Second Lieutenant. Killed at Grovetown, Va., August 29, 1862.

Murchison, Roderick, Second Lieutenant. Promoted from Third Lieutenant, 1862. Resigned and joined Kirk's Cavalry. Dead.

Murphy, Duncan, Lieutenant. Promoted from First Sergeant, May, 1864. Killed at Spottsylvania, May 6, 1864.

Butler, Gilbert, First Sergeant. Wounded Wilderness. Promoted from Sergeant. Died, 1866, from effects of wound.

Blue, William, First Sergeant. Promoted, 1863. Killed at Wilderness.

McKellar, John D., First Sergeant. Promoted from Corporal. Died East Tennessee, March 10, 1864.

McInnis, Daniel, Second Sergeant. Died at home, 1868.

McCall, Nathan, Third Sergeant. Died at home, 1862.

Carmichael, Malcolm C., Fourth Sergeant. Promoted from Corporal, 1864. Living.

Campbell, Daniel, Fifth, Sergeant. Promoted from Corporal, 1864. Living.

Carmichael, Daniel A., Corporal. Died at Charleston, August 28, 1862.

McCormac, John H., Corporal. Living.

A HISTORY OF MARION COUNTY.   597

Lofton, John H., Corporal. Killed at Richmond, 1864.

McInnis, Murdock, Corporal. Wounded Fredericksburg, 1862. Died of wounds at hospital, January 13, 1862.

Brigman, Arthur P., Corporal. Exchanged.

Privates.

Ammons, Philip.

Ammons, Asa. Died at hospital, 1863.

Bailey, Christopher. Wounded Lookout Valley, October 23, 1863. Living.

Bethea, Holden. Living.

Bolton, Britton. Died at hospital, 1864.

Butler, Eli T. Living.

Butler, Alfred W. Living.

Buie, William H. Died Newman, Ga., October, '63.

Bundy, John A. Living.

Burnett, John. Living.

Carmichael, Alex. J. Wounded Manassas, August 30, 1862. Died of wounds, Virginia, January 30, 1863.

Campbell, John C. Wounded Spottsylvania, May 6, 1864. Came home on wounded furlough, and killed by mistake for deserter.

Clark, Kenneth. Died in hospital, Virginia, December, 1862.

Cottingham, Stewart. Wounded Grovetown, Va., August 29, 1862. Died, 1874, from effect of wounds.

Crawford, James D. Living.

Coward, Abner. Died at home, 1866, from disease.

Coward, Ansel.

Dillon, William. Died, 1879.

Easterling, Henry. Killed Fort Harrison, October 2, 1864.

Evans, William T. Exchanged to Gregg's Battery, 1863. Living.

Fitzgerald, Robert E.

Fore, Tracy. Exchanged to 8th Regiment. Living.

Garner, James. Died Charleston, August, 1862.

Gaddy, Ithanner J. Living.

Graham, Dugald. Died in hospital, Virginia, November 16, 1862.

Gray, Franklin. Living.

Gray, Henry. Living.

Hamilton, Tobias. Exchanged to 23d Infantry, 1864. Living.

Hamilton, Tristram. Died Charleston, S. C., June 22, 1862.

Hamilton, Whitton. Living.

Horton, Thomas T. Living.

Hargrove, Isaac H. Killed East Tennessee, January 17, 1864.

Herring, Harmon. Living.

Herring, Edward. Living.

Herring, Daniel M. Died at home.

Herring, Samuel. Living.

Hyat, Soloman. Living.

Hyat, John C. D. Living.

Hyat, James K. Died Charleston, 1862.

Hyat, John. Living.

Hyat, Hugh. Discharged Charleston, 1862. Died at home, 1866.

Hyat, David. Died of disease in Maryland on a march.

Hulon, Wylie. Living.

Hamilton, John. Wounded at Richmond, December 10, 1864. Died at home, January, 1868.

Jackson, Warren A. Died hospital, 1862.

Jackson, Charles T. Living.

Jackson, James R.

Jackson, John T. Died at hospital, 1863.

Jackson, John C. Wounded Lookout Valley, 1863.

McCall, John C. Living.

McDaniel, Amos. Killed at Spottsylvania, May 6, 1864.

McDaniel, Joseph. Died Charleston, S. C., 1862, August.

McDaniel, Randall. Wounded Lookout Valley, October 28, 1863. Died, 1868, from effects of wounds.

McArthur, James. Died near Culpeper, December, 1862.

Owens, Redin. Dead.

Paul, William. Died near Winchester, October 15, 1862.

Stackhouse, William R. Dead.

Stackhouse, Tristram F. Living.

Sherwood, Richard. Died Columbia, June 2d, 1862.

Surles, Archibald. Living.

Taylor, Ephraim. Living.
Townsend, Daniel A. Living.
Turner, John C. Living.
Turner, Joel. Living.
Walter, Philip D.

Roll of Company L, Tenth Regiment Infantry, South Carolina Volunteers, in the Confederate States Provisional Army:

McMillan, S. E., Captain, Marion. Not re-elected in 1862.

Ford, A. H., Captain, Marion. Promoted from First Lieutenant, 1862.

Harrelson, D. J., First Lieutenant. Promoted from Second Lieutenant, 1862. Wounded Atlanta.

Stackhouse, R. B., Second Lieutenant. Not re-elected in 1862.

Russ, T. B., Second Lieutenant. Promoted from First Sergeant. Wounded, Atlanta.

Giles, W. H., Second Lieutenant. Promoted from ranks. Killed Atlanta, July 28, 1864.

McDuffie, D. D., Sergeant. Promoted First Lieutenant Co. G.

Smith, T. A., Sergeant. Mustered out, over age.

Murphy, N. C., Sergeant. Promoted Second Lieutenant Co. F.

Munnerlyn, W. H., Sergeant. Promoted Second Lieutenant Co. D.

Smith, A. N., Sergeant. Promoted from Corporal. Captured at Missionary Ridge.

Coleman, W. D., Corporal. Promoted from Corporal. Wounded at Chickamauga.

Lee, H., Corporal. Discharged at Georgetown.

Hayes, T. B., Corporal. Discharged at Georgetown.

Miller, L. W. Died of disease in South Carolina, on march to Charleston.

Collins, D. F., Corporal. Died of disease in Georgetown.

Johnson, T. H., Corporal. Promoted from ranks.

McCall, D. N., Corporal. Promoted from ranks.

McIntyre, W. W., Corporal. Promoted from ranks.

Privates.

Adkinson, J. A.
Adkinson, B. F.
Aymet, W. D. Wounded Chickamauga.
Barber, William. Captured at Nashville.
Boatright, J. A.
Benjamin, S. Mustered out, under age.
Brown, G. R. W. Wounded at Murfreesboro. Lost a leg.
Brown, R. M. Died at hospital.
Brown, J. L. Died at hospital.
Brown, L. Died at hospital.
Brown, W.
Brogsden, E. Discharged.
Collins, A. J. Died at hospital.
Collins, J. D. Died at hospital.
Collins, R. Wounded Chickamauga.
Collins, S. Wounded Missionary Ridge.
Collins, J. G. Died at hospital.
Campbell, G. F. Died at hospital.
Carmichael, J. L. Died at Franklin, of wounds.
Cameron, D. C. Mustered out, under age.
Coleman, Jessee.
Croker, H. Died at hospital.
Clark, H. S. Discharged, Prussian subject.
Deaver, A., Marion. Wounded Murfreesboro. Lost a leg.
Flowers, B. A. Wounded Resaca. Died of wounds at Murfreesboro.
Flowers, B. Died at hospital.
Flowers, N. Died at hospital.
Ferguson, M. M. Detached, hospital steward.
Gregg, A. E.
Gregg, William.
Gregg, R. W. Mustered out, under age.
Giles, A. J. Captured Missionary Ridge.
Giles, R. J.
Giles, J. B. Died, hospital.
Harrelson, G. W.
Hertz, H. Discharged, Prussian subject.
Holden, E.

Holden, J.
Horn, J. M. Died at hospital.
Huggins, T.
Huggins, A. H. Died at hospital.
Huggins, N. C. Killed at Nashville.
Huggins, J.
Jasper, A. W. Killed at Murfreesboro.
James, G. T.
Johnson, A. P. Wounded at Murfreesboro.
Johnson, G. W. Wounded at Murfreesboro.
Lane, J. Mustered out, under age.
Lane, G. W. Transferred.
Lambert, B. F. Discharged.
Mearse, P. L. Died at hospital.
Miller, N.
Miller, James.
Miller, Thompson.
Middleton, J. E. Wounded Chickamauga, lost leg. Living.
Murphy, J. B.
McCall, J. Killed at Bentonville.
McDaniel, A. Died at hospital.
McKenzie, W. T. Discharged.
Nance, A. Discharged.
Owens, N. R., Marion.
Page, A. Wounded Resaca.
Price, J. C. Wounded Chickamauga.
Price, B. T. Wounded. Captured Missionary Ridge.
Richardson, F. M. Died at hospital.
Richardson, J. G.
Rogers, W. H. Captured Missionary Ridge.
Rogers, J. D.
Sawyer, T.
Snipes, J. Killed at Franklin.
Smith, G. W. Transferred to Gregg's Battery.
Smith, J. F.
Stephens, W. T. Mustered out, under age.
Shelley, J. T. Captured Missionary Ridge.
Sweet, W. P. Died at hospital.
Tabler, W. Captured.

Thompson, W. M.   Killed at Murfreesboro.
Wall, S. B.
Waller, G. W.
Wallace, W. J.   Captured in Kentucky.
Wiggins, J. B.   Died in hospital.

Roll of Company L, Eighth Regiment Infantry, South Carolina Volunteers, in the Confederate States Provisional Army:

Stackhouse, E. Thomas, Captain, Marion. Wounded at Sharpsburg, Gettysburg, Deep Bottom. Transferred from Co. I. Promoted Major, Lieutenant Colonel and Colonel. Dead.

Carmichael, William D., Captain, Marion. Wounded at Malvern Hill, Gettysburg, Petersburg. Promoted Captain at Gettysburg. Surrendered at Greensboro. Living.

Huggins, George W., First Lieutenant, Marion. Surrendered at Greensboro. Living.

Clark, John Calvin, Second Lieutenant, Marion. Promoted from ranks Co. I. Killed Deep Bottom.

Carmichael, Duncan D., First Sergeant, Marion. Surrendered Greensboro. Living.

Ayers, Enoch S., Second Sergeant, Marion. Surrendered Greensboro. Living.

Rogers, Ebenezer, Third Sergeant, Marion. Killed Gettysburg.

Mannings, Eli, Fourth Sergeant, Marion. Transferred to Spark's Cavalry. Dead.

Murchison, Duncan, Fifth Sergeant, Marion. Wounded Gettysburg. Surrendered Greensboro. Dead.

Carmichael, Alexander, First Corporal, Marion. Killed Harper's Ferry.

Page, Joseph N., Second Corporal, Marion. Surrendered Greensboro. Dead.

Roberts, James H., Third Corporal, Marion. Killed Savage Station.

Barfield, Thompson, Fourth Corporal, Marion. Transferred from Co. I. Wounded Chickamauga, lost a leg. Discharged. Dead.

A HISTORY OF MARION COUNTY. 603

Privates.

Alford, Robert H., Marion.
Alford, Artemus, Marion. Died near Richmond.
Alford, W. McD., Marion. Surrendered Greensboro. Living.
Ammons, J. Duncan, Marion. Wounded Gettysburg. Living.
Ayers, D. Dwight, Marion. Died near Richmond.
Barfield, R. Talley, Marion. Wounded twice at Cold Harbor. Transferred from Co. I. Living.
Barfield, Marsden, Marion. Living. Surrendered Greensboro. Transferred from Co. I.
Barfield, Harllee, Marion. Wounded Deep Bottom. Surrendered Greensboro. Living.
Bethea, J. Frank, Marion. Transferred to Medical Department.
Bethea, Henry P., Marion. Died in Union Prison.
Brigman, Arthur P., Marion. Discharged. Transferred from Co. I. Living.
Byrd, Hugh G., Marion
Carmichael, Archibald, Marion. Wounded Deep Bottom. Transferred from Co. I. Surrendered Greensboro. Living.
Carmichael, Alex., Jr., Marion. Wounded Deep Bottom. Transferred from Co. I. Surrendered Greensboro. Living.
Carmichael, Duncan C., Marion. Transferred from Co. I. Living.
Cottingham, Conner, Marion. Died near Richmond.
Candy, Samuel, Marion. Died at home.
Clark, R. Knox, Marion. Wounded Malvern Hill. Discharged. Died since war.
Crowley, William C., Marion. Transferred 23d Infantry.
Coward, Harvey, Marion. Died in Virginia.
Cook, John, Marion.
Harper, John M., Marion. Wounded. Living.
Herring, Samuel, Marion. Discharged. Living.
Huckabee, John, Marion. Transferred to Co. K.
Hicks, John C., North Carolina.
Huggins, William E., South Carolina. Surrendered Greensboro. Living.

Huggins, Doc., South Carolina. Surrendered Greensboro. Living.

Hunt, James E., South Carolina. Died in Virginia.

Herring, Ebby B., South Carolina. Died in Virginia.

Irwin, James R., Darlington. Killed Deep Bottom.

Jackson, Robert, Marion. Wounded Beans Station. Surrendered Greensboro. Living.

Jackson, Malcolm, Marion. Surrendered Greensboro. Living.

Jackson, Levi, Marion. Surrendered Greensboro. Living.

Jackson, Nicholas, Marion. Wounded Cold Harbor. Surrendered Greensboro. Dead.

Lane, Samuel, Marion. Wounded Fredericksburg. Surrendered Greensboro. Living.

Lane, Evander, Marion. Killed North Anna River.

McPhaul, Daniel, Marion. Died near Richmond.

McRae, Colin, Marion. Wounded Savage Station. Died near Richmond.

McRae, Norman, Marion. Died in Virginia.

McRae, Roderick, Marion. Surrendered Greensboro. Living.

McRae, Franklin, Marion. Transferred to Co. K.

McGill, Colin, Marion. Died in Virginia.

McLaurin, Duncan, Marion.

Morgan, W. Colin, Marion. Wounded Malvern Hill. Died at hospital.

McGill, David, Marion. Wounded Chickamauga. Surrendered Greensboro. Living.

Owens, Shadrack S., Marion. Transferred to Co. I.

Page, David N., Marion. Died in Virginia.

Page, Doc. T., Marion.

Rogers, Thompson, Marion.

Rogers, John J., Marion. Killed at Malvern Hill.

Rogers, Allen, Marion. Surrendered at Greensboro. Living.

Rogers, William D., Marion. Surrendered at Greensboro. Dead.

Rogers, Ervin B., Marion.

Rogers, Lot B., Marion. Surrendered at Greensboro. Living.

A HISTORY OF MARION COUNTY. 605

Stocks, John, North Carolina.
Sarvis, John, Marion.
Turner, John C., Marion. Transferred to Co. I.
Turbeville, Calvin, Marion. Died in Williamsburg.
Waters, John W., Marion.
Watson, John R. Killed Malvern Hill.
Watson, Quinn, Marion. Killed Savage Station.
Watson, Lindsay, Marion. Died in Virginia.

Roll of Company I, Twenty-first Regiment Infantry, South Carolina Volunteers, in the Confederate States Provisional Army:

Woodberry, Evander M., Captain, Marion. Resigned March 1, 1862, and died at home soon after.

Howard, Richard G., Captain, Marion. Captured Morris Island, July 10, 1863. Surrendered at Florence. Dead.

Gasque, Henry A., First Lieutenant, Marion. Discharged, May 1, 1862. Dead.

Cannon, Henry M., First Lieutenant, Marion. Discharged, May 1, 1862. Dead.

Shelley, David, Second Lieutenant, Marion. Captured Petersburg, June 24, 1864. Died Point Lookout, 1864.

Jordan, A. Bennett, Bv. Second Lieutenant, Marion. Resigned, May 1, 1862. Living.

Jarrat, J. Allston, Second Lieutenant, Darlington. Died of disease at Charleston.

Altman, William T., Second Lieutenant, Marion. Wounded Petersburg. Promoted May, 1863. Died since war.

Chappell, Henry C., Second Lieutenant, Alabama. Died of wounds at Petersburg.

Noble, J. Hardy, First Sergeant, Marion.

Gasque, C. Marion, Second Sergeant, Marion. Wounded Morris Island. Killed City Point, June, 1864.

McDaniel, John R., Third Sergeant, Marion. Captured Petersburg. Died Elmira.

Jordan, George S., Fourth Sergeant, Marion. Living.

Cannon, George H., Fifth Sergeant, Darlington. Living.

Hucks, John R., Sergeant, Marion. Discharged, over age. Dead.

Dozier, J. Valentine, First Corporal, Marion. Killed Morris Island, July 10, 1863.

Cannon, William H., Second Corporal, Darlington. Living.

Wright, John W., Third Corporal, Marion. Killed Petersburg, June 24, 1864.

Altman, J. Hamilton, Fourth Corporal, Marion. Living.

Privates.

Avant, Orlando R., Marion. Died Columbia.

Altman, Samuel S., Marion. Died Georgetown, April, 1862.

Altman, J. Benjamin, Marion. Died Georgetown, March 28, 1862.

Altman, J. Wesley, Marion. Died Georgetown, March 26, 1862.

Bone, John, Marion. Died at home, 1862.

Bone, Robert G., Marion. Discharged, 1862, over age. Living.

Bailey, G., Marion. Discharged for disability, November 19, 1863.

Boatwright, Robert S., Marion. Wounded Morris Island. Lost a leg. Captured, July, 1863. Living.

Brown, George W., Marion.

Brown, Henry, Marion. Living.

Brown, Jessee C., Marion. Died at home, 1863.

Brown, William J., Marion. Wounded Petersburg, 1863. Lost a leg. Living.

Brown, Evander, Marion. Captured Petersburg, May 9, 1864. Died at Elmira, 1864.

Bellflowers, Jessee, Marion. Killed Battery Wagner, July 12, 1863.

Burroughs, Thomas, Williamsburg. Discharged, 1862, over age.

Cannon, Samuel W., Marion. Living.

Collins, Valentine, Marion. Living.

Cook, James Ervin, Marion. Died Georgetown, 1862.

Davis, James H., Marion.

Davis, H. Foster, Marion. Died of wounds, Petersburg, July, 1864.

Dozier, John F., Marion. Captured Morris Island, July 10,

1863. Discharged Point Lookout at close of service. Living.

Dozier, Tully, Marion. Captured Fort Fisher, where he was discharged at close of service. Dead.

Foxworth, Ervin J., Marion. Died at home, 1862.

Foxworth, Joseph B., Marion. Killed Drewry's Bluff, May 16, 1864.

Gasque, Ervin A., Marion. Killed Gaines Mill, June 5, 1864.

Gregg, Thomas C., Marion. Transferred to Co. B.

Gregg, Wesley L., Marion. Attached to Ambulance Corps. Living.

Gunter, William, Marion. Wounded Port Walthall, May 7, 1864. Died Port Walthall, May 9, 1864.

Ham, Charles W., Marion. Died Georgetown, April 25, 1863.

Herrin, Allison W., Marion. Died at home, 1863, of disease.

Herrin, David F., Marion. Died Georgetown, 1863, April, 25th.

Hewett, Thomas, Marion. Living.

Hewett, Joseph R., Marion. Living.

James, James V., Marion. Hospital Steward, October 20, 1862. Living.

Jarratt, James B., Darlington.

Jarratt, Chas. Ed., Darlington. Discharged, 1863, under age.

Jordan, W. King, Marion. Captured Petersburg, June 24, 1864. Died Elmira, 1864.

Lowrimore, John, Marion. Died Fort Reliance, Pee Dee, June 15, 1862.

Lowrimore, Moses, Marion. Discharged, December 24, 1862, for disability.

Lowrimore, Hanson L., Marion. Died at home, 1862.

Marlow, R. William, Marion. Killed Petersburg, 1864.

Martin, Stephen H., Marion. Died March, 1867.

Martin, ——, Marion. Living.

McClellan, Daniel B., Marion. Living.

McClellan, Enos, Marion. Living.

McDaniel, J. Randall, Marion. Living.

Miller, John P., Darlington. Discharged, December.

Pace, James A., Marion. Captured Morris Island, July 10, 1863. Died Point Lookout, 1864.

Powell, Noah P., Marion. Killed Petersburg, June 18, 1864.

Parker, Thomas, Marion. Captured, 1863.

Prior, William M., Georgetown. Discharged for disability, April 23, 1863. Living.

Rogers, Thomas G., Marion. Died Fort Fisher, January 16, 1865.

Rogers, J. Benjamin, Marion. Died, 1879.

Richardson, Pinckney G., Marion. Died, 1876.

Richardson, E. Franklin, Marion. Discharged, July 22, 1862, for disability. Died, 1881.

Richardson, Thomas, Marion. Died Charleston.

Richardson, David W., Marion. Killed Swift Creek, May 9, 1864.

Richardson, J. Graves, Marion. Living.

Richardson, James H., Marion. Living.

Richardson, Thomas J., Marion. Wounded Petersburg, severely. Living.

Rowell, James W., Marion. Wounded Morris Island. Died at home, 1868.

Rowell, David A., Marion. Died Morris Island, May, 1863.

Rowell, Valentine, Marion. Living.

Rowell, William P., Marion. Wounded Port Walthall, May 7, 1864. Died of wounds Port Walthall, May 9, 1864.

Stanley, John F., Marion. Died of wounds Port Walthall, May 9, 1864. Wounded Port Walthall, May 7, 1864.

Sampson, Joseph, Georgetown. Detailed Qr. Mas. Dept.

Sampson, Samuel, Georgetown. Transferred, April, 1862.

Shelley, John C., Marion. Living.

Shelley, Zachariah, Marion.

Sineath, Joseph P., Marion. Died Morris Island, 1863.

Shackelford, Stephen P., Marion. Living.

Tindal, Emanuel, Marion. Living.

Tindal, Solomon, Marion. Died at home, February 13, 1863.

Tucker, John, Marion. Wounded Morris Island. Discharged, disabled, July 10, 1863.

Turbeville, Asa, Marion. Wounded Petersburg. Living.

Williams, Henry S. B., Marion. Wounded Port Walthall, May 7, 1864. Died, May 9, 1864.

Williams, John C., Marion. Died Georgetown, March 25, 1862.

Williams, Jacob H., Marion. Living.

Williams, Jordan, Marion. Discharged, February 1, 1862, over age.

White, James H., Marion. Died Petersburg, June, 1864.

Whaley, John H., Marion. Died at home, November 17, 1862.

Whaley, William M., Marion. Died at home, February 10, 1862.

Wall, Lawson J., Marion. Living.

Wallace, John J., Marion. Died at home, 1862.

Roll of Company E, 23d Regiment, South Carolina Volunteers, in the Confederate States Provisional Army:

Fladger, Chas. J., Captain. Killed by deserter, at home.

Finklea, James C., Captain. Resigned, July 17, 1864. Living.

Covington, Harris, First Lieutenant. Resigned.

Moody, R. B., First Lieutenant. Wounded Petersburg. Died since war.

Bethea, B. J., First Lieutenant. Living.

Crawford, W. H., Second Lieutenant. Dead.

Moody, A. C., Second Lieutenant. Resigned. Living.

Bethea, J. C., Third Lieutenant.

Bethea, A. J., Third Lieutenant. Dead.

Carmichael, D., Third Lieutenant. Died, 1864.

McIntyre, D. A., First Sergeant.

Hayes, S. P., Second Sergeant.

Benjamin, E., Second Sergeant. Died, 1869. Promoted.

Wilson, J. T., Third Sergeant. Wounded Second Manassas, August 30, 1862. Living.

Whittington, C. C., Third Sergeant. Promoted from ranks. Living.

Price, H. G., Third Sergeant. Promoted from ranks. Living.

McIntyre, J. C., Third Sergeant. Promoted from ranks.

Smith, H., Fourth Sergeant. Promoted from ranks.

Jackson, S. S., Fourth Sergeant. Promoted from ranks.

Berry, D. F., Fifth Sergeant. Promoted from ranks. Dead.

Braswell, J. R., Fifth Sergeant. Promoted from ranks. Living.

Tart, J. W., First Corporal. Promoted from ranks. Dead.

Smith, F. D., First Corporal. Promoted from ranks. Wounded. Living.

Blackman, Wm., First Corporal. Promoted from ranks. Living.

Owens, D. F., First Corporal. Promoted from ranks. Living.

Crawford, G. G., Second Corporal. Promoted from ranks. Living.

Hays, J. D., Second Corporal. Living.

Hays, Wilson, Third Corporal. Living.

Hearsey, W., Fourth Corporal. Living.

Smith, J. R., Fourth Corporal. Living.

Sanderson, D., Fourth Corporal. Detached service.

Owens, Willis, Fifth Corporal. Living.

Privates.

Allen, J. W. Living.
Bethea, E. A. Transferred. Living.
Bethea, M. S. Died at home.
Bethea, J. K. Dead.
Bailey, J. R. Living.
Broachman, J. K. Dead.
Broachman, S. C. Dead.
Broachman, ———.
Berry, J. Living.
Berry, L. Living.
Bullard, Wm. Lost in action, January 17, 1864.
Brigman, ———. Died, 1864.
Cottingham, T. F. Dead.
Christmas, J. L. Living.
Campbell, W. P.
Campbell, E.
Campbell, E. A.
Crawford, A. B.
Coats, John.
Campbell, S. A.

Daniel, N. Dead.
Driggers, R. S. Discharged.
Fladger, Hugh G. Dead.
Freeman, F. Discharged. Disability.
Freeman, F.
Godbold, J. Dead.
Godbold, J. G. Living.
Gaddy, R. W. Living.
Gaddy, T. C. Dead.
Godbold, Hugh. Living.
Godbold, H. L. Living.
Greenwood, W. D.
Hayes, H. Killed Petersburg, Va.
Hamer, J. H. Living.
Hayes, Wm. Living.
Hays, J. Living.
Hyatt, Isaac. Dead.
Hyatt, William H. Dead.
Hargrove, N. N. Living.
Hearsy, Wm. H. Living.
Hulon, William. Living.
Hulon, E. Living.
Huggins, Thomas. Dead.
Harper, J. M. Wounded at 2d Manassas.
Harper, G. W.
Hubbard, J. G.
Hays, D. H.
Hays, W. H.
Huggins, T. F.
Hunt, J. E.
Hearsy, W. Wounded.
Hays, N. Died August 1, 1864.
Jackson, A. J.
Jackson, John. Wounded Petersburg, Va.
Jackson, B. F. Dead.
Jackson, A. W. Living.
Jackson, F. M.
Jackson, B. B.
Jackson, S. S.

Jones, D. M.
Jones, H. B.
Jones, James A.
Jones, J. L.
Jones, ——, Marion. Killed Petersburg, Va., June 17, 1864.
Kersey, H., Marion.
Kersey, M., Marion.
Kersey, J., Marion.
Kersey, S. D., Marion.
Keefe, W.
Little, D. Dead.
Little, C. M. Discharged.
Lester, R. H. Living.
Lane, J. V. Dead.
Lane, J. O. Wounded. Dead.
Lane, L. L.
Love, R. Dead.
Lee, W. F. Wounded.
Lee, T. T.
Mooneyham, William W. Killed Petersburg, Va.
Mooneyham, John.
Mooneyham, Tobias.
Mooneyham, T. C.
Mooneyham, James.
Moore, A. B.
McIntyre, A. C.
Moody, W. H.
Norton, Thomas.
Norton, J. C. Dead.
Owens, J. W.
Owens, J.
Price, J. H. Dead.
Price, M. R. Dead.
Powers, Jeff. Wounded. Died.
Powell, J.
Powell, D.
Sweat, N. Wounded. Living.
Smith, J. K. Living.
Snipes, R. S. Died, August 25, 1864.

Turner, W.
Turner, A.
Turner, W. S.
Turner, E.
Turner, J.
Turner, S. D.
Turner, L.
Taylor, J. R.
Wise, E. T.
Wilson, J.
Whittington, J. G.

The following appear as supplementary, by G. G. Crawford, from memory:

Calder, Joel.
Carter, Henry.
Carter, Joe.
Fladger, James.
Hayes, Joe. Dead.
Hamer, R. P. Living.
Horton, Nicholas. Living.
Hunt, Cornelius. Living.
Kitchen, Eli.
Owens, Willis.
Price, H. G.
Power, Malcolm.
Power, J. H.
Rodgers, Henry. Dead.
Smith, H. L.
Sanderson, Daniel. Dead.
Turner, Richard.
Turner, Stephen.

Roll of Gregg's Battery, Co. D, Manigault's Battalion Artillery, South Carolina Volunteers, in the Confederate States Provisional Army:

Matthew, B. Stanley, Captain, Marion. Resigned, May 14, 1863.

Thos. E. Gregg, Captain, Marion. Promoted from First Lieutenant, May 14, 1863.

Wm. W. Braddy, First Lieutenant, Marion. Resigned, January 20, 1863.

David W. Edwards, First Lieutenant, Marion. Promoted from Second Lieutenant, May 14, 1863. Resigned, September 1, 1864.

Chas. E. Gregg, First Lieutenant. Promoted from First Sergeant, May 13, 1863. Died, July 7, 1878.

Smilie, A. Gregg, First Lieutenant, Darlington. Wounded Petersburg, April 10, 1865. Promoted from private, November 2, 1864.

F. M. Godbold, Second Lieutenant, Marion. Resigned, May 2, 1863.

David G. Marshall, Second Lieutenant, Chesterfield. Promoted for gallantry, March 2, 1865.

John L. Collins, Sergeant Major, Marion.

Alexander Page, Quartermaster Sergeant, Marion. Promoted from ranks.

Cyrus B. Haselden, Sergeant, Marion.

Robert C. Rogers, Sergeant, Marion. Wounded Battery Wagner, August, 1863.

John E. Perritt, Sergeant, Marion.

Spencer G. Cain, Sergeant, Marion. Transferred to Sharpshooters.

G. Thos. Gibbes, Sergeant, Marion.

Thomas D. Moody, Sergeant, Marion.

Chesley D. Jones, Sergeant, Marion.

David N. Bethea, Sergeant, Marion. Died February 12, 1901.

Henry L. Richardson, Sergeant, Marion.

Hardy Johnson, Sergeant, Marion.

Richard J. Edwards, Corporal, Marion.

Benjamin L. Fry, Corporal, Marion. Discharged, April 16, 1863.

Jas. C. Campbell, Corporal, Marion. Discharged, April 16, 1863.

Stephen Altman, Corporal, Marion. Discharged, April 16, 1863. Dead.

John W. Tart, Corporal, Marion. Dead.

Solomon Bryant, Corporal, Marion.

A HISTORY OF MARION COUNTY. 615

James Carmichael, Corporal, Marion. Discharged. Dead.
Samuel Bellflowers, Corporal, Marion.
George W. Smith, Corporal, Marion.
Mitchell R. Powers, Corporal, Marion.
Wm. J. Edwards, Corporal, Marion.
Berry A. Shooter, Corporal, Marion. Dead.
Wm. T. Evans, Corporal, Marion.
Joe Garner, Bugler, Marion.
Percival Sessions, Bugler, Marion.
Wm. Richardson, Bugler, Marion. Wounded Battery Hampton.

Privates.

Ammonds, D. Pinkey, Marion. Discharged, February 10, 1863.
Ard, Andrew J., Marion.
Ard, Laney, Marion.
Atkinson, Jacob, Williamsburg.
Ammons, Hamilton A., Marion.
Ard, General, Marion.
Ammonds, Benjamin, Marion.
Altman, John J., Williamsburg.
Bellflowers, Henry, Marion.
Broach, Robert R., Marion. Discharged.
Brown, Stephen, Marion.
Bryant, David, Marion.
Bryant, John Wesley, Marion.
Baxley, Solomon, Marion.
Barnes, Henry L., Marion.
Bond, Henry J., Marion. Dead.
Barrett, Isaac, Charleston. Transferred to Captain Charles' Battery.
Bostick, Paul J., Marion.
Baxley, Joseph, Marion.
Baxley, Joseph, Marion.
Bryant, James, Marion.
Brown, Hugh, Marion.
Bragdon, Manly, Marion.
Berry, Henry T., Marion.
Bostick, Joseph, Marion.

Collins, Samuel, Marion.
Cain, David, Marion.
Campbell, John C. Discharged, November 30, 1863.
Capps, Richard, Marion.
Colcutt, James W., Marion. Selected as one of four to receive reward for bravery. Noticed for gallantry, August 17, 1864, Davis Farm.
Collins, Owen R., Marion.
Creel, Samuel E. Mc., Marion. Wounded Davis Farm, August 20, 1864.
Campbell, Simeon, Marion. Discharged.
Campbell, Theophilas, Marion. Dead.
Collins, Benjamin J., Marion.
Church, James, Marion.
Capps, Francis.
Collins, Thomas J.
Collins, Stephen R.
Collins, Uriah H.
Cook, Wm. H., Marion.
Cohen, Joseph, Charleston.
Campbell, Ebenezer, Marion. Discharged, November 30, 1863.
Cook, Berry
Collins, Gregory.
Creel, John J.
Collier, Thomas.
Daniels, John L.
Drew, William, Marion.
Edwards, Cary, Marion.
Edwards, Richard M., Marion.
Edwards, Albert P., Marion.
Ellis, Hugh G.
Foxworth, Andrew J., Marion.
Foxworth, A. C.
Foxworth, Henry.
Godbold, Chas. F. Dead.
Garris, Elias.
Goodyear, Elias.
Gibbs, Joseph S.

Gilbert, James.
Harrellson, Geo. W.
Harrelson, Thomas.
Harrellson, Ed. H.
Harrellson, Stephen.
Harrellson, John C.
Huggins, Bird.
Huggins, Levi.
Hoges, Pinckney.
Herrin, Chestley.
Horn, Neal.
Horn, Wm. Pinckney. Killed Davis Farm, August 18, 1864.
Huggins, John J.
Herring, Miles.
Huggins, Neal C. Killed Davis Farm, August 18, 1864.
Hutcherson, Ed. B.
Hulon, Elijah.
Hannah, John G.
Hill, Edward. Shot as a deserter by parties at home.
Hodges, John H.
Hutcherson, John W.
Johnson, David. Dead.
Jones, Ebenezer L. Dead.
Jones, Wm. N.
Keefe, D. Frank.
Kennedy, Evander. Died at Charleston of disease.
Keefe, Ervin H.
Lewis, Joseph. Died Charleston.
Lewis, Baker.
Lewis, Zion.
Lamb, Wm. D. Discharged.
Lloyd, William. Died Charleston.
Lupo, Allen C.
Lupo, Thos. A. Died Charleston.
Lupo, Wm.
Lambert, Wesley.
Lambert, E. H.
Lane, James M.
Lane, Wm.

Lester, Robert H. Transferred to Smith's Battery.
Martin, Ed. B.
Martin, Ed. W.
Martin, Stephen B.
McDaniel, Wm.
Moody, John Thomas. Selected as one of four the bravest to receive reward.
Munn, Malcolm L.
Martin, Alex. H.
Mears, Wm.
McDaniel, Joseph.
Munn, Geo. W.
Nance, Atckerson. Discharged.
Perritt, Tristram.
Perritt, Needham.
Pace, Wm. J.
Perritt, David.
Paston, J. Rayford. Discharged.
Poston, Reddick.
Poston, Simon.
Powers, Christopher.
Powell, J. Matthew.
Paston, Daniel.
Page, Wm. H.
Page, Maston.
Paston, Robt. T.
Roberts, Duke M.
Perritt, Bennett. Discharged.
Perritt, David B.
Rogers, Francis.
Richardson, Arrey.
Richardson, W. Hamilton.
Richardson, Jas. W.
Rogers, Alex., Sr.
Rogers, Alex., Jr.
Rogers, David. Selected as one of four to receive reward for bravery.
Rogers, Robbin. Died at Charleston.
Rogers, George W.

Richardson, J. Richard.
Rogers, Cade.
Rogers, Ebenezer.
Rogers, Johnson.
Rogers, James.
Rogers, Jessee. Dead.
Roberts, Rolin Q. Transferred to Pee Dee Battery.
Rogers, H. D.
Rogers, John.
Rogers, Tristram. Dead.
Richardson, Wm. R.
Rogers, Jas. J. Dead.
Rogers, Tristram B. Dead.
Rogers, Pinckney.
Snipes, Daniel.
Snipes, Perry. Died Charleston.
Stone, Samuel J. Dead.
Smith, Calom M. Wounded Davis Farm and Wagner.
Sutton, John E.
Smith, Daniel.
Sexton, Oliver M.
Syphrett, J. W. W. Killed Charleston.
Stephens, Wm. T.
Sutton, Wm. H.
Smith, John J.
Singletary, Wm. J.
Stephens, Barney.
Thomas, Nelson.
Thomas, Patrick.
Turbeville, Richard.
Turbeville, Jas.
Turner, Jas.
Turner, Wm.
Tart, Jas. H.
Tart, Henry H. Selected as one of four to receive reward for bravery. Notice for gallantry, August 17, 1864, Davis Farm.
Taylor, John E.
Towlson, Geo. W.

Tart, John M.
Walker, Henry.
Wiggins, Ed.
Watson, Jas. R.

Roll of Company H, Twenty-third Regiment Infantry, South Carolina Volunteers, in the Confederate States Provisional Army:

John Roberts, Captain, Marion. Wounded at 2d battle of Manassas, Va. In recognition was elected Lieutenant Colonel. Died of wounds at Marion.

Solon A. Durham, Captain, Marion. Wounded at Goldsboro, N. C. Promoted to Major in C. S. A., and transferred. Dead.

W. Warren Hamilton, Captain, Marion. Wounded at 2d battle of Manassas. Captured at Five Forks, Va., and surrendered at John's Island. Promoted to Captain from Third Lieutenant, and from First Sergeant to Third Lieutenant. Living.

Kendre Nichols, First Lieutenant, Marion. Killed at 2d Manassas.

Richard W. Hale, Second Lieutenant, Marion. Resigned at Wilmington, N. C. Living.

Asa Perritt, Third Lieutenant, Marion. Wounded at Crater, Petersburg, Va. Promoted Second Lieutenant from Third Sergeant. Living.

John D. Huggins, Third Lieutenant, Marion. Captured at Five Forks. Surrendered Johnson's Island. Promoted from Orderly Sergeant. Living.

Edward Carmichael, Orderly, Marion. Promoted from Third Sergeant. Surrendered Point Lookout. Dead.

William G. Lindsey, Second Sergeant, Marion. Wounded 2d Manassas. Died of wounds at Farmville, Va.

Daniel Page, Third Sergeant, Marion. Wounded Goldsboro, N. C. Transferred to Hampton Legion, June 14, 1864. Dead.

William S. Turbeville, Fourth Sergeant, Marion. Dead.

Elly B. Greenwood, Fifth Sergeant, Marion. Wounded

Petersburg, Va. Surrendered Five Forks, 1st April, 1865. Living.

Alfred Fore, Fifth Sergeant, Marion. Died in hospital, Va.

Evander P. Ellis, Fifth Sergeant, Marion. Transferred to Hampton Legion, June 6, 1864. Living.

James V. Roulle, Fifth Sergeant, Marion. Captured 17th June, Petersburg, Va., 1864. Died Elmira, N. Y.

Wm. Hyatt, Corporal, Marion. Wounded Petersburg, Va., January 12, 1865. Dead.

Joseph Smith, Corporal, Marion. Transferred to Hampton Legion, June 14, 1864. Living.

Hardy D. Smith, Corporal, Marion. Surrendered Appomattox. Living.

John C. Bass, Corporal, Marion.

Joseph W. Allen, Corporal, Marion. Surrendered Five Forks, Va., 1st April, 1865. Dead.

John Smith, Corporal, Marion. Surrendered Appomattox. Living.

Hugh G. Bryant, Corporal, Marion. Surrendered Appomattox. Living.

William R. Graham, Corporal, Marion. Surrendered Appomattox. Dead.

D. F. Lane, Corporal, Marion. Surrendered Appomattox. Living.

Peter P. Hyatt, Corporal, Marion. Surrendered Appomattox. Living.

Elias Grantham, Corporal, Marion. Discharged, over age, 1862. Dead.

William R. Martin, Corporal, Marion. Captured, June 17, 1864, and never heard of since.

John Sanger, Corporal, Marion. Surrendered Five Forks, April, 1865. Dead.

Privates.

Allen, William, Marion. Died hospital, Morris Island.

Ammons, Levi, Marion.

Ammons, Daniel P., Marion.

Arnett, K., Marion. Died, August 15, 1864.

Bryant, Pinckney, Marion. Surrendered Appomattox. Living.

Bryant, James C., Marion. Living.

Britt, J. L., Marion. Died field hospital, June, 1864.

Braswell, Jack G., Marion. Died North Carolina hospital, 1862.

Biggs, Richard, Marion. Living.

Bailey, Samuel, Marion. Discharged, over age, 1862. Living.

Calder, Duncan, Marion. Surrendered Five Forks.

Calder, Peter, Marion. Transferred from Hampton Legion. Living.

Calder, Nias, Marion. Discharged, 1862, over age.

Caine, Kinion W., Marion. Discharged. Dead.

Coats, John, Marion. Surrendered. Living.

Capps, John W., Marion. Discharged, over age, 1862. Dead.

Cater, John W., Marion. Transfarred to 21st S. C. Regiment. Living.

Calder, William C., Marion. Died of wounds hospital, Va.

Dew, Christopher I., Marion. Living.

Dew, Samuel, Marion. Killed Goldsboro, N. C.

Dozier, Griffin, Marion. Killed Goldsboro, N. C.

Ednars, Matthew H., Marion. Killed Second Manassas.

Edwards, Solomon M. Surrendered Appomattox. Died, 1875.

Ellis, Hugh G. Discharged, under age, 1862. Dead.

Fogleman, James G., Hospital Steward. Discharged November 30, 1863. Disability.

Fowler, Benjamin. Discharged, over age, 1862.

Fore, H. James. Imprisoned Point Lookout. Surrendered Five Forks. Living.

FitzGerald, Robert.

Grantham, E. Bright. Wagon driver. Surrendered Appomattox.

Grantham, Pinckney. Discharged. Dead.

Granger, Samuel P., Horry.

Graves, George S., Marion. Dead.

Graves, Anseyer, Marion.

George, W. J., Marion. Left sick in Virginia, supposed dead.

George, Henry J., Marion. Dead.

Graham, William H., Horry. Transferred from Hampton Legion.

Gibson, Jessee L., Marion. Transferred from Hampton Legion, May 26, 1864. Surrendered Five Forks, Va. Living.

Gibson, James H., Marion. Transferred from Hampton Legion, May 26, 1864. Wounded Petersburg, Va., and discharged. Surrendered Five Forks, Va. Dead.

Gibson, Allen, Marion. Transferred from Hampton Legion, May 26, 1864. Surrendered Point Lookout. Living.

Greenwood, James L., Marion. Captured. Surrendered Five Forks. Living.

Gaddy, Tritcan C., Marion. Captured. Surrendered Five Forks. Dead.

Hodges, Robert, Marion.

Herrin, A. W., Marion. Over age, 1862. Living.

Hyatt, James R., Marion. Killed Second Manassas.

Hyatt, Oliver, Marion. Surrendered. Dead.

Hyatt, Thomas R., Marion. Died on march in Virginia, 1862.

Hyatt, Ervin, Marion. Living.

Harrellson, Brigan J., Marion. Surrendered Five Forks. Living.

Harrellson, John B., Marion. Killed Second Manassas.

Hays, Alexander G., Marion. Surrendered Five Forks. Living.

Hays, Nicholas W., Marion. Living.

Hays, T. B., Marion. Living.

Hays, Willson, Marion. Transferred from 6th S. C. Cavalry. Dead.

Hamilton, Tobias, Marion. Imprisoned Point Lookout. Surrendered Point Lookout. Died Horry County.

Jackson, William J., Marion. Living.

Jackson, Selkirk, Marion. Killed Petersburg, Va., 1864.

Johnson, Carey, Marion. Over age. Living.

Johnson, Hugh G., Marion. Discharged. Living.

Johnson, Zeus, Marion. Living.

Johnson, Samuel S., Marion. Died in hospital, Virginia, August 5, 1864.

Jones, John S., Marion.
Jones, Wesley, Marion. Killed Petersburg, Va.
Kersely, William, Marion. Killed Goldsboro, N. C.
Kersely, Evin, Marion.
Kitchen, Chas. E., Marion. Surrendered Point Lookout.
Lane, Addison L., Marion. Surrendered Five Forks, April, 1865. Living.
Lane, George W., Marion. Living.
Lee, R. W., Marion. Living.
Lee, John E., Marion. Dead.
Lee, James W., Marion. Surrendered Goldsboro, N. C. Living.
Lee, Christopher, Marion. Discharged, September, 1863. Living.
Lewis, William E., Marion. Surrendered, under age, 1862. Living.
Lewis, J. W. P., Marion. Surrendered Five Forks. Dead.
Locklier, John, Marion. Discharged, 1862.
Locklier, Gibbert, Marion. Discharged, 1862.
Locklier, Washington, Marion.
Locklier, W. E., Marion. Discharged.
Lane, Stephen L., Marion. Killed Appomattox, Va.
Miller, William, Marion.
Miles, Nathan, Marion. Discharged. Dead.
McKenzie, Alfred, Marion. Surrendered Five Forks, Va. Living.
McKenzie, Willie T., Marion. Surrendered Five Forks, Va. Living.
Mincey, Patrick, Marion. Discharged, June 16, 1864, Petersburg. Dead.
Mincey, Jessee, Marion. Surrendered, April, 1865. Dead.
Mincey, George,. Surrendered, April, 1865. Living.
McCormick, Peter P. Wounded Second Manassas. Living.
Martin, Alex. H. Discharged, 1862. Living.
Martin, William R.
McMillan, John A. Surrendered, 1865. Dead.
Nichols, Benjamin.
Owens, Walter. Discharged, 1862. Living.

Owens, William R., Marion. Surrendered, 1865. Dead.
Page, William, Marion. Surrendered, 1865, Appomattox. Living in Horry.
Page, Harrison, Marion. Killed Second Manassas.
Page, Abraham, Horry. Surrendered, 1865. Living in Horry.
Page, Return, Horry. Surrendered, 1865. Living in Horry.
Peter, James H., Marion. Living.
Peter, Nicholas T., Marion. Discharged. Dead.
Price, ——, Marion. Killed Boonsboro, Md.
Rogers, Roblin W., Marion. Surrendered Virginia, 1865. Living.
Rogers, William J., Marion.
Rogers, Thernas, Marion. Dead.
Rogers, Wade, Marion. Dead.
Rogers, John, Marion. Died Virginia.
Rogers, Willis, Marion. Supposed dead, left in Mississippi.
Rogers, Timothy, Marion. Killed Goldsboro, N. C.
Rowell, David, Marion. Living.
Rowell, John H., Marion. Living.
Rowell, Jessee, Marion. Living.
Rogers, John R., Marion. Died Florence, S. C.
Strickland, Ervin, Horry. Discharged, over age. Dead.
Strickland, Ros., Horry. Killed Second Manassas.
Smith, John, Marion. Surrendered Appomattox. Living.
Smith, Hardy D., Marion. Surrendered Appomattox. Living.
Smith, Hugh G., Marion. Surrendered, Five Forks. Captured, April, 1865. Living.
Souls, J. W., Horry.
Sawyer, John, Marion. Surrendered. Dead.
Turbeville, Geo., Marion. Surrendered Five Forks. Living.
Turbeville, Albert B., Marion. Living.
Turner, Joseph, Marion. Discharged.
Taylor, John M., Marion. Died of wounds Petersburg, Va.
Taylor, Benj. B., Marion. Died Point Lookout.
Vantep, William, Marion. Killed Second Manassas, Va.

Wiggins, John, Marion. Living.
Wise, Bradley, Marion. Dead.
Walsh, James B., Marion. Left in Mississippi, supposed dead.
Watson, Barney, Marion. Dead.
Watson, Merideth, Marion. Dead. Surrendered 1865.
Ward, Colin, Marion. Dead. Surrendered 1865.

Roll of Company D, Tenth Regiment Infantry, South Carolina Volunteers, in the Confederate States Provisional Army, from Marion County:

Godbold, Z., Captain. Resigned 1862.
Harllee, R. Z., Captain. Wounded Atlanta, 1864. Promoted from First Lieutenant, 1862.
Munnerlyn, W. H., First Lieutenant. Killed Atlanta, July 22, 1864. Promoted from Second Lieutenant.
Boothe, R. A., Second Lieutenant. Resigned.
Williamson, D. J., Second Lieutenant. Resigned.
Blackman, H. J., Second Lieutenant. Promoted from Sergeant. Died at hospital July, 1862.
Kimball, R. H., Second Lieutenant.
Coleman, G. B., Sergeant. Wounded Murfreesboro, Chickamauga.
Lloyd, J. J., Sergeant.
Williamson, J. B., Sergeant.
Bird, S., Sergeant. Wounded Chickamauga. Promoted from ranks.
Coleman, W. J., Corporal.
Cook, W. H., Corporal.
Wiggins, J. B., Corporal.
Hodges, J., Corporal. Wounded Atlanta. Lost right arm.

Privates.

Ammons, A. R. Discharged 1862.
Altman, W. T. Wounded Murfreesboro.
Avant, A. Died in hospital.
Baxley, B. Died in hospital.
Baxley, W. Wounded Chickamauga.

Baxley, L. Wounded at Murfreesboro.
Beverly, F. Died hospital.
Beverly, D. Died hospital.
Bird, H. G. Died Franklin.
Bird, J. Died Kentucky.
Blackman, K. C. Died hospital.
Boatright, J.
Brown, J.
Carmichael, D. Killed Murfreesboro.
Clark, W. P.
Coleman, J. W. Died at hospital.
Collins, D. Died at hospital.
Collins, W.
Drew, N. Killed Murfreesboro.
Flowers, G. S. Killed Chickamauga.
Flowers, E.
Gasque, E. Died at hospital.
Gunter, D. Wounded Chickamauga.
Gerald, S. W. Died at hospital.
Harrell, M. W. Killed Chickamauga.
Herren, J. P. Died at hospital.
Herren, W. P. Died at hospital.
Jones, J.
Jones, J. J.
Lambert, P. Died at hospital.
Lambert, D. H. Wounded Murfreesboro.
Lambert, J. H.
Legette, W.
Lloyd, J. Died at hospital.
Lloyd, T. M.
Marlor, W. Died at hospital.
McMeenee, W. Killed at Resaca.
Moore, S. Killed at Atlanta, July 22, 1864.
Moore, E. Wounded Murfreesboro.
Nobles, H. Died at hospital.
Nobles, J. W. Missed at Chickamauga, supposed killed.
Nobles, N. Missed at Atlanta, supposed killed.
Owens, R. H. Died at hospital.
Owens, M. Killed Kennesaw Mountains.

Owens, E. Died at hospital.
Owens, S. Died at hospital.
Porte, Jehu. Died at hospital.
Porte, L. Died at hospital.
Rogers, J. L. Died at hospital.
Rogers, C. C.
Sanders, J.
Shelley, J. G.
Shaw, E. Died at hospital.
Stephens, J. W. Died at hospital.
Tart, C. Died at hospital.
Thomas, S. Killed Chickamauga.
Thomas, E. Died at hospital.
Thomas, H. Died at hospital.
Turner, J. Died at hospital.
Turbeville, F. Died at hospital.
Turbeville, P. Died at hospital.
Turbeville, W.
Ward, W. Died at hospital.
Woodad, L. Killed Murfreesboro.
Wright, G. W.
Wright, W. C. Died at hospital.
Wiggins, J. W. Died at hospital.

Roll of Company F, Tenth Regiment Infantry, South Carolina Volunteers, in the Confederate States Provisional Army, from Marion County:

Miller, E., Captain. Not re-elected 1862. Appointed Surgeon Western Army, in field and hospital.

Bostick, F. J., Captain. Wounded Chickamauga, Missionary Ridge. Promoted from First Lieutenant.

Davis, J. F., First Lieutenant. Resigned.

McWhite, L. T., Lieutenant. Not re-elected 1862.

Bragdon, J. T., Lieutenant. Not re-elected 1862.

Belin, J. H., Lieutenant. Wounded Murfreesboro. Promoted from Sergeant. Dead.

Murphy, N., Lieutenant. Promoted from Co. L.

Coleman, G. W., Sergeant. Discharged.

Belin, C., Sergeant. Wounded Nashville, Resaca, Atlanta.

Shaw, H., Sergeant. Transferred and promoted Lieutenant Co. "M." Dead.
Brown, M., Sergeant. Killed in battle at Atlanta.
Prosser, J. L., Lieutenant. Wounded Murfreesboro. Died Tompkinsville, Tenn.
Lewis, T. J., Corporal. Killed Chickamauga.
Bostick, J. N., Corporal Color Guard. Captured Missionary Ridge.
Foxworth, R. W., Corporal. Died Tupelo, Miss.
Collins, J. B., Corporal. Died Tiner's Station, Tenn.
Ard, A. J., Corporal. Died Saltillo, Miss.
Johnson, F. A., Corporal. Died Tupelo, Miss.
Glisson, E. B., Corporal. Killed Chickamauga.
Williams, J. J., Corporal. Died at home.

Privates.

Adkinson, P.
Brach, R. Died at hospital.
Brown, J. Discharged.
Bartell, H Wounded Atlanta twice, Resaca.
Bartell, J. R.
Bellflower, J. J. Died Corinth, Miss.
Curry, G. W. Captured Missionary Ridge.
Curry, D. Died at home.
Curry, J. Died at home.
Cannon, R.
Cox, S. C. Captured Missionary Ridge.
Collins, J. E. Wounded Murfreesboro, Chickamauga.
Collins, S. J. Discharged, over age.
Crossby, T. E. Atlanta.
Crossby, J. W. Died in Mississippi.
Crossby, J. L. Died at home, on sick furlough.
Cox, John.
Daniels, J. G. Died South Island.
Dimary, J. T.
Evans, N., Marion. Died in Mississippi.
Foxworth, A. B. Captured Missionary Ridge.
Gasque, J. Discharged on account of disability.
Gunter, H. Died at hospital.

Goff, J.
Hinds, S. O. Died at Columbus, Miss.
Hinds, H. N. Died at home.
Hogg, M. T. Wounded Murfreesboro.
Hutcherson, N. P. Died at home.
Hyman, William. Died at hospital.
Hawkins, H.
Jarrall, J. J. Died at home, on sick furlough.
Johnson, P. C. Died at Tupelo, Miss.
Johnson, J. J. Captured Missionary Ridge.
Johnson, T. H. Captured Missionary Ridge.
Kenner, G. W. L. Discharged on account of disability.
Keefe, W. E. Captured at Chickamauga.
Keightley, J. G.
Lewis, J. R. Died Knoxville, Tenn.
Lee, N. C.
Marler, J. R.
Marler, V. A. Died Corinth, Miss.
Miller, E. Missing.
McNeill, J. Died at South Island.
Nobles, J. P. Died Tupelo, Miss.
Parker, S. F. Captured Missionary Ridge.
Pace, R. W. Died at hospital.
Phillips, F. M. Discharged.
Powell, A. E. Wounded Chickamauga.
Powell, W. M. Discharged.
Powell, M. B.
Poston, G. W. Wounded Chickamauga, Atlanta.
Richardson, A. J., Marion.
Rowell, R. R. Wounded Murfreesboro, Chickamauga.
Smith, J. B. Killed at Franklin, Tenn.
Shaw, J. H. Wounded Resaca.
Stone, R. W. Died Glasgow, Kentucky.
Taylor, R. W. Died Mississippi.
Turbeville, S. Died home. Wounded Atlanta.
Turner, G. W.
Turner, R. H. Died Corinth, Miss.
Turner, T. D. Died in prison. Wounded.
Wall, C. M. Died Tupelo, Miss.

Wall, S. J.
Wall, J. C.
Wall, J. W.   Killed at Chattahoochie, on picket line.
Williams, D. N.   Died in Kentucky.

Company I, 6th Regiment Cavalry, South Carolina Volunteers, in the Confederate States Provisional Army:

Whitaker, J. C., Captain, Marion.   Wounded Beams Station.
Jenkins, Robert, First Lieutenant, Marion.   Wounded Beams Station.   Promoted Captain.
DeBerry, Ed., Second Lieutenant, Marion.
McClenaham, Honorine, Third Lieutenant, Marion.
Fladger, H. G., First Sergeant, Marion.   Wounded Trevillian Station.
Friar, Andrew, First Corporal, Marion.
Cain, J. H., Second Corporal, Marion.
Boatright, Thos., Third, Corporal, Marion.
Bass, A. W., Second Sergeant, Marion.

Privates.

Atkinson, Benjamin, Marion.
Atkinson, Jessee, Marion.
Atkinson, John, Marion.
Bragdon, Jas., Marion.
Bethea, Edward, Marion.
Brown, Samuel, Marion.
Campbell, John C. C., Marion.
Campbell, Jas. W., Marion.   Wounded Fayetteville, N. C.
Cameron, Don., Marion.
Cox, Samuel, Marion.
Cox, George, Marion.
Cusack, Samuel, Marion.
Deas, John, Marion.
Dill, Bright, Marion.
Egerton, Evander, Marion.
Egerton, Samuel, Marion.
Richardson, J., Marion.
Rodgers, ———, Marion.

Stewart, Ran., Marion.
Signer, Joe, Marion.
Taylor, John, Marion.
Wilson, Alex., Marion.
Wurrell, Jas., Marion.
Wurrell, Jas., Jr., Marion.
Woodrow, William, Marion.
Whittaker, ——, Marion.
Dargan, L. O., Darlington.
McCall, S. A., Darlington.
Cook, Henry, Darlington.
Boswell, Samuel, Darlington.
Coker, Harmon, Darlington.
Coker, Sandy, Darlington.
Plummer, Hugh, Darlington.
Polk, James, Darlington.
Stokes, John, Darlington.
Thomas, E. R., Darlington.
Tedder, W. J., Darlington.
Windham, George, Darlington.
Young, J. D., Darlington.

The foregoing roll was made from memory, by Sergeant S. A. McCall.

Roll of Company D, Twenty-fifth Regiment Infantry, South Carolina Volunteers, in the Confederate States Provisional Army, from Marion County:

McKerrall, William Jasper, Captain. Captured W. & W. R. R., and imprisoned at Point Lookout and Fort Delaware. Died since war.

Haselden, James, First Lieutenant. Died 1900.

McKay, Daniel J., First Lieutenant. Wounded Petersburg. Promoted from Second Lieutenant. Living.

Bethea, Pickett P., Second Lieutenant. Killed Weldon R. R.

Smith, Marcus L., Second Lieutenant. Wounded Drewry's Bluff. Promoted from Orderly Sergeant. Living.

Alford, Artemas, Sergeant. Wounded Weldon R. R. Surrendered City Point. Living.

Richard, Meyer, Sergeant. Living.

McIntyre, Joseph, Sergeant. Wounded Drewry's Bluff severely and captured. Living.

Barfield, Jessee, Sergeant. Living.

Sweet, David, Corporal. Died in Virginia 1864.

Cox, Lewis J., Corporal. Killed at Petersburg.

Greenwood, E. B., Corporal. Living.

Herring, John C., Second Corporal. Killed Weldon R. R.

Herring, Marcus C., Corporal. Living.

Turbeville, George, Corporal. Wounded Drewry's Bluff. Promoted from ranks. Living.

Privates.

Allen, John. Living.
Atkinson, Talley.
Barrentine, Wilson.
Berry, Nathan.
Blackman, David.
Barrentine, Nelson. Killed James Island.
Bullard, P. D. B. Living.
Barnett, D. Wounded Weldon R. R.
Beverly, Douglass. Killed Swift Creek.
Coward, Ansel.
Calder, William. Died since war.
Calder, Noah. Died since war.
Cook, Hiram. Living.
Coates, Evander.
Cottingham, Wesley.
Coats, James.
Calder, William, Sr. Died on James Island.
Coleman, Louis.
Clark, Johnson. Living.
Carter, Henry. Killed Swift Creek.
Daniel, Harllee. Died since war.
Drew, R.
Daniel, Dargan.
Dew, Turrentine.
Dew, John W.
Edge, John. Died since war.

Edge, Hamilton. Died hospital.
Foxworth, John.
Foxworth, W. K., Color-bearer. Killed Weldon R. R.
Freeman, Robt. Killed Swift Creek.
Freeman, Robert. Killed Drewry's Bluff.
Gaddy, J. J.
Graham, James. Killed Battery Wagner.
Godbold, James P. Died since war.
Graves, W. M. Killed Petersburg, 1862.
Godbold, Eli. Wounded Petersburg.
Graham, E.
Hoyt, Hugh.
Hoyt, Washington.
Herring, D. M.
Hamilton, Whitner, Jr.
Hunt, George.
Hunt, Charles.
Hunt, P. O.
Hays, W. M. Died in Virginia.
Hays, Nicholas W. Surrendered James Island.
Hays, W. C. Killed at James Island.
Hays, H. R. Living.
Hays, R. H. Killed James Island.
Hays, A. G. Imprisoned at Point Lookout till close of war. Died since.
Hays, Jessee H. Surrendered at Charleston.
Hays, E. W. Killed Weldon R. R.
Hays, C. Died in Union Prison, New York.
Hargrove, William. Died James Island.
Hargrove, W. H. Living.
Haselden, James. Dead.
Hyatt, Hugh.
Hyatt, John.
Herlong, James. Imprisoned at Point Lookout.
Ikner, James. Wounded Petersburg. Living.
Johnson, J. F.
Jordan, Jacob. Killed Drewry's Bluff.
Jackson, J. R.
Johnson, George.

Johnson, Barney. Killed Drewry's Bluff.
Jones, F. D.
Keever, Daniel A. Killed Weldon R. R.
Kennedy, Evander. Died of disease Elliott Cut, Stono.
Lane, Ferdinand. Died in prison.
Lane, Franklin.
Lundy, John.
Lovell, J. W. Living.
Lane, Robert. Living.
Lane, S. D. Dead.
Lundy, William. Living.
McCorkle, J. F. Surrendered James Island.
Meekins, Philip B.
Meekins, Oscar.
McKnight, J. E.
Moore, G. W. Wounded Drewry's Bluff. A soldier of Mexican War. Was severely wounded, furloughed home, and killed at Little Rock by parties unknown.
Norton, Sandy. Killed in Virginia.
Nees, John. Wounded Weldon R. R.
Owens, Hewitt. Living.
Owens, Lot. Killed in Virginia.
Ransom, John.
Rushing, James. Died Fort Delaware.
Riley, D. S.
Redman, Jake. Killed.
Rucker, Ruff.
Smith, J. K. Surrendered James Island.
Turner, Willis, Jr.
Turner, Martin. Died since war.
Turner, Joel.
Tart, G. Died Petersburg.
Whittington, W. G. Living.
Watson, David. Living.
Wilkes, James. Died at hospital.
Wilkinson, James. Died since war.
Wood, John. Killed James Island.
Yates, William. Died Charleston.

Roll of Company C, Twenty-sixth Regiment Infantry, South Carolina Volunteers, in the Confederate States Provisional Army, from Marion County:

Rowell, C. D., Captain. Promoted Major 1863, and resigned 1864.

Lofton, A. M., Captain. Promoted from First Lieutenant 1863.

Rogers, R. H., Captain. Promoted from Second to First Lieutenant 1863, and Captain 1865. Served in 8th Regiment short time.

Page, P. C., Second Lieutenant. Promoted from Sergeant 1863. Died Jackson, Miss., 1863.

Hayes, A. T., Second Lieutenant. Promoted from Sergeant 1863. Killed Petersburg 1864.

Wilkerson, J. R., Second Lieutenant. Wounded Appomattox C. H. Promoted from Sergeant 1865.

Platt, J. B., Second Lieutenant. Resigned June, 1864.

Cuisack, J. H., Sergeant. Discharged Mount Pleasant.

Allen, J. C., Sergeant. Discharged McLendonville.

Campbell, Samuel, Sergeant. Promoted from ranks 1863.

Davis, J. H., Sergeant. Promoted from ranks 1863.

Gerry, J. H., Sergeant. Promoted from ranks 1863.

Steel, Samuel, Sergeant. Promoted from ranks 1864.

Wiggins, J. M., Sergeant. Promoted from ranks 1864.

Miller, H. W., Corporal.

Phillips, H. G., Corporal. Killed Jackson, Miss.

Collins, F. A, Corporal.

Potter, James, Corporal. Discharged Charleston.

Harrellson, Sim, Corporal. Promoted from ranks 1864.

Rogers, Barfield, Corporal. Promoted from ranks 1864.

Privates.

Anderson, J. M.
Abbett, Simeon.
Bullock, Joel.
Britt, E. I.
Brewer, H. C.
Bigham, ——.
Bailey, Sam.

Bailey, J. R.
Byrd, Joseph. Died McLendonville.
Berry, Joseph.
Collins, Mack.
Collins, Evander.
Collins, Frank. Died Mt. Pleasant.
Cooper, Fry. Died Petersville, Va.
Cooper, E. W. Captured at Five Forks 1865.
Campbell, Daniel. Died at Mt. Pleasant.
Campbell, J. C. Transferred to Cavalry 1863.
Carmichael, Archie.
Carmichael, John. Died at Petersburg.
Cain, R. M.
Cain, W. E. Died at Petersburg.
Cain, S. J.
Cain, T. C. Died at Petersburg.
Cain, J. C.
DeBerry, R. M. Transferred to Cavalry 1864.
Dillard, E. Captured 1864.
Dillard, John.
Davis, Henry.
Davis, Frank. Captured Petersburg 1864.
Dewitt, Peter.
Dewitt, John. Died of disease at Petersville.
Dew, F. C. Died of disease at Church Flat.
Elmore, P. J.
Elmore, D. W.
Elvington, Joel. Died at Savannah.
Flowers, Nicholas. Died at Petersburg of wounds.
Flowers, Robert. Captured at Petersburg 1864.
Glison, J. H. Captured at Five Forks 1865.
Goodyear, ——. Died of wounds at Petersburg.
Grimsley, James.
Hayes, Robert R. Wounded Burgess Mill. Captured 1865.
Hayes, William B. Tranesferred to Artillery.
Lofton, John.
Moody, Enos.
Moore, Robert.
Miller, Pitman.

Miller, John C.
Miller, W. W.
Miller, H. B.
Miller, George.
Miller, John. Captured at Five Forks. Died at Charleston.
Oakley, William. Captured at Five Forks.
Oakley, Daniel. Captured at Five Forks.
Phillips, F. Marion.
Phillips, Benjamin.
Phillips, Isham.
Phillips, Isaac.
Powell, Robert. Captured at Petersburg.
Powell, Mat. Captured at Five Forks.
Poston, Bryant. Captured at Petersburg. Killed Burches Mill.
Pauley, Robert.
Platt, John.
Pittman, Thomas.
Rogers, Hinyard. Died at Charleston.
Rogers, William. Killed Jackson, Miss.
Robins, Robert M.
Sturges, Samuel.
Scott, Allen. Died wounds at Iron Bridge.
Sanderson, John W.
Stephens, Allen. Captured at Five Forks 1865. Killed Bermuda Hundred.
Turner, John K. Captured at Five Forks 1865.
Turner, Moses. Captured at Five Forks 1865.
Turner, Robert. Captured at Five Forks 1865.
Tanner, John L. Captured at Five Forks 1865.
Hayes, Hardy.
Hayes, Allen. Killed at Petersburg.
Hayes, Elly. Wounded Bermuda Hundred.
Hayes, Daniel S. Captured at Deep Bottom. Killed at Petersburg.
Herring, Frank.
Herring, John T.
Herring, Arthur. Captured at Petersburg.
Herring, Edmund.

Herring, James. Killed at Petersburg.
Harrellson, W. W. Captured at Five Forks.
Harrellson, James. Wounded Iron Bridge.
Harrellson, E. Preston.
Haselden, Stephen F. G. Wounded Jackson, Miss.
Haselden, Edward. Captured at Five Forks.
Haselden, William W.
Heyman, John.
Heyman, Gilbert. Captured at Petersburg.
Heyman, Benjamin.
Heyman, Ephraim.
Hutchinson, Wm. J. D. Captured at Five Forks.
Herring, McSwain. Died at Jackson, Miss.
Herring, Clinton.
Herring, Daniel M. Died at Charleston, S. C.
Israel, Ancil. Captured at Five Forks 1865.
Israel, Wright. Captured at Five Forks 1865.
Jackson, Reuben. Captured at Five Forks 1865.
Lovett, Kinchan. Wounded Church Flat.
Lupo, Malcolm. Killed Bermuda Hundred.
Lupo, James. Died Mt. Pleasant.
Lupo, William. Discharged.
Lupo, Evan. Died at Petersburg.
Thomas, James H. Captured at Five Forks 1865.
Tart, James. Transferred to Artillery.
Timmons, Luther. Died of disease at McClendenville.
Timmons, Burnett.
Williams, Thomas.
Williams, Silas. Captured at Petersburg 1864.
Williams, George.
Wall, Albert.
Wall, Henry. Died of disease at Petersburg.
Wiggins, W. Henry.
Wiggins, C. W.

Roll of Company I, Tenth Regiment Infantry, South Carolina Volunteers, in the Confederate States Provisional Army, from Marion County:

Lofton, H. M., Captain. Resigned.

McWhite, B. B., Captain. Promoted from First Lieutenant. Wounded Murfreesboro. Living.

Gasque, S. S., First Lieutenant. Not re-elected in 1862.

Poston, Andrew, First Lieutenant. Promoted from Sergeant and Second Lieutenant. Wounded at Chickamauga.

Poston, Benjamin, Second Lieutenant.

Bostick, T. J., Second Lieutenant. Promoted from Sergeant. Died of wounds at Franklin.

Finklea, G. C., Second Lieutenant. Promoted from Sergeant. Captured Missionary Ridge.

Bartell, William, Sergeant. Died in Tennessee.

Bartell, Jasper, First Sergeant. Mustered out, over age.

Hyman, W. L., Sergeant. Wounded at Murfreesboro.

Myers, A. A., Sergeant. Promoted Regimental Color Sergeant 1864.

Turbeville, R., Corporal. Killed at Murfreesboro.

Hicks, N. C., Corporal. Died in Kentucky.

McWhite, W. H., Corporal. Wounded at Murfreesboro, Franklin, Atlanta.

Poston, Daniel, Corporal.

Flowers, J. H., Corporal.

Privates.

Altman, W. S.

Altman, C. T. Died of wounds at Chickamauga.

Adkisson, Jacob. Mustered out, over age.

Askins, J. A. Died in Mississippi.

Ard, Barnabas.

Andrews, D. J. Died of wounds at Resaca.

Barnes, B. J. Died of wounds in Atlanta.

Bostick, J. H. Died in Kentucky.

Bragdon, J. B. Wounded at Chickamauga.

Cooper, Levi. Mustered out, over age.

Cooper, Simon.

Caulcutt, James.

Cain, E. E. Died in Georgia.

Cain, William.

Creel, N. B. Died in Mississippi.

Carter, W. E. Died in Georgia.

Campbell, W. D.   Wounded at Jonesboro, Ga.
Eaddy, Gregory.   Died in Mississippi.
Finklea, Robert.
Finklea, W. E.
Foxworth, C. B.   Wounded Chickamauga.
Flowers, Clayton.   Mustered out, over age.
Glisson, G. W.
Gordon, A. B.   Mustered out, over age.
Gordon, J. J.   Surrendered and discharged at South Island.
Holland, J. H.
Haines, J. B.   Wounded at Missionary Ridge.
Huggins, W. S. A.
Hanna, J. B.   Died at South Island.
Hanna, D. P.   Died in Kentucky.
Hanna, Ervin.   Wounded Missionary Ridge.
Hutchison, E. B.
Hutchison, L. N.   Wounded Atlanta.
Hutchison, John.   Died in Kentucky.
Hyman, J. L.   Mustered out, over age.
Lee, J. W.
Lee, W. A.   Died in Mississippi.
Munn, G. W.
Munn, W. J.   Killed at Murfreesboro.
McGee, W. A.
McKissick, A. W.
McDaniel, Enos.   Mustered out, over age.
Marree, Thomas.
Myers, G. H.   Wounded Missionary Ridge.
McWhite, G. W.   Died in Mississippi.
Parker, G. R.
Prosser, Nathan.   Died in South Carolina.
Prosser, M. V.
Powell, J. S.
Poston, Hampton.   Died in South Carolina.
Poston, Christopher.   Died in Tennessee.
Poston, Joseph H.   Died in Tennessee.
Poston, M. M.
Poston, F. L.
Poston, T. W.   Mustered out, over age.

Poston, B. D.
Poston, John L. Wounded at Chickamauga.
Poston, W. H. Killed at Missionary Ridge.
Poston, William.
Poston, Hugh.
Powell, S. C. Mustered out, over age.
Smith, D. C.
Sturges, S. B.
Turner, Lewis. Died in Georgia.
Tanner, W. N.
Tanner, John.
Woodrow, D. M. Died in Georgia.
Wiggins, E. J.
Williams, Samuel. Died in Georgia.
Williford, A. S.
Williford, R. J.

Roll of Company D, 7th Battalion, South Carolina Reserves, Major J. M. Ward, of Timmonsville, commanding; attached to the brigade commanded by Brigadiar General Albert Z. Blanchard, of New Orleans, La.:

Captain, W. H. Crawford. Dead.
First Lieutenant, Henry B. Cook. Dead.
Second Lieutenant, Neill McDuffie.
Third Lieutenant, Alfred B. Gordon.
Sergeant, Alexander C. Carmichael.
Sergeant, Stephen G. Owens. Dead.
Sergeant, Salathiel S. Moody. Dead.
Sergeant, Thomas L. James.
Corporal, Alfred Edens. Dead.
Corporal, M. H. Martin. Dead.
Corporal, Charles G. Collins.
Corporal, Daniel Little. Dead.
Corporal, T. G. Davis, Jr.
Company Clerk, John Wilcox, afterwards Sergeant Major of battalion.
Company Commissary, N. B. Goddard. Dead.

Privates.

Alford, John C.
Alford, John D.
Alford, Wm. Mack.
Alford, Walter S.
Altman, James D.
Avant, Jordan G.
Bailey, ———.
Baker, B. B.
Berry, Clinton.
Berry, Samuel. Dead.
Bethea, D.
Bethea, James D.
Brown, Edward.
Brown, Henry.
Brown, John.
Brown, W. K. Dead.
Bryant, Henry.
Bryant, Samuel.
Bryant, Stephen S.
Byrd, Huger.
Burriss, Robert L.
Capps, John H.
Carmichael, John.
Coleman, Franklin D.
Collins, Benjamin F.
Collins, Barny P.
Cribb, Thomas.
Cuddle, James R. Dead.
Dickson, W. J. Dead.
Eaddy, Trezevant.
Edwards, George. Dead.
Edwards, Wm. G.
Evans, Josiah.
Evans, Thomas.
Finnagan, Patrick.
Ferrel, James.
Finklea, J. Wesley.
Finklea, Samuel B.
Foxworth, W. C. Dead.
Fowler, Joseph.
Gibson, John.
Godbold, Robert. Dead.
Greenwood, James L.
Gregg, Francis M.
Gregg, Wm. B.
Godbold, Ervin. Dead.
Hairgrove, Stephen A. Dead.
Harrington, John T. Dead.
Hatchel, B. Pleasant.
Hatchel, ———.
Haynes, James W.
Hudson, Eli T.
Huggins, Enos T.
Hutchinson, Rix.
Hyman, Causea.
Jordan, John D. Dead.
Jordan, John J.
Lee, Curtis.
Lewis, John. Dead.
Lewis, W. Evan.
Lewis, Wm. S. Dead.
Lowrimore, Collin W.
Marlow, David.
Matthews, ———.
Moore, John Beaty.
McCormac, P.
McDaniel, B. F.
McInnis, Laurin.
McKenzie, Eli.
McNeill, Simon P.
Owens, William.
Parker, Robert.
Parker, Stephen.
Poston, Francis.

Poston, J. McK.
Poston, Thomas.
Proctor, Thomas.   Dead.
Prosser, Job.
Reaves, J. Robert.
Reaves, Robert H., Jr.
Richardson, John M.
Rogers, E. W.
Rogers, Henry.
Rogers, John H.   Dead.
Rowell, Jesse C.   Dead.
Rowell, Wm.
Salmons, Samuel.   Dead.
Sawyer, Willis.
Singletary, Hamer.
Smith, Anderson.
Smith, Jacob W.
Smith, Nathan.
Smith, Thomas.
Smithey, G. W.
Stafford, Neill.
Tart, E. Murchison.
Tart, Henry.
Taylor, James.
Timmons, Wm.
Turbeville, Wm.   Dead.
Waters, Willis.   Dead.
Welsh, James E.   Dead.
White, John.
White, W. Coke.
Williams, Geo. N.
Williams, James A.
Wise, Wilson D.   Dead.

Roll of company of militia last called into service:

Captain, W. J. Davis.
First Lieutenant, J. B. Shackleford.
Second Lieutenant, A. McGoogan.
Third Lieutenant, W. McDaniel.
First Sergeant, T. F. Brown.
Second Sergeant, W. W. Braddy.
Third Sergeant, W. H. Witherow.
Fourth Sergeant, John Mace.
Fifth Sergeant, H. B. Wheeler.
First Corporal, W. S. Shackleford.
Second Corporal, W. W. Mullins.
Third Corporal, H. H. Singletary.
Fourth Corporal, J. F. Gasque.

Privates.

Alford, Walter.
Altman, W. J.
Alford, John D.
Allen, W.
Allen, John.
Altman, W. C.
Avant, A. N.
Bird, James.

Boker, J. R. M.
Brown, Alex.
Brown, Lex.
Brown, W. T.
Bailey, W.
Bethea, G. J.
Blackman, Campbell.
Barfield, A.
Berry, J. S.
Berry, S. A.
Costen, W.
Collins, Shade.
Cooper, John.
Campbell, William.
Campbell, Robert.
Collins, Thomas.
Cook, W.
Cribb, Joseph.
Campbell, Andrew.
Calder, Henry.
Calder, Joseph.
Coleman, S.
Calder, M.
Collins, A. H.
Clark, M. L.
Cannon, J. B.
Drew, Thomas.
Davis, S. J.
Dill, D. M.
Davis, E. J.
Dove, J. D.
Davis, E. M.
Edwards, John.
Floyd, Charles.
Freeman, George.
Fladger, R. B.
Gasque, F.
Groom, M.
Gaddy, Herod.

Greggs, E. E.
Greenwood, J. R.
Gasque, J. H.
Hunter, T.
Haynes, James.
Harrelson, Hugh.
Harper, Isaac.
Hays, J. D.
James, J. H.
Jackson, Alex.
Jackson, Jeff.
Jones, Elijah.
Lupo, John.
Lawrimore, Gus.
Leggett, A. R.
Lane, C. C.
Montgomery, J. D.
Moody, Hugh.
Miller, Levi.
Manning, T. J.
McPherson, Samuel.
McInnis, Neal.
McEachern, Neal.
McLellan, Preston.
Owens, W.
Owens, Z.
Page, W. B.
Perritt, John.
Parker, Allen.
Powers, E.
Pitman, I.
Pierce, Robert.
Pierce, Dr.
Rogers, R. J.
Rogers, L. B.
Rogers, C. B.
Ross, A. W.
Rit, D. E.
Stephens, Jessie.

Shelly, C. W.
Stevenson, J. N.
Smith, Willis.
Snipes, J. S.
Stubbs, J. W.
Shaw, A. B.
Turbeville, Pinckney.
Tiler, J. M.
Tiler, George.
Turbeville, Samuel.
Tart, Nathan.
Turbeville, Lemuel.
Williamson, J. W.
Wall, W. A.
Williamson, L. J.
White, Evander.
Worrell, John.
Williamson, James.
Whittington, J. N.
Watson, I. H.
Wagner, A. C.
Flowers, B.
Davis, W. M.
Davis, William.
Munn, A. B.
Kirton, H. P.
Moody, E. J.
Berry, Elihu.

Goodyear, A. M.
Harrell, S. A.
Gasque, Gehu.
Lawrimore, John.
Head, Wellington.
Jackson, L.
Jackson, W.
McKenzie, Robert.
Spivey, D. E.
Turner, William.
Watson, Isham E.
McKnight, J. E.
Shelly, David.
Holden, James.
Lewis, J. J.
Proctor, J. T.
Sherwood, T. C.
Williams, S. J.
Timmons, J. C.
Walker, H.
White, W.
Hatcher, R.
Hargrove, A. L.
Braddy, W. M.
Johnson, H. R.
Jackson, J. K.
Fore, Edward M.

Such as I know to be dead I have so marked; there may be others of them dead.

Besides, there was a company of Citadel Cadets, commanded by Maj. J. B. White, in which company there were three from Marion District: R. K. Clark (dead), John C. Sellers and James A. Ferrell.

Just before completing the foregoing, the author was stricken with a fatal malady, cancer on the face, and after a lingering illness of several months which he bore with uncomplaining fortitude, he died on Good Friday, the 28th day of March, 1902, being 84 years and one day old, and was buried Easter Sunday in the Dothan Church Cemetery by the side of his wife, who had preceded him to the grave nine years. At the time of his death he was perhaps the oldest active Mason in the county, having joined that order in early life. At different times he had served as Worshipful Master of Mackey Lodge No. 77, of Little Rock, now the Dillon Lodge, of Clinton Lodge No. 60, at Marion, and of Dalcho Lodge No. 160, at Latta, and at the time of his death was an honorary member of Dalcho Lodge. These three lodges, with members from every lodge in the county, paid the last tribute of respect to their venerable Past Master, according to the beautiful and impressive ritual of the order of Ancient Free Masons. A large concourse of people from nearly every section of the county was present, and the commodious church could only seat a part of the crowd present. The church services were conducted by the Rev. Dove Tiller and Rev. C. C. Herbert, of the Methodist Church, of which church the author had been a member nearly seventy years. At the conclusion of the church services, Maj. J. Monroe Johnson, Past Master of Clinton Lodge No. 60, was introduced and paid an eloquent tribute to the character and worth of his departed brother and lifelong friend. He spoke of him as a Mason, a lawyer and as a man, and dwelt particularly upon these marked characteristics of the deceased:

1. His phenomenal memory.
2. His untiring industry and energy.
3. His heroic independence.
4. His sturdy honesty.
5. His marked individuality.

A Masonic procession was then formed and the body carried to the nearby cemetery, where it was buried in accordance with the beautiful ceremonies of Freemasonry.

Index

ABBETT, SIMEON	636	. NEILL	152,219,282-284	. MARY ROBERTS	211
ABBOTT,	425		293,362	. NANCY WATSON	202
. ADA LOCKE	329	. ROBERT	282-283	. SALLIE ROBERTS	211
. WILLIAM	329	. ROBERT H.	603	. THOMPSON	171,354,562
ADAMS,	150	. SALLIE BETHEA	417	. W.	644
. ANNE	277	. SION	290,292	. W.C.	50
. DORA	269,278	. W.	582	. WILLIAM	202,621
. ELIAS	277	. W. McD.	283,567,603	ALLISON,	135,137-138,398
. ELLEN	277	. W. WARREN	578		448
. ELLEN HARLLEE	343	. WALTER	644	. JAMES H.	138
. JAMES H.	570	. WALTER L.	282	ALLSTON, R.F.W.	139
. JOHN	83	. WALTER S.	283,643	. WILLIAM	139
. MARY MACE	221	. WARREN L.	284	ALSTON, JOSEPH	569
. SARAH JANE HAYES	269	. WILLIAM MACK	643	. R.F.W.	570
. WILLIAM	343	. WILLIAM McD.	282	ALTMAN,	434,458
ADKINSON, B.F.	600	ALFROD, ELLA	282	. BENJAMIN E.	457
. J.A.	600	. MACK	282	. C.T.	640
. P.	629	. PLUMMER	282	. CHARLES	298
ADKISSON, JACOB	640	. ROBERT	282	. ELIZABETH DOZIER	456
AIKEN, WILLIAM	569	. WILLIAM	282	. FRANCES MAURICE-HARREL	456
ALDRICH, A.P.	72	. YANCY	282	. J.	593
ALFORD,	319	ALLEN,	228,341	. J. BENJAMIN	606
. ALTHEA	284,286,370	. ALBERT	211	. J. HAMILTON	606
. ANN	290	. ALICE	202-203	. JACK	457
. ARTEMAS	632	. ALICE ALLEN	203	. JAMES D.	457,643
. ARTEMUS	603	. ALMIRA BETHEA	229	. JAMES G.	456
. AUGUSTUS	262	. AMANDA FORE	154	. JAMES S.	456
. BETTIE McKAY	293	. ANNA MARIE	399	. JOHN	257,456-457,586
. BETTIE WALTERS	295	. ANNIE	202	. JOHN J.	615
. CLARKEY McKAY	293	. ANNIE MARIA	203	. M.F.	457
. DANIEL M.	283	. BETTIE	391	. MANILA McEACHERN	298
. DANIEL W.	295,578	. D.S.	473	. PRESTON	457
. DELLA	284	. DAVID E.	202-203,391	. REBECCA ROWELL	468
. DIAN	284	. DAVID S.	154	. SAMUEL S.	606
. DIANNA	284	. ELIAS	171	. STEPHEN	457,614
. DOCK	284	. ELIZABETH BETHEA	203	. THOMAS	456-457,468
. DOUGLASS	578	. ELIZABETH SMITH	498	. W.C.	644
. DUCK STACKHOUSE	362	. ELMORE	211,281	. W.J.	644
. FRIERSON	283	. ELMORE C.	211	. W.S.	640
. HARRIETT	152	. EUGENIA	202-203,273	. W.T.	626
. HENRY	282-283,293	. FRANK	202-203	. WILLIAM	456-457,520
. J.	582	. FURMAN	203	. WILLIAM J.	605
. JAMES L.	282-284	. HELEN BASS	202	AMMONDS, BENJAMIN	615
. JOHN	282-283	. HEROD W.	236,326	. PINKEY D.	615
. JOHN C.	643	. J.C.	636	AMMONS,	467,489
. JOHN D.	643-644	. J.W.	610	. A.R.	626
. JOHN K.	293,417	. JAMES	202	. ASA	597
. KATIE	292	. JOEL	97,171,202-203, 273,399,406,562,567	. BENJAMIN	529
. LODERICK B.	284	. JOEL I.	202,227-229	. DANIEL P.	621
. LODWICK B.	282, 286,370	. JOHN	633,644	. EMALINE SNIPES	529
		. JOSEPH	229,236	. H. CALHOYN	573
. MALCOLM	578	. JOSEPH W.	621	. HAMILTON A.	615
. MANTON	283	. LAURA BETHEA	354	. J. DUNCAN	603
. MARY HENRY	262	. LULIE MEREDITH	202	. JOHN T.	578
. MOSES	578	. MARIA	202	. JOSHUA	178
. NEIL	283	. MARY	154,473	. LEVI	621
		. MARY ANN COLEMAN	473	. M.	582

. PHILIP	597	. MARY	490	BACOT,ANNE COX	330
. THOMAS	178	. MINNIE	490	. CYRUS	330
. W. EDWARD	573	. OLIVE GASQUE	375,490	BAGGETT,HENRY	42-43
ANDERSON,	211,455,462	. REBECCA GASQUE	376	. J.H.	43
. H.J.	582	. RICHARD	298	. PETER	42-43
. J.M.	636	. SARAH ANN	489	BAILEY,	227,643
. JAMES R.	573	. TALLEY	633	. ALICE	245
ANDREWS,D.J.	640	. THOMAS	275-276,489-490	. CHRISTOPHER	597
APPLEWHITE,		. THOMAS J.	489	. G.	606
FANNIE EVANS	134	. VIOLA	489	. HENRY	571
ARCHDALE,JOHN	568	. W.B.	176,275	. J.R.	610,637
ARD,A.J.	629	. WILLIAM B.	490	. JOHN	593
. ANDREW J.	615	. WILLIAM J.	256,489	. SAM	636
. BARNABAS	640	ATTMAN,DAVIS	474	. SAMUEL	622
. GENERAL	615	. PRESTON	474	. SILSY ROWELL	496
. . LANEY	615	. STEPHEN	474	. W.	645
ARMFIELD,A.L.	593	AUGUSTINE,	109	BAILY,BENJAMIN	578
ARNETT,	178	AVANT,	210,222,243,422	. D.	582
K.	621		454,464-465,473,532	. ERVIN	582
ARNOLD,F.W.	571	. A.	626	. LIAS	573
ASBURY,	476,505,544,561	. A.N.	644	. MATHEW	573
. FRANCIS	136	. ANNA LEWIS	222	. MINEOLA DAVIS	450
ASHLEY,ANTHONY LORD	2	. ANNE LEWIS	482	. R.	582
ASKINS,J.A.	640	. CATHERINE BAKER	445	. THOMAS P.	450
ATCHISON,	349	. ELIZABETH	470,525	. WESLEY	573
ATKINS,DOW	152	. IRA	454	BAKER,	126,134,258
. EMMA BERRY	152,269	. JORDAN	573		292-293,434,449,470
. MONTCALM DOW	269	. JORDAN G.	643		525
ATKINSON,	241,376,458	. JOSHUA	445	. A.M.	290
	460,467	. JULIA	449	. ADDIE L. DAVIS	447
. ANN ELIZA DEW	275	. MARION	222,482	. ADGER	448
. ANNIS	489	. ORLANDO R.	606	. ALBERT M.	289,291
. BENJAMIN	631	. SARAH DAVIS	454	. ALEX T.	448
. CELIA ANN	490	. THOMAS	470	. ANN	470
. CELIA GASQUE	375	. WILLIE	223,482	. ANNA M.GRAHAM	446
. CELIA SMITH	264	AYCOCK,NORA	347	. ANNA MONROE	526
. CHARLOTTE	489	AYERS,D. DWIGHT	603	. ANNE GADDY	446
. EBBIE	375	. ENOCH S.	591,602	. ANNE M. GRAHAM	447
. EBBY	489-490	. JOSEPH	573	. ANNE MONROE	446
. ELIZA ANN	489	. THOMAS	573	. ANNIS	381-382
. ELIZA DEW	489	. WILLIAM D.	573	. ANNIS GILES	445,447
. ELIZABETH	489	AYMET,W.D.	600	. ANNIS PHILIPS	445,447
. GEORGE	489	AYRES,ADDIE	163	. ANNIS PHILLIPS	381
. HUGH	489-490	. ALICE McMILLAN	421	. ANNISE	132
. HUGH J.	489	. CATHERINE	166-167	. ARCHIE	382
. JACOB	615	. DARIUS	166-167	. B.B.	643
. JAMES	256	. ELIAS	166	. BENJAMIN	446
. JANE	489	. ENOCH S.	166	. BENJAMIN B.	447-448
. JESSEE	488-491,631	. ERMA	166		573
. JESSIE	376	. JACK	166-167	. BILL	471
. JOHN	275,631	. JOHN	166	. BOYD	447
. JOHN A.	465	. LENNON	166	. BROCKINTON	448
. JOHN W.	489-490	. MARTHA A.-		. CARRY	447
. JULIA	469	WILLIAMSON	430	. CARY LENORA	448
. LILLA	489	. PENDLETON G.	166,421	. CATHERINE	445
. MARGARET		. ROBERT	166	. DAVID GORDON	446
CAVE	489-490	. SALLIE	166	. EDMUND	290
. MARTHA DEW	275,490	. SUSAN PAGE	166	. ELIZA	382,447
. MARTHA J.-		. THOMAS W.	163,166,430	. ELOISE	448
HARRELSON	489	. WILLIAM	166-167	. ELWOOD DAVIS	448

. GERTRUDE	447	. T.F.	382	BASS,	139,147,193,228
. HANNIBAL	447	. THOMAS	531,586		557
. HERBERT	448	. THOMAS D.	447-448	. A.W.	631
. IMO	448	. THOMAS WILSON	448	. ADAREZER	226,230
. J.E.	447	. W.B.	381,447	. ADDISON	202
. J.G.	51	. W.J.	445	. ADDISON L.	226
. JAMES	95,290,382	. W.W.	63,382,462	. AMELIA MOODY	226
	445-448	. WARREN CALDWELL	446	. ANNA	230-231
. JAMES D.	447	. WILLIAM	126,132,381	. ARAMINTA	226
. JAMES G.	446,526		445,447	. BEULAH McCOLL	232
. JAMES M.	446	. WILLIAM B.	372,430,447	. BRYANT	226,230,331
. JAMES OSCAR	446		572	. C.G.	226-228,339
. JAMES R.	447	. WILLIAM D.	449	. CARL	227
. JAMES T.	526	. WILLIAM J.	382,445,447	. CORNELIUS G.	228
. JEANNETTE	291	. WILLIAM W.	446,572	. DAVID S.	229-230
. JENNETTE	382,447-448	BALLARD,		. DICEY	231
. JENNETTE BAKER	448	. MATTIE COLEMAN	473	. EDGAR	226,231
. JOHN	445,447-448,591	. QUINCY	473	. ELIZABETH	226,399
. JOHN D.	291	BALLOON,LIZZIE	110	. ELIZABETH A.	229
. JOHN E.	447,573	BALLOONE,JOANNA	356	. ELLEN WATSON	202,226
. JOHN TENNENT	446	. LIZZIE	355	. ENOS	226,228
. JOSEPH A.	177,382,446	BARBER,C.H.	51	. GEORGE F.	226,232
	586	. WILLIAM	600	. HANNAH JANE	
. JOSEPH MARY	446	BARFIELD,	427	BETHEA	228,397
. KATIE EVANS	447	. A.	645	. HARRIET	226,229,401
. LAURA DAVIS	449	. APPY	192	. HELEN	202,226-227
. LENORA	448	. BARRETT	191		229-230,367
. LEOLA	448	. HARLLEE	586,603	. HORTENSIA WATSON	200
. LILLIAN	446	. HENRY	590		226
. LIZZIE	448	. JESSEE	633	. J. EDGAR	301,439
. LOU LEGETTE	447	. MARSDEN	603	. J.W.	228,232
. LOVEDY McPRIEST	291	. MARY	179	. JAMES W.	41,226-227
. MARION TAYLOR	447	. THOMPSON	427,602		229,231,339
. MARTHA CAROLINE	381	. WRIT	191-192	. JANE	331
	382	BARNES,	426	. JANE ROGERS	230
. MARTHA CAROLINE-		. B.J.	640	. JOHN	229
BAKER	382	. HARRIET	346	. JOHN C.	226,228-230
. MARTHA TENNENT	446	. HENRY	298		397,621
. MARY	381-382,446-448	. HENRY L.	615	. JOSEPH	146,224-231
. MARY E.	430	. LAURA McCORMICK	298		386-387
. MARY ELIZABETH	447	. MARY	486	. JOSEPH D.	40,332
. MARY J. GRAHAM	446	. MARY LEWIS	481	. JOSEPH R.	226,399,401
. MARY MONROE	447	. MOSLEY	486	. LABENNON	224
. MARY R.	447	. RANDAL	481	. LAURA	226,229
. MATTIE	447-448	BARNETT,D.	633	. LAURA BASS	229
. MATTIE CARRIE-		BARNWELL,R.W.	84	. LEBANON	226,230
SNIPES	531	BARRENTINE,	281,543	. LOUISA	164,230
. MATTIE SNIPES	448	. NELSON	633	. LUCIUS	226,232
. MOLLIE DEW	274	. WILSON	633	. LUCY MOODY	226,339
. MOURNING ELIZ.	117	BARRETT,ISAAC	615	. LULA DEER	228,339
. NEILL	290-291,448,578	BARRY,	71-72	. LUTHER	227
. NEILL A.	291	BARTELL,H.	629	. MAHALA DEER	231
. PAULINE	447	. J.R.	629	. MASSEY	230
. POLLY	447,471	. JASPER	640	. MASSEY CRAWFORD	226
. POLLY McARTHUR	290	. WILLIAM	640	. MERCY CRAWFORD	146
. REBECCA	447-448	BARTLEY,CHARLES	593	. MILLEY MOODY	332
. ROBERT	448	. EDWARD	593	. NANCY	231
. SUSAN	382,447-448,466	. HENRY	593	. NETTIE McINTYRE	301
. SUSANA C.	447	. J.G.	593		439
. SUSANNAH	449	BASLY,WILLIS	375	. ROBERT	226,231

. ROBERT A.	232,334	
. ROSA	226	
. ROSE	199	
. RUFUS	226	
. T. LEON	226,232,538	
. T.R.	567	
. THOMAS	227	
. THOMAS J.	200,226-227	
. THOMAS R.	97,226,228	
. TRACY	227	
BAXLEY,	472,528,543	
. ALICE COLEMAN	473	
. ANNE COLEMAN	473	
. B.	626	
. BARNY	504	
. CELIA	473	
. HARLLEE	473	
. JOSEPH	615	
. L.	627	
. MARTHA	504	
. PATSY	460	
. RILEY	582	
. SOLOMON	615	
. W.	626	
. WILLIAM	582	
. WILLIE	473	
BAXLY,LEAH	474	
BAXTER,DAVID	586	
. GEORGE W.	586	
. JOHN	566	
BEACH,	378	
BEATY,	490	
. JAMES	355	
. JAMES C.	124	
. L.F.	490	
. MATTIE	124	
. THOMAS	573	
BECKWITH,MARTHA	295	
BEDFORD,JOHN	586	
BEECHER,	350	
BEGHAM,		
. FLORENCE GASQUE	376	
. R.H.	376	
BELIN,	451	
. C.	628	
. J.H.	628	
BELK,FRANCOIS	431	
. JULIUS	431	
BELL,	510	
BELLAMY,		
. HATTIE HARLLEE	352	
. MARSDEN	352	
BELLFLOWER,J.J.	629	
BELLFLOWERS,H.	593	
. HENRY	615	
. JESSEE	606	
. SAMUEL	615	
BENJAMIN,E.	609	
. S.	600	

BENNETT,	164	
. JOHN	234	
BENSON,JACOB	582	
BENTHAN,	571	
BENTON,GEORGE W.	591	
BERKLEY,JOHN LORD	2	
. WILLIAM	2	
BERRY,	138,148,164,219	
	231,333	
. ADDIE	269	
. AMANDA		
GREENWOOD	285	
. ANDREW	148,150-151	
	156-157,271,274	
. ANDREW STEPHEN	149	
. ASHTON	152,217	
. AURELIA		
GEORGE	278,285	
. BLANCHE DEER	339	
. BRIGHT	150	
. BRIGHT W.	489	
. CADE	151	
. CHARITY CRAWFORD	146	
	151	
. CHARLES	149	
. CLINTON	643	
. CLOSE	150-151	
. CROSS ROADS		
HENRY	149	
	150-153,155-156,204	
	220,268,271,274,284	
	340,414,562	
. D.F.	150,609	
. DANIEL F.	305,514,565	
. DAVID	150	
. DENNIS	148-149,391,498	
. DOWNING	152	
. E. BURKE	239	
. E.B.	556	
. ED LIDE	152	
. EDMUND BURKE	153,217	
. EDWARD BURKE	152	
. ELIHU	133,151-153,218	
	269,646	
. ELIHU LIDE	269	
. ELIZABETH	148-149,244	
. EMMA	152,269	
. ETTA	152	
. EUGENE	152	
. EUPHEMIA WATSON	153	
. FAMA	148-149,157	
	196-197	
. FAMA WATSON	204,244	
. FLORENCE	152	
. FRANK A.	149,202	
. G. RAYMOND	156,302	
. GEWOOD	50,151,153,217	
. HARRIETT ALFORD	152	

. HENRY	39,146,148-153	
	155-157,182,197,204	
	220,244,247,268,271	
	274,278,284-285,340	
	414,562	
. HENRY SLAUGHTER	149	
. HENRY T.	615	
. J.	610	
. J.S.	645	
. JAMES	151-152,226,233	
	283,414,461	
. JAMES H.	152-153,219	
	362	
. JANE		
HASELDEN	152-153	
	225	
. JANIE	153	
. JOANNA ELLERBE	217	
. JOANNE ELLERBE	151	
. JOHN	157	
. JOHN H.	152,199-200	
	217	
. JOSEPH	150,637	
. JULIA	152,233,461	
. L.	610	
. LEILA	152	
. LUCY	152	
. MADGE FORE	153	
. MADISON	157	
. MARTHA	148	
. MARY	148,150,153-154	
	182,220	
. MARY BURKE	368	
. MARY C. HAMER	461	
. MARY CUTTING-		
CARMICHAEL	302	
. MARY ELIHU	368	
. MARY ELLEN HAYES	269	
. MARY ELLEN HAYS	152	
. MARY HAMER	233	
. MARY MANNING	153	
. MARY NEILL	368	
. MARY OLIVER	368,462	
. MARY QUINCE	368	
. MARY STACKHOUSE	362	
. MOLLIE MANNING	239	
. MOLLIE		
STACKHOUSE	153	
. NATHAN	150-151,633	
. NEIL A.	152	
. NEILL	233,461	
. NEILL A.	40	
. NELLIE WATSON	202	
. PATTIE	148,150	
. QUINCY	152,368,462	
. REBECCA	153	
. ROBERT A.	152	
. ROBERTA DEW	273	
. S.A.	645	
. SALLIE	152-153,218	

. SAMUEL 272,643
. SAMUEL J. 157
. SLAUGHTER 148
. STEPHEN 148-149,151
153,157,194,204,244
271
. STEPHEN F. 150,156,181
235,247
. SUE 133,152-153
. TELATHA 152,155,220
269
. THOMAS 269
. THOMAS
WICKHAM 152-153
217,239
. TIGHT 150-151
. TOMMIE
MANNING 153,239
. VERZILLA 222
. VERZILLA WATSON 202
. VIRZILLA 155
. WADE HAMPTON 156
. WILLIAM 194
. WILLIAM E. 152,217
. WILSON 157,235,268
. WYLIE 156,273
BERTHIER, 395
BEST,JOHN J. 504
. SUSAN 504
BETHEA, 89,200,278,421
498,546
. A.J. 609
. ABSALA 324,396-398
. ABSALA PARKER 396
. ADALINE 397
. ADDIE 200,229
. ADGER 406
. ALEXANDER 420
. ALFRED 415-416
. ALFRED W. 415-416
. ALICE 390,403
. ALICE ROGERS 181,415
. ALMIRA 229
. ALONZO 418-419
. AMANDA 237,239,398
. ANDREW 203,399
. ANDREW J. 203,399
. ANDREW PEARCE 399
. ANN ELIZA
GODBOLD 398
. ANNA 406
. ANNA J. SELLERS 399
. ANNA JANE 412
. ANNA LAVAL 399
. ANNA M. SMITH 391
. ANNA MARIE ALLEN 399
. ANNA
SHREWSBERRY 405
. ANNA SMITH 403
. ANNIE 154

. ANNIE ELIZA-
GODBOLD 121
. ANNIE MARIA ALLEN 203
. ARCHIE 415
. ARTHUR 404,408
. ASA 398
. AUGUSTA 383,404
. AUGUSTA B. 403,407
. AUGUSTUS B. 407
. B.J. 609
. BELLE 398,409
. BENJAMIN 404
. BENJAMIN PARKER 354
413
. BESSIE 418
. BETTIE 391
. BETTIE ALLEN 391
. BLANCHE 154
. CADE 39,193-194,249
363,414-415,417-418
419
. CALVIN 417,419
. CALVIN C. 419
. CAROLINE 417,419
. CAROLINE BETHEA 419
. CARRIE 229,360,404,418
. CARRIE
BETHEA 229,360
. CARRIE HONOUR 405
. CARRIE SESSIONS 406
. CATHARINE 397,399
. CATTIE 399-400
. CATTIE MAY 399-400
. CHALMERS 397
. CHARLES 154,404,413
415
. CHARLOTTE 262,397
399-400,415,417
. CLARA 154,240,408-409
. CLARENCE 403,405
. CLARISSA 403,410
. CLAUDIS 399
. CLAUDIUS 401
. CURTIS 405
. D. 643
. D. McL. 154,219,240
. D. McLEOD 408
. D.N. 243
. D.W. 50,146,240,385
417
. DALLAS 404,415-416
. DANIEL 311-312,420
. DAVID 399,401,419-420
. DAVID A. 399-400
. DAVID N. 399,614
. DAVID W. 415-416,567
. DEBORAH 399
. DEBROAH 401
. E. 248
. E.A. 610

. E.C. 40,390
. EDITH 408
. EDWARD 631
. EDWIN 397
. EDWIN A. 121,424,573
. EDWIN ALLISON 398
. ELISHA 25,31,396,400
404-405,408,413-414
419
. ELISHA C. 38,383
403-407,417
. ELISHA PICKET 403
. ELIZABETH 203,398,406
420
. ELIZABETH A. 417
. ELIZABETH A. BASS 229
. ELIZABETH A.-
BETHEA 417
. ELIZABETH ANN 403
. ELIZABETH BASS 399
. ELIZABETH BETHEA 406
. ELIZABETH
HARLLEE 354,413
. ELIZABETH
ROBERTS 354
. ELLA 397
. ELLA EASTERLING 146
385
. ELLEN 398
. ELLIE SHERWOOD 397
. ELOISE 408
. EMMA 403
. ERNEST 406
. ESTELLE 154
. EUGENE 405,408
. EVA 405
. EVA MANNING 203,219
. EVANDER R. 360,417-418
. EVANDER S. 397-398
. FARQUEHARD 415
. FESTUS 418
. FET 361,418
. FLORA 232,272,311-312
401,416
. FLORA BETHEA 416
. FLORA FORE 154,408
. FLORA J. 399
. FLORA MARG.-
CAMPBELL 320
. FLORENCE 404
. FLORENCE ALLINE 154
. FLORENCE FORE 154
. FLORENCE
JOHNSON 408
. FRANK 241,396-397
415-416
. FRANKLIN 416
. G.J. 645
. GARY 397
. GEORGE 397,403,405

- GEORGE C. 369,391
- GEORGE J. 165,237,320 396-397,443
- GEORGIA 203,400
- GEORGIA BETHEA 203,400
- GOODMAN 414,420
- HANNAH 16,415,417
- HANNAH JANE 228,397 415
- HANNAH JANE BETHEA 415
- HANNAH WALKER 415
- HARLLEE 211,354,413
- HARRIET 181,354,399 401,417,419
- HARRIET BASS 229,401
- HARRIS C. 229
- HENRIETTA 398
- HENRY 3 97,414,416-417 419
- HENRY L. 397
- HENRY P. 603
- HERBERT 203,219 398-399,406
- HETTIE 398,415
- HETTIE BETHEA 398,415
- HOLDEN 181,415,597
- HORACE 398
- HUGH GOODMAN 414
- IDA 154
- IRENA PAGE 397
- ISABELLA 409
- J. FRANK 603
- J.C. 609
- J.F. 180,233,309,407 415-416,559,567
- J.J. 367,556
- J.K. 610
- J.R. 408-409
- J.T. 571
- JAMES 396,399,401-403 405,414,419
- JAMES A. 403-404
- JAMES D. 154-155,408 643
- JAMES EARLE 399
- JAMES R. 10-11,13,40 145,240,333,402-403 407,409,567
- JAMES STEPHEN 154
- JANE 385,399
- JANE SMITH 391,403
- JASPER 360,398,418
- JESSE 10,418
- JESSEE 417,419-420
- JESSIE 408,414-415 418-419
- JESSIE CRAWFORD 145 404
- JOHN 25,31,66-67,180 236,238,242,249,358 392,395-397,399-400 403,407,410,413-414 415,417-420
- JOHN B. 406,415,417
- JOHN C. 10,38,66,87-89 143,235,396,398,407 414-415,452-454,566 567
- JOHN CRAWFORD 89
- JOHN D. 165,238,241 398,419
- JOHN F. 415
- JOHN J. 259,391-392 403
- JOHN L. 420
- JOHN R. 40,200,399,401
- JOHN T. 229
- JOHN W. 417-419
- JOHNSON 408
- JOSEPH J. 229,360
- JOSEPHINE 360,418
- JULIA WAYNE 369,391
- JULIAN 392
- JULIUS 406
- JULIUS N. 403,405
- KATE 402,408-409
- KEMPER 154
- KITTIE 398,417
- KITTIE BETHEA 417
- L. ASBURY 391
- LAURA 354
- LAURIN 418
- LAWRENCE 392
- LEON 416
- LEONA 408
- LEROY 146,240,385,416
- LESLIE 154
- LEVI 228,262,281 396-397,417
- LEWIS S. 211,229
- LILIAN 391
- LILLIAN 399
- LONNIE 154
- LOUISA 281,397,399,401
- LUCILE 418
- LUCINDA 399-401
- LUCRETIA 358,399,402
- LUTIE 154
- M. ISABELLA 408
- M.S. 610
- MAGGIE 154
- MARGARET 399-400,403 410
- MARGARET COCKRANE 399
- MARIA 354
- MARKELY 408
- MARTHA 249,281
- MARTHA A. 546
- MARTHA ANN 403,411
- MARTHA ANN WALTERS 403
- MARY 10-11,154,311-312 397-398,403,409,415
- MARY ANN 262,281,363 397,415,417,419
- MARY ANN BETHEA 397 417
- MARY ANN MILES 401
- MARY ANN- STACKHOUSE 360 418
- MARY ANN THOMAS 405
- MARY BETHEA 398,403 415
- MARY McLEOD 407-408
- MARY PLATT 415
- MARY POLLY 232
- MARY POLLY- SHECKELFORD 396
- MARY ROGERS 181,399
- MATTIE 404
- MATTIE MAY 406
- MAUDE 154
- MINNIE 259,392
- MIRANZA ROGERS 181,399
- MISSOURI 233,397
- MOLLIE 396
- MORGAN 403-405
- MORRISON 405
- NANCY 399,401
- NANNIE 180,360,391,400 418
- NANNIE BETHEA 360,400
- NELLIE 154,219,240,248 404
- NETTIE 203
- NOAH 420
- OSCAR 405
- P.P. 51
- PARKER 181,354,396 413-414
- PATTIE 396,420
- PEARL 392
- PERCE 203
- PERCY 399
- PHILIP 42,63,66-67,396 402-403,407,410-411 414-415,419-420,546 566,571,578
- PHILIP OSBORNE 399
- PHILIP P. 341
- PHILIP W. 203,391,403
- PHILIP Y. 43,395,408
- PICKETT 391,405
- PICKETT K. 405

. PICKETT P. 632	. W.T. 203	. HAMILTON 389
. POLLY 403	. W.W. 398	. JACK 388-390
. POWER 405	. WALKER 405	. JOHN 245,388-390,578
. PRESTON 416	. WALTER E. 229	582
. PRESTON L. 415-416	. WILLIAM 143,263,281	. JOSEPH A. 389-390
. RACHEL 235,399,402	311-312,324,396-397	. K.C. 627
. RACHEL COCHRANE 403	398-399,407,414-415	. STEPHEN 389
. REBECCA 311,397-398	416-417,419-420	. WILLIAM 389,610
. REBECCA MANNING 241	. WILLIAM A. 165,398	BLACKSHEAR,PATTY 309
397	. WILLIAM C. 221,417,419	BLACKWELL,R.J. 538
. REDDEN 578	. WILLIAM ELLIS 402,404	. SAMUEL A. 424
. REDDICK 419	. WILLIAM HENRY 397	. SUE McMILLAN 424
. REDDIN 211,413	. WILLIAM S. 233,396-397	. ZILPHA HUGGINS 244
. ROBERT 397,403-404	491	BLAKE,JOSEPH 568
. ROBERT C. 403-404	. WILLIAM T. 399	BLAKENY, 571
. ROBERT LUCIEN 408	. WILLIAM THADDEUS 399	BLANCHARD,
. ROBERTA FLOYD 229	400	ALBERT Z. 642
. ROBERTS ROBERTS 211	. WILLIAM W. 398,403,405	BLUE, 293,314,320,422
. ROSA CARNES 408	415	. ALEXANDER 289-290
. RUTH 392	. WILMINA R. 403	. ANN ALFORD 290
. S.J. 203,229,272	. WILMINA RACHEL 407	. ANNA M. EVANS 130
399-401,419	. WILSON 397	. CATHERINE 289
. SALLIE 145,396,399,401	BETHUNE, 415	. DANIEL 289-290
405,415,417,424	BETTS,CHARLES 304,494	. EFFA 371
. SALLIE ELLIS 404	. MARTHA 304	. EFFIE 131
. SALLIE	. PATTIE 494	. FLORA 289
MANNING 241,398	BEVERLY, 492	. HETTIE 131
. SALLIE MORRISON 405	. D. 627	. IDA 131
. SAMUEL J. 40,181,196	. DOUGLASS 633	. J.G. 567
358,360,385,399-400	. F. 627	. JENNIE BUTLER 328
. SAMUEL STOLL 399	BIGGS,ALFRED 422	. JOHN G. 130,371,567
. SARAH 180,399-400,420	. CHALMERS 154	571
. SARAH ANN 397	. MARY McMILLAN 422	. KATE 131
. SARAH ANN DAVIS 398	. MAUDE BETHEA 154	. MARTHA ANN 289
452	. RICHARD 622	. MARY 289
. SARAH ANN	BIGHAM, 636	. MARY ANN 290
DEBERRY 397	. L.S. 567	. NANCY 289
. SARAH JANE 399	. SAMUEL 565	. RUPERT 131
. SARAH JANE	. W. HARVEY 591	. SALLIE 131
MANNING 240	BIRD,CLAUDIUS 477	. SARAH 289
416	. H.G. 627	. VICTOR 131
. SIMEON 419	. HUGH 196,389	. WILLIAM 289-290,328
. SOPHIA 397,415,417,497	. HUGH G. 573	596
. STEWART 408	. J. 627	. WILLIAM E. 131
. SUMTER 407	. JAMES 644	BOATRIGHT,J. 627
. SWINTON LEGARE 399	. JOE 389	. J.A. 600
. T.C. 181	. JOSEPH 196	. THOMAS 631
. THEODORE 405	. M.M. 477	BOATWRIGHT, 460,472,522
. THOMAS 419-420	. MARY 477	. ELI 524
. THOMAS C. 181,229,399	. MARY PROCTOR 487	. FOSTER 520,524,586
414	. S. 626	. JOHN 524
. TRISTRAM 232,239,249	. SARAH NORTON 477	. LIZZIE 469
396,403,414-417,419	BLACK,C.H. 161	. ROBERT S. 606
420	BLACKMAN, 159-160,393	. T. 582
. VERZILLA MACE 221	. CAMPBELL 645	. THOMAS W. 265,524
. VICTOR 415	. CAROLINE MEARS 390	BOKER,J.R.M. 645
. VICTORIA	. ELIZABETH 389,473	BOLTON,BRITTON 597
McCORMICK 312	. ELIZABETH LANE 389	BOND,BERNARD 368
. VIRZILLA MACE 419	. H.G. 582	. HARPER 368
. W. ELLIS 146	. H.J. 626	. HENRY J. 615

Name	Page
. JAMES	368
. LIZZIE	372
. O.J.	368
. ROBE	299
. SARAH WAYNE	368
BONE, JOHN	606
. ROBERT G.	606
BONHAM, MILLEDGE L.	570
BOONE, DANIEL	159-160
. THOMAS	569
BOOTH,	172,462
BOOTHE, R.A.	626
BOSTICK,	453
. F.J.	628
. J.H.	140,640
. J.N.	629
. JOSEPH	615
. PAUL J.	615
. T.J.	640
BOSWELL, SAMUEL	632
BOWEN,	245
. HATTIE JONES	244
BOYD, CARRIE	371
. J. MARION	371
. R.W.	572
BOYLSTON, R.B.	571
BRACH, R.	629
BRACY,	290
. W.C.	184
BRADDY,	163
. ADOLPHUS	249-250
. ALICE	249-250
. ANNE NICHOLS	190,250
. DANIEL McK.	249-250
. EDGAR	251
. ELIZABETH	249,251
. ETHEL	251
. HARRIET	132,134,249
	251-252
. HATTIE	251
. JOHN	39,249-251,420
. JOHN B.	249
. KITTIE	249
. LIZZIE EVANS	133,250
. LUTON C.	249-250
. MARTHA BETHEA	249
. MARY CRAWFORD	249
. OSCAR	190,250
. PATTIE BETHEA	420
. R.B.	250,293
. RHODA	249
. ROBERT	250,577
. ROBERT B.	249
. SUE	133
. SUSAN	250
. T.B.	163,190,249-250
. TRISTRAM B.	249
. W.M.	646
. W.W.	133,250,565,644
. WALKER	133,250
. WIGHTMAN	133,250
. WILLIAM	250
. WILLIAM W.	249-250,614
BRADSHAW, JOHN	578
BRADY,	377
BRAGDON, J.B.	640
. J.T.	628
. JAMES	631
. MANLY	615
BRAGG,	349
BRANTLEY, MARTHA	470
BRASSWELL, MILLY	329
. POLLY	328
BRASWELL,	
. EFFA McEACHERN	436
. EFFIE McARTHUR	299
. GADI	299
. ISLA	436
. J.R.	610
. JACK G.	622
. JEFFERSON	377
. MARY	436
. RICHARD	436
. RICHARD H.	299
BRAWLER, JACOB	518-520
BRAYDON, J.J.	593
BREEDEN,	234
. ABSALA	324
. ADALINE CAMPBELL	324
	325
. APPEY	324
. J.B.	324
. JACKEY	324
. JOHN A.	11,324,359
. JOSEPH	324
. MOLLIE	324,359
. PETER L.	546
. VICTORIA GODBOLD	121
	324
. W.H.	121
. WILLIAM H.	325
. WILLIAM HUGH	324
BREVARD, JOSEPH	73
BREWER, H.C.	636
BRIDGES,	
. LUCINDA BETHEA	401
. WILIE	401
BRIGMAN,	610
. ARCHIBALD	591
. ARTHUR P.	597,603
. EVANDER	332
. SMITHY MOODY	332
. THOMAS	236
BRITT,	369
. E.I.	636
. J.L.	622
. MOLLY	518
BRITTON,	108-110,135,137
	356,448,458
. MARGARET	
WOODBERRY	110,355
. THOMAS	355
. TOM	110
BROACH, G.W.	593
. ROBERT R.	615
BROACHMAN, J.K.	610
. S.C.	610
BROADHURST,	
GEORGE	464
. GERTRUDE CRAVEN	464
BROCK,	453
BROCKINTON, JOHN	455
. LAURA	455
BROGSDEN, E.	600
BROUGHTON, THOMAS	569
BROWN,	207,355,359,378
	483,493
. ALEXANDER	645
. ALLISON H.	379
. ANN	378,380
. ANNA MARIA	
COLEMAN	474
. ANNE COX	330
. ANNIE	380
. ASA	582
. C.B.	495
. CAROLINE	504
. CHARLES V.	379
. CHARLOTTE	378
. D.	582
. EDITH GASQUE	374,380
. EDWARD	245,259,643
. EDWARD W.	379
. ELIZA CLARK	253
. ELIZA CLARKE	381
. ELIZABETH	504
. ELIZABETH	
WILLIAMSON	431
. EVANDER	380,606
. FANNIE	378
. FRANCES	378-379
. G.R.W.	600
. GEORGE	483
. GEORGE W.	606
. HARRIET	380
. HENRIETTA	378-379,504
. HENRY	606,643
. HUGH	474,615
. J.	627,629
. J. GRAHAM	577
. J.C.	582
. J.L.	600
. J.O.	381
. JAMES	380
. JAMES T.	50,381
. JANE	379
. JANE TART	195
. JEREMIAH	51,380
. JERRY	380

. JESSEE C. 606	. W. 600	. REBECCA
. JOHN 245,288,349	. W.A. 42,380,430,567	MILLER 197,476
378-379,643	. W.J. 378	. SAMUEL 643
. JOHN O. 381,573	. W.K. 643	. SARAH ANN NORTON 476
. JOHN S. 380	. W.T. 645	. SOLOMON 187-188,197
. JOSEPH 378,380	. WASHINGTON 380	. 578,614
. JOSHUA 378	. WILLIAM 50,245,378,380	. STEPHEN 197-198
. JULIA 380-381,463	504,573	. STEPHEN S. 643
. JULIA DAVIS 380,453	. WILLIAM A. 245,253,379	. WILLIAM 197-198,332
. JULIA WOODBERRY 40	381,567-568	. 394,476
. KATE 495	. WILLIAM E. 181-182	BUCHANAN, 422
. L. 600	. WILLIAM J. 378,606	BUCK,W.L. 537
. LEWIS 378-379,504-505	. WILLIAM M. 274	BUIE, 312
. LEX 380,645	BROWNFIELD,SUSAN 449	. A.S. 298,321,328
. LOUISA BRUNSON 381	BROWNLOW,PARSON 86	. AMARANTHA 298
. LOUISE DURANT 381	BRUCE,JOSEPH 333	. LOUISA 328
. M. 629	. SUE MOODY 333	. MARGARET C. 441
. MARTHA CAROLINE-	BRUNSON, 241,417	. WILLIAM H. 597
BAKER 381	. HAROLD 450	BULL,WILLIAM 569
. MARY 378	. J. BOYD 593	BULLARD,P.D.B. 633
. MARY JANE 274	. LOUISA 381	. WILLIAM 610
. MARY PACE 378	. MARY DAVIS 450	BULLOCK, 481
. MARY SNIPES 529	. R.A. 295	. ALICE 351
. MATTIE BAKER 447	. ROBERT A. 418	. JOEL 591,636
. MINNETTA 504	. WILLIE WALTERS 295	BULTER,PIERCE M. 569
. MOLLIE 378	BRYAN, 201	BUNDY,JOHN A. 597
. MOURNING 374	. CELIA MOODY 332	. MARTHA ANN ELLEN 238
. NANCY 374	. LIZZIE A. MOODY 332	. WILLIAM 238
. NANCY JONES 245	. QUINCY 332	BURCHES, 638
. NELLIE GASQUE 374,380	. WILLIAM 332	BURGESS, 637
. PAT ROGERS 379	BRYANT, 333,489,544	BURGOYNE,JACK 503
. PATSY 378	. ALICE EDWARDS 187	BURNETT,JOHN 597
. PATTIE 378	. BETHEL 578	. THOMAS 569
. PATTY 528	. CELIA MOODY 332	BURNEY, 189
. PINCKNEY 380	. CURTIS 197	BURR,AARON 83
. R.M. 600	. DAVID 197,394,615	BURRISS,ROBERT L. 643
. RACHEL 467	. ELI 197	BURROUGHS,THOMAS 606
. RACHEL	. EMALINE EDWARDS 187	BUTLER, 170,181
FLOWERS 379,505	. EVAN 578	. ABY 518
. RANSOM 582	. EVANS 476	. ALFRED 329
. REBECCA 378,380,421	. F.D. 198,571	. ALFRED W. 327,597
. RICHARD 378,504	. HENRY 643	. ANNIE 327
. ROBERT 431	. HUGH 187,197	. CHARITY 328
. SAMUEL 631	. HUGH G. 621	. DEMPSY 327-329
. SARAH E.-	. JAMES 615	. ELI T. 597
WILLIAMSON 430	. JAMES C. 622	. ELIAS 340
. SARAH ROWELL 468	. JESSE 197-198	. FLORA A. 328
. SOLOMON 582	. JOHN M. 197-198,394	. GILBERT 321,327-328
. STEPHEN 378-379,468	. JOHN WESLEY 615	596
582,615	. LIZZIE 474	. ISHAM 327-328
. SUSAN A. 381	. LIZZIE A. MOODY 332	. JAMES 329
. SUSAN TART 194	. LIZZIE MOODY 342	. JANE DAVIS 329
. T. FOSTER 463	. M.Q. 332	. JENNIE 328
. T.F. 356,381,447,453	. MARVIN 332	. JESSE 258
456,644	. MARY NORTON 476	. JOHN A. 591
. TEMPERANCE 378-379	. MILLEY 374	. KATIE McEACHERN 327
. THOMAS 378-379	. McQUINCY 342	. LANEY 327-329
. TRAVIS FOSTER 380	. PINCKNEY 197,621	. LANEY BUTLER 327-329
. VICTORIA MARTIN 245	. QUINCY 332	. LOUISA BUIE 328
259	. REBECCA 394	. LOUISA CAMPBELL 321

. MARY	328	. D.C.	600	. J.C.	637
. MARY ROGERS	328	. DON	631	. JAMES	322,325,327,486
. MILLY BRASSWELL	329	. HECTOR	423		488,578
. NATHAN	329	CAMPBELL,	121,176,211	. JAMES C.	614
. OBEDA	340		288,290,299,367,436	. JAMES S.	460
. PATIENCE	327		471,485-486,495-496	. JAMES W.	631
. PIERCE M.	84		563	. JEANETTE	287
. POLLY	327	. A.	324	. JEREMIAH	488
. POLLY BRASSWELL	328	. ABSALA		. JERRE	486-487
. SAMUEL	329	BETHEA	324,398	. JERRY	175
. SILAS	327	. ADALINE	324-325	. JOHN	327,486,488
. SILAS W.	591	. AGNES	443	. JOHN C.	141,196
. SOLOMON	328	. ALEXANDER	322,324		325-326,597,616
. STEPHEN	327-328	. AMELIA TART	196,326	. JOHN C.C.	631
. SUSAN	327	. ANDREW	645	. JOHN EDWARD	321
. THOMAS	327-328	. ARCHIE	322	. JOHN J.	322,439,590
. VINEY	329	. BENJAMIN F.	487	. JOHN P.	322
. WILLIAM	578	. BRYON	326	. JOHN S.	460
. ZILLA	327	. CAPERS	488	. JOSEPHINE	
BYERS,E.H.	436	. CHARLES FLETCHER	487	HUGGINS	487
BYRD,	435	. CHARLOTTE LANE	486	. K.M.	175
. HUGER	643	. CHLOE ROGERS	486	. KENNETH	487
. HUGH G.	603	. DANIEL	320,327,439,596	. LILLY	300
. JOSEPH	637		637	. LOUISA	321,488
CADELL,		. DANIEL M.	320	. MAGGIE	488
. SARAH ELLEN -		. DANIEL WALKER	308,321	. MALCOLM C.	320
LEGETTE	204	. DAVID	322,325	. MARGARET	321
CAESAR,JULIUS	306	. DORA	488,546	. MARGARET	
CAIN,	204	. DUNCAN	287,320-322,325	McEACHERN	320
. CHURCH	593	. DUNCAN M.	321	. MARTHA	439,487
. DAVID	616	. E.	610	. MARTHA J.	
. E.E.	640	. E.A.	610	McCOLLUM	320,443
. J. COON	593	. EBBY	486	. MARY	321,325,486
. J.C.	637	. EBENEZER	616	. MARY ANN	325
. J.H.	593,631	. EDWARD	320,397	. MARY ANN FORE	220
. J.J.	593		442-443	. MARY BARNES	486
. K.S.	593	. ELI	487	. MARY McLELLAN	320
. R.M.	637	. ELIZA CARMICHAEL	321	. MARY NORTON	476,487
. RIX M.	593		439	. MIKE C.	573
. S.G.	593	. ELIZABETH	486-487	. MIRANDA CRIBB	488
. S.J.	637	. ELLA McDONALD	299	. MOSLEY BARNES	486
. SPENCER G.	614	. ELY	175	. NANCY	321
. T.C.	637	. EMALINE	487	. NANCY ANN	486
. W.E.	637	. EMMA HUGGINS	488	. NEILL MURDOCH	321
. WILLIAM	640	. ERASMUS D.	590	. OSCAR	321
CAINE,KINION W.	622	. ERVINIA		. PATIENCE	
CALDER,BOAH	633	RICHARDSON	460	SCOTT	175,486
. DUNCAN	622	. ETTA	488	. PATSY BROWN	378
. HENRY	845	. FLORA	325-326,394	. PEGGY	322
. JOEL	613	. FLORA MARG.	320	. PETER	322-323,325
. JOSEPH	645	. FRANK	326,486	. PRESTON	326
. M.	645	. G.F.	600	. ROBERT	645
. NIAS	622	. GADI	263,476,486-488	. ROBERTA	326
. PETER	622	. GEORGE	486	. ROMINE	326
. WILLIAM	633	. GEORGE R.	299	. S.A.	610
. WILLIAM C.	622	. HUGH	321-322,324-325	. SAMUEL	220,325-326,394
CALDERS,	543		327,398		636
CALDWELL,	178	. IVERSON	488	. SARAH ANN	322
CAMERON,		. J.A.	460	. SIMEON	476,616
. ALEXANDER W.	590	. J.B.	451,460-461	. SPENCER	486

. SUE 321,327	. ALEXANDER A. 310	. EDNA 436,439
. SUE CAMPBELL 321,327	. ALEXANDER C. 642	. EDWARD 620
. THEOPHILAS 488,616	. AMANDA 311,439	. EDWARD D. 315,439,443
. THEOPHILUS 263	. AMANDA	. ELIZA 321,439
486-487	CARMICHAEL 311	. ELLEN 441
546	439	. EMALINE 301,439
. THOMAS LEGRAND 326	. ANGUS 444,477,482	. EVANDER 442,574
. VALCOUR 326	. ANN MURPHY 311	. FANNIE 443
. W.D. 641	. ANNE 443	. FLORA 311,440,444,481
. W.J. BEAUREGARD 326	. ANNE CARMICHAEL 443	. FLORA C. 311
. W.J.B. 325	. ARCHIBALD 603	. FLORA
. W.P. 565,610	. ARCHIBALD B. 573	McLELLAN 310,442
. WARREN W. 487	. ARCHIE 301,318,436-438	. FRANKLIN 442,572,574
. WILLIAM 394,569,645	440-441,443-444,574	. GADDY 439
. WILLIAM P. 322-324	637	. GILBERT 442-444
. WILLIAM S. 184,323	. ARCHIE B. 438	. HATTER JOHN 298,311
325-326,394	. ARCHIE M. 302	315,318,321
. WILLIAM	. AUGUSTA 444	. HATTIE McLELLAN 441
SIMEON 321,327	. B.M. 444	. HETTIE 441
CANBY, 513-514,565	. BAKER 443	. IDA 442
CANDY,SAMUEL 603	. BENJAMIN M. 260	. J.B. 574
CANNON, 356	. CALVIN C. 321,441	. J.L. 600
. AMELIA 352	. CAROLINE 439-440	. JAMES 439,444,615
. GEORGE H. 605	. CATHARINE 311,440-442	. JEFFERSON D. 302
. HENRY M. 605	. CATHARINE-	. JENNETTE 439
. J.B. 645	CARMICHAEL 440,441	. JENNIE 298,443
. R. 629	. CATHERINE 310	. JESSIE 351
. SAMUEL W. 606	. CHALMERS 442	. JOEL 441
. WILLIAM H. 606	. CHARLOTTE 310	. JOHN 298,311,315,318
CANTEY, 450	. CHARLOTTE-	321,437-441,444,637
CAPET,	CARMICHAEL 310	643
. MAGGIE MAY	. CHRISTIAN 437,442-443	. JOHN C. 441,443
JOHNSON 357	. CHRISTIAN-	. JOHN L. 310-311
. THOMAS J. 357	CARMICHAEL 437	. JOHN R. 402,440-441
CAPPS, 109	. CIVIL 441	. JOHNY 281,402,441
. ANN BROWN 378	. CIVIL EDWARDS 188	. JUDSON D. 574
. CALEDONIA SNIPES 529	. CLYDE 439	. JULIA M. WRIGHT 441
. DAVID 378	. COY 441	. KATIE 315
. FRANCIS 616	. D. 609,627	. LANIER B. 442
. FRANK 378	. DANIEL 310,437-438,440	. LEMANTHA WALTERS 310
. HAMILTON 529	442-444,586	. LILLY MACK 441
. JOHN H. 643	. DANIEL A. 596	. LIZZIE GADDY 177,439
. JOHN W. 622	. DANIEL ARCHIE 436,439	. LORETTA 302
. RICHARD 616	. DANIEL FRANK 302	. LOU 441
. WILLIAM W. 586	. DANIEL M. 431,441-442	. LOUISE 302
CAREW, 71-72	574	. LOUISE
CAREY,SAMUEL 540	. DANIEL W. 188,439,443	CARMICHAEL 302
CARMICHAEL, 188,266	. DAVID 441	. LOUISE McEACHERN 436
427,558-559,563	. DOUGALD 302,442-444	439
. A. 565	477,481	. LUTHER 443
. A.B. 45,177,438-439	. DOUGALD A. 310	. MACK 440
. AGNES CAMPBELL 443	. DOUGALD B. 310-311,316	. MAGGIE WILLIAMS 260
. AGNES HARLLEE 351	442	444
. ALBERT 444	. DUGAL 187	. MALCOLM 318,441
. ALBERT E. 311	. DUGALD B. 317	443-444
. ALBERT J. 441	. DUGALD C. 183	. MALCOLM C. 310,439,596
. ALEX 603	. DUNCAN 317,440-443	. MARGARET 315,441
. ALEX J. 597	. DUNCAN C. 310,439,603	444-445
. ALEXANDER 402,441-442	. DUNCAN D. 441,602	. MARGARET C. BUIE 441
444,591,602	. E.D. 567	

. MARGARET CAMPBELL	321	
. MARGARET M.R.-McCAULL	351	
. MARGARET McDUFFIE	315	
. MARGARET McLEOD	439	
. MARTHA	311,440,443-444	
. MARTHA CAMPBELL	439	
. MARTHA CARMICHAEL	444	
. MARTHA J. McCOLLUM	442,443	
. MARY	302,311,318 440-441,444	
. MARY ANN	310,316	
. MARY CARMICHAEL	441	
. MARY CATLING	302	
. MARY CUTTING	302	
. MARY POLLY	442	
. MASTON	443	
. MASTON NEILL	443	
. MATILDA	442	
. MICHAEL	443-444	
. MONROE	441	
. McCOY	402	
. NANCY	315,317,440-444 477	
. NANCY CARMICHAEL	440	
. NANCY McDUFFIE	318	
. NEILL	267,437-438,440 443-444	
. NEILL C.	207,311,442	
. NEILL J.	310,439	
. NEILL M.	302,440-442	
. NETTIE	444	
. NINA	436,439	
. OLIVER	443	
. ORELLA	302	
. PENCIE LEWIS	444	
. PENNSY LEWIS	482	
. PENSY	477	
. POLLY	443-444	
. R.J.	439	
. REBECCA	443	
. RED DUNCAN	439	
. SALLIE McKINNON	310	
. SAMUEL	443	
. SARAH	444-445	
. SARAH A.	302	
. SARAH HARRELSON	440	
. SOLON	444	
. SUSAN	443-444	
. SUSANNAH	477	
. SUSANNAH-WILLIAMSON	431	
. T.W.	50	
. VIOLA	442	
. W.D.	284,317,327,351 436	
. WALTER	311	
. WILLIAM	440-441	
. WILLIAM D.	50,351,436 439-441,444,590,602	
CARNES, . ROSA	239 408	
CARPENTER,	152	
CARR,	570	
CARSON,	12	
CARTER,	205,228,464	
. AMELIA SNIPES	529	
. CHARLOTTE BROWN	378	
. HENRY	613,633	
. JAMES	378,583	
. JOE	613	
. JOHN	378,529,574	
. NANNETTE GREGG	510	
. NANNIE	460	
. SUSAN	457	
. W.E.	640	
. W.J.	246	
CARTERET,	4	
CASH,	381	
CASTLES,LOUISA	531	
CATER,JOHN W.	622	
CATTEL,	23	
CAULCUTT,JAMES	640	
CAVE,MARGARET	489-490	
CHAMBERLAIN,	101,103	
. D.H.	96	
. DANIEL H.	100,570	
CHAPPEL,	273	
CHAPPELL,HENRY C.	605	
CHARLES,	615	
CHERRY,	262	
. RACHEL	143	
. SARAH JANE	370	
CHEVES,LANGDON	73	
CHINA,	446	
CHINNIS,	459	
CHREITZBERG,	261	
. CATHERINE M. WAYNE	368	
. GEORGIA GAME	487	
. LULA	487	
. OSGOOD A.	368	
. ROBERT	487	
CHREITZBURG,BOND E.	50	
CHRISMAN,F.M.	262	
CHRISTMAN,JARROTT	593	
CHRISTMAS, J.L.	393 610	
CHURCH,JAMES	616	
CLAFF,MAPP	107	
CLARK,	269,536-537	
. ANGUS J.C.	583	
. DORA	253	
. ELIZA	253	
. H.S.	600	
. JOHN	42,254,578	
. JOHN C.	41
. JOHN CALVIN	41-42 252-253,602
. JOHNSON	633
. KENNETH	252,254,377 597
. KNOX	359
. LILLY	253,494
. LUTHER	42
. M.L.	645
. MALCOLM	252-254,317
. MARGARET	317
. MARTIN LUTHER	252-253
. NANNIE	253
. NANNIE STACKHOUSE	42 253,359
. PINCKNEY	254
. PINK	254
. R. KNOX	603
. R.K.	41-42,391,494,646
. ROBERT C.	573
. ROBERT KNOX	252-253
. W.P.	627
CLARKE,ELIZA	381
. MALCOLM	377
. R.K.	381,565
CLAY,HENRY	85,88
CLEVELAND,	245,285
CLINTON,	405
COACHMAN,FRANK	353
. HELEN	353
. MATTIE HARLLEE	353
COARY, . ANNIS WILLIAMSON	430
. N.D.	430
COATES,EVANDER	633
COATS,JAMES	633
. JOHN	610,622
COBB,THOMAS	579
COBURN,	136
COCHRANE,RACHEL	403
. THOMAS	235,403
COCKRANE,MARGARET	399
. THOMAS	399
COHEN,DAVID	592
. ISAAC	574,592
. JOSEPH	616
COIT,	570
COKER,HARMAN	632
. SANDY	632
COLCOCK,C.J.	84
. CHARLES JONES	73
COLCUTT,JAMES W.	616
COLE,ANN ELIZA EVANS	134
. E.	574
. MARY MARTIN	260
COLEMAN,	106,109
. ALICE	473

. ALMA PEARCE	473	. JOHN D.	154,274,389		. CATHERINE DAVIS	451	
. AMOS	472		472-473		. CHARLES G.	642	
. ANGELINA SMITH	473	. JOHN W.	472-473		. D.	627	
. ANNA	473	. JOSEPH	472-473		. D.F.	599	
. ANNA JONES	472	. JULIUS	473		. DAVID C.	573	
. ANNA M.	473	. LAURA GODBOLD	474		. DEUTERONOMY	513	
. ANNA MARIA	474	. LEAH BAXLY	474		. DORA OWENS	467	
. AUGUSTUS	472	. LENA	472		. E.C.	582	
. BEDA ROGERS	473	. LIDE	474		. EDWARD	515	
. BETSY WHALEY	472	. LIZZIE BRYANT	474		. EDWARD C.	370,515	
. BETTIE	472	. LOUIS	633		. EDWARD H.	592	
. CANTEY	472	. MAJOR	473		. ELIZABETH PHILIPS	466	
. CAROLINE TART	474	. MAMIE COOK	473		. ELSY PHILIPS	465	
. CATHERINE FLOYD	472	. MARTHA	430		. EVANDER	637	
. CELIA BAXLEY	473	. MARTHA J.	473		. F.A.	636	
. CHARLOTTE	473	. MARTHA WALLER	472		. FRANK	637	
. CORA	474	. MARY	472		. GREGORY	616	
. CORNELIUS	473	. MARY ALLEN	154,473		. H.G.	431,583	
. D.V.	172	. MARY ANN	472-473		. HOOK	380	
. D.W.	583	. MARY DREW	473		. HUGH	513	
. DANIEL	472-473	. MARY ELIZ.	530		. J. BURT	515	
. DAVID	472-473	. MARY SMITH	474		. J.B.	629	
. DAYTON	473	. MATTIE	472-473		. J.D.	600	
. DONNELLA	472	. MATTIE HAYS	172		. J.E.	629	
. DORA	473	. MOSES	261,457,474-475		. J.G.	600	
. E.J.	473-474		484		. JAMES	514	
. EDWARD	474-475	. NANCY SHELLY	472		. JANE A.	430	
. ELIZABETH		. NINA	472		. JOEL B.	573	
BLACKMAN	389,473	. POLLY SASSER	473		. JOHN	451,512-513	
. ELIZABETH		. PRESSLY	472-473		. JOHN E.	515,578	
FLOWERS	474	. ROSA B.	532		. JOHN J.	342,430,515	
. ELLY	474-475	. S.	645		. JOHN L.	614	
. EMMA R.	473	. SAMPSON	474-475		. JOHN W.	573	
. ENOS	474	. SAMSON J.	572		. JONAH	512,514	
. EUGENIA	472	. SARAH	473		. LAWRENCE	370	
. EULA	472	. SUE BRADDY	133		. M.H.	380	
. FONTAINE	472	. SUE LANE	474		. MACK	637	
. FRANK	473	. SUSAN BRADDY	250		. MARGARET		
. FRANKLIN D.	643	. VIRGINIA PEARCE	473		SMITH	495,513	
. G.B.	626	. W.D.	475,599		. MARTHA		
. G.W.	628	. W.J.	626		WILLIAMSON	431	
. GARY	472	. WALKER	250		. MARY	469	
. GRIFFIN	472,474	. WESLEY	473		. MARY LEGETTE	370	
. GRIFFIN B.	472-473	. WILLIAM	472		. OWEN	513	
. HANNAH DREW	473	. WILLIAM J.	472		. OWEN R.	616	
. HOWARD	472	. WILLIAMSON	474		. PERRY	579	
. I.M.	583	. WILLIE	473		. PRUDENCE		
. IDA SHELLY	473	COLLETON, JAMES	568		HARRELSON	515	
. IRIS	472	. JOHN	2		. R.	565,583,600	
. ISAAC M.	472	COLLIER, HTOMAS	616		. RICHARD	466,573	
. J.P.	473,583	COLLINS,	368,375,467,495		. ROBERT	432,512,514	
. J.T.	50,250,475		497,514,516		. ROMNEY	513	
. J.W.	627	. A.H.	645		. S.	600	
. JACOB	472,474	. A.J.	600		. S.J.	629	
. JAMES	430,472,474	. AMANDA WALL	432		. S.T.	583	
. JANE FLOWERS	474	. BARNEY	432,513		. SAMUEL	512,616	
. JESSEE	474,600	. BARNY P.	643		. SHADE	645	
. JOEL S.	473	. BENJAMIN	514		. SHADRACH	514-515,573	
. JOHN	473-475	. BENJAMIN F.	643		. SOLOMON	512-513	
		. BENJAMIN J.	616		. STEPHEN R.	483,616	

. STEPHEN T.	495,513	. HENRY C.	14	. WILLIAM H.	463-464
. SYDNEY	513	. J.C.	246	. WILLIAM LORD	2
. THOMAS	512,514,645	. JANE HARLLEE	343	CRAWFORD,	89,126,140,158
. THOMAS J.	616	. LILA	52		196,221,223,262,333
. URIAH H.	616	. STEWART	247,592,597		374,396,398,422,457
. VALENTINE	606	. T.F.	610		551
. W.	627	. THOMAS	247,343,487	. A.B.	610
. W.S.	97,567	. THOMAS F.	592	. ALBERT	146,339
. WILLIAM	430,465,469	. WESLEY	633	. C.J.	91,567
	483,514	. WILLIAM	246	. CARRIE R.-	
. WILLIAM T.	572	. YATES	14-15,247	McPHERSON	145
. WOODSON	515	COUCHMAN,	571	. CHAPMAN J.	88-89
. ZILPHA	430	COUNCIL,	403		142-144
CONNELLY,	231	COVINGTON,	240	. CHARITY	146,151
CONNERLY,	162	. B.H.	347	. CYPE	145-146
CONNOR, WILSON	578	. BENJAMIN HARLLEE	348	. DOCK	146,339
CONTENT, GEORGE	2	. FRANK F.	347	. G.C.	402
COOK,	543	. HALLIE	348	. G.G.	146,610,613
. BERRY	616	. HARRIS	43,410,609	. GADI	146
. CATHERINE AYRES	167	. J.E.	347	. GEORGE	144
. H.B.	13,167,522	. MARY ANN HARLLEE	347	. GIBSON C.	409
. HENRY	632	. NORA AYCOCK	347	. GIBSON G.	145,401
. HENRY B.	590,642	. PET STACKHOUSE	362	. HAL	146,221
. HIRAM	633	. T.C.	219,362	. HARDY	142,145,401-402
. JAMES C.	583	COWARD, ABNER	597	. HARDY B.	145,592
. JAMES ERVIN	606	. ANSEL	597,633	. HENRY L.	586
. JOHN	603	. HARVEY	603	. JAMES	62,142-146,333
. MAMIE	473	. SARAH	393		389
. W.	645	. WILSON	393	. JAMES C.	402
. W.H.	626	COX,	202,348,481,528	. JAMES D.	597
. WILLIAM H.	616	. ANNE	330	. JAMES G.	145
COOPER, BRUNSON	593	. ELIZABETH WALL	433	. JAMES HARDY	401
. E.W.	637	. GEORGE	631	. JESSIE	145,402,404
. FRY	637	. GEORGE B.	592	. JOHN	142,145-146,339
. JOHN	645	. HUGH	579	. JOHN H.	146
. LEVI	640	. J.T.	593	. KATE BETHEA	402,409
. RALPH	573	. JOHN	629	. MARGARET	145-146
. ROBERT D.	593	. LEWIS J.	633		401-402
. SAMUEL	564,568	. MARTHA WALL	432	. MARY	145-146,249,340
. SIMON	640	. N.D.	583		402
. THOMAS	8	. S.C.	629	. MARY POLLY MACE	221
. WITHERSPOON	593	. SAMUEL	631	. MASSEY	226
COPER, LELIA SMITH	265	. SARAH	120,330	. MATTIE E. ROWELL	471
. P.S.	265	COXE,		. MERCY	146
CORBIN, H.C.	94	. ADAREZER BASS	230	. RACHEL	143
CORNWALLIS,	343	. EDWIN	231	. RACHEL NEVILS	143
COSTEN, W.	645	. JAMES	231	. RHODA	145-146,385
COTESWORTH,		. JAMES E.	230		401-402
. CHARLES	22	. NANCY BASS	231	. SALLIE	144,333,402
. ELIZA LUCAS	22	. ROBERT	231	. SALLIE BETHEA	145,401
COTTINGHAM,	156,333	CRAVEN, ANNE WALL	463	. SAMUEL B.	145-146,402
. A.J.	246	. BOYD	463	. SARAH ANN MOODY	146
. A.J.C.	246,559	. CHARLES	463,569		339
. ANDREW	246	. CLAUDE	463	. THOMAS C.	145,401-402
. CONNER	246,603	. GERTRUDE	463-464		586
. D.S.	204	. HENRY	463	. W.H.	39,609,642
. DANIEL	246,273	. JULIUS EDWARD	463	. WILLIAM	144-145,401
. DANIEL C.	246	. LANE	463	. WILLIAM H.	138,143-144
. ELKANAH	246	. LULA	463	. WILLIS	145-146,401-402
. HENRY	247	. PRESTON	463	. WILLIS G.	145,385

Name	Page
CREEL, JOHN J.	616
. N.B.	640
. SAMUEL E.	616
CRIBB, ALICE	459
. ANTHONY	170,258
. CAROLINE	459
. DEMPSEY	258,586
. DEMPSY	170
. GEORGE T.	170
. GEORGE TALLEY	586
. JOSEPH	645
. LEONARD	476
. LEVI	592
. MARGARET	482
. MARY JANE-HARRELSON	256
. MIRANDA	488
. NANCY NORTON	476
. REBECCA	459
. THOMAS	643
. W. THOMAS	586
. W.T.	170,256
CRIDDLE, JAMES R.	573
CROCKETT, DAVID	115
. DAVY	115-116
. JAMES	107,114
CROFT,	570
CROKER, H.	600
CROMWELL,	22
CROSBY,	138,141
. WILLIAM	142
CROSS, KATE EVANS	130
W.H.	130
CROSSBY, J.L.	629
. J.W.	629
. T.E.	629
CROSSWELL, J.J.	114
W.J.	114
CROUCH,	
. ELLA WOOD NORTON	479
CROWLEY, WILLIAM C.	603
CRUMPLER, ISLA DEW	274
CUDDLE, JAMES R.	643
CUISACK, J.H.	636
CULBREATH, BEVERLY	141
CULPEPPER, GEORGE	593
CURRIE,	283
CURRY, D.	629
. G.W.	629
. J.	629
. MARY ELLEN	350
CUSACK, GEORGE W.	591
. SAMUEL	631
. SAMUEL C.	591
CUSAIK, JOSEPH	578
DAGGETT,	102
DAIVS,	375
DANIEL,	126
. CHESLEY D.	566
. DARGAN	633
. EMMA MARTIN	259
. HARLLEE	633
. J. OSCAR	259
. KATIE	259
. LOUISA MARTIN	259
. MARY	259
. MINNIE BETHEA	259,392
. N.	611
. ROBERT	259,569
. ROBERT M.	392
. SOPHRONIA	189
. W.H.	259,392
DANIELS, CHARLEY	570
. CHARLEY D.	566
. J.G.	629
. JOHN L.	616
. W.H.	200
DANSEY,	465
DARGAN,	250,352
. G.W.	570
. GEORGE W.	73,434
. JULIUS	118
. JULIUS A.	182,571
. L.O.	632
DAVID, FRANK B.	401
. J.E.	571
. J.H.	239,401,559
. LETTIE MANNING	239
. WILLIAM J.	283
DAVIS,	107-108,127,134-135,137,188,375,405,433,448,458,520,570
. A.G.	449
. ABRAHAM	452
. ABRAM	450
. ADDIE	451,460
. ADDIE L.	447
. ALVA	452
. ANN SHAW	520
. ANNA MARIA	451
. ANNE	433
. ANNE DAVIS	433
. ANNE KEENE	449
. ANNIE WHITE	454
. ARGENT GERALD	452
. ARTHUR	579
. B.F.	40,251,361,445,449-451,539,567
. B.F.W.	455
. BEN	433
. BENJAMIN	450,454
. BENJAMIN F.	449
. BENJAMIN S.	449,451
. C. KEENE	455
. C.L.	449
. CANTEY	450
. CATHERINE	449,451
. CHRISTIANNA	449
. CLAUDIS	449
. CORA	450
. CORINNA McCORMIC	450
. CORNELIA RAYSOR	455
. DANIEL	449,454
. DAVID	451-454
. DESDA	110,355
. E.M.	51,645
. EDWARD WILLIAM	451
. ELBERT	133
. ELI	449
. ELIHU	449
. ELIZA	449,451
. ELLA	455
. ELLA DAVIS	455
. ELLA JENKINS	40,449
. ELWOOD	448
. EMMA	449-450
. ERVIN	451-452
. ERVINIA RICHARDSON	451,460
. EUGENIA RICHARDSON	452
. EUNICE	421
. EVA	450
. EZRA M.	306
. FONTAINE	449
. FOSTER	452
. FRANK	452-453,637
. GARY	455
. GEORGE	433,454
. GEORGE PIERCE	455
. H. FOSTER	606
. HANNAH	110,356
. HARRY	449,451-452
. HENRY	87-88,452-454,565-567,637
. HENRY GRADY	450
. HICKS	133
. HUGH	222,454
. HUGH G.	454
. IDA	457
. IDA MAY	455
. IDA MAY DAVIS	455
. J. CLEMENT	373
. J. PRESTON	445,449-450
. J.F.	628
. J.G.	593
. J.P.	567
. J.R.	583
. J.W.	133,152,250,269
. JACKEY	380,451-452
. JACKSON	451-452
. JACKY	381,449,454
. JAMES	449,451-452,454
. JAMES C.	451
. JAMES H.	606
. JANE	329
. JEFFERSON	433
. JENNIE	455

. JOHN	449,454	. SUSAN B.	449	. ANNE LANE	273
. JOHN C.	453,455	. SUSAN B. DAVIS	449	. BENJAMIN O.	156
. JOHN H.	153	. SUSAN BROWNFIELD	449	. CAD	274
. JOHN R.	454	. SUSANNAH BAKER	449	. CALVIN	245,274
. JOHN W.	457	. SUSIE	381	. CHARITY	271-272
. JOSEPH	449-451,453,460	. T.G.	642	. CHRISTOPHER	185,245
. JOSEPH P.	453	. TELATHA BERRY	152,269	.	267,271-272,274
. JULIA	380,449-450,453	. THEODORE G.	451	. CHRISTOPHER I.	622
	465	. THEODORE		. CHRISTOPHER T.	271
. JULIA AVANT	449	GOURDIN	451	. D.M.	556
. JULIA DAVIS	453	. VIOLA	455	. DENNIS	274
. JULIA F.	451	. VIOLA DAVIS	455	. DORA	273
. JULIA F. AVANT	449	. W.J.	449,644	. DUNCAN M.	273
. JULIUS	454	. W.M.	448,567,646	. ELIZA	489
. KATE McINTYRE	450	. WALKER BRADDY	133	. EUGENIA ALLEN	203,273
. KEENE	449-450	. WARDLAW	453	. F.C.	217,637
. L. FONTAINE	450,463	. WILLIAM	449,451,454	. FLORA BETHEA	272
. LAURA	449		579,646	. FRANK	274,279
. LAURA BROCKINTON	455	. WILLIAM G.	451,455,460	. FREDERIC C.	245
. LIZZIE	449-450	. WILLIAM J.	380,445,447	. H.C.	156
. LORINE	452		449,451,453-454	. HARTWELL C.	273-274
. LOUISA	449	. WILLIAM M.	450-451	. HARVEY	274
. MAGGIE McWHITE	452	. WILLIAM PRESTON	455	. HENRIETTA	271-272,393
. MAMIE SMITH	452	. WILLIE	133,334	. ISLA	274
. MARIA	449	DEAS,JOHN	631	. JAMES L.	247
. MARION	452	. JONAS	98-99	. JANIE	274
. MARTHA	451	. SIMON	593	. JOHN	271,274
. MARVIN		DEAVER,A.	600	. JOHN A.	245,268,579
WARREN	449-450	DEBERRY,ARTEMISSIA	509	. JOHN FOSTER	245
. MARY	449-451	. ED	631	. JOHN L.	273,556
. MARY L. GODBOLD	124	. EDMUND	501	. JOHN W.	633
	455	. HENRY	509	. JOSEPH H.	50,273
. MARY STEVENSON	463	. R.M.	637	. JULIAN	52,274
. MATILDA McINTYRE	306	. SARAH ANN	397	. LAWTON	274
. MAUDE	433-434	DECK,	459	. LEONARD M.	274
. MAY	452	DEENS,STEPHEN R.	586	. MARINA	267,271-272
. MINEOLA	450	DEER,	152	. MARTHA	274-275,490
. NICHOLAS	433	. BLANCHE	339	. MARY	185
. NICHOLAS CALVIN	451	. CHERRY	201	. MARY JANE BROWN	274
. NIMROD	566	. ELIZABETH ANN	174	. MARY POLLY	271-272
. OLIVER	451-452	. JOHN	165,387	. MARY POLLY LANE	273
. ORILLA	454	. JOSEPH	165,174,201	. MISSOURI JACKSON	279
. ORION	452	. JULIA MOODY	339	. MOLLIE	274
. PRESTON	453	. LULA	228,339	. NANCY	271-272
. R. MEANS	51	. MAHALA	231	. PHILIP	245
. RACHEL	449,451	. WILLIAM P.	165,339,586	. PRESTON L.	203,273
. RANDALL	454	DENNIS,GEORGE W.	574	,.ROBERTA	273
. RICHARD	124	DESAUSSURE,	571	. SAMUEL	622
. RICHARD F.	455	. HENRY WILLIAM	69,73	. TURRENTINE	633
. RICHELIEU	452	DEVEAUX,	22	. WILLIAM	274-275
. ROBERT L.	449-450	DEVON,	375	.	489-490
. S.J.	645	DEW,	393	. WILSON	268,271-272
. S.U.	568	. ABASLOM	271	DEWITT,JOHN	637
. SALLIE	449-450	. ABRAHAM	271-272	PETER	637
. SARAH	452,454	. ABSALOM	274	DEWS,	157
. SARAH ANN	398,452	. ALEXANDER	274	DICKSON,BONNA	510
. SARAH WALL	433	. ANN ELIZA	274-275	. IDA	510
. SHEP U.	452	. ANN ELIZABETH-		. JAMES J.	510
. STEPHEN	452	HAYES	268	. MAXCY	510
. SUSAN	449,451	. ANNE	274	. W.J.	643

. WESLEY	510	. JOHN	379	. GREGORY	641
. WILLIAM J.	510	. MARY	473	. HENRY	583
DILL,	264,458	. N.	627	. TREZEVANT	643
. BRIGHT	524,631	. POLLY	459	EAGARTON,	465
. D.M.	645	. R.	633	EAGERTON,	433
. FRANK	524	. THOMAS	645	. HENRY	593
DILLARD,E.	637	. WILLIAM	616	. MARGARET P.	
. J.H.	583	DRIGGERS,R.S.	611	MOORE	473
. JOHN	637	DUBOIS,	546	. ROBERT	473
DILLON,		. ETTA	424	EARLE,JOSEPH H.	480
. BLANCHE BETHEA	154	. EUGENIA POTTER	424	EASTERLING,	416
. DAN	154	. HATTIE	424	. CELIA	199,386
. J.W.	141,295,327,559	. J.T.	412,424	. ELLA	146,385
. WILLIAM	141,597	. KATE	424	. ENOS	384,386
DIMARY,J.T.	629	. M. SUE	412,424	. FLORENCE	146,385-386
DONALDSON,		. META	424	. FRANK	146,165,202,385
. BESSIE WILLSON	461	. SALLIE	424	. HENRY	146,202,384-386
. T.Q.	461	. WILLIAM J.	424		402,597
DOUGLAS,		DUBOSE,	161,283	. J. FRANK	146
. LIZZIE BOND	372	DUDLEY,	153,261	. JAMES	384
DOVE,HUGH	325	. C.W.	571	. JAMES F.	384,386
. HUGH G.	592	. JAMES	153	. JANE	385
. J.D.	645	. JANIE BERRY	153	. JANE BETHEA	385
. JOHN W.	592	. REBECCA	225	. JANE STACKHOUSE	402
. MARY ANN		DUDNEY,JAMES	487	. JOHN	384
CAMPBELL		. MARTHA CAMPBELL	487	. LUCRETIA A.	385
DOZIER,	374-375,467,472	DUFFIE,EMERSON M.	154	. MAGGIE PAGE	165
	572	. IDA FORE	154	. MAGGIE	
. A.W.	522,571	DUNBAR,J.C.	359,559	WATSON	202,385
. ANNIS	469	DUNCAN,	72,544,571	. MARTHA	385
. BETTIE STEVENSON	313	DUNKIN,B.F.	73,570	. McPHERSON	386
. DAVID	375,521	. C.J.	570	. RHODA	
. ELIZA ROWELL	469	. CHANCELLOR B.F.	72	CRAWFORD	146,385
. ELIZABETH	456,504	DUNLAP,J.E.	306		402
. GRIFFIN	622	. REBECCA McINTYRE	306	. RUPERT	202,385
. HENRY	521	DUNSFORD,ASA	579	. SALLIE	386
. IRIS GRICE	521	DUPRE,		. SILAS	384,386
. J. TULLEY	504	. CAROLINE BETHEA	419	. THOMAS	146
. J. TULLY	505	. JAMES	269,419	. THOMAS C.	385
. J. VALENTINE	606	. SARAH JANE HAYES	269	. TRISTRAM	384-385,402
. J.T.	209,500,505	DURANT,	551	. W.C.	204
. JAMES T.	520	. ELLEN GRICE	208	. WILLIS C.	146,385
. JAMES TULLY	521	. FLORENCE	127	EDENS,ALFRED	642
. JOHN	469,564	. H.H.	144	. FRANK	301,324
. JOHN F.	521,606	. LOUISE	381	. JACKEY BREEDEN	324
. JULIA SHAW	520	. THADEUS	209	. JOE	315
. LEONARD	565,568	. W.L.	119	. SALLIE SINCLAIR	315
. LUCY ANN FLOWERS	505	. W.W.	91,208,507,567	EDGE,HAMILTON	634
. MARY GASQUE	375	. WILLIAM L.	586	. JOHN	633
. McROY	520	DURHAM,	97,551	EDINO,SALLIE	295
. T.J.	313,522	. CICERO A.	132	EDNARS,MATTHEW H.	622
. TULLY	500,607	. EUNICE	132	EDWARD,ALBERT	439
. WILLIE	474	. KATE McKERALL	132	. HAMILTON	397
DRAKE,JOHN	293	. MARGARET EVANS	132	EDWARDS,	222
DRAYSPRING,		. MARGUERETTE	132	. ALBERT	186,210
. ETTA BERRY	152	. S.A.	97,132,184,221	. ALBERT P.	616
DRAYTON,JOHN	569		303,491,551	. ALICE	186-187
DREW,	197,528,543	. SOLON A.	620	. AMANDA	545
. FRANCES BROWN	379	DUSENBERRY,	217	. ANDREW	186-187
. HANNAH	473	EADDY,	466	. ANNE MARTIN	259

. AUSTIN	187,189,400,443	
. B.F.	187,189	
. B.T.	45	
. B.W.	572	
. BONNIE	186	
. CAREY	186	
. CAROLINE MARTIN	187	
. CARRIE	156	
. CARY	187,222,616	
. CATHERINE	187	
. CHARLES	545	
. CIVIL	188	
. D.S.	440	
. D.W.	11	
. DAVID	183,185-187,197	
. DAVID S.	45,188,260 331,440,464	
. DAVID W.	187,445,614	
. E.C.	187,445	
. ELIZABETH	186,188	
. ELIZABETH OWENS	466	
. EMALINE	186-187	
. ENOS	186	
. FRANK	189	
. G. EMORY	188	
. G.E.	51,440	
. GEORGE	187,482,643	
. GOLDHEADED DICK	188 189	
. GOLDHEADED RICHARD	186	
. HAMILTON	186	
. HARRIET	186-187,331	
. HENRY	186,189	
. HENRY A.	156	
. IDA SMITH	186	
. JAMES	187-188	
. JAMES W.	545	
. JANE	187	
. JOHN	187-188,645	
. L.M.	186,189,210,260 276	
. LEVI	189,483	
. LEVI H.	586	
. LUCINDA M. MACE	156	
. MAGGIE	156	
. MARGARET-CARMICHAEL	445	
. MARION	186	
. MARTHA	183,186-187	
. MARTHA CARMICHAEL	440,443	
. MARTHA MACE	187,222	
. MARY	156,186,188,225 340	
. MARY MOODY	332	
. MARY SELLERS	545	
. MELVIN	187,445	
. MELVINA	187-188	
. NANCY	186,188	
. NANCY OWENS	187	
. OLIN	172,186	
. ORILLA HAYS	172	
. P.H.	51,186	
. PATIENCE FOWLER	483	
. REBECCA CARMICHAEL	443	
. RENSELAER	188	
. RICHARD	185-187,259 466	
. RICHARD J.	614	
. RICHARD M.	616	
. RICHARD W.	574	
. ROBERT	186-187,222,482	
. SALLIE	186-187	
. SALLIE ROWELL	469	
. SAMUEL	156,186,188,260 484	
. SAMUEL W.	443	
. SANDY	482	
. SARAH LEWIS	187,222 482	
. SOLOMON	172,188-189	
. SOLOMON M.	622	
. STANLY	187	
. THOMAS H.	571	
. WILLIAM	186-187	
. WILLIAM G.	156,643	
. WILLIAM J.	615	
EDWNS,	361	
EGERTON,C.B.	583	
. EVANDER	631	
. SAMUEL	631	
ELERBY,JOHN	213	
. OBEDIENCE-GILLESPIE	214	
. THOMAS	213-214	
. WILLIAM	214	
ELFORD,NELLIE	215	
ELLEN,AMANDA BETHEA	237,398	
. DAVID	178,237-238	
. ELIJAH	237	
. ELIJAH J.	592	
. JAMES	238	
. JOHN H.	178,238,331	
. MARGARET LITTLE	237	
. MARTHA ANN	237-238	
. MARY JANE	237-238	
. MARY POLLY	238	
. MARY POLLY-McKENZIE	237	
. MARY WILSON	237	
. RITTA	237	
. ROBERT M.	237	
. SOPHIA MOODY	331	
. W.B.	165	
. WESLEY	237	
. WILLIAM B.	237,398	
. ZIMRI	237	
ELLERBE,	133,145,196,281 326,480	
. CASH	216-217	
. E.B.	121,494	
. EDWARD B.	214,217	
. ELIZA	338	
. ELIZABETH LAMB	217	
. ESTELLE	216	
. EVA	217	
. HENRIETTA BETHEA	398	
. HENRIETTA ROGERS	214	
. HERBERT	216	
. ISLA	494	
. J.E.	51,215-217,567	
. JOANNA	214,217	
. JOANNE	151	
. JOHN	213	
. JOHN C.	39,151,214,217	
. JULIA	214,217,225	
. LUCY	120	
. MARY	216	
. MARY ELLERBE	216	
. NELLIE ELFORD	215	
. OBEDIENCE-GILLESPIE	214	
. OMEGA	216	
. RICHARD P.	214,217	
. SALLIE	120,214	
. SARAH GODBOLD	121,217	
. SARAH HASELDEN	214,225	
. THOMAS	213-214,216	
. W.H.	398,570	
. W.M.	51,216	
. W.S.	120,151,216,218 239,338,381	
. WILLIAM	214	
. WILLIAM H.	40,214-215	
. WILLIAM S.	99,214	
ELLIOTT,	366,378	
. B.F.	259	
. IDA MARTIN	259	
ELLIS,ARAMINTA BASS	226	
. B.S.	397	
. EVANDER P.	621	
. GINSEY SMITH	498	
. GINSY	404	
. HUGH	226	
. HUGH G.	616,622	
. SALLIE	404	
ELMORE,D.W.	637	
. F.H.	84	
. P.J.	637	
. WILLIAM J.	586	
ELVINGTON,	162,171	
. APPIE	175	
. DAVID	586	
. DENNIS	592	

. ELIZABETH ANN
   DEER 174
. ELIZABETH PAGE 165
. GEORGE W. 174
. GILES 174
. HUGHEY 174
. JACK 174
. JESSE 175
. JESSEE 174-175,178,540
. JOEL 637
. JOHN 174-175,178,263
   587
. JOHN E. 165,174,431
. L.M. TULULAH 431
. L.M.T. 431
. MARY ANN PAGE 174
. NATHAN 587
. OWEN 174,587
. SALLIE 175
. WILLIAM 174
. ZADOC 178
EMANUEL,BEULAH 199
. FRANK 579
. THEODOCIA 199
ERVIN,ERASMUS 571
. J.R. 570
. JAMES 566,570
. JOHN F. 85
. JOHN T. 12
. SAMUEL 571
. SUSAN GASQUE 375
. VAL DOZIER 375
EVANS, 126,132,142,145
   402,449,476,491,493
   505,570
. A.L. 128
. ALFRED 126,128
. AMELIA 130
. AMELIA
   LEGETTE 129,372
. ANN ELIZA 132,134
. ANN M. 129
. ANNA M. 130
. ASA 126
. BETTIE 127
. BEVERLY 126,128
. C.D. 38,51,224,571
. CATHARINE 129
. CHARLES E. 129,307
. CHESLY D. 126-127
. DAVID 125-127
. DIXON 129-130,509
. EDNA 251
. ELIZA BAKER 382,447
. ELIZA JANE 129
. ELIZA JANE EVANS 129
. EMMA 133
. FANNIE 132,134,251-252
. FLORENCE DURANT 127
. FRANK 127

. GAMEWELL 126
. GARY LEE 133
. HARRIET
   BRADDY 132,134
   251-252
. J. HAMILTON 50
. JACKSON 126,128
. JAMES 126
. JAMES AUBREY 133
. JAMES E. 128
. JAMES
   HAMILTON 129,372
. JANE
   HASELDEN 127,224
. JENNIE 378
. JOHN GARY 127,215,570
. JOSEPH 130
. JOSEPH J. 73
. JOSIAH 643
. JULIUS 132,134,251
. JUNIUS H. 127,571
. KATE 130
. KATIE 447
. LAWRENCE 132,134
   251-252
. LEON 127
. LIZZIE 132-133,250
. LOUISA 129-130
. LUCY 133
. MAGGIE HASELDEN 133
. MAMIE 133
. MARGARET 129,132
. MARTHA 132,134,251
. MARY 129
. N. 629
. N. GEORGE 127
. N.G. 38,128
. N.J. 574
. NATHAN 38,66,125-127
   129,132-134,180,250
   251,366,382,445,447
   510
. NATHAN G. 126
. NELLIE 133
. NELSON 579
. PAT 132,134
. ROSA 129,132,304
. SAMUEL 127
. SARAH 126
. SARAH ANN
   GODBOLD 129
. SHANKS 127
. SOLON 579
. SOPHIA McINTYRE 307
. SOPHIE MILES 130
. SUE BERRY 133,153
. THOMAS 64,125-126,128
   369,510,551,566,568
   571,643
. THOMAS BAKER 133

. TRIS MAGISTAS 127
. W. BOYD 133
. W.B. 51,153,251,581
. W.T. 129,378,435,502
   566
. WALKER 127
. WILLIAM 11,38,84,99
   125-126,128-129,132
   180,304,366,369,511
   566-567
. WILLIAM B. 132-133
. WILLIAM BOYD 133
. WILLIAM T. 597,615
. WILLIAM THOMAS 129
. WOODSON 126,128
EWART,SALIE 474
FAIRLEE, 290,297-298,314
   328
. G.M. 51
. GEORGE M. 485,577
FALCONER,WILLIAM 570
FALK, 169
. MAYRANT A. 421
FANNING, 380
FARLEY, 557
. BLANCHE McINTYRE 439
. HENRY 439
. JAMES 376
. MARTHA ANN
   GASQUE 376
FAULK,CARL 312
. FLORA BETHEA 312
. LILLY 300
. MARY BETHEA 312
. RICHARD 312
FENAGAN,JAMES 591
FERDON, 570
FERGUSON,M.M. 600
FERREL,JAMES 643
FERRELL,JAMES A. 646
FIERSON,J.M. 574
FINAGAN,PATRICK 415
FINKLEA, 218,334,411
. ALFRED 223,579
. ARTER WILLIS 410
. ELIZABETH FORE 220
. FRANCES 525
. FRANKY 221
. G.C. 640
. HARDY 223,579
. HUGH 220,223,579
. J. WESLEY 643
. J.C. 124,223
. JACK 194
. JAMES C. 410,609
. JOANNA ROBERTS 212
. JOHN 223,593
. LUCINDA 410-411
. MARGARET 224,411

. MARGARET	. CLAYTON 641	. CHARLES 645
AGNES 410-411	. E. 627	. CHARLES P. 211
. MARGARET BETHEA 410	. ELIZABETH 474	. DICEY 481
. MARTHA 221	. ELIZABETH BROWN 504	. FAULK 324
. MARY E. HUNT 124	. ELIZABETH DOZIER 504	. GILES R. 211
. NEILL 223	. ELIZABETH KEEFFE 502	. H.B. 288
. ROBERT 641	. ELIZABETH MARLOW 504	. HARMAN 176,553
. SALLIE 224,410-411	. ELLY 504,574	. HENRY BASCOM 211
. SAMUEL B. 643	. ERVIN HUGER 502	. JUGH JAMES 451
. THOMAS 212,223	. EVERETT 504-505	. PEARL 324
. W.E. 641	. G.S. 627	. ROBERTA 229
. WILLIAM 410-411,579	. HENRIETTA BROWN 379	. ZILPHA 172
. WILLIS 194,212,221,223	504	. ZILPHA ROBERTS 211
340,377,410-411	. HENRY 502-505,583	FOGLEMAN,JAMES G. 622
FINNAGAN,PATRICK 643	. J.A. 583	FOLEY,CIVIL 546
FINNEGAN,	. J.H. 583,640	FOLK,
. MARY ANN GEORGE 278	. JACOB 502	. SARAH JANE
. MICHAEL 278	. JAMES 502	BETHEA 399
FITZGERALD,ROBERT 622	. JAMES J. 504,587	FOLSTON,GEORGE 593
. ROBERT E. 597	. JANE 474	FORD, 164,192,540
FLADGER, 108,135,137,177	. JOEL 504	. A.G. 494
448	. JOHN 502,504-505	. A.H. 599
. ANNA MARIA DAVIS 451	. JOHN H. 502,505	. ALLEN 168-169
. C.J. 40,43,137,233,253	. JOHN J. 502	. BAKER 52
410,488	. JOHN JEREMIAH 472	. C.R. 554
. CHARLES 525	. JULIA 472	. C.T. 52,165,169,186
. CHARLES J. 491,609	. LOVE 379,474,503-505	. CAROLINE 168,485
. FANNIE 233	. LUCY ANN 504-505	. CHARLES 168-169
. H.G. 631	. MARGARET A.	. CHARLES P. 587
. HENRY 491-492	JAMES 504	. DAVID 168
. HUGH 451,460,491-492	. MARTHA BAXLEY 504	. ELIAS B. 155,163
579	. MARTHA PARKER 504	168-169,318-319,562
. HUGH G. 611	. MARY JAMES 504	. ELIZABETH 168,170-171
. JAMES 613	. MINNETTA BROWN 504	. FANNIE 318
. LIZZIE 488	. MOLLIE 502	. GEORGE 169-170,485
. R.B. 645	. N. 600	. GEORGE W. 587
. SALLIE MARIA 137,491	. NANCY 502	. H. PINCKNEY 587
. SARAH 491	. NATHAN 504	. HARDEE 587
FLAGDER,HUGH 270	. NICHOLAS 637	. HARDY 170
FLEMING,	. OLIVE 502	. HELEN PITTMAN 169
FLEMING, 571	. OLIVIA 502	. JAMES 167,562
FLETCHER,JOHN 386	. PATSY SAVAGE 502	. JANE HERRING 168
FLOOD,MARY NORTON 476	. RACHEL 379,504-505	. JESSE 485
FLOWERS, 122,277,435,483	. SALLIE 502	. JESSEE 168-169,171,566
561-562	. SAMUEL S. 504-505	. JOHN 62,255,566
. A. LOVE 504	. SARAH ANN JAMES 504	. LIZZIE 318
. ANN JAMES 504	. SUSAN BEST 504	. MARY 168,170,176
. ANN LAMBERT 504	. TELATHA 262,502	. MARY E. SMITH 494
. ANN MARLOW 504	. W.D. 593	. NELSON 170
. ANNE 502,505	. WILLIAM 502,504-505	. PENELOPE 319
. ANNE FLOWERS 502	574	. PERSERVED 168
. ANNIE 467,502	. WILLIAMSON 504	. RAMSAY 167
. ANNIE PAYNE 502	FLOYD, 398,415,472,515	. RUFUS 52,169
. ANNIS 502	. ABSALA BREEDEN 324	. SALLIE 169,206
. ARCHIE 502	. APPEY BREEDEN 324	. SANDY 168
. B. 600,646	. BATTIE 211	. THOMAS 168
. B.A. 600	. C.P. 211	. VIRGINIA 168
. BARNY 504	. CATHERINE 472	. WATSON 168
. BENNETT 502,504	. CATHERINE DAVIS 451	. WILLIAM 11,168-170
. BETSY 502	. CATHERINE N. 464	. ZARV 168-169
. CAROLINE BROWN 504		

. ZAW	562	. TRACY	153,218,268,597	. LUCY	522
. ZILPHA	229	. TRACY R.	153,199,218	. MARY	374
FORE,	195,326	. WILLIS	153,155,218-220	. MATILDA	527
. A.M.	220		270	. R.W.	629
. ALFRED	218,220,621	FORT,	186	. S.	583
. AMANDA	153-154	. JANE	527	. SALLIE	376,522
. ANN ELIZA-		. KIRKLAND	172,188	. SERENA GREGG	510,522
STACKHOUSE	525	FOSS,I.I.	559	. STEPHEN	522-523
. ANNIE	153-154,201	FOUNTAIN,	456	. T.	583
. BAKER	155,220	FOWLER,	466	. THOMAS	522
. CLARENCE	153,155	. BENJAMIN	622	. TRUMAN	122,523,527
. CROMWELL	155	. FURMAN	483	. W.C.	178,305,643
. DANIEL	218-219,306,315	. JAMES F.	574	. W.K.	634
	377,525	. JESSE	484	. W.S.	500,520
. EDWARD M.	218-219,646	. JESSEE	431,483	. WESLEY	527
. ELIZABETH	220	. JESSIE	378	. WILLIAM	523
. ELIZABETH ANN	218-219	. JOSEPH	375,483,643	. WILLIAM C.	376,510,522
	361	. MAGGIE	484		524
. ELLY	218	. MARTHA	483	. WILLIAM CAPERS	522
. EUGENIA	218-219	. MARY	483	. WILLIAM S.	523
. FLORA	153-154,408	. MATTIE GASQUE	375	FRANKLIN,DEAS	574
. FLORENCE	153-154	. MOLLIE BROWN	378	FREEMAN,F.	611
. GEORGE	153,155,169	. PATIENCE	483	. GEORGE	645
. H. JAMES	622	. SARAH	483	. JOSEPH	592
. HENRIETTA LANE	218	. STEPHEN	483	. ROBERT	634
. IDA	153-154	. TRECIA	431	FRIAR,ANDREW	631
. J. RUSSEL	155	. WILLIAM	483	FRIERSON,D.E.	303
. J. RUSSELL	153	FOXWORTH,	123,125,224	FRY,BENJAMIN L.	614
. JAMES	194,218		457,460,493,520,522	FRYE,	377
. JANIE	218	. A.B.	629	. MARTHA GASQUE	374
. JENNIE LASSITER	155	. A.C.	616	FRYER,ANDREW J.	592
. JOEL	218-220,525	. ANDREW J.	616	FULLER,	400
. JOHN	218	. ANN WOODWARD	527	. ELIZABETH WAYNE	368
. JOHN A.	220	. ANNIS McWHITE	523	. FRANK	368,370,515
. JOSEPH	155	. B.F.	583	. GEORGE	368
. KATE	155	. BENJAMIN	523	. SALLIE	368,462
. KATE WATSON	199,218	. C.B.	641	. WYATT	341,368,462
. LINWOOD	153,218	. CAROLIN GASQUE	527	FULMORE,	311-312
. MADGE	153	. CAROLINE GASQUE	374	. ALEXANDER	417
. MAGGIE HASELDEN	219	. CHARLES	583	. ANN	349
. MARTHA ANN MACE	220	. CHARLEY	577	. CHARLOTTE BETHEA	417
. MARTHA ANN MILES	221	. CHARLEY J.	523	. HANNAH BETHEA	417
. MARY	525	. EDWARD	522	. ZACK	417
. MARY ANN	220	. ELI	527	GADDY,	168,175,178,191
. MARY BERRY	153-154,	. ELIZA	527		257,391,427,496,518
	220	. ELIZA FOXWORTH	527		540,562
. MARY McDUFFIE	315	. ELIZABETH	527	. ALLEN	39,176-178,182
. OLIVER CROMWELL	153	. ELIZABETH WHITE	527	. ANN	176
	155	. ERVIN J.	607	. ANNA JANE	177
. REBECCA	218,270	. GEORGE	522	. ANNE	446
. REBECCA J.	248	. HENRY	527,616	. CHARITY	177
. REBECCA JANE	218-219	. JACK	523	. CHARITY PITMAN	176
. RICHARD	525	. JAMES	523	. CHARLES B.	176,212
. SALLIE BERRY	153,218	. JIMMY	522	. CHERRY GODBOLD	503
. STEPHEN	40,153-155,201	. JOB	516,522-523,527	. DUNCAN	177,426
	218,220,408	. JOHN	634	. ELIZABETH	176,178
. TELATHA		. JOSEPH B.	607	. ELIZABETH JONES	177
BERRY	155,220	. JUDAH	516		243
. THOMAS	218-219,248,361	. JUDITH	527	. ELLEN	278
. THOMAS E.	194,218	. KITTIE SMITH	500,523	. HARDY	176-177,273

Name	Page(s)
. HENRY	439
. HEROD	177,181,645
. ISRAEL	176
. ITHAMER	171,176-178, 358
. ITHANNER J.	597
. J. MASTON	177,503
. J.J.	634
. JAMES	176-177,243,427
. JAMES M.	446,526
. JOHN	278
. JOHN I.	168,176
. JOHN W.	178
. JOSEPH	176
. LEVI	176,578
. LIZZIE	177,439
. MARY	176-178,358
. MARY FORD	168,176
. NICHOLAS	176
. NICHOLAS W.	177
. POLLY	176,178
. R.C.	273
. R.W.	611
. RHODA	525
. RICHARD M.	177,592
. ROXANNA	309
. SALLIE JONES	176,243
. SAMUEL T.	45,176,275,490
. SARAH	176-177,308
. SILAS	176,178
. T.C.	611
. TRISTRAN	178
. TRITCAN C.	623
. WALKER	176
. WILLIAM	176-177,243,308
. WILLIAM D.	592
. WINNIE HUMPHREY	177
GAILLARD,C.C.	400
. LUTHER	400
. MAGGIE	400
. THEODORE	69
GAINES,	297,579,581
. JOHN	579
GAINEY,FANNIE	469
. JUDITH	525
GALIVANT,	264,284,458
GALLOWAY,HENRY	281,397
. JAMES	281,397
. JAMES F.	397
. JAMES T.	281
. JOHNY CARMICHAEL	281,441
. JOSEPH	281
. LOUISA BETHEA	281,397
. MARY	397
. RACHEL	397
. REBECCA	397
. REBECCA TOWNSEND	281
. SALLIE	397
. SAMUEL	441
. SAMUEL T.	281
. WILLIAM	281
GAME,	122
. ELIZABETH CAMPBELL	487
. GEORGIA	487
. HATTIE	487
. JOSEPH	222
. JOSEPH BETHEA	488
. LILA	487
. LIZZIE FLADGER	488
. MARY	487
. MINNIE	488
. MORGAN	488
. R.B.	137,487
. ROBERT B.	261
. ROBERT G.	488
. ROBERTA	487
. SIMPSON	488
. SUSAN WHITE	222
GARDNER,DANIEL	574
GARNER,JAMES	597
. JOE	615
GARRETT,W.	583
GARRIS,ELIAS	616
GARRISON,E.J.	560
GARY,	127
. F.B.	128
GASQUE,	218,458
. A.M.	572
. ABASLOM	469
. ABSALOM	374-375,377,490
. ADDISON	374
. ADDISON L.	377
. ALFRED	374,377
. ANDREW STOKES	376
. ANN	374-375,469
. ANN ROWELL	375
. ANN WATSON	375
. ANNA M. PHILIPS	465
. ANNA SMITH	376,501
. ANNIE WILLIAMSON	430
. ARCHIE	374-375
. ARCHIE B.	375-376
. ARNY	205
. ARNY M.	375
. BETTIE	375
. BOND	377
. BOYD	375
. BOYD R.	376
. CAROLIN	527
. CAROLINE	374
. CAROLINE GASQUE	374
. CARROLL	376
. CELIA	375
. CHARLES W.	376
. CHARLOTTE	376
. CICERO	375-376
. CLAUDIA	376
. CORA	376
. DAVID	376,501
. DAVID A.	375
. DAVIS	574
. DOCK	376
. E.	627
. E.H.	376,501,522,551
. EDITH	374,380
. EDNA	376
. ELI	376
. ELI H.	376-377
. ELIZABETH	374
. ELIZABETH WALL	434
. ELLY	374,376,378,380
. ELLY A.	378
. ELMORE	375
. EMMA	205,375
. ERVIN A.	607
. EUGENIA	205,375
. EVELINE LEGETTE	372
. F.	645
. FLORENCE	375-376
. FLOSSY	376
. FRANCES	375
. FRANKLIN J.	375-376
. GEHU	646
. GEORGE K.	377
. HANNIBAL L.	375
. HARRIET PORTER	376
. HATTIE	376
. HENRY	374,376-378,380,574
. HENRY A.	375,490,605
. HENRY E.	376,511
. HENRY I.	129,378
. HENRY LITTLE	376
. HERBERT	376
. IDELLA	375
. J.	629
. J. F.	434
. J. MASTON	574
. J.F.	421,644
. J.H.	645
. JAMES	377
. JAMES C.	374,465
. JAMES W.	375
. JANE	376
. JENNETTE	375
. JENNIE EVANS	378
. JOHN	374,377,434
. JOHN D.	375
. JOHN O.	376
. JOSEPH H.	376
. JULIA	375
. KITTY	376
. L.M.	372,567

. LEVI	181-182	. BENJAMIN	87-88,110,355	. ALLEN	161-162,200,372
. LIZZIE	372		454,462-463,568		623
. LONNEY M.	376	. JOHN	110,355	. ANNA PHILIPS	465
. LOVE	374,377	GEDDES,JOHN	569	. CONSTAINE-	
. LUCY	376	GEE,E.	570	McCLENAGHAN	160
. MARION	375	GEORGE,	268	. DAVID	161,465
. MARTHA	374	. AGENORA	278	. DESDA	429
. MARTHA ANN	376	. AGENORA A.		. FERDINAND S.	160-161
. MARY	375-376,469	JACKSON	278		566
. MARY		. AURELIA	278,285	. GIDEON	147,159-160
McMILLAN	376,421	. DELLA	278	. JAMES	161
. MASTEN	364	. DORA ADAMS	269,278	. JAMES H.	623
. MASTIN	374,377	. ELLEN GADDY	278	. JAMES S.	160-161
. MASTON	220	. HENRY	279	. JESSE	200
. MATTIE	375	. HENRY J.	623	. JESSEE	161-162
. MILLEY BRYANT	374	. J.J.	278	. JESSEE L.	623
. MONETTA	375	. JASPER C.	269,278	. JESSIE H.	40
. MOURNING BROWN	374	. JOHN J.	11,13,278,404	. JOHN	159-161,566,643
. McB. R.	375		409	. JOHN S.	575
. NANCY	119,374,377	. MARY ANN	278	. JORDAN	159-160
. NANCY BROWN	374	. MATTIE BETHEA	404	. KNIGHT	161
. NANNIE	376	. NANCY	181	. MARY E. WATSON	40
. NANNIE GREGG	376,511	. PERCY	278	. MARY WATSON	200
. NELLIE	374,380	. W.J.	622	. NATHAN S.	161
. OLIVE	374-375,490	. W.W.	556	. OSCAR E.	574
. OLIVIA	464	. WILLIAM WARREN	278	. ROBERT W.	574
. PHILIP	375	GERALD,	189,464	. ROGER	159
. POLLY	375	. ARGENT	452	. SARAH WATSON	200
. R.K.	377	. CATHARINE	430	. SQUIRE DAVID	161
. RANDOLPH	377	. CATHERINE	466	. STEPHEN	66,159-160
. REBECCA	374,376	. ELIZABETH O.-		. TOBIAS	159-160
. RENA	376	WILLIAMSON	429,430	GILBERT,JAMES	617
. ROBERT	377	. HANNAH	527	. WILLIAM	579
. ROBERT K.	252	. HANNAH F.-		GILCHRIST,	383,426,481
. S.S.	640	WILLIAMSON	430	. A.E.	407,582
. SALLIE	375,377	. HARDY	481	. ALICE	383
. SALLIE FOXWORTH	376	. JOEL	481	. ARCHIE	383
	522	. JOHN	574	. ARCHIE HILL	383
. SALLIE GASQUE	375,377	. JOHN L.	430	. AUGUSTA B.	
. SAMUEL	373-375,377	. JONATHAN	481	BETHEA	407
. SAMUEL O.	574	. KATE E.	430	. AUGUSTA BETHEA	383
. SARAH	375	. LEVI	429-430	. BESSIE	383
. SUMTER	374	. MARTHA ANN	430	. BETTIE McDUFFIE	383
. SUSAN	375	. S.W.	627	. CHARLES	383
. SUSAN ROGERS	377	. SAMUEL	429	. CHARLES B.	383
. THOMAS	579	. SAMUEL W.	430	. CLAUDIUS	383
. TROY	375	. SARAH	430	. D.E.	383-384,583
. VIRGINIA	376	. WILLIAM	481	. DANIEL	87,382,384,454
. W.B.	374	. ZILPHA LEWIS	481	. EUGENE C.	383
. W.B.R.	377	GERGG,JOHN	568	. GEORGIA	383
. W.E.	430	GERRY,J.H.	636	. IDA	383
. WESLEY	375-376	GEVE,	444	. JOHNSON	318,383
. WESLEY E.	375,574	GIBBES,	265	. MARY	383
. WILLIAM B.	374,377	. G. THOMAS	614	. THOMAS	312
. WILLIAM B. ROWELL	375	. ROBERT	569	. VAN	383
. WILLIAM B.R.	574	GIBBS,JOSEPH S.	616	. VIRGINIA	383
. WILSON	374,377	GIBSON,	140,142,158-159	GILES,	67,108,135,448
GASQYE,C. MARION	605		240	. A.J.	600
GAUSE,	527	. ALBERT	161-162,220,572	. ABRAM J.	471
				. ANNIS	445,447

. ANNIS PHILIPS	465	
. ANNIS PHILLIPS	381	
. CATHARINE	471	
. CATHERINE	472	
. EDWARD	471	
. ELIZA FRANCONIA	472	
. FRANCONIA	472	
. HUGH	63,66,135,381,445	
	447,465,471,568	
. J.B.	600	
. JEANNETTE	472	
. JOHN B.	472	
. POLLY BAKER	447,471	
. R.J.	600	
. REBECCA	471	
. ROBERT	135	
. ROBERT B.	472	
. SARAH	471	
. W.H.	599	
. WILLIAM H.	471	
GILESBORO,	66	
GILLESPIE,	570	
. OBEDIENCE	214	
GIST,WILLIAM H.	570	
GLEN,JAMES	569	
GLISON,J.H.	637	
GLISSON,ANN	469	
. E.B.	629	
. G.W.	641	
GLOVER,AMELIA EVANS	130	
GODBOLD,	126,438	
	490-491,526,546	
. ABRAHAM	123	
. ABRAM	117	
. ALEXANDER	119	
. ALICE	120,527	
. ANN	502-503	
. ANN ELIZA	398	
. ANNA	124,413	
. ANNE	117,120	
. ANNIE	121	
. ANNIE ELIZA	121	
. ASA	38,118-121,123-124	
	217,325,330,337,398	
	400,455,564,568	
. AUGUSTA RICHARDSON	40,461	
. BESSIE	120,413	
. CADE	117,123	
. CELIA ANN ATKINSON	490	
. CHARLES	38,51,118-119	
. CHARLES F.	374,616	
. CHERRY	502-503	
. CHRISTOPHER C.	490	
. D.E.	122-123,503,538	
. DAISY	120	
. DAVID	117,119,121-122	
	502-503,593	
. EBBY	490	
. ELI	489-490,634	
. ELIZA	120	
. ELIZABETH	117,223,526	
. ELIZABETH McGURNEY	117	
. ELLY	11,38,117-119,121	
	123,125,177,182,409	
	502-503,514,527,565	
. ERVIN	125,284,523-524	
	643	
. ERVIN M.	121,123,125	
. F. MARION	120	
. F.M.	41,121,614	
. H.L.	611	
. HUGER	122,488,502-503	
	523,527,575,581	
. HUGH	38,87,108,117-118	
	146,249,454,519,611	
. J.	611	
. J.G.	611	
. JAMES	117,120,123,456	
	461	
. JAMES C.	120	
. JAMES H.	40	
. JAMES P.	634	
. JEHU	119	
. JESSE	117,123	
. JOHN	66,108,117-119	
	121,123,125	
. JULIA YOUNG	538	
. JULIUS	527	
. LAURA	474	
. LAWRENCE	120	
. LEILA	527	
. LIZZIE JONES	527	
. LUCY	333	
. LUCY ELLERBE	120	
. LUTHER	120	
. MAGGIE	502-503,527	
. MARTHA ANN	120	
. MARTHA HERRON	117-118	
. MARY	224	
. MARY E.	124	
. MARY E. HUNT	124	
. MARY JANE	120,455	
. MARY L.	124,455	
. MARY O. SELLERS	413	
. MARY SELLERS	124,136	
. MARY WHITE	527	
. MATTIE	124,463	
. MATTIE BEATY	124	
. MOLLIE	120,400	
. MOURNING ELIZ.- BAKER	117	
. NANCY	551	
. NANCY GASQUE	119,377	
. OLIVIA	503	
. OLIVIA FLOWERS	502	
. PRISCILLA JONES	117	
. RHODA CRAWFORD	146	
. ROBERT	119,124,456,527	
	643	
. SALLIE ELLERBE	120	
. SARAH	120-121,217	
. SARAH ANN	129	
. SARAH ANN ATKINSON	489	
. SARAH COX	120,330	
. SARAH FLADGER	491	
. STEPHEN	117,119,121	
	428-429	
. STEPHEN G.	119,330	
. STEPHEN T.	123	
. SUSY	503	
. T.W.	551	
. THOMAS	11,117-121	
	123-125,129,223-224	
	377,460,491,524,565	
	568,575	
. THOMAS CARROLL	124,413	
. THOMAS N.	124,413	
. THOMAS W.	120-121	
. TOM CAT	125	
. VICTORIA	120-121,324	
. VINCENT	460,474,489	
. W.H.	413	
. WADE	461	
. WALTER	120	
. WARREN	461	
. WATIES	122,527	
. WILLIAM	120	
. WILLIAM ELI	490	
. WILLIAM H.	120,124,411	
	429,455,463	
. WILLIE	216	
. WILLIE A.	333	
. Z.	583,626	
. ZACHARIAH	117,122-123	
. ZACK	502-503	
GODDARD,	523	
. N.B.	642	
GODFREY,	9,77,160,451	
. RICHARD	565	
GOFF,AZARIAH	578	
. HENRY	579	
. J.	630	
. JAMES	579	
GOODMAN,EDITH	136	
GOODYEAR,	193,637	
. A.M.	646	
. ELIAS	192,616	
. ELIZABETH FORD	170	
. GRACE	192	
. HARMAN	192	
. JOHN	174-175,178,192	
. JOHN EMORY	587	
. LOVE	191-192	

Name	Page
. MADISON	192
. SALLIE	210
. WILLIAM	170,192,210
GORDON,	446
. A.B.	641
. ALFRED B.	642
. J.J.	641
GORE,	266
GORHAM,	221
GOUD,S.	583
GOURDIN,	570
. E.H.	567
GRAHAM,	465,571
. ANNE M.	447
. ANNIE BROWN	380
. C.	143,456,551
. DUGALD	597
. E.	634
. ELLEN HARLLEE	348
. HERBERT C.	143
. JAMES	446,527,568,634
. JOHN	380
. JOHN M.	595
. MARY J.	446
. R.F.	97,567,571
. REBECCA BROWN	380
. RHODA WHITE	527
. ROBERT F.	348
. SARAH JANE	143
. WILLIAM H.	623
. WILLIAM R.	621
GRAINGER,	192
. LEVI	167
GRANER,JOHN	579
GRANGER,SAMUEL P.	622
GRANT,	486,570
GRANTHAM,	518
. ANNE	499
. BRIGHT	500
. E. BRIGHT	622
. ELIAS	176,621
. ELIZABETH ANN-GADDY	176
. ELIZABETH GADDY	178
. HENRY	531
. JULIA SNIPES	531
. OWEN	178,499
. PINCKNEY	622
. WILLIAM B.	175
GRANVILLE,	4
GRAVES,	107-108,135,137,448
. ANSEYER	622
. GEORGE	579
. GEORGE S.	622
. W.M.	634
GRAY,	463
. FRANKLIN	597
. HENRY	598
. J.	579
GREELEY,HORACE	144,250
GREEN,	99
GREENE,	462
. NATHANIEL	545
GREENWOOD,	
. ADDIE BERRY	269
. ADDIE HAYES	285
. AMANDA	285
. DAWSON	284
. DONALDSON	285
. E.B.	633
. ELLY	275
. ELLY B.	285,620
. FRANK	284-285
. J.R.	645
. JAMES	269,285
. JAMES L.	623,643
. MARY	284
. NANCY NICHOLSON	275
. W.D.	611
. WILLIAM	284
GREGG,	25,52,108,159,177,193,491,494,503,518,613
. A. STUART	591
. A.E.	600
. ALEXADNER	503
. ALEXANDER	566,568
. ALEXANDER L.	84
. ANN	356,510
. ANN GODBOLD	503
. ANNA	510
. BELLE	510
. BISHOP	29-30,75-78,105,107,110,117-118,125,135-140,142,147-148,158-159,197,213,241,242,386-388,445,448
. C.E.	51
. CHARLES E.	614
. CHERRY GODBOLD	503
. D. REESE	51
. DIXON	463
. E.	585
. ED W.	539
. ELEANOR	366
. ELIZABETH McMILLAN	425
. EVANDER	51
. EZRA M.	51
. FRANCIS M.	643
. G. COOPER	51
. HEZEKIAH	539
. J. ELI	539
. JIMMY	511-512
. JOHN	566
. JOHN W.	593
. KEENE	539
. LENA	511
. LIZZIE	510
. MAXCY	120,455,485
. MELVINA	456
. McFADDEN	593
. NANNETTE	510
. NANNIE	376,511
. O.S.	51,456
. R.J.	126,356,463,512,522
. R.W.	600
. ROBERT	425,503
. ROBERT E.	510
. ROBERT EVANS	510-511
. ROBERT H.	51
. ROBERT J.	510
. ROBERT JAMES	510
. S.A.	51
. SERENA	510,522
. SMILEY A.	593
. SUSAN	463
. SUSAN STEVENSON	463
. THOMAS	511
. THOMAS C.	592,607
. THOMAS E.	613
. W.C.	425
. WALTER	51,593
. WESLEY	510
. WESLEY L.	607
. WESLEY W.	366
. WILLIAM	510,600
. WILLIAM B.	643
. WILLIAM W.	585
. WILLIAM WESLEY	510
GREGGS,E.E.	645
GRICE,	165
. A.E.	521,566,571
. AUGUSTUS E.	209
. ELLEN	208
. GEORGE	579
. IRIS	521
. MOURNING LEWIS	481
. PERSEUS L.	209
. W.H.	208,427,481,551,566
. WILLIAM H.	88,209
GRIFFIN,ALLEN	430
. EMMA J. WILLIAMSON	430
. JAMES	583
. MARY	207
. STEPHEN	583
GRIFFITH,	205
GRIMES,	436
GRIMSLEY,JAMES	637
GROOM,M.	645
GUERARD,BENJAMIN	569
GUERY,ALBERT	450
. EVA DAVIS	450
GUNTER,D.	627
. H.	629
. WILLIAM	607

GURLY, ANN	352	
. JOSEPH	352	
GUY, J.H.	595	
GUYTON, ELLA	457	
HAGOOD,	350,596	
. JOHNSON	570	
HAINES, J.B.	641	
HAIR, JAMES	575	
HAIRGROVE,		
HULDAH	276,490	
. MARY JACKSON	276	
. STEPHEN A.	275-276,489	
	643	
. THOMAS H.	276	
HALE, RICHARD W.	620	
. SAMUEL	579	
HALL,	284	
. MARK	578	
HAM, CHARLES W.	607	
. KITSEY	206	
. SMITHY	206	
HAMER,		
. ALICE RICHARDSON	40	
	233,461	
. ANNIE PRICE	202	
. BROOKS	234	
. CHARLES	235	
. E.R.	346	
. ED	40	
. ED R.	152	
. EDWARD R.	461	
. ELIZABETH ANN	232	
. FANNIE FLADGER	233	
. FANNIE LYLES	233	
. J.H.	611	
. JAMES	234	
. JESSE	235	
. JOHN	232-233,235,403	
	461	
. JOHN B.	156,235	
. JOHN DAVID	233	
. JOHN H.	40,50,232-233	
	239,385,461	
. JOHN J.	397	
. JULIA BERRY	152,461	
. L.D.	232	
. M.R.	346	
. MARY	233	
. MARY C.	461	
. MARY POLLY		
BETHEA	232	
. MISSOURI	237	
. MISSOURI BETHEA	233	
	397	
. MISSOURI R.	50,280	
. MISSOURI ROBERT	233	
	397	
. MOLLIE THOMPSON	232	
. ORIANNA	239,461	
. OVIANNA	461	
. P.B.	568,571	
. POLLY BETHEA	403	
. R.C.	348	
. R.P.	291,294,308,327	
	343,559-560,613	
. ROBERT C.	232-234	
. ROBERT P.	51,232-234	
	348,364	
. TRISTRAM	232,461	
. TRISTRAM B.	40	
. W.M.	51	
. WILLIAM M.	234	
HAMILTON,	249	
. ALEXANDER	82-83	
. ALLEN	247	
. ARTHUR	247	
. BERTHA	404	
. BRYANT	247	
. DAYTON V.	247	
. EDWARD	579	
. IRA	247	
. JAMES	569	
. JASPER	248	
. JOHN	247-248,598	
. JOHN H.	247	
. NELLIE BETHEA	248,404	
. PAUL	569	
. PERRY	247	
. REBECCA J. FORE	248	
. REBECCA		
JANE FORE	219	
. SALLIE	404	
. STEPHEN	247	
. THOMAS	219	
. THOMAS F.	248	
. TOBIAS	247-248,623	
. TOBIS	598	
. TRISTRAM	248,404,598	
. W. WARREN	620	
. W.W.	219,249	
. WARLEY	248	
. WHITNER	634	
. WHITTINGTON	247-248	
	280	
. WHITTON	598	
. WILLIAM	247-248,280	
	331	
. WILLIAM K.	247	
. WILLIAM W.	248	
. WILLIAM WARREN	247	
HAMMOND, J.H.	569	
HAMPTON,	96,102-103	
. G.W.	583	
. GEORGE	595	
. THOMAS	595	
. W.	583	
. WADE	101,104,358,570	
HANNA, ERVIN	641	
. J.B.	641	
. W.J.	571	
HANNAH, JOHN G.	617	
HARGOOD,	289	
HARGROVE, A.L.	646	
. ASA	295	
. FLORA McCORMICK	295	
. ISSAC H.	598	
. JOHN C.	295	
. KENNETH	237	
. N.N.	611	
. THOMAS	222	
. W.H.	634	
. WILLIAM	634	
HARLEE, ANNE	345	
. DAVID S.	345	
. ELIZABETH	345	
. HARRIET	345	
. JOHN	345	
. JOHN ANNE	345	
. LUCRETIA	345	
. PETER	345	
. ROBERT	345	
. THOMAS	345	
. W.W.	571	
. WILLIAM W.	345	
HARLEY,	345	
. PETER	342	
. ROBERT	342,345	
. THOMAS	62	
HARLLEE,	14-15,101,117	
	342,362,414,507	
. A.T.	287-288,291,293	
	317,320,351,354	
. AGNES	351	
. ALICE BULLOCK	351	
. AMELIA	351	
. AMELIA CANNON	352	
. AMELIA HOWARD	352	
. ANDREW C.	351	
. ANDREW T.	349,590	
. ANN ELIZA	351	
. ANN FULMORE	349	
. ANN GURLY	352	
. ANN LEAKE	343	
. ANNE	349	
. ANNIE	353-354	
. ARTHUR	352	
. BETTIE	351	
. CHARLES STUART	353	
. D.S.	38,347-348,565	
. DAVID	582	
. DAVID S.	347	
. DAVID STUART	346	
. EDWARD PORCHER	353	
. ELIZABETH	347,353-354	
	413	
. ELIZABETH STUART	344	
. ELLEN	343,348	
. FLORENCE	353	
. HARRIET	354	
. HARRIET BARNES	346	

. HARRY T.	352	HARRALSON,E.		. JULIA ANN	
. HATTIE	352	PRESTON	592	ROBERTS	210
. HORACE E.	351	. M. JACKSON	592	. LEWIS	255,257,566
. JAMES	353	HARREL,	453,466	. MACK	421
. JAMES J.	262,346,348, 571	. ANNA ISGAT	456	. MARTHA J.	489
. JANE	343	. ANNIE GODBOLD	121	. MARY JANE	256
. JOHN	343-344,351	. ELIZABETH JONES	456	. PERCY	487
. JOHN W.	288,349-350, 596	. EMMA BETHEA	403	. PRUDENCE	256,515
		. EPHRAIM	456	. PRUDENCE-WILLIAMSON	431
. JULIA	348	. FRANCES MAURICE	456	. SAMUEL	256
. LIZZIE	353	. FRANK	374	. SARAH	440
. LOUISA	352	. FRED	374	. STEPHEN	257
. MARGARET McCOLL	347	. GEORGE W.	456	. STEPHEN H.	258
. MARTHA SHAKELFORD	353	. JAMES	121,374	. THERESA	256
		. JOE	374	. TIMOTHY	575
. MARY ANN	347	. LEVI	456	. ZEPHANIAH	257
. MARY ELLEN CURRY	350	. MARY FOXWORTH	374	HARRINGTON,	25,119
. MARY SCARBOROUGH	262	. SAMUEL	456-457	. JOHN T.	207,643
		. WILLIAM	403	. MARY GRIFFIN	207
. MATTIE	353	HARRELL,EPHRAIM	575	HARRIOT,	570
. PETER	342-343,348-351, 441	. M.W.	627	HARRIS,MARIA BETHEA	354
		. S.A.	646		
. PETER S.	591	HARRELLSON,		HARRISON,	285
. PETER STUART	351	BRIGAN J.	623	. WILLIAM HENRY	86
. PETER ZACK	349	. E. PRESTON	639		453-454
. R. ARMSTRONG	591	. ED H.	617	HARRLESON,CHARLES	256
. R.Z.	111,626	. GEORGE W.	617	. JOHN	256
. ROBERT	38,91,144,345, 352,427,434,566,568	. JAMES	639	. LEWOS	256
		. JOHN B.	623	. MAHALA ROGERS	256
. ROBERT ARMSTRONG	352	. JOHN C.	617	HASELDEN,	491
		. SIM	636	. ALONZO	217
. ROBERT E.	349	. STEPHEN	617	. ANNA	224,239
. ROBERT Z.	349	. THOMAS	617	. ANNE	217
. SALLIE	349,352	. W.W.	639	. C. EDGAR	217
. SUSAN A. MUNNERLYN	349	HARRELSON,	182,309,370, 392,441,443,485,487	. C.B.	224
				. CARRIE	41,225
. THOMAS	11-12,39,84-85, 160,247,277,294,343, 344,348-349,352-353, 354,413,564,566,568	. A.H.	210	. CHARLES	217,219, 224-225
		. ALFRED H.	257		
		. BENJAMIN	62,255,257, 575	. CYRUS B.	223-224,230, 319,411,614
		. D.J.	599		
. THOMAS HENRY	347	. DAVID J.	256	. CYRUS COX	330
. THOMAS M.	349	. G.W.	600	. DELLA GEORGE	278
. W.W.	11-12,38,71,101, 157,277,315,348,352, 566-568	. GEORGE	256	. EDWARD	639
		. H.G.	431	. ELIZABETH GODBOLD	223,526
		. HAM	257		
. WALTER C.	352	. HUGH	255-257,645	. FANNIE	224,411
. WILLIAM C.	351	. HUGH G.	256	. FRANK	224,411
. WILLIAM F.	347	. HUGH H.	489,515	. GUY	217
HARNAGOR,	453	. J.C.	264	. H.G.	583
HARPER,	268,288	. J.D.	457	. HUGH	341
. G.W.	611	. JACK	257	. HUGH G.	223-224
. ISAAC	645	. JAMES W.	257	. J. DUDLEY	156,225
. J.M.	611	. JESSEE	584	. J.D.	41,560,567
. JOHN M.	603	. JOEL	257,591	. J.G.	41,567,583
. WILLIAM	73,84	. JOHN C.	498	. JAMES	39,133,214,217, 223-225,239,245,329, 567,632,634
HARRAL,EPHRAIM	595	. JOHN E.	256-257,284		
. N.W.	595	. JOHN ELLIS	256	. JAMES DUDLEY	225
. W.T.	595	. JOHN R.	257	. JAMES G.	145,224-225

. JANE	127,152-153	. G.	268	. C.	634
	223-225	. H.	611	. D.H.	611
. JOHN	223-224,278,329	. HAMILTON R.	268	. DAVID PINCKNEY	587
	411	. HARDY	638	. E. WILAON	172
. JULIA ELLERBE	217,225	. HENRY	267,271	. E. WILSON	171
. L.B.	41	. HENRY C.	269	. E.W.	258,634
. L.M.	41	. HUMBERT	268	. EBBEN	96,567
. LABENNON BASS	224	. IDA	270	. ELIZABETH ANN-	
. LAWRENCE BENTON	225	. JAMES	267-268,270-271	ROGERS	171
. LEBANON BASS	230	. JAMES ADGER	268	. ELIZABETH	
. LIZZIE	529	. JAMES N.	268	FORD	168,171
. LUCY	224,411	. JAMES S.	269	. ELIZABETH	
. LUTHER M.	225	. JESSEE H.	268	ROBERTS	172,212
. MAGGIE	133,219,224,319	. JOE	613	. FANNY	172
	411	. JOHN	267-268,270,276	. GAMEWELL	171
. MARY	217	. JOHN C.	269,277-278	. H.R.	153,634
. MARY EDWARDS	156,225		285	. HAMILTON R.	400
. MARY GODBOLD	224	. JOHN DAVID	268	. HENRY	211
. MARY WHITE	527	. JOHN G.	267	. INA	172
. REBECCA DUDLEY	225	. JOSEPH D.	268	. INA REMBERT	172
. ROSA SNIPES	529	. L.G.	268	. J.	611
. SALLIE FINKLEA	224,411	. LEVI G.	268	. J.D.	610,645
. SAMUEL	217	. LEVI H.	267-268	. JAMES	171
. SARAH	214,224-225	. LEWIS E.	269	. JAMES S.	156
. STEPHEN F.G.	639	. MARINA DEW	267	. JESSEE	171,340,587
. THOMAS	217	. MARY	270	. JESSEE H.	634
. WILLIAM	223-224	. MARY ANN STUBBS	269	. JOHN C.	152-153,199
	329-330,527,529	. MARY ELLEN	269		402
. WILLIAM E.	225	. MILLS	267	. JOSEPH B.	171-172,178
. WILLIAM W.	639	. NEWTON	269		188,212,484
HATCHEL,B. PLEASANT	643	. NICHOLAS W.	268	. L.B.	583
. CHARLOTTE		. REBECCA FORE	270	. LEVI	246
COLEMAN	473	. RICH	268,272	. LEVI H.	166,171-172
. JANE GASQUE	376	. ROBERT H.	268		178,326
. JOHN	473	. ROBERT R.	637	. LEWIS	171
. JOHN A.	376	. RUTHERFORD B.	103	. MARY	199
HATCHELL,BENJAMIN	376	. S.P.	609	. MARY ELLEN	152
. MARTHA ANN		. SARAH JANE	269	. MATTIE	172
GASQUE	376	. T.B.	599	. MURRAY	172
HATCHER,R.	646	. THOMAS C.	269	. N.	611
HAUSEA,HESTER	532	. WILLIAM	267-268,270	. NICHOLAS W.	623,634
HAWES,	581-582		611	. O.C.	171
HAWKINS,H.	630	. WILLIAM B.	637	. ORILLA	172
HAY,	435,437	. WILSON	268	. R.H.	634
HAYES,A.G.	268	HAYNE,H.E.	96	. R.R.	179
. A.T.	636	. HENRY E.	94-95,97,568	. REBECCA BERRY	153
. ADDIE	285	. ROBERT Y.	84,569	. SALLIE	390,498
. ALLEN	638	. W.A.	567	. SARAH NANCE	172
. ANN ELIZA	260	. W.E.	99	. T.B.	45,171-172,186
. ANN ELIZABETH	268	. WILLIAM E.	99		212,623
. B.F.	272	HAYNES,JAMES	645	. TRISTAM	172
. BENJAMIN F.	268	. JAMES W.	643	. W. DWIGHT	587
. CHARLES W.	268	HAYS,	148,153,157,186	. W.B.	166,326
. COBURN	269	. ALECK	171	. W.C.	634
. DANIEL S.	638	. ALEXANDER	212	. W.D.B.	211,354
. DAVID S.	269-270	. ALEXANDER G.	623	. W.H.	611
. DWIGHT	267	. ANNIE	172	. W.M.	634
. EBBEN	267-268,271	. BEN	390	. WALKER	172
. ELLY	638	. BENJAMIN	170,172,178	. WALKER HAYS	172
. ERASTUS W.	268		258,498	. WILLIAM	485

. WILLIAM B.	172,178,404	. EDWARD	598	. JAMES	646
. WILLIAM H.	168,171	. FRANK	638	. JERRY	516
. WILLSON	623	. HARMON	598	HOLLAND,GEORGE	595
. WILSON	149-150,172,210	. JAMES	639	. J.H.	641
	584,610	. JANE	168	. J.S.	595
HAYWOOD,JAMES	575	. JOHN	424	HOLLIDAY,J.G.	450
. JOHN W.	575	. JOHN C.	633	. JESSEE G.	450
HAZELTON,HUGH	579	. JOHN T.	638	. SALLIE DAVIS	450
HEAD,WELLINGTON	646	. KATE DUBOIS	424	HOLT,	571
HEARSEY,W.	610	. MADGE McDUFFIE	319	HOME,WILLIAM	579
HEARSY,W.	611	. MARCUS C.	633	HONEYCUT,	476
. WILLIAM H.	611	. MILES	617	HONOUR,CARRIE	405
HEMINGWAY,	490,570	. McSWAIN	639	. JOHN H.	405
. WILSON	566	. PINCKNEY L.	575	HOOD,	244,545
HENAGAN,B.K.	88-89	. SAMUEL	603	HOOK,	
	214-215,539,568-569	HERRON,MARTHA	117-118	LENNIE I. ROWELL	471
HENDERSON,		HERTZ,H.	600	HORN,	162,178
ALEXANDER	248	HESELDEN,LUTHER M.	51	. DANIEL	48
. ROBERT	354	HEWETT,THOMAS	607	. ELGAT	48
HENDRICKS,		. W.C.	581	. ELGATE	174
THOMAS A.	350	HEWIT,LOLA JONES	190	. J.M.	601
HENEGAN,B.K.	42	. W.L.	243	. NEAL	617
. BOB	43	. WILLIAM E.	190	. WILLIAM PINCKNEY	617
. J. HAMILTON	577	HEYMAN,BENJAMIN	639	HORRY,	112,491,528,533
. R.Y.	42-43	. EPHRAIM	639	HORTON,NICHOLAS	613
HENRY,	497	. GILBERT	639	. THOMAS T.	598
. CHARLOTTE BETHEA	262	. JOHN	639	HOWARD,A.H.	567
	397	HEYWARD,	133	. A.J.	50
. D.S.	502	HICKS,JOHN C.	603	. AMELIA	352
. DAVID S.	262-263	. N.C.	640	. ANTHONY	99
. ELLA	263	HILL,	268,426	. CHARLES	352
. JACK	262	. ADALINE	266	. MELVINA	352
. JOHN	261-262	. CHARLES	266	. R.	583
. JOHN E.	261-263,397	. EDWARD	617	. R.G.	11,51,99,515
	502	. ELIZABETH			567-568
. MARY	262	HUGGINS	266	. RICHARD	303
. PATRICK	262	. JAMES	587	. RICHARD G.	352,605
. SHEPPARD	262	. JOHN	266	. SOPHIA	303
. TELATHA FLOWERS	262	HILLSBORO,	558	HOYT,HUGH	634
	502	HINDES,ALEXANDER	579	. WASHINGTON	634
HENSEY,	393	HINDS,H.N.	630	HUBBARD,J.G.	611
HERBERT,C.C.	647	. J.D.	583	HUCKABEE,JOHN	603
HERLONG,JAMES	634	. R.	583	HUCKS,	356
HERREN,J.P.	627	. RESTER	578	. A.P.	380
. W.P.	627	. S.O.	630	. ARTHUR	356
HERRIN,A.W.	623	HINTON,JESSEE W.	592	. JOHN R.	116,605
. ALLISON W.	607	HODGE,CHARLES	579	. MARTHA	
. CHESTLEY	617	. SAMUEL	207	WOODBERRY	356
. DAVID F.	607	HODGES,	450,508	. OLIVE GASQUE	374
HERRING,	247,279-280,340	. BARNEY	595	. ROBERT	116
	425	. J.	626	. W.W.	116
. ARTHUR	638	. JOHN	588	HUDSON,ELI T.	643
. C.S.	424	. JOHN H.	617	. J.H.	571
. CHARLES	424	. ROBERT	623	. JOSHUA H.	298
. CLINTON	639	. SAMUEL	506	. RICHARD	68
. D.M.	634	HOGES,PINCKNEY	617	HUETT,WILLIAM L.	470
. DANIEL M.	598	HOGG,M.T.	630	HUGER,	559
. EBBY B.	604	HOLDEN,	467,543	HUGGINS,	468,497,524
. ED B.	592	. E.	600	. A.H.	601
. EDMUND	638	. J.	601	. BIRD	617

. CAROLINE NORTON 266
                           478
. CHARLES   244
. CHRISTOPHER   572
. CHRISTOPHER C.   588
. D.A.   267
. DOC   604
. DOCK   244
. E.T.   357
. EBBEN   263-264
. ELIZABETH   266
. EMMA   488
. ENOS   263-264
. ENOS T.   643
. FRANK   184
. GEORGE   263
. GEORGE W. 244,264,591
                       602
. HENRY   174,263
. J.   601
. JACK   244,263,475
. JASPER A.   588
. JESSE   266
. JOHN   244,263-264
       266-267,392,486,498
. JOHN C.   475
. JOHN D.   620
. JOHN J.   617
. JOSEPHINE   487
. JUDSON   267
. LEVI   617
. LEWIS   266,476,478
. LOU   244
. LOUISA   244
. MARTHA   263
. MARY CAMPBELL   486
. MARY JONES   244,264
. MARY POLLY   264
. MEILL   267
. N.C.   601
. NANCY   266,477
. NANCY ANN
       CAMPBELL   486
. NEAL C.   617
. NEILL C.   267
. OLIVE NORTON   476
. POLLY   265-266,392,498
. R.   584
. S. LEWIS   575
. SALLIE JOHNSON   357
. SOLOMON   243,263
. T.   601
. T.F.   611
. THEOPHILUS   263-264
. THOMAS   611
. THOMAS A.   263
. W.S.A.   641
. WESLEY   575
. WILLIAM D.   575
. WILLIAM E.   603

. WILLIS   263,266,477,486
. ZILPHA   244
HUGHES,   462
. GEORGE W.   593
. R.D.   595
HULIN,   193,386
HULON,   139
. E.   611
. ELIJAH   617
. WILLIAM   611
. WYLIE   598
HUMPHREY,WINNIE   177
HUNCHY,ELIZABETH   545
HUNT,CHARLES   634
. CORNELIUS   613
. GEORGE   634
. J.E.   611
. JAMES E.   604
. MARY E.   124
. P.O.   634
HUNTER,   106,109,338
. ANGELINE WHITE   526
. COSTA JONES   204
. COSTARICCA JONES 526
. DAWSON   595
. HATTIE GAME   487
. J.   583
. JAMES   526
. JOSEPH   526
. MARY   526
. ROBERT   135,137-138,448
. STEPHEN   526
. T.   645
. WILLIAM   526
HURSEY,J.H.   559
HUTAFF,LUCY
    FOXWORTH   522
HUTCHERSON,ED B.   617
. JOHN W.   617
. N.P.   630
HUTCHINSON,ARTHUR   376
. JOHN   191
. MARY GASQUE   376
. RIX   643
. WILLIAM J.D.   639
HUTCHISON,E.B.   641
. GEORGE   595
. JOHN   641
. L.N.   641
. SAMUEL   595
. W.C.   595
HUX,   433,520
. SARAH WALL   432
. WILLIAM R.   432
HYAT,DAVID   598
. HUGH   598
. JAMES K.   598
. JOHN   598
. JOHN C.D.   598
. SOLOMAN   598

HYATT,   247
. ERVIN   623
. HUGH   634
. ISAAC   611
. JAMES R.   623
. JOHN   634
. OLIVER   623
. PETER P.   621
. THOMAS R.   623
. WILLIAM   621
. WILLIAM H.   611
HYMAN,BENJAMIN   595
. C.E.   595
. CAUSEA   643
. J.L.   641
. W.L.   640
. WILLIAM   630
IKENOR,CHARITY   532
IKNER,JAMES   634
INGLIS,   182
. JOHN A.   72-73,571
. W.C.   571
INMAN,
. ANNA JANE GADDY   177
. MARY GADDY   177
IRBY,   398
IRWIN,JAMES R.   604
ISEMAN,   71-72
. I.   551
. LIGHTFOOT   551
. M.   551
ISGAT,ANNA   456
ISRAEL,ANCIL   639
. WRIGHT   639
IVEY,   266
. BERRY   588
. MAGGIE   150
. SARAH   477
. W.A.   299
JACKSON,   268,345
. A.J.   611
. A.W.   611
. AGENORA   277
. AGENORA A.   278
. ALEXANDER   645
. AMELIA   277
. ANDERSON W.   277
. ANDREW   84,115
. ANDREW K.   579
. ANNE   279
. ANNE ADAMS   277
. ARTHUR   279
. ASBURY   443
. B.B.   611
. B.F.   611
. BILL   249
. CHARLES T.   598
. DILLA McKENZIE 237,280
. EDWARD   236,276
                   279-280

. EDWARD M. 276-277	. J.H. 645	. E.W. 566
. ELIZABETH 237	. JAMES V. 607	. EDWARD EVANDER 357
. ELLEN ADAMS 277	. JOSEPH 588	. EDWARD W. 539
. EMERY 236	. MARGARET A. 504	. ELIZA DAVIS 451
. ERVIN 276,280-281	. MARY 504	. ELIZA NORTON 478
. ERVIN M. 236-237,280	. MARY BROWN 378	. ELIZABETH ANN-
. F.M. 611	. PRESTON 378,579	WOODBERRY 356
. FRANK M. 279	. ROBERT 579,592	. ELLA PAGE 357
. HENRY 248,280	. SARAH ANN 504	. EMMA RICHARDSON 461
. J.K. 646	. SIMPSON T. 588	. F.A. 629
. J.R. 634	. THOMAS L. 642	. FLORA 461
. JAMES 279-280	. WILLIAM 588	. FLORENCE 408,516
. JAMES R. 277,598	. WILLIAM P. 575	. G.W. 601
. JEFF 645	. WILSON 378	. GEORGE 634
. JEFFERSON A. 277	JARNIGAN,	. GILBERT D. 478
. JOHN 276,279-280,611	. ALICE BAILEY 245	. H.R. 646
. JOHN C. 598	. B.W. 245	. HARDY 197,540,614
. JOHN M. 279-280	. J.E. 147,245,568	. HEZEKIAH 51
. JOHN R. 280,436	. MARY POLLY JONES 245	. HUGH G. 623
. JOHN T. 598	. SARAH ELLEN 245	. HUGH R. 104,110,244
. L. 646	JARRALL,J.J. 630	357,478
. LEVI 248,604	JARRAT,J. ALLSTON 605	. J. MONROE 647
. MALCOLM 248,604	JARRATT,CHARLES ED. 607	. J.F. 634
. MARY 276	JAMES B. 607	. J.J. 630
. MISSOURI 277,279	JASPER,A.W. 601	. J.M. 98,369,461,571
. NICHOLAS 604	JEFFERSON,THOMAS 83	. J.W. 400,571
. OWEN 172,237,248,276	JENKINS, 107,111-113,288	. JAMES 400,451
280	. ELLA 40,449	. JOHN M. 461,567
. PRESTON B. 277	. JAMES 40,110,114,355	. JOHN W. 567
. REUBEN 276,279,639	357,449	. JOSEPH 451,538-539
. REUBEN B. 236,331	. JIMMY 505	. LEWIS 540,542
. ROBERT 248,604	. MARTHA 466	. LILLY SNIPES 531
. S.S. 609,611	. MARY 429	. LOUISE 461
. SALLIE McEACHERN 436	. ROBERT 631	. MAGGIE MAY 357
. SARAH A. McKENZIE 280	. ROBERT W. 591	. MARGARET F. 104
. SARAH ANN	JERNAGEN,CEILA 309	. MARGARET F.-
McKENZIE 236,237	JOHN,IDA BLUE 131	WOODBERRY 357
. SELKIRK 623	. JAMES 131	. MARY L. SNIPES 531
. SUSAN CARMICHAEL 443	. PETER 131	. MARY
. SYDNEY E. 269,277	. SALLIE BLUE 131	THOMPSON 541-542
. THOMAS 236,280	JOHNS,JAMES H. 81	. NATHANIEL 35,569
. W. 646	JOHNSON, 75-76,212,383	. P. 584
. WARREN A. 598	392,395,431,518,523	. P.C. 630
. WARREN R. 276-279	593,595	. PALMER 461
. WILLIAM 248,276	. A.G. 538-539	. PETER P. 143
279-280	. A.P. 370,515,531,601	. PRUDENCE
. WILLIAM J. 623	. ALEXANDER 48,540-542	HARRELSON 256,515
. WILLIAM R. 276	. ALGERNON SYDNEY 477	. RICHARD M. 86
. WILLIAM T. 237	. ALICE 461	. RICHARD OLIN 357
JACOBS,M. 575	. ALLEN 540,542	. RICHARDSON 461
JAMES, 125,142,378,431	. ANDREW 59-60,87,307	. ROBERT 3,461,569
473	316,570	. ROLLIN KEMBALL 531
. ADDINGTON 466	. ANNE 540	. SALLIE 357,458-459
. ANN 504	. BARNEY 635	. SAMUEL 141
. BENJAMIN 457	. BRIGHTY EVELYN 531	. SAMUEL A. 357
. CELIA PHILIPS 466	. CAREY 540,623	. SAMUEL CAREY 540
. G.T. 601	. CHARLOTTE	. SAMUEL S. 623
. H.L. 584	STANLEY 461	. SARAH 110,356
. HENRY 504	. DAVID 73,197,539-540	. SUSANNA 194
. HENRY L. 504	569,617	. SUSANNAH 540

. T.H.	599,630	. JAMES A.	243,263,575	. W.		612	
. THOMAS	539		612	. W.E.		630	
. W.D.	99,400,567,571	. JAMES E.	149,244-245	KEEFFE,ELIZABETH	502		
. W.R.	507,539	. JAMES R.	171	KEELYN,JOHN G.	588		
. WHITEFORD F.	357	. JENNETTE GASQUE	375	KEENE,		539	
. WILLIAM	516,539,588	. JEPTHA	464	. ANNE		449	
. WILLIAM H.	356	. JESSEE	592	. BROCKINGHAM	491		
. WILLIAM R.	91,451,538	. JOHN	176-177,225	. ROCKINGHAM	167		
	567-568		241-243,245,375	KEEVER,DANIEL A.	635		
. WILLIAM		. JOHN D.	243-244	. ELLEN		434	
WOODBERRY	357	. JOHN S.	624	. SALLIE		470	
. ZENO	540	. JOHN THOMAS	243	KEIGHLY,		138,141	
. ZEUS	623	. JOSEPH	242	KEIGHTLEY,J.G.	630		
JOHNSTON,	133	. KENDREE	190,243	KEITH,		184,422,434	
. JOB	72-73,84	. LIZZIE	527	. DAVID L.	586		
. JOE	278	. LOLA	190	. ELI		589	
JOLLY,	380	. LUCY ELLEN	190	. EVANDER	588		
JOSEPH	143,454,567	. MARTHA HUGGINS	263	. JAMES		589	
JONES,	156,472	. MARY	243-244,264	. JESSEE		589	
. ALICE	205,368,462	. MARY POLLY	244-245	. PATIENCE FOWLER	483		
. ALLEN	527	. MATTHEW	171	KELLEY,JOHN A.	571		
. ANNA	472	. MINERVA LEWIS	483	KELLY,		123	
. BEVERLY	190,243	. NANCY	149,244-245	. DANIEL	579		
. BRYANT	148-149,200,225	. POLLY	149	. JOHN A.	43		
	241,243-245,272	. PRESLEY	204	KENADY,SALLIE	236		
. CHARLES	244	. PRISCILLA	117	KENEDY,		318	
. CHESLEY D.	475,614	. R. BOYD	243	KENNEDY,		353	
. CORA	205	. REAVES	171	. ALFRED	595		
. COSTA	204	. ROBERT BOYD	190,374	. ANDREW	595		
. COSTARICCA	526	. SALLIE	176,205,243	. EVANDER	617,635		
. D.M.	612	. SALLIE NICHOLS	243	KENNER,G.W.L.	630		
. EBBY	486	. SAMUEL	243-244	KERCHNER,F.W.	228		
. EBENEZER L.	617	. SARAH	190	KERSELY,EVIN	624		
. ELI	190,243	. SARAH ANN LANE	395	. WILLIAM	624		
. ELIJAH	645	. SARAH JONES	190	KERSEY,E.	595		
. ELIZABETH	177,200	. THEODOCIA	205	. H.		612	
	243-245,456	. THOMAS M.	241,243,245	. J.		612	
. ELIZABETH BERRY	148	. THOMAS N.	225	. M.		612	
	149,244	. W.D.B.	171	. S.D.		612	
. EUPHEMIA WATSON	153	. WESLEY	579,624	KERSHAW,	353		
. EVANDER	190,243,579	. WILLIAM	584	KIBBER,		106,109	
. F.D.	149,153,635	. WILLIAM N.	617	KIBLER,		106,109	
. FAMA WATSON	204,244	JORDAN,	252,444,477,495	KILGO,NETTIE BETHEA	203		
. FANNIE	243	. A. BENNETT	605	. PEARCE	399		
. FRANK	244	. BENNETT	220	. PIERCE F.	203		
. FRED D.	204,244,262	. ELIZABETH FORE	220	KIMBALL,			
	368,526	. GEORGE S.	605	. MARY WOODBERRY	356		
. FREDERIC D.	244,575	. JACOB	634	. R.H.		626	
. H.B.	612	. JOHN D.	431,643	. ROLLEN	356		
. H.D.	457	. JOHN J.	643	KINARD,JANIE DEW	274		
. HATTIE	244	. MARTHA EVANS	134,251	KING CHARLES,	2,113		
. HENRY	149,171	. MARY	429	KING GEORGE,	3,160,388		
. HENRY B.	244	. PAT EVANS	134	KING,		222,338,526,570	
. J.	627	. RICHARD	134,251	. SIMEON	584		
. J. THOMAS	190	. SARAH A.-		KINNEY,JOHN T.	411		
. J.J.	627	WILLIAMSON	431	. LUCINDA FINKLEA	411		
. J.L.	612	. W. KING	607	. MARY POLLY	238		
. J.O.	243	. WILLIAM	575	KINTON,STEPHEN	584		
. J.R.	263-264	KEEFE,D. FRANK	617	KIRBY,JOHN G.	272		
. J.T.	470	. ERVIN H.	617	KIRK,		596	

KIRLE, RICHARD	568	
KIRTON,	465	
. CATHERINE N. FLOYD	464	
. ELIZABETH	464-465	
. H.P.	646	
. HANNAH PHILIPS	464	
. HANNAH SINOTH	464	
. HENRY	464-465	
. JOHN	464	
. MARY	464-465	
. OLIVIA	465	
. OLIVIA GASQUE	464	
. PHILIP	464	
. SAMUEL	464-465	
. THOMAS	464	
. THOMAS H.	464-465,472,589	
. WILLIAM	464	
KIRVEN, ALFRED	185	
KIRVIN,	218	
. ALFRED	194	
. ELIZABETH TART	194	
. LUCINDA	194	
KITCHEN, CHARLES E.	624	
ELI	613	
KOLB,	242-243,387-388	
KOLLOCK,	570	
KYLE,	411	
LABORDE, JOHN B.	571	
LABRUCE, . HELEN COACHMAN	353	
LAMB,	333	
. ELIZABETH	217	
. LIZZIE MOODY	339	
. THOMAS A.	326	
. W.D.	339	
. WILLIAM D.	617	
LAMBERT,	466	
. ANN	504	
. B.F.	601	
. D.H.	627	
. E.H.	617	
. HARRISON	483	
. J.H.	627	
. JAMES	504	
. JERRY	184,495	
. JERRY H.	531	
. P.	627	
. ROBERT	575	
. SERENA ADELAIDE-SNIPES	531	
. WESLEY	617	
LAMMOND, . FLORA McMILLAN	422	
. HUGH	422	
LANDING, ELIZA	468	
LANE,	403-404,498	
. ADDISON	197	
. ADDISON L.	624	
. ALEXANDER	389,393-394
. ANNE	273
. BRYANT	218,271-274,393
. C.C.	645
. CHARITY GADDY	177
. CHARLOTTE	486
. CHARLOTTE GASQUE	376
. CORA COLEMAN	474
. CRAWFORD	394
. D.F.	621
. DAVID	389,395,579,589
. ELISHA	393
. ELIZABETH	389
. EVANDER	604
. FERDINAND	635
. FLORA	200
. FLORA BETHEA	272,401
. FLORA CAMPBELL	325-326,394
. FLORA ELLEN	273-274
. FRANK	376
. FRANKLIN	635
. FREDERIC	393
. G.W.	601
. GEORGE	188
. GEORGE W.	624
. HAPSEY	394
. HENRIETTA	218
. HENRIETTA DEW	271-272,393
. HENRY J.	395
. J.	601
. J.O.	612
. J.V.	612
. JAMES	326,389,394-395
. JAMES C.	312,394-395,415
. JAMES M.	617
. JIM	288,350
. JOHN	389,392
. JOHN G.	392
. JOHN O.	394
. JOSEPH	272-273,393
. JOSEPH V.	572
. KESIAH	273,389-390
. KITTY GASQUE	376
. L.L.	612
. LEMUEL	589
. LEONARD	394
. MARY EDWARDS	188
. MARY POLLY	273
. MITCHEL	377
. ORPHEA	394-395
. OSBORNE	142,386-390,392-395,415,497
. POLLY	415
. PRISCILLA	394-395
. R.C. GADDY	273
. R.L.	177,273
. ROBERT	389,393,395,635
. ROBERT L.	272-273,575
. S.D.	272,635
. SAMUEL	326,376,393,604
. SARAH ANN	395
. SARAH ANNE	394
. SARAH COWARD	393
. STEPHEN	326,389,395
. STEPHEN D.	272-273,393
	401
. STEPHEN L.	325,394,624
. SUE	474
. THOMAS	389,392-393
. VERNER	273
. WILLIAM	325,389,393,395,617
. WILLIAM B.	393
LASSITER, JENNIE	155
LATTA, JOHN H.	51
LAW, C.C.	429
. DESDA GIBSON	429
. E.A.	571
. JUNIUS H.	143
LAWRIMORE, GUS	645
. JOHN	646
LAWSON, . HALLIE COVINGTON	348
. LUCY NICHOLS	190
. WILLIAM	348
LEACH, DUNCAN N.	589
. JAMES MADISON	589
. JOHN	589
. JULIUS	595
LEAKE, ANN	343
LEDINGHAM, ELIZABETH	373
. T.J.	373
. THERESA ANN-LEGETTE	373
LEE,	64,313,350,381,486
. BENJAMIN	542
. BETSY SMITH	496
. CALVIN	238,375,496
. CHRISTOPHER	624
. CURTIS	643
. ELLY	496
. FRANCES GASQUE	375
. H.	599
. HIRAM	172,481
. J.W.	641
. JAMES	496
. JAMES W.	238,624
. JOHN	394
. JOHN E.	624
. LIZZIE	496
. MASON	517
. N.C.	630
. R.W.	624
. ROBERT E.	477

. T.T.	612	. MARY ADELAINE-		. DICEY FLOYD	481
. TELATHA	496	WAYNE	368	. DIO	481
. W.F.	612	. MARY JANE		. EBBEN	526
. WILLIS	496	McARTHUR	299	. ELIZA JANE-	
LEGETTE,	146,376,435,455	. MARY WATSON	204	STACKHOUSE	482
	462	. MAY	372	. ERNEST	482
. A.S.	303	. MELVINA	369-370	. EVAN	222,482-483
. ABNER	369-370,373	. MORGAN	369,578	. FERABA	
. ALTHEA		. NELSON	373,460	STRICKLAND	482
ALFORD	284,370	. RINGOLD	373	. FLORA	481
. AMELIA	129,372	. ROBERT	372	. FLORA CARMICHAEL	444
. ANDREW	204	. SALATHIEL	204		481
. ANN	367,371-372	. SALLIE	309	. HARDEE	589
. ANNA	182,369-370	. SARAH ELLEN	204	. HARDY	481,501
. ANNE	303	. T.J.	299	. HERBERT	481
. ARMAN C.	373	. THERESA A.	373	. ISAAC	481
. ARMAND C.	368	. THERESA ANN	367,373	. J. WESLEY	482
. ASHLEY S.	373	. THERESA ANNA	371	. J.J.	646
. CHARLOTTE-		. VIRGIE	297	. J.R.	630
RICHARDSON	460	. VIRGIL	373	. J.W.P.	624
. CIVIL	300	. W.	627	. JAMES	481
. CLARA L.	370	. WILLIAM	373	. JANIE STACKHOUSE	361
. DAVID	129,367,369-373	. WOODSON	373	. JOEL	222,476,481-483
	447,460	LEGGETT,A.R.	645	. JOEL J.	482
. EBBY	551	LEIGH,		. JOEL W.P.	481
. EBENEZER	367,371	. BENJAMIN WATKINS	85	. JOHN	589,643
. ELIZABETH	371,373	LEITH,EMMA MARTIN	259	. JONATHAN	481-483
. ELIZABETH M.	367	. WILLIAM	259	. JOSEPH	617
. ELIZABETH W.	372	LEITNER,C.C.	51	. LEON	482
. EUGENE	372	C.H.	51	. LEONARD	486
. EVELINE	372	LESLIE,	94	. LIZZIE	481
. HANNIBAL	371,381,572	LESTER,	335	. MAGGIE	482
. HASKELL	372	. HUMPHREY	195	. MARGARET	481
. HENRY C.	566,575	. JANE TART	195	. MARGARET CRIBB	482
. J.B.	584	. MARY	195,360	. MARION	481
. J.G.	584	. R.H.	612	. MARVIN	482
. JACK	373	. ROBERT H.	195,618	. MARY	463,481
. JAMES B.	204,246,269	. W.M.	51	. MINERVA	483
	385	. WILLIAM BRADDY	291	. MOURNING	481
. JAMES S.	282	LEVY,	570	. MOURNING VAMPELT	480
. JANE	367,371-373	LEWELLYN,JESSEE B.	595	. ODELL	482
. JANE LEGETTE	373	LEWIS,	150,162,186,264	. PATRICK	481
. JESSE	369,371,373		445,465	. PENCIE	444
. JESSEE	367,371,460	. ADALINE	482	. PENNSY	482-483
. JESSIE	372-373	. ADDIE	482	. PENNSYLVANIA	482
. JOHN	373,580	. ADDIE POTTER	222	. PENSY	477
. JOHN C.	142,404	. ALLEN	264	. POLLY	481
. KOSSUTH	371	. ALLEN C.	481,589	. RHODA MACE	222,482
. LANGDON	372	. ANGUS	481,589	. RUPERT	482
. LEVI	38,126,182,284	. ANNA	222	. RUTH NORTON	476,483
	369-370,515,530,567	. ANNE	222,482	. SARAH	187,222,482
	575	. BAKER	379,617	. SARAH CARMICHAEL	445
. LOU	447	. BETSY	481	. SOLON	401
. LOUISE	299	. CARRIE	482,526	. SOLON A.	481
. MARJORY	371	. CATHARINE	481	. SUSANNAH PORTER	482
. MARTHA		. CELIA	501	. T.J.	629
RICHARDSON	460	. CHARLES	222	. TAYLOR	482
. MARY	369-370	. DANIEL	445	. TEMPERANCE	
. MARY A. WAYNE	373	. DEMPSEY	482	BROWN	379
		. DEMPSY	45,361,485	. VICTOR	482

. W. EVAN	482,643	
. W.A.D.	481	
. W.A.D. MARION	481	
. W.L.	444	
. WESLEY	222	
. WILLIAM	480-481	
. WILLIAM E.	624	
. WILLIAM L.	481	
. WILLIAM S.	222,482,643	
. WILSON	174	
. ZILPHA	481	
. ZION	617	
LIDE,	119,208	
LINCOLN,ABRAHAM	87	
LINDSAY,	269	
. MARY ANN STUBBS	269	
LINDSEY,WILLIAM G.	620	
LINTON,MARGARET	465	
LISTER,WILLIAM B.	579	
LITTLE,C.M.	612	
. D.	612	
. DANIEL	642	
. JOHN R.	237	
. L.M.	195	
. LEWIS H.	335	
. MARGARET	237	
LITTLETON,		
. WILLIAM HENRY	569	
LLEWELLYN,B. FRANK	592	
LLOYD,HENRY	592	
. J.	627	
. J.J.	626	
. T.M.	627	
. WILLIAM	617	
LOCKE,ADA	329	
. BENJAMIN	329	
. GERIAH	329	
. JOHN	3	
. SALLIE	329	
. VINEY BUTLER	329	
. WILLIAM	329	
. WILLIE	329	
LOCKEY,BENJAMIN B.	589	
LOCKLIER,GIBBERT	624	
. JOHN	624	
. W.E.	624	
. WASHINGTON	624	
LOFTON,AM.M	636	
. H.M.	639	
. JOHN	637	
. JOHN H.	597	
LONGSTREET,	426	
LORD,	71	
LOVE,	265	
R.	612	
LOVEJOY,GUY	152	
. TELATHA BERRY	152	
LOVEL,MARY ATKINSON	490	
LOVELL,	469	
J.W.	635	
LOVET,	258	
. LEVIN	589	
LOVETT,KINCHAN	639	
LOWNDES,RAWLINS	569	
LOWRANCE,LAWRENCE	580	
LOWRIMORE,	105,108-111,114	
. COLLIN W.	643	
. HANSON L.	607	
. JOHN	607	
. M.M.	104,106-108,137	
. MOSES	607	
. ROBERT	105,108	
. W. JAMES	105	
LOWRY,	338	
LOYD,ELIZABETH	531	
. MELVINA LEGETTE	370	
. WILLIAM	370	
LUCAS,	125,142,454	
. ELIZA	22	
. GEORGE	22	
. JESSEE	584	
. MAGGIE	527	
. MARIA	520	
LUDWELL,PHILIP	568	
LUNDY,JOHN	635	
. WILLIAM	635	
LUPO,	170,178	
. ALLEN C.	617	
. ELIZABETH HUGGINS	266	
. JAMES	639	
. JOHN	645	
. MALCOLM	639	
. THOMAS A.	617	
. W.S.	45	
. WILLIAM	617,639	
LYLES,FANNIE	233	
. JAMES	451	
. SUSAN DAVIS	451	
M.GRAHAM,ANNA	446	
MACDUFFIE,GEORGE	84	
MACE,	526,546	
. BOYD	375	
. CORNELIUS	205	
. DRUSILLA	419	
. DRUSILLA MILES	221	
. ELIZABETH	205,221,340	
. EMMA	375	
. EMMA GASQUE	205	
. EUGENIA GASQUE	205,375	
. FRANKY	212,221-222	
. FRANKY FINKLEA	221	
. GREGG	221,577	
. JAMES	221-222	
. JAMES C.	592	
. JANE WATSON	205	
. JOHN	155,221-223,411,644	
. JOHN C.	205	
. JOHN M.	205,434	
. JULIA PHILIPS	205	
. LENA GASQUE	375	
. LUCINDA M.	155-156	
. MAGGIE E.	411	
. MAGGIE ELLEN	155-156	
. MARTHA	187,221-222	
. MARTHA ANN	220	
. MARTHA FINKLEA	221	
. MARY	205,221	
. MARY POLLY	221	
. MASSEY	221-222	
. MATTHEW	221	
. MOSES	39,205,220-221,223,375,419	
. NEILL	205	
. PHILIP	375	
. RHODA	221-222,482	
. SALLIE	221-222,528	
. SAMUEL	205	
. STEPHEN	205	
. THADEUS	205,375	
. VERZILLA BERRY	222	
. VIRZILLA	419	
. VIRZILLA BERRY	155	
MACFARLAN,ROBERT	572	
MACKEY,	94	
. E.W.M.	103	
MADAN,	570	
MAGRATH,A.G.	570	
MAHONEY,	296-297	
MALLOY,	196,239,492-493	
MANIGAULT,	319,349,613	
MANNING,	276,279,558	
. A.S.	50	
. AMANDA BETHEA	239	
. ANN	384	
. ANNA HASELDEN	239	
. AUSTIN	219,240,556	
. CLARA BETHEA	240,409	
. ELI	239	
. EVA	203,219,240	
. FRANK	239,241	
. GERONA	239,241	
. HOLLAND	239-240	
. HOLLARD	409	
. HOPE	409	
. HOUSTON	203,219,239-240,362	
. IRA	238	
. JAMES	238-240	
. JAMES H.	216,239	
. JOHN	209,238-239,241,284	
. JOHN L.	570	
. LAWRENCE	40,233,239-240,461	

. LETTIE	239	
. LISHA	238	
. LISHIA	209	
. MARTHA J.-		
STACKHOUSE	240	
. MARTHA		
STACKHOUSE	358	
. MARY	153	
. MARY BELLE	409	
. MARY POLLY		
KINNEY	238	
. MATTIE		
STACKHOUSE	362	
. MAURICE	154,219,240	
. MEALY	416	
. MEELY	238-241	
. MOLLIE	239	
. NELLIE BETHEA	154,219	
	240	
. ORIANNA		
HAMER	233,239,461	
. REBECCA	241,301,397	
. RICHARD J.	569	
. ROBERT	241	
. SALLIE	241,398	
. SARAH JANE	239-240,416	
. T.J.	645	
. T.L.	51	
. THOMAS B.	239	
. THOMAS J.	153,239	
. TOMMIE	153,239	
. WILLIAM	239-240,288	
	358	
. WILLIAM L.	596	
. WILLIE	240,358-359	
. WOODWARD	11,238,241	
	301,341,397-398	
MANNINGS,ELI	602	
MANSHIP,	178	
. CHARLES	384	
MARCE,	465	
MARION,	107,112,114,533	
. FRANCIS	491	
MARLER,J.R.	630	
. V.A.	630	
MARLOR,W.	627	
MARLOW,ANN	504	
. DAVID	643	
. ELIZABETH	504	
. POLLY	529	
. R. WILLIAM	607	
MARREE,THOMAS	641	
MARSHALL,DAVID G.	614	
MARTIN,	186,392,443,459	
. A.	186	
. AARON	188,258-260,484	
. ALEXANDER	258	
. ALEXANDER H.	618,624	
. ANNE	259	
. CAROLINE	187	
. CELIA	431	
. CHARLES	258	
. CHARLES B.	375,475	
. CHARLES BETTS	261	
. CLYDE	259	
. CUFF MOSE	458	
. DANIEL	261,475,487	
. DAVID	187,260	
. DON	478	
. DONALD	259	
. ED B.	618	
. ED W.	618	
. EFFA	426	
. ELIZABETH KEEFFE	502	
. EMMA	259	
. FLORENCE OWEN	259	
. GEORGIA GAME	487	
. IDA	259	
. JAMES	580	
. JOHN	171,258,260,266	
. JOSEPHINE MOODY	260	
	331	
. JULIA	261	
. KATE	259,478	
. LEASY	458	
. LILLY	259,478	
. LIZZIE	265	
. LIZZIE SMITH	259	
. LOUISA	259	
. M.H.	642	
. MAC F.	575	
. MACK	187,231,260,331	
. MAGGIE	259,478	
. MARGARET NORTON	259	
	478	
. MARTHA	431	
. MARY	260	
. MATTHEW	172,188,258	
	260,275,484,502	
. MAY	259,478	
. MITCHEL	259,498	
. MITCHEL M.	258	
. MITCHELL	259,264	
. MOSES	167	
. NORMAN	426	
. PENSY	259,478	
. ROBERT	260	
. SALLIE EDWARDS	187	
. STEPHEN B.	618	
. STEPHEN H.	187,258,260	
	607	
. SUE	260	
. TALLEY	247	
. VALENTINE	258-259,476	
	478	
. VANCE	259	
. VICTOR	259	
. VICTORIA	245,259	
. W.P.	474	
. WILLIAM	261,474,584	
. WILLIAM P.	261	
. WILLIAM R.	621,624	
MATHESON,A.J.	245	
. SARAH ELLEN-		
JARNIGAN	245	
MATHIS,	570	
MATHISON,DONALD	571	
MATTHEW,B. STANLEY	613	
MATTHEWS,	643	
. FRANK	593	
. JOHN	68,569	
. NANNIE GASQUE	376	
. SAMUEL P.	575	
. WALKER	376	
MAXWELL,H.J.	94	
MAYRANT,C.	570	
MEANS,JOHN A.	570	
MEARES,	523	
. ANTHONY	476	
. JERUSHA NORTON	476	
MEARS,CAROLINE	390	
. WILLIAM	618	
MEARSE,P.L.	601	
MEDLEY,	347	
MEEKINS,AARON	402	
. ANN ELIZA HAYES	269	
. E.J.	441	
. ENOCH	402	
. ENOCH J.	294	
. LUCRETIA	358	
. LUCRETIA BETHEA	402	
. OSCAR	635	
. PHILIP B.	269,402,592	
	635	
. RACHEL BETHEA	402	
MEGGS,JOEL	268	
. JOHN L.	268	
. W.H.	268	
. WILLIAM	580	
. WILLIAM H.	268	
MELICHAMP,	570	
MELLICHAMP,	366	
MELTON,W. JOSEPH	165	
MENDENHALL,	124	
MEREDITH,LULIE	202	
MICHALL,	107	
. JOHN	107-108	
. WILLIAM	107	
MICHALLS,	105	
MIDDLETON,ARTHUR	569	
. HUGH	569	
. J.E.	601	
MIKELL,	107,221	
. JOHN	107-108	
. WILLIAM	107	
MILES,	149,217	
. CHARLES	269,279,401	
. D.F.	119,130,219,221	
	307,329,361,368,466	
	565,567	

. DAVID 148,221,279
. DAVID FRANKLIN 119
. DRUSILLA 221
. F.A. 97,567
. FRANCES A. 119
. FRANCIS A. 279,330
. FRANK 307
. FRANK A. 221
. GREGORY 221
. JAMES 221
. JOHN M. 148,221,274
. LANNEAU 307
. LILLIAN 466
. MARTHA ANN 221
. MARTHA BERRY 148
. MARY 219,221,361
. MARY ANN 401
. NATHAN 624
. PATTIE BERRY 148,150
. S.A.C. 216
. S.G. 524
. SALLIE McINTYRE 307
. SAMUEL A.C. 119
. SOPHIE 130
. STEPHEN C. 119
. STEPHEN G. 64,216
. VERILLA 221
MILLEN,JOHN 587
MILLER, 177,427,442,476
 511
. ALEXANDER
 CARSON 426
. ALLEN 426
. BEMNA BENTON-
 McGIRT 426
. C.W. 571
. CHARLES W. 575
. DAVID 425
. DIANA 426
. E. 628,630
. EDMUND 425-427
. EDWARD 426
. EFFA MARTIN 426
. ELIAS 475,488
. GEORGE 425-427,638
. GUNGER BILL 425-427
. H.B. 638
. H.W. 636
. HENRY 425
. HEZEKIAH 425-427
. JAMES 601
. JESSE 426
. JESSEE 425,427
. JOHN 425-427,638
. JOHN C. 638
. JOHN P. 607
. LEVI 645
. MACK PIPKIN 426
. MARTHA 475-476
. MARY 425

. N. 601
. NAT 488
. NATHANIEL 475
. PITMAN 637
. REBECCA 197,475-476
. ROBERT 425
. ROBERT H. 426
. STEPHEN D. 84,569
. T.W. 599
. THOMPSON 601
. W.W. 638
. WILLIAM 425-426,624
. WILLIAM H. 592
MILLICHAMP,
. ANNE PEARCE 352
MILLING,D.C. 143
MILLS,LAWRENCE 98
MILLSAPS,JOHN 291
. MARY McARTHUR 299
. MARY McKAY 291
. RICHARD J. 299
MINCEY,GEORGE 624
. JESSEE 624
. PATRICK 624
MIRAN,NANCY BLUE 289
MIXON,MICHAEL 167
MONROE, 41,72,332,440
. ANNA 526
. ANNE 446
. CARRIE LEWIS 482,526
. CLEMENT 526
. D. 581
. DAVID 222,224,447
 525-526
. ELIZABETH
 GODBOLD 526
. F.M. 40,224,446,482
. FANETTA WHITE 525-526
. FRANCIS MARION 526
. JAMES 224,526
. MAGGIE 525-526
. MARY 447,525-526
. MARY
 McMILLAN 423,525
. MASSEY MACE 222
. McCOY 526
. McKAY 526
. NANCY CAMPBELL 321
. RHODA GADDY 525
. ROBERT 321,446,525
. SALLIE 525-526
. THOMAS 177,525
. W.M. 423,525
. WALTER 525
. WALTER S. 525
. WILLIAM M. 525
MONTAGUE,
. CHARLES GEVILLO 569
MONTGOMERY, 265
. ANNA STACKHOUSE 362

. J.D. 200,378,645
. JANIE WATSON 200
. W.J. 50,219,361-362
 378,567-568,571
MOODY, 66-67,89,196,337
 476,551
. A.C. 609
. ALBERT C. 333,338
. AMELIA 226
. BARFIELD 88-89,144,146
 226,330-331,333-334
 338-339,401,564,566
 567
. BARTOW 333
. BETSY 340
. CALVIN C. 589
. CELIA 330,332
. CHARLES 165,201
 330-331
. CLARENCE 333
. CORNELIUS G. 335
. CURTIS 589
. DANIEL 340
. DAVID 331
. DELILAH WYCHE 334
. E.J. 16,147,193,195
 306,326,335,360,492
 498,509,646
. ELIZA ELLERBE 338
. ELIZABETH 226
. ELIZABETH
 MACE 221,340
. ELIZABETH SMITH 330
 497
. ENOS 317,340,637
. EVALINE 330,332,342
. EVALINE
 MOODY 332,342
. EVANDER J. 333
. FLORENCE 333,335,509
. FLORENCE
 SMITH 333,498
. HARRIET EDWARDS 187
 331
. HELEN 331
. HUGH 230,248,330-331
 645
. J.H. 315
. JAMES A. 330,332,342
. JAMES C. 333
. JAMES R. ERVIN 340
. JANE BASS 331
. JANE TART 195,335
. JENNIE 306
. JESSEE 342
. JOHN B. 592
. JOHN H. 221,340,577
. JOHN THOMAS 330-331
 618
. JOHN W. 341,485

. JOSEPHINE 260,331	. JAMES 612	. FRANK K. 509
. JOSHUA T. 332,341	. JOHN 612	. GUERRY 508
. JOSHUA W. 183	. T.C. 612	. HENRY 51,506,508-509
. JOSIAH 341	. TOBIAS 612	571
. JULIA 338-339	. WILLIAM W. 612	. IDA 467,506
. LIZZIE 338-339,342	MOORE, 313	. J.C. 335,509
. LIZZIE A. 332	. A.B. 612	. JAMES C. 276,506,509
. LUCY 226,333,338-339	. ALFRED 204	. JOHNSON 509
. MAGGIE 195,335	. ANGUS 248	. JULIA 508-509
. MARTHA 331	. BLANEY 593	. LIZZIE 508
. MARTHA SHOOTER 485	. C.R. 473	. MAGGIE McKERALL 508
. MARY 330,332	. CLANCY 400	. MARY 305,508
. MARY CRAWFORD 340	. E. 627	. R. RANDOLPH 509
. MARY EDWARDS 340	. E.L. 244,559	. RANDOLPH 335
. MASSEY SMITH 331	. ELIZABETH	. W.S. 305,467,507,509
. MILLEY 332	McLELLAN 312	571
. MILLY 330	. EMMA R. COLEMAN 473	. W.W. 644
. NANCY BETHEA 401	. G.W. 635	. WILLIAM L. 508
. NEILL 335	. IDA HAYES 270	. WILLIAM S. 91,97,506
. NEILL C. 195	. J.B. 120	508,567
. OBEDA BUTLER 340	. JAMES 3,400,569	. WOODS 335
. OLIVER 589	. JAMES B. 400	MUNN,A.B. 646
. POLLY BUTLER 327	. JOHN B. 270	. G.W. 641
. POLLY PLATT 341	. JOHN BEATY 643	. GEORGE W. 618
. R.B. 609	. JOHN S. 536	. MALCOLM L. 618
. RHETT 333	. LACOSTE 400	. W.J. 641
. RICHARD 187,238	. LORENA 400	MUNNERLYN, 106
330-331	. MARGARET P. 473	. B.A. 111
. RICHARD J. 331	. MINNIE 536	. JAMES 167
. ROBERT 232,330-333,497	. MOLLIE GODBOLD 400	. SUSAN A. 349
. ROBERT B. 333,335,580	. ROBERT 637	. THOMAS M. 111,349
. SALATHEL 401	. S. 627	. W.H. 599,626
. SALATHIEL 231,260	. SARAH BETHEA 400	MUNRO,R. 571
330-331	MORGAN, 145	MUNSHIP,CHARLES 238
. SALATHIEL S. 642	. CALVIN 444	MURCHISON, 538
. SALLIE CRAWFORD 144	. SUSAN CARMICHAEL 444	. DUNCAN 280,440,602
333	. W. COLIN 592,604	. JOHN D. 440
. SANDY 333	MORRIS, 181	. MARY CARMICHAEL 440
. SARAH ANN 146,331	MORRISON, 293	. RODERICK 596
338-339	. SALLIE 405	. WILLIAM 440,568
. SARAH ANN MOODY 331	MORTON,JOSEPH 1,568	. WILLIAM L. 596
. SMITHY 330,332	MOSES, 94	MURDOCH, 304
. SOPHIA 331	. F.J. 95,103,570-571	. ALEXANDER 366
. STEPHEN 327,340	. FRANKLIN J. 100	. JOHN 366
. SUE 333	MOULTRIE,WILLIAM 569	. KENNETH 366
. T.C. 64,98,216,338,564	MUCKENFUSS, 348	. MARTHA WAYNE 366
567-568	MULDROW, 570	MURFEE, 138,140-141,158
. TAPLEY 330,339-340	MULLINS, 306,507,523	. ARLINE 147
. THEODORE 333	. ARTEMISSIA	. MALACHI 30-31,147
. THOMAS C. 333-334	DEBERRY 509	. MAURICE 147,159
. THOMAS D. 331,614	. B.R. 130,435,509,566	. MICHAEL 147
. THOMAS E. 195,335	. BENJAMIN R. 509	. MOSES 147
. VIRGINIA 195,335	. CHARLES 508	MURPHY, 160,389,438-439
. W.H. 11,140,612	. CHARLES WOODS 509	. ARCHIBALD 443
. WESLEY 340	. EDWARD 508	. ARCHIE 317
. WILLIAM 333	. EMILY PRICE 508	. ARLINE 147
. WILLIAM H. 333	. FLORENCE 335,509	. CAROLINE-
MOONEYHAM,	. FLORENCE	CARMICHAEL 440
. ARLINE MURFEE 147	MOODY 335,509	. DUNCAN 288,317,443,596
. ARLINE MURPHY 147	. FRANK 335,508	. EDWARD 318

Name	Page
. EDWARD J.	317
. J.B.	601
. JOHN	317,443
. JOHN C.	592
. JOSEPH	440
. MALACHI	30
. MALCOLM	317
. MARGARET McDUFFIE	317
. MARY E. REAVES	207
. MARY REAVES	204,318
. MAURICE	159,388
. N.	628
. N.C.	204,443,599
. NANCY CARMICHAEL	317, 443
. NEILL C.	317
MURRAY, JOHN W.	184,444
MYERS,	312
. A.	570
. A.A.	567,595,640
. G. MATTHEW	593
. G.H.	641
. GEORGE J.	567
. JOHN E.	592
. WILLIAM	595
McALISTER,	219,361
McALL,	105
McARTHUR,	289,293,297, 300
. ALEXANDER	299
. EFFIE	299
. JAMES	297,299,598
. JENNIE	299
. JOHN	299
. KATIE	299
. MARGARET	302
. MARY	299
. MARY JANE	299
. POLLY	290
. SARAH McDONALD	299
McCALL,	352,539
. BARNEY	575
. C.S.	525
. CAROLINE	354
. D.N.	599
. DUNCAN N.	289
. GEORGE I.W.	354
. HANNAH JANE	354
. HARRIET HARLLEE	354
. J.	601
. JOHN	584
. JOHN C.	598
. JOHN N.	348,571
. JULIA HARLLEE	348
. L. ALLSBROOKS	592
. MARY BLUE	289
. NATHAN	596
. REBECCA	354
. S.A.	632
. SALLIE	298
. WILLIAM	234-235,580
McCANTS,	449
McCAULL, JOHN A.	351
MARGARET M.R.	351
McCHESNEY,	152
McCLANNAGHAN, JOHN C.	304
McCLELLAN, DANIEL B.	607
. ENOS	607
. GEORGE B.	87
McCLENAGHAN, . CONSTAINE	160
. GEORGE S.	585
. HONORINE H.	591
. HORATIO	128
. J.C.	51
McCLENAHAM, HONORINE	631
McCOLL,	303,436,443,529
. A.M.	314
. BEULAH	232
. C.J.	164,231
. C.S.	314
. CATHARINE-CARMICHAEL	442
. D.D.	571
. EMELIA	213
. FANNIE	213
. J.G.B.	314
. JOHN L.	314
. JOHN M.	212
. JOHN N.	567
. LOUISA ROBERTS	212
. MARGARET	347
. MILLE	213
. NANCY SINCLAIR	314
. RICHARD	442
. T. DICKSON	314
. WILLIAM	347
McCOLLUM, BROWN	234,252,303
. DOUGALD	320
. EFFIE	303
. MARTHA J.	320,442-443
. MATILDA CARMICHAEL	442
. WILLIAM	442
McCORD,	517
McCORKLE, J.F.	635
McCORMAC, JAMES	580
. JOHN H.	596
. NATHANIEL	580
. P.	643
. PETER P.	178
. REBECCA MANNING	241
. SIMEON P.	241,587
. THOMAS	580
McCORMIC,	307,518
. ADALINE HILL	266
. CORINNA	450
. PETER PARLEY	331
McCORMICK,	292,329
. A.P.	295
. ADA	296
. ALLEN	294
. ARCHIE	294
. BETTIE	297
. CHARLES	329
. DANIEL	297
. DRUSILLA	297
. DRUSILLA McCORMICK	297
. DUNCAN E.	294-296
. ELLEN	296
. FLORA	295
. FLORA A.	297,309
. FRANK	297
. GENERAL	295
. GEORGIANNA	295
. HARRIET RIDGELL	295
. HARRIET WALTERS	295
. JAMES	297,312
. JAMES A.	299
. JAMES HUNT	309
. JOE	297
. JOHN	293,295-297,329
. KATIE McDONALD	297
. LAURA	298
. LITTLE MACK	293, 296-297
. MALCOLM	294
. MANILA	298
. MARTHA BECKWITH	295
. MARY	295
. MARY BUTLER	328
. NATHAN	328-329
. NEILL	294,297-298
. PETER P.	624
. PHILIP	295
. RANDALL	297
. REBECCA	301
. THOMAS	297
. VICTORIA	312
. VIRGIE LEGETTE	297
. WARREN ALFORD	297
. WILLIE LOCKE	329
. WYLIE	297
McCOWN, MAXCY	281
McCOY,	488
McCRACKEN, MARTHA	462
McCRACKIN, . TELATHA LEE	496
McDANIEL, A.	601
. AMOS	598
. B.F.	643
. CATHARINE LEWIS	481
. DANIEL	580
. ENOS	641

. J. RANDALL	607
. J.B.	348
. JAMES	580
. JOHN R.	605
. JOSEPH	598,618
. PRESTON	580
. RANDAL	481
. RANDALL	598
. W.	644
. WILLIAM	618
McDONALD,	197,286,551
. A.J.	286
. BETTIE McCORMICK	297
. D.J.	39,143-144,567
. ELLA	299
. FLORA	297
. HUGH A.	297-298
. JAMES	286
. JOHN H.	39
. KATIE	297
. NEILL	299
. SARAH	299
McDOUGAL,	127
McDUFFIE,	155,200,329
. A.B.	440
. A.Q.	39,43,50,98,220
.	315-316,365,384,513
	571
. ALEXANDER	315-318
. ARCHIE	252,315
. ARCHIE B.	318
. BETTIE	383
. D.D.	45,169,440,599
. D.K.	319
. DALLAS	316
. DANIEL	290,315-316,320
. DANIEL Q.	591
. DOUGALD	316-317
. DUNCAN	200,252,315
	317-319,440
. DUNCAN D.	319
. ELLERBE	319
. EMERSON	319,425
. FANNIE FORD	318
. FLORA	317
. GEORGE	315-316
	319,569
. GEORGE ALEXANDER	319,440
. JASPER	319
. JENNETTE	316
. JENNETTE McQUEEN	315
. JENNIE	316
. JOHN	316
. JULIUS	319
. KATIE	317
. LIZZIE	316
. LIZZIE FORD	318
. MADGE	319
. MAGGIE HASELDEN	319
. MARGARET	298,315,317
. MARGARET CLARK	317
. MARTHA	317
. MARY	315
. MARY ANN-CARMICHAEL	310,316
. MARY CARMICHAEL	318
	440
. N.C.	182,438,565
. NANCY	317-319
. NEIL C.	440
. NEILL	298,309-310,316
	320,327,642
. NEILL C.	169,318-319
	323-324,381,513,572
. PENELOPE FORD	319
. SALLIE	317
. WATSON	319
. WILLIAM	43,50,290,320
McEACHERN,	299
. AMARANTHA BUIE	298
. BENJAMIN	436
. DANIEL	435-436,439
. DUNCAN	294,435-436
. EDEARD	437
. EDMUND	436
. EDMUND BISHOP	298
. EDMUND Q.	298
. EDWARD	436
. EFFA	436
. EFFA McKELLAR	435
. ELIZABETH	435
. FLORA	298
. FLORA C.	437
. GILBERT	296,435
. JENNETTE-CARMICHAEL	439
. JENNIE CARMICHAEL	298
. JOHN	435-436,580
. JOHN B.	327,435-436
. JOHN C.	298,439
. JOSEPH	435
. JOSEPH A.	299
. KATIE	327
. LILLY	130
. LOUISA EVANS	130
. LOUISE	436,439
. LOUISE LEGETTE	299
. MANILA	298
. MANILA McCORMICK	298
. MANILLA	437
. MARGARET	320,436
. MARGARET ANN	296
. MARGARET McDUFFIE	298,317
. MARY ANN McGILL	435
. NEAL	645
. NEILL	298,435-436
. NEILL DUNCAN	298,317
. PETER	436-437
. PETER G.	298
. ROBERT	436
. ROBERT BRUCE	298
. SALLIE	435-436
. SALLIE McCALL	298
. WILLIAM	298,436
McFADDEN,	251
McFAIL,	283
McGEE,W.A.	641
McGILL,COLIN	604
. DAVID	604
. MARY ANN	435
McGILVRAY, CATHARINE	314
McGIRT,BEMNA BENTON	426
. JAMES	402
. JOE	426
. JOHN	295
. MARY McCORMICK	295
McGIST,	290
McGOOGAN,A.	644
McGRAMS,JOHN	566
McGROGAN,ARCHIBALD	43
McGURNEY,ELIZABETH	117
McILVEEN,	
. AGNES WOODBERRY	356
McINNIS,	6,285,444
. ALTHEA ALFORD	284,286,370
. DANIEL	181,596
. DUNCAN	286-287
. JAMES P.	284,286,370
. JOHN L.	286-287,578
. LAURIN	643
. MILES	286-287
. MURDOCK	597
. NEAL	645
. NEILL	286,580
. NORMAN	580
. WILLIAM	286
McINTYRE,	156,231,380
	431,563
. A.C.	612
. ANNE LEGETTE	303
. ARCHIBALD	304,585
. ARCHIE	300-301,303-307
	430,494,508
. BLANCHE	301,439
. CELESTIA	302
. CIVIL LEGETTE	300
. CORA	302
. COUSAR	300
. D.	51,285
. D.A.	609
. DANIEL	300,302-303
. DELIA	302
. DONALD	302
. DOUGALD	300-303,421

. DOUGALD C. 300	. REBECCA	. JOHN 292
. DOUGALD W. 302	McCORMICK 301	. JOHN D. 596
. DOUGLAS 195,220,303	. RICHARD 303-304	. PETER 291-292,298,580
306,315,335	. ROBERT C. 303	. TRAWICK 291
. DUGAL C. 210	. ROBERT	. WILLIAM 291
. DUNCAN 132,300-301	CHARLES 304,366	McKENZIE,A.C. 302
303-304,373,439,580	. ROSA EVANS 132,304	. ALFRED 624
593	. ROSANNA 302	. ALLEN 236
. DUNCAN A. 302-303	. S. 567	. ASA 235,237
. DUNCAN E. 300-301	. SALLIE 303,307	. DAVID 236
. EFFIE McCOLLUM 303	. SARAH 300,421	. DAVID J. 236,308
. ELIZABETH 300,302	. SARAH A.-	. DILLA 235,237,280
. EMALINE	CARMICHAEL 302	. ELI 236,643
CARMICHAEL 301,439	. SOPHIA 307	. ELISHA 236,248
. EMMA YOUNG 305,538	. SOPHIA HOWARD 303	. EMERY JACKSON 236
. FANNIE WILLIS 300	. THERESA ANN-	. FLORENCE 308
. G.A. 450,463,522,538	LEGETTE 373	. FRANK 236
. GEORGE A. 303,305,585	. VIRGINIA	. JACKEY 236
. ISLA 301,439	MOODY 195,335	. JAMES 236
. J.C. 609	. W.M. 301	. JOHN 235-236
. JAMES 241,300-301	. W.W. 599	. JOHN W. 236
. JANIE 195	. WALLACE 301	. MARGARET
. JENNETTE 300,302	. WILLIAM WALLACE 300	McINTYRE 302
. JENNIE 306,488	301	. MARTHA MOODY 331
. JENNIE MOODY 306	. WOODWARD	. MARY POLLY 235,237
. JOHN A. 300	MANNING 241	. ROBERT 235-237,280,646
. JOHN B. 300,421	McIVER,A. 571	. SALLIE 237
. JOHN C. 302	. EVANDER R. 566	. SALLIE KENADY 236
. JOSEPH 300-301,303,305	. HENRY 571	. SARAH A. 280
439,508,580,633	McKAY, 250	. SARAH ANN 236-237
. KATE 450	. ALFORD 292	. W.T. 601
. KATIE McLELLAN 301	. ARCHIE 292-293	. WILLIAM 331
. KATIE ROBERTS 302	. BETTIE 292-293	. WILLIE T. 624
. KITTIE 302	. CLARKEY 292-293	McKERALL, 405
. LAYTON 439	. D.J. 289,291-293,297	. KATE 132
. LIEGHTON 301	. DANIEL 292	. MAGGIE 508
. LILLIAN 307	. DANIEL J. 632	. W.J. 43,132,508,571
. LILLY 300,302	. EVALINE STAFFORD 289	McKERRALL, 292
. LILLY CAMPBELL 300	292	. WILLIAM JASPER 632
. LILLY FAULK 300	. FLORA ANN 292	McKETHAN,
. LIZZIE 301,439	. G.W. 292	ALEXANDER 457
. LIZZIE MULLINS 508	. GILBERT W. 291,341,577	McKIBBEN,BENJAMIN 283
. LUCY MOODY 333	. HECTOR T. 293	McKINLEY, 285
. MARGARET 300,302	. JANIE 293	McKINLY,
. MARGARET	. JEANNETTE BAKER 291	. CATHARINE McNISH 307
McARTHUR 302	. JOHN 292-293	. D.C. 177
. MARTHA BETTS 304	. JOHN J. 293	. DANIEL 307
. MARY 300,303,307	. JOHN W. 291	. DUNCAN 307-308
. MARY CARMICHAEL 302	. KATIE ALFORD 292	. DUNCAN C. 308
. MARY K. 430	. MARY 291	. FLORENCE
. MARY MULLINS 305,508	. WILLIAM 291	McKENZIE 308
. MATILDA 303,306	McKELLAR, 291,293,297	. JENNETTE 307-308
. NANCY 300,302	. A. 291	. JOHN 177,307-308
. NETTIE 301,439	. ARCHIE 291	. JOHN D. 308
. PALMER 302	. EFFA 435	. LEONORA 308
. PATTIE 494	. ELMYRA 292	. MARY 307-308
. R.C. 51	. FLORA C.	. NEILL 307-308
. REBECCA 303,306	McEACHERN 437	. SARAH GADDY 177,308
. REBECCA MANNING 241	. FLORA McEACHERN 298	. WILLIAM 177
301	. JAMES 437	. WILLIAM D. 308

McKINNON,	249,293	. PETER	312,394	. REBECCA BROWN	421	
. MARY	308	. PRESTON	645	. ROBERT	423	
. SALLIE	310	. REBECCA		. S.A.	423,556	
McKISSICK,A.G.	595	BETHEA	311,398	. S.E.	423-424,525,599	
. A.W.	641	. REBECCA BRYANT	394	. SALLIE BETHEA	424	
. MURCHISON	595	. ROBERT	309	. SARAH	421,423,425	
McKNIGHT,J.E.	635,646	. ROXANNA GADDY	309	. SARAH		
McLAURIN,	286,418	. SALLIE LEGETTE	309	McINTYRE	300,421	
. CLARENCE	284	. SARAH	310	. SARAH WILSON	422	
. D.W.	190,250,417,567	. T.R.	297	. SUE	423-424	
. DUNCAN	295,557,604	. TIMOTHY R.	301,309,439	. SUE ROGERS	423	
. GEORGIANNA-			441	. SYDNEY	423-424	
McCORMICK	295	. TRISTRAM	310	. SYDNEY E.	423	
. HARRIET BETHEA	419	McLEOD,	416	. W.C.	121,423-424,551	
. JAMES	419	. MARGARET	439	. WALTER	423	
. JOHN L.	480	. MARY	407	. WILLIAM C.	423	
McLEAN,	282	. N.C.	268	. WILLIAM CICERO	423	
. AILSEY SMITH	496	McLUCAS,	283	McNAIR,		
. DIAN ALFORD	284	. J.S.	51	. BETTIE SINCLAIR	290	
. DIANNA ALFORD	284	. JENNETTE	314	. ELIZABETH		
. GERONA MANNING	241	. JOHN D.	568,571	HARLLEE	347	
. HUGH	308	McMEENEE,W.	627	. HARLLEE	347	
. JOHN W.	300	McMILLAN,	166,203-204	. NATHANIEL	290	
. LEONORA McKINLY	308		318,546	. NEILL	347	
. MARY McINTYRE	300	. ALICE	421	McNEILL,	422,506	
. R.B.	231	. BARBARA		. ANNIE HARLLEE	354	
McLELLAN,	313	PATTERSON	422	. DANIEL	382	
. ALEXANDER	308-311	. BELLE	423	. FANNIE McCOLL	213	
. ANGUS	312	. DANIEL	422	. J.	630	
. ANN M.		. EDWIN	423	. JOHN	354	
CARMICHAEL	311	. ELIZ. S.-		. LAVINA WATSON	199	
. ARCHIBALD K.	181	WILLIAMSON	430	. SIMON P.	643	
. ARCHIE	312	. ELIZABETH	423,425	McNISH,CATHARINE	307	
. ARCHIE K.	308-310	. ELIZABETH-		McPHAUL,	283	
. CEILA JERNAGEN	309	WILLIAMSON	421	. DANIEL	604	
. COLIN	308,311,398	. EMMA	423	. MILTON	289	
. DANIEL	48,308-309	. EUNICE DAVIS	421	. SARAH BLUE	289	
. DUNCAN	308-309	. FLORA	422	McPHERSON,	229,282,402	
. ELIZABETH	312	. FLORA PATTERSON	422	. C. ERVIN	412,593	
. ENOS	312	. FRANK	423	. CARRIE R.	145	
. F. TRISTRAM	309	. HAMPTON	264	. FLORENCE-		
. F.T.	48	. HECTOR	422	EASTERLING	146,386	
. FLORA	308,310,442	. JANE	422	. HARRIET J.	412	
. FLORA A.		. JOHN	421-425,430	. JAMES	566	
McCORMICK	297,309	. JOHN A.	624	. ROBERT	146,304,386	
. HANNAH WIGGINS	310	. JOHN C.	423-424	. SAMUEL	11,645	
. HARRIET		. JOHN P.	423-424	McPRIEST,		
ROGERS	181,309	. JOHN W.	300	ALEXANDER	291	
. HATTIE	441	. LEX	423	. KATIE	291	
. JOHN	308,312	. LOUISE	423	. LOVEDY	291	
. JOHN B.	309	. MALCOLM	421-422,430	. MARY ANN	291	
. JOHN ROBERT	310	. MARGARET	422	. PETER E.	291	
. KATIE	301	. MARY	376,421-423,525	McQUEEN,	251,464	
. MALCOLM	308-309	. MARY WILLIAMSON	421	. CATHARINE-		
. MARGARET	310		430	CARMICHAEL	310	
. MARY	320	. MATTIE PORTER	423	. FLORA C.-		
. MARY ANN	310	. MATTIE ROBSON	424	CARMICHAEL	311	
. MARY McKINNON	308	. NEILL	422	. IDA CARMICHAEL	442	
. MORANZA	310	. NEILL V.	421	. JAMES R.	315	
. PATTY BLACKSHEAR	309	. PALMER	424	. JENNETTE	315	

. JOHN	571	. FANNIE	190,391	. JERUSHA	476
. NEILL B.	258,310	. KENDRE	620	. JERUSHA REAVES	476
. S.A.	311	. KENDREE	189	. JOHN	259,266,475
. WILLIAM	442	. LUCY	190		477-478,483,487
McRAE,	347,440	. MARY	190,200,319	. JOHN CLARENCE	478
. ALEXANDER	347	. McKENDREE	189	. JOHN W.	266,444
. COLIN	28,604	. POLLY LEWIS	481		476-477,483,587
. ELIZABETH	346	. REBECCA	190	. LIZZIE	266
. ELIZABETH		. SALLIE	243	. LONNEY	477
HARLLEE	347	. SOPHRONIA DANIEL	189	. MABEL	478-479
. FRANKLIN	604	NICHOLSON,	186,285	. MARGARET	259,477-478
. JAMES	293,416,567,592	. ARCHIBALD	275	. MARTHA	212,476-477
. JOHN	62,564	. ARCHIE	258	. MARY	476,487
. JOHN A.	348,515	. DUNCAN	275-276,481	. MARY	
. JOHN D.	322	. FRANCIS	569	ELIZABETH	477-478
. MALCOLM D.	515	. JOHN M.	275	. MATTIE	478
. NORMAN	604	. NANCY	275	. MILTON	477,487
. RICHARD	380	. WALTER	275-276	. MINNIE	266,477
. RODERICK	604	NOBLE,J. HARDY	605	. NANCY	266,476
McREE,	180	. PATRICK	215,569	. NANCY	
. J.J.	568	NOBLES,H.	627	CARMICHAEL	477
. JOHN	566	. J.P.	630	. NANCY	
McSWEENEY,M.B.	570	. J.W.	627	HUGGINS	266,477
. MILES B.	215	. JOHN B.	587	. OLIVE	476
McWHITE,A.A.	595	. N.	627	. PENNSY LEWIS	483
. ANNIS	523	NORMAN,		. PENSY CARMICHAEL	477
. B.B.	640	. CHARITY BUTLER	328	. PENSY LEWIS	477
. E.	593	. JEREMIAH	110,355	. PRISCILLA LANE	395
. G.W.	641	. MARY	355	. RACHEL	156,412
. L.T.	628	. SAMUEL	110,355	. RACHEL C.	
. MAGGIE	452	. WASHINGTON W.	328	SELLERS	479
. W.H.	640	NORTH,	571	. RELDA	
NANCE,	264,498	NORTON,	489,544,546	PROCTOR	477,487
. A.	601	. ANNA ROLAND	476	. RUTH	476,483
. ATCKERSON	618	. BESSIE	477	. SANDY	395,635
. AVERITT N.	399	. CAROLINE	266,477-478	. SARAH	476-477
. CATHARINE BETHEA	399	. CATHARINE	477	. SARAH ANN	476
. DANIEL	399	. COLIN MURCHISON	477	. SARAH IVEY	477
. EVERETT	172	. DAISEY	478	. SOLOMON	475-476
. PRUDENCE	429-431	. DAVID	475	. SUSANNAH-	
. SARAH	172	. ELIZA	477-478	CARMICHAEL	477
NAPIER,	268	. ELLA POWELL	478	. THOMAS	612
NASH,BEVERLY	94	. ELLA WOOD	478-479	. VAN	478
NEES,JOHN	635	. EVAN	477,479,587	. VIRGINIA	477
NESBIT,	456	. EVAN LEWIS	412,479	. W.F.	265
NEVILS,RACHEL	143	. FLORENCE		. WILLIAM	475-476
NEWSOM,	383	SMITH	265,412,479	. WILLIAM FITZROY	412
NEWSON,JAMES	451	. H.H.	539		479
. RACHEL DAVIS	451	. HENRY	476-477	. WOODBERRY	178,395
NEWTON,H.H.	315,571	. HOLLAND	395	NORWOOD,G.A.	538
. JAMES W.	584	. HOUSTON	395	. GEORGE A.	508
. KATE SINCLAIR	315	. IRA	266	. SAMUEL A.	508
NICHOLS,	16,497-498	. IRES	477	NOTT,ABRAHAM	73
. A.B.	191,554	. IVA	444	NYE,	264
. ALICE	163	. J.C.	612	OAKLEY,DANIEL	638
. ANNE	190,250	. J.O.	478	. ROBERT N.	580
. AVERETT	163,189	. J.W.	477	. WILLIAM	638
. AVERITT	190,250,481	. JAMES	212,266,412	ODOM,LEVI	396
. AVERITT BURNEY	189		475-480,483,487,567	. SALLIE BETHEA	396
. BENJAMIN	624		587	OKES,	106,110

OLIVER,	152,376	. DANIEL	466-467,484	. SHADRACH S.	592
. A.C.	210,431	. DAVID	432,466-467	. SHADRACK	175,467
. A.R.	372,450,462	. DAVID J.	431	. SHADRACK S.	604
. AARON	164,266,478	. DAVID R.	284-285,467	. SHIVER BILL	467
. ALEXANDER R.	576,587		592	. SOLMON	467
. ALICE JONES	205,368	. DOCK	467	. SOLOMON	431,466-467
	462	. DORA	467		502
. AMANDA PITTMAN	169	. E.	628	. STEPHEN G.	284,642
. ANNE STEVENSON	462	. E.B.	467,506,513,582	. SUSAN BAKER	382,447
. AVA PAGE	163	. ELIJAH	467	.	466
. CIVIL PAGE	163	. ELISHA	467	. W.	645
. D.J.	152	. ELIZABETH	466	. WALTER	624
. DANIEL	462	. EZEKIEL	467	. WATTIE	467
. DANIEL J.	368	. GABRIELLA WALL	433	. WESLEY	467
. J.D.	462	. GAUSE	467,489	. WILLIAM	467,643
. JAMES D.	163	. GOURDIN	467	. WILLIAM J.	466
. JAMES R.	169	. HEWITT	635	. WILLIAM R.	625
. JAQUILINE	413	. IDA MULLINS	467,506	. WILLIE J.	466
. JOSEPH R.	45,163	. J.	612	. WILLIS	610,613
. L. WYATT	368,462	. J.W.	612	. Z.	645
. L.W.	205	. JAMES	176	PACE,	460
. LIZZIE NORTON	266	. JOSEPH	466	. ANN	459
. MARY	368,462	. JOSEPH W.	466	. CHARLES	380
. MARY A.	431	. L.R.	285,432-433	. JAMES A.	607
. MARY ELIZABETH-		. LAMAR	466	. JOSEPH	380
NORTON	478	. LEONARD R.	284-285,467	. JULIA BROWN	380
. SALLIE FULLER	368,462	. LEONORA	467	. MARY	378
. SAMUEL	462	. LILLIAN MILES	466	. R.W.	630
. SAMUEL L.	585	. LILLIAN McINTYRE	307	. WILLIAM J.	618
. SHEPHERD	318	. LOT	175,468,635	PAGE,	171,200,390
. SQUIRE D.J.	152	. LOUISA BETHEA	401		497-498,540
. W.A.	567	. M.	627	. A.	601
. WILLIAM A.	163,174,318	. MAGGIE	467	. ABRAHAM	625
. WILLIAM H.	163	. MAGGIE FOWLER	484	. ABRAM	162-163
ONEALL,JOHN		. MARTHA	429,466	. ABRAM B.	163
BELTON	72-73	. MARTHA A.R.-		. ADDIE AYRES	163
ONEILL,JOHN	580	WILLIAMSON	431	. ALEXANDER	614
ORR,	290-291,297,314,577	. MARTHA JENKINS	466	. ALICE NICHOLS	163
. JAMES L.	513,570	. MARTHA		. AUGUSTUS	163-164
. JOHN	62	WILLIAMSON	466	. AVA	163
OSBORNE,CHARLES	546	. MARY	432	. AVERETT	163
. CIVIL FOLEY	546	. MARY GREENWOOD	284	. CIVIL	163
. JOSEPH	546	. MARY PALMER	466	. DANIEL	620
. MARY	545	. MEMMINGER	467	. DAVID	162,164
OSSAUWATOMIE,	349	. MOLLIE BETHEA	396	. DAVID N.	163,604
OULDFIELD,JOHN	79	. N.R.	601	. DOC T.	604
OWEN,FLORENCE	259	. NANCY	187,465-466	. DOCK	163,166
. JOHN	259	. NEDDIE	467	. ELI	164
OWENS,	189,433,456,465	. NEWETT	467	. ELIZABETH	165
. ABSALA BETHEA	396	. NEWTON	401	. ELLA	357
. ALBERT	466	. PAUL	285	. ELLENORA	165
. ALBERT P.	587	. R.H.	627	. ERNEST	165,202
. ALEXANDER	382,447,466	. RACHEL BROWN	467	. HARRISON	625
. ANNIE FLOWERS	467	. REDDIN	175,468	. HETTIE SMITH	392
. ANNIS FLOWERS	502	. REDIN	598	. IRENA	397
. AVANT	467	. ROBERT	467	. J. LAWRENCE	165
. BILL	467	. S.	628	. J.K.	201,560
. CATHERINE	466	. S.G.	125,250,433,467	. JAMES E.	164
. CATHERINE GERALD	466		524,565	. JANE	496
. D.F.	610	. SHADRACH	468	. JOHN F.	164

. JOHN K.	164-165,202	. WILLIAM	598	. CHALMERS	466	
. JOHN S.	164,230-231, 496	. ZILLA BUTLER	327	. CLARISSA WALL	465	
		PAULEY,ROBERT	638	. CORA	466	
. JOHN W.	162-163	PAWLEY,	115	. DAVID	465	
. JOSEPH	162-164,174	. TORY	115	. DELTA	466	
. JOSEPH N.	163,169,540, 602	. TROY	107	. ELIZA WALL	434	
		PAYNE,ANNIE	502	. ELIZABETH	465-466	
. LOUISA BASS	164,230	. EMILY	347	. ELSEY	465	
. MARY ANN	174	PEABODY,CHARLES	580	. ELSY	465	
. MASTON	618	PEARCE,ALMA	473	. F. MARION	205	
. P.C.	636	. ANNE	352	. F.M.	434	
. PINCKNEY	164	. J.F.	352	. FRANCES	429-430,465	
. PINCKNEY C.	357,392	. JAMES F.	501,591	. FRANCIS		
. RETURN	625	. JAMES H.	501	MARION	465-466	
. S.L.	164	. LOUISA HARLLEE	352	. HANNAH	464-465	
. SAMUEL	165,202,254	. R.H.	595	. HUGH G.	465	
. SAMUEL T.	164,323	. ROBERT H.	352	. ISAAC	465	
. SOLOMON	162,164	. SALLIE HARLLEE	352	. ISHAM	425	
. SOPHRONIA WATSON	202	. VIRGINIA	473	. ISSORA	466	
		PENNIWELL,	517	. J. BENJAMIN	466	
. SUSAN	166	PEPPER,	259	. JANE	465	
. THOMAS	162,164-165	PERRIT,NEEDHAM	331	. JOCKEY	465	
. TIMOTHY	162,166	PERRITT,A.J.A.	184	. JOCKEY JOHN	465	
. W.	584	. ADDISON	394	. JOHN	465	
. W.B.	645	. ARVINGTON	184	. JULIA	205,466	
. W.J.	199	. ASA	183-184,620	. JULIA DAVIS	465	
. WILLIAM	164-166,172, 230,397,497,625	. BENNETT	183-184,331, 618	. MARGARET LINTON	465	
				. MARTHA FLEETWOOD	466	
. WILLIAM H.	618	. CHLOE	496			
. WILLIAM J.	164-165,172	. DAVID	183-185,325,394, 496,618	. McGEE	466	
PALMER,	462,468			. N.	88	
. DAVID	87-88,423,454, 460,566	. DAVID B.	183,187,618	. NANCY OWENS	465-466	
		. ELIZABETH TART	185,194	. PALMER	465	
. ELIZABETH	460	. EVÁNDER	375	. PERCIVAL	466	
. MARY	466	. HETTIE	496	. REBECCA	465,468	
. THERESA ANN-LEGETTE	367	. JAMES	394	. REMINGTON	466	
		. JESSE	183-185,272	. THOMAS	465	
PARKER,	106,109,413	. JESSEE	194	. THOMAS H.	465	
. ABSALA	396	. JOHN	183,185,645	. VERNULL	466	
. ALLEN	645	. JOHN E.	183-184, 325-326,439,614	. WILLIAM	465-466	
. E.	584			. WILLIAM L.	465-466	
. G.R.	641	. JOSEPH	183,185	. ZACK	465-466	
. MARTHA	504	. MARTHA EDWARDS	183,187	PHILLIPS,	375	
. ROBERT	643			. ANNIS	381	
. S.G.	630	. MARY CAMPBELL	325	. BENJAMIN	638	
. STEPHEN	643	. MARY DEW	185	. F. MARION	638	
. THOMAS	608	. MARY POLLY DEW	272	. F.M.	630	
PARNELL,	180	. MORGAN	184	. H.G.	636	
PASTON,DANIEL	618	. NEEDHAM	183,618	. ISAAC	638	
. J. RAYFORD	618	. TRISTRAM	618	. ISHAM	638	
. ROBERT T.	618	. WILLIAM	183-184	PICKENS,	350	
PATE,ALICE GODBOLD	120	PERRY,B.F.	59,316,508,570	. ANDREW	569	
. J. THOMAS	120	PETER,JAMES H.	625	. FRANCIS W.	570	
. JOHN A.	315	. NICHOLAS T.	625	PIERCE,	127	
PATTERSON,	422	PETTIGRU,J.L.	571	. DR.	645	
. BARBARA	422	PHILIPS,ANNA	465	. FRANKLIN	92	
. FLORA	422	. ANNA M.	465	. J.F.	567	
. JOHN J.	94	. ANNIS	445,447,465	. ROBERT	645	
PAUL,	322	. BENJAMIN	222	PINCKNEY,	23,83	
. REUBEN	327	. CELIA	465-466	. CHARLES	22,569	

. CHARLES C.	84	. CHRISTOPHER	641	. ANNIE	202		
. ELIZA LUCAS	22	. DANIEL	618,640	. ANNIE HAMER	202		
. THOMAS	84,569	. F.L.	641	. ANNIS ATKINSON	489		
PIPKIN,	181,361	. FRANCIS	643	. B.T.	601		
. MACK	426	. G.W.	630	. CIVIL SELLERS	546		
PITMAN,	542	. HAMPTON	641	. CONNERLY	540		
. ALFRED	199	. HUGH	642	. D.S.	161,508,510		
. CHARITY	176	. J. McK.	644	. EMILY	508		
. DAVID	584	. J. RAYFORD	618	. H.G.	609,613		
. DAVID G.	576	. JOHN L.	642	. HENRY	481		
. H.M.	582	. JOSEPH H.	641	. HUGH	184		
. HARDY	176	. M.M.	641	. HUGH P.	237,280,489		
. I.	645	. REDDICK	618	. IDA DICKSON	510		
. MARTHA WATSON	199	. ROBERT T.	618	. ISAAC	237		
PITTMAN, AMANDA	169	. SIMON	618	. J.C.	505,601		
. HELEN	169	. T.W.	641	. J.H.	612		
. THOMAS	638	. THOMAS	644	. JESSEE	489		
PLATT,	145,402	. W.H.	642	. JOHN	481		
. D.W.	165	. WILLIAM	642	. JOSEPH M.	261,475,546		
. DANIEL	231,341,415,566	POTTER, ADDIE	222	. JULIA MARTIN	261		
. DANIEL A.	150,181,285	. EUGENIA	424	. LIZZIE LEWIS	481		
. ELIZABETH ROGERS	181	. EVANDER	425	. M.R.	612		
. J.B.	636	. JAMES	424,576,636	. MARGARET LEWIS	481		
. JOHN	638	POUNCY, JOHN A.	571	. MARTHA A. BETHEA	546		
. JOHN B.	165,265	POWELL,	513,515	. MILTON F.	540,546		
. LUCRETIA A.-		. A.E.	630	. PAULINE WATSON	202		
EASTERLING	385	. D.	612	. PETER	237		
. MARY	415	. ELIZABETH	516	. RACHEL FLOWERS	505		
. POLLY	341	. ELLA	478	. RITTA ELLEN	237		
. POLLY LANE	415	. J.	612	. RUFFIN	546		
. R.B.	165,231,258	. J. MATTHEW	818	. STEPHEN H.	489		
. ROBERT B.	417	. J.S.	641	. WILLIAM	588		
. SOPHIA BETHEA	417	. JESSEE	587	. WILLIE	201		
. WILLIAM	385	. M.B.	630	PRINCE ALBERT,	144		
PLUMMER, HUGH	632	. MAT	638	PRINGLE,	570		
POLK, JAMES	632	. NOAH P.	608	PRIOR, WILLIAM M.	608		
. JAMES K.	88	. ROBERT	638	PROCTOR,	195		
POLSON,	468	. S.C.	642	. EMALINE CAMPBELL	487		
POND, FOSTER	580	. W.M.	630	. FANNIE	487		
POPE, VENETIA		. WILLIAM	576	. GEORGE	488		
WOODBERRY	356	POWER, J.H.	613	. J.T.	646		
PORT,	453	. JOHN M.	130	. JANIE McINTYRE	195		
PORTE, JEHU	628	. LILLY McEACHERN	130	. JENNIE McINTYRE	306		
L.	628	. LOUISA EVANS	130		488		
PORTER,	532	. MALCOLM	613	. LOUISA CAMPBELL	488		
. CATHARINE NORTON	477	. W.C.	130	. MARY	487		
. HAPSEY LANE	394	POWERS,	229	. RELDA	477,487		
. HARRIET	376	. ADALINE	496	. ROBERT	195,306,488		
. JAMES	394,452,576	. CHRISTOPHER	618	. SARAH	487		
. JOHN A.	244,423	. E.	645	. THOMAS	488,644		
. LORINE DAVIS	452	. ELIZA WIGGINS	516	. THOMAS A.	487-488		
. MATTIE	423	. JEFF	612	PROSSER, J.L.	629		
. ROBERT P.	143,394	. JOSEPH	516	. JOB	644		
. S. GOSS	576	. MITCHEL	194	. M.V.	641		
. S.G.	477	. MITCHELL	184	. MICHAEL	595		
. SUSANNAH	482	. MITCHELL R.	615	. NATHAN	641		
POSTON, ANDREW	640	PRICE,	201,247,467,518	PRUITT, ASA	188		
. B.D.	642		625	. NANCY EDWARDS	188		
. BENJAMIN	640	. ALONZO	584	QUARRY, ROBERT	568		
. BRYANT	638	. ANNE JOHNSON	540	QUEEN ANNE,	342		

QUEEN VICTORIA, 144	. A.J. 630	. JAMES H. 608
RAMSAY, 4-5,21,35,82,547	. ALICE 40,233,458	. JAMES J. 460
562	460-461	. JAMES W. 618
RAMSEY,RICHARD 580	. ALICE CRIBB 459	. JENNETTE GILES 472
RANSOM,JOHN 635	. ALICE SANDERS 460	. JESSE 459
RAY, 106,111	. ALLEN 459	. JOHN 371,457-458
. A. 595	. AMANDA WALL 435	460-461,491,576
. JOHN 588	. ANDREW	. JOHN B. 472
RAYSOR,CORNELIA 455	JACKSON 460,462	. JOHN CALHOUN 460
REAVES, 206,558	. ANN ELIZA 459	. JOHN H. 233
. AUGUSTUS 208	. ANN PACE 459	. JOHN M. 458-459,644
. CHARLES 204,207	. ARNA 459	. JOHN P. 569
. CHARLES W. 586	. ARNY 459	. JOHN PETER 570
. CHRISTIAN-	. ARREY 618	. JOHN S. 73
CARMICHAEL 443	. AUGUSTA 40,460-461	. JULIA BERRY 233
. EDWARD 207	. AVERY 459-460	. LEASY MARTIN 458
. ELIZABETH WATSON 203	. BENJAMIM 375	. LEE 459
207	. BENJAMIN 458	. LENA 459
. GEORGE 259	. BETSEY 458	. MARION 459
. GEORGE R. 207	. BETSY 458	. MARTHA 458,460
. GEORGE W. 203,207-208	. BOYD 460	. MARY 233,460-461
318,380,443,484	. BRADLEY 460	. MARY JANE ROWELL 468
. HENRY 208	. BYRD 459	. MATTHEW 459
. J. ROBERT 164,421,644	. CAROLINE CRIBB 459	. MAUDE DAVIS 434
. J.L. 582	. CATHERINE 458	. MILLY 459
. J.R. 203-204,254	. CHARLOTTE 460	. MILLY RICHARDSON 459
. JAMES 208	. CHARLOTTE	. MINNIE ATKINSON 490
. JAMES ROBERT 207	STANLEY 456	. NANCY 458,460
. JERUSHA 476	. CORDE 459	. NANCY RICHARDSON 460
. JOHN 207	. CORNELIUS 459	. NANCY ROBERTS 458
. KATIE DANIEL 259	. COY 459	. NANNIE CARTER 460
. MARY 204,318	. DAVID W. 608	. ORIANNA 233
. MARY E. 203,207	. E. FRANKLIN 608	. PATSY BAXLEY 460
. MARY GRIFFIN 207	. EBBY 458	. PINCKNEY G. 608
. R.H. 551	. EDDY 459	. POLLY 458
. ROBERT 203-204	. EDWARD 459	. POLLY DREW 459
. ROBERT H. 207-208,572	. EDWARD R. 233	. POLLY GASQUE 375
644	. ELIZABETH PALMER 460	. PRESTON 458
. S.W. 50,204	. EMMA 460-461	. REBECCA CRIBB 459
. SALLIE 208	. ENGLISH 459	. RICHARD 458
. SAMUEL W. 204	. ERVIN 434,459	. ROBERT 460
. SARAH McMILLAN 421	. ERVINIA 451,460	. SALLIE
. SOLOMON 207	. EUGENIA 452,459	JOHNSON 458-459
. THOMAS 208	. F.M. 601	. SARAH ANN 458
. WILLIAM 207	. FRANCONIA GILES 472	. STEPHEN 576
REDMAN,JAKE 635	. FRANKLIN 459	. SUMTER 460
REEVES,CHARLES	. GRAVES 458	. SUSANNAH LEE 459
J.W. 584	. HAMPTON 459-460	. SYDNEY 380,458,460
. ENOS 98	. HARDY 458	. THOMAS 458,580,608
REGAN,CHARLEY F. 457	. HENRY 458-459	. THOMAS J. 608
. FRANCES 457	. HENRY L. 614	. TRISTRAM 233
REMBERT,INA HAYS 172	. HOPKINS 458-459	. TROY 459
RENFROE, 166	. J. 631	. VALENTINE 460
REQUIER,A.J. 129	. J. GRAVES 608	. W. HAMILTON 618
. MARY EVANS 129	. J. RICHARD 619	. W.F. 40,120,461
RICE, 432,465	. J.G. 601	. WALTER 459
. ELIZABETH PHILIPS 465	. J.J. 435,456	. WASHINGTON 458
RICHARD,MEYER 633	. JACKSON 458	. WESLEY 468
RICHARDSON, 71,380,433	. JAMES 458-459	. WILLIAM 457-460,615
463,472,491,570	. JAMES B. 569	

. WILLIAM F. 233,371,451
460-462
. WILLIAM R. 619
RICHBURG,T.S. 559
RIDGELL,HARRIET 295
RIE,JAMES 62
RILEY,D.S. 635
RIT,D.E. 645
ROBBINS, 570
. JOHN B. 591
ROBERTS, 186,201,213
413-414
. BENJAMIN
FRANKLIN 588
. BETTIE WATSON 211
. CARRIE 211
. CORNELIA 211
. DUKE M. 618
. ELIZABETH 172,212,354
. ELLIOTT 211
. FRANKY MACE 212,222
. GILES 209-210
. HENRY 210
. JAMES 209-210,486
. JAMES H. 602
. JANIE 531
. JOANNA 212
. JOHN 172,176,210,222
476,620
. JOHN M. 209,212
. JOSEPHINE 486
. JUDSON 211
. JULIA ANN 210
. KATIE 302
. LAMAR 211
. LISHA MANNING 238
. LISHIA MANNING 209
. LISPIA 210
. LOUISA 212
. MARTHA ANN 212
. MARTHA
NORTON 212,476
. MARY 211
. MARY SMITH 210,498
. MINNIE 211
. NANCY 458
. NORTON 209,212,476
. PENELOPE 210
. PINCKNEY 210
. PINCKNEY J. 588
. REDDEN 209
. REDDIN 210-212,354
. ROBERTS 211
. ROGER 210,212
. ROGER R. 580
. ROLIN Q. 619
. ROWLAND 201,209-211
. SALLIE 211
. SALLIE GOODYEAR 210
. SAMUEL 186,210

. STEPHEN 210
. WILLIAM 209,238,257
. WILLIAM D. 209-210,341
. ZILPHA 211
ROBERTSON,L.D. 576
ROBINS,ROBERT M. 638
ROBINSON,L.D. 584
ROBSON,MATTIE 424
ROCKWELL, 166
RODGERS,HENRY 613
ROGERS, 126,178,393,445
469,496,631
. ADALINE TOWNSEND 183
. ALBERT 156,354,441,487
. ALBERT S. 181
. ALEXANDER 618
. ALFRED 179
. ALICE 181,415
. ALLEN 588,604
. ANNA 181,370
. ANNA LEGETTE 182
369-370
. ANNA ROGERS 181,370
. ANSON 580
. B. 584
. BARFIELD 45,179,636
. BEDA 473
. BENJAMIN 468
. BETHEL 474,483-484,576
. C.B. 645
. C.C. 628
. CADE 619
. CADE B. 181,328
. CAMBYSES 595
. CARY 576
. CATHERINE
EDWARDS 187
. CHALMERS 265-266,391
498
. CHARLES 182
. CHARLEY 216
. CHLOE 486,546
. COLEMAN 474
. D.S. 181
. D.W. 187
. DAVID 618
. DAVID S. 181,354,392
. DENNIS 588
. DEW 179,186,191,540
. DORA ROWELL 469
. E. 584
. E.W. 644
. EBBEN 369-370
. EBEN 580
. EBENEZEER 591
. EBENEZER 179,191,602
619
. EDWARD 474
. ELI 230
. ELIZABETH 181

. ELIZABETH ANN 171,182
. ELIZABETH BETHEA 398
. ELLEN CARMICHAEL 441
. ERVIN 588
. ERVIN B. 604
. EVAN 181-182
. F.G. 584
. FANNIE
CARMICHAEL 443
. FERDINAND 45,484
. FRANCIS 618
. FRANK 182
. FRANKLIN 176
. FRED G. 576
. GEORGE 498
. GEORGE W. 264-265,618
. H.D. 619
. HAMPTON 478,487
. HARRIET 181,309
. HARRIET
BETHEA 181,354
. HENRIETTA 214
. HENRY 13,179,214,398
477,644
. HENRY G. 181
. HERBERT 50,172,485
. HINYARD 638
. HUGH G. 577
. J. BENJAMIN 608
. J. DEW 588
. J. MARION 51,172,484
. J.D. 601
. J.L. 628
. J.R. 51
. JAMES 588,619
. JAMES J. 546,619
. JAMES S. 11,180
. JANE 230
. JESSE 179,181,354
. JESSEE 370,580,619
. JESSIE 415
. JOHN 207,258,484-485
512,619,625
. JOHN B. 180
. JOHN H. 644
. JOHN J. 604
. JOHN R. 625
. JOHN W. 484-485,576
. JOHNSON 546,619
. JOSEPH 527,581
. JOSEPH B. 580
. L. 580
. L.B. 567,645
. LAURA 498
. LAURA SMITH 266,391
498
. LEROY 265-266
. LEVIN 469
. LOT 126,180,182

. LOT B.	150,171,181-183	. WILLIAM	148,150,180	. EMALINE	469
	423,604		182-183,360-361,366	. EVA	469-470
. LOUISA	530		580,638	. FANNIE GAINEY	469
. LUCEAN	265	. WILLIAM D.	604	. GRADY	470
. MAHALA	256	. WILLIAM J.	625	. HERBERT	469
. MARGARET	182	. WILLIAMS	580	. HUGH G.	469
. MARY	181,328,399,477	. WILLIS	487,625	. JACOB	468
. MARY ANN	182,360	. ZANY	29,179	. JAMES	469
. MARY BARFIELD	179	ROLAND,ANNA	476	. JAMES V.	471,496
. MARY		ROPER,JOHN	360	. JAMES W.	608
BERRY	148,150,182	. NANCY	358	. JEREMIAH	471
. MARY GAME	487	. POCAHONTAS-		. JERRY	496
. MILLINGTON	595	SINCLAIR	315	. JESSE C.	644
. MIRANZA	181,399	ROSIER,SOOKEY	28	. JESSEE	469,625
. NANCY	182	. SUSAN	28	. JESSIE C.	374
. NANCY GEORGE	181	ROSS,	143	. JOHN	469,471
. NANNIE BETHEA	180	. J. NEWTON	590	. JOHN H.	625
. NATHAN	377	ROTHMAHLOR,	570	. JOSEPH	469-470
. OWEN M.	576	ROTHWELL,JONATHAN	544	. JULIA ATKINSON	469
. PAT	379	RHODA SELLERS	544	. JULIUS	469
. PENSY MARTIN	478	ROULLE,JAMES V.	621	. KEEVER	470
. PHILIP B.	150,182-183	ROUSE,	229	. LAURA WALL	434,469
	278,280,361	. PHILIP	329	. LENNIE I.	471
. PINCKNEY	619	. SALLIE LOCKE	329	. LINNIE I.	470
. R.H.	45,169,191,350	ROWELL,A.V.	434	. LIZZIE	
	391,562,567,636	. AGNES	468	BOATWRIGHT	469
. R.J.	477,645	. ALBERT	469	. MAMIE	470
. R.L.	51	. ALEXANDER-		. MARTHA BRANTLEY	470
. R.R.	584	VALENTINE	469	. MARTHA ELIZA	470
. RHERNAS	625	. ALICE	470	. MARTHA ELIZA-	
. ROBBIN	618	. ALICE REBECCA	469	ROWELL	470
. ROBERT C.	390,614	. ALPHEUS	469	. MARY A.	470
. ROBERT H.	29,179,590	. ANN	375	. MARY COLLINS	469
. ROBERTA GAME	487	. ANN BAKER	470	. MARY GASQUE	469
. ROBLIN W.	625	. ANN ELIZA	469	. MARY JANE	468
. SALIE EWART	474	. ANN ELIZABETH	470	. MATTIE E.	470-471
. SAMUEL	487	. ANN GASQUE	374-375	. MAXCY	470
. SARAH BETHEA	180,420		469	. MELVIN L.	470-471
. SILAS	180	. ANN GLISSON	469	. OLIVER	469
. SIMEON	487	. ANNIS DOZIER	469	. PAUL	469
. STACY ANN ROWELL	468	. ARCHIE	470	. PERCIVAL E.	470-471
. SUE	423	. ARTHUR	470	. R.F.	584
. SUSAN	377	. BENJAMIN	468-469	. R.R.	630
. SUSAN SELLERS	546	. BRUCE	470	. R.W.D.	470-471
. T.	576	. C. THOMAS	470	. REBECCA	468-469
. T.B.	45,172,485	. C.D.	470-471,636	. REBECCA PHILIPS	468
. TARLETON	179,186	. CARRIE	469	. RICHARD	468
. THOMAS	484,580	. CLARA	470	. ROBERT	434
. THOMAS G.	608	. CLAUDIUS	469	. ROBERT	
. THOMPSON	604	. DAVID	426,468-469,471	CHARLES	469-470
. TIMOTHY	180-181,309		625	. SALLIE	469
	377,399,420,625	. DAVID A.	608	. SALLIE KEEVER	470
. TRESTRAM B.	180	. DAVID J.	375	. SAMUEL	469
. TRISTRAM	619	. DAVID OSCAR	470	. SARAH	468
. TRISTRAM B.	484,619	. DORA	469	. SARAH ANN SMITH	496
. VIRGINIA NORTON	477	. ELIZA	469,525	. SILSY	496
. W.H.	601	. ELIZA LANDING	468	. SIMPSON WALL	434,470
. W.R.	485	. ELIZABETH	468	. STACY ANN	468
. WADE	625	. ELIZABETH AVANT	470	. SUSAN	469
		. ELLEN	470	. THOMAS	469

. VAL	468	
. VALENTINE	468-470,483	
496,514,566,576,608		
. W.B.	38,470-471	
. WILLIAM	468-469,496	
	576,644	
. WILLIAM B.	470,525	
	566-567	
. WILLIAM DAVID	469	
. WILLIAM L.	468	
. WILLIAM P.	608	
. WILLIE	470	
ROWLAND,ALFRED	292	
. FLORA ANN McKAY	292	
. JOHN A.	292	
ROZIER,S.S.	28	
RUCKER,RUFF	635	
RUSHING,ARCHIBALD	588	
. HENRY	261,588	
. JAMES	635	
. WILLIAM	588	
RUSS,JOHN	581	
. R.B.	599	
. ZACK	581	
RUTLEDGE,EDWARD	569	
. HUGH	73	
. JOHN	68,73,569	
SAINTCLAIR,J.W.	405	
SALMON,JOSEPH	581	
SAMUEL J.	577	
SALMONS,SAMUEL	644	
SAMPSON,JOSEPH	608	
SAMUEL	608	
SANDERS,ALICE	460	
. J.	628	
. JOHN	142	
. PETER	142,581	
SANDERSON,D.	610	
. DANIEL	613	
. JAMES	184	
. JOHN W.	638	
. SOLOMON	588	
SANGER,JOHN	621	
SARVIS,CORNELIUS	462	
. JOHN	605	
SASSAR,BENJAMIN	581	
SASSER,POLLY	473	
SAUNDERS,	138,140-142	
	158,435	
. CAROLINE McCALL	354	
. GEORGE	157-158	
. JOHN	157-158	
. JORDAN	158	
. MOSES	158	
. NATHANIEL	158	
. REBECCA McCALL	354	
. SMITHEY	158	
. THOMAS	158	
. TOBIAS	158	
. WILLIAM	157	
SAVAGE,	160	
. PATSY	502	
. SAMUEL S.	565	
SAWYER,JOHN	576,625	
. T.	601	
. THOMAS	331,576	
. WILLIS	644	
SAYLE,	2	
. WILLIAM	1,547,568	
SCARBOROUGH,A.L.	346	
. ADDISON L.	87,262,454	
. LEWIS	282	
. LOU	282	
. MARY	262	
. MARY F.	262	
. R.B.	282	
. RICHARD	143,262	
SCOTT,	94,356	
. ALLEN	638	
. ANDREW	588	
. APPIE ELVINGTON	175	
. AQUILLA	588	
. ELI	174	
. ELY	175	
. ERVIN	175	
. GILES	175	
. JAMES	174-175	
. JOHN L.	175	
. JOHN W.	589	
. PATIENCE	175,486	
. PHARAOH	175	
. PHAROAH	486	
. R.K.	96	
. ROBERT K.	570	
. SALLIE ELVINGTON	175	
. THOMAS	175	
. WILLIAM	175	
SEABROOK,		
WHITEMARSH B.	570	
SEELY,ALLEN	310	
. MARGARET		
McLELLAN	310	
SELLERS,	107,392,420,543	
. AGNES LEONA	412	
. ANNA J.	399	
. ANNA JANE	411,546	
. ANNA JANE BETHEA	412	
. ANNIE	156	
. ANNIE R.	411-412	
. B.B.	51,393	
. BENJAMIN	476,544,546	
. BENJAMIN B.	156,202	
	411-412	
. BENJAMIN D.	544	
. BENJAMIN MORGAN	411	
. BRYANT J.	545	
. CHLOE ROGERS	546	
. CIVIL	545-546	
. DORA CAMPBELL	488,546	
. ELISHA	544	
. ELIZABETH HUNCHY	545	
. ETTA	412	
. HARRIET J.- McPHERSON	412	
. HARRY	202,412	
. HENRY	544	
. JACOB	544	
. JAMES F.	546	
. JAMES JORDAN	545	
. JAMES O.	545	
. JAQUILINE OLIVER	413	
. JOEL	544	
. JOHN C.	43,51,97,155	
201-202,266,411,413		
546,560,567,571,646		
. JOHN DUBOIS	412	
. JOHN M.	411	
. JORDAN	235,544-545	
. LELIA	156	
. LEVIN	235-236,544	
. LUCY	156	
. LUCY B.	201,411-412	
. LUKE	544	
. M. SUE DUBOIS	412,424	
. MAGGIE E. MACE	411	
. MAGGIE ELLEN	156,412	
. MAGGIE ELLEN MACE	155,156	
. MAGGIE LEILA	411-412	
. MARGARET ELLEN	202,412	
. MARTHA ANN BETHEA	411	
. MARVIN McSWAIN	412	
. MARY	124,136,545-546	
. MARY O.	411,413	
. MARY OSBORNE	545	
. MATTHEW	544	
. MILDRED EUGENIA	412	
. NORMA WATSON	202,412	
. P.B.	424,571	
. PEARL	156,412	
. PHILIP B.	51,411-412	
	546	
. PHILIP BRUCE	412	
. RACHEL	546	
. RACHEL C.	411,479	
. RACHEL ELISE	412	
. RHODA	544	
. RUTH NORTON	476	
. SION	544	
. SUSAN	545-546	
. T.W.	488	
. THOMAS W.	546	
. W.W.	40,71,98,411-413	
	546,571	
. WALLACE D.	51,156	
. WALLACE DUNCAN	411-412	

. WILLIAM	544	. WILLIE	41,424	. WILLIAM	485-486
. WILLIAM MAYNARD	412	SHELBY,	463	. WILLIAM N.	486,589
. WILLIAM W.	411	SHELLEY, DAVID	605	. WILLIAM P.	170,455
. WRIGHT	544	. J.G.	628	SHREWSBERRY, ANNA	405
SESSIONS, CARRIE	406	. J.T.	601	. EDWARD C.	405,415
. CLYDE	367	. JOHN C.	608	SHULER,	488
. JANE TREZEVANT-WAYNE	367	. JOSEPH G.	576	SIGNER,	632
. ZACHARIAH			608	SIMMONS, E.B.	570
. JEREMIAH	367	SHELLY,	467,495	. JAMES	508
. JOHN D.	256,406	. BOYD	469	. KEATING L.	570
. LAURENS TREZEVANT	367	. C.W.	646	SIMONTON, C.H.	101
. DAVID			472,646		507-508
. LAWRENCE	230,487	. DAVID H.	431	SIMPSON, W.D.	101
. LAWRENCE T.	367	. IDA	473	SIMS, A.D.	571
. LAWRENCE TREZEVANT	367	. JAMES	469	SINCLAIR,	99,246,275
. MARIA			531	. A.C.	290-291,314
. PERCIVAL	615	. MARY ANN COLEMAN	472	. ARCHIBALD C.	577
. PERCY	367	. MARY ROWELL	469	. ARCHIE	314-315
. WESLEY W.	581	. NANCY	472	. BETTIE	290
SESSOMS,	244,428	. REBECCA ROWELL	469	. CATHARINE-McGILVRAY	314
SEXTON, OLIVER M.	619	. STARR	375		
SHACKELFORD,		. SUSAN GASQUE	375	. D.C.	314
. STEPHEN P.	608	. SUSAN ROWELL	469	. DANIEL C.	314
SHACKLEFORD, J.B.	644	. SUSAN WILLIAMSON	431	. DUNCAN	314
. JOHN B.	576	SHEPHARD, JOHN C.	570	. JENNETTE McLUCAS	314
. W.S.	644	SHERMAN,	254	. JENNIE CARMICHAEL	443
SHAFFER,	508	SHERWOOD,	423		
SHAKELFORD, MARTHA	353	. CADE	282	. JOHN C.	314
SHARP,	350	. ELLIE	397	. KATE	315
SHAW,	166,408,454,510	. JAMES	281-282	. MALCOM G.	581
. A.B.	646	. JOHN	281-282	. MARY	314-315
. A.J.	98-99,571	. LOU SCARBOROUGH	282	. MARY ANN BLUE	290
. ANN	520	. MARTHA BETHEA	281	. NANCY	314
. ARMSTRONG	520	. POSTELL	282	. POCAHONTAS	315
. BAKER	581	. RICHARD	598	. SALLIE	315
. BENJAMIN A.	576	. T.C.	646	SINEATH, JOSEPH P.	608
. BETSEY TANNER	520	SHHOTER,	494	SINGLETARY,	315
. CHARLEY	520	SHOOTER, ALBERT	210	. A.G.	50
. CLARENCE	520	. ALBERT H.	485-486	. ARCHIE G.	383
. DANIEL	520,581	. B. FRANK	486	. H.H.	644
. E.	628	. BENJAMIN	170,341	. HAMER	644
. EDWARD BAKER	520		484-486	. J.W.	383
. EVANDER	520	. BENJAMIN FRANKLIN	485	. JOSEPH W.	383-384
. H.	629			. R.L.	126,593
. HENRY	432,520	. BERRY A.	485,615	. SARAH EVANS	126
. J.H.	630	. CAROLINE FORD	168,485	. W.J.	51
. JOHN D.	518,520-521			. WILLIAM J.	571,619
. JOSEPH	520	. CHARLES F.	589	SINOTH, HANNAH	464
. JULIA	520	. EVANDER C.	485-486,585	SISTRUNK,	453
. MARIA LUCAS	520	. GEORGE E.	168,257	SMALLEY, ISAIAH	593
. MERDOCK	376	. GEORGE W.	485	SMILIE, A. GREGG	614
. SARAH WALL	432	. JOHN MILTON	485-486	SMITH,	65-66,232,256,388
. STEWART T.	520	. JOSEPHINE ROBERTS	486		416,467,502,536,551
. THOMAS	516,520				571,618
. WILLIAM	518-520	. MARTHA	485	. A. JACKSON	501
. WILLIE	520	. MARY	484,486	. A.J.	582
SHECKELFORD, JOHN B.	41	. MARY FORD	170	. A.N.	599
	449	. W. PINCKNEY	485	. ADALINE POWERS	496
. MARY POLLY	396	. W.P.	50,170,305,478	. AILSEY	496
. SUSAN DAVIS	449	. WASHINGTON P.	585	. ALBERT	390

. ALICE BETHEA 390	. ENOCH 576	. JOHN 67,193,492-493
. ALONZO 190	. EUGENE 265	495-496,500-501,584
. ANDERSON 644	. F.D. 610	621,625
. ANGELINA 473	. FANNIE	. JOHN A. 390
. ANNA 376,403,494,501	NICHOLS 190,391	. JOHN ALBERT 391,497
. ANNA BASS 231	. FLEMING 265	. JOHN B. 397
. ANNA M. 391,497	. FLORENCE 265,333,412	. JOHN G. 493,495
. ANNE GRANTHAM 499	479,498	. JOHN J. 619
. ANNE TURBEVILLE 496	. FOSTER 496	. JOHN L. 164,390-392
. ARCHIE 422	. FRANK 495	403,497,502
. ARTEMISSIA-	. FRENCH 495	. JOHN M. 376,501
WILLIAMSON 431	. G.W. 601	. JOSEPH 231,496,621
. AUGUSTUS 264,496,498	. GEORGE 495,500-501	. JULIA ANN 196
524	. GEORGE W. 264,392,481	. KATE BROWN 495
. B. GAUSE 165,392,412	498,615	. KEENE DAVIS 495
479,498	. GILMORE 500	. KESIAH LANE 390
. BENJAMIN	. GINSEY 498	. KITTIE 500,523
GAUSE 264,590	. GUERY 496	. L. BOYD 265
. BESSIE 265	. H. 609	. L.B. 51
. BETSY 496	. H.E.K. 273	. LAURA 266,391,498
. BETTIE SMITH 500	. H.L. 613	. LEGRANDE 495
. BILLY 523	. HAM E.G. 495	. LEILA 367
. BONHAM 264	. HARDY 496	. LELIA 265
. C. 97	. HARDY D. 621,625	. LEONARD 492-493
. C.C. 568,571	. HARRIETT 496	. LIDE 495
. C.W. 500	. HARVEY 500	. LILLY CLARK 253,494
. CALOM M. 619	. HELEN BASS 230,367	. LIZZIE 259
. CELIA 264	. HENRY 391,498-500	. LONZO 556
. CELIA LEWIS 501	. HENRY E.K. 397	. M.L. 494
. CHARLES 500	. HENRY W. 521	. MAMIE 452
. CHARLES B. 494	. HETTIE 391-392,497	. MARCUS L. 390-391,397
. CHLOE PERRITT 496	. HETTIE PERRITT 496	497,632
. CHRISTOPHER 585	. HUGH 183,495-496	. MARGARET 493,495,513
. COLIN 501	. HUGH G. 496,625	. MARGARET
. D. ASBURY 407	. HUGH GODBOLD 492-493	McMILLAN 422
. D.C. 642	495,513	. MARY 210,391,474,498
. DANIEL 501	. HUGH H. 493	. MARY E. 494
. DANIEL ASBURY 390-391	. IDA 186	. MARY EDWARDS 188
497	. ISAIAH 501	. MARY J. 497
. DAVID 493	. ISLA ELLERBE 494	. MARY POLLY
. DAVID A. 585	. J. ALBERT 42,367,565	HUGGINS 264
. DORA DEW 273	. J. EMORY 264-265,392	. MARY SMITH 391
. E. 584	431,498	. MASSEY 331
. E. KIRBY 477	. J.B. 630	. MAXCY 390
. E.B. 253,305,494-495	. J.F. 601	. MITCHELL ANDREW 496
567	. J.G. 584	. MOLLIE 501
. EBB 188	. J.K. 612,635	. MOSES 500-501
. EBBY 492,498	. J.R. 610	. N.P. 584
. EBENEZER 264,392	. J.W. 423,556-557,567	. NAT P. 499
. EDGAR 495	. JACOB W. 190,390-391	. NATHAN 644
. EDWARD 493,495,584	497,644	. NATHANIEL P. 499-500
. EDWARD B. 493	. JAMES 492,495,499,501	. NEILL 577
. EDWIN 290	584	. O.R. 64
. ELI 584	. JAMES D. 481	. PATTIE BETTS 494
. ELIZABETH 330,497-498	. JANE 391,403	. PATTIE McINTYRE 494
500	. JANE PAGE 496	. POLLY 265
. ELLISON H. 495	. JENNIE 391	. POLLY
. ELLY 495-496	. JENNIE SMITH 391	HUGGINS 265,392,498
. ELLY D. 532	. JERRY 493	. R. 584
. ELMIRE 496	. JIMMY 500	. R. BARNWELL 84

. REDDEN 531
. REDDIN W. 38,184,391
. REDDING 493,495
. REDDING W. 495
. REMBERT 265
. RHETT 84
. RHODA WHITE 527
. RICHARD 494
. ROBERT 496
. ROBERT J. 501
. S. 584
. S. ELMORE 264-265,392
498
. S. WHITEFORD 264-265
498
. S.W. 392,524
. SALLIE 496
. SALLIE HAYS 390,498
. SALLY H. 494
. SALLY H. SMITH 494
. SAMUEL 164,171,210,231
330,332-333,390,492
496,498
. SAMUEL O. 397,400
. SARAH ANN 496
. SCOTCH 502
. SOPHIA BETHEA 397
. STEPHEN 259,264-265
390,392,497-498,527
. STEPHEN LANE 400
. STONEWALL
JACKSON 495
. T.A. 599
. TELATHA FLOWERS 502
. THOMAS 568,644
. TILLMAN 495
. W.B. 584
. W.H. 230
. WESLEY 584
. WHITEFORD 265
. WILBUR F. 50,390,392
497-498
. WILLIAM 397
. WILLIAM B. 397,499-500
. WILLIAM H. 331,367,498
. WILLIS 496,646
. WILLIS G. 492-493
. ZACH 585
. ZACK 494
SMITHEY,G.W. 493,644
. J.W. 493
. JOHN 493
SNIPES, 534-536
. ADDISON 474
. ADDISON J. 370
. ADDISON JONATHAN 530
. ALLEN 529,532,589
. AMELIA 528-529
. ANNE 531

. ARCHIE GILCHRIST 531
532
. AUGUSTUS-
BEAUREGARD 530,531
. BARNES 529
. BENJAMIN
FRANKLIN 531,532
. BERTIE FAY 531
. BESSIE LOUISA 529
. BLAKELY 530
. CALEDONIA 528-529
. CALHOUN 530
. CARL 530
. CHARITY IKENOR 532
. CHARLES 529
. CHARLEY 529
. CHESLEY 532
. CHRISTOPHER 532
. CLYDE 531
. DANIEL 484,495,528-529
531-532,560,619
. DANIEL
PRESTON 531-532
. DAVID 528-529
. DOCTOR 529
. EDITH XIMENA 531
. EDWARD 532
. EDWIN 530
. ELIZABETH LOYD 531
. EMALINE 528-529
. ETHEL MILLISSA 531
. EVAN 530
. HENRY RUFUS 531
. HESTER HAUSEA 532
. J. 601
. J.S. 646
. JAMES 528-529,532
. JANE 528
. JANIE ETHEL 532
. JANIE ROBERTS 531
. JESSIE PEARL 532
. JIMMIE 529
. JOE 528-529,533,560
. JOE HOOKER 531-532
. JOHN 528,531
. JOSEPH 528
. JULIA 530-531
. JULIA ANN 529
. LILLY 531
. LIZZIE HASELDEN 529
. LOUISA 531
. LOUISA CASTLES 531
. LOUISA ROGERS 530
. MABELL 531
. MARIA SHELLY 531
. MARTHA 528
. MARY 528-529
. MARY ELIZ.
COLEMAN 530

. MARY
ELIZABETH 530-531
. MARY LUCRETIA 531
. MATILDA STANLY 529
. MATTIE 448,529
. MATTIE CARRIE 530-531
. MAY WALLER 531
. MICHAEL 529,532,593
. MINNIE C. TIMMONS 531
. MINNIE STEPHENS 529
. MONROE 531
. MOSES 576
. NELSON 528-529
. PATTY BROWN 528
. PERRY 529,532,619
. POLLY MARLOW 529
. POLLY VENTERS 529
. R.S. 612
. RALPH VINCENT 531
. RICHARD 529,532
. ROBERT 529
. ROBERT CHARLES 531
. ROSA 529
. ROSA B. COLEMAN 532
. RUFUS 531
. SERENA ADELAIDE 530
531
. TELATHA 528
. THOMAS 528-529,531-532
. VIOLA 531
. WADE HAPTON 529
. WILLIAM 528-530
. WILLIE 474
. WILLIE MAUDE 531
. WILSON 448,474,529-532
. WINFRED HUBERT 531
. WYATT ENSE 531
SNOW, 426
. ANN LEGETTE 367,372
. IDA 372
SNOWDEN, 414
SOTHEL,SETH 568
SOULS,J.W. 625
SPAIN,A.C. 71,571
SPARKMAN,
. GEORGE R. 593
. LEVI 591
SPARKS, 204
SPEARS,ANDREW J. 401
. DEBROAH BETHEA 401
. EDWIN A. 401
. JAMES 401
SPENCER, 427
. HENRY 428
. J.F. 428-429
. JOHN 428-429
. JOHN F. 119,428
. NATHAN 119,428
. THOMAS 428-429
. WILLIAM 428-429

. REDDEN	531
. REDDIN W.	38,184,391
. REDDING	493,495
. REDDING W.	495
. REMBERT	265
. RHETT	84
. RHODA WHITE	527
. RICHARD	494
. ROBERT	496
. ROBERT J.	501
. S.	584
. S. ELMORE	264-265,392
	498
. S. WHITEFORD	264-265
	498
. S.W.	392,524
. SALLIE	496
. SALLIE HAYS	390,498
. SALLY H.	494
. SALLY H. SMITH	494
. SAMUEL	164,171,210,231
	330,332-333,390,492
	496,498
. SAMUEL O.	397,400
. SARAH ANN	496
. SCOTCH	502
. SOPHIA BETHEA	397
. STEPHEN	259,264-265
	390,392,497-498,527
. STEPHEN LANE	400
. STONEWALL JACKSON	495
. T.A.	599
. TELATHA FLOWERS	502
. THOMAS	568,644
. TILLMAN	495
. W.B.	584
. W.H.	230
. WESLEY	584
. WHITEFORD	265
. WILBUR F.	50,390,392
	497-498
. WILLIAM	397
. WILLIAM B.	397,499-500
. WILLIAM H.	331,367,498
. WILLIS	496,646
. WILLIS G.	492-493
. ZACH	585
. ZACK	494
SMITHEY,G.W.	493,644
. J.W.	493
. JOHN	493
SNIPES,	534-536
. ADDISON	474
. ADDISON J.	370
. ADDISON JONATHAN	530
. ALLEN	529,532,589
. AMELIA	528-529
. ANNE	531
. ARCHIE GILCHRIST	531
	532
. AUGUSTUS-BEAUREGARD	530,531
. BARNES	529
. BENJAMIN FRANKLIN	531,532
. BERTIE FAY	531
. BESSIE LOUISA	529
. BLAKELY	530
. CALEDONIA	528-529
. CALHOUN	530
. CARL	530
. CHARITY IKENOR	532
. CHARLES	529
. CHARLEY	529
. CHESLEY	532
. CHRISTOPHER	532
. CLYDE	531
. DANIEL	484,495,528-529
	531-532,560,619
. DANIEL PRESTON	531-532
. DAVID	528-529
. DOCTOR	529
. EDITH XIMENA	531
. EDWARD	532
. EDWIN	530
. ELIZABETH LOYD	531
. EMALINE	528-529
. ETHEL MILLISSA	531
. EVAN	530
. HENRY RUFUS	531
. HESTER HAUSEA	532
. J.	601
. J.S.	646
. JAMES	528-529,532
. JANE	528
. JANIE ETHEL	532
. JANIE ROBERTS	531
. JESSIE PEARL	532
. JIMMIE	529
. JOE	528-529,533,560
. JOE HOOKER	531-532
. JOHN	528,531
. JOSEPH	528
. JULIA	530-531
. JULIA ANN	529
. LILLY	531
. LIZZIE HASELDEN	529
. LOUISA	531
. LOUISA CASTLES	531
. LOUISA ROGERS	530
. MABELL	531
. MARIA SHELLY	531
. MARTHA	528
. MARY	528-529
. MARY ELIZ. COLEMAN	530
. MARY ELIZABETH	530-531
. MARY LUCRETIA	531
. MATILDA STANLY	529
. MATTIE	448,529
. MATTIE CARRIE	530-531
. MAY WALLER	531
. MICHAEL	529,532,593
. MINNIE C. TIMMONS	531
. MINNIE STEPHENS	529
. MONROE	531
. MOSES	576
. NELSON	528-529
. PATTY BROWN	528
. PERRY	529,532,619
. POLLY MARLOW	529
. POLLY VENTERS	529
. R.S.	612
. RALPH VINCENT	531
. RICHARD	529,532
. ROBERT	529
. ROBERT CHARLES	531
. ROSA	529
. ROSA B. COLEMAN	532
. RUFUS	531
. SERENA ADELAIDE	530
	531
. TELATHA	528
. THOMAS	528-529,531-532
. VIOLA	531
. WADE HAPTON	529
. WILLIAM	528-530
. WILLIE	474
. WILLIE MAUDE	531
. WILSON	448,474,529-532
. WINFRED HUBERT	531
. WYATT ENSE	531
SNOW,	426
. ANN LEGETTE	367,372
. IDA	372
SNOWDEN,	414
SOTHEL,SETH	568
SOULS,J.W.	625
SPAIN,A.C.	71,571
SPARKMAN,	
. GEORGE R.	593
. LEVI	591
SPARKS,	204
SPEARS,ANDREW J.	401
. DEBROAH BETHEA	401
. EDWIN A.	401
. JAMES	401
SPENCER,	427
. HENRY	428
. J.F.	428-429
. JOHN	428-429
. JOHN F.	119,428
. NATHAN	119,428
. THOMAS	428-429
. WILLIAM	428-429

. MARTHA		
McCRACKEN	462	
. MARY	463	
. MARY LEWIS	463	
. MATTIE	463	
. MATTIE		
GODBOLD	124,463	
. ROBERT	463	
. SAMUEL	63,313,463	
. SAMUEL M.	462	
. SUSAN	463	
. SUSAN GREGG	463	
. WILLIAM	462	
STEWART,ARCHIE	310	
. MARY ANN		
McLELLAN	310	
. ORELLA		
CARMICHAEL	302	
. PETER	302	
. RAN	632	
STITH,	129	
STJOHN,	76	
. JAMES H.	79	
STOCKS,JOHN	605	
STOEBER,E.M.	567	
STOKES,JOHN	632	
STONE,F.F.	596	
. R.W.	630	
. SAMUEL J.	619	
. W.C.P.	593,596	
. WILLIAM	584	
STRICKLAND,ERVIN	625	
. FERABA	482	
. ROS.	625	
STRINGFELLOW,	349	
STROBEL,SALLIE	408	
STROBHART,	427	
STROUD,JOHN H.	554	
STUART,DAVID	344	
. ELIZABETH	344	
. HARDY	344	
STUBBS,	269	
. J.W.	646	
. MARY ANN	269	
STURGES,	356	
. S.B.	642	
. SAMUEL	638	
STURGIS,	452	
. MORGAN W.	452	
SUMMERFORD,WILLIAM	576	
SUMMERSET,	526	
SURLES,ARCHIBALD	598	
SURLS,A.B.	247	
SUTTON,JOHN E.	619	
. WILLIAM H.	619	
SWAILS,S.A.	94,96	
SWEAT,	543	
. GEORGE	394	
. N.	612	
SWEET,DAVID	633	

. EBENEZER L.	572	
. GAUSE	382	
. GOSPERO	447,566	
. MARY BAKER	382,447	
. W.P.	601	
SYPHRETT,J.W.W.	619	
TABLER,W.	601	
TANNER,	209,516	
. ANN SHAW	520	
. BETSEY	520	
. JOHN	642	
. JOHN L.	638	
. ROBESON	520	
. TOM	585	
. W.N.	642	
TART,	125,194,218,242	
. AMELIA	196,326	
. ANDREW	268,400	
. C.	628	
. C. MURCHISON	492	
. CAROLINE	474	
. CARRIE BETHEA	404	
. DICEY BASS	231	
. DOG ENOS	196	
. E. MURCHISON	644	
. ELIZABETH	185,194	
. ENOS	64,149,185	
	193-197,492,540,565	
	566,568	
. ENOS MURCHISON	196	
. FAMA	148,150,270,474	
. FAMA BERRY	148-149	
	157,196-197	
. G.	635	
. GADIE	149	
. H. TART	149	
. H.H.	150	
. HENRY	644	
. HENRY J.	619	
. J.W.	610	
. JAMES	39,196,326,400	
	492,639	
. JAMES H.	149,619	
. JANE	149,194-195,335	
. JOHN	193,196,400,404	
. JOHN M.	620	
. JOHN W.	196,400-401	
	481,614	
. JULIA ANN SMITH	196	
. LISPIA ROBERTS	210	
. MARGARET	401	
. MARGARET BETHEA	400	
. NATHAN	148-149,193	
	195-197,646	
. RUSSELL ENOS	197	
. SUSAN	194	
. SUSANNA JOHNSON	194	
. SUSANNAH		
JOHNSON	540	
. THOMAS E.	149,195,210	

TATUM,		
. JESSIE		
CARMICHAEL	351	
. WALTER	351	
TAYLOR,	120,382,570	
. ANN ELIZABETH-		
ROWELL	470	
. AQUILLA	589	
. ARCHIE	472	
. BENJAMIN B.	625	
. CATHERINE GILES	472	
. CHARLES	198,210	
. CHARLOTTE J.	472	
. D.J.	11,470	
. DAVID	589	
. DAVID J.	446	
. E.P.	51	
. EDWARD E.	472	
. EPHRAIM	14,599	
. GEORGE	581	
. HUGH G.	472	
. J.R.	613	
. JAMES	644	
. JAMES ROBERT	472	
. JENNETTE		
ELIZABETH	472	
. JOHN	569,632	
. JOHN E.	619	
. JOHN M.	625	
. JOSEPH	589	
. JOSEPH A.	472	
. JULIA DAISY	472	
. JULIA FLOWERS	472	
. MARY ELIZA	472	
. MORGAN	14	
. PENELOPE ROBERTS	210	
. R.W.	630	
. ROBERT	472	
. SARAH ANNIS	472	
. THOMAS	14	
. WILLIAM	581	
TEDDER,DANIEL M.	576	
. W.J.	632	
TEMPLE,L.W.	163	
TENHET,EDGAR	251	
. ETHEL	251	
. J.R.N.	251	
. OTHO	251	
TENNENT,MARTHA	446	
TESKY,MARY		
McEACHERN	130	
THOMAS,	539	
. CADE	375,589	
. DAVID	589	
. DRURY	374	
. E.	628	
. E.R.	632	
. H.	628	
. JAMES	451,590	
. JAMES H.	639	

Name	Page	Name	Page	Name	Page
. JOSEPH	581	TILLER,DOVE	647	. JOH	540
. MARTHA ANN		TILLMAN,	490	. JOHN	140-141
WIGGINS	516	. B.R.	338	. JOSEPH	496
. MARTHA DAVIS	451	. BENJAMIN R.	570	. LEMUEL	496,646
. MARY ANN	405	TIMMERMAN,		. LIZZIE LEE	496
. MARY DAVIS	451	. CHARLOTTE		. NED	141
. NANCY GASQUE	374	THOMPSON	233	. ORPHEA LANE	395
. NELSON	619	. P.N.	233	. P.	628
. PATRICK	619	TIMMONS,ANNIE	452	. PINCKNEY	646
. S.	628	. BURNETT	639	. RICHARD	619
. SAMUEL B.	576	. J.C.	646	. ROBERT	141
. SAMUEL W.	590	. LUTHER	639	. S.	630
. TRISTRAM	451	. MINNIE C.	531	. SALLIE SMITH	496
. YANCY	516	. WILLIAM	644	. SAMUEL	141,646
THOMPSON,	169,171,192	TINDAL,EMANUEL	608	. SOLOMON	590
	426,571	. SOLOMON	608	. STEPHEN	141,245
. ARCHIE	172	TODD,ALVA	457	. W.	628
. B.A.	567	TOLAR,JOHN H.	577	. WILLIAM	139-141,197
. B.F.	96	. SARAH FOWLER	483		496,644
. CHAPMAN	464	TOUCHBERRY,		. WILLIAM S.	620
. CHARLOTTE	233	JERRY	106,109	TURNER,	543
. ELIZ.	233	TOWLSON,GEORGE W.	619	. A.	613
. ELIZ. THOMPSON	233	TOWNSEND,	168-169,233	. E.	613
. ELIZABETH A.			417,425	. G.W.	630
HAMER	232	. ADALINE	183	. J.	613,628
. ELIZABETH		. C.P.	571	. JAMES	619
EDWARDS	188	. D. LATTA	478	. JOEL	599,635
. FLORA BETHEA	232,416	. D.A.	183	. JOHN	581
. HOWARD	464	. DANIEL A.	599	. JOHN C.	593,599,605
. HUGH S.	570	. DAVID	233	. JOHN K.	638
. J.C.	490	. ELIAS	185,194,348	. JOSEPH	625
. J.H.	430	. ELIZABETH TART	194	. L.	613
. JAMES T.	576	. FRANCIS M.	576	. LEWIS	642
. JEFFERSON	464	. JABISH	281	. MARTIN	635
. JESSE	464	. JACOB	183	. MOSES	638
. JOHN	188,232	. LIGHT	286	. R.H.	630
. JOHN C.	464	. MATTIE NORTON	478	. RICHARD	613
. LEMUEL	233	. MEEKIN	281	. ROBERT	638
. LEMUEL S.	364	. REBECCA	281	. S.D.	613
. LEWIS	179	. S.J.	571	. STEPHEN	613
. LUCY	364	TRAVIS,JOSEPH F.	38	. T.D.	630
. MARTHA ANN-		TRAWICK,DAVID	292	. W.	613
WILLIAMSON	430	. ELMYRA McKELLAR	292	. W.S.	613
. MARTHA		. MACK	292	. WILLIAM	619,646
WILLIAMSON	464	. WILLIAM	292	. WILLIS	635
. MARY	233,541-542	TREZEVANT,ESTHER	366	TWIGGS,DAVID E.	345
. MOLLIE	232	. LEWIS	366	TWINING,	
. ROBERT	233	TUCKER,JOHN	608	. HATTIE GASQUE	376
. SOPHIA BETHEA	497	TURBEVILLE,	140,429	TYLER,	108,135,137,166
. STEPHEN	464	. ABSALOM	140-141,540		448
. TRISTRAM	232,416	. ALBERT B.	625	. JOHN	86-87,375,454
. W.H.	457	. ANNE	496	. RICHARD	576
. W.M.	602	. ASA	140,608	. SARAH GASQUE	375
. WILLIAM	464,541	. B.	640	TYRREL,	456,560-561
THORNTON,	273	. BETHEL	141	TYUTE,EDWARD	569
THORNWELL,		. CALVIN	605	VAMPELT,MOURNING	480
. CHARLES A.	571	. EDWARD	141	VAN BUREN,MARTIN	453
THWING,	181	. F.	628	VAN DORN,EARLE	477
TILER,GEORGE	646	. GEORGE	141,496,625,633	VANBUREN,	87-88
. J.M.	646	. JAMES	515,619	. MARTIN	86

VANCE, 41,121	. SAMUEL 434	. JANE TART 149
. ZEB 379	. SARAH 432-433	. JOHN W. 605
VANDERHORST,A. 569	. SIMPSON 433-434,470	. WILLIS 149,644
VANTEP,WILLIAM 625	. W.A. 646	WATIES,THOMAS 73
VAUGHT, 432,515	. W.B. 582	WATSON, 112-113,221,243
. ELIZABETH-	. WASHINGTON 432,520	333,391,431,433,443
LEDINGHAM 373	. WILLIAM A. 432,434,566	522,526,543
VENTERS,POLLY 529	. WILLIAM B. 433-434	. ADDIE BETHEA 200,229
VERDRIES, 570	. WILLOUGHBY 448	. AGNES ROWELL 468
VONKOLNITZ, 366	. WILMAR 434	. ALBERT 201
WAGNER,A.C. 646	. WRIGHT 432,435	. ALMA 154
WALKER,A. 585	WALLACE,JOHN J. 609	. ANN 375
. H. 646	. W.J. 602	. ANNIE FORE 154,201
. HANNAH 415	. WILLIAM H. 103	. BARNABAS 199
. HENRY 620	WALLER, 219,543	. BARNEY 205-206,626
WALL, 285	. G.W. 602	. BARNY 199
. ALBERT 433,639	. HENRY 379	. BETTIE 211
. AMANDA 432,435	. JANE BROWN 379	. BEULAH EMANUEL 199
. ANNE 463	. MARTHA 472	. BUCK 167
. BEATY 448	. MAY 531	. BURKE 154
. C.M. 630	WALLING, 199	. CELIA EASTERLING 199
. CHAPMAN 434	WALPOLE,ROBERT 95	386
. CLARISSA 465	WALSH,GEORGE C. 510	. CHARLES 200
. COLUMBUS 432	. HENRY 590	. CHERRY DEER 201
. EDWIN 433-434	. J.T. 571	. CICERO 200
. EDWIN J. 349	. JAMES B. 626	. D. MAXCY 201,412
. ELIZA 433-434	. TRACY R. 38,263	. D.I. 195,335
. ELIZABETH 432-434	WALTER, 283	. DAVID 635
. ELIZABETH MACE 205	. AUGUSTUS J. 581	. DAVID E. 199,226,590
. ELLEN KEEVER 434	. JOHN R. 581	. DRUSILLA 200
. ESTELLE 448	. PHILIP D. 599	. DUNCAN I. 200
. F.M. 448	. WILLIAM B. 581	. DUNCAN J. 319
. FURMAN 205,433-434	WALTERS, 244	. ED B. 229
. GABRIELLA 432-433	. AUGUSTUS J. 295	. EDWARD B. 200
. GEORGE 285,432,513,520	. BETTIE 295	. ELIZABETH 199,203,207
. H. 585	. ELIZABETH BETHEA 420	. ELIZABETH JONES 200
. HENRY 433,639	. HARRIET 295	245
. HUGH G. 432-433	. JEREMIAH 403,420	. ELLEN 201-202,226
. ISAIAH 432,434-435	. LEMANTHA 310	. ENOS 199
. J.C. 631	. LEONARD 321	. EUPHEMIA 153
. J.W. 631	. MARTHA ANN 403	. FAMA 199,204,244
. JAMES 432,434	. MARY CAMPBELL 321	. FANNIE
. JIM 585	. SALLIE EDINO 295	STACKHOUSE 288
. JOHN 432	. TRISTRAM B. 294	. FLORA ELLEN LANE 274
. JULIUS 434-435	. WILLIAM 295	. FLORA LANE 200
. LAURA 433-434,469	. WILLIE 295	. FURMAN 201
. LAWSON 432,435	WANNAMAKER, 390,497	. GEORGE E. 200
. LAWSON D. 434-435	WARD, 425,531	. GEORGE ELMORE 319
. LAWSON J. 609	. COLIN 626	. GREEN 327
. MARION 433-435	. J.M. 642	. HENRY 199
. MARTHA 432	. W. 628	. HORTENSIA 199-200,226
. MARY ELLEN 434	WARDLAW,D.L. 72-73	. HOYT 154
. MARY OWENS 432	. F. 72	. I.H. 565,646
. NEVADA 448	. F.H. 84	. ISHAM 39,153,199-200
. PETER 432	. FRANK 73	202-206,270,276-277
. PRESSLY 434-435	WARING, 43	. ISHAM E. 199,646
. REBECCA BAKER 448	WARLEY,F.F. 571	. ISHAM H. 190,199-200
. S.B. 602	WASHINGTON, 343,545	319,323,440
. S.J. 631	. GEORGE 113	. JAMES 40,162,199-200
. SALLIE HARLLEE 349	WATERS, 248	245

. JAMES R.	274,620	
. JANE	199,205	
. JANIE	200	
. JASPER	154	
. JOHN G.	201	
. JOHN R.	169,206,593	
	605	
. JOSEPH	398	
. JOSEPH F.	200	
. JULIAN	154	
. KATE	199,218	
. KERIGAN	206	
. KITSEY HAM	206	
. KITTIE BETHEA	398	
. LAVINA	199	
. LAWTON	154	
. LINDSAY	605	
. LUCY B.	393	
. LUCY B. SELLERS	201	
	412	
. M.M.	300	
. MAGGIE	165,200,202,385	
. MAGGIE MOODY	195,335	
. MARK	280	
. MARTHA	199	
. MARY	199-200,204	
. MARY E.	40	
. MARY HAYES	270	
. MARY HAYS	199	
. MARY NICHOLS	190,200	
	319	
. MATTHEW	199,218,226	
	386	
. MELTON	200-201	
. MEMORY	154	
. MEREDITH	205,325,332	
	394	
. MERIDETH	626	
. MICHAEL	206	
. MILTON	332	
. NANCY	199,202	
. NANCY McDUFFIE	319	
. NEEDHAM	206	
. NELLIE	199,202	
. NORA	154	
. NORMA	201-202,412	
. PATIENCE BUTLER	327	
. PAULINE	154,201-202	
	518	
. PRATT	154	
. QUINN	593,605	
. ROBERT	199	
. ROSA BASS	226	
. ROSE BASS	199	
. S.C.	200-201	
. S.P.	165,200-201	
. SALLIE FORD	169,206	
. SAMUEL	146,165,199-202	
	210	
. SARAH	200	

. SCAREBOOK	168	
. SEACEBOOK	206	
. SILAS	199	
. SMITHY HAM	206	
. SOPHRONIA	165,200,202	
. STONEWALL	288	
. STONEWALL C.	165	
. TELATHA	200	
. THEODOCIA EMANUEL	199	
. THOMAS	206	
. TONY	468	
. VERZELLA	199	
. VERZILLA	202	
. W. JOSEPH	165	
. W. JOSEPH MELTON	165	
. W.J.	200	
. WICKHAM	206	
. WILLIAM	154,165,167	
	199,201-202,226,339	
	412,518	
. WILLIAM E.	201	
. WILLIE	154	
WAYNE,	391,510,536	
. ANTHONY	366	
. ASBURY	366	
. CAROLINA ANNA	367	
. CATHERINE M.	368	
. DANIEL G.	366	
. DAVID	581	
. ELEANOR GREGG	366	
. ELIZABETH	368	
. ELIZABETH M.- LEGETTE	367	
. ELIZABETH W.- LEGETTE	372	
. ESTHER TREZEVANT	366	
. F.A.	367,369	
. FRANCIS A.	372,586	
. FRANCIS ASBURY	366,369	
. GABRIEL I.	369,391	
. JANE TREZEVANT	367	
. JULIA	369,391	
. MARTHA	366	
. MARY A.	373	
. MARY ADELAINE	368	
. SARAH	368	
. WILLIAM	366	
WEATHERBY,COLON W.	416	
WEATHERFORD,BEN	596	
. W.S.	596	
. W.T.	585	
WEBB,JOHN	576	
WEEMS,M.L.	112	
. MASON L.	528,533	
WELLS,	127	
. G.H.	585	
. WALTER H.	51	

WELSH,		
. CHARLOTTE ATKINSON	489	
. JAMES E.	644	
WESLEY,CHARLES	135,449	
. JOHN	448	
WEST,JOHN	457	
. JOSEPH	1,547,568	
. RUTH BETHEA	392	
WETHERFORD,	272	
WHALEY,BETSY	472	
. D.B.	457	
. ELLA GUYTON	457	
. F.D.	457	
. FRANCES REGAN	457	
. GEORGE	581	
. H.J.	457	
. IDA DAVIS	457	
. JOHN H.	457,609	
. M.F. ALTMAN	457	
. SUSAN CARTER	457	
. W. MANLY	457	
. WILLIAM M.	609	
WHATCOAT,	505	
WHEELER,	333,369,493	
. CARRIE BOYD	371	
. CLARA L. LEGETTE	370	
. E.B.	11,38,120,344,370	
	515,564	
. E.H.	493	
. ED B.	143	
. ED. B.	371	
. EDWARD B.	131,568	
. EFFA BLUE	371	
. EFFIE BLUE	131	
. H.B.	644	
. J. HAMILTON	143	
. JAMES HAMILTON	370	
. LISTON C.	371	
. O.P.	143,262	
. SARAH JANE CHERRY	370	
. SARAH JANE GRAHAM	143	
. TISTON C.	143	
WHILDEN,	538	
WHIPPER,W.J.	94,100	
WHITAKER,J.C.	631	
WHITE,	82,220,444,460	
	475,483,529	
. ADA McCORMICK	296	
. ALICE	525	
. ANDREW	525	
. ANGELINE	525-526	
. ANN ELIZA	527	
. ANN ELIZA- STACKHOUSE	525	
. ANNIE	454	
. AUGUSTUS K.	572	
. BENJAMIN	525,527	

Name	Page
. CHARLOTTE	525
. ELIZA ROWELL	525
. ELIZABETH	525
. ELIZABETH AVANT	525
. EUGENIA	525
. EVANDER	527,646
. FANETTA	525-526
. FANNIE	527
. FRANCES FINKLEA	525
. HANNAH GERALD	527
. HUGH	527
. HUGH L.	86
. J.B.	646
. JAMES	222,525,527-528
. JAMES H.	609
. JANE FORT	527
. JOHN	525,644
. JOSEPH	525,527
. JUDITH GAINEY	525
. MAGGIE LUCAS	527
. MARTHA	222,525
. MARY	525-527
. MARY FORE	525
. MATTHEW	525
. NELSON	525
. NELSON J.	590
. RHODA	525,527
. SALLIE	222,525
. SALLIE MACE	222,528
. SILAS	525,527
. STEPHEN	122,503 525-528
. SUSAN	222
. T.C.	433
. W.	646
. W. BOONE	296
. W. COKE	644
. W.S.	582,585
. WESLEY	222,454,466,527
. WHITBY	525
. WILLIAM	222,525,590
WHITEHART,CORDE	516
. VIRGINIA WIGGINS	516
WHITEHEARTE,	
. FILMORE	500
. JIMMY SMITH	500
WHITNER,	337,379
. JOSEPH N.	593
WHITNEY,ELI	19-21,24
WHITTAKER,	632
WHITTEMORE,B.F.	95
WHITTER,	379
WHITTIER,	379
WHITTINGTON,	268
. C.C.	609
. J.G.	613
. J.N.	646
. MOSES	581
. W.G.	635
WICHAM,THOMAS	566
WICKHAM,THOMAS	62
. THOMAS J.	214,568
WIGGINS,	454
. ABY BUTLER	518
. BAKER	516-517,520,581
. BENJAMIN	516-517
. C. WESLEY	518
. C.W.	639
. CALVIN	581
. CHARLES	516,518
. CHARLES W.	202
. DANIEL	516
. E.J.	642
. ED	620
. ELIAS	516
. ELIZA	516
. ELIZABETH POWELL	516
. FLORENCE JOHNSON	516
. FRANCIS MARION	516
. H.	585
. HANNAH	310
. HARMAN	516
. HENRY	518
. HENRY HOUSTON	516
. J.B.	602,626
. J.M.	636
. J.W.	628
. JASPER	516
. JOHN	626
. JOHN M.	518
. JUDAH FOXWORTH	516
. MARION	518
. MARTHA ANN	516
. MICAJAH	516
. MOLLY BRITT	518
. NATHAN	369
. PAULINE WATSON	202,518
. STEPHEN	516
. SUSAN	516-517
. VIRGINIA	516
. W. HENRY	639
WILCOX,	513,551
. CAROLINA ANNA-WAYNE	367
. CLARK A.	536
. EDWARD T.	536-537
. GEORGE	367
. HENRY	537
. HENRY M.	50,536
. JAMES C.	536
. JOHN	367,391,498 536-537,565-566,568 642
. LEILA SMITH	367
. MINNIE MOORE	536
. P.A.	51,536-537
WILDER,A.J.	585
WILDS,S.	570
. SAMUEL	73
WILKERSON,J.R.	636
WILKES,JAMES	635
WILKINS,	570
WILKINSON,	294
. JAMES	635
WILLARD,A.J.	103
WILLIAMS,	111,120,288 464,543
. ADDIE LEWIS	482
. BENJAMIN	251
. CALEB	387
. D.N.	631
. DAVID R.	569
. ELIZABETH BRADDY	251
. ELIZABETH ROWELL	468
. FRANCES PHILIPS	465
. GEORGE	639
. GEORGE N.	644
. GREEN	468
. HENRY	596
. HENRY S.B.	608
. J.B.	190,243,289
. J.J.	629
. JACOB H.	609
. JAMES A.	644
. JEFFERSON	251
. JOHN	465
. JOHN C.	608
. JORDAN	609
. KATIE MARTIN	259
. LILIAN BETHEA	391
. LUCY ELLEN JONES	190
. MAGGIE	260,444
. MARY BRASWELL	436
. NANNIE BETHEA	391
. OLIVER	482
. PERRY J.	187,259-260
. R.L.	596
. S.B.	596
. S.J.	646
. SAMUEL	642
. SARAH PROCTOR	487
. SILAS	639
. SUE MARTIN	260
. THOMAS	596,639
. THOMPSON	436
WILLIAMSON,	256,375,432 444
. ADRA	430
. ALICE	430
. AMBROSE	431
. ANNIE	430
. ANNIS	430
. ARTEMISSIA	431
. ARTIMISSIA M.	430
. BERTHA	431
. BRIGHT J.	430-431,577
. CELIA MARTIN	431
. CHARLEY	431

. CHARLIE 431	. MARY 421,430	. SAMUEL 355,422
. CRISTIE 431	. MARY A. OLIVER 431	. SARAH 422
. D.J. 585,626	. MARY E. BAKER 430	. WILLIAM T. 87,454
. D.V. 582	. MARY ELIZ. BAKER 447	WINDHAM,GEORGE 632
. DANIEL 483	. MARY JENKINS 429	WISE, 297
. DANIEL J. 430-431	. MARY JORDAN 429	. A.G. 272
. DANIEL L. 430	. MARY K. McINTYRE 430	. AQUILLA 272
. DAVID C. 430-431	. MARY McINTYRE 303	. BRADLEY 626
. DAVID R. 429-430,577	. MODANZA 431	. CHARITY DEW 272
. ELIZ. A. 430-431	. MONROE 431	. E.T. 613
. ELIZ. A.-	. OVERTON 431	. EMMA 429-430
WILLIAMSON 430,431	. PRUDENCE 431	. FINKLEA G. 272
. ELIZ. S. 430	. PRUDENCE ANNE 430	. J.M. 576
. ELIZABETH 421,431	. PRUDENCE	. JAMES C. 272
. ELIZABETH ANNIE 430	NANCE 429-431	. MARTHA MILLER 476
. ELIZABETH O. 429-430	. REMBERT 431	. MOSES 429,476
. ELIZABETH S. 430	. ROBERT L. 429-430,572	. THOMAS AQUILLA 272
. EMMA J. 429-430	. RYAN 431	. WILSON D. 644
. EMMA WISE 429-430	. SAMUEL W. 429-430,577	WISHART, 250
. EULAH 431	. SARAH A. 431	WITHEROW,W.H. 38,644
. FERDINAND 430-431	. SARAH ANN 430	WITHERSPOON,GAVIN 566
. FRANCES PHILIPS 429	. SARAH E. 430	. JOHN D. 30
430	. SIDI 431	WOLLING, 425
. FRANCOIS BELK 431	. SOL M. 577	WOOD,JOHN 635
. GROVER 431	. SOLOMON M. 429-430	WOODAD,L. 628
. GUSTAVUS A. 430-431	. SUSAN 431	WOODBERRY, 48,106,110
. HANNA F. 430	. SUSANNAH 430-431	. AGNES 356
. HANNAH F. 430	. SYDNEY G. 430-431	. ANN BROWN 380
. J.B. 626	. TRECIA FOWLER 431	. ANN GREGG 356,510
. J.W. 308,646	. VELNA 431	. BENJAMIN G. 380
. JAMES 646	. W. LAWRENCE 430-431	. BENJAMIN
. JANE A. COLLINS 430	. WALTER 431	GAUSE 355-356
. JESSEE 431	. WILBORN 431	. DESDA DAVIS 110,355
. JOHN 421,429-430,466	. WILLIAM D. 429-431	. DORA 356
. JOHN B. 430	. WILLIAM J. 174,430-431	. EDWARD 356
. JOHN C. 430-431	. WILLIAM L. 447	. ELIZABETH ANN 356
. JOHN J. 429-431,447	. WILLIE 431	. ELOISE 355
. JOSEPH 166,265,429-430	. ZILPHA COLLINS 430	. EVANDER M. 605
. JOSEPH M. 429-431,577	WILLIFORD,A.S. 642	. EVANDER McIVER 356
. JOSEPH W. 303,321,430	. R.J. 642	. FANNIE 110,355
. JUNIUS 431	WILLIS, 310,545	. FRANKLIN 355
. L.J. 646	. FANNIE 300	. G.W. 40,380-381
. L.M.T. ELVINGTON 431	WILLSON,BESSIE 461	. GEORGE W. 355
. LAYTON 431	. JOHN O. 461	. GEORGE
. LEONARD 572	. MARY RICHARDSON 461	WASHINGTON 356
. LEONARD S. 431	WILSON, 223,397,571	. HANNAH DAVIS 110,356
. LEONORA S. 430	. ALEXANDER 632	. HARRIET BROWN 380
. LOLAH 431	. ANNE HARLLEE 349	. HARRISON 356
. LONNIE 431	. ANNE LEWIS 482	. JAMES 356
. LUNA 431	. FANNIE WOODBERRY 110	. JOANNA BALLOONE 356
. MARCELLUS 431	355	. JOHN 88,110,355-356
. MARTHA 431,464,466	. J. 613	510
. MARTHA A. 429-430	. J.T. 609	. JONAH 110,355,358
. MARTHA A.R. 430-431	. JOHN A. 482	. JOSEPH A. 356
. MARTHA ANN 430	. JOHN B. 237	. JOSEPH ALSTON 356
. MARTHA COLEMAN 430	. JOHN L. 569	. JULIA 40,356
. MARTHA FOWLER 483	. JOHN LIDE 84	. LIZZIE BALLOON 110
. MARTHA MARTIN 431	. JOSEPH O. 349	. LIZZIE BALLOONE 355
. MARTHA OWENS 429,466	. MARY 237	. MARGARET 110,355
. MARTHA P. 431	. SAM 110	. MARGARET F. 356-357

. MARTHA	355-356	WOODS,C.A.	537,571	WRIGHTSON,	447
. MARY	356	. JACK	476	WURRELL,JAMES	632
. MARY NORMAN	355	WOODWARD,	444	WYCHE,DELILAH	334
. NORMAN	355	. ANN	527	YATES,WILLIAM	635
. RICHARD	110,355-356	. CHARLOTTE	489	YEAMAN,JOHN	546-547,568
	358	. ELIZABETH		YEAMANS,JOHN	1-2
. SARAH		ATKINSON	489	YOUNG,	123,368,551,557
JOHNSON	110,356	. WILLIAM	489	. CELESTE	538
. TRAVIS FOSTER	356	. WILLIAM J.	590	. EMMA	305,538
. VENETIA	356	WOOLVIN,	354,413	. FRANK	538
. WADDY	356	WORREL,JAMES	577	. HAL	538
. WASHINGTON	110	WORRELL,JOHN	646	. J. BLAKE	538
. WILLIAM	11,24,104,110	WRIGHT,	157	. J.B.	503,538
	355-357,565-566	. DANIEL	581	. J.D.	632
. WILLIAM D.	572,593	. G.W.	628	. JOHNSON B.	305,537-538
WOODLEY,	233	. J.J.	103	. JULIA	538
WOODROW,D.M.	642	. JOHN W.	606	. TEXIA	359
. JOHN E.	591	. JULIA M.	441	. WILLIE	538
. WILLIAM	632	. W.C.	628	YOUNGBLOOD,	571
. WILLIAM J.	593				

www.ingramcontent.com/pod-product-compliance
Lightning Source LLC
Chambersburg PA
CBHW031356290426
44110CB00011B/191